Quality Assurance for Textiles and Apparel

Quality Assurance for Textiles and Apparel

Sara J. Kadolph
IOWA STATE UNIVERSITY

FAIRCHILD PUBLICATIONS
New York

Editor: Chernow Editorial Services, Inc.
Interior Design: UG, Inc.
Cover Design: WHIZBANG! Studios

Library of Congress Catalog Card Number: 97-78089

ISBN: 156367-144-1

GST R 133004424

Printed in the United States of America

BRIEF CONTENTS

EXTENDED CONTENTS

PART II
MATERIALS TESTING .103

PREFACE

The idea for this book developed as a result of my consulting activities within the textile industry complex, readings in quality management and quality control, research in quality assurance, discussions with students who had interned in quality assurance or quality control areas, meetings with and phone calls from graduates, observations made during industry tours of manufacturing facilities and testing laboratories, and discussions with professionals at trade meetings. For several years, I combined and honed these ideas and concepts in my textile product quality assurance classes at Iowa State University. *Quality Assurance for Textiles and Apparel* is the result of that work.

PHILOSOPHY

The book integrates a traditional textile testing approach with a broader focus on the product and target market and such approaches to managing quality as total quality management, statistical process control, quality function deployment, and zero defects management. The book is based on the basic premise that quality is developed into a product from the inception of the idea to its delivery to the ultimate consumer. I have tried to reflect the best practices and most practical efforts used in the industry to provide products of an identified and consistent quality that meets the customer's needs.

It is important to recognize that the term quality is used differently by the consumer and the industry professional. Based on my research, I believe that the industry is concerned with quality from a combination of three perspectives: identification of product standards and specifications that define in detail the desired appearance, performance, size, and so on, of the finished product; consistency between identical products so that variations among products is minimal; and providing products that meet known or perceived customer needs.

Similarly, within the industry, customers and consumers are not synonymous. Customers are businesses who buy products or materials from suppliers and perhaps also consumers, who are the ultimate users of finished textile products. Consumers look at quality from many different perspectives—excellence in construction, good performance at a reasonable price, exquisite materials with a good hand, high fashion, good fit and function, nice or unique detailing, unusual trims, recognized brand or store name, and other characteristics. Retailers, on the other hand, are concerned that the product looks good, is suitable for their consumer (this could mean fashion, fit, price, performance, and so on) and is priced so that it will sell. Thus, quality means different things to the various parts of the industry and the consumer.

However, there are several aspects of quality for which the focus is in agreement—product appeal and satisfactory product performance. Both influence customer satisfaction with the product. If the product is not appealing, it will not sell; if it performs in an unsatisfactory fashion, consumers will not be happy with it. Unfortunately, all too often the industry does not recognize consumer satisfaction as an important issue and does not include it in its product development activities. Assessment of material interactions in a product is an example of testing that is often omitted in product development.

The emphasis here is on the product and the consumer. This is a critical omission in materials analysis (textile testing) books and classes. Often, the emphasis has been on testing only the fashion, shell, or exterior fabrics using a variety of standard test methods without recognizing the specific needs and expectations of a stated target market and the unique characteristics and interactions inherent in the finished textile product. This book includes materials analysis, but only as one stage in developing a textile product that meets identified standards and specs based on the needs and expectations of a known target market in a consistent fashion. This book expands beyond textile testing to include other textile and nontextile materials; it includes information for writing specs and standards for most materials used in apparel and furnishings and some industrial goods; it discusses such critical aspects of textile products as appearance, construction, workmanship, fit, function, size, zones, and material and styling interactions; it describes inspection types and methods of taking samples; it examines total quality management from a textile industry perspective; and it incorporates a discussion of statistical process control.

This book assumes that the reader has a basic understanding of textiles, manufacturing techniques, identification and characterization of target markets, statistics, and fashion terminology. Students may need access to textbooks and other course materials from these classes to refresh their memories. Access to a product evaluation lab, equipment, and manuals is also critical. Products cannot be developed or evaluated without experience in a laboratory. Although some educational institutions may have only a few key pieces of equipment and other institutions a wider variety of equipment, all students should acquire experience with the basic elements involved in evaluating product quality.

The basic elements of materials assessment and inspection include fiber type (qualitative and quantitative), yarn structure, fabrication method, stage of coloration, fabric mass, grain (bow or skew), inspection for patent defects of materials, and selected performance measures (abrasion or strength, colorfastness to cleaning and some use dimensions, dimensional stability, hand or stiffness, and comfort elongation and recovery). Additional material assessments are ideal if time, space, and equipment allows. The basic elements of product assessment include size, appearance, construction, workmanship, interaction of materials (seams, interlinings and support materials, trims, closures) in cleaning and performance, and assessment of patent defects in the product by zone.

It is important for students to work with sample products for an identified target market so that they have experience in identifying specs and standards for a specific audience. Without that grounding and orientation, results of textile testing are difficult to comprehend and apply. Students also need to work with several identical products so that they see firsthand the minor variations possible within identical products and have experience assessing product consistency within a small sample and matching product characteristics and performance to standards and specs.

It is not easy for students to develop standards and specs for products for a specific target market, but this experience helps them focus on key elements within the product and the most important features from the target market's perspectives. Once they have developed specs and standards, they are more focused on the meaning of the results of testing and evaluation and are better able to discuss their product's success or failure.

This book requires the integration of a significant number of concepts and ideas presented in other classes. For this reason, the book is most appropriate for upper level students who have had significant experience in the integration of ideas, application of concepts, critical thinking, and problem solving. All these things are involved in quality assurance.

ORGANIZATION AND FEATURES OF THE TEXT

The book is organized in four parts. Part I, Understanding Quality Assurance, consists of four chapters and includes a discussion of quality from many perspectives; connects products, quality, and consumers; defines and discusses standards and specifications; and describes professional organizations and introduces basic concepts related to testing of materials and products.

Part II, Materials Testing, focuses on materials and consists of five chapters. First, materials are specified in terms of characteristics, quality, and performance. Four of the chapters examine how materials are measured in a specialized or dedicated laboratory. Specific standard test methods and nonstandard industry techniques are discussed. Photographs of selected equipment are included so that students can relate the equipment to the performance or characteristic being assessed. These photos are especially important because many educational institutions do not have a complete range of equipment used in testing materials.

In Part III, Product Specifications and Analysis, the focus expands to consider the complete textile product. This part is probably the most unique component of the book. It consists of four chapters that integrate products with materials and consumers. It includes chapters on developing specs and standards for products, inspection processes, product testing, and taking samples.

Finally, Part IV, Integration and Data Analysis, consists of two chapters that apply total quality management to the textile industry complex and discuss statistical process control using selected methods to present and manipulate data.

Each chapter includes objectives, key words, review questions, references, tables, illustrations, and photographs. Appendices facilitate use of the book in quality assurance with sample forms and assessment guides and lists of standard test methods, provide assistance for scientific notation and converting from one unit to another, identify equipment sources and testing laboratories, and present guidelines for ethical behavior for quality assurance professionals. In addition, an index developed by the author and a glossary are included so that the book is of use to professionals working in the industry.

ACKNOWLEDGMENTS

An endeavor of this magnitude cannot be completed without the help of many people. I thank my colleagues at Iowa State University (faculty, staff, and students) for their support, encouragement, and assistance in developing the concepts and providing a semester leave to make this book a reality. Sandra Chisholm, Grace Kunz, and Ruth Glock were especially helpful as I developed basic concepts. My experimental subjects (students in my TC 305 and 505 classes) helped integrate and formalize vague concepts into concrete ideas.

Graduates of the department in professional positions were most helpful in facilitating research visits: Beth Teggatz at Lands' End, Dodgeville, Wisconsin; Jackie Myers at L. L. Bean in Maine; Rita Ostdiek at JCPenney in Carrollton, Texas; Annette Tetmeyer, formerly with Rite Hite in Dubuque, Iowa; and Dana Rupe, formerly with Lortex in Des Moines, Iowa.

The readers selected by the publisher helped me expand the focus of the book, incorporate additional ideas and concepts, provide more concrete examples to illustrate and clarify ideas and concepts, and generally improve the book. They included: Catherine Burnham, Brigham Young University; Sally Fails Brittain, Oregon State University; Elizabeth Csordas, Marist College; Elizabeth Easter, University of Kentucky-Lexington; Maureen Grasso, UNC-Greensboro; Christine M. Ladisch, Purdue University; Carla J. Perez, Florida State University; Ann Beth Presley, Auburn University; Lydia L. Roper, University of Alabama; Carolyn Schactler, Central Washington University; and Janis Shaffer, Indiana University. Your comments were invaluable in writing and revising. I thank you for your time!

The efforts of several graduate students currently enrolled in the Department of Textiles and Clothing demand special recognition. A special thanks to Vicki Dirksen for her generous assistance with over 50 photographs! Her professional assistance with the photography is greatly appreciated. Thanks to Brecca Farr and Betsy Chew for demonstrating the contributions a fit model and fit specialist make to product quality.

My family, friends, and support staff at home and on the farm (Molly, Fuff, Boom, Cube, Bear, Shorty, and all the others) also deserve great thanks for encouraging me to write the book and providing the distractions that kept me sane during the process.

UNDERSTANDING QUALITY ASSURANCE

Quality is such an important commodity to both consumers and producers that it has become a goal within many companies. Two approaches to ensuring quality have evolved. Some companies view quality as a factor or a group of factors that can be controlled by inspecting finished products. Satisfactory or acceptable products pass inspection; unacceptable products are sold as seconds at a lower price. Other companies have defined a level of quality for any output, which ensures that all efforts are directed toward achieving these specific goals. These companies are more likely to test and inspect materials during production, so that a higher percentage of acceptable products are manufactured. These two approaches illustrate the importance of quality in the marketplace and in the manner in which products are manufactured and services are delivered.

Part I focuses on several of the initial steps involved in the textile quality assurance process, including:

- *presenting a model of quality assurance,*

- *defining quality and quality assurance,*

- *understanding how to evaluate the factors that define quality,*

- *understanding target markets and their expectations for textile products,*

- *understanding standards and specifications that reflect target market expectations at appropriate price levels, and*

- *examining the ways textile products can be evaluated to see if they meet required quality levels.*

Chapter 1

INTRODUCTION TO QUALITY ASSURANCE

OBJECTIVES

- To describe the textile industry complex.
- To define quality assurance.
- To introduce a quality assurance model that presents factors of importance assuring the quality of products or services.

KEY TERMS

textile industry complex

raw materials

processed materials

materials

sewn product manufacturers

retailers

consumers

customers

textile quality assurance

quality control

Quality is a necessary, but elusive, element that applies to all aspects of conducting business in today's market. For individuals interested in learning about and pursuing careers in the textile industry complex, quality includes understanding the way in which product development and production are integrated, so that products satisfy consumer expectations. Everyone talks about quality, but successfully planning for and manufacturing quality in products requires access to knowledge, as well as the development and coordination of wide-ranging and multifaceted skills in all areas of the textile industry complex. The development of a quality assurance program is therefore a driving force in many industries, especially because producing quality products at a competitive price is a major factor in world markets.

The approach to achieving quality in a product or service is not uniform. The factors of importance vary among industries. For example, training, equipment, and materials are quite different between the steel industry and the food processing industry. Nevertheless, some basic concepts related to internal operations, identifying customers' needs, and meeting business goals are common to all industries. The manner in which a company's management views quality will influence almost every activity it undertakes. Some companies and industries are more advanced in their approach to quality; others take a more traditional approach. The textile industry complex tends to be more traditional.

THE TEXTILE INDUSTRY COMPLEX

The textile industry complex has often been compared to a pipeline, which implies that the steps in the process of designing, producing, and selling a product are sequential and linear. In many instances, this no longer provides a realistic view of the industry. Many activities and production processes occur simultaneously, sometimes within the same company.

The **textile industry complex** includes suppliers of raw and processed materials, sewn product manufacturers, wholesalers, and retailers. Companies may focus on providing fabrics or other materials used in making finished textile products, on producing specific types of textile products, or on producing selected fabrics and such related products as polo shirts. Other companies focus on selling products to individuals. Companies may sell products they purchase from producers or products they design and for which the production is contracted to a producer. All companies involved in processing or producing raw materials, constructing and finishing products, and selling goods to customers comprise the textile industry complex.

Raw materials include the unprocessed components used to produce a product. **Raw materials** include fibers, yarns, dyes, finishing chemicals, and such other materials as plastics and metal that are processed into buttons, zippers, and other items that are used to produce finished products. As the term suggests, raw material requires additional processing before it can be used in the production of a finished product. Bales of cotton fiber are a good example. Woven and finished cotton fabric is an example of a **processed material,** which means that the item requires no additional processing before it can be used in the production of textile products. Processed materials are often referred to simply as **materials** and include fashion and support fabrics, thread, zippers, and other items used in making up or constructing textile products.

Sewn product manufacturers make apparel, furnishings, and industrial products. These manufacturers often incorporate other activities, such as fusing and dyeing, into the production process. They may sell their products to wholesalers or directly to retailers who then sell the merchandise directly to consumers. **Retailers** encompass a variety of store types, including department, discount, and specialty stores, as well as catalog companies. **Consumers** are the individuals who use or wear finished textile products. **Customers** include consumers, companies, such as sewn product manufacturers, who buy fabric and other materials, and retailers who buy quantities of identical products for sale to the consumer.

The term textile industry complex will be used throughout this book to refer to industries that work together to produce the materials used in textile products, to sew the textile products, and to market these finished products to individual consumers. This book focuses on quality assurance as used by forward-thinking companies within the textile industry complex, with an emphasis on sewn product manufacturers and retailers.

Some firms in the textile industry are vertically integrated. This means that they may be involved in production of materials and products or in production and retailing. For example, some knitwear companies buy fiber, spin yarns, knit and finish jersey or fleece fabric, and cut and sew such apparel items as casual shirts and active sportswear. Other companies sew apparel and sell it to consumers directly. Many manufacturers and retailers have off-shore production facilities or work with contractors who produce goods off-shore. The use of off-shore facilities can create special problems, especially when language and units of measure differ between the production facility and the design or product development and management teams. However, the need for quality assurance exists regardless of the separation of design, product development, production, and management.

TEXTILE QUALITY ASSURANCE

Textile quality assurance is the process of designing, producing, evaluating, and checking products to determine if they meet the desired quality level for a company's target market. It involves many activities that are based on a knowledge of textiles, design, merchandising, production, consumer behavior, product and process evaluation, marketing, and statistics. Although individual employees in many firms have titles that incorporate the word quality, no one person is completely and solely responsible for the quality of finished products.

One common misunderstanding is that quality can be assessed after production of the textile product. While this may be so, the implications of this approach can be expensive, particularly when resources, such as labor and materials, are invested in producing a product that turns out to be unacceptable. For example, companies can miss shipping deadlines due to products that did not pass inspection. In addition, this post-production quality control approach increases the possibility that an unacceptable product will reach a consumer. This approach is often referred to as **quality control.** In this process, quality is controlled after production by inspecting the goods and sorting them into acceptable and unacceptable groupings. Because unacceptable products may be passed over or missed during inspection, it is more likely that a consumer will purchase an item that is not satisfactory.

Companies that approach quality from a different perspective tend to do a better job of manufacturing products to a desired level of quality on a consistent basis. According to these companies, quality is inherent in a product and is incorporated into the product during product development, production, and marketing. Many departments within a single company interact to help ensure that the final product is of the appropriate quality for the market. When quality is considered from this perspective, it is vitally important that the departments or individuals involved understand their roles in terms of quality and work to meet expectations for product quality. In addition, these companies ensure that their suppliers use appropriate quality materials to create the product. Thus, textile quality assurance considers not only the quality of the finished product, but also the actions and interactions of the departments, materials, and processes involved in production.

THE MODEL

The conceptual model that is used as the framework for this book is presented in Figure 1-1. The model describes the components that contribute to quality of the finished textile product, the interactions among factors of the product, and the communication and activities within companies and with suppliers and buyers. Another important aspect of the model is that it indicates the connection between customers and business objectives. The key elements of the model and their relationship to quality are discussed in detail throughout the book. This model is based on the practices used by many companies that make up the textile industry complex.

The outermost circle represents the materials, processes, and product characteristics and features that are combined in a finished textile product. This circle assumes that the quality of a product is related to these three factors and their interactions.

The next circle indicates that the three factors must be defined, evaluated, inspected, and analyzed to be sure that they are satisfactory. Writing standards and specifications and developing acceptance criteria that reflect customer expectations for the product are critical in quality assurance. In

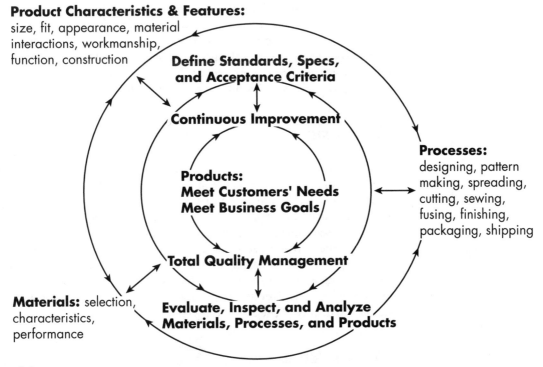

Product Characteristics & Features:
size, fit, appearance, material interactions, workmanship, function, construction

Define Standards, Specs, and Acceptance Criteria

Continuous Improvement

**Products:
Meet Customers' Needs
Meet Business Goals**

Processes:
designing, pattern making, spreading, cutting, sewing, fusing, finishing, packaging, shipping

Total Quality Management

Materials: selection, characteristics, performance

Evaluate, Inspect, and Analyze Materials, Processes, and Products

Figure 1-1
Quality assurance as applied to the textile industry complex.

addition, the materials, processes, and products must be evaluated and inspected to ensure that they meet specific criteria defined by the company. Analysis can be simple or complex depending on the data collected.

The innermost circle indicates that quality assurance is a never-ending process. Changes in the product are implemented as a result of sales, customer feedback, changes in the marketplace, technological advancements, and fashion. Continuous improvement and total quality management are basic approaches to quality. Continuous improvement assumes that the company is constantly working to improve itself. The focus might be on decreasing customer returns, decreasing seconds, or increasing material utilization rates. Total quality management focuses on continuous improvement and on satisfying customer expectations. As customer feedback is received in terms of complaints, comments, or sales, this information is used to make adjustments in the process, product, or materials.

The center of the model presents the two basic goals of quality assurance. One goal is to provide products that meet or exceed customers' needs in terms of performance, fashion, timely delivery, or any other criteria of importance. A second goal is to sell products that enable the company to meet its business objectives in terms of productivity, profit, product mix, or other criteria.

The arrows within the model indicate that communication among departments, team members, vendors, and customers is needed to assure that the desired level of quality is achieved. Arrows also imply interactions among the elements that influence the quality of and the customer's satisfaction with the product or service. The concentric circles of the model suggest interactions and connections among adjacent circles.

CONCLUSION

This chapter introduced the basic concepts necessary for understanding quality assurance and the textile industry complex. It is important to recognize that a basic knowledge of textiles, manufacturing, and design will help the reader understand how the different factors influence product quality. Throughout subsequent chapters, the reader will find frequent reference to the two approaches to quality assurance, which were introduced and compared in this chapter, as well as to the conceptual model that provides the framework for this book. It is important to understand the integration among the various parts of the model and their relationship to assuring the quality of products and services.

SUGGESTED READINGS

Apparel Quality Committee. (1985). *Elements of an Apparel Quality Control Program.* Arlington, VA: American Apparel Manufacturers Association.

Brown, Patty. (1992). *Ready-to-Wear Apparel Analysis.* New York: Macmillan.

Carruthers, Hamish. (1991). Design for the market. In *Textile World at Crossroads.* Manchester, England: Textile Institute.

Chisholm, Sandra Flora. (1995). Textile Quality Assurance: A Comparison Between Education and Industry. Unpublished Master's Thesis, Iowa State University, Ames, IA.

Crosby, Philip B. (1979). *Quality Is Free: The Art of Making Quality Certain.* New York: McGraw-Hill.

Glock, Ruth E., & Grace I. Kunz. (1995). *Apparel Manufacturing: Sewn Products Analysis,* 2nd ed. Englewood Cliffs, NJ: Prentice-Hall.

Juran, J. M., & Frank M. Gyrna. (1993). *Quality Planning and Analysis: From Product Development Through Use.* New York: McGraw-Hill.

Karnes, Carol L., & John J. Karnes. (1994, February). How the Apparel Industry Measures Up to Quality Standards. *Quality Progress, 27,* 25–29.

Lupo, John. (1995). Wal-Mart: Building Better and More Effective Partnerships. Paper presented at the 1995 Apparel Research Conference, Atlanta, GA, November, 1995.

Peters, M. M. (1983). Fabric for Garments: Quality, Design, and the Purchaser. In The Textile Institute (ed.), *Quality, Design, and the Purchaser.* Manchester, England: Textile Institute.

Powers, Mary E. (1984). Textiles from the Consumer's Viewpoint. *Textile Chemist and Colorist, 16,* 228–231.

Rabolt, Nancy J., Katrina Bothwell, Judith Forney, & Mary Barry. (1988). Quality Control in Overseas Apparel Manufacturing. *Journal of Consumer Studies and Home Economics, 12,* 389–397.

Roach, A. R. (1994). Meeting Consumer Needs for Textiles and Clothing. *Journal of the Textile Institute, 85(4),* 484–495.

Scheller, Heidi P. (1993). The Meaning Of Apparel Quality Through the Perceptions of Apparel Production Managers and Operators. Unpublished Master's Thesis, Iowa State University, Ames, IA.

Scherkenback, William W. (1986). *The Deming Route to Quality and Productivity: Road Maps and Roadblocks.* Washington, DC: Ceep Press.

Shishoo, Roshan L. (1995). Interactions between Fabric Properties and Garment Making-up Processes. In the Textile Institute (ed.), *Textiles: Fashioning the Future*. Manchester, England: Textile Institute, pp. 337–358.

Technical Advisory Committee. (1994). *New Yardsticks for Apparel*. Arlington, VA: American Apparel Manufacturers Association.

Weir, George. (1995, June). Management by Knowing: My Customer Doesn't Know Quality. *Knitting Times*, 43.

Winchester, S. C. (1994). Total Quality Management in Textiles. *Journal of the Textile Institute, 85(4)*, 445–459.

Wood, Freddie. (1993, September). Succeeding in Textiles in the Nineties. *Textile World*, 45, 51, 53, 54, 56–59.

REVIEW QUESTIONS

1. Why is an understanding of quality important in today's market?

2. Define the terms given below and explain how they relate to product quality.
   a. textile industry complex
   b. materials
   c. quality assurance

3. Explain the connections between customers and product quality.

4. Describe how the quality of a product affects customer satisfaction.

5. Explain the model shown in Figure 1-1.

ACTIVITIES

1. Describe how a specific textile product would relate to the model shown in Figure 1-1.

2. Discuss the role of the designer, production engineer, merchandising specialist, or product development specialist in assuring product quality.

3. Suggest how the courses required in your degree program will provide you with knowledge and skills in terms of quality assurance.

4. From a quality assurance perspective, analyze the service you receive when you go to a restaurant, check out a book, take a class, visit the dentist or doctor, use public transportation, or buy something in a store. Identify the ways in which the service was acceptable and the ways in which it could be improved. Describe how these issues relate to quality assurance.

5. Discuss how an individual could implement a quality assurance perspective in terms of his or her work or education.

6. Read the article (Rabolt, Nancy J., Katrina Bothwell, Judith Forney, & Mary Barry. [1988]. Quality Control in Overseas Apparel Manufacturing. *Journal of Consumer Studies and Home Economics, 12*, 389–397) and discuss its relationship to quality assurance.

Chapter 2

LINKING PRODUCTS, QUALITY, AND CUSTOMERS

OBJECTIVES

- To understand how quality is defined.

- To apply definitions of quality to product development, product evaluation, and customer satisfaction.

- To integrate an understanding of specific target markets with product quality.

- To identify product attributes that contribute to product quality.

- To relate customer expectations to satisfaction with textile products.

KEY TERMS

quality	product attribute	comfort
product quality	target market	care
first-quality product	serviceability	appearance retention
substandard product	aesthetics	customer satisfaction
total quality management	durability	product development
	cost	

The concept of quality has become very important within the textile and apparel industry. Employees refer to quality when they talk about the operating structure of their company, work with suppliers or vendors, sell to customers, and promote their products. Why has quality become so important?

Consumers are increasingly demanding in what they look for in textile products and discriminating in what they find acceptable. Quality is one important factor that consumers use in making decisions regarding textile product purchases. Consumers are more likely to purchase a product that they perceive to have good quality than a product that they find lacking in quality. Thus, to satisfy the consumer and remain competitive, a company must consider quality when the product is developed, produced, and marketed.

The global marketplace has increased competition throughout the textile industry. This increased competition affects materials producers, manufacturers of sewn products, retailers, and consumers. The products now on the market are from many countries and vary significantly in product cost, characteristics, and attributes. To survive in this highly competitive climate, companies need to maintain quality. Companies that consistently produce substandard products or products that do not meet their target market's expectations do not survive.

As a result of the growing global market, a wide variety of products are available from many sources. These products represent a range of fibers, fabric structures, styles and fashions, construction methods, appearance standards, and performance levels. Because these variables combine to create products at many quality levels, it is challenging for consumers to differentiate among products to determine which will be satisfactory. Thus, consumers have become more dependent on experts who work with and assess the quality of textile products. These experts are expected to assure consumers that products in the marketplace are of satisfactory quality. Unfortunately, quality is a nebulous characteristic that is not easy to define.

Interest in quality has become pervasive within the business world. Companies must recognize the importance of incorporating quality in standard day-to-day business practices to do business with other companies and customers. Companies demand quality in materials received from suppliers and service providers, such as shipping and computer maintenance providers. It is becoming standard practice for issues related to quality to be incorporated into contracts. For example, vendor contracts often refer to manuals that offer detailed descriptions of expectations concerning product characteristics related to many factors, including seam types, color matching of materials, and inspection methods.

Textile, apparel, and furnishing companies are competing in a market that has changed considerably in the past few decades. Improving product quality is one way a company can improve its ability to survive. Companies use quality assessments to promote their products. Unfortunately, the industry and the customer do not always agree on the characteristics of quality and the ways in which quality should be measured or judged. This mismatch leads to customer complaints, distrust, and incorrect perceptions of standard business practices. This chapter examines how quality experts define quality, what customers look for in terms of quality of textile products, and how customer satisfaction relates to the perception of product quality. In addition, a brief overview of product development will help focus attention on how quality is incorporated into a product from the initial planning stages of the process.

DEFINING QUALITY

Quality is a complex concept. No single definition addresses all the dimensions, areas of impact, and concerns related to quality. The term itself is used in many ways for many reasons. Each use reflects a different perspective based on philosophy, economics, consumer behavior, production and engineering, and value systems. Definitions may focus on a holistic perspective, the impact of quality on the organization's income, the changing marketplace, the nature of a product or service, the way a product or service conforms to specifications, or the ability of a product or service to meet customers' needs and satisfy their demands. Companies and their employees need to understand how quality affects organizations, standard practices within organizations, consumer behavior, customer purchases and satisfaction, and competition within the marketplace.

DEFINITIONS OF QUALITY

Holistic Perspective

Webster's dictionary (1977) defines quality as "that which belongs to something and makes or helps to make it what it is; characteristic element; any character or characteristic which may make an object good or bad; the degree of excellence which a thing possesses." This is a good beginning point, because it helps us look at quality from a holistic perspective and implies that even if quality is not the same for all things, it is still inherent in all objects and actions.

Thus, quality is defined as the total of the characteristics that help describe the overall object or service. The assumption is that "you will recognize quality when you see it." This naive approach is still widely held by many experts and consumers, but it does not address many important contemporary business issues, such as understanding the components that contribute to quality, engineering quality into a product, measuring a product's quality, and improving quality of a product or process. Cotton provides a good illustration of these issues. Many individuals assume that cotton is the best fiber on the market, even though its production and processing have inherent environmental drawbacks and cotton does not perform as well as synthetic fibers for many end uses. In addition, many types and quality levels of cotton exist. Some have less environmental impact than others. Some are stronger and have greater fiber length than others. However, cotton is not always a good choice for many textile products. Imagine, for example, how different undergarments and support garments would be if they were manufactured without the synthetic fiber spandex.

Product Perspective

Product quality is represented by the total of a set of precise and measurable characteristics or components of a finished product. Differences in product quality can be attributed to differences in components or characteristics. A continuum can be developed on which the quality of any one characteristic can be precisely located. Consider, for example, two measures used to characterize the quality of woven fabrics: weight in ounces per square yard (oz/yd^2) and yarns per inch for warp and filling. One assumption is that the greater the weight within a given range or the higher the count of yarns, the better the quality of the fabric. Figure 2-1 illustrates one continuum for a fabric. The characteristics of weight and count are linked to yarn and weaving costs, but do not necessarily imply better products. For example, greater weight may mean that the fabric does not drape as well as a lighter weight fabric. Therefore, in products where drape is a critical factor, lower weight may be preferred. Similarly, finer yarns may be less abrasion resistant than coarser yarns. Thus, for products where high abrasion resistance is required, coarser yarns may be preferred. Clearly, these common measures of quality are not necessarily directly related to consumer satisfaction.

Producer Perspective

From a producer's or manufacturer's perspective, quality is often defined as consistent conformance to specifications and standards. Thus, when a product meets a company's standards and specifications, it has achieved the desired quality level. This desired level may be high, low, or at any point in between the extremes of the continuum. By this definition, quality is achieved when products consistently fall within a range of acceptable measures for all dimensions of quality. An example of quality in terms of consistent conformance includes buttons that are within a narrow range of the specifications for diameter, thickness, and color, and have the appropriate number and size of holes for sewing to a shirt. These characteristics are especially important in factories in which buttons are attached to product

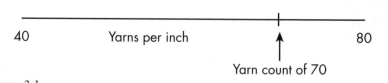

Figure 2-1

One continuum for yarn count in a fabric. Because the mark indicating yarn count is fairly close to the high end, this fabric would be considered fairly high quality.

components by automatic button setting machines. These buttons may or may not perform in a satisfactory fashion for the consumer, but they satisfy the manufacturer's expectations for quality and performance. This producer-oriented definition of quality suggests that manufacturers will not stay in business if too many products fail to meet standards and specifications, but it does not address consumer expectations.

The producer's definition of quality addresses a company's ability to produce products that consistently meet predetermined criteria and can be sold in the market at full price. The emphasis here is on consistently meeting stated expectations. A hidden assumption is that products that meet this level of quality will produce the greatest income and profit for the company. Thus, a company with this perspective ideally should meet its business objectives.

Philip Crosby, a well-known quality expert, states that quality is free. He means that production costs are the same for items that do and those that do not meet specifications and standards. Hence, Crosby says that production and material costs are the same for **first-quality products** (those that meet the standards) as for **substandard products** (those that do not meet standards). Crosby's 14 steps to quality improvement are listed in Table 2-1

Table 2-1
CROSBY'S 14 STEPS TO QUALITY IMPROVEMENT

1. Make it clear that management has a long-term commitment to quality.

2. Form cross-departmental quality teams.

3. Identify where current and potential problems exist.

4. Assess the cost of quality and explain how it is used as a management tool.

5. Increase the quality awareness and personal commitment of all employees.

6. Take immediate action to correct problems identified.

7. Establish a zero defects program.

8. Train supervisors to carry out their responsibilities in the quality program.

9. Hold a zero defects day to ensure all employees are aware there is a new direction.

10. Encourage individuals and teams to establish both personal and team improvement goals.

11. Encourage employees to tell management about obstacles they face in trying to meet quality goals.

12. Recognize employees who participate.

13. Implement quality councils to promote continual communication.

14. Repeat everything to illustrate that quality improvement is a never-ending process.

(Reprinted from Philip B. Crosby, Quality is Free: The Art of Making Quality Free, 1979, McGraw-Hill, with permission of The McGraw-Hill Companies.)

(Crosby, 1979). The costs to the company are constant regardless of how much first-quality salable merchandise has been produced. In other words, the cost to produce 100 items is the same regardless of whether 100, 75, or 50 items are first quality. Companies have the same investment in a substandard product as in a first-quality product. However, the return from the substandard product will be substantially different from that of the first-quality product. Companies lose money on substandard products, even when those products are reworked so that they meet first-quality standards. Thus, efforts to improve quality emphasize reducing substandard products or defects. Sometimes this approach is referred to as zero defects management, because the goal is to have zero defects in production.

Customer Perspective

From a customer's perspective, quality depends on the dimensions of a product or service that are of importance to that user. These dimensions will differ by product or service type, as well as by customer. Returning to the button example may help clarify this point. The customer could be the manufacturing company who buys buttons to attach to shirts, or it could be the individual consumer who wears and cares for the shirts to which the buttons have been attached. Thus, both customers should be considered when button quality is defined and assessed.

This perspective recognizes the primary role of the customer in determining whether or not a product or service meets or exceeds expectations. However, quality is not in a steady state; from a customer's perspective, quality reflects an everchanging marketplace and satisfies the everchanging needs of the customer in that market. Thus, the buttons should not be adversely affected by any chemical or abradant finishing the shirt receives. In addition, companies need to respond to changes in expectations and needs by maintaining contact with their customers.

One difficult aspect of examining quality from the customer's perspective is understanding and incorporating the characteristics that the customer finds desirable at a price that is acceptable. For example, the price-conscious consumer might find superior colorfastness to washing and abrasion desirable, but may not be willing to pay a higher price for a product that exhibits these characteristics. From the manufacturing perspective, customers desire consistency of fabric width and color, ease of spreading, and freedom from visible fabric defects. But with the exceptions of consistency of color and freedom from visible defects, consumers generally are not concerned with the other fabric characteristics that are very important to manufacturers. Hence, a company needs a good understanding of the wants of the immediate customer and the ultimate consumer.

This focus on customers and their satisfaction is a basic underlying principle of **total quality management** (TQM). Several definitions of TQM exist. All focus on an integrated, continuous improvement process that involves everyone in the organization. In TQM, all of the company's

Figure 2-2
Satisfying business objectives forms the foundation for customer satisfaction. *(Based on the model from Card, 1992, pp. 101–102.)*

actions are directed toward producing a quality product for the target market, satisfying the target market, and meeting the company's business objectives. Although business objectives generally focus on financial and market growth, these objectives must include customer satisfaction. Satisfying business objectives forms the foundation for customer satisfaction (see Figure 2-2). Customer satisfaction will not occur if the company keeps in contact with customers only through complaint departments, satisfaction surveys, and warranties.

Each functional area of the company should focus on satisfying the customer. A management system that involves all parts of the company in improving customer satisfaction is therefore necessary. Many companies assume that they understand their customers, but they really have a distorted perspective. Companies must understand all interactions customers have with the company and use that information to improve the system. For example, if a customer complaint is handled only by the complaint department and no further effort is taken to prevent the problem from recurring, the problem remains and overall customer satisfaction does not improve. Many companies within the textile industry have adopted a TQM approach to minimize problems with customer satisfaction. Figure 2-3 illustrates a system-wide approach used within a dyeing operation. Many companies within the industry use similar systems.

One of the first individuals to recognize the need to focus on quality in production and product development was W. Edwards Deming (1982), who maintained that quality is the responsibility of management. Deming's management principles include 14 points (see Table 2-2) that relate to adopting a philosophy of improving products and services, remaining competitive, staying in business, and providing jobs. One principle involved building quality into products from inception of the idea. Deming focused on minimizing total cost and constantly improving the system. Continuous training on the job and innovative leadership are crucial. Cross-functional teams, so common in today's textile industry complex, facilitate communication across departments and help companies reach their quality goals. Deming's 14 points continue to have a significant impact on the quality movement within the U.S. industry. The Deming cycle (Figure 2-4), which links production, target markets, and

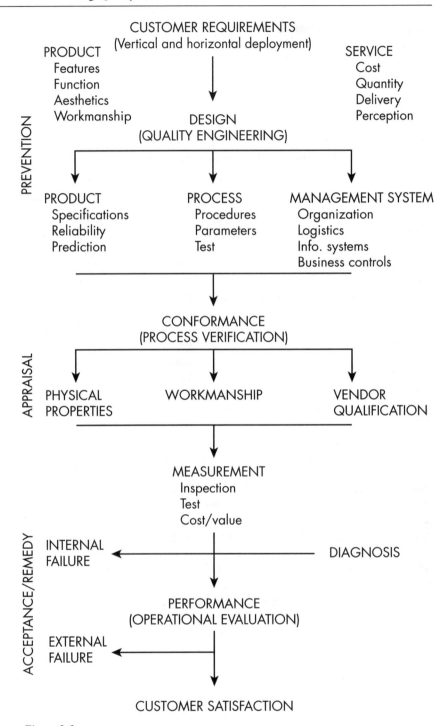

Figure 2-3

Total quality value system. (Reprinted from Textile Chemist and Colorist, Vol. 24, No. 10, October 1992. Published by the American Association of Textile Chemists and Colorists, P. O. Box 12215, Research Triangle Park, NC 27709.)

Table 2-2
DEMING'S 14 POINTS

1. Create constancy of purpose for improvement of product and service.
2. Adopt the new philosophy.
3. Cease dependence on mass inspection.
4. End the practice of awarding business on the basis of price tag alone.
5. Improve constantly and forever the system of production and service.
6. Institute training.
7. Adopt and institute leadership.
8. Drive out fear.
9. Break down barriers between staff areas.
10. Eliminate slogans, exhortations, and targets for the work force.
11. Eliminate numerical quotas for the work force.
12. Remove barriers that rob people of pride of workmanship.
13. Encourage education and self-improvement for everyone.
14. Take action to accomplish the transformation.

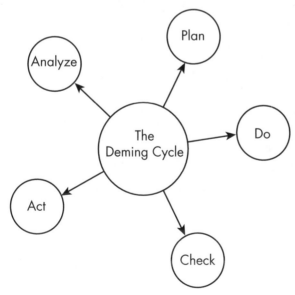

Figure 2-4
The Deming Cycle.

business objectives, can be summarized as a five-step approach (Goetsch & Davis, 1994):

1. Conduct consumer research. Use the results in planning the product (plan).

2. Produce the product (do).

3. Check the product to make sure it meets criteria identified in the plan (check).

4. Market the product (act).

5. Analyze how the product is received in the marketplace in terms of quality, cost, and other criteria (analyze).

Many companies follow these steps as they develop, produce, market, and evaluate or analyze their products. The need for communication within the company and with customers is vital for survival in today's market.

Joseph M. Juran is another quality pioneer, who developed ten steps to quality improvement (see Table 2-3). Juran's (1989) approach, another example of zero-defects management, concentrates on eliminating the relatively few sources that cause the majority of problems. Once again, the

Table 2-3
JURAN'S TEN STEPS TO QUALITY IMPROVEMENT

1. Build awareness of both the need for improvement and opportunities for improvement.

2. Set goals for improvement.

3. Organize to meet the goals that have been set.

4. Provide training.

5. Implement projects aimed at solving problems.

6. Report progress.

7. Give recognition.

8. Communicate results.

9. Keep score.

10. Maintain momentum by building improvement into the company's regular systems.

(Adapted with the permission of The Free Press, a Division of Simon & Schuster from JURAN ON LEADERSHIP FOR QUALITY: An Executive Handbook by J. M. Juran. Copyright © 1989 by Juran Institute, Inc.)

focus is on understanding customers, communication within the company and with customers, and continuous improvement.

Value-Based Perspective

From a value-based approach, quality products are those that perform at acceptable prices or conform at acceptable costs (Winchester, 1994). Thus, value and excellence are combined in a concept that is referred to as afford-able excellence (Garvin, 1984). Here, value is expanded to incorporate ser-vice, delivery, and financial arrangements. But, this concept is more diffi-cult to assess than several of those discussed previously. Silverman and Propst (1996) expand the scope and define value as the customer's percep-tion of total lifetime benefits minus total lifetime costs. Thus, when bene-fits exceed costs, the customer is satisfied and the quality level is perceived as good. When costs exceed benefits, the customer is not satisfied and quality is perceived as poor.

Summary

Quality is a dynamic state associated with products, services, people, processes, and environments that meets or exceeds expectations (Goetsch & Davis, 1994). For TQM, the customer's perspective (including the need for consistency in products and the expectation that products meet stan-dards and specifications) defines quality for the company. Companies are organized to address the customer's expectations for quality, and their business plans reflect that focus on customer satisfaction.

DIMENSIONS OF QUALITY

In addition to defining quality, the characteristics or conditions that are of importance when quality is of interest need to be established. Garvin (1984, 1987) has identified eight dimensions related to quality: perfor-mance, features, reliability, conformance, durability, serviceability, aesthet-ics, and perceived quality. An understanding of these eight dimensions will provide a better understanding of product quality.

The dimension of *performance* combines product and user-based ap-proaches and focuses on measurable **product attributes.** However, Garvin maintains that this dimension is influenced by semantics. Some attributes may be used to describe quality, while others describe product categories. For example, because woven and knit fabrics tend to be used for different product categories, it would be difficult to determine which of the two represents better quality. Thus, type of fabric structure may not be a reli-able measure of product quality, but it may be a way to differentiate among product categories. With some imports, fabric structure is used to separate textile products into categories.

In addition, performance differences may be perceived as quality differences by some customers, but not by others. For example, heavier weight fabrics tend to be stronger and more abrasion resistant, but are also stiffer and less fluid in drape. One customer might prefer the heavier and more durable fabric; another might prefer the less durable, but more fluid fabric for a similar product. In their assessments of the products, each customer would probably refer to quality in describing their assessment of the product. Both customers would have salient points, but their descriptions would differ significantly.

Features are secondary characteristics that supplement a product's basic function. Many style and design aspects, especially for fashion products, would be categorized as features. The impact of features on quality is affected by individual preferences. For example, some women insist that their skirts and pants have side pockets; other women do not want extra bulk in the hip area and avoid side pockets almost entirely. Features for fashion products change more quickly than features for basic products. For fashion products, features and their contribution to quality are very dependent on current fashion trends. A feature that is assessed as of low quality or out of fashion at one time, may be assessed as of high quality or in fashion at another time.

Reliability describes the likelihood that a product will fail within a given time period. Reliability is more important with durable goods and less important with nondurable goods. Textile products are often categorized as semidurable goods, because many are used or worn numerous times before they are discarded or used up, but their normal life span is shorter than that for durable goods. Reliability for textile products may mean the use of an item for one or more seasons before failure occurs. Failure with textile products refers to actual failure of some physical component of the product, such as fabric, seams, zippers, or buttons. Discarding or deciding not to wear or use a textile product because the consumer deems it to be out of fashion is not a measure of reliability.

Conformance describes the degree to which a product's design and function match standards and specifications. Reliability and conformance are related to manufacturing-based approaches to quality and tend to focus on objective measures of quality. Design, technical design, and engineering specialists describe in detail the desired construction and materials performance, such as fabric strength, matching of plaids at center front seams, and matching of trim and fabric in terms of color. When a product meets or exceeds these standards and specifications, it is in conformance.

Durability describes how long a product will be suitable for its end use. Durability has both economic and technical dimensions. With textile products, individual consumers determine when a product has deteriorated to the point where it is no longer suitable for its original end use. Deterioration includes both physical measures of quality, such as colorfastness and abrasion resistance, and less measurable dimensions, such as fit, style, and fashion. A product's life span may well vary for different consumers. Products are purchased for various reasons. Consumers might have different expectations for products purchased to be worn at home compared with products to be worn at work. Durability and reliability may be related, but not always directly.

In Garvin's model, *serviceability* is related to product repair. Because product repair is of little importance for most textile products, the definition needs to be adjusted. For textiles, serviceability probably most closely relates to the "clean-ability" of the product: Can it be cleaned and restored to its new or near-new condition? This perspective of serviceability integrates the cleaning process with product performance during cleaning. It includes such factors as dimensional stability, colorfastness, soil-release, and wrinkling. If the process was done incorrectly, if inappropriate materials were used, or if incompatible materials were combined in the product, it may no longer be useable after care. For example, if the wash water is too hot, dye bleed may be permanent.

Aesthetics tends to be more subjective than any other measure of quality. Aesthetics describes how one's physical senses of sight, sound, and touch perceive the product. The focus is on textile and product aspects, including hand, weight, texture, color, and fashion. Aesthetics reflects individual preferences. For example, some people decorate with pastels; others never use pastels. Some people like to dress in loose, relaxed clothing; others prefer body-hugging styles and fabrics.

Perceived quality is another strongly subjective area. Customers rarely possess complete information about a product at point of purchase. They often have little knowledge of the materials combined in the product or the processes used to make the product. Hence, they tend to rely on nebulous factors, such as brand name or advertising, in making their purchase decisions. These incorrect perceptions regarding product quality may be a significant factor when they are not satisfied with a product.

DETERMINING PRODUCT MARKETS

As a company develops its product concept, it must also visualize its target market. A **target market** is a group of customers or a segment of the population that is interested in and likely to purchase a particular product. Many beginning entrepreneurs find it difficult to identify and define their target market. They may not understand the importance of focusing on one particular target market, or they define their market too broadly. Companies that try to be all things to all people frequently fail, because they spread their limited resources too widely and fail to earn a profit. Frequently these companies also fail to satisfy the needs of any subset of the population, because they have not tried to satisfy the needs of any specific group of individuals. Identifying a target market will help the company direct products toward that market, assess their ability to sell to that market, identify how to market their product to that population, and identify the size and location of their market.

IDENTIFYING TARGET MARKETS

To identify a target market, a company needs to analyze carefully customer characteristics according to demographics, lifestyle factors, and psychographics. These factors help define the members of the target market, how they use textile products, and the importance of textiles to them and to their lifestyles. Once a company has identified these factors about its target market, it will have a better understanding of the type of product that will appeal to this group, how to market to this group, and the characteristics that must be incorporated in a product for this market.

Demographics

Demographics include factors that describe the target market. Gender is one significant factor, especially in terms of apparel. Clothing appropriate for males and females may be similar for some product types, such as blue jeans and tee shirts, but the physical shapes of these products often differs. For example, patterns for women's jeans incorporate different hip shapes and waist circumferences than for men's jeans.

Age and stage of the life cycle help define the kinds of products consumers purchase. For example, individuals in their early teens look for different product attributes than individuals in their thirties. Single, working people have different needs compared to families with young children. Family size is also significant. Larger families have different demands on money across most budget categories. Thus, the money available for apparel, furnishings, and other textile products may be more limited in larger families.

Education level and socioeconomic status strongly influence purchases; this may be the result of income, occupation, or workplace requirements. For example, the move by many businesses to a casual Friday look has had a major impact on the profit margin for some producers of tailored suits. Factory employees buy different items for work compared to office workers. People who work in design companies may dress differently than those who work in insurance or accounting companies.

Geographic location influences customer's purchases. Requirements for winter clothing vary with climate. Recreational activities are often determined by geographic location. For example, people who live near large bodies of water may spend more of their leisure time at the beach or on the water and wear clothing specifically selected for those activities.

Ethnicity and cultural membership also may influence textile purchases. Personal coloring is a factor in selecting the color of apparel. Cultural membership may influence type, fabric patterns, color combinations, and accessories for furnishings and apparel.

Finally, physical abilities and limitations affect what a consumer may look for when considering purchases of textile products. For example, if an individual has limited range of motion in the shoulder, back closures in apparel are not as desirable as front closures.

Lifestyle Factors

Lifestyle factors include such things as social activities, entertainment preferences, membership in groups and organizations, shopping habits, hobbies, spending and saving habits, and gift giving. Sports activities influence the purchase of textile products. Individuals who play tennis on a regular basis have different needs compared to those who ride horses. The tennis player would require clothing, shoes, tennis racket and balls, and a racket case. The rider would need different clothing, boots, and special textile products for the horse, such as a saddle, bridle, and horse and saddle blankets.

Travel and vacation plans also influence purchases. Individuals who travel to island resorts to relax and enjoy themselves require different products than those who enjoy cycling and pack their clothes and other vacation supplies on a bike as they ride from place to place.

Wardrobe size and variety also affects needs and expectations. One person may own four or five pairs of black slacks or pants, with each pair differing in weight, texture, styling, and fabrication. Someone else may own only one pair of black slacks, and a third person might own several identical pairs of black slacks. Each of these individuals has developed a wardrobe to meet particular needs.

The manner in which individuals clean, repair, and store textiles influences purchases. For example, women often pay more when blouses are dry cleaned compared to the costs for cleaning men's shirts. Alterations of women's apparel tends to be more expensive than that for men's apparel. Some individuals replace an item when they lose a button. Someone else might replace the lost button or replace all the buttons on a product if they are unable to match the lost button. Both ways of dealing with the lost button have an impact on the market.

Psychographics

Psychographics is a more difficult aspect of target markets to define. Psychographics describes the social and psychological aspects of apparel, furnishings, and other textile products. Important factors include individual self-concept and self-esteem, body image, personal values, interest in and attitude toward fashion, standard of living, and religious beliefs.

Environmental attitudes may force individuals to modify their purchases so that they only buy certified organic cotton in natural fiber colors, thus minimizing the environmental impact of their purchases. Individuals concerned with the quality of the environment may consider how products are packaged when looking for textiles. They also may decide to limit their purchases because the production of every product and the way it is used, cared for, and disposed of puts demands on the environment.

A background in textiles and apparel may make shopping more challenging, as knowledge of products increases and the desirable characteristics of textile products become more precisely defined. As a result, individuals become more demanding of certain characteristics and more discriminating in what they find acceptable.

Personal likes and dislikes influence shopping preferences, choice of store, and product type. Some individuals are far more likely to purchase products in pastel colors; others avoid pastel colors at all times. Some individuals prefer shopping at discount stores, some at specialty stores, some at outlet malls, and still others from catalogs in the comfort of their home.

RELATING TARGET MARKET TO PRODUCT ATTRIBUTES

A company needs to identify its target market in terms of demographics, lifestyle, and psychographics before it can begin to translate these factors into product and serviceability attributes. The ability to translate target market characteristics into product attributes for a specific product is difficult.

Let us consider a target market defined as a family of limited income, with some vocational education, parents in their early twenties, one or more small children, northern Midwest suburban location, a moderate interest in fashion, and conservative attitudes. Family members are avid watchers of televised team sports, situation comedies, and children's programs, and they are interested in crafts. This market may be more interested in products that are relatively low cost, durable, and easy care. Thus, a company that produces for this group would need to be extremely price conscious. Their products would probably incorporate cotton, cotton/polyester, or all polyester in fabrications that have good abrasion resistance, are strong, and do not require special care in laundering. Products would need to be constructed in a durable fashion and not incorporate any components that required dry cleaning. These products would probably be somewhere in the middle of their fashion cycle, but the fashion component would be modified to appeal to the more conservative nature of this target market. Because of the interest in crafts, a special trim, applique, embroidery, or screen print might appeal to this group provided that the addition did not add too much to the cost or affect care or durability.

Let us expand this to a specific product: tee shirts for a five-year-old kindergarten girl. This customer would likely shop at a discount mass merchandiser in the suburban community. The merchandiser is known for its everyday low prices and reasonably durable products. The tee shirts are made of either all cotton or cotton/polyester blends and are machine washable. Some of the tee shirts are solid colors, some have lace trim and ribbons or embroidery, and some incorporate screen prints of currently popular children's cartoon characters. No doubt this customer would find at least one product in this retailer's offerings that would satisfy requirements for a girl's tee shirt.

Product attributes are driven by a need or an expectation that a customer has for a product. Thus, it is extremely important for companies to recognize customer expectations. Conformance to product requirements may not be sufficient, especially if specific customer needs are not recognized. However, the company's business objectives also must be met during this process or the company will not be successful.

IDENTIFYING PRODUCT ATTRIBUTES

Once a company has a clear understanding of its target market, it can begin to define or describe the attributes of specific textile products that would appeal to that market. **Serviceability** describes how well a product satisfies customer needs. Serviceable textile products are those that meet customer needs and performance expectations.

Customer needs may include physical characteristics that can be measured in a laboratory using a specific piece of equipment following a detailed written procedure. Abrasion resistance of fabrics is an example of such an attribute. Many specialized procedures and pieces of equipment have been developed to measure abrasion resistance. Other physical characteristics can also be assessed in a specialized lab. These characteristics and evaluation procedures will be discussed in greater detail in Part II.

Customer needs also include less measurable components, such as fit. The fit of a garment varies from customer to customer. Although two customers may have the same circumference measurements, a garment may fit one customer but not another. Garment fit is one of the attributes an individual evaluates when trying on a garment. Some customers are more critical in terms of fit than others. Customer needs also relate to unmeasurable attributes, such as fashion. Customers indicate the success or failure of this attribute by the degree to which they purchase a particular style.

The components of serviceability include aesthetics, durability, cost, comfort, care, and appearance retention. These same components are often used as the basis for understanding textile materials because they address customer needs and expectations for textile products. This discussion will be expanded beyond that generally included in a textile book because the approach is to look at the entire product, not just at the textile materials used to produce the product.

Aesthetics

Aesthetics describes how a textile product satisfies the customer's needs in terms of appearance, fashion preferences, fit, and styling. Customers who value high fashion are interested in items at the forefront or beginning of the fashion cycle. Customers who prefer classic fashions may never be interested in a particular style or may be interested in a less extreme version of a particular style. Aesthetics includes characteristics related to how the components work together, and their impact on the overall appearance of the product. For example, does the interlining alter the way the collar rolls? Does the padding create unattractive lumps under the chair's upholstery, or is the heading stiff enough to support the draperies?

Aesthetics integrates many factors that deal with a customer's perception of the product. The pattern from which the components are cut is important. The various parts of the product must physically fit together so that the overall structure has integrity and creates an attractive or suitable appearance. In addition, the components must work together in such a way that the product creates an aesthetic appropriate for its end use. For example, does the facing extend far enough into the jacket front to support the collar and buttons? Does the wrap skirt fall open when the wearer sits? Is the pocket designed so that the facing does not show during wear and that contents do not spill out when the wearer sits or walks? Does the upholstery fabric extend far enough under the cushions so that the support fabric does not show when the sofa is being used?

Aesthetics includes workmanship. How was the item constructed? This includes, for example, how the pleats fall on a skirt or set of draperies, how well the plaid or fabric motif matches at seams or overlaps, the way buttons and buttonholes line up on a shirt or jacket, and the degree to which the dimensions of a symmetrical product are identical between its right and left sides.

Durability

Durability refers to how long a textile product will be usable for its intended purpose. Durability incorporates an element of time into the assessment. Some textile manufacturers have addressed this customer need in guarantees for their products for a specific time period, such as 12 months. In addition, some retailers have developed guarantees and company policies that focus on product durability and customer satisfaction. However, many textile products have no written guarantee.

Durability can be influenced to a substantial degree by how the item is used, cleaned, and stored. Hence, durability is difficult to define in absolute terms. Because of these issues, measures of strength and structural integrity are often used to assess durability. For example, fabric durability may be assessed in terms of strength and resistance to abrasion, pilling, snagging, and deformation. For carpeting, resistance to soiling, pile matting, and pile crushing may be measured.

The type of use and the kind of treatment a product receives influences how it wears. Expectations for durability may differ depending on whether an item is a high-fashion or a basic product. Compare the differences in a customer's durability expectations between a rug in the living room and a rug to be used as a bed for the family pet. For the living room, durability issues probably relate to maintaining its structural integrity: minimal shedding of fibers, good abrasion and snag resistance, and not buckling with use. Other performance issues might include color permanence and appearance and relate to such issues as no fading, soiling, pilling, or matting of surface yarns. For the pet rug, durability may relate to withstanding regular machine washing and surviving wear and tear from the pet. It is not likely that most consumers would consider the same rug for both uses.

Equally important is the durability of all components used in a product: fashion fabric, thread, buttons, zippers, lining, support fabrics, padding, and other materials. Durability is influenced by selection of the appropriate stitch and seam type to produce the performance expected for the product. Customers expect that seams will not distort or rupture with use. However, many customers would prefer that the seam rupture before the fabric tears because seams are fairly easy to repair.

Stitch and seam type frequently change from one part of a product to another because the stress on seams and performance expectations differ throughout the product. Several seam and stitch types are used because they differ in their production requirements, ease of production, costs, or performance. For example, the crotch seam in a pair of jeans experiences different forces and customers have different expectations for them compared to seams in the belt tabs on the same pair of jeans.

Other examples of durability factors include the bond strength of fusible interlinings or fusible support fabrics, the ability of elastic components to be stretched repeatedly without losing either elongation or elasticity characteristics, and the ability of zippers to be used repeatedly without disintegrating.

Cost

Cost refers to the amount of money exchanged for a textile product. Cost or price is used to differentiate and categorize many textile products. Mass merchandise price lines of better, bridge, moderate, and budget for many apparel and furnishing products suggest to customers that the cost of a product and its quality are directly related. Thus, better price lines are assumed to be the best quality and budget price lines are assumed to be the lowest quality. Customers have been led to believe that cost is an indicator of quality regardless of the quality of design, materials, or production.

Because of this implied relationship between cost and quality, cost may be a factor in how the customer assesses satisfaction with a textile product. Customers tend to have higher expectations for more expensive products. However, a common misconception is that better quality products are more expensive than lower quality ones. Customers may have unrealistic expectations for expensive goods and may not understand other factors that affect the cost of a product. Many studies have found that price is not necessarily related to quality. Often moderately priced goods are better in quality than higher-priced goods. In fact, customers of nondurable goods, including apparel, who rely on price as an indicator of product quality are recognized as engaging in a high-risk strategy (Riesz, 1978).

Customers assume that the price of a product is directly related to the inherent value of the item. Although this may be true in terms of intangibles, such as fashion and brand name, it does not mean that quality is equal to value or that quality is equal to durability. Often moderately priced products produce the greatest value for the amount paid.

Cost depends on many factors—the materials used to produce the product, labor, indirect factors, and overhead. It also includes fees for registered trademarks and licensing of copyrighted materials, such as emblems and cartoon characters. In addition, costs include advertising, services provided by retailers, such as alterations, and the ambiance within the retail store, including decor, music, computer animations, and videos. Thus, although cost may be related to product quality, it is not necessarily a direct or an obvious relationship.

Comfort

Comfort describes how the textile product interacts with the body. People most often think of comfort in terms of apparel, but comfort also is related to furnishings and some industrial products. Items that are comfortable allow consumers to use or wear them without thinking about them or being annoyed or made uncomfortable by them.

Comfort includes how the textile product affects heat loss or heat gain (insulate) and is important for apparel, especially active sportswear and outerwear, bedding, draperies, and insulation materials used in homes, offices, and factories. A product's ability to absorb moisture is important for apparel, toweling, and industrial wipes. Products such as umbrellas, awnings, and some outerwear are designed to be water resistant or water repellent. Some industrial products, such as awnings and pavilions, are used for protection from sun and rain and must be resistant to sunlight damage, mold, rot, and mildew.

Static build-up is a comfort problem that develops with some apparel, carpeting, and upholstery. It also creates problems in the production of textile materials and textile products. For these reasons, the ability of a fabric to develop static charges or static cling is an area that may be assessed by manufacturers.

Fabric hand is another factor related to comfort. Fabrics that will be in direct contact with the skin tend to have a softer hand compared to fabrics that will not come in contact with the skin. Comfort includes using materials in such a way that they do not create discomfort for the user or wearer. How often have people torn out care labels because they are stiff, uncomfortable, and irritating even though the labels are supposed to remain permanently attached to a garment?

Comfort is also influenced by how the item has been assembled. For example, seams that are excessively bulky can be uncomfortable, especially in certain areas of a garment. Stiff threads, such as the clear plastic threads used in some items, are extremely irritating when the cut edge comes in

contact with the skin. Rivets used in some denim garments and metal zippers can become very hot when dried in a drier or exposed to radiant heat
from the sun or a campfire.

Fit is also related to comfort. When fit is evaluated using fit models, it
is important for the model to walk, sit, and go through a normal range of
body motions while wearing the item. For example, coats that restrict arm
movement may make it difficult to drive while wearing them.

Care

Care describes how the product responds to the procedure(s) recommended for returning a soiled item to its clean and as near-to-new condition as possible. The effect of cleaning a product is evaluated from many
perspectives. For example, product dimensions are important: How much
does the product change in dimensions following cleaning and drying? Although shrinkage is most common, some items can stretch in one or both
directions.

Care also addresses how color is affected by cleaning procedures.
Problems include bleeding, fading, and migration. Pilling, snagging, fabric distortion, and yarn slippage can also occur during cleaning as a result
of the abrasion to which the products are subjected during agitation.
Metal zippers and buttons may tarnish with some compounds used in
cleaning.

The ability of fabrics to resist soil is an important attribute in carpets,
rugs, upholstery, and fabrics with wrinkle-free resin finishes. The way fabrics with wrinkle-free finishes respond to cleaning is also important, as
these fabrics tend to hold on to oily soils tenaciously. Ring-around-the-col-
lar is an example of a soil that is difficult to remove from cotton shirts that
have been treated to be wrinkle free.

Changes in product features, such as pleats, creases, seams, pockets,
collars, and plackets, are also important. Some of these features can undergo drastic changes during cleaning. Some plackets and collars become
very soft and lose most of their aesthetic appeal after washing. Although
care labels are required for many textile products, some labels are not correct for the item. Others may be unrealistic or confusing. For example,
how should a consumer clean a red-and-white striped tee shirt with a care
label that reads "wash bright colors separately?"

Appearance Retention

Appearance retention describes the degree to which a textile product retains its original appearance during storage, use, and care. Performance
characteristics include resistance to color change regardless of any degrading factors to which a product may be exposed. One problem that occurs
fairly frequently with some product or fabric types is yellowing. This problem can develop before the consumer ever sees the product. Some early

abraded denim jeans turned yellow or developed a green cast while in the distribution center waiting to be shipped to the retailer or consumer.

Aging of components can distract from the appearance of the item. For example, adhesives used in applying fusible interlinings may darken and stiffen with age. Wrinkling in use and care is another appearance-retention factor. Creases from packaging of some items may be difficult to remove either by retailers, as they prepare items for display on the selling floor, or by consumers after purchase of an item.

Also of importance is the relationship among the fabric structure, the way the fabric was used in the product, and the storage method. For example, when placed on hangers, knit and bias-cut garments may stretch, while bulky loose knits are likely to develop a shoulder bubble.

CUSTOMER PERCEPTIONS OF QUALITY

Customer perceptions of quality consider the materials and production techniques used in the product, the uniformity or consistency across similar products, the fashion statement inherent in the design of the product, and the cost or price of the product. Of these factors, the least valid in terms of product quality is cost. In spite of several studies that have demonstrated that product cost does not reflect product quality (Dardis, Spivak, & Shih, 1985; Gerstner, 1985; Norum & Clark, 1989), individual consumers continue to rely on price as an indicator of product quality.

Companies need to recognize the existence of this cost-quality perception when developing business plans and studying their customers. Each company considers a specific target market as its customer. Quality is as important for the industry customer as it is for the consumer who buys the finished product for personal use. For example, a company that produces buttons is a customer of metal, plastic, leather, wood, and other materials used in buttons; the equipment used to produce the buttons; materials used to package buttons for sale to the target market; and services, such as shipping, collection of recyclable materials, and data processing. The button producer has certain expectations for the quality of the materials, equipment, and services it uses. The target market for buttons may include apparel manufacturers, furniture manufacturers, wholesalers for fabric and craft stores that sell to individuals, and other companies that use buttons in making products. Button producers that sell to apparel manufacturers produce buttons of a very different nature from those sold to manufacturers of upholstered furniture. Button producers often do not describe the individual consumer as their target market nor do suppliers commonly sell directly to individuals, except to dispose of odd lots or seconds. However, successful companies consider the needs of the individual consumer, so that the buttons meet the ultimate customer's expectations. From a consumer's perspective, button failure could include cracking, chipping, breaking, tarnishing, rusting, bleeding, fading or discoloring, or shanks cutting through sewing threads.

Regardless of the company, customer satisfaction must be based on an understanding of the target market. Although the button supplier has no control over the other materials used in the finished textile product or over the assembly of that product, the supplier does have control over the buttons and must ensure that the button's attributes are satisfactory to both the direct customer (the apparel or furniture producer) and the ultimate consumer. If the button fails in the ultimate consumer's hands, the entire product may be assessed as unsatisfactory by that consumer. Failure of one component or material can result in failure of an entire product, regardless of the success of the many other components or materials used in the product.

PERFORMANCE EXPECTATIONS

Deming states that quality is measured by the interaction among three participants: the product, the user, and training of the user or support during the life of the product. Product refers to the textile product. User refers to the way the product is used and cared for and the expectations the user developed for the product as a result of external factors. Training and support refer to instructions for use or care, service for repair, and availability of replacement parts. Figure 2-5 illustrates the connections between consumer (customer) expectations and perceptions of product performance.

Customers tend to develop expectations for a product based on a holistic perspective that includes numerous factors, such as cost, comfort, durability, fashion, end use, and perceptions of others. This holistic perspective is especially true of textile products, where fashion for apparel and furnishings is an important element. Customers develop their performance expectations based on previous experiences with similar products, information from family members and friends, and assumptions regarding trade names, brand names, fiber content, fabric type, and color.

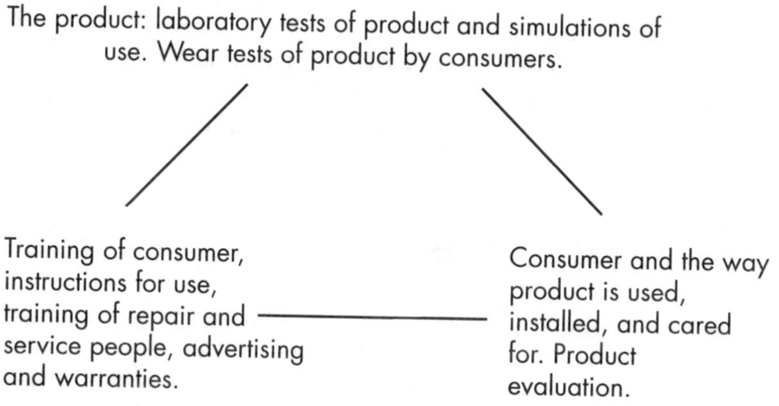

The product: laboratory tests of product and simulations of use. Wear tests of product by consumers.

Training of consumer, instructions for use, training of repair and service people, advertising and warranties.

Consumer and the way product is used, installed, and cared for. Product evaluation.

Figure 2-5
The three corners of quality. (Based on the model in Deming, 1986, p. 177.)

One of the problems with customer expectations is that many customers have an extremely limited knowledge of textiles. Some of that knowledge may be incorrect. In addition, customers may be somewhat biased in their perspective on textiles and textile products. Thus, their expectations for product performance might be skewed in unrealistic directions. For example, when acid-washed denims were first introduced, manufacturers did not help customers understand how the fashion look was achieved. Thus, customers unrealistically expected that the frosted denim jeans would perform as well and last as long as untreated denim jeans. This was not the case; zipper tape disintegrated, fabric turned yellow or green, and severe fraying occurred at the fly area and along seams, hems, and pockets. Customer satisfaction with the performance of cotton denim jeans plummeted. However, because the frosted look was a significant fashion look, customers continued to buy products with this finish and the industry learned to modify the finish so that customers received reasonable performance from the product. Customer satisfaction with this fashion product increased.

PRODUCT PERFORMANCE IN CUSTOMERS' HANDS

The customer remains the ultimate judge of product quality and performance. One of the major problems that businesses have is understanding what customers look for, how they evaluate tangible and intangible attributes of a product, and what their evaluation means in terms of both satisfaction and market behavior. Customer perception of product performance may change as information, experience, and other factors accumulate.

Assessment of performance is related not only to physical attributes, but also to other, more abstract factors. Fabric, for example, is a physical attribute that contributes to more abstract concepts in terms of product satisfaction. Something as apparently simple as fabric durability can have far-reaching consequences. Fabric that is perceived to be durable may also be perceived as contributing to saving money, being worn for a longer time period, and helping the wearer develop a better feeling of self and positive self-esteem, looking good to others, and receiving respect from them (Hines & O'Neil, 1995).

These more abstract factors that are related to product performance and customer satisfaction are hard to define. Customers remain the ultimate judges of market success and failure. They are the ones who decide what to purchase and where to purchase it.

CUSTOMER SATISFACTION

Customer satisfaction is an attempt at assessing how well a product or service meets customer expectations. In TQM, customer satisfaction is a primary objective of a successful company. Thus, the company needs to know who its customers are in order to satisfy their needs. In addition, the company needs to have a good sense of what the customer wants in a product. Unfortunately, with many textile products, an assessment of product performance may not be developed before the product is offered on the market. Companies need to be sure that their business objectives do not conflict with customer satisfaction. Figure 2-2 shows that the customer evaluation process begins with the purchase process and continues throughout use of the product. Receiving high value for what is perceived to be a low price contributes to a satisfied customer. This is especially true if the customer evaluates product performance higher than originally expected. Figure 2-6 examines the effects of expectation and performance on overall consumer satisfaction with a product. Consumers tend to be most satisfied when performance significantly exceeds expectations.

One of the difficulties in achieving high customer satisfaction is that customers are often unable to articulate the product attributes that are most important to them. Customers frequently judge products while working with a limited amount of knowledge regarding the product and its set of attributes.

Unfortunately, an attribute that may be deemed of little importance in producing satisfaction may be of great importance in producing dissatisfaction (Swan & Combs, 1976). For example, zipper function may be of little importance when a customer assesses satisfaction with a pair of jeans. However, if the zipper fails, the customer might express great dissatisfaction with the jeans regardless of how the jeans performed otherwise. A major challenge faced by design companies and others who develop products is translating consumer or customer expectations into descriptions, characteristics, and performance requirements for the products they sell.

Customer satisfaction surveys attempt to identify issues related to products or services that did not meet customer expectations. The difficulty is in assessing how good is good enough for any particular product or service. Companies may ask customers to assess their performance on several levels: customer service, friendliness, availability of merchandise, low prices, product durability, and so on. When the assessment is based on a scale where 5 is good and 1 is poor, a rating of 4.2 might lead the company to conclude that

Figure 2-6
The effect of expectations and performance on satisfaction.

it has a well-satisfied customer base. However, surveys of this nature have three inherent problems: measures of dissatisfaction are very difficult to interpret, very little information is collected regarding market actions because of satisfaction levels (do customers adjust their purchase behavior based on individual assessment?), and surveys do not address critical issues related to sources of satisfaction or dissatisfaction (Goodman, Broetzmann, & Adamson, 1992). Thus, numerical surveys of customer satisfaction probably provide little useful information to a company. Surveys of this type do not ask the right types of questions and do not collect information that addresses issues related to customer satisfaction from a broader perspective.

Another difficulty in understanding customer satisfaction with textile products is that many of these products have a relatively short life span. Even basic goods may change as fashion changes or with the seasons of the year. Rapid product change is a given for many textile products, especially goods with a high focus on fashion. Rapid product change makes it extremely difficult to conduct a full customer satisfaction assessment; several seasons or years may elapse before the results of such a study are available. By that time, most textile companies would have changed their product line significantly as a result of changes in fashion, availability of materials, and consumer expectations. The results, therefore, would have little application.

Among textile companies, mail order retailers and companies that produce basic products are more likely to devote time to assessing customer satisfaction. For example, many mail order retailers focus on returned products. They recognize that return rates will be fairly high because the customer did not have the opportunity to assess hand, color, fit, texture, construction, and other attributes before purchase. Thus, these retailers often have lenient return policies, pay for return mailing of merchandise, and include instructions for returns with the initial shipment.

Mail order companies routinely compile reasons for returns by merchandise type and product category. Reports identifying the reason why each product was returned are shared with product development or product management teams to assess where or how a product can be improved to minimize future returns. For example, a mail order company may suddenly see an increase in the number of knit shorts being returned because of loss of elasticity in the waistband. The team may request that shipment of a specific style be stopped on future orders so that the cause of the problem can be identified and solved before more unsatisfactory products end up in customers' hands.

The American Society for Quality (ASQ) and the National Quality Research Center (NQRC) at the University of Michigan have developed an American Customer Satisfaction Index (ACSI) that attempts to address customer perceptions of the quality of goods and services that are used or sold in the United States and are available from selected companies and government agencies (Becka, 1994). This index is expected to help companies assess how well they are meeting customer expectations and identify where expectations are not being met. Other countries, including Sweden, Germany, Japan, and Singapore, have developed or are developing similar indices. Unfortunately, the ACSI includes only a few companies that produce textile products, so its application beyond those companies is limited.

PERFORMANCE MEASURES FOR COMPANIES

Companies measure their performance on a regular basis as part of their business plan to determine where they are and where they are going. They may assess gross income, sales figures by dollar or number of merchandise turns, productivity levels in manufacturing facilities, percent of seconds versus percent first quality in production, or some other measure that is designed to help them determine if they are making progress toward meeting their business goals. Performance measures are necessary to determine where a company is in relationship to its goals and determine what actions need to be taken. Companies need to be sure that the performance measures focus on gathering information that reflects real performance. For example, retailers that focus on counting number of units of merchandise sold and dollar amounts may not be gathering data that helps them plan for the future. Retailers that assess the type of merchandise that is selling versus the type of merchandise that is not selling may be gathering data that helps them plan for future action.

PRODUCT QUALITY

Product quality is one measure of a company's performance that should be assessed. Although product quality is defined in many ways, companies need to develop a method of incorporating a desired level of quality into the products they sell. They also need to develop a means of assessing their performance in meeting that defined level of quality. Aspects related to measuring performance in terms of quality issues will be addressed in future chapters.

PRODUCT DEVELOPMENT

Product development is the planned integration of creative, technical, and managerial processes resulting in products that are serviceable, producible, salable, and profitable (Kunz, Kadolph, & Fiore, 1997). Product development specialists must keep in mind the need to satisfy the target market and meet the company's business goals as they develop new products. When a company focuses on incorporating quality into the textile product from the initial design and engineering stages, several key elements must be incorporated into the process: pattern characteristics, materials, product specifications, fit, styling, company standards related to appearance and performance, and assembly methods. These key elements must be integrated throughout the process in order to produce a product that meets the desired quality level.

Although this list, at first glance, may appear to relate only to apparel, these elements relate to almost any textile product. Consider an upholstered chair. If the pattern pieces from which the upholstery and support fabrics are cut are incorrect, the textile components will not cover the frame and padding completely or correctly. This lack of attention to pattern pieces and fit may create a poorly fitting cushion or side panel and an unacceptable chair. The pattern for a loading dock cover of coated vinyl fabric has similar general demands for pattern and fit.

Each key element will be discussed in detail in later chapters, but it is essential that evaluation and assessment be integrated throughout the process. In some cases, evaluation and inspection occur within the company. In other cases, outside agencies, service or supplier companies, and customers are involved in the process. This product development process builds on the five-step Deming cycle and has become a fundamental practice of companies that compete in the market using product quality as a base.

CONCLUSIONS

For companies to compete in the marketplace, they must have an understanding of their target market, incorporate appropriate dimensions of quality for their product and target market, and maintain good contact with their customers. Good communication with a company's target market allows the company to respond quickly and efficiently to changes in the market. For companies to remain competitive, they must be customer sensitive and agile, and maintain a knowledge-based approach within the market. The company must be able to reconfigure products, services, and integrate expertise from other organizations. Many companies are addressing quality issues throughout the organization. Most of this book will focus on the ways companies define quality; incorporate quality into their products; evaluate materials, products, and processes; and work with their customers to improve satisfaction with both the products and services.

SUGGESTED READINGS

Abraham-Murali, Liza, & Mary Ann Littrell. (1995). Consumers' Perceptions of Apparel Quality over Time: An Exploratory Study. *Clothing and Textiles Research Journal, 13(3)*, 149–158.

ANSI/ASQC A3-1978. (1978). *Quality System Terminology*. Milwaukee, WI: American Society for Quality Control.

Bicknell, Barbara A., & Kris D. Bicknell. (1995). *The Road Map to Repeatable Success: Using QFD to Implement Change.* Boca Raton, FL: CRC Press.

Bradbury, Mike, & John Kent. (1994, May/June). Dynamic Response: Its Impact on the Textile Marketing Chain.

Part 1. The Fabric Supplier, Garment Maker, and Retailer. *Journal of the Society of Dyers and Colourists, 110*, 173–175.

Brecka, Jon. (1994, October). The American customer satisfaction index. *Quality Progress, 27*, 41–44.

Brown, Patty. (1992). *Ready-to-Wear Apparel Analysis*. New York: Macmillan.

Card, David. (1992, March). Beyond Quality to Customer Satisfaction. *IEEE Software, 9*, 101–102.

Carruthers, Hamish. (1991). Design for the Market. In *Textile World at a Crossroads*. Manchester, England: Textile Institute.

Crosby, Philip B. (1979). *Quality Is Free: The Art of Making Quality Certain*. New York: McGraw-Hill.

Dardis, Rachel, Steven M. Spivak, & Chi-Mei Shih. (1985). Price and Quality Differences for Imported and Domestic Men's Dress Shirts. *Home Economics Research Journal, 13(9)*, 391–399.

Deming, W. Edwards. (1982). *Quality, Productivity, and Competitive Position*. Cambridge, MA: Massachusetts Institute of Technology, Center for Advanced Engineering Study.

Deming, W. Edwards. (1986). *Out of the Crisis*. Cambridge, MA: Massachusetts Institute of Technology, Center for Advanced Engineering Study.

Garvin, David A. (1984, Fall). What Does "Product Quality" Really Mean? *Sloan Management Review, 26*, 25–43.

Garvin, David A. (1987, November/December). Competing on the Eight Dimensions of Quality. *Harvard Business Review, 65*, 101–109.

Gerstner, Eitan. (1985, May). Do Higher Prices Signal Higher Quality? *Journal of Marketing Research, 22*, 209–215.

Glock, Ruth E., & Grace T. Kunz. (1995). *Apparel Manufacturing: Sewn Products Analysis*, 2nd ed. Englewood Cliffs, NJ: Prentice-Hall.

Goetsch, David L., & Stanley Davis. (1994). *Introduction to Total Quality: Quality, Productivity, Competitiveness*. New York: Merrill.

Goodman, John A., Scott M. Broetzmann, & Colin Adamson. (1992, May). Ineffective—That's the Problem with Customer Satisfaction Surveys. *Quality Progress, 25*, 35–38.

Hines, Jean D., & Gwendolyn S. O' Neal. (1995). Underlying Determinants of Clothing Quality: The Consumers' Perspective. *Clothing and Textiles Research Journal, 13(4)*, 227–233.

Juran, Joseph M. (1989). *Juran on Leadership for Quality: An Executive Handbook*. New York: Free Press.

Koksal, Gulser, William A. Smith, & C. Brent Smith. (1992). A System Analysis of Textile Operations: A Modern Approach for Meeting Customer Requirements. *Textile Chemist and Colorist, 24(10)*, 30–35.

Kunz, Grace I., Sara J. Kadolph, & Ann Marie Fiore. (1997). Product Development. Unpublished manuscript. Ames, IA: Iowa State University.

McKechnie, Jean L. (ed.). (1977). *Webster's New Twentieth Century Dictionary*. New York: Collins World, p. 1474.

Norum, Pamela S., & Lee Ann Clark. (1989). A Comparison of Quality and Retail Price of Domestically Produced and Imported Blazers. *Clothing and Textiles Research Journal, 7(3)*, 1–9.

Powers, Mary E. (1984). Textiles from the Consumer's Viewpoint. *Textile Chemist and Colorist, 16*, 228–231.

Riesz, Peter C. (1978). Price Versus Quality in the Marketplace, 1961–1975. *Journal of Retailing, 54(4)*, 15–28.

Rose, Kenneth H. (1995, February). A Performance Measurement Model. *Quality Progress, 28*, 63–66.

Scheller, Heidi P. (1993). The Meaning of Apparel Quality Through the Perceptions of Apparel Production Managers and Operators. Unpublished Master's Thesis, Iowa State University, Ames, IA.

Silverman, Lori L., & Annabeth L. Propst. (1996, July). Where Will They Fit in? *Quality Progress, 29*, 33–34.

Swan, John E., & Line Jones Combs. (1976, April). Product Performance and Consumer Satisfaction: A New Concept. *Journal of Marketing, 40*, 25–33.

Turner, R. Carroll. (1990). Wall-to-wall consumer expectations. *ASTM Standardization News, 18(7)*, 42–45.

Weir, George. (1995, June). Management by Knowing: My Customer Doesn't Know Quality. *Knitting Times*, p. 43.

Winchester, S. C. (1994). Total Quality Management in Textiles. *Journal of the Textile Institute, 85*, 445–459.

Zangwill, Willard I. (1994, June). Ten Mistakes CEOs Make about Quality. *Quality Progress, 27*, 43–48.

REVIEW QUESTIONS

1. Why is an understanding of quality important in today's market?

2. Differentiate among these definitions of quality:
   a. holistic perspective
   b. product perspective

    c. producer's perspective
    d. consumer's perspective
    e. value-based perspective

3. Describe two different target markets and describe how their expectations for a towel might differ.

4. For each of the products listed below, identify aspects of quality that would be important for one or more target markets.
    a. hazard fence of polypropylene
    b. study or reading pillow
    c. napkin for a formal restaurant
    d. slippers for use at home
    e. upholstery for a veterinarian's waiting room

5. Identify how consumers define their expectations for each of these dimensions of performance:
    a. aesthetics
    b. durability
    c. cost
    d. comfort
    e. care
    f. appearance retention

6. Discuss consumer satisfaction and how it relates to product quality.

7. Describe several ways in which consumers assess product performance. How do these assessments relate to product quality?

ACTIVITIES

1. Select a textile product and develop definitions for its quality based on these approaches: holistic, product, producer, consumer, and value-based.

2. Interview members of a selected target market and develop a definition of quality for a specific textile product.

3. Interview members of two different target markets using the same textile product and identify differences and similarities between the definitions.

4. Apply the Deming Cycle (Figure 2-4) to a project or assignment for a class.

5. Use a textile product you own and analyze your level of satisfaction with it based on Figure 2-6. Explain how the application of the Deming Cycle during the development of the product could have altered your satisfaction with the product.

6. Discuss the article (Weir, George. [1995, June]. Management by Knowing: My Customer Doesn't Know Quality. *Knitting Times*, p. 43) and what it suggests in terms of quality assurance and working with customers.

Chapter 3

UNDERSTANDING STANDARDS AND SPECIFICATIONS

OBJECTIVES

- To know organizations and agencies involved in developing, assessing, and verifying product quality and performance.

- To understand standard documents.

- To understand standards and specifications and their uses.

- To use appropriate information sources while developing standards and specifications.

- To understand the relationships among standards, specifications, and cost.

KEY TERMS

American Association of Textile Chemists and Colorists (AATCC)

American Society for Testing and Materials (ASTM)

American Society for Quality (ASQ)

American Apparel Manufacturers Association (AAMA)

Textile/Clothing Technology Corporation [(TC)²]

American National Standards Institute (ANSI)

International Organization for Standardization (ISO)

standard

standardization

test method

specification

practice

terminology

guide

classification

company standard

industry standard

voluntary standard

mandatory standard

international standards

minimum

tolerance

open specification

closed specification

target specification

functional specification

product specification

materials specification

process specification

inspection specification

test specification

acceptance specification

installation specification

use specification

maintenance specification

disposal specification

procurement specification

In an industry with so many segments, each with its own interests, communicating quality requirements and supplying goods of the appropriate quality level are difficult. As a result, individuals and companies with similar interests have formed professional and trade organizations that enable them to educate their members and enhance communication among industry segments. These organizations focus their efforts on identifying and defining terms, developing consistent practices within the field for describing and evaluating materials and processes, encouraging fair trade practices, developing technological advances to maintain competition in the world market, and promoting the U.S. textile industry complex.

To communicate their needs and expectations to the appropriate segment of the industry, many companies use documents called standards and specifications. These documents help them define and produce quality products, receive materials appropriate for their products, incorporate appropriate production methods, and meet their target market's needs.

ORGANIZATIONS

Professional and trade organizations engage in specific activities related to their objectives. Each organization focuses on a specific segment of the industry or on an issue that cuts across many segments. Although several major organizations are discussed in this section, other organizations may also be of interest in some product categories.

AMERICAN ASSOCIATION OF TEXTILE CHEMISTS AND COLORISTS

From its founding in 1921, the American Association of Textile Chemists and Colorists (AATCC) has focused on the dyeing and finishing of textiles. AATCC, sometimes referred to as A^2, is the world's largest association devoted to textile chemistry and the wet processing industry. It holds an annual international conference and exhibition. There are more than 7,500 members from 63 countries, 13 local sections throughout the United States, and 25 student chapters at colleges or universities. AATCC has approximately 90 national administrative and technical research committees that deal with various professional concerns, including performance and measurement procedures and technology.

AATCC develops internationally recognized standard test methods used by the industry, governments, researchers, and others. It develops procedures to assess the characteristics of materials and their performance in the areas of wet processing, dyeing, care, biological properties, and other related factors. These procedures are sometimes described as wet tests because liquids, such as water or other solvents, are used in preparing specimens or in the procedure.

AATCC maintains a cooperative relationship with other organizations and agencies and participates in activities with the International Organization for Standardization (ISO) to bring about uniformity in testing procedures worldwide. Many members work with other organizations, such as the American National Standards Institute (ANSI), the joint AATCC-ASTM Committee on Textile Testing, the Inter-Society Color Council, and the United States National Committee of the Commission Internationale de l'Eclairage (CIE). AATCC publishes *Textile Chemist and Colorist,* a monthly journal that includes current trade information and research articles, an annual *Buyer's Guide* that includes names and addresses of chemical suppliers to the textile industry, an annual *Technical Manual* of testing procedures, an annual *Membership Directory,* conference and symposia papers, filmstrips, quality assurance aids, and specialized reference books for the wet processing industry. AATCC also offers workshops related to wet processing and product or process evaluation. AATCC and its sister society in England, The Society of Dyers and Colourists, collaborate in publishing the *Colour Index,* a standard reference book that includes information on dyes and pigments.

AATCC standard test methods are developed by research committees after extensive investigation and interlaboratory comparisons. Development or extensive revision of a procedure reflects several years of work. Test methods are approved by a three-level hierarchy before they are published in the *Technical Manual.* A test method is reviewed annually for its first three years of existence. After that, it is reviewed every five years and is reaffirmed, revised, or withdrawn.

AMERICAN SOCIETY FOR TESTING AND MATERIALS

The American Society for Testing and Materials (ASTM) is the world's largest nongovernmental standards writing body. ASTM is an organization that deals with materials used in many industries, and its interests extend beyond textiles into such areas as medical devices, building materials, and water and environmental technology. Established in 1898, ASTM is one of the oldest professional organizations in the United States. ASTM consists of more than 130 technical committees, is international in scope, and supports the work of the National Institute of Standards and Technology. ASTM publishes an *Annual Book of Standards* of one or more volumes for each of its 16 major interest areas, a monthly magazine, *Standardization News,* several technical journals, and special technical publications.

ASTM Committee D-13 focuses on textiles; other committees focus on other materials or products, such as leather and building materials. ASTM procedures are used to identify physical characteristics and assess performance related to physical-mechanical procedures. These procedures are often referred to as dry procedures because the materials are most often tested in the dry state and performance related to most wet-processing finishing and dyeing procedures is not part of ASTM's area of interest. The organization also works with industry, government, and others interested in developing uniform standards.

ASTM standards are full-consensus standards. This means that a standard results when a full consensus of all concerned parties is met. Proposed standards and revisions are voted on by ASTM voting members. Once the standard has been approved, it is included in the *Annual Book of Standards.* All interested individuals participate in the development and/or use of the standard. ASTM requires that all standards be reviewed by the appropriate committee every five years, so that each standard reflects current thinking and practices within the industry. During the review process, the committee recommends that the standard be reaffirmed, revised, or withdrawn. Once again, before any action can occur, full consensus must be attained. Standards are used voluntarily and are not legally binding unless they become incorporated in laws or regulations or are cited in contracts.

ASTM has no certification program, but standards sometimes are used in certifying products. Products may carry labels indicating that a product was certified following an ASTM procedure. This means that a standard ASTM procedure was followed and that the product met or exceeded a minimum level of performance established by another group completely separate from ASTM.

AMERICAN SOCIETY FOR QUALITY

The American Society for Quality (ASQ) (formerly the American Society for Quality Control (ASQC)) is an organization of professionals who work to improve the quality of manufactured goods, services, and related factors. ASQ has developed a professional code of ethics to guide professional practices (see Appendix F). It has 15 divisions; the Textile and Needle Trade division deals with textile products. ASQ has eight technical committees and a certification program for professionals. The Society publishes a newsletter, *On Q,* ten times a year; *Quality Progress,* a monthly journal that includes articles on quality methods and important quality issues; and several quarterly journals that examine technical, theoretical, and practical issues related to quality. In addition, ASQ also publishes books related to quality issues. Two annual conferences are held:

one is a technical conference and the other deals with measuring customer satisfaction and quality.

AMERICAN APPAREL MANUFACTURERS ASSOCIATION

The American Apparel Manufacturers Association is a national organization that deals with issues of interest to the sewn products industry. AAMA holds an annual trade meeting called the Bobbin Show. It has several professional committees; the Education Committee helps educational institutions provide current information to and experiences for their students. The Education Committee also certifies colleges and universities that meet their standards in terms of courses, equipment, and faculty experience. The Apparel Research Committee reports on state-of-the art technology.

TEXTILE/CLOTHING TECHNOLOGY CORPORATION

The Textile/Clothing Technology Corporation $(TC)^2$ was established in 1981 as a coalition of leaders in the U.S. textile and apparel industry, labor unions, and government organizations; it currently has more than 185 member and associate member companies. $(TC)^2$'s focus is on improving the sewn products industry in the United States to make it more productive, competitive, and cost effective. It works with manufacturers to develop new processes, equipment, and implementation procedures.

$(TC)^2$ provides internships for faculty and students in production at $(TC)^2$'s National Apparel Technology Center. Innovations are shared with the industry at the Bobbin Show and other trade shows, through professional seminars and workshops, during on-site training visits to the center, and via its educational materials and computer simulations. $(TC)^2$ has been innovative in interactive video training that shows specific procedures and methods for technicians and equipment operators. It has also developed partnerships with several other professional organizations, including the American Apparel Manufacturers Association (AAMA), the National Center for Manufacturing Sciences (NCMS), the Association for Manufacturing Excellence (AME), and the American Textile Partnership (AMTEX).

AMERICAN NATIONAL STANDARDS INSTITUTE

The American National Standards Institute (ANSI), which is a federation of many organizations, agencies, and groups, coordinates all national voluntary agencies that develop standards. It has an accredited certification program. Certification attests that a product has been tested and meets specified requirements. These requirements are usually based on minimum performance characteristics and often relate to such health and safety issues as strength of structural steel components used in bridges and buildings.

Many ASTM procedures have been approved by the ANSI, and this is indicated in the designation of the test method. Very few textile products go through a professional certification program such as that offered by ANSI.

INTERNATIONAL ORGANIZATION FOR STANDARDIZATION

The International Organization for Standardization (ISO) coordinates many voluntary standardization organizations worldwide. Two ISO programs have a major impact on international trade.

The ISO 9000 quality management standards are accepted in many parts of the world. In many countries, a company must be ISO 9000 certified in order to trade. Many companies in the United States and other countries have become ISO 9000 certified just to maintain access to these markets. Certification indicates that a company has met the criteria for a quality system that is well understood by all employees of the company. Documentation exists for various activities, including design, purchasing, process control, inspection, record keeping, delivery, and storage. Outside audits are conducted periodically to evaluate the system. Benefits of ISO certification include eliminating unproductive work, reducing costs, providing a competitive advantage for companies, promoting teamwork within the company, and developing a better understanding of processes and responsibilities throughout the company.

The ISO 14000 environmental management program enables any organization or company to formulate, implement, and audit policies related to their impact on the environment. Companies use ISO 14000 registration as a means of showing regulatory compliance with and commitment to environmental protection.

OTHERS

The National Institute of Standards and Technology (NIST) is a federal agency that coordinates activities related to science and technology. Working with the development of standards is one area of interest to the NIST.

The American Textile Manufacturer's Institute, Inc. (ATMI) represents textile producers from fiber producers to fabricators and finishers to marketing companies. ATMI's areas of interest include government relations, international trade, and economic and educational information. ATMI works with other organizations, such as AATCC and AAMA. It also sponsors an annual textile tour for educators in textiles and clothing.

The Industrial Fabrics Association International (IFAI) represents the industrial fabrics industry. This group includes companies that produce fabric structures, sails, tarpaulins, sleeping bags, conveyor belts, and other industrial products. These products are sewn products and deal with many quality issues similar to those of interest to apparel and furnishing companies.

The International Fabricare Institute (IFI) deals with issues related to commercial dry cleaning and laundering of apparel and furnishings. IFI issues technical bulletins, offers classes on dry cleaning and industrial or commercial laundering, and has a research lab that deals with complaints and process improvements for the commercial care industry.

STANDARDS AND SPECIFICATIONS

Many companies have established sets of expectations for the products they produce or sell. These expectations describe various factors, including the sizes or size range, features or style components, appearance aspects, materials, and performance. Expectations may exist in a written and organized form, in a series of memos from various individuals within the company, or in an unwritten form. These expectations may be stated in general terms, or they may incorporate very specific numerical descriptions. Companies that are committed to quality are far more likely to have compiled their expectations in an organized, detailed written quality assurance manual. Quality assurance manuals may be used within the company, by outside vendors or suppliers, by both groups, or by companies that have no connection with the author company. Companies such as the JCPenney Company are so well known within the industry that their standards have been adapted for use by many companies beyond those with which it does business.

STANDARDS

Standards are commonly agreed upon aids for communication and trade. **Standards** are "a set of characteristics or procedures that provide a basis for resource and production decisions" (Glock & Kunz, 1995, p. 133). The term standard can be used to describe a wide range of things. A standard language is a common language that promotes the exchange of information. Whenever you study a new subject, you begin by learning the terminology and language of that field. For example, with a beginning course in textiles, you have begun to learn the terms that are used to communicate specific information about textiles.

Standards are used in defining weights and measures. For example, one calorie is equal to the amount of heat needed to raise the temperature of one gram of water one degree centigrade. **Standardization** is the process of developing and applying rules for a consistent and uniform approach to a specific activity for the benefit and with the cooperation of all concerned. Thus, standardization involves a series of actions by a group of individuals who work toward a specific goal. Developing a consistent and uniform way of presenting data in tables for a paper written as a team project for a class is an example of standardization.

Standards are used to set forth practices and expectations in the field. They are used to describe characteristics of a product in a precise and consistent fashion. They help describe a minimum level of performance and a minimum level of safety. Standards for seat belts have been developed to minimize the potential for injury or death in case of a vehicular accident. Stop lights and stop signs have been standardized so that almost everyone immediately understands the meaning conveyed by their combination of color, shape, and arrangement.

Standards facilitate commercial communication because they convey information about a product or material in a consistent manner. When technological advances are incorporated into standards, they are more readily adapted and used by others. For example, VICS (Voluntary Interindustry Communication Committee) has been instrumental in advancing the use of bar coding of products and the standardization of electronic data transmission. Bar coding helps companies locate products in distribution centers and keep track of inventory.

Production efficiency is enhanced by standardization of parts, processes, and products, because it enables economies of scale in production. Identical parts are interchangeable among products. Theoretically, parts cut from the same pattern are interchangeable. With multiple layer spreading and cutting in the sewn products industry, part A from the top layer should be interchangeable with part A from the eighth or any other layer. This efficiency benefits consumers. For example, when it is time to replace a lightbulb, we do not take the lamp to the store to check that the bulb will fit. Time is saved during production because various parts are used to produce a product, but the operators do not need to combine parts cut from the same layer of fabric.

Standardization allows for enhanced competition. When products and features conform to one standard, it is easier for consumers to compare products. Competition is sharper and companies work harder to remain competitive. Process management is also enhanced. Design is done according to standards. In addition, the company is organized so that its products meet standards.

Public welfare also benefits. Standards are used to protect health and environmental quality and promote safety. For example, federal laws have defined acceptable flammability performance standards for selected textile products.

Developing Standards

Standards are developed with the cooperation of various interest groups, such as producers, suppliers, manufacturers, government agencies, and consumers, because a need is perceived within an industry, a company, or another area of interest. Often a standard reflects one company's interest that has been adapted or widened to reflect a wider range of applications. Standards within an industry reflect a consensus of opinion among the interested parties about procedure, application, analysis, and related factors. Standards are examined, evaluated, and revised many times before they are acceptable to all groups. Periodic review, modifications, and revisions reflect changes in approaches, related procedures or documents, instrumentation, and customer expectations.

Types of Standards

ASTM develops six types of full-consensus standards: test methods, specifications, practices, terminology, guides, and classifications. Table 3-1 provides definitions of each type. It is important that you know their differences and similarities, as these terms will be used throughout this book. In addition to these six standards, other standards are used in industry.

A **company standard** reflects a consensus among employees for products or services provided. Company standards are used throughout the company in product development, production, purchasing, and quality assurance. Company standards often describe general characteristics or features of a product or service or they describe a required level of performance. A company standard for a knit shirt might incorporate many details, such as the expectation that all shoulder seams include a reinforcing tape to minimize stress damage. Company standards often include fabric characteristics, materials used in the product, fit of the product, and production methods used to make the product. A company standard for service might include the expec-

---

Table 3-1
ASTM FULL CONSENSUS STANDARDS

test method: a definitive procedure for the identification, measurement, and evaluation of one or more qualities, characteristics, or properties of a material, product, system, or service that produces a test result.

specification: a precise statement of a set of requirements to be satisfied by a material, product, system, or service that indicates the procedures for determining whether each of the requirements is satisfied. They often are given as numerical requirements with appropriate units and within reasonable limits.

practice: a definitive procedure for performing one or more specific operations or functions that does not produce a test result. These are not down-graded tests. They include statistical procedures, writing statements on precision, and selecting, installing, and operating equipment.

terminology: a document comprising definitions of terms; descriptions of terms; and explanations of symbols, abbreviations, or acronyms.

guide: a series of options or instructions that do not recommend a specific course of action. Guides suggest approaches, offer guidance for a procedure, increase awareness of available techniques and provide information regarding evaluation and standardization.

classification: a systematic arrangement or division of materials, products, systems, or services into groups based on similar characteristics such as origin, composition, properties, or use. Examples include fiber and yarn classification charts used in beginning textiles classes.

(Reprinted with permission, from the ASTM Form and Style Manual, 10th edition, 1996, copyright American Society for Testing and Materials, 100 Barr Harbor Drive, West Conshohocken, PA 19428-2959.)

tation that all phones are answered within three rings. Many companies that make materials for the textile industry or produce or sell finished goods have developed company standards for their merchandise or services.

Industry standards reflect consensus among many companies in an industry or among individuals members of a profession. Industry standards are not common in the textile industry in terms of product performance. Very few industry-wide standards exist for performance of materials, in spite of what vendors may indicate. For example, although some suppliers may state the industry standard for the shrinkage of rayon challis is 15 percent, no industry standard has been established for shrinkage performance for a specific fabric type. Standards are much more common in terms of materials. Many definitions of materials, such as the definition for a basic fabric like jersey, reflect industry standards. Another example is printcloth. There are several standard types on the market, so that companies can buy the type and quality needed for their products.

Voluntary standards allow individuals or companies to determine on their own whether to adopt a standard. ASTM standards are examples of voluntary standards. No organization or group forces adoption of these standards. However, voluntary standards may become incorporated into laws, regulations, or contracts.

With **mandatory standards,** adoption is required, generally by a law or regulation. Most mandatory standards relate to safety or health issues. For example, with textile products, children's sleepwear has to meet mandatory standards in terms of its minimal burning behavior. Any item of children's sleepwear sold in the United States must meet this performance requirement.

International Standards

Because standards have become so important to many industries worldwide, standards are used internationally to facilitate trade and technology transfer among nations. **International standards** describe a situation in which a majority of the products or services conform to the same standard regardless of where a product was produced or a service was performed. This situation usually implies that an agreement has been reached by the various companies, organizations, and governments involved. The goal of international standardization is to enhance product quality and reliability at reasonable prices; improve health, safety, and environmental protection; reduce hazards; produce greater compatibility of goods and services; simplify and improve product and service usability; and increase distribution efficiency (International Organization for Standardization, 1997). These goals are aimed at reducing technical barriers to and facilitating international trade.

International standards exist for many industries including information processing, banking, energy production, communication, and textiles. Often, standards that are widely used by one country involved in international trade become part of international standards simply because they are widely used in many parts of the world. These standards may be modified slightly or significantly in the process.

More than 80 organizations are involved in developing international standards. Examples of national standards organizations that work with ISO include the Japanese Industrial Standards Committee (JISC), the Standards Council of Canada (SCC), American National Standards Institute (ANSI), Standards New Zealand (SNZ), and British Standards Institution (BSI). Many of these organizations work with standards related to the textile industry complex. One of the benefits of international standards is that the variety of test methods, equipment, and staff expertise for evaluating materials and products is decreased.

CEN (European Committee for Standardization) includes the national standards organizations of the European Union (EU) and the European Free Trade Area (EFTA). CEN/TC248 is the committee that works with textiles and textile products. Although most international standards are voluntary, CEN/TC248 must replace conflicting national standards (Hall, 1994). Because CEN/TC standards are not necessarily ISO standards, a potential for conflict and trade difficulties exists when the organizations do not agree.

Application to the Textile Industry Complex

Standards reflect business objectives that deal with meeting target market needs and expectations. Thus, similarities in standards must exist among producers, suppliers, vendors, retailers, and consumers. Standards guide product development, materials selection, prototype analysis and refinement, production, finishing, labeling, packaging, shipping, and other activities within a company. They also reflect the characteristics that define quality for that company and are used to market products to consumers.

National standards relate to labeling and supplying information for consumers at point of purchase. International standards relate to information necessary to do business in a global market. ISO 9000 standards are one example. Companies may decide to write their documents in languages other than English and include measurements in both metric and U.S. units. Although the United States does not use the metric system, almost all other countries do. Thus, a company might need to describe filament yarn size in both denier and tex or dtex and fabric mass in oz/yd^2 and g/m^2 (grams per square meter).

Although many individuals talk about developing quality standards, that approach makes little sense. The purpose of standards and specifications is to incorporate the desired quality into the products that are produced based on those documents and requirements. Thus, one does not develop or write quality standards, but appropriate aspects of quality are incorporated into standards and specifications as they are developed. This perspective is key in developing products and services with a designed and built-in quality level. Quality cannot be added to products after production, so quality standards enforced at that stage merely separate first-quality merchandise from second-quality merchandise.

Thus, the company's focus needs to be on what factors contribute to a quality product and how to incorporate standards that address those concerns. A company needs to examine each element of its product and relate those elements to consumer expectations and satisfaction. Many divisions of a company will be involved in the process of developing and continuously examining and refining company standards. Marketing provides feedback from customers and may seek out information from consumers. Production analyzes the requirements and capabilities related to equipment, skills and training, costs, and quantity. Merchandising examines product requirements in terms of materials, products, and customer expectations. This information is pulled together and integrated to form the standards related to the product line. A company is likely to develop standards for size based on its basic blocks for patterns, grading rules to be used in developing the size range for each style, expectations for fit, performance of materials used in the product line, basic elements regarding the construction of the product line, special needs of the user, appearance of finished products, and packaging.

Product size is also based on basic pattern blocks. The basic block is important regardless of whether the company is producing apparel or not. The basic block is the starting point for developing the pattern for a specific style. It is the block and the grading rules used to increase or decrease the size that determine the dimensions of the finished product. A consumer may discover that one company's basic block fits her/his figure better than another company's basic block. The rules used within the company to adjust patterns for different sizes influence how a product fits. Many companies have developed dimensions that are acceptable for each size. These dimensions incorporate a plus/minus tolerance or range of acceptable dimensions for a size. Unfortunately, the plus/minus tolerance can overlap into adjacent sizes. Companies that produce children's wear and other small products must be especially sensitive to this problem. For example, if the chest measurement of a child's garment size 6 is 24 inches with a tolerance of ± 1 inch, then any chest measurement between 23 and 25 inches would be acceptable. If the company's size 5 has a chest measurement of 23 and the size 6X has a chest measurement of 25, a significant problem may result with overlap between these sizes.

In terms of product fit, companies may develop standards that describe a loose or tight fit, or they describe a combination of fit characteristics that focus on incorporating growth features for children's wear, aspects unique to petite figures, and so on. Fit standards must be consistent, so that the target market finds that the product fits in a constant and consistent manner. Some companies may combine some aspects of fit with some appearance aspects. For example, a company may have a standard that all side seams are perpendicular to the floor. This means that requirements for pattern, fit, and construction should address meeting this standard.

Performance of materials and product may be addressed by standards. In some companies, only materials performance is addressed. The assumption is that if materials meet the standard, then products will also meet the standard. That is not necessarily the case, because materials may interact in ways that decrease performance. Materials performance may focus on requirements for care; ability to be spread, cut, sewn, and finished in the production facility; durability; comfort; and appearance retention.

Terms commonly used by consumers may be included in standards. For example, care may be addressed by terms such as easy care, machine washable and dryable, or dry cleanable. Durability requirements may use terms such as strong, abrasion resistant, pill resistant, and long wearing.

Construction standards may address how components are assembled. Standards might be listed as: shirts always have a separate collar stand, hems are circular (side seams are produced first, then the garment is hemmed); and elastic is stitched in place. Construction standards may indicate that no exposed seams have raw edges or that all shirts have seven-button fronts. Construction standards do not describe the specific steps in production, but they address expectations for product characteristics and performance for consumers.

Special consumer needs may be addressed in company standards. For example, companies that produce trunk liners for cars may work with materials that are not sensitive to heat and cold, resistant to soil, and mold well to the shape of the trunk. Companies that produce buttons for men's shirts may focus on producing buttons that do not crack when subjected to pressure, heat, and steam in commercial laundry presses. Companies that produce children's wear may focus on incorporating features that enable children to dress themselves.

Company standards may also address the appearance of the finished product. Standards may be as simple as stating that fabric and thread colors match; buttons are always imitation tortoise shell, or hems do not roll. Because product appearance is one of the first characteristics that attracts the attention of the individual consumer, appearance should address those characteristics the consumer may consider in assessing products. These characteristics may be factors that the consumer conscientiously looks for, or they may include more subtle aspects. For example, consumers generally examine a product to verify that all parts look as if they have the same color and texture. If differences are too noticeable, consumers will not purchase the product.

Packaging is another area that standards may address. Many companies are developing packaging standards that follow environmentally friendly practices: fewer materials, more recycled or recyclable materials, and plastic bags and films of a certain type and weight of plastic. In addition, with increasing use of EDI (Electronic Data Interchange), use of bar code labeling is increasing. Standards in terms of location of bar codes and information incorporated in the bar codes is becoming more significant.

Standards are important for all companies, but even more so for companies that sell their products through print or electronic catalogs. For these companies, the written description and picture of the product must sell the product to the customer. Information that describes the product must be accurate and as straightforward as possible. Customers can develop a very good sense of company standards by reading catalog copy carefully.

Retail buyers accept vendor's standards when they buy merchandise or they negotiate changes in the vendor's standards when contracting for private label merchandise. The vendor is responsible for product consistency, and the buyer has recourse to the vendor if inconsistencies arise. One important observation is that many desirable characteristics of a product or service are not obvious or visible. These aspects require careful attention to detail, and in-depth knowledge of the target market, the product, and the process of getting the product from the design stage to the retail customer.

SPECIFICATIONS

A **specification,** or spec, is a precise statement of a set of requirements to be satisfied by a material, product, system, or service that indicates the procedures for determining whether each of the requirements is satisfied. Several key elements within that definition need to be emphasized.

Requirements indicate that these expectations are nonnegotiable. Requirements must be met for the specifications to be satisfied. For example, educational institutions have requirements for graduation in each major area of study. The requirements specify the number of credit hours to be earned, courses to be taken, and a minimum overall acceptable performance level or grade point average. Sometimes course substitutions and transfer credits may be negotiated, but the other two requirements remain firm. Students do not graduate unless they have taken all the courses listed (or acceptable substitutes), earned the minimum number of credits for graduation, and earned at least the minimum grade point average.

Specifications describe requirements. In other words, specific terms and numerical values with measurement units are listed so that it is clear what issues are considered important. The expectation for performance, quality, or condition is expressly defined. For example, if a specification addresses durability performance, a statement will describe a specific aspect of durability and a numerical value for that aspect. If abrasion resistance is the aspect of durability of interest, the numerical value might be set at a minimum of 350 cycles. This numerical value indicates that the fabric should not exhibit a hole until the fabric has been subjected to at least 350 cycles of abrasion. Fabrics exhibiting performance of 250, 300, or even 325 cycles would not be acceptable.

The numbers that describe expectations also address two important elements in specifications: minimums and tolerances. A **minimum** is the least or lowest acceptable value for any given parameter or dimension. In the abrasion resistance example, the minimum is 350 cycles. Anything less than 350 would not be acceptable. Establishing minimums can be a very difficult task because it is these values that encompass performance, appearance, and quality of the product.

A **tolerance** describes the range of acceptable values, or, in other words, it describes allowable deviations from specified values. In the abrasion resistance example, the range would be anything above 350 cycles. Tolerances may be listed in several ways: as a range from X to Y, as a plus/minus value such as $X \pm Y$, or as a minimum with any value greater than the value listed as being acceptable. Fabric mass often is listed as a range: 6.0 to 7.0 oz/yd^2. Any fabric that weighs between 6.0 and 7.0 oz/yd^2 would be acceptable. Fabric mass also might be listed as a plus/minus value: 6.5 $oz/yd^2 \pm 0.5$ oz/yd^2. To determine the effective range, 0.5 oz/yd^2 would be subtracted from and added to 6.5 oz/yd^2. Thus, the acceptable range would include any fabric weighing from 6.0 to 7.0 oz/yd^2. Fabric mass also might be listed as 6.0 oz/yd^2 or greater, indicating that any mass greater than 6.0 oz/yd^2 would be acceptable. Although minimums are more common in terms of performance, they are rarely used to describe the physical parameters or character of a product because there is usually an upper or lower limit that cannot be exceeded in terms of drape, cost, or other pertinent factor. For fabric mass, fabrics greater than 7.0 oz/yd^2 would be too heavy, costly, and bulky for a product that requires fabric ranging from 6.0 to 7.0 oz/yd^2.

A major problem with tolerances is that they can accumulate or stack up in a product. The result is an unacceptable product, even though no single specification is outside the acceptable limit. If a product or material consistently pushes the lower limit for performance, the final product may not satisfy consumer expectations. Thus, many companies require that their products and vendors meet specifications exactly. Vendors may receive a warning if a product drifts too far from the spec too often, even if it remains within listed tolerances. Tolerances are included when a range is acceptable. Not all specs will include tolerances.

The final key element in specifications is the inclusion of procedures for determining if the requirements have been met. The procedure, test method, or process must be identified in detail in the specification. In terms of materials performance, this detailed procedure can refer to a standard test method, such as those developed by ASTM or AATCC. In terms of other aspects, such as product dimensions, diagrams and detailed explanations or procedures may need to be included. Identification of procedures is critical, because they ultimately measure whether the product conforms to specifications and is acceptable to the company and its target market.

Types of Specifications

Companies develop specifications for a product or a material as either an open specification or a closed specification. An **open specification** allows for consideration of multiple vendors and includes a description of the character and/or performance desired in the product or material to be purchased. An open specification describes what is wanted and leaves the field open to any supplier who thinks that it can meet the requirements specified. Open specifications can include general information or very specific information regarding fabric mass, resistance to fading, or whatever performance and design features are required. An example of an open specification for fiber might be listed as 100 percent polyester, trilobal cross-section, 2.0 denier, delustered, crimped, and 1.25 inches in length. Any fiber manufacturer who produces a polyester with these characteristics could submit a bid. Open specifications are used to locate appropriate materials for production or sale that would satisfy the target market. Sourcing agents work with open specifications because they are looking for companies to supply materials or products that meet certain required characteristics and delivery requirements.

A **closed specification** specifies the exact material, component, or product by manufacturer or vendor and includes style numbers, trade names, or other specific identifiers. All producers or vendors except for the one specified are restricted from submitting a bid. Let us use the fiber example again. A closed specification might be Dacron ™ polyester, with a type number identified. The type number would be one that DuPont uses to describe fiber characteristics, including denier, fiber brightness, cross-section, length, and crimp. This would be a closed specification, because only the DuPont Company produces polyester under the Dacron ™ tradename. All other producers of polyester would be excluded. Closed specifications are used for production purposes, pricing, and for items that must incorporate specific materials.

Table 3-2 lists 13 types of specifications used by various industries. Some of these have little relation to textile products. Others may be combined when dealing with textile products. The importance of others depends on the company.

Target specifications relate to understanding the company's focus in terms of product type, price point, and target market needs and expectations. Target specifications for textile products may be stated in nebulous terms in the company's mission and philosophy statement. For example, a company that describes its mission as "We provide high-fashion, upscale furnishings for the discriminating consumer" incorporates some general aspects related to their target market and types of products produced.

Functional specifications for textile products relate to performance requirements. Recognizing customer expectations for products will assist in developing functional specifications. In addition, several laws and regulations incorporate functional specifications that must be met. For example, functional requirements in terms of flammability are defined by federal law for mattresses and mattress pads.

Product specifications include elements related to production: seam and stitch type, equipment to be used for each operation, and the aspects related to quality. This would include a description of each seam, the thread to be

Table 3-2
TYPES OF SPECIFICATIONS

Target: details the principal elements that should be considered during the design stage. Probably prepared by the marketing division.

Functional: describes the intended functional requirements for a product and may identify limitations. Probably prepared by the marketing division.

Product: describes the product to the extent necessary to make it. Includes details required of the various departments involved in the product's manufacture. Probably prepared by the engineering or production division.

Materials: includes details of materials used to produce a single product. Might include any associated processes. Will closely relate to target and functional specifications. Probably prepared by the design or product development division.

Process: describes actions that need to be performed during the processing of materials to bring them to final product stage. Probably prepared by the engineering or production division.

Inspection: describes the details of the various inspections that have to be carried out on the product at various stages of production. Based on the details in the target and functional specifications. Probably prepared by the production division.

Test: details any tests that may be required during decision making, manufacturing, and inspection stages. Need to pay close attention to the target and functional specifications. Probably prepared by the production, merchandising, or product development division.

Acceptance: identifies various criteria that will govern the acceptance of a product at various stages of production and at final acceptance upon completion of production. Probably prepared by the product development, engineering, or design division.

Installation: details instructions necessary for installing products on site ready for use. Probably prepared by the design or product development and engineering divisions.

Use: includes information and special instructions that users will need to enable them to use the product in its intended manner. Probably prepared by marketing with assistance from design and engineering divisions.

Maintenance: details the procedures to be followed to ensure that the product receives correct maintenance at required intervals. Probably prepared by the design and marketing divisions.

Disposal: identifies any special requirements in terms of disposal of the product. May be included with recyclable materials. Probably developed by the design and engineering divisions.

Procurement: provide a total picture of the what, where, when, and how expected of the product so that prospective suppliers know what is expected of them. Used by buying organizations to procure relatively complex products that must meet a variety of requirements related to materials, functional, inspection, test, and acceptance areas. Probably developed by the design, product development, and engineering divisions.

(Reprinted from Max McRobb, SPECIFICATION WRITING AND MANAGEMENT [Quality & Reliability Series: Volume 20], Marcel Dekker Inc., NY, 1989, by courtesy of Marcel Dekker Inc.)

used, seam type, stitch type, stitch density, and specifications related to the degree of matching required for plaids or when seams meet. For example, when arms-eye and sleeve seams meet at the underarm, should all four seams come together within ¼ inch, or is ½ inch acceptable (see Figure 3-1)?

Materials specifications for textile products combine identification of the characteristics of each material (its type, quality characteristics, description, and condition) with functional or performance aspects. For materials, this would focus on how the materials react to various conditions of use. Note that the focus is on assessing the materials, not on assessing the entire product. Functional specifications tend to focus on the product.

Process specifications address all processes, including pattern and marker making, spreading, cutting, sewing, finishing, packaging, and shipping the product. For example, what criteria are used to determine when a marker is acceptable? Product specifications should address issues related to product quality. For example, specifications for packaging might incorporate instructions regarding how many items should be placed in a box and what kind of labels are needed on the exterior of the box. These criteria are important for large companies that operate from distribution centers because of the space available, conveyor belt size restrictions when merchandise is moved from storage areas to loading docks so that orders can be filled, and in keeping track of merchandise deliveries.

Inspection specifications tend to be one of several types: in-process inspection, final inspection, or acceptance inspection. These specifications, which describe how and when to inspect products, will be discussed in Part III.

Test specifications may be incorporated with functional and materials specifications. Test specifications describe the procedures to follow in evalu-

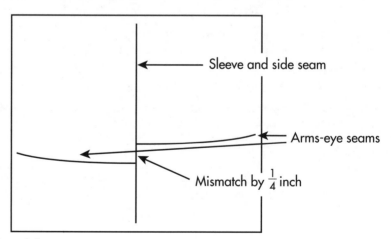

Figure 3-1
Product specifications: alignment tolerances for underarm seams.

ating the process or the product before, during, or after production. Testing done before production focuses on the materials—their character and performance. Testing done during production focuses on the processes and most often occurs during the finishing of textile materials. For example, production testing may be done in dye houses to evaluate color consistency and its fastness characteristics. Testing done after production often focuses on performance. Companies verify that the process and materials used have produced products that are consistent with those produced at an earlier time. For example, testing after production is common in yarn spinning facilities to assure that the yarns produced today are consistent in performance with the yarns produced yesterday, last week, and last year.

Acceptance specifications describe the frequency, type, and location of defects that will or will not be acceptable in the finished product. Acceptance specifications often address aspects related to appearance, performance, labeling, and packaging. For example, some flaws in a product might be acceptable if they occur on the underside of a collar, but would not be acceptable if they appear on the right side of the collar. Many companies have developed extensive acceptance specifications for textile products that incorporate great detail and clearly define acceptable limits for products. Table 3-3, for example, describes some defects that would be unacceptable for a towel. Appendix C, Assessment Guides, presents a more complete list of acceptance specifications.

Installation specifications most often relate to the installation of contract and home furnishings and industrial products. The type of carpet padding, the hanging of draperies and wall coverings, the way in which upholstery is cut all influence the customer's satisfaction with the product.

Table 3-3
PARTIAL LIST OF UNACCEPTABLE DEFECTS FOR A TOWEL

Any hole or tear in the fabric.

Any spot, stain, or soil.

Any irregularities of yarn or fabric structure that could result in a hole or product return.

Fabric must conform to stated performance requirements.

Stitching must be uniform, even, and conform to product specifications.

All thread ends must be clipped even with the hem; no stitch run-off allowed.

Incorrect labels in terms of information or placement.

Color should match the standard or fall within acceptable shade bands.

No roped hems.

For example, if a velvet upholstery fabric is used, the pile of the pieces must be cut in the same direction. If a print has an obvious up and down pattern, specifications regarding the way the material is cut and installed must be included. With many industrial products, the installation must be correct or the product will not work. For example, if a fan belt is installed incorrectly in a car, the fan will not run or the belt will break quickly.

Use specifications may not be included for apparel and furnishing textiles, but are often included with industrial products. Instructions for using textile products generally relate to safety and health issues. For example, tow ropes may include instructions for use. Air bags in vehicles should not be used with children or small or frail adults.

Maintenance specifications most often relate to furnishings and industrial products. This is especially true of frequency and type of cleaning for contract furnishings used in businesses and office buildings. Carpeting and upholstery often include maintenance specs.

Disposal specifications may be included for packaging materials used with textile products. Some products that can be recycled may also include specifications that facilitate this process. For example, some carpets made of 100 percent recyclable materials include disposal information.

Procurement specifications are a growing area for textile products. Retailers recognize the importance of quality and offer merchandise of a known quality level. They are beginning to accept responsibility for the quality of the merchandise offered for sale by their companies. Catalog retailers have been developing procurement specifications for several years. Other retailers, especially those who provide private label or store brands, are developing procurement specifications. These companies recognize that they need to be able to evaluate a vendor's ability to meet contract requirements in terms of delivery, quantity, and quality. The ability of a retailer to assess these aspects of a vendor are critical. Procurement specifications help retailers recognize critical aspects to be evaluated in order to identify vendors who can meet their criteria.

Application to the Textile Industry Complex

Specifications are used to describe the materials, procedures, dimensions, and performance for a particular product or style. They are more specific than standards, but reflect the standards. For example, if a company has a standard that all knit shirts for children will be machine washable, the specification describes the actual performance that will be acceptable. These specifications probably relate to aspects including, but not necessarily limited to, acceptable limits for materials in terms of dimensional change, color change, staining, and wrinkling and for products in terms of appearance of seams and collars, interactions of materials, minimal twisting of the shirt body, and no rolling of hems or collar points. Thus, the standard for machine washability has been translated into very definite and measurable specifications.

In developing specifications, the characteristics and the performance of the materials and the product should be addressed. It is not uncommon for specifications to focus on easily measurable characteristics that have little to do with the performance of the materials in production, the ultimate satisfaction of the consumer, or any other truly relevant point. For example, tensile strength is included in many product or materials specifications because it is easy to do and because many labs are equipped to assess strength. In addition, strength measures produce a good indication of batch-to-batch variation with yarns and fabrics even though the end product may have little need of that degree of tensile strength (Skelton & Petterson, 1983).

Specifications require a great deal of time and expertise to develop. It is important that specifications reflect company standards, costs, customer needs and expectations, and implementation abilities. Specifications that are inappropriate for the target market, vendor, or internal operations are a waste of time and skills, and can create significant problems in working with vendors and other outside companies. They need to be strict enough to produce the appropriate type of product, but not so strict that they make it impossible to work with vendors, find appropriate materials, or meet cost requirements.

As communication tools, specs describe the product in very detailed terms in a way that produces consistent products of a desirable quality. Specifications are used to negotiate bids and contracts. They describe what is needed, when it is needed, how it should be delivered, and what kinds of information should be included when delivery is made. They also describe how something should be done. After vendors have examined a specification document, they may request a meeting with the company to discuss it. Vendors may propose another material or process to be used. Sometimes vendor's suggestions are acceptable; sometimes they are not.

Specifications are used to purchase materials for use in producing the textile product. They describe the nature or characteristics of the material, its desired quality level, and its expected performance. Performance can relate to production aspects or its use in consumers' hands.

Specifications are used to communicate production requirements to production workers. Workers need to be informed of the requirements related to product quality, trained to produce that quality, and rewarded for production that meets that quality. This communication issue applies to all individuals who work with materials and processes involved in producing the finished goods.

Suppliers and vendors of materials use specifications to advertise their product lines and services. For example, it is not uncommon for vendors to indicate that they supply well-known retailers or manufacturers with materials or that they are certified suppliers for these companies. This information is used to demonstrate that a vendor or supplier has met the requirements of a large company. The implication is that they will be able to satisfy the requirements of other companies as well.

With private label merchandise, retailers set the standards and develop specifications to establish consistency. Figure 3-2 is a sample spec form that includes a variety of information related to private label merchandise. Contractors or vendors are responsible only for items or characteristics included in the specifications. Thus, characteristics, performance measures, production requirements, and all other details of importance must be addressed in specifications, because it is the specifi-

DL Sportswear

43874-V-neck Basketball Jersey with 4" Side Inserts - inches										6/1/97
	36	**38**	**40**	**42**	**44**	**46**	**48**	**50**	**52**	Tolerance
Chest Width	18 1/2	19 1/2	20 1/2	21 1/2	22 1/2	23 1/2	24 1/2	25 1/2	26 1/2	1/2"
Length - From HPS	32 3/8	32 5/8	33 7/8	34	35 3/8	35 5/8	35 7/8	36	36 3/8	1/2"
Length - From CB	30 7/8	31	32 1/4	32 1/2	33 3/4	34	35 1/4	34 1/2	34 3/4	1/2"
Hem Width	19	20	21	22	23	24	25	26	27	1/2"
Across Shoulder Width	10 1/8	10 1/8	10 1/8	10 1/8	10 1/8	10 1/8	10 1/8	10 1/8	10 1/8	1/2"
Neck Opening Width - CB to CF Curve	12	12	12	12	12	12	12	12	12	1/4"
Neck Opening Width - HPS to HPS	6 3/8	6 3/8	6 3/8	6 3/8	6 3/8	6 3/8	6 3/8	6 3/8	6 3/8	1/4"
Neck Drop	5 5/8	5 5/8	5 3/4	5 3/4	5 3/4	5 3/4	5 3/4	5 3/4	5 3/4	1/4"
Armhole	23 3/8	24 1/4	25 1/4	26 1/8	27 1/4	28 1/4	29 1/4	30 3/8	31 3/8	1/4"
B03 Braid (3/8" Wide) on a Roll										
K26 (2 3/8" Wide) Knit for Neck - cut 1	23	23	23	23	23	23	23	23	23	
K26 (2 3/8" Wide) Knit for Arm - cut 2	20	20	23	23	23	26	26	26	26	
Care Label	One per Jersey									
2" × 3" Size Label	One per Jersey									

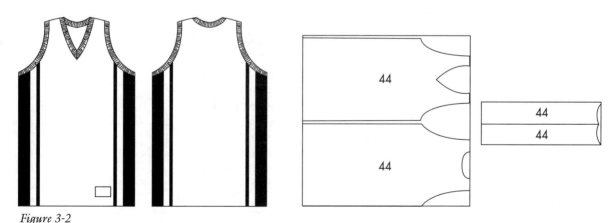

Figure 3-2
A specification form for private label merchandise that includes a product sketch and information related to product size, dimensions, construction, and materials.

cation that provides control over and determines the quality of the product or service.

Specifications are used to determine if a product meets requirements in terms of performance, size, appearance, construction, fit, freedom from defects, and so on. When they are complete and written at the appropriate level, they result in fewer rejected goods or seconds, less waste of fabric and other materials, reduced labor costs, more timely deliveries, and more satisfied customers. They are used as the basis of product evaluation and product inspection. More information on product inspection will be included in Part III.

DL Sportswear

Bill of Material   **6/1/97**
Style #: 43874
Description: Men's V-neck Basketball Jersey with 4" Side Inserts
Size Range: 36–52

Vendor Name	Material Description	Use	QTY	Color Codes
Game Time	100% Antron Nylon (DL #419)	Body		
DL Sportswear	3/8" Wide Braid (DL B03)	Decoration		Match Insert
DL Sportswear	2 3/8" Wide Knit (DL K-26)	Neck Opening	1.00	
DL Sportswear	2 3/8" Wide Knit (DL K-26)	Armhole Opening	2.00	
DL Sportswear	100% Nylon International Care & Content Label **Must Include Country of Origin	Lower Left Side Seam	1.00	
DL Sportswear	2" × 3" Size Label	Lower Left Front	1.00	

Figure 3-2 (continued)

DL Sportswear

43874   Men's Basketball Jersey, 100% heavy weight double knit Nylon

STANDARD: *Knit V-neck*
Coverstitched Neck & Arm Trim
Contrasting 4" Self-material Side Insert
3/8" Solid Braid (along both sides of insert)

SIZE RANGE: 36 – 60

CONSTRUCTION DETAILS:

STANDARD STITCH LENGTH: 8 stitches per inch   SEAM TYPE: 3 thread overcast (1/4")

LABELS: DL SPORTSWEAR SIZE LABEL: Set on lower left front panel 2" from front/insert seam & 2 1/4" from hem. Lockstitch all sides of label. CARE LABEL: Top edge of label caught in left front/insert seam 5 1/2" from bottom hem.

NECK OPENING: V-NECK RIB KNIT COLLAR: 3 thread overcast knit; clean finish rib seam. 2 needle coverstitch-1/4" gauge, straddle seam. 3/8" horizontal bartack on front body at point of mitered "V to reinforce.

ARMHOLE OPENING: 3-thread overcast knit; clean finish rib seam. 2 needle coverstitch-1/4" gauge, straddle seam. Set armhole rib seam at middle of side insert.

SIDE INSERTS: 2 needle coverstitch-1/4" gauge, straddle front/insert & back/insert seams.

BRAID: 3/8" braid set 3/4" from insert seams on front & back body with a 2 needle lockstitch-1/4" gauge.

BOTTOM HEM: 5/8" turn, 2 needle coverstitch-1/4" gauge, set 3/8" up from fold.

DL Sportswear

43874

OPERATIONS	MACHINE REQ.	COMMENTS
Cut & Bundle Knit Trim	Manual	
Piece V-neck Collar	Single Needle Lockstitch	
S/N Pre-set V-neck Collar	Single Needle Lockstitch	
Join Shoulders	3-Thread Overcast	
Close Sides	3-Thread Overcast	Care label in left side seam
Set Collar	3-Thread Overcast	
Set Side Braid	2 Needle Lockstitch	
Set Arm Trim	3-Thread Overcast	
Turn	Manual	
Coverstitch Insert	2 Needle Coverstitch	
Coverstitch Neck & Arm Trim	2 Needle Coverstitch	
Hem Bottom	2 Needle Coverstitch	
Bartack V-neck	Bartacker	One bartack
Set Label	Single Needle Lockstitch	
Inspect & Fold	Manual	
Bag to Shipping	Manual	

Figure 3-2 (continued)

SUGGESTED FABRIC SPECIFICATION DATA SHEET

To be prepared by fabric supplier and given to buyer at the time of sample submission.

Fabric Manufacturer: _____ Contract No.: _____ Date:_____

Fabric Brand Name: _____ Construction Name: _____

Fiber Content: _____ Special Finish: _____

YARNS:

Generic Title: _____ Size of Yarn(s): Warp/   Fill/

         Wales: _____Course: _____

No. of turns per inch: Warp/Wales: _____ Course/Fill: _____

Texture Type: Warp/Wales: _____ Course/Fill: _____

Construction Description:

Warp/Wales: _____ Course/Fill: _____ Finished Width _____ ± _____

Weight: Per sq. yd. _____oz. ± _____ Per linear yd. _____ oz. ± _____

End use of the fabric: _____

Property	Performance Level		Test Method
STRENGTH: Tensile (W/F) Tear (W/F) Bursting	Average	Minimum	ASTM-D 1682 ASTM-D 1424 ASTM-D 231
STRETCH: (W/F) %			ASTM-D 2594

SHRINKAGE:
1. Hothead Pressing (W/F)
2. Home Laundry &
   Tumble Dry (W/F)
			1. As agreed between
			   buyer and seller
			2. AATCC-124

ABRASION: Describe Method: 1. _____ 2. _____ 3. _____			ASTM-D 1175

Figure 3-2 (continued)

WRITING STANDARDS AND SPECIFICATIONS

Writing standards and specifications requires a thorough understanding of the product, the company, and the target market. It requires careful attention to detail, an integration of the impact of standards and specifications on product cost and quality, good writing skills, and the ability to function within a team. Standards and specifications are almost always written by teams of individuals who bring specific areas of expertise to the process. When developing standards and specifications, most companies make use of a database that includes all kinds of information about their products, sample products of competitors, and the cumulative experience and knowledge of their staff. Standards and specifications are never considered finished documents, but they undergo periodic revisions as changes occur in the products, the target market and its expectations, production methods, materials and equipment, regulations, and other factors.

SOURCES OF INFORMATION FOR SPECIFICATIONS AND STANDARDS

Numerous sources of information exist for developing and refining specifications and standards. Textbooks and reference books related to textiles, design, product development, flat pattern, and manufacturing include a great quantity of information. In some cases, the information may be basic, but it often includes specific details to illustrate concepts or give examples. For example, some introductory textiles books include information related to yarn size, yarn twist, and fabric weight for many basic fabrics.

A source of information related to performance of materials is ASTM. ASTM includes many recommended performance specifications for fabrics used in many product categories, ranging from apparel to furnishings to uniforms and career apparel to the textiles used in the hospitality industry to fabrics used for awnings and canopies (see Appendix G). These documents include several performance characteristics related to durability, care, appearance retention, and safety (flammability). Appropriate test methods and minimum numerical values are included for these selected performance characteristics. Because of the significant differences between woven and knit fabrics, separate values may be listed for these two major fabric types. Of course, individual companies are free to set their own values for any performance characteristic. However, it is helpful to see what values are recommended by a group of professionals. Many companies set their company specifications higher than these recommendations because their target market expects higher performance levels. It is important to recognize that these ASTM documents focus on materials used in these products. These documents provide no information in terms of product design, construction, appearance, size, fit, or interaction of materials combined in products.

Standard test methods also help in writing specifications related to the characteristics, quality, and performance of materials because these documents identify the information to be collected in performing the testing and the form and type of information to be reported when the testing has been completed. For example, when colorfastness to laundering is of interest, it is helpful to examine the appropriate test method to understand that the specimens should be evaluated for both color change and staining. In addition, test methods describe other information that should be identified in the results. Generally, when a test method specifies information to be included in the results, that information should be considered when developing specifications for performance.

Other reference materials include fabric handbooks such as the *Wellington Sears Handbook of Industrial Fabrics* and the *Swirle's Handbook of Basic Fabrics*. These two sources provide very detailed information regarding specific fabrics or applications. Dictionaries and encyclopedias are sources of basic information: *Fairchild's Dictionary of Textiles, Fairchild's Dictionary of Fashion, Hoechst-Celanese's Dictionary of Fiber and Textile Terminology,* the Textile Institute's *Textile Terms and Definitions,* and Grayson's *Encyclopedia of Textiles, Fibers and Nonwoven Fabrics*. These sources provide basic information regarding fabric types and definitions of terms.

Excellent sources of information are the products and the materials from which they are made. Sample fabrics and other materials can be used to develop basic descriptions of desirable materials. Sample products (those produced in-house, as well as competitors' products) can be used to develop standards and specifications. Many companies use sample or prototype products to develop their standards and specifications, especially in terms of materials, fit, size, and production. Understanding the materials used in a competitor's products and how those products are made also helps companies modify their products to remain competitive. It also helps the firm identify areas in which minor improvements could have a significant impact on product quality and business objectives. Finally, it gives them a better understanding of their competition.

Sample and prototype products are especially helpful in terms of identifying standards and specs for appearance, fit, size, and production. Standards and specs based on sample products undergo significant refinements and modifications as the product line changes and as the designer, product development team, and engineers who work with the products become more familiar with specs, standards, their product line, and their target market.

Another excellent source of information comes from the experience of the individuals involved in developing the specifications. Experience often incorporates significant professional knowledge and personal use of textile materials. Personal experience with textile products is of most help when the individual also reflects characteristics of the company's target market.

Vendor recommendations may be of use, but it is important to keep in mind that vendors may have a different objective when specifications are discussed. Vendors may be considering their capabilities and current operations and may be attempting to modify specifications so that they are required to make fewer changes.

A final and important source of information is the target market. Understanding what customers want in terms of product characteristics, quality, and performance is critical in terms of meeting their needs and satisfying their expectations. It is important to recognize two critical factors here. One, customers may not be able to articulate their needs in concrete terms. Thus, it is very difficult to develop standards and specs that truly reflect customer expectations. Products that have been returned by individual consumers can provide much helpful information in terms of areas for improvement. Unfortunately, this source of information may be lost between the retailer and the product development team. Some firms keep records regarding returns, complaints, and other problems, and consult these records when developing new products or when modifying existing products so that problems, shortcomings, other areas of concern, and wishes are addressed.

A second factor is that customer satisfaction surveys may not provide much useful information. Satisfaction surveys seldom provide sufficient opportunity for customers to describe in detail what they do or do not like about a product. In addition, it may be difficult to determine how the company can better satisfy customer needs using the results of such surveys.

POTENTIAL PROBLEM AREAS

Specifications can be the source of many problems. Faults with specifications relate to three major areas: words, ideas, and presentation (McRobb, 1989). Table 3-4 identifies types of faults in each area.

The quality of specifications can be judged based on their use and the ability of others to understand them. If a specification has been in use for some time and no problems related to use and interpretation have developed, the specification is probably of good quality. It is a good idea to circulate specifications to individuals inside the organization so that they can comment on the document. Sometimes outside comment is also helpful, but outside assistance may jeopardize security of the document.

The specification must clearly state requirements in a way that is easy for the user to understand. This is difficult to do. Often diagrams, illustration, photographs, samples, definitions, and examples are used to clarify specifications. But, care must be taken to assure that these aids do not confuse the issue. It is important that any labels, arrows, and other clarifications in documents are correct.

When words cause problems with specifications, it may be the result of poor sentence structure, the use of passive voice, or incorrect use of a word. For example, it is important that sentences be written so that the meaning is clear. Dangling participles, imprecise antecedents, and excessive jargon

Table 3-4
PROBLEMS WITH UNDERSTANDING AND INTERPRETING SPECIFICATIONS

Words	Ideas	Presentation
The use of words in nonstandard meanings	Lack of clarity/confused statements	Lack of consideration for the user
Changing meanings of technical words	Repetition	Unbelievable examples
Inconsistency in the use of words and phrases	Contradiction	Untrue statements
Grammar	Nonsense statements	Philosophizing
Incorrect text references	Dangerous extracts from other documents	"Reading across" and illogical ordering of contents in a specification system
Definitions		
Ambiguity	Excessive requirements	
	Multiple mixed specification systems	Poor visual material
	Chain specification systems	Unsatisfactory proofreading
	Multiple authors	Lack of an index in larger specifications
	Omissions	

(Reprinted from Max McRobb, SPECIFICATION WRITING AND MANAGEMENT [Quality & Reliability Series: Volume 20], Marcel Dekker Inc., NY, 1989, p. 18, by courtesy of Marcel Dekker Inc.)

make it difficult to comprehend the meaning and intent of specifications. When a term is used to refer to a specific parameter, it is important to avoid using the same term for another parameter. For example, in textiles, bursting strength and tearing strength refer to different measures. They are not synonymous terms. Terms that have meanings distinct to the specification should be defined. Once defined, they should be used only in that context.

Incorrect text references also create problems. For example, if a specification for fabric performance refers to section 7, then section 7 should deal with fabric performance. Otherwise, the user will have difficulty determining where the information is located. This is especially true if the user is not familiar with performance measures.

Ideas create problems with specifications when terms are repeated in the document with slightly different usages, statements contradict each other, or sections simply do not make sense. Word processing makes it easy to generate documents by copying and inserting sections from one document to another, but it also can create problems. The author should verify that the new section is appropriate, uses terms in the way they have been defined in the first document, and does not include sections of the previous document that do not relate to the current document.

Multiple authors can contribute to problems in the presentation of ideas. A single writer or final reader should be used to minimize these problems. Although errors may occur when specifications are developed, proofreading helps assure that the final document is error free. It is not wise to rely solely on a spell checker, because this component of any word processing program does not check for context and does not catch typographical errors if the misspelled word is itself a valid word. All parts of a specification that deal with the same topic should be incorporated together. Aspects related to performance testing of materials should be in the same section of the document. Parts related to product dimensions should be in another part of the document. Finally, for large specifications, an index is beneficial, especially because a user may be reminded of something stated in an earlier section of the document.

Presentation can create problems with specifications, especially if on first examination, the specifications appear impossible to achieve or make no sense. The credibility of the specification can be questioned if unbelievable examples or incorrect parameters are included. For example, if a fabric mass is specified as 50 oz/yd^2 ± 10% for a shirt, no one who works with fabric mass will believe it. The omitted decimal point created a problem in credibility. The correct mass should have been 5.0 oz/yd^2 ± 10%.

Valid specifications must meet the needs of the customer. Customer research will help identify and define their needs. Analysis and testing will determine if the product is able to meet those needs. Responsibility for each detail in a specification must be identified if the specification is to effectively achieve the desired product with the desired quality level.

EFFECTS OF STANDARDS AND SPECIFICATIONS ON COST

Standards and specifications for products and materials have a significant impact on final costs. For example, when specifications indicate a high level of performance in terms of durability, the fabrics, fasteners, thread, and other materials must be selected to meet that level of performance. Costs for materials of greater durability will probably be higher and, thus, the final cost for the product will be high. The same thing applies to standards. If production standards require that all shoulder seams be taped, then additional cost must be computed for materials (the tape), labor, and attachments for machines. In addition, costs for operator training and time to meet these standards must be included.

When minimum levels of performance or characteristics are high, costs tend to be higher. When minimum levels are lower, costs tend to decrease. Thus, the level at which minimums are set may have a significant impact on the cost of the product.

When specs are tight, costs are increased. Tight specs incorporate narrow tolerances or allow for very little acceptable variation. Tight specs may result in rejection of acceptable merchandise. Loose specs allow for a wide range of variations within the product. Loose specs decrease costs because more products are acceptable. However, loose specs may allow for acceptance of poor- or low-quality merchandise. In addition, there is less consistency among products, so consumers may be confused as to what commitment the company has toward product quality.

Managing standards and specifications can be a time consuming task. Managing includes developing, maintaining, publishing, and administering standards and specs. It involves editing and proofreading documents to see that terms, references, and examples are correct and consistent. It also involves constant checking to determine where errors, ambiguous statements, poor illustrations, and unclear language create problems with understanding and implementing standards. Many large companies have separate divisions that are responsible for managing standards and specifications. Thus, costs related to managing standards and specifications occur and must be considered as part of the costs of doing business.

CONCLUSIONS

Standards and specifications are used to define and describe the quality of the product. Because quality has become such an important factor in the success or failure of a company, it is necessary to understand how companies establish these standards and specifications that define product quality. Several organizations focus on textile products and contribute to standard practices that are used to define and measure the quality of products. Standards and specifications that help companies define quality for their products must be developed carefully, so that the information is clearly expressed and understood by readers. Companies must understand the impact that these documents have on their interactions with suppliers and customers and on the cost of their products.

SUGGESTED READINGS

American Apparel Manufacturers Association. (1978). *Guidelines for Purchasing by Specification and Vendor Evaluation & Rating System*. Arlington, VA: Author.

American Association of Textile Chemists and Colorists. (1996). *AATCC Technical Manual, 71*. Research Triangle Park, NC: Author.

American Association of Textile Chemists and Colorists. (1996). Buyer's Guide. *Textile Chemist and Colorist, 28(7)*. Research Triangle Park, NC: Author.

American Society for Testing and Materials. (1996). *Annual Book of ASTM Standards, Vol. 7.01 & 7.02*. West Conshohocken, PA: Author.

Benson, Roger S., & Richard W. Sherman. (1995, October). ISO 9000: A Practical Step-by-Step Approach. *Quality Progress, 28*, 75–78.

Clark, Mark H. (1995). Founding the American Association of Textile Chemists and Colorists: Louis Atwell Olney and the Professionalization of Dyeing. *Textile Chemist and Colorist, 27*, 14–18.

Corrigan, James, P. (1994, May). Is ISO 9000 the Path to TQM? *Quality Progress, 27*, 33–36.

Criqui, Francis L. "Tex." (1995, December). Competitiveness, Standards and the U.S. Automobile Industry. *ASTM Standardization News, 23*, 20–25.

Dale, Barrie, & John Oakland. (1991). *Quality Improvement through Standards.* Cheltenham, England: Stanley Thornes.

Davis, Helen. (1990, February). Standardization in Europe. *ASTM Standardization News, 18,* 34–37.

Ellis, Wayne. (1992, September). "Standard" Terminology: Definitions Alternatives. *ASTM Standardization News, 20,* 21.

Float, Leslie W. (1994, May). Quality Control: What Is a Standard? *Metal Finishing, 92,* 19–21.

Ford, J. E. (1993). Textile Product Specifications. *Textiles, 22(3),* 23–25.

Gavlak, Martin. (1984, September). Product Performance Specifications: A Retailer's Perspective. *ASTM Standardization News, 12,* 16–18.

Glock, Ruth E., & Grace I. Kunz. (1995). *Apparel Manufacturing: Sewn Products Analysis,* 2nd ed. Englewood Cliffs, NJ: Prentice-Hall.

Gompert, David C., & F. Stephen Larrabee. (ed.). (1997). *America and Europe: A Partnership for a New Era.* New York: Cambridge University Press.

Hall, Alan J. (1994, May). Developing International and European Standards. *Textile Chemist and Colorist, 26(5),* 17–18.

Hansen, Steven W. (1996, February). Using Standards in Defending Product Liability Cases. *ASTM Standardization News, 24,* 40–43.

International Organization for Standardization. (1997, June 9). Information obtained from the world wide web at http://www.iso.ch/infoe/stbodies.html.

International Standards, Conformity Assessment, and U.S. Trade Policy Project Committee, National Research Council. (1995). *Standards, Conformity Assessment, and Trade.* Washington, DC: National Academy Press.

Kalogeridis, Carla. (1995, September). Getting Committed to Textile Standards. *America's Textiles International, 242,* 244.

Line, Henry. (1993, November). Industry Standards: A Key Factor for Market Success. *ASTM Standardization News, 21,* 32–41.

Ludolph, Charles M. (1997, May). Winds of Change in Europe: Commerical Implications for U.S. Companies. *Textile Chemist and Colorist, 29(5),* 9–11.

McRobb, Max. (1989). *Specification Writing and Management.* New York: Marcel Dekker.

Merkel, Robert S. (1991). *Textile Product Serviceability.* New York: Macmillan.

Musser, Linda. (1989, October). Fibers &

Fabrics: Tracking Down Specs, Standards. *Industrial Fabric Products Review, 17,* 40, 42.

Musser, Linda. (1989, April). Identifying Standards: How to Find Out If a Standard Exists. *ASTM Standardization News, 18,* 44–47.

O'Grady, Joseph G. (1990, February). The Challenge of Standards and Trade: Can They Exclude Your Product? *ASTM Standardization News, 19,* 24–25.

Peters, M. M. (1983). Fabrics for garments: Quality, Design, and the Purchaser. In *Quality, Design, and the Purchaser.* Manchester, England: Textile Institute.

Pitt, Hy. (1981, July). Specifications: Laws or Guidelines. *Quality Progress, 14,* 14–18.

Pratt, Herbert T. (1984, September). Managing Textile Terminology. *ASTM Standardization News, 12,* 22–23.

Randall, Janet. (1993, April/May). Standard Time. *Canadian Textile Journal, 110(3),* 10–12.

Ricci, Patricia L. (1990, June). Standards Sources and Resources. *ASTM Standardization News, 18,* 54–59.

Roach, A. R. (1994). Meeting Consumer Needs for Textiles and Clothing. *Journal of the Textile Institute, 85(4),* 484–495.

Schuler, Charles A., Jesse Dunlap, & Katherine L. Schuler. (1996). *ISO 9000: Manufacturing, Software, and Service.* Albany, NY: Delmar.

Skelton, J., & D. R. Peterson. (1983). The Specification and Design of Industrial Fabrics. In *Quality, Design, and the Purchaser.* Manchester, England: Textile Institute.

Spivak, S. M. (1994). The Role of Standards for Textiles. *Journal of the Textile Institute, 85(4),* 441–444.

Struebing, Laura. (1996, January). 9000 Standards? *Quality Progress, 29,* 23–28.

Swirles, Frank M. (1962). *Swirles Handbook on Basic Fabrics,* 2nd ed. Los Angeles, CA: Swirles.

Tortora, Phyllis G., & Robert S. Merkel. (1996). *Fairchild's Dictionary of Textiles,* 7th ed. New York: Fairchild.

Villa, Kay M. (1996, November). Weaving a Fabric Cooperation: ASTM and ATMI's Relationship. *ASTM Standardization News, 24,* 19–22.

Warren, J. R. (1994). The Use of ISO 9000 in the Textile Industry: The DuPont Experience. *Journal of the Textile Institute, 85(4),* 460–468.

Weston, F. C. (1995, October). What Do Managers Really Think of the ISO 9000

Registration Process? *Quality Progress,* 28, 67–73.

Wilson, Lawrence A. (1996, January). Eight-Step Process to Successful ISO 9000 Implementation: A Quality Man-agement System Approach. *Quality Progress,* 29, 37–40.

Zuckerman, Amy. (1997). *International Standards Desk Reference: Your Passport to World Markets.* New York: Amacon.

REVIEW QUESTIONS

1. Identify the specific focus of each of the following organizations and its relationship to quality assurance.
   a. AATCC
   b. ASTM
   c. ASQ
   d. AAMA
   e. (TC)^2
   f. ISO

2. Define and give an example of each term:
   a. voluntary standard
   b. mandatory standard
   c. standards
   d. standard test method
   e. classification
   f. guide
   g. practice
   h. terminology
   i. specification

3. Explain the differences and similarities between these pairs of terms.
   a. standards and specifications
   b. voluntary standards and mandatory standards
   c. open specifications and closed specifications
   d. specifications and tolerances
   e. minimums and tolerances

4. Identify sources of information that will help you answer Question 3. What information do you expect to find in each source?

5. Select a textile product you own and develop standards and specifications related to its size, appearance, style, characteristics, and performance.

ACTIVITIES

1. Search the world wide web for information related to standards and specs. Key words that might be useful are: standards, specifications, international standards, textiles, industrial textiles, apparel industry, and

contract furnishings. Record the search engine and key words used and the addresses in case you want to share this information with others or visit the site again.

2. Examine textile products, vehicles, and other property for information related to industry and company standards. How is that information used to promote products and assure customer satisfaction?

3. Compare two products of the same type such as pillows or shirts and write company standards that reflect the characteristics, performance, and quality of each product. What are the differences and similarities between your standards? What would they mean in terms of product promotion, retail presentation, target market, and customer satisfaction?

4. Write target, functional, and product specifications for a specific textile product. (Using a sample or prototype makes this an easier task.)

5. Read this article (Roach, A. R. [1994]. Meeting Consumer Needs for Textiles and Clothing. *Journal of the Textile Institute, 85(4),* pp. 484–495) and discuss its relationship to standards, specifications, international trade, and quality assurance.

Chapter 4

INTRODUCTION TO TESTING

OBJECTIVES

- To understand the dimensions of testing of materials and products.

- To understand how testing is used in assessing and measuring performance and characteristics of materials and products.

- To use testing for product development, verification of information, and satisfying customer expectations.

- To understand the components of a standard test method.

- To know standard conditions for testing of textile materials and products.

- To understand characteristics and applications of materials testing and product testing.

KEY TERMS

testing	accuracy	moisture equilibrium
laboratory testing	reliability	comparative testing
specimens	bias	materials testing
supplier testing	calibration	product testing
in-house testing	verification	wear testing
independent or contract testing	standard calibration fabric	service testing
		prototype testing
test method	pass/fail scales	controls
standard test method	standard atmosphere	lifetime testing
precision	moisture regain	guarantees

The goal of a company committed to quality is to manufacture, sell, or provide products that meet customer expectations. Manufacturers need to be sure that the materials they work with, the processes they use, and the finished products they sell meet that goal. Retailers need to be able to assess that the products they buy meet their expectations in terms of performance, size, fit, and consistency. Companies need some way to assess the characteristics and performance of the materials and the quality of the finished product.

Failure of a product, which can be caused by a single factor or an accumulation of many factors, results in customer dissatisfaction. It can be a result of poor materials performance, unsatisfactory materials interactions, poor fit, unacceptable appearance, or inconsistencies among supposedly identical products. Testing is a common practice within the textile industry complex to assess materials and products in an effort to minimize product failure and improve customer satisfaction.

Testing is the analysis and evaluation of a material or product to assess its characteristics, quality, or performance. A material or product may be examined in its original condition or it may be subjected to one or more procedures before a measurement of its performance is made. Testing is conducted so that a material or product is evaluated in a controlled and planned manner. This approach minimizes omission of any critical factor or step and decreases inconsistencies in the evaluation.

WAYS OF TESTING

Textile materials and finished products can be assessed in several different ways. Each provides valuable information, but the type of information differs in its nature and application. Companies may use one way to identify the appropriateness of materials or production procedures for the product's end use. They will probably use a different way to identify product adherence to company standards and specifications, appropriateness of design or materials, and the target market's assessment of and satisfaction with the product.

LABORATORY TESTING

Laboratory testing is sometimes referred to as accelerated testing because the goal is to assess characteristics and performance quickly. It is most often used to assess materials. The results of laboratory testing are assumed to describe in some fashion the serviceability of the materials from which the product is made. It is also assumed that the performance of the materials predict the serviceability of the finished product. This may not always be the case. A limited number of standard test methods work with specimens that combine two or more materials to assess their interactions. A few standard test methods evaluate the manner in which a completed product performs. These tests usually relate to functional or protective clothing or furnishings such as mattresses or upholstered chairs.

Laboratory testing is defined as evaluating characteristics or performance of materials using standard procedures in a specialized facility. The facility could consist of a separate room or rooms or a separate building on the site. Because a controlled atmosphere is desirable for many procedures, space for laboratory testing is not often shared with other workspace. Standard test methods are used in assessing characteristics, quality, and performance. Trained technicians or specialists conduct the procedures. The majority of the equipment that is used may be specialized for each measurement of the material or product. For example, when measuring resistance to pilling, a piece of equipment designed to subject fabric to conditions where pills are likely to form is used in this performance evaluation.

The tests are conducted using one or more **specimens,** which are small pieces of the material cut or removed from a larger piece of fabric or a product. The nature and dimension of the pieces to be tested relate to the specific test method to be followed. Often a **cut** or sample fabric piece of three to five yards is provided by suppliers. These sample pieces are tested for conformance to specified requirements for material characteristics, quality, and performance.

Results of testing are available fairly quickly because many procedures do not take long to perform. An entire procedure—from start to finish—can often be done in a working day, provided the material or product has been conditioned appropriately. When items need to be conditioned before testing, the procedure may take more time. Often results are available immediately or following some relatively simple calculation. Most procedures done in a laboratory are based on standard test methods from AATCC, ASTM, other groups, or on company procedures. Precision and accuracy for some procedures are known. These laboratory tests may be used for research, product development, end-use performance testing, materials or product analysis, or performance assessment.

AATCC, ASTM, FTMS, and company procedures are examples of laboratory tests. These procedures check for conformance to specifications in terms of characteristics, quality, and performance as indicated in supplier or vendor agreements. Testing may be done to verify performance and product quality and to provide information for product promotion, catalog copy, certification requirements, licensing agreements, or hangtag claims. Testing may also be done during production to assure that quality standards are being met or to verify that labels and product performance meet the requirements of government laws and regulations for such things as fiber content, care, and flammability. Evaluating products to determine reasons for consumer complaints and returns and to identify performance and characteristics of competitor's products are other applications of laboratory testing.

Laboratory testing is used extensively in research because its approach is organized, systematic, and carefully planned. These are some of the criteria that must be met for research studies to be credible and accepted by other researchers.

Finally, forensic testing also requires that the results be ascertained in a repeatable and consistent fashion that reflects industry wide agreement in terms of process. Forensic refers to collecting information that might be used in either civil or criminal trials.

Supplier Testing

In **supplier testing,** the company that supplies a material or a product tests it to make sure that it meets the requirements listed in the contract or agreement with the buyer. Suppliers often test their products as part of their quality assurance program to ensure that what they are producing is consistent in quality, characteristics, and performance. Suppliers may take shortcuts with standard practices, especially if they are determining values for use within the company. When outside companies rely on suppliers to test the materials or products for adherence to requirements, they need to recognize that supplier's results may reflect an inherent bias to make sure that their goods are acceptable to buyers. Most companies that rely on supplier testing periodically check the results to make sure that no bias is present. Manufacturers often rely on suppliers for materials testing. Some problems with poor performance of products can be traced to this practice. Supplier testing is especially problematic when buyers fail to check the reliability and accuracy of the supplier's test results.

Although most suppliers are reputable and stand behind their products, suppliers' information should be evaluated periodically within the company or by an independent lab. Many companies that have worked with an individual supplier for years form a formal or informal partnership with the supplier. Even so, they check the accuracy of the information on an irregular basis just to be sure that the quality is consistent and the information is accurate. Companies that are beginning relationships with suppliers will want to check the information provided on a more regular basis until a level of confidence has been established.

In-House Testing

In-house testing involves evaluating the materials or products within the company that has produced them. In-house testing is common with both large and vertically integrated companies because they can afford the costs associated with maintaining specialized testing facilities and employing trained staff. The lab supports the firm's reputation for a high-quality product, obtains repeat business, provides a dependable source for solving problems, and maintains control of production quality. In-house testing often works with selected procedures that are done on a regular basis by technicians who have training in conducting those tests. Companies often contract certain procedures with outside testing labs when tests are beyond the capability of the equipment and staff or when requests for procedures occur with such low frequency that it is cheaper to have an outside lab do the testing.

In-house testing is also used to verify the performance of selected materials provided by suppliers. Often these companies certify their suppliers based on the quality of the materials received over an extended time span. For example, if a supplier has provided the quality and amount of material as specified in the agreement for ten consecutive shipments and the information about the material is acceptable, it may be appropriate to certify that supplier. The supplier must be able to document its quality assurance procedures and be willing and able to maintain records to verify that it is meeting the buyer's expectations and requirements. Even with supplier certification, verifying the materials is a necessary component for companies with a commitment to quality.

Independent Testing

Independent or contract testing is performed by a separate business organization that specifically tests materials and products for other companies. These businesses may specialize in particular procedures or types of materials. Independent labs must be reliable, have trained personnel, current copies of appropriate industry test methods, appropriate equipment, and the ability to respond quickly for contracted services. Many companies work with the same independent testing lab on a regular basis.

Using independent labs can be time consuming and expensive, but it may be cheaper than providing a specialized lab in-house. In addition, technicians in the testing lab tend to specialize in certain areas or techniques. For example, identification of fibers can be an expensive and detailed process regardless of who does the work. People who have extensive experience and work with fiber identification on a regular basis will be more precise and accurate in their work than will those who analyze fiber content occasionally. Expenses can increase quickly. For example, a simple test on one specimen may cost $15 or more. If multiple fabrics or specimens are needed, additional expenses are accrued.

When working with an independent lab, all requested procedures and presentations of results should be specified in the service agreement or contract. There are many independent testing labs that specialize in testing textile materials in the United States, the Far East, Europe, and elsewhere. Appendix J presents information sources that provide lists of independent testing labs, their specialties, and locations.

TEST METHODS

A **test method** is a definitive procedure for the identification, measurement, and evaluation of one or more qualities, characteristics, or properties of a material, product, system, or service that produces a test result

(ASTM, 1996). **Standard test methods** are test methods that have been approved by specific organizations, such as ASTM and AATCC. The textile industry complex uses standard test methods to identify the materials used in a product, key elements regarding its physical structure, such as yarn type, and the performance that can be expected from that material. Companies also use standard test methods to evaluate products, but fewer standard test methods exist for product evaluation for several reasons. With the enormous range of products on the market, it is difficult to standardize procedures. With fashion goods, changes may occur so quickly that consensus standards cannot be reached before one product has been replaced by another. Finally, and probably most importantly, most products are evaluated based on in-house procedures and companies are not willing to share their procedures with competitors.

The test results for materials and products are used in assessing how well contract conditions have been met, in determining appropriateness of materials for products and performance for the target market, and in working with consumer complaints and returns. Because of these applications, it is very important that the procedures meet certain criteria in terms of precision, reliability, and validity. These three measures are addressed during the development of standard test methods, and they are considered very carefully when decisions are made regarding approval of a test method as a standard, its use by individual companies, and its modification.

DEVELOPMENT OF A STANDARD TEST METHOD

When standard test methods are developed, care is taken that the method will be useful in a variety of locations, applications, and circumstances. Test methods are developed to reflect a need recognized by individuals, companies, or groups of individuals representing several companies. A great deal of effort, research, and time is spent on developing and refining test methods so that they represent current practices and address recognized needs. Several key criteria are considered when any test method is developed.

Precision

Precision refers to the degree of agreement within a set of observations or test results obtained as directed in a method (ASTM, 1996). Sometimes the terms "repeatable" and "reproducible" are used to address this agreement of results. Precision addresses the ability of a procedure to give essentially the same results regardless of who does the testing, where it is done, why it is done, or when it is done. Generally, results are most similar when the same individual does the procedure in the same lab with the same piece of equipment. Because tests are done by different operators and at various laboratories or time frames, the carefully written procedure minimizes variation.

Accuracy

Accuracy refers to the agreement between the true value of the property being tested and the average of many observations made according to the test method, preferably by many observers. In other words, are the results of the test a reflection of the real performance of the material being tested? Test methods are designed to reflect behavior of materials in customer use. Most test methods use an instrument or piece of equipment to measure a property or a characteristic. For example, a scale is used to measure mass or determine the weight of an object.

Anyone who uses an instrument to measure some characteristic of an object assumes that the instrument is accurate. For example, when a child is ill, parents use a thermometer to check the child's temperature. If the reading is excessive, say 102 °F or higher, they are more likely to consult a doctor than if the temperature is only slightly elevated, say 99.5 °F. Parents assume that the thermometer's reading is accurate, that it is recording a true measure of the child's temperature.

Reliability

Reliability refers to the ability to repeat the process and get the same or very similar results. One of the advantages of a standard test method is that it has been developed to meet this requirement. Technicians and consumers expect that the instrumentation they use on a regular basis produces reliable results. For example, drivers expect that the car's speedometer correctly reflects the speed at which the car is moving. If the speedometer is not reliable, the driver risks getting a speeding ticket one day and irritating other drivers by driving too slowly the next day, even though the speedometer indicates the car is traveling at the same speed both days.

Application

Precision, accuracy, and reliability are concerns in all performance testing and in measuring characteristics of materials and products. Efforts to minimize problems with these three dimensions are addressed in the detail included in standard test methods and procedures, in statements regarding calibration, and in the training of operators and technicians. For example, when using a balance, the operator should always verify the zero reading of the balance to ensure that results will be correct. In addition, the operator must be careful that the numbers are read from the correct angle. Some balances are designed so that the operator must be standing directly in front of it and reading the values at eye level to be sure that the results are precise, accurate, and reliable.

Bias refers to a constant and systematic error in results. For example, if the operator reads the balance at too high an angle, that is the operator's eyes were above the optimum angle, the results might be consistently low or the mass consistently recorded as being lighter than it is (see Figure 4-1).

Technician and operator training helps ensure that results are reliable. Most laboratories require that individuals follow a standard test method. Although these individuals may do a certain test many times each week, they need to be sure that they are following the procedure indicated in the standard document. When a process is performed repeatedly, shortcuts may develop without the individual realizing the problem. Checking the test method on a regular basis minimizes errors in the process. It is important that operators never rely on memory for conducting a test, because important details may be incorrect, omitted, or ignored.

Equipment and instruments must be properly maintained. A basic task in operating a testing lab is to keep the equipment clean and working properly. Periodic maintenance is necessary. In addition, most equipment must be calibrated or verified before use. In calibrating or verifying equipment, the piece of equipment is checked to be sure that the results are accurate. **Calibration** is the process of fixing, checking, or correcting the gradations of a measuring instrument. Verification is another term used to

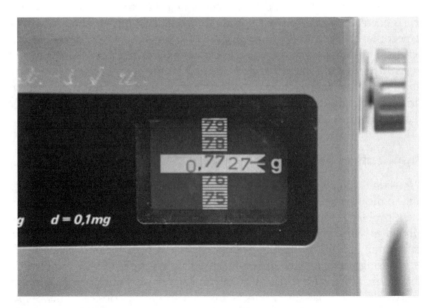

Figure 4-1

The angle at which the numbers are viewed makes a difference in the results of weighing an object. With this balance, the most accurate reading occurs when the operator is standing directly in front of the balance so that the center line in the window is at the same level as the operator's eyes.

describe this process. Technically, calibration occurs at the factory when the instrument is new. **Verification** is done periodically with the instrument in its use location. Most equipment is designed so that accuracy can be adjusted as needed.

The bathroom scale provides a simple example. Most scales of this nature are equipped with a tiny knob that can be adjusted so that the scale reads zero when not in use and the assessment of mass (weight to the consumer) is accurate. Consumers can check the accuracy of the scale by weighing something that is sold by weight, such as a three-, five-, or ten-pound sack of flour, potatoes, or cat food. Technicians in the lab do the same kind of thing with laboratory equipment and instruments.

Sometimes, because of the way the equipment operates, it is necessary to use a standard calibration fabric to be sure that the equipment is operating properly. **Standard calibration fabric** is used because the operator knows the results that should be obtained with the fabric, and adjusts the equipment accordingly. These fabrics are used in procedures ranging from testing colorfastness to light and snagging to agitation of washing machines.

In addition, the environment in which the testing is done has an effect on the results. Conditions within the laboratory are carefully controlled to reduce the variation resulting from environment.

PARTS AND COMPONENTS

Test methods are organized and written in a somewhat consistent and logical sequence, so that information can be found quickly. The organizations and agencies that develop standard test methods may present the information in slightly different sequences or may use different terms to describe similar components.

The purpose of the procedure is identified in a brief statement at the beginning of the test method. The scope or range of its application and any restrictions or limitations for its use may also be listed. Safety statements may be included as a safeguard against legal liability.

Some methods identify the scientific principle under which the test method operates. Procedures for sample or specimen preparation describe limitations for making or taking specimens, as well as provide directions describing how to cut and otherwise prepare specimens. Procedures for determining the number of specimens to use in the procedure may be included.

A major concern in specimen preparation is that the fabric pieces used in the procedure should be representative of the actual product material. Specimens should be selected as randomly as possible to minimize inherent bias in the results. For example, some procedures related to durability restrict specimens being taken from fabric within 10 percent of the selvage, because selvages may vary in their structure, yarn type, yarn density, or finish. Other procedures may specify that the specimens be cut so that the same warp or filling yarns are not represented in more than one specimen (see Figure 4-2). For tests that focus on the performance of warp yarns more than filling yarns, taking two specimens that represent the same warp yarns would not provide any additional information. Taking specimens side by side would incorporate different warp yarns and increase information regarding the fabric's performance. Since many standard test methods focus on materials assessment, companies, independent testing labs, and others who work with finished products may need to develop specific criteria for removing specimens from products when product or component testing is to be done.

Requirements for conditioning specimens before testing are described. Apparatus and reagents needed for the procedures are identified. Suppliers for both equipment and reagents are included in endnotes or footnotes. This is especially true for unusual equipment and chemicals that may be provided by only one or two suppliers. Procedures for verifying equipment or instruments (often referred to as calibration) help ensure that the equipment is prepared for the procedure and working properly. A summary of the procedures helps operators understand the test method before they read the detailed procedures. A detailed procedure instructs the operator on how to conduct all parts of the test. Evaluation, analysis of results, or calculations sections explain how to calculate final values using the data collected.

The test method will identify applicable documents that operators might want to consult while preparing or conducting the test, define terms used in the test method, discuss the application of results, and explain how the report should be written. There may also be special notes on the proce-

Figure 4-2
Specimens A and B will incorporate the same filling yarns, while specimens A and C will incorporate the same warp yarns. When a test method restricts using two specimens incorporating the same warp yarns, both specimens A and C could not both be used, but specimens A and B would be acceptable. When the test method restricts specimens from the portions within 10 percent of the selvages, then the fabric within that area should not be used for specimens.

dure, safety precautions, comments on working with reagents, information on taking and using any necessary control specimens, and a statement regarding the precision and accuracy of the test method.

AATCC test methods often include these parts: purpose and scope statement, scientific principle, specimen preparation, apparatus and reagents, equipment calibration, procedure, evaluation of results, safety precautions, use of controls, and special notes related to the procedure, reagents, or sources. ASTM test methods often include these parts: scope, applicable documents, definitions, summary, uses and significance, apparatus, sampling information, number of specimens, conditioning requirements, procedure, calculations, report writing, precision and accuracy, calibration of equipment, and preparation and evaluation of specimens.

PASS/FAIL SCALES

Pass/fail scales describe the level of performance that meets or exceeds acceptable limits for a characteristic or condition, as well as the level of performance that does not meet the requirements. Pass/fail scales incorporate descriptions and physical measures of characteristics, quality, and performance in terms of numbers and units. These scales identify the minimum levels that would meet the requirements. Any value below that minimum level fails the procedure. For example, a manufacturer of canvas bookbags may establish a strength requirement of 150 pounds of force for the fabric. Fabrics that rupture above this value are acceptable for use in the bookbag; fabrics that rupture below this value are not.

Standard test methods never include descriptions or levels of performance that are acceptable or those that are not acceptable. They explain how to do the procedure; they do not judge if the performance is or is not acceptable. The acceptance or rejection of a material or product based on a test result is a decision that must be made by the parties involved. Thus, individual companies may develop pass/fail scales for materials or products to meet customer expectations, but these scales are not found in standard test methods.

For products that may affect public health and safety, pass/fail scales are included in most laws and regulations. An example relating to textile product safety is children's sleepwear. The pass/fail criteria are carefully identified to exclude products that are determined unsafe for consumer use. Producers and retailers of such products must ensure that the product and materials are acceptable according to these pass/fail scales.

STANDARD CONDITIONS FOR TESTING

Because some materials exhibit different performance behaviors under different environmental conditions, especially those related to temperature and humidity, it is important that materials be tested under similar conditions regardless of when the testing is conducted or where the lab is located. These conditions are often connected to the testing of textile materials and products and reflect the fact that many textile fibers behave differently as environmental conditions change. Tests should be performed under constant and nonchanging conditions. ASTM D 1776, Standard Practice for Conditioning Textiles for Testing, is a very detailed discussion of conditioning and preconditioning textiles in order to test them. **Standard atmosphere** for testing textiles is defined as air maintained at a relative humidity of 65 ± 2 percent and a temperature of 21 ± 1 °C (70 ± 2 °F). Standard atmosphere is also referred to as standard conditions or standard environment. The room where the conditions are controlled and where testing is conducted sometimes is known as a standard environment room (SER) or standard environment chamber (SEC).

Materials and products must be tested under these conditions, especially when they have high regain values. This is because their behavior can change as they pick up moisture from or lose moisture to the environment. **Moisture regain** is the amount of water in a material determined under prescribed conditions and expressed as a percentage of the mass of the water-free material. Moisture regain, usually expressed as a percentage, can be calculated by weighing a material when it is completely dry and then again when it has reached moisture equilibrium within a new environment, usually standard conditions (see Equation 4-1). ASTM D 2654, Moisture in Textiles, is the procedure most often used to assess moisture regain and related aspects for textile materials. Specimens are heated in an oven set at 105°C until the loss in mass between consecutive weighings is minimal. The reading from the last weighing is the dry weight used in Equation 4-1. Specimens must be handled carefully to avoid loss of fibers or yarns and to avoid moisture absorption during the process.

Equation 4-1   Moisture regain

$$R = 100(B-D)/D$$

where, R is the moisture regain listed as a percentage (%)
    B is the mass of the material (weight) in moisture
    equilibrium at specified conditions, and
    D is the mass of the material (weight) dried under specified
    conditions

Moisture equilibrium is the condition reached by a specimen when it no longer takes up moisture from or gives up moisture to the surrounding atmosphere. Moisture equilibrium occurs when successive weighings of the material do not show a progressive change in mass greater than the tolerances established for various textile materials. In other words, the mass of the material does not change between weighings or the change is so slight that it is acceptable within the limits established for the procedure. For most textiles, it takes several hours for moisture equilibrium to be reached. Eight hours, overnight, or even longer may be needed, especially if materials or products consist of several layers, compact fabrics, or are located in still air.

STANDARDIZED TESTS

Standardized tests are developed by professional organizations, government agencies, and individual companies. These procedures are generally compiled in a book so that they are readily available to interested parties. Knowing where to look for specific procedures will facilitate the testing process. Understanding their arrangement and their components is also important.

INDUSTRY PROCEDURES

AATCC test methods are organized in the *Technical Manual* by numeric order. The number of the test method is a one-, two-, or three-digit number followed by a dash and a four-digit year. The number before the dash is the number of the test method. The number after the dash indicates the year the test method was developed, revised, or reaffirmed.

In the front of the technical manual, AATCC includes a table of contents, a numerical list of test methods and procedures followed by an alphabetical list, a summary of changes from the previous volume, and a preface. Even if only the number of a test method is known, users can find the full title of the procedure in the table of contents. Standard test methods comprise the majority of the volume, but other information is also included, such as evaluation procedures, nomenclature for subjective rating processes, and a glossary of standard terminology.

Most ASTM test methods related to textile products are included in Volumes 7.01 and 7.02. Other procedures may be found in Volume 15.04 (leather) and Volumes 4.07, 1.03, and 12.02 (some furnishings). The test method number is either a three- or four-digit number followed by a dash and a two-digit number. The first number is the number of the test method. The second number describes the year the test method was adopted or revised. Some procedures are followed by a number in parentheses, which gives the year of the last revision of the test method.

Approximately 30 percent of each ASTM volume is new or revised. Test methods are organized alphanumerically by their ASTM designation. Each volume includes a foreword, a list of sections and volumes, a list of subjects, and a table of contents for that volume listing standards by numerical designation and by subject. Thus, one can find the full title and designation if only one component is known. The last few pages list a subject index of the standards included in each volume.

Other industry procedures may be of interest for some product types. For instance, the National Fire Protection Association (NFPA) develops procedures for assessing the flammability and burning characteristics of various products and materials including textiles and textile products. Other organizations that sponsor test method development include the Upholstered Furniture Action Council (UFAC), the Industrial Fabrics Association International (IFAI), and the Business and Industrial Furniture Manufacturers Association (BIFMA).

GOVERNMENT PROCEDURES

The federal government and some state, city, and county governments may develop procedures for evaluating materials and products. These procedures are cited most often in regulations relating to health and safety. For example, some states have developed procedures for assessing the flammability of sleeping bags and tents. Cities and counties may develop procedures for testing safety of furnishing textiles.

Test methods and standards used by the federal government to assess the quality and performance of textile products purchased for government use are included in the **Federal Test Methods and Standards** (FTMS). Many of these procedures resemble standard test methods developed by AATCC, ASTM, and other organizations. FTMS procedures may be shorter and include fewer parts and details. FTMS procedures are designated by a three- or four-digit number, a decimal, and usually a one-digit number. The number before the decimal is the number of the procedure. The number after the decimal is the number of the revision or modification to the procedure.

Other government agencies also develop test methods for some textiles and textile products. The Consumer Product Safety Commission (CPSC) deals with safety issues, such as flammability. The Federal Aviation Administration (FAA) focuses on furnishings and other textiles used in aircraft. The Department of Transportation (DOT) deals with furnishings and other textiles used in vehicles. The National Institute of Standards and Technology (NIST) considers upholstered furniture and building materials.

COMPANY PROCEDURES

Company procedures are developed by individual companies to address special concerns within the firm. Some of these procedures are refined and revised and become standard ASTM or AATCC procedures. The key concern in developing a company procedure is to address the issues related to validity, precision, and reliability. For example, a company producing hunting boots may be interested in developing a procedure for consistently testing materials to meet or exceed the performance expectations of hunters. This probably would include procedures related to insulation, waterproof behavior, traction on various surfaces, and comfort. Let us focus on comfort. In many areas, hunters walk through very rough country. When walking through areas with plants or trees that produce large thorns, hunters want to prevent the thorn from penetrating through any part of their boot and puncturing the skin. Besides the discomfort, holes also negate the waterproof characteristics of the boot. The company might focus on developing a specific procedure related to the issue of thorn penetration. The procedure, which would attempt to duplicate what might happen in actual use, can be repeated many times in the lab with very similar results. The company would use this information to establish minimum standards in performance that would produce a reasonably accurate assessment of performance in the field.

TESTING APPLIED TO PRODUCT DEVELOPMENT AND OTHER ACTIVITIES

Results of testing have many applications and are of use to several divisions within a company. These results are used in developing new products, improving current products, modifying standards and specifications, providing information to buyers, meeting labeling and certification requirements, establishing criteria for guarantees, and dealing with complaints.

Tests are used to ensure that products or materials conform to requirements. Materials and products are evaluated to ensure that they are free of defects and they are consistent in characteristics and quality.

Testing of materials and products is often used to select the most appropriate material or product when several similar items are available. In **comparative testing,** a company may test two or more products from the same plant, from different plants owned by the same company, or from competitors. Comparative testing may be done to ensure that the quality and performance of materials and products are consistent over time and among production facilities. This is especially important when coordinating products are produced in different facilities or when components are purchased at different times. For example, if a customer purchases one piece of soft-sided luggage one year, the company needs to be sure that the customer's next purchase will be consistent in materials, appearance, construction, and performance with the first piece.

Comparative testing is also used to verify that a company's product compares reasonably well with its competitors' products, particularly if prices are similar or, even more importantly, if a competitor's prices are slightly lower. Competition has become so tight with some product types that changes in one firm's product produces very quick and similar improvements in a competitor's product.

MATERIALS TESTING

Materials testing evaluates each material used in a product to determine its characteristics, quality, and to measure its response to selected performance tests. This type of testing has traditionally been referred to as textile testing, because such testing originally emphasized the evaluation of the characteristics and performance of the major textile fabric or the fashion fabric. Fashion or shell fabric refers to the fabric that is seen when the product is used or worn. In terms of cost and quantity, it often constitutes the largest percentage of materials used in the product. Hence, quality and performance of the fashion fabric is a significant factor in producing goods that appeal to the target market. However, customer satisfaction is based on the characteristics and performance of all materials used within a product, not just the fashion fabric. All materials should be evaluated for their characteristics and performance.

Materials testing normally identifies the characteristics and performance of materials in isolation. That is, the material is tested by itself, and not in combination with any other material. For example, interlinings and fashion fabric are tested separately, rather than after they have been fused or stitched together. Materials testing rarely assesses how two or more materials interact when combined in a product. Materials testing focuses on laboratory testing and should not be confused with other types of testing, in which the product is evaluated, it is worn or used by individuals or the components of finished products are tested.

Most materials performance testing focuses on assessing performance of one selected dimension at a time. Thus, elongation of a fabric or trim may be evaluated. But, this elongation testing does not factor in conditions that may be present during actual product use—conditions such as perspiration and body heat.

Use of Materials Testing

Companies need to determine the nature, structure, and quality of the materials that form any physical component of a textile product. This assessment serves several purposes. It helps identify the type of materials with which a company is working, which is an important step in product development. It helps manufacturers combine appropriate materials into a single product. For example, if a product includes a wool fashion fabric that must be drycleaned, other non-machine washable items, such as shoulder pads and interlinings can also be used. By combining materials with similar care requirements, the potential for customer dissatisfaction is reduced.

Information about the physical materials helps companies to determine the conditions of manufacture. If a material is heat sensitive, a range of acceptable temperatures can be identified so that surfaces are not melted or glazed during pressing. Identification of materials also tells companies more about the nature of the material. For example, materials analysis of woven fabrics can determine the number of yarns per inch in warp and filling directions. This detailed description of the fabric can be used to guarantee the purchase of additional fabric that is identical in structure. Conversely, the information about yarns per inch can be modified if performance problems or quality issues develop.

Analysis of materials identifies the presence and frequency of defects and irregularities. Thus, materials with physical defects can be isolated so they are not incorporated into products. If the frequency and type of defects are excessive, this information can be used to adjust payment for materials received and to determine future purchases.

When companies use the nature of a product's material in advertising, product descriptions, or product guarantees, the information must be accurate. Materials testing helps companies verify the accuracy of their claims. For example, when a company claims that buckles used in belts are all brass, they need to be able to demonstrate that the claim is true.

Most companies keep records of materials testing to document their efforts to provide accurate information to customers. The records are used to track performance of suppliers, record the materials combined in a product, and deal with consumer complaints and liability situations.

Performance assessment measures a material's behavior in relation to selected performance dimensions. Specific procedures are used to determine the way a material performs. Results from these procedures are used to determine if a material meets target market expectations for performance. Many companies have identified numerical measures of performance that reflect their target market's expectations. In other words, if a target market expects high durability for a product, a company might translate that general statement into a strength measure of at least 150 pounds of force before a fabric ruptures. No two companies are likely to define customer expectations precisely the same way.

One of the most difficult and complex issues in quality assurance is translating customer expectations into technical specifications. There are no simple solutions or equations that provide the answer. Knowledge of the target market and experience with the product are two factors that contribute to assigning real values to customer expectations. However, specifications are adjusted based on customer complaints, if new materials appear on the market, or if new processes are used. Thus, it is important to recognize that specs are likely to change over time. It is equally important to recognize that the use of materials to satisfy performance requirements does not guarantee that the product will also satisfy customer requirements.

Companies use measures of performance to establish standards and make sure that their products are consistent in performance. Results of performance testing cannot be translated directly into specific performance behaviors or duration of use by the consumer. For example, a company standard for shrinkage of 2 percent following washing and drying during performance testing does not guarantee that the fabric will not shrink more than 2 percent in the hands of a consumer. If however, the consumer washes the fabric under the same conditions used in the testing lab, shrinkage of the material should be approximately no more than 2 percent. But, if the consumer uses hotter water or greater agitation, shrinkage may increase. It is likely that a product may shrink a small amount each time it is washed and dried for the first several wash-dry cycles. The 2 percent shrinkage performance required by the company may represent only one wash and dry cycle, not several cycles. Finally, the 2 percent value may only represent the fashion fabric. Other materials, such as lining, thread, trim, and zipper tape may not have been tested, and each material may exhibit different amounts of shrinkage compared to that of the fashion fabric. Thus, even though the fashion fabric may not exceed the 2 percent value, the product may be unacceptable because of the shrinkage exhibited by one or more of its component materials.

Performance assessment is based on specific conditions of testing and focuses on one performance dimension at a time. This means that only one stress is applied to the material at a time. For example, in strength testing, the new fabric is stressed until it pulls apart and the force at which it tore is recorded. This is a situation contrary to most conditions of use. When consumers use a product, it is being subjected to many factors simultaneously. For apparel, these factors probably include some stress due to fit on the human form, movement and heat of the body, moisture from perspiration, and current atmospheric conditions. Furthermore, except for the first time some products are used, most textiles continue to be used after they have been cleaned. Changes in the product because of wear accumulate as product use increases. Thus, product failure is generally the result of an accumulation of many factors related to use, cleaning, and storage. In the strength example, a fabric may tear the eighteenth time it is used as a result of abrasion from each of the previous uses, numerous washings, stress because it is too small, and minor damage from a fall during the thirteenth use.

When a performance dimension is evaluated in the lab, most of the conditions of wear are not present. For example, in assessing laboratory resistance to pilling, the fabric is tumbled in a chamber with loose fiber for a specified length of time in controlled conditions of temperature and humidity. In actual use, the fabric may pill more slowly or more quickly depending on how it is used. Some parts may exhibit more pilling, and some may exhibit less pilling. Consider the differences in pilling among the various parts of a sweater: more pilling under the arm and on the forearm of the sleeve and less pilling at the center front and back of the sweater's body.

Materials testing provides a uniform way of measuring material performance, so that the results from a variety of materials that were tested in the same way can be compared. A decision concerning material selection can then be based on comparative results from the same procedure. Results from laboratory testing allow for a comparison of performance across time. Although no defined correlation exists between lab results and consumer wear, experience has indicated that when minimum acceptable performance is met in laboratory tests, consumers tend to be satisfied with the performance of the textile product. Most companies that have established minimum performance requirements for their products guard that information closely.

The performance dimensions that are measured depend on the target market, product type, and materials used. For example, assessment of elongation and recovery from elongation may be more important for companies that deal with knit products than for companies that deal with woven products. This is especially true if the product is expected to stretch as the body moves and recover from stretch when the body stops moving.

Application to Product Development

Materials testing is a key element in product development. Ideally, the assessment of materials occurs early in the product development process. That way, companies can verify that appropriate materials are being used. The materials selected will influence pattern development, fit, styling, production, cost, handling, performance, labeling, advertising claims, guarantees, and customer satisfaction. Thus, evaluation of the materials used to create the final product is a significant factor in meeting the quality and performance expectations of the target market.

Selecting materials is one step in product development. Materials are selected based on their availability, quality, and performance of materials and the product category (for example, shirts for formal, casual, or work activities), costs, target market characteristics and expectations, and fashion trends. It is crucial to select materials that will result in products that satisfy customer needs and meet customer expectations.

Testing can be conducted by the supplier of the materials, an independent lab that specializes in testing materials, or a specialized team within the firm. Testing usually provides a fairly detailed description of the material, an assessment of selected performance dimensions, inherent physical characteristics, and quality. For example, when fabrics are assessed, fabric description often includes fiber content based on percentage by mass, yarns per inch, yarn size, fabric width, presence and length of flaws, and designators that describe the fabric's print, style, color, or pattern. Performance aspects might include fabric strength, colorfastness to laundering and crocking, abrasion resistance, shrinkage, and pilling. A description of trim may include trim width, type, color, style, treatment (for example, folded), and fiber content. Performance aspects for trim would likely be more limited and might include colorfastness during laundering and shrinkage.

Performance assessed during the product development process minimizes the company's commitment to unacceptable or substandard materials and decreases the possibility of producing or selling products that incorporate substandard materials. It also will ensure that the products meet the company's minimum expectations for materials performance. For example, if a red print fabric is of interest to the product development or design team, the material should be tested to be sure that it meets their requirements for durability, colorfastness, and care. If the fabric does not meet company's expectations, the company should look for a similar fabric with better performance or eliminate the red print from the potential product line for that season. A company that continues with a fabric that does not meet its performance requirements fails to meet its business objectives and quality commitment. It is likely to suffer losses because of returns, complaints, and loss of image with its target market.

PRODUCT TESTING

In **product testing,** the finished product is the focus of analysis and evaluation. Product testing can relate to apparel, furnishings, functional and protective clothing, and industrial textile products. Although materials testing is able to assess some performance parameters, success of a product is based not only on the materials used in a product, but also on the design of the product, how it was produced, how it looks and fits, and how the materials interact. Products may be tested to evaluate materials interactions in use and cleaning. Fit, size, and design may be evaluated using mannequins. When a live fit model is used, a more realistic assessment of fit, function, and mobility is possible compared to the use of a stationary mannequin.

After production, product testing is done to ensure that production or shipping lots meet standards and specifications. A few products may be selected from the lot for evaluation of appearance, construction, size, and other selected measures. If these sample products do not meet the criteria, the buyer may refuse the entire lot or it may evaluate each product in the lot, accepting those that meet the criteria and rejecting those that do not. This type of product testing can be a tedious and time-consuming process.

WEAR TESTING

One specialized category of product testing combines the interaction of products with target market individuals. In **wear or service testing,** the product is put to use or worn by individual consumers. Wear testing is often used to refer to this manner of testing of apparel and service testing to describe this testing for furnishings and industrial products. For ease of understanding and readability, wear testing will be used in this discussion, but its use should not be construed as referring only to the testing of apparel products. A subdivision of wear testing is prototype testing. In **prototype testing,** sample products, prototypes, or several products from a limited production run are used or worn by a small group of users. Except for the selection of the product, wear and prototype testing are identical.

ASTM D 3181, Practice for Conducting Wear Tests on Textiles, provides information in terms of designing and planning for wear testing, conducting the wear test, identifying parameters to be evaluated at the conclusion of the wear period, and evaluating the results. The focus of this procedure is apparel, but the basic principles can be applied to product tests for any textile product. Use of controls may be helpful, especially if performance measures are to be collected at the end of the wear test. **Controls** or control textiles are textiles or textile products that have a known history, the performance of which in a specific end use has been established previously, and which is used as a standard of comparison. Controls help identify when differences in performance are the result of product wear. In wear testing, controls receive no wear or use and function as reference standards. Products returned after testing are compared to these unused products so that the effects of use can be ascertained.

Wear testing is more expensive and time consuming than other types of product testing. First, more products may be required. Then, individuals must be contacted and agree to participate in the product test, products must be delivered to them, and they must be trained or given instructions regarding the test's parameters. The training of participants tends to be relatively brief and in no way compares to the training of technicians for laboratory testing. The conditions of use must be of sufficient duration and of sufficient rigor to provide a reasonable range of possibilities in terms of use and performance. Conditions of use are likely to vary widely among participants. Precision is not known, but accuracy is high because the products experience real-world conditions of use and abuse by consumers. There are some additional problems with product testing. Some participants may disappear or drop out during the test. Some products may be destroyed and not be available for analysis. Some participants may not fulfill the requirements of the agreement in terms of use and care of the product.

Several means of locating test participants are used. Some companies work with businesses in their region who have working conditions that meet their criteria. Companies find participants among employees, their friends, or family members. Some companies place ads in local papers. Others use consultants to locate participants. Some catalog retailers contact customers who have a long history with the company to test specific products. For example, if a catalog retailer is interested in refining a product that has been a steady seller for several seasons, the company may select a few customers who have purchased several items at different times from previous catalogs and ask them to test a new prototype for a specified time period.

Participants receive a product and instructions to use it under a prescribed set of circumstances. Instructions might address frequency of use, length of time of each use, cleaning or not cleaning the product, and types of activities, such as work or leisure. At the end of the use period, participants might be asked to fill out a questionnaire, respond to an interviewer's questions, return the item to the company for laboratory analysis, or some combination of these assessments. Sometimes they keep the item; sometimes they are paid a fee for their time.

Participants are often asked to assess their experience with the product by responding to open-ended questions. This minimizes bias on the part of the supervisor of the product test. An open-ended question is one where the participant is not restricted to a set of predetermined responses. An example of an open-ended question is, "tell me the features you liked most about the product." After the testing is concluded, skilled interviewers question the participants to be sure that no information is lost. This is especially important if target market individuals do not possess the specialized language to describe performance parameters, likes, and dislikes in technical terms. In addition, participants may use expressions that mean different things to them and the wear test supervisor. The interviewer needs to be sure that different meanings of words or expressions are made clear to all involved.

Many companies conduct wear testing because it provides them with information that is not available by any other process. Wear testing during product development is used to refine product characteristics, dimensions, and features. It helps product development specialists understand how the target market would use the product and what their expectations are for the product. It also helps identify the range of uses and conditions within the target market. For example, a manufacturer of boots for cold weather wear may ask a small group of people who work in refrigeration conditions, such as meat packing plants and ice cream production facilities, to test the boots for comfort, foot and arch support, insulation, traction on wet and dry surfaces, and water resistance. Wear testing helps companies correct problems with products and continually refine and improve products due to input from target market individuals.

Another type of product testing, lifetime testing, differs substantially from the others. In **lifetime testing,** the product remains in use until the user decides it is no longer serviceable. Lifetime testing is not often done because of the time involved and because the most important information from product testing does not relate to the length of time the product is serviceable, but rather to factors that influence the use of materials, product design and fit, production processes, and other aspects related to consumer use and satisfaction.

LABELS

Many labels are used on textile products to provide fiber content, RN number, country of origin, care, size, and manufacturer or retailer identification. Some of this information is required by federal law or federal regulations. Other information is provided to promote the manufacturer or retailer. Still other information, such as size, is designed to help the customer select an appropriate product. Some of the information must be available to the consumer at point of purchase, but does not necessarily have to be sewn into the product. Other information must be on a permanent, sewn-in label. Evaluation and analysis procedures are used to ensure that the information provided on labels and hangtags is correct and accurate. It is the responsibility of the manufacturer and retailer to ensure that all information required by federal laws and regulations is accurate and meets the specified criteria.

Required Information

Required information can be divided into two categories: that available at point of sale and that permanently attached to the product. Federal law requires that fiber content information be provided at point of purchase for garments. Although it is not required to be sewn in, many companies have selected to include fiber content information on permanently attached, sewn-in labels. Required fiber content information includes fiber content by generic fiber name as a percentage by mass (weight) in descending order, manufacturer's identification by name or registered number (RN or WPL), and country of origin. The Textile Fibers Product Identification Act addresses most apparel and some furnishing products, defines generic fibers, and identifies restrictions on the use of trade names and trademarks on labels. The Wool Products Labeling Act and the Fur Products Labeling Act address products made of wool, wool blends, and fur, defines terms, and restricts use of misleading words on labels.

Recommended care information must be sewn into the product at a specified location as a permanent label and using defined terms or symbols. Information on the care label must address cleaning, use of such special cleaning aids as bleach if their use is likely, pressing or ironing, drying, dry cleaning, and any other necessary treatments. More information on care labeling will be discussed in Chapter 8.

Information regarding the specific information and its format for each law and regulation is available from the Federal Trade Commission. In addition, introductory textile books often discuss these laws and regulations in detail.

Voluntary Information

Some information on labels is voluntarily provided by manufacturers and retailers. This information often relates to size of the product, claims regarding product performance, certification, brand names, union labels, disclaimers related to appearance or performance, price, color, and style. Size, product claims, certification, brand names, and price provide information to the customer that assist in making purchase decisions. Certification indicates that the product has met a specified condition or level of performance. For example, products that carry the cotton seal of approval must be made of 100 percent U.S. grown cotton. The union label indicates that union labor was used to make the product. Brand names indicate the company that made or sold the product. Brand names help sell merchandise to brand-conscious consumers.

Disclaimers can include comments regarding irregular color, warnings regarding hazards such as the tendency for surface fibers on some fuzzy fabrics to ignite quickly, and appearance alterations as a result of abrasive finishes. Color and style information can be used in distribution or catalog centers and stores. This information helps the staff or customer select the style and color needed. Catalog distribution centers that select items for individual customers find that color, size, and style labeling is especially important in correctly filling orders and quickly shipping them.

GUARANTEES

A **guarantee** is a pledge or an assurance that a product is accurately represented and will be replaced if it does not meet specifications. Guarantees can be either implied or written. Implied guarantees are based on an assumption of reasonable expectation of performance and are present with most textile products. Written guarantees are less common. Some companies have developed written guarantees that are posted in the store or included in a catalog. Many high-ticket furnishings, such as carpeting and upholstered furniture, include written guarantees of performance and appearance. Written guarantees for textile products generally identify a specific time frame, such as 12 or 18 months, during which the product should maintain a satisfactory appearance and give acceptable performance. Written guarantees may describe how the product should be used or installed and the type of care required to maintain the guarantee. Incorrect installation or care can void the guarantee.

CUSTOMER COMPLAINTS

Customers set the standard for product satisfaction. When a product does not meet their expectations, they may complain to the retailer or manufacturer. Many manufacturers and retailers do their best to satisfy customer complaints. Testing may be used to determine why a product failed and if that failure extends to a larger group of products resulting in a number of dissatisfied customers.

When customer complaints occur, companies check their documentation to identify if the product was produced by the firm, when and where the product was produced, and the materials used in its production. In addition, companies that are interested in continuous product improvement compile information from consumer complaints and returns. They examine this information to identify problem areas, trends, and issues related to quality. These results are used to improve products or to remove potentially problem products from the market.

LAWSUITS

Information from testing can be used as important evidence in criminal and civil lawsuits. In addition, in civil cases resulting from product failure, assessment of the type of materials and product features may provide significant information. Personal injury, wrongful death, and failure to meet guarantees are common reasons for civil cases.

It is important that companies maintain accurate records of testing. Accurate records are especially critical when the claim attributes significant financial loss, personal injury, or death to the textile product.

CONCLUSIONS

Testing is a critical step in incorporating quality into a product. Test methods are documents that have been carefully developed to address all aspects involved in carrying out the procedure. Test methods include a number of components to facilitate understanding and conducting the procedure. Precision, accuracy, and reliability are elements that influence the development of test methods.

Product development specialists need to know what the materials are and how they will perform for the target market. These specialists also need to know how the various materials used in a textile product interact and how the product fits and functions. In addition, buyers need to know if products meet their specifications and standards. Assessment of quality, characteristics, and performance can be based on standard test methods of materials and products and wear tests. Product testing provides additional information that can benefit product development efforts. It is also used to ensure that products are acceptable to customers. Wear tests are used to assess suitability for the target market and the likelihood of consumer acceptance. Wear tests provide information used to modify and improve products.

SUGGESTED READINGS

American Association of Textile Chemists and Colorists. (1996). *AATCC Technical Manual, 71*. Research Triangle Park, NC: Author.

American Society for Testing and Materials. (1996). *Annual Book of ASTM Standards, Vol. 7.01 & 7.02*. West Conshohocken, PA: Author.

Anfuso, Dawn. (1994, July). L.L. Bean's TQM Efforts Put People before Processes. *Personnel Journal, 72*–83.

Anon. (1987, December). Quality Assurance through Commercial Laboratories and Consultants. *Food Technology*, 110–127.

Bona, Mario. (1990). *Textile Quality: Physical Methods of Product and Process Control*. Rome: Texilia.

Brown, Patty. (1992). *Ready-to-Wear Apparel Analysis*. New York: Macmillan.

Dickerson, Kitty G., Christopher C. Hooper, & Robert D. Boyle. (1995, April). The New Approach for Manufacturers. *America's Textiles International*, 28–30, 32.

Fortess, Fred. (1986, August). No Inspection Required. *Bobbin Magazine, 27*, 54–56, 58, 60.

Glock, Ruth E., & Grace I. Kunz. (1995). *Apparel Manufacturing: Sewn Products Analysis*, 2nd ed. Englewood Cliffs, NJ: Prentice-Hall.

Hallgarth, D. S. Lawrance. (1989). The Evolution and Development of Supplier Quality Assurance. In *Textiles Towards World Class*. Manchester, England: Textiles Institute.

Mehta, Pradip V. (1992). *An Introduction to Quality Control for the Apparel Industry*. Milwaukee: ASQC Press.

Merkel, Robert S. (1991). *Textile Product Serviceability*. New York: Macmillan.

Paluchowski, T. D. (1989). Quality and the Retailer. In *Textiles Towards World Class*. Manchester, England: Textiles Institute.

Patterson, Anne. (1987, September). The Future of Textile Testing. *American Dyestuff Reporter, 76*, 20.

Reda, Susan. (1994, March). Quality Con-

trol: K-Mart Commits to Product Testing. *Stores*, 47–49.

Tortora, Phyllis G., & Robert S. Merkel.
(1996). *Fairchild's Dictionary of Textiles*,
7th ed. New York: Fairchild.

Tyson, Samuel E. (1986, January). The In-
House Laboratory. *ASTM Standardization News, 14*, 40–41.

REVIEW QUESTIONS

1. Define testing and give examples of its use in the textile industry complex.

2. Describe circumstances under which a company might select one of the following.
   a. supplier testing
   b. in-house testing
   c. independent laboratory testing

3. Define precision, accuracy, and reliability.

4. Select five general parts of a test method and explain why that part or component is included in a standard test method.

5. Explain the differences between material and product testing.

6. Suggest four ways that the results would differ between laboratory and wear testing for bed linens.

7. Explain how materials testing and wear testing contribute to product development.

ACTIVITIES

1. Tour a testing lab and talk to the staff about the materials or products with which they work and the procedures they use.

2. Check information found on hangtags and labels and in catalogs for information regarding standards and specifications.

3. Analyze shops and businesses where goods are sold by weight and volume. Check the measurement devices to see how frequently their accuracy is verified by state or federal agencies.

4. Check the accuracy of your bathroom scale and correct its accuracy, if necessary.

5. Visit web sites related to product and materials testing, such as the one for JCPenney (http://www.jcpenney.com) that includes a tour of its product evaluation facilities.

6. Identify procedures related to materials testing, product testing, and wear testing for a selected textile product. Explain why you made those choices.

7. Read this article (Reda, Susan. [1994, March]. Quality Control: K-Mart Commits to Product Testing. *Stores*, 47–49) and discuss how testing is used in this company to meet customer expectations.

Part II

MATERIALS TESTING

This part focuses on the materials used to produce a textile product and includes discussions of fashion, lining and support fabrics, closures, trims, elastics, threads, and other materials. Materials testing incorporates many procedures to evaluate the nature, characteristics, and performance of different materials and their interactions. A knowledge of materials testing is necessary to write product specifications, so that the desired material is used and the materials used deliver satisfactory performance for the product type and target market.

Chapters 5 through 8 identify materials and assess their performances. These chapters present theory and describe standard and nonstandard procedures. Other important issues include sample or specimen preparation, equipment and instrumentation used in assessments, and interpretation of results. Chapter 9 examines the complexities of shade sorting and color matching.

Thus, Part II focuses on:

- *specifying materials used in textile products,*

- *describing desired characteristics, quality, and performance levels for these materials, and*

- *understanding evaluation and testing procedures used in the assessment of materials.*

Chapter 5

SPECIFYING AND EVALUATING MATERIALS

OBJECTIVES

- To describe materials used in specific textile products.

- To understand units and terms used in material specifications.

- To understand procedures used to identify the nature and characteristics of materials.

- To write specifications describing desired characteristics and quality of materials for specific products and target markets.

- To interpret specifications for materials.

KEY TERMS

Worth Street Textile Market Rules	put-up	defect point
fiber analysis	width	demerit point
qualitative procedures	bow	penalty point
quantitative procedures	skew	closures
yarn number	crimp	sewing thread
twist	takeup	trims
yarn defects	barré	elastic
threshold levels	finishes	interlining
fabrication	coloration	lining
fabric density	fabric quality	strike-through
count	defect	support materials
fabric mass per unit area	patent defects	labels
length	latent defects	hangtags
	grade	packaging

The materials used in a product have a significant impact on the appearance, structure, appeal, and performance of that product. Materials specifications are therefore an important factor in determining the quality of a textile product. Materials specifications are used to describe each physical component that will be used in a product or style, including the type, quality, and characteristic of materials needed and the required performance for specific aspects of interest to the company and its target market. Although materials specs often focus only on the fashion fabric, they should also address all other materials because all materials influence the appeal, cost, and performance of the product.

In many companies, materials specs are listed in descending order, from the component that comprises the greatest percentage of material used, or the most expensive, to the component that represents the lowest percentage, or least expensive. Thus, specs may begin with the fashion fabric and then address lining fabrics, support fabrics, trims, closures, elastics, and thread, in that order. Although the order of the specs may not be critical, the information is.

Nature is a general term that describes the chemical type of material, such as fiber content or metal, and its physical structure, such as woven, cast, or laminated. Characteristics is another general term that describes the physical aspects of materials, such as their weight and finish, and dimensional aspects, such as their length and width. Quality refers to desirable physical aspects of a material, including regularity or variability of characteristics, freedom from defects, and adherence to a standard type for that material. For example, most standard plain weave fabrics are expected to have essentially the same number of yarns in the warp direction anywhere across most of the width of the fabric, regardless of where a count of yarns is made. If the number varies substantially from one area across the fabric's width to another area, the fabric is lower quality than a fabric where the warp yarn density is consistent across the fabric. The number of yarns per inch is another measure of fabric quality. This and several characteristics that describe quality can be placed on a continuum that ranges from lower levels of quality to higher levels of quality.

Each material used in textile products will be presented in terms of its nature, characteristic, and quality measures; standard procedures; example results with appropriate units; and an interpretation of the results. General comments regarding working with data and presenting results are included to introduce basic concepts. In addition, reference to basic business and industry practices are also discussed.

MANIPULATION, ORGANIZATION, AND PRESENTATION OF DATA

Whenever a measurement of a material, product, or process is made, the results describe some important factor relating to product quality, productivity, or performance. However, the individual numbers are not always of immediate use. Some data manipulation or data organization is often required to make the information easier to understand and more useful for decision making.

In many instances, repeated measurements assess variability in a material, product, or process. This knowledge helps companies implement procedures to reduce excessive variation and decrease the risk of dissatisfied customers. For example, the number of warp and filling yarns are counted at least five times at different locations in the fabric. The average values and variation (standard deviation) are calculated using the individual numbers to provide more useful information. Average and standard deviation are more representative of the material and are compared to specifications to determine the acceptability of the material.

Companies often compare information measured at different facilities and times to ensure product and process consistency and to access the affects of process improvements, changes in materials or design, or other relevant factors. The data are organized and presented in a chart or diagram. Visual presentation quickly demonstrates trends, adherence to standards and specifications, or problems. Ways of presenting data in a visual form vary based on how the data was collected, its use, or its type. Because of this, it is important to select the most appropriate presentation method for the data. Chapter 15 focuses on commonly used methods for data analysis, organization, and presentation.

WORTH STREET TEXTILE MARKET RULES

The **Worth Street Textile Market Rules** (1986) are a standard code of practices for marketing textile materials in the United States. These rules describe the point at which ownership transfers, arbitration of disputes, contractual features, buyer's and seller's rights, and other issues related to fair business practices. In addition, tolerances, deficiency limits, and allowances for specified fabric types and yardages are described. Basic terms related to trade are defined, such as assortments, rejections, quantities, defect types, and seconds.

Many practices addressed in this book are standardized procedures based on the Worth Street Rules. Such practices include identifying fabric quality, grading, defects, width, count, mass per unit area, length, and several performance measures. For example, threads per inch or count is determined by counting warp and filling yarns in at least five different places no nearer the selvage than one-tenth the fabric width without duplicating the information (that is, not counting the same yarn twice). The average is determined and the fabric is considered acceptable if it is within tolerances (± 2 percent in the warp and ± 5 percent in the filling). Standard practices help ensure that companies evaluate materials in the same way, use terms in the same manner, and are held to the same expectations. These practices facilitate trade by promoting fair business practices.

FABRICS

A fabric is a planar structure consisting of yarns or fibers (ASTM, 1996), solutions, fabrics, or any combination of these (Kadolph & Langford, 1998). Fabrics include several types of materials that are likely to be combined in a textile product. Besides the fabric often referred to as the fashion fabric, fabrics are used for trims, elastics, linings, and support in the finished product. Fabrics used in a narrow form are often referred to as narrow fabrics. Much of the basic specification information included under this heading applies to these fabrics, too. In addition, more specific information for some of the specialized narrow fabrics will be discussed later in this chapter.

Specifying fabrics often incorporates information about each component used to produce the final fabric. Thus, fiber, yarn, fabrication method, and finishes should be considered when developing specifications for fabric. It might be helpful to consult a basic or introductory textiles book if terms used in this discussion are not clear.

FIBERS

Many factors related to fibers are important in terms of specifying the materials to be used in a textile product. Much of this information may be specified by a fabric supplier and may not be provided automatically to the buyer unless specifically requested. Suppliers use some of this information to ensure that a material is consistent in its characteristics from one time period to another. Often the information used by the yarn producer and fabrication mill are of minimal concern to the sewn products manufacturer or retailer, unless some inconsistency in the material becomes apparent as a result of problems in production, poor performance in testing, or complaints from consumers.

Fiber Characteristics

Numerous fiber characteristics need to be determined to produce appropriate yarns for weaving, knitting, or other methods of fabric production. These characteristics are useful in combining fibers of the same or different generic types. For example, self-blending of cotton from several bales where fibers from each bale demonstrate slightly different characteristics is done to minimize variation in fibers resulting from different growing conditions, variety of cotton fiber, or some other variable. It is important to recognize that measuring these characteristics provides information used in yarn spinning, weaving, knitting, and other materials facilities.

Specialized ASTM procedures are used to evaluate selected aspects of many fibers and some nonfibrous materials, such as plumage (down and feathers). Some procedures focus on specific products, such as rope or batting. Other procedures determine fiber characteristics, so that fiber combinations produce the appropriate fabric performance.

Breaking strength and other tensile properties help evaluate fiber performance and quality and are used in the selection of appropriate combinations of fibers to produce desired durability characteristics in finished fabrics. ASTM procedures for determining characteristics related to cotton grades include fiber maturity, color of raw fibers, nonlint content (soil and plant debris), and micronaire readings. Moisture content based on an ASTM method is used in determining commercial weights in buying and selling fiber. This is important because many materials are sold at a set price per unit mass. When the amount of moisture in the atmosphere varies, the mass and the market value of materials also varies. Thus, a means of adjusting mass is a necessary trade practice in marketing fibers.

Fiber characteristics that are important in yarn production include fiber cohesion, fiber crimp, and staple length. Cohesion of fibers is critical in producing spun yarns. ASTM procedures are used to determine fiber cohesion for such yarn precursors as sliver, roving, or top. Because crimp is added to most synthetic fibers before they are cut into staple form to be used in spun yarns, consistency of crimp is one measure of fiber quality. Also, because staple length contributes to characteristics of spun yarn fabrics, determining the distribution and uniformity of staple fiber lengths must also be determined. ASTM procedures are used to evaluate crimp and length of manufactured staple fibers.

Fiber Content

Identifying the generic fiber types present and their percentage distribution in the product at point of sale to consumers is required by such federal laws as the Textile Fiber Products Identification Act and the Wool Products Labeling Act. In addition, fiber content helps determine characteristics that are important in handling of materials, temperature concerns related to pressing and finishing steps, and product finishing steps. Product cost is significantly influenced by fiber cost. Fiber content is also critical in terms of many characteristics of the product that are important to the customer.

Some fiber content information is used in marketing the product. For example, trade names, such as Thinsulate™, which is often associated with performance outerwear, are used to promote textile products. Often products made of materials that carry trade names must meet specific characteristics or performance measures to use the trade name. Fiber type also may be used in promoting products. For example, terms such as pima, Peruvian, and Egyptian that describe different types of cotton are used in product promotion.

Two dimensions related to fiber content must be included in information available to the consumer at point of purchase. It includes the types of generic fibers present and their amount or percentage by weight.

Qualitative Procedures

Identification of the generic fiber types present in the textile product can be made using **qualitative procedures.** Two documents—AATCC 20, Fiber Analysis: Qualitative, and ASTM D 276, Identification of Fibers in Textiles—include a number of techniques. Both documents recommend using several procedures until enough information has been obtained to make a reasonable assessment as to the fiber type or types present.

The specimen for fiber analysis might come from fiber bales, yarns, or fabrics. Each document identifies issues related to taking a representative specimen in terms of intimate blends or mixtures, differences among yarns in a fabric, and union or cross-dyed fabrics. Thus, for example, the analyst needs to look for the presence of more than one fiber type in all procedures used and to examine both parts of a two-ply yarn, all yarn colors in yarn-dyed striped or plaid fabrics, and both warp and filling yarns in a woven fabric. As experience in analysis increases, accuracy of the results increases.

In microscopy, a few representative fibers are used to prepare each slide. If the analyst is working with a yarn, the yarn must be untwisted or otherwise separated so that fibers, not yarns, are examined. Magnification of at least 100x (100 times that of the unaided eye) helps in seeing physical structure, such as cotton's convolutions, linen's nodes, and wool's scales. Microscopy is used to make details along the length and in the cross-section of the fiber visible. Figure 5-1 illustrates both views of a cotton fiber—cross-section and lengthwise. Microscopy is the best way to identify natural fibers because these fibers possess unique physical structural aspects that are discernible with the microscope. Specialized techniques and microscopes may be needed to differentiate among such animal fibers as wool, mohair, and cashmere. Microscopy does not work well for identifying synthetic and manufactured fibers because their structure can be modified extensively during fiber spinning and finishing and many of them possess no unique structural feature. Microscopy will identify that these fibers are not natural fibers, but it will not identify the specific synthetic or manufactured fiber.

Solubility of fibers is another common identification technique. Because of the unique chemical nature of many fibers, a fiber will dissolve in one solvent, but not in another. This information is used to create a flow chart that starts with an unknown fiber and systematically exposes specimens of the fiber to a series of carefully selected solvents. Behavior in terms of the fiber's reaction to each solvent (soluble, insoluble, formation of a precipitate or a plastic mass) is compared to the chart to determine the fiber present. If the fiber content is known or suspected and the analyst is interested in verifying the fiber content, an abbreviated group of solvents

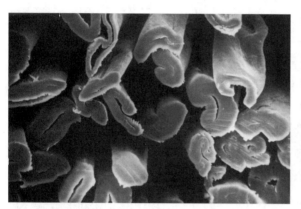
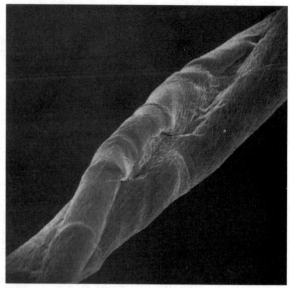

Figure 5-1

Photomicrographs of cotton: cross-sectional (left) and lengthwise (right). Convolutions of cotton and its cross-sectional shape help identify cotton. (*Courtesy of the USDA Southern Regional Research Center*)

can be used in the determination. Solubility is one of two methods for determining manufactured fibers. It is not as good for identifying natural fibers because it is not able to discriminate between fibers of similar chemical nature. For example, protein fibers, such as wool and mohair, exhibit the same solubility behavior. The same kind of problem occurs with cellulosic fibers, such as cotton, ramie, and flax.

In spectrophotometry, a visual representation of the fiber's molecular components is produced. The word spectrophotometer was coined from spectra (energy at different wavelengths) plus photo (light) plus meter (measuring). Thus, a spectrophotometer measures the amount of each different wavelength of light energy that passes through or is absorbed by a liquid. The energy of interest for fiber analysis is present at many different wavelengths in the infrared region. A carefully controlled beam of energy shines through a liquid in which the fiber has been dissolved and the results are recorded on a chart or spectrum (several are called spectra). An organic compound, such as a fiber, produces a unique "signature" that is demonstrated by a series of peaks or valleys in the chart at specific wavelengths. When the results are printed out in a continuous spectrum, the shape is unique for each generic type. The spectrum is examined and matched to a standard decision chart or spectrum of a known fiber to determine the fiber present. Figure 5-2 shows spectra for nylon 6,6 and nylon 6. Although spectrophotometry is preferred for identifying manufactured and synthetic fibers, the equipment is expensive and the technicians

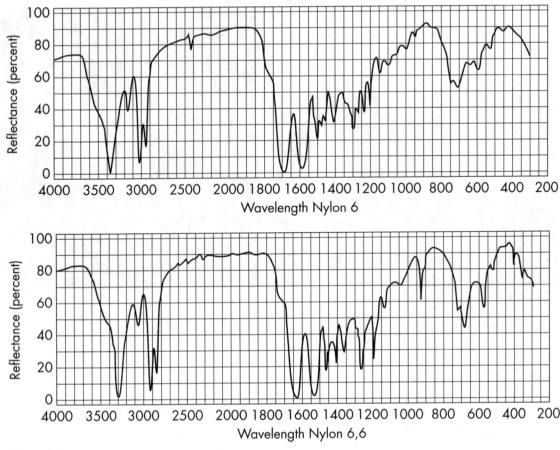

Figure 5-2
Infrared absorption spectra for nylon 6 and nylon 6,6.

require training in using this instrument and in analyzing the results. In addition, the different varieties within a single generic type may produce slightly different results. For example, the several varieties of nylon 6,6 that exist will produce slightly different spectra. Thus, experience in interpreting and reading the spectrum helps in achieving reliable results.

Another procedure is the burn test, in which a small tuft of fibers is placed in the point of a pair of tweezers and brought toward a flame. Fiber behavior as the tuft approaches the heat, the way the fibers burn, the odor and color of smoke produced, and the type and color of ash are compared to a table in the test method to identify the fiber.

Additional procedures may help in fiber identification. Several possible techniques can be used to assess fiber density. Melting point is valid only for those fibers that melt when exposed to heat. Fibers that do not melt will not produce useable results. In refractive index, the change in the speed of light as it passes through matter is used. As light is slowed by matter, it is deflected from a straight line. Liquids of known refractive index are used to identify fibers. In birefringence, a light ray is split into different components transmitted at different velocities and from different directions. Fibers that exhibit birefringence will appear very bright; fibers that exhibit weak birefringence will appear dim; and fibers that exhibit no birefringence will be dark. Fiber type can be determined following the instructions for refractive index and birefringence and consulting the reference table included in the test method.

The final two identification procedures are used primarily to differentiate among bast fibers. Stain tests work with fibers that are naturally light in color. In this procedure, a few fibers are placed on a microscope slide along with a special chemical reagent. The resulting fiber color is used to identify the fiber present. In the drying twist test, a few parallel fibers are dipped in water. The free ends of the fibers are held over a hot plate in warm air and the rotational direction of the fibers identifies the specific bast fiber present.

Quantitative Procedures

Quantitative procedures determine the percentage by weight of each generic fiber present in blends. AATCC 20A, Fiber Analysis: Quantitative, and ASTM D 629, Quantitative Analysis of Textiles, are two standard procedures used. Precautions regarding working with finishes and special blends are discussed. Techniques to remove dyes, finishes, soils, and nonfibrous materials that may interfere with the process are also described. Procedures include chemical analysis, mechanical separation, and microscopic techniques. In each procedure, the first step is to dry and weigh a representative specimen.

Chemical procedures are based on dissolving one component of a fiber blend. After dissolving the component, the remaining fiber is washed, dried, and weighed. The percentage is calculated using Equation 5-1. The percentage of the remaining fiber is calculated by subtracting the percentage of the fiber dissolved from 100.

Equation 5-1

$$\text{Fiber dissolved, \% dry} = 100 \ (F{-}G/F)$$

where, F is the original dry specimen mass (g) and
    G is the extracted dry residual mass (g)

Mechanical separation is used for mixtures and combinations in which yarns of different generic fibers are present in a fabric. Several possibilities exist. One fiber type may be used in the warp direction and a second fiber type in the filling direction. Yarns of one fiber type may be dyed one color and yarns of another fiber type another color. For example, red yarns might be cotton and blue yarns might be polyester. Or, ply yarns are used, with each ply being a different fiber type. For example, a spiral yarn has one ply of mohair and the second ply of a metallic monofilament. In each situation, the analyst can physically separate the components, dry them, weigh them, and calculate the percentages based on the original weight of the specimen (see Equation 5-2).

Equation 5-2

$$\text{Fiber type 1, \% dry} = 100 \ (A/B)$$

where, *A* is the dry specimen mass (g) of fiber 1 and
      B is the original dry specimen mass (g)

In the microscopic technique, the analyst counts the number of fibers of each identifiable type present in a sample. This technique is used when fibers cannot be separated by chemical methods, but they differ in microscopic appearance, such as a cotton and ramie blend. Percentages are calculated based on the number of each fiber type counted, the average fiber diameter, and each fiber's specific gravity.

Quality Measures

Fiber quality is generally of greatest interest to yarn spinners and nonwoven producers. However, fiber quality will have a significant influence on yarn and fabric production costs, as well as the quality of the resulting fabric. Thus, a basic understanding of the factors that describe fiber quality is important. Characteristics will differ depending on whether the fiber is natural or manufactured. These characteristics differ for each natural fiber type as well. Specialized equipment has been developed for each fiber type and for various fiber characteristics used in the process of grading or evaluating fiber quality. ASTM procedures are used to assess the quality characteristics of fibers.

The grade of cotton is a measure of the overall quality of the fiber. Grade is based on fiber color, fiber fineness, fiber strength, maturity, convolutions, amount and type of impurities or trash, including plant matter and soil, the ginning process, where fiber and seed are separated, and fiber length (Bona, 1990; Kadolph & Langford, 1998). Dead fibers will not take dye, and they create problems in spinning processes. Presence of and amount of dead fiber are further quality indicators. These factors are used to select parameters for spinning cotton yarns and in blending cotton with other fibers.

The grade of wool is also a measure of its overall quality. Grade is based on fiber color and fineness, crimp, amount and type of impurities or trash, including plant matter and grease from the animal, fiber strength, and fiber length (Bona, 1990; Kadolph & Langford, 1998). In addition, felting and compression characteristics of wool may also be used in determining the quality of the fiber and its appropriateness for certain applications.

Similar aspects of importance exist for other commonly used natural fibers. With manufactured fibers, fiber characteristics can be engineered based on the expected end use. Methods for evaluating the presence and consistency of these characteristics were discussed briefly at the beginning of this section.

YARNS

Because yarns are the basic structure for many fabrics used in textile products, significant factors that describe yarns may be included in specifications for materials. Note that this discussion will focus on yarns for producing fabrics; threads are a special type of yarn that will be discussed later in this chapter.

Yarn Type and Structure

Specifications for yarn type and structure include information related to how the yarn was made, the components used to produce the yarn, and the nature or character of the components.

Yarn characteristics differ depending on the physical nature of the fibers used in the yarn. Fiber length, fineness, longitudinal and cross-sectional shape affect yarn performance and cost. When fiber content or a fiber trade name is identified in specs, it includes assumptions about the character of the yarn. For example, if specs for a cotton fabric identify pima or Egyptian cotton, they incorporate factors related to fiber length, fiber fineness, and cross-sectional shape.

ASTM D 123, Standard Terminology Relating to Textiles, includes definitions of basic yarn types. Other sources of information regarding yarn types include basic textiles books, books that specialize on yarns and yarn production, and textile dictionaries. When writing specs for yarns, it may also be necessary to indicate the method used to produce the yarn, yarn bulk, or texture, because different yarn production techniques result in yarns with different characteristics in relation to cost, production, and performance in manufacturing and in consumers' hands. For example, some knit goods are made from ring spun yarns because these yarns produce a smoother and more uniform, but more expensive, fabric compared to fabrics made using open-end spun yarns.

ASTM D 1244, Designation of Yarn Construction, helps standardize descriptions of yarns. This procedure is used to describe single, plied, and cable yarns of filament or spun fibers, but it is not broad enough to include novelty or core spun yarns. Notation information is used by yarn producers and by manufacturers who work with the finished yarn or fabric made from the yarn. Information should address the yarn number and numbering system used and the direction and amount of twist. Additional information, including generic fiber type and percentage, linear density, fiber length, fiber modifications, and fiber denier, may need to be included. For a yarn described as 20 c.c. Z 18 tpi (cotton), 20 is the yarn size, c.c. refers to the cotton count system, Z is the twist direction, 18 tpi is the twist amount, and the fiber is cotton.

Yarn Number or Yarn Size

The size of the yarn can be a critical aspect for the fabric. **Yarn number** is a general term that describes the size of the yarn. Yarn number sometimes is referred to as yarn count, but that term is a dated one. Different yarn numbering systems have developed for various fibers. These systems can be described as direct systems, in which the number increases as the size of the yarn increases, or as indirect systems, in which the number decreases as the size of the yarn increases. Information in terms of yarn size used in standard basic fabrics is included in some introductory textile books.

Direct systems, which are sometimes referred to as fixed weight systems, include denier and tex. With these systems, the yarn number is the same as the weight of a specified length of yarn. For example, in the denier system, the yarn number is equal to the mass in grams of 9000 meters of yarn. As the size of the yarn increases, its weight and yarn number increase. Thus, if 9000 m of yarn weighs 27 g, then the yarn size in the denier system is 27. The tex system works with a shorter length of yarn, 1000 m. Tex values tend to be small, because the yarn length is much shorter. As a result, dtex or deka tex is used. Dtex is 10 times larger than tex. Examples of yarn sizes include 75 denier for warp, 150 denier for filling in taffeta, 75 denier for warp, and 200 denier for filling in faille. Sometimes direct systems describe both the size of the yarn and the number of filament fibers present because those factors help determine performance in relation to comfort and durability. This information may be represented by listing the yarn number first, a slash, and then the number of filaments. For example, 100/50 indicates that the yarn is 100 denier and has 50 fibers present. The denier of each filament can then be determined by dividing the size of the yarn by the number of filaments. In this example, the size of each fiber is 2 ($100 \div 50 = 2$).

Indirect systems, which are sometimes referred to as fixed length systems, include cotton, woolen, worsted, and other natural fiber systems. With these systems, the yarn number is the number of yarn lengths (or hanks) of a given measure that will weigh one pound. Thus, for example, in the cotton system, hanks are 840 yards long. If a yarn has a yarn number of 23, then 23 hanks of yarn, each measuring 840 yards in length, will weigh one pound. As yarns increase in size, it takes fewer hanks of yarn to weigh one pound. Thus, as yarn size increases, the yarn number decreases.

If a yarn is made of one strand, it is a single yarn and may be designated by the small letter s after the yarn number, that is, 23s. A yarn that contains 2 plies is designated by the yarn number, a slash, and the number of plies, that is, 23/2. Some examples of yarn numbers include 70s for warp and 100s for filling in lawn, 30s for warp and 42s for filling in printcloth, 13s for warp and 20s for filling in cotton suiting, and 7s to 16s for warp and 8s to 23s for filling in denim.

ASTM D 1059, Yarn Number Based on Short-Length Specimens, is used to determine yarn number for yarns removed from yarn packages or fabrics. Because the yarns are short, this method produces results that are only approximations. Factors related to fabrication, finishing, and dyeing or printing may shrink, swell, or stress yarns, thereby changing their size. Thus, the number calculated for the yarn removed from the fabric and the number of the yarn used to produce the fabric may not match. ASTM D 2258 Practice for Sampling Yarn for Testing describes yarn selection for analysis.

Each test method describes the procedure in detail. This discussion will summarize the procedures for working with yarns removed from fabrics, because that is the form with which much materials analysis of and for sewn products is conducted. In testing for yarn size, yarns are carefully removed from the fabric. Yarns representing each component should be tested. For example, several specimens of reasonable length for both warp and filling yarns should be tested for woven fabrics. Yarn is placed in a twist tester (see Figure 5-3) with sufficient tension to remove any crimp

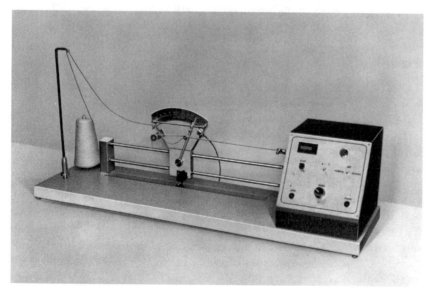

Figure 5-3

Twist tester used to determine several characteristics of yarns. *(Courtesy of SDL International Ltd)*

from the yarn. Most twist testers are equipped with a tensioning device that provides a means of measuring yarn length in a reliable and precise way. The straightened yarn's length and weight are measured. Based on fiber and yarn type, yarn number is calculated using the appropriate option (see Equation 5-3). For example, the cotton system is used for yarns of all cotton, cotton blends, and other fibers in which the resulting look resembles cotton. The woolen system is used for bulky wool and wool-like fabrics. The worsted system is used for compact wool and wool-like fabrics. Denier is most often used for bulk and smooth filament. Tex can be used for any yarn. ASTM D 1907, Yarn Number by the Skein Method, works well for yarns removed from packages or cones.

Equation 5-3

$$\text{Yarn number, indirect system} = [454(1 + C)/(G \times L)]Y \times P$$
$$\text{Yarn number, direct system} = (G \times D)/(1 + C)Y \text{ or }$$
$$(G \times F)/(1 + C)M$$

where, D = constant for direct system (Tex = 1093.5, Denier = 9842.5)
   F = constant for direct system (Tex = 1000, Denier = 9000)
   G = mass conditioned yarn
   L = number of yards in 1 pound (Cotton = 840,
      Woolen = 1600, Worsted = 560)
   P = number of plies
   M = length of the specimen in meters
   Y = length of the specimen in yards
   C = change in length per unit length of yarn in untwisting

Yarn Twist

Twist describes the number of times the fibers in the yarn turn around the lengthwise central axis per unit measure. Twist helps control fiber-to-fiber cohesion in yarns, yarn bulk, and yarn hairiness. Twist is usually reported as turns per unit measure and can be reported as turns per inch (tpi) or turns per meter (tpm). Twist varies with the type of fabric and its intended end use. Typical amounts of twist for basic fabric types are included in most basic textile books. Examples of twist in terms of fabric and yarns include 18 tpi for warp and 6 tpi for filling for flannelette, 25 tpi for warp and 20 tpi for filling for printcloth, and 2 tpi for warp and filling for taffeta. Twist is either S or Z, with Z being more common. Direction of twist is important in terms of consistency among yarns in a fabric (yarns of one type having the same direction of twist) or deliberate combinations of S and Z twist to create subtle difference in color or texture.

ASTM D 1422, Twist in Single Spun Yarns by the Untwist-Retwist Method, and ASTM D 1423, Twist in Yarns by the Direct-Counting

Method, are two standard procedures used. Yarns must be handled carefully to avoid loss of twist before testing. In the untwist-retwist procedure, a length of yarn is clamped in a twist tester, straightened, and the yarn is untwisted until it has been untwisted completely and an equal amount of twist in the opposite direction has been inserted. The number of twists on the counter, direction of twist, and specimen length are recorded. Twist is calculated using Equation 5-4.

Equation 5-4

$$T = R/2L$$

where, T = twist (tpi or tpm)
    R = counter reading
    $1/2$ = the correction for twist–retwist
    L = specimen length

In the direct counting procedure, both yarn ends are fixed in position, and the number of rotations of one end are counted until the fibers between the clamps are parallel and untwisted as assessed by use of a teezing needle. Twist is calculated by using Equation 5-5.

Equation 5-5

$$T = R/L$$

where, T = twist (tpi or tpm)
    R = counter reading
    L = specimen length (inches or meters)

Yarn Defects

Yarn defects refer to irregularities within the yarn that are not deliberately a part of the yarn. Yarn appearance procedures, for example ASTM D 2255, Grading Spun Yarns for Appearance, use photographic standards so that the appearance of yarns can be evaluated by trained observers who compare appearance of yarn specimens wound on cards to the standards and assign a value based on their perception of the closest match between the specimen and the standards. Observers look for such problems as fuzz, neps, slubs, and thick or thin places in yarns. Other yarn defect scales, such as the Sears scale for knots and slubs shown in Figure 5-4, are plastic replicas showing several sizes of these common yarn flaws in fabrics. **Threshold levels** are used in yarn and other specs in describing the greatest degree of irregularity that would be acceptable in materials or finished products.

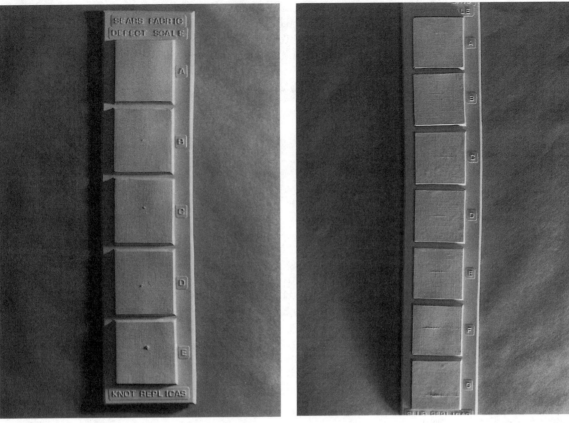

Figure 5-4
Sears yarn defect scales for knots (left) and slubs (right). (*Courtesy of Sears, Roebuck and Co., Product Quality Assurance*)

Yarn Quality

The presence or absence of localized or periodic faults in the yarn is one measure of yarn quality. However, several other measures are also indicators of quality. ASTM procedures assess yarn strength and elongation performance, bulk properties of textured yarns, shrinkage of yarns, yarn evenness, and friction coefficient. Bulk properties of textured yarns are measures of yarn shrinkage or crimp recovery when the yarns are exposed to steam or dry heat, such as during finishing of fabrics or products. Other ASTM procedures describe assessing tolerances for spun and filament yarns related to linear density, tenacity, elongation, twist, and weight.

Additional ASTM procedures address several performance aspects and properties unique to some yarns. Examples include deformation of elastic yarns, in which the elastomeric fiber is used as a bare continuous filament yarn under tension. Appropriate applications might include such products as support garments, hosiery, and exercise apparel. Fabrics woven from stretch yarns can be tested for stretch, growth, and recovery characteristics. These fabrics are used in body-contouring and body-hugging garments.

Finally, ASTM D 2260, Conversion Factors and Equivalent Yarn Numbers Measured in Various Numbering Systems, is a useful source of information for converting yarn numbers from one system to another.

FABRIC CHARACTERISTICS

Fabric characteristics is a general term that refers to how various components are combined to create a fabric. These dimensions contribute to fabric cost, quality, appearance, performance, and production aspects. Many types of fabrication methods are used to produce fabric. Each method uses different technology and terminology. ASTM D 4850, Standard Terminology Relating to Fabric, defines terms of interest in this section, as do various basic textile books.

Fabrication Method

Fabrication method refers to the technique used to produce the fabric. Many possibilities exist. Some are more common than others, but all are presently available. Fabrics can be made from polymer solutions (films and foams), fibers (fiber webs or nonwovens), yarns (wovens, knits, braids, laces, and others), fabrics (quilted and bonded fabrics), and composites that combine at least two or more components into one fabric (coated, poromeric, foam and fiber, and so on). Thus, materials specs need to identify in an unambiguous way the fabric desired.

Fabrication method can be general or more specific. For example, a general method would include describing a fabric as a plain weave. A more specific description might describe that fabric as a balanced plain weave. In some cases, the type of selvage would also need to be specified because of the way the fabric is handled or the product made.

Fabric Density

Fabric density is a general term that describes the number of components in the fabric per unit measure. Probably the most common measure of fabric density is fabric count, or simply **count,** which is the number of yarns in the lengthwise and crosswise direction of the fabric in one unit of measure (that is, inch or centimeter). When using ASTM D 3775, Fabric Count of Woven Fabric, the fabric within one-tenth of the fabric's width closest to the selvage is not included, because the count may vary slightly in these areas depending on how the selvage was produced. Both warp and filling yarns are counted at five locations within the fabric, sampling as many different shuttle changes as possible. Figure 5-5 illustrates an example of locations where count was measured. Figure 5-6 shows a pick counter often used for count determinations.

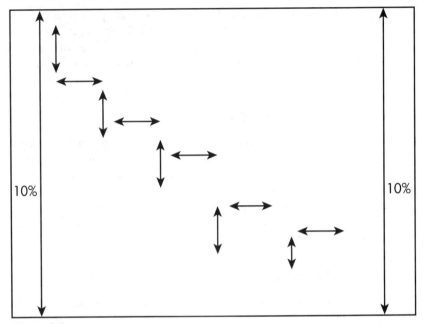

Figure 5-5
Measuring fabric count of a woven fabric.

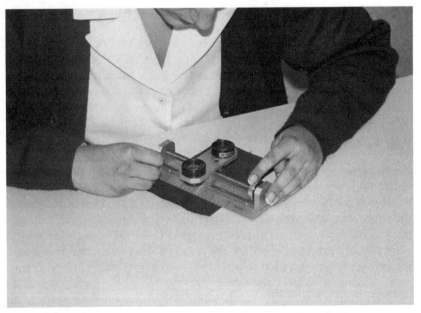

Figure 5-6
Pick counter used to determine count in woven fabrics. (*Courtesy of SDL International Ltd*)

When count of woven fabrics is assessed, the procedures differ depending on the complexity and width of the fabric. For fabrics less than 5 inches wide, the entire fabric width is counted. For fabrics with a low count (fewer than 25 yarns per inch or 1 yarn per mm), each count is made over a 3-inch width. For dense fabrics (more than 25 yarns per inch), the count is made for 1 inch. With fancy patterns, the count is made for full pattern repeats. With some fabrics in which yarns may not be distinguishable, such as with meltons, unraveling the fabric may be needed to obtain an accurate count of yarns. In all cases, the count per inch is calculated.

Woven count is reported as whole numbers with the warp listed first. For example, 40 × 80 would be read as forty by eighty. Forty describes the number of warp yarns per inch and eighty the number of filling yarns per inch. Example counts for woven fabrics include 88 × 80 for lawn, organdy, and batiste; 80 × 80 to 76 × 76 for printcloth; 144 × 76 for combed broadcloth; 56 × 30 for wool flannel; 60 × 36 for denim; and 200 × 65 for satin.

Gauge or cut refers to the needles per inch of the knitting machine used to knit the fabric. Although there is a connection between gauge and fabric density, the two terms are not synonymous because fabrics relax after knitting and finishing altering the density of the structure. With knits, density is a measure of the wales and the courses per inch. Figure 5-7 illustrates the shape and direction of courses and wales. Wales are reported first, then courses. Examples of fabric density for knit fabrics include 32 ×

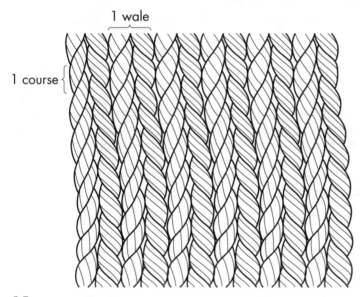

1 wale

1 course

Figure 5-7
Close-up of knit fabric: the counter needle moves across to count wales and up/down to count courses.

40 for jersey, 6×12 for a coarse stockinette, and 12×25 for a fine stockinette.

Fabric Mass Per Unit Area

Fabric mass per unit area, or weight, is an important factor in determining fabric amount, cost, and quality. ASTM D 3776, Mass per Unit Area (Weight) of Woven Fabric, is used to assess this characteristic. Several options related to the length and width of the fabric are included. In the bolt or roll method, fabric length and width are measured, the bolt is weighed, and the weight calculated as mass per unit area (ounces per square yard (oz/yd^2) or grams per square meter (g/m^2)), mass per linear yard or linear meter, or linear yards per pound or linear meters per kilogram. In the full-width sample option, a sample or specimen cut from a roll or bolt is used and its length and width are measured. In the small-swatch option, a piece of fabric is cut and weighed. Calculations are listed in Equation 5-6 for mass per unit area for this option.

Equation 5-6

$$\text{Mass per unit area (oz/yd2)} = 45.72 G/L_S W$$
$$\text{Mass per unit area (g/m2)} = 106 G/L_S W$$

where, G = mass of specimen in grams
W = width of specimen in inches
L_S = length of specimen in inches

Fabrics that weigh less than 4.0 oz/yd^2 are considered light weight fabrics and are often used for blouses, shirts, and sheer draperies. Fabrics that weigh between 4.0 and 7.0 oz/yd^2 are considered medium weight fabrics and are used for many pants, skirts, suits, some draperies and upholstery fabrics, curtains, and sheets. Fabrics that weigh more than 7.0 oz/yd^2 are considered heavy weight and are used for heavier and more durable suits, pants, upholsteries, draperies, and many industrial products.

Fabric Packaging

Because rolls or bolts of fabric used in production facilities are bulky and heavy, specs regarding the maximum allowable weight or length on a single bolt or roll are often identified. Additional specs regarding the minimum allowable inner diameter for the cardboard tube on which the fabric is rolled may be dictated by the dimensions of the forklift's lifting arms. When bolts weigh several hundred pounds, they will not be moved by hand by individual employees. Finally, packaging materials used with fabric may be specified to facilitate recycling and minimize disposal costs. Packaging specs include the type of plastic wrap used to protect the fabric from stains and soil during storage, shipping, and handling and the grade and weight of cardboard tubes.

Length and Width

Because sewn product manufacturers buy large quantities of fabric, it is not practical to measure the fabric length by hand. **Length** is used to describe the linear quantity of fabric delivered or used. ASTM D 3773, Length of Woven Fabric, describes four ways of determining the length of fabric. In the hand method, the fabric length is measured under no tension. The hand method is the most accurate, but also the most time consuming. In the drum method, fabric is wound onto a measuring drum that has a synchronized counting mechanism for recording meters or yards. With the clock method, wheels equipped with a counting mechanism measure the length. The folding method is used to measure the **put-up,** or length of fabric on the roll or bolt with lighter weight, soft fabrics that weigh less than 6 oz/yd^2. Several folds are measured and the fabric length is calculated by multiplying the number of folds by the average fold length.

Fabric width is critical in terms of marker making and cutting. **Width** describes the full useable width of the fabric from one edge to the other. Fabric width needs to be as specified and must be consistent. Width requirements and tolerances are affected by the product, pattern requirements, and equipment available in cutting facilities, including fabric spreaders, tables, and automatic cutters. Some products, such as bedding, require exceptionally wide fabric because seams are unacceptable. With some products, styling features may require wide pattern pieces, but equipment needs within a cutting facility are probably a stronger factor in influencing fabric width. Two methods of determining width are identified in ASTM D 3774, Width of Woven Fabric—the full bolt or roll method and the short specimen method. The fabric is placed on a flat horizontal surface, and its width is measured perpendicular to selvages to the nearest 1 mm, using a measuring stick or steel tape measure. Fabric or plastic tape measures are not recommended because they distort with use or age.

Bow and Skew

Bow and skew describe two ways a crosswise yarn or yarn path can be distorted from a straight perpendicular line. In **bow,** the crosswise yarn forms one or more arcs as it moves across the fabric. Examples are illustrated in Figure 5-8. In **skew,** the crosswise yarn forms some angle other than 90° as it moves across the fabric (see Figure 5-9). Bow and skew occur with both woven and knitted fabrics. These off-grain problems can develop while the fabric is being produced, as in skew with knits, or while the fabric is being finished, as with some types of skew or most types of bow. Both bow and skew create problems in spreading and cutting fabrics, matching seams or pattern as in plaids or stripes, distortion of seams or fabric patterns, and in the way the finished product falls or drapes (see Figure 5-10).

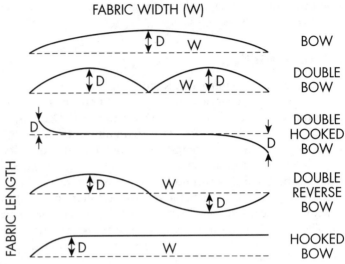

Figure 5-8
Examples of bow.

Bow and skew should be small, generally less than 1 percent, in order to minimize problems with the fabric in production or satisfaction with the product in use. Better quality fabrics are not bowed or skewed, or the amount is very small. ASTM D 3882, Bow and Skewness in Woven and Knitted Fabrics, is used to measure this potential distortion. The difference between the two measurements is based on the yarn path in the fabric. Usually, a straight perpendicular line is traced across the entire width of a fabric, starting at the place at which a specific filling yarn or course meets the selvage. The actual path that the yarn or course takes across the fabric is traced, and the greatest difference between the perpendicular path and the actual path is measured. Thus, if multiple bow is identified, measure all instances, but use only the greatest value in the calculation. Calculations for bow are made using Equation 5-7. Skew is calculated using Equation 5-8. Bow and skew are reported as a percentage, such as 2 percent bow.

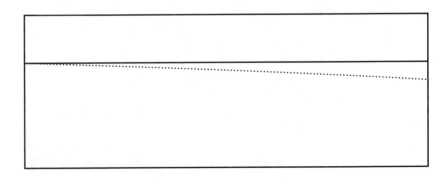

Figure 5-9
Skew in a fabric: solid line is perpendicular to the selvages; the dotted line shows the skewed yarn or course.

Equation 5-7

$$\text{Bow, } \% = 100(D/W)$$

where, D is the maximum bow and W is the width of the
fabric where the measurements are taken

Equation 5-8

$$\text{Skew, } \% = 100(O/W)$$

where O is the difference between the perpendicular line
and the actual yarn path; W is the width of the fabric where
the measurements are taken

Other Fabric Deformations

Other problems with fabric deformation occur when the fabric is rolled
onto a tube. Fabrics can buckle or be rolled unevenly when they are packaged at the mill or finishing plant. As layers of fabric on a roll accumulate,
stress on each layer can be substantial. These stress marks and buckles may
be permanently "set" into the fabric. In addition, depending on the cohe-
siveness between the layers on the roll and the roll's orientation, problems
can occur during handling, storage, and shipping. Orientation of the roll
refers to whether it is resting on its side so that it takes on a flattened appearance over time, or whether it is resting on one end of the cylinder,
which can cause the fabric to slouch down over time.

Buckling and unevenness contribute to problems in spreading, cutting, and making up of products. Because of these problems, some manufacturers specify the maximum amount of fabric allowed per roll, handling
of the roll, and its orientation during storage and shipping.

Crimp and Takeup

Crimp and takeup (ASTM D 3883, Yarn Crimp or Yarn Takeup in Woven
Fabrics) describe the relationship between the length of a piece of fabric
and the length of a yarn removed from that fabric. **Crimp** deals with the
additional amount of yarn needed to interlace with other yarns. **Takeup** is
the additional length of yarn needed to produce a piece of fabric. The two
values deal with different perspectives of the same issue. Yarns in a fabric
are not perfectly straight; they move away from straight whenever they interlace or interloop with other yarns in the fabric. For both crimp and
takeup, a length in a fabric is marked so that the marks are visible on the
yarns when they have been removed from the fabric (see Figure 5-11). The
distance between the marks in the fabric should be measured precisely at
10 inches. The yarn is removed from the fabric, placed under tension, and
subjected to tension until it is straight (such as in a crimp tester) and the

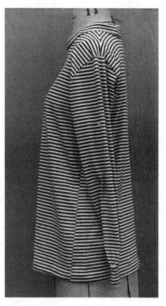

Figure 5-10
Skew causes this side seam to
twist to the front.

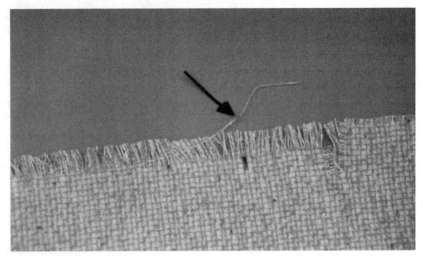

Figure 5-11
This fabric is ready to assess crimp and takeup. Note the mark on the fabric and the mark on the yarn partially removed from the fabric.

---

straightened length measured. Equation 5-9 is used to calculate yarn crimp; Equation 5-10 is used to calculate yarn takeup.

Equation 5-9

$$\text{Yarn crimp, } C, \% = 100(Y - F)/F$$

where, F = distance between marks in the fabric
        Y = distance between the same two marks on the yarn removed from the fabric

Equation 5-10

$$\text{Yarn Takeup, } T, \% = 100(Y - F)/Y$$

where, F = distance between marks in the fabric
        Y = distance between the same two marks on the yarn removed from the fabric

Barré

Barré is the "optical result of physical or dye differences in the yarns, geometric differences in fabric structure, or any combination of the differences" (AATCC, 1996, p. 335). This problem is often seen as a subtle stripe or shade variation in materials and products. The presence of barré is detected by using AATCC 178, Barré: Assessment and Grading. In the assessment process, a roll or bolt of three or more products is evaluated by

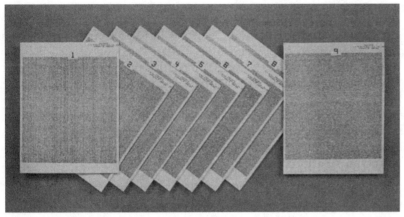

Figure 5-12
The Uniform Reference Scale used in assessing barré. (*Reprinted with permission from the American Association of Textile Chemists and Colorists, P.O. Box 12215, Research Triangle Park, NC 27709*)

three or more trained observers using standard lighting conditions. Each observer compares the specimen to the steps of the Uniform Reference Scale and assigns the number of the step that most closely matches (see Figure 5-12 and Figure 5-13). Besides reporting the numerical step, a term describing the barré pattern is also reported.

Figure 5-13
Barré marks in a fabric. The arrow marks the first of several barré marks.

FINISHES

Finishes are a fabric characteristic that may be identified when a fabric is named or described. For example, flannelette implies a napped finish on the fabric. However, since flannelette may be napped on one or both sides of the fabric, more information may be needed when writing specifications. Other finishes, for example soil resistance, need to be identified by name when an order is placed. Often a supplier will provide the fabric with a specific combination of finishes applied to a basic or standard fabric. For example, a cotton sateen may be Schreiner calendered and singed to provide the smooth regular surface expected with that fabric.

Presence of Finishes

Several AATCC procedures are used to identify the finishes, particularly chemical finishes, present on a fabric. Mechanical-physical finishes, such as napping, are easier to identify based on the hand, texture, or appearance of the fabric. AATCC 94, Finishes in Textiles: Identification, is used to assess chemical finishes, dyes, and pigments present. This procedure subjects the fabric specimen to sequential solvent extraction to remove chemicals. The extract is subjected to sophisticated instrumental or wet-chemical analytical procedures to identify warp sizes, dyes, optical brighteners, fabric softeners, flame retardants, durable press compounds, and other general or special purpose finishes.

The dye or pigment used to add color to textiles is important in terms of the product's final color, cost, processing requirements, and fastness characteristics. However, identifying the specific dye is a tedious process that involves spectrophotometric techniques similar in a general sense to those discussed for quantitative fiber analysis. For many textiles, the color is the result of a combination of dyes or pigments. Thus, many companies evaluate fastness characteristics with other techniques to be discussed later. Companies may specify a general dye class, such as reactive dye or vat dye, but they do not specify the precise dye to be used to achieve a color.

The stage in which the colorant is applied to the textile component is a common specification. Stage of coloration relates to cost, quality, design, and production. For example, fiber dyed is expensive, but produces a visual characteristic that is not possible with other techniques. Greater variation in color among the fibers is tolerated, but the overall color perceived in the fabric must fall within the specified range. Color matching and shade sorting will be discussed in a later chapter.

The color or pattern of the fabric is included in the specifications. This information may be described in terms of the suppliers' name or code for the fabrics they produce, a standard color chip such as that produced by Pantone, a name or term, or a sample of fabric, paper, or other material. Visual samples or a standard color chip make color specs much easier to meet than a descriptive term. For example, what color is moss green?

Performance of Finishes

Most finishes are used to enhance performance, hand, or other characteristic of a fabric. Many standard test methods are used to evaluate the effectiveness of these finishes. For example, the effectiveness of a durable press finish can be assessed using an AATCC procedure. Later chapters will discuss how the performance of many finishes are assessed. Other AATCC procedures are used to assess the presence of certain chemicals, such as formaldehyde, that may contribute to health and environmental problems or permanganate that may contribute to yellowing of fabric.

FABRIC QUALITY

Fabric quality is based on the quality of each component used to produce and finish the fabric, as well as the way in which the various components interact. Thus, fabric quality is cumulative and has the potential to produce a synergistic or an antagonistic affect.

A **defect** is defined as the departure or nonconformance of some characteristic from its intended level or state (ASTM, 1996). Examples of fabric defects are included in Figure 5-14. Illustrations of other defects can be found in Powderly (1987), Goldberg (1957), or ASTM 3990 (1996).

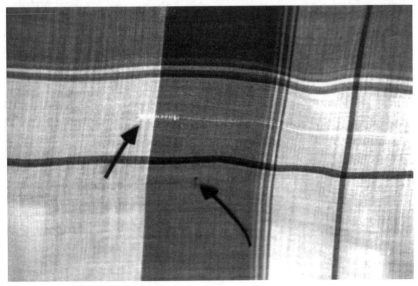

A

Figure 5-14
Fabric defects: (a) slubs; (b) missing warp; (c) reed marks; (d) hole; (e) dark yarn.

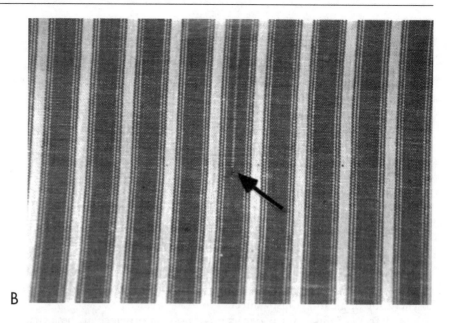

B

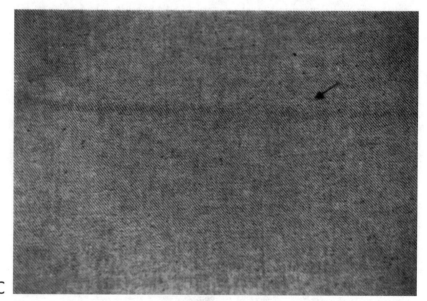

C

Figure 5-14 (continued)

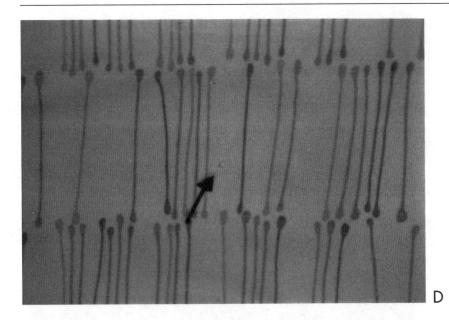

D

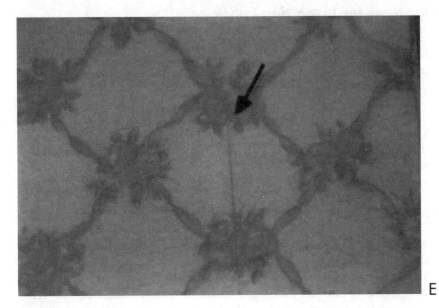

E

Figure 5-14 (continued)

Definitions of Patent and Latent Defects

There are two basic types of defects related to materials and products. The discussion here focuses on materials, but these definitions also apply to products. **Patent defects** are those flaws and irregularities that can be perceived during examination or inspection of the material. Patent defects are visible and may be defined by the buyer. Thus, one company may identify something as a defect, while another company might not find that particular irregularity a defect. Many companies have gone to great expense to develop a list of defects, along with visual examples of acceptable variations in appearance and unacceptable defects. These are used to identify the visual aspects that will contribute to acceptance or rejection of materials or products.

A **latent defect** is a hidden problem that is not apparent no matter how carefully the material or product is examined. Latent defects most often relate to performance problems or problems that develop with storage or aging. These defects become apparent with age, testing, or use.

Patent defects are identified by inspection; latent defects can only be detected by testing the fabric's performance characteristics.

Systems for Inspecting Fabric

Fabric is inspected to identify the type, number, size, and location of defects. The cumulative total of these defects is then used to determine the grade of the fabric and its acceptability for the production of finished products.

A **grade** is a numerical value assigned to a fabric based on the number, size, and severity of defects seen during a visual inspection. ASTM D 5430, Visually Inspecting and Grading Fabrics, is used to inspect and grade fabrics. ASTM D 3990, Standard Terminology Relating to Fabric Defects, is a source of information for identifying and naming defects in woven and knitted fabrics. Inspection is done using a fabric inspection machine that moves the fabric lengthwise across the viewing surface from the beginning to the end of the roll or bolt (see Figure 5-15). Speed of viewing is negotiable between buyer and vendor. Some inspection machines are able to produce a map of the fabric that identifies the location and type of each defect. The map aids in spreading and cutting so that fabric defects are less likely to be incorporated into product parts.

Several options for assigning points to defects exist. **Defect, demerit, or penalty points** are based on the length of the defect. Longer defects are assigned more points because their existence presents more significant problems in terms of fabric usage. In all options, fabric width less than the minimum specified also is considered a defect.

In one option, the greatest number of points assigned to any one defect is 4. A maximum of 4 points can be assigned to any one yard of fabric, regardless of the number and length of defects. Short defects up to 3 inches in length are assigned 1 point; defects 3 to 6 inches in length, 2

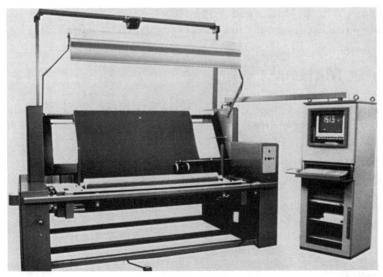

Figure 5-15
Fabric inspection machine. (*Photo courtesy Joseph Pernick Manufacturing Corporation. © 1997 Joseph Pernick Manufacturing Corporation, Glendale, NY*)

points; 6 to 9 inches in length, 3 points; and greater than 9 inches, 4 points.

In a second option, the maximum number of points is greater and the defect length is based on increments of 9 inches. For example, a defect up to 9 inches in length is assigned 1 point, but a defect between 18 and 27 inches is assigned 3 points.

In a third option, the points assigned to a defect differ between warp and filling with up to 10 points assigned to any one defect. Points are reported per 100 meters or yards or 100 linear meters or yards using one of the four equations listed in Equation 5-11.

Equation 5-11

$$\text{Points for fabric defects}$$
$$\text{Points}/100 \text{ m}^2 = 100{,}000P/WL$$
$$\text{Points}/100 \text{ yd}^2 = 3{,}600P/WL$$
$$\text{Points/linear m} = 100P/WL$$
$$\text{Points/linear yd} = 100{,}000P/WL$$

where, P = total points assigned
W = Fabric width (*millimeters or inches)
L = fabric length examined (meters or yards)

Most inspection is done by trained inspectors. Efforts to standardize inspection have focused on training personnel and on developing computerized, or automated inspection systems. Although not yet a standard practice, computer inspection can be used for woven fabrics.

OTHER MATERIALS

Because many other materials beyond fabric are used in textile products, understanding their basic characteristics is important when writing specifications.

CLOSURES

Closures include zippers, buttons, hooks and eyes, hook and loop fasteners, and snaps. Each type uses unique terms and has characteristics that should be considered when developing specs.

Zippers

Zippers close an opening in a product when two rows of stringers (teeth, scoops, or coils) interlock as they pass through a slider. Zippers make closer fitting garments possible, accept seam stress better than other openers, and produce a smoother and flatter appearance at the zipper compared to other closures. Zippers are sometimes selected for their aesthetic contribution to the product's appearance because they can be produced with decorative pulls and tapes and color-coordinated parts. Zipper failure may result in product failure and rejection by the consumer.

The various parts of a zipper may differ with the type, design, and function. Zippers can be made in varying strengths; they can be decorative, hidden, heavy, light, and open at one end, both ends, or neither end. Thus, specs need to address the principle parts of the zipper, its overall length, its open length, its materials, and other relevant factors (see Figure 5-16). ASTM D 2050, Standard Terminology Relating to Zippers, is an excellent source of information for these specs. With some products, the dimensions of major components, such as chain length, chain thickness, and slider mouth width, are also important. Overall assembled zipper length, the effective length of the opening, and zipper width are usually included in specs because these dimensions are related to the product type or style and the demands placed on the zipper. ASTM D 2060, Measuring Zipper Dimensions, explains the procedure for determining basic dimensions. ASTM D 3657, Standard Specifications for Zipper Dimensions, is a source of information for standard zipper sizes and standard dimensions for component parts. ASTM D 4465, Standard Performance Specification for Zippers for Denim Dungarees, is the only spec that is available for use in specifying zippers for a particular product type.

Materials used to produce zippers include synthetic polymers, such as polyester and nylon, that are used to produce zipper teeth, tape, sliders,

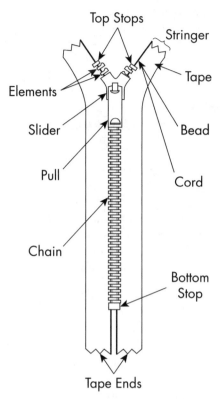

Top Stops

Stringer

Tape

Elements

Slider

Bead

Pull

Cord

Chain

Bottom
Stop

Tape Ends

Figure 5-16
Major parts of a zipper.

and other parts. Synthetic materials used for the chain tend to be more flexible, are lighter weight, and will not rust or corrode. These materials can be produced in colors to match the other parts of the zipper and other materials used in the product. They do not feel cold or hot. If the zipper is made with synthetic coils for the chain, a split zipper may be made useable by forcing the slider over the split area.

Metal, such as brass, nickel, steel, or zinc, may be used in zipper teeth, sliders, and other parts. Sometimes, brass plating is used over a base metal. One drawback is that metal components may corrode or rust. This can be a problem with products that are wet processed or chemically treated after production with some abrasive finishes or product dyeing. Of all metals, brass and stainless steel are less likely to corrode or rust during these processes. Metal zippers are stronger, stiffer, heavier, and more abrasive than synthetic polymer zippers; the teeth can be removed during application in production without damaging the zipper tape. Although various types of sliders are produced, most are made of metal. Metal sliders may be coated with enamel so that they coordinate with the other parts of the zipper, but enamel is not necessarily as permanent as dyeing or mass pigmentation of the synthetic polymer parts. Continuous chain zippers are available by the reel and are cut to the appropriate length as it is applied during production. Sliders and stops are purchased in bulk and combined with the chain during production to produce a workable, inexpensive zipper of the appropriate weight, type, and length. These bulk zippers are widely used by manufacturers of basic goods and industrial products because they minimize stocking a variety of zippers and provide flexibility in production because zipper length can be adjusted for a particular product style or size.

Zipper tapes are narrow, tricot knit or twill weave fabrics of cotton, synthetic fibers, or a fiber blend. Tapes come in a variety of widths and densities depending on the product and performance expectations for the zipper. Durability of the tape is an important contributor to the durability of the zipper. Low density tapes are less expensive, but may fail under stress during use. Tapes made of synthetic fibers are stronger, lighter weight, more stable to washing or dry cleaning, and more abrasion resistant. Cotton tapes tend to be used in all cotton products, but may exhibit shrinkage and be more sensitive to abrasive and chemical washes used in some product finishing.

Buttons

Buttons are small knobs or disks of materials that are used with corresponding slits or buttonholes as a unit to secure two parts of a product together or close an opening in a product. Unlike zippers, buttons do not create a continuous closure, but rather are placed at specified distances throughout the length of an opening. Buttons are attached by thread that passes through either shanks on the back of the button or holes in the visible knob or disk of the button.

Performance of the button-buttonhole unit depends on its materials and structure and its compatibility with the product. An endless variety of shapes, sizes, and colors of buttons made of many materials in many styles are available. Buttons can be made singly or in small lots by artists and craftpersons or in large lots by manufacturers. Buttons can be strictly utilitarian applications or can add interest, color, texture, identification, or style to a product. Some buttons support other buttons, especially those of greater value and larger size or those used under greater stress. Because button loss is a problem for consumers, many products include replacement buttons at point of sale. If products are to be sold with replacement buttons, extra buttons will need to be purchased for this service.

Many materials are used to produce buttons. The type of material will probably relate to the product type, style, and cost, as well as the target market. Buttons are made from naturally occurring materials, including wood, leather, bone, shells, rocks, horns, and hulls of nuts, that incorporate natural variations in color and texture. These buttons may be considered to be environmentally friendly, but that is not always so. After all, if a button is made from a seashell, the animal living in the shell has been, at the very least, removed from its home. Natural materials may be hard to dye, inconsistent in performance, or brittle. Some wooden or nut-hull buttons may swell and split if they remain in water for too long, for example, if the product is soaked overnight to remove stains.

Synthetic materials, including polyester, nylon, and acrylic resins, are used to imitate natural button materials. For example, the tortoise shell button on the market today is a synthetic resin; trade of tortoise shell is banned because it comes from an endangered species. Synthetic materials are also used to make plastic buttons. Some of these materials are thermoset; others are thermoplastic. Thermoset buttons include polyester, melamine, and urea. These buttons cannot be melted after they are produced and are less likely to be damaged during production and pressing when exposed to high heat. Nylon buttons are thermoplastic, and they will melt if the temperature exceeds the melting point for that type of nylon. Plastic buttons are usually either cast or molded. Cast buttons tend to be less expensive than molded buttons.

Metal buttons can be made from base metals, such as nickel or tin; alloys, such as brass or pewter; or precious metals, such as silver. Brass plating may be used with a base metal to give the appearance of a better quality button. Metal buttons may need to have a clear finish applied to minimize problems with tarnish, rust, and corrosion.

Glass and pottery buttons are sometimes considered to be made from natural materials, but these materials require extensive processing to be useable in button form. Buttons of these materials are more sensitive to shattering, cracking, or breaking than many other materials.

The manner in which the material of the button is finished will affect aesthetics and performance. Button finishes range from dull and matte to shiny and glossy. Shiny buttons that become dull in an irregular fashion may create problems with customer satisfaction. This is especially true if the texture of the button was an important component of the aesthetics of the product. If button finish is important to its appearance or that of the product, then the type of finish needs to be specified.

Button structure describes not only how the button is made, but how many parts will be needed. Some buttons combine different parts that may be made of different materials. Parts may be clinched, clamped, glued, soldered, or molded together. The permanence of the joints is critical in terms of button performance. For example, glues that are soluble in hot solvents may dissolve in dry cleaning, causing the components to separate and creating problems with consumer satisfaction. In addition, button design may be related to end use. For example, buttons that will receive significant abrasion in use may be designed with a deep thread groove. This minimizes abrasion of the thread thereby reducing the possibility that the button will separate from the product.

Button color is another criterion to consider when developing specifications. Some producers do not match button color to the fashion fabric. All products have the same basic beige or neutral button attached. This practice minimizes inventory, but color matching of materials is a characteristic used to define high product quality. Better quality products are made with buttons that match the color of the fashion fabric. This creates problems in terms of identifying when colors match and whether the color of the fashion fabric and the button will react to age, storage, use, and care in a similar fashion. In other words, will the button's color still match the fabric's color in six months, or after use and cleaning?

Some button raw materials have had the color added just before extrusion for molding or casting, such as mass pigmentation of synthetic resins or coloring of glass. Other button materials have the color added during finishing, as with glazed pottery or clay buttons. Still other button materials can be dyed after production, but some dyes are not fast and some processes may weaken the buttons. Buttons to be used on products that will be dyed after production probably should not absorb color during this process. It is not likely that buttons and fabric will absorb dye in a similar manner and produce an acceptable product.

Button size is based on several dimensions. Diameter is based on lignes, a unit of measure equal to 1/40 of an inch. Other dimensions of importance include thickness; the number of holes and their diameter and spacing; shank type and bridge (distance from shank end to hole edge); and depth. Button size requirements are determined by the product and its style, fashion, appearance, the number of buttons, and holding strength. It is not uncommon for a product to use different sizes of the same type, style, and color of a button in different areas. For example, a blazer may use one size down the front, another size on the sleeves, and a third size on the collar or pockets. Consistency of size is important when automatic machines are used to apply the button. In addition, if the button has a definite top and button, then application costs may increase because the operator needs additional time to apply each button in its correct orientation, that is, right side up.

Hooks and Eyes

Hooks and eyes (bars) are paired metal fasteners often used on waistbands of garments. The type used in manufacturing facilities is usually held in place by a clinch plate inside the waistband. The prongs on the hook, or bar, clamp around the plate and hold each part of the pair in place. Hooks and eyes are generally made of a noncorrosive metal. Because they are used to form hidden closures, finishes such as enamel coatings are seldom used.

Hook and Loop Fasteners

Hook and loop fasteners, such as Velcro®, are contact fasteners made from paired nylon tapes; one tape is covered with tiny hooks and the other with tiny loops. When the two tapes are pressed together, many hooks catch on opposing loops and hold the tapes together. If greater pressure is applied when closing the tapes, a more powerful hold is created. Closed tapes are separated by a peeling action. The tapes are available in many colors (dyed) and weights, and as continuous tapes or various shapes that have been die cut. Holding power is also affected by the structure of the tape and its application method. Important factors include tape size, hooks per square inch, hook strength, and hook length. Tapes can be woven or knit pile fabrics that are heat set to retain the shape of the hook or loop. Back coating minimizes yarn slippage, a tendency with tapes made of smooth filament yarns. Back coating can include an adhesive to facilitate application. Solvent- or heat-activated and pressure-sensitive adhesives are available.

Snaps

Snaps are another type of mechanical fastener that produces a noncontinuous closure. They produce a less formal look and are often used on outerwear, active sportswear, and other casual apparel. Snaps, which are sized by lignes, should be easy to quickly press closed and pull open. They require more precision in matching the two parts and greater strength to operate than buttons. The gripping power of snaps increases with size; larger snaps have more gripping surface. Snaps may be used for such products as billfolds and belts that are stiffer or bulkier than other textile products. Most snaps are made of metal components, such as brass, steel, and nickel, but plastic snaps are used in children's wear, rainwear, and some packaging. Plated snaps are also available. Caps, the outer covering used to dress up snaps, add an aesthetic component to the snap and are available in materials similar to those used for buttons. Caps of various colors or pressed logos or designs are used to add a design element to many products. Caps made of various synthetic materials similar to those used in buttons are available; fabric caps are also used.

THREAD

A **sewing thread** is a special type of yarn that will pass through a sewing machine rapidly, form a stitch efficiently and consistently, and perform adequately in a textile product. It influences the quality of stitches and seams, product performance, aesthetics, and cost. Thread connects product parts, finishes edges, attaches other materials, and adds aesthetic appeal. It may be dyed to match the color of other materials in the product. They are selected based on function, appearance, and performance expectations in terms of strength, abrasion resistance, elongation and elasticity, colorfastness, stability, chemical and heat resistance, and flammability.

Thread failure may mean failure of the entire textile product. Sewing problems related to thread include breakage, skipped or irregular stitches, partial fusing or melting, and seam pucker. Sewability of threads is related to consistent loop formation and resistance to breakage and other problems involved in passing through the machine and needle. High-quality thread is uniform in its characteristics and dimensions, can be used on a variety of machines with a variety of fabrics, and minimizes problems with breakage, incorrect stitches, and fabric damage.

Most threads are cotton, polyester, nylon, or rayon. Specialty threads of silk, linen, spandex, aramid, or other fibers are available for products requiring special performance characteristics. Thread characteristics are similar to fiber characteristics. For example, cotton thread is moderately strong and absorbent, exhibits poor elasticity, and dyes well. Polyester thread is strong and heat sensitive, but not absorbent. Cotton threads are a standard by which other threads are judged in terms of loop formation and sewability. However, cotton thread is becoming less popular as synthetic threads improve in quality. In some hot and humid climates, cotton and rayon threads may rot in storage.

Threads are available in a wide variety of sizes and styles. They can be made from staple fibers, filament fibers, or combinations of both. Spun threads generally consist of two to six single plies that are twisted together. As a result, they have good stability and holding power. Filament threads are stronger than spun threads. The three major types are smooth multifilament, textured filament, and monofilament. Smooth multifilament threads are used when high strength is needed for such products as shoes, saddles, and tents. Textured filament threads are often used as the looper thread for cover stitches. They have a softer luster and more cover, but are more prone to snagging during sewing and use. Monofilament thread is a neutral color, strong, uniform, stiff, and inexpensive thread with limited holding power. It is not often used in apparel because of problems with comfort and holding power. Corespun thread combines staple and filament fibers with the filament fibers at the center of the thread for strength and the staple fibers on the exterior for comfort and sewability.

Threads are similar to yarns in terms of twist type. Most threads are Z twist because S twist threads untwist during stitch formation. Thread must have a correct and stable twist balance so that it does not kink or snarl during sewing. A variety of finishes are used to enhance their sewability or performance in use. Finishes include mercerization of cotton to increase strength, luster, and dyeability; glazing to increase abrasion resistance; bonding to increase ply security and smoothness; and lubrication to reduce friction and minimize the affect of needle heat during sewing.

Thread size describes the diameter of the thread. Finer threads result in fewer distortion problems. This is especially important for dense, fine yarn fabrics such as taffeta and satin. Thread size is most often indicated by ticket number, which is an indirect system. (See the discussion of yarn size earlier in this chapter for a description of indirect sizing systems.) Threads with higher numbers are finer and yield more length of thread per given unit of weight. Thread packages describe the type of container on which the thread is wound and is related to type of thread, machine, and sewing requirements. Thread is normally sold by length, not weight.

ASTM D 3693, Sewing Thread, Labeled Length per Holder, is also used to assess length of thread. ASTM D 3823, Determining Ticket Numbers for Sewing Threads, is used to convert from yarn number to ticket number.

ELASTICS

Elastic is a narrow fabric used to create an expandable opening in a product. Elastics expand under stress and recover well from stress. Some elastics are used because they have good holding power or high retractive forces. The degree of elongation, elasticity, and holding power varies with its type and structure. However, the rigidity of the fabric to which the elastic is attached will determine the maximum amount the combined materials (elastic and fabric) can be stretched. Elastics require little force for elongation, but tend to have low holding power. Elastics with good elasticity are used to gather fabric or shape garment parts. Elastics with good holding power are used to support or shape body parts.

Elastics may be covered or encased in another material or used uncovered. In some cases, the elastic component may come into direct contact with the skin, such as with waistbands elastics in some underwear. Some elastics also trim and shape garment areas, such as waistbands. The design in trim elastics can be structural (jacquard woven patterns for logos) or applied design (printed). With some fabrics, like tricot and single jerseys, that tend to curl or roll, elastic helps retain shape at fabric edges.

Materials

Elastics incorporate an elastomeric material, such as spandex or synthetic or natural rubber. Rubber is less expensive than spandex, but yellows and loses its stretch and recovery characteristics as it ages. It is more sensitive to damage from heat and chemicals, including perspiration, dry cleaning solvents, and chlorine bleach. Spandex is more expensive, but has better holding power and elasticity in smaller deniers. It is slightly more comfortable when in contact with the skin and more tolerant of heat and chemicals than rubber. Fiber modifications include resistance to chlorine, ultraviolet light, and salt water for swimwear and beach cover-ups. Elastomers are often combined with other fibers, including nylon, polyester, acetate, rayon, and cotton, to produce elastic fabrics. The percentages of fibers in the blend relate to comfort, durability, cost, and aesthetic requirements.

Elastics are available in both narrow fabrics (generally fabrics less than 15 inches wide) and broad fabrics (greater than 15 inches wide) that can be cut and sewn as with other fabrics. Elastic thread is also available and is usually either a monofilament elastomeric fiber covered with a yarn of cotton or acetate, or it is a core spun thread with a central core of elastomeric fiber covered with spun cotton or acetate. Narrow strips of film elastomer are used in some products, where they are encased in thread or covered with fabric.

Elastics can be made in several ways. Braided elastics have a high degree of elongation, but they narrow when stretched. This may contribute to recovery problems if they are stitched in place while stretched. Woven elastics are among the heaviest types. They are more stable in the width direction, are less likely to fold over during use, and have greater holding power. They maintain an attractive appearance longer than other types and are often used in products with more rigid specifications, such as for the military. Woven elastics are more expensive to purchase because production rates are lower. Several structural types are available including plain, satin, and simple patterned weaves, as well as types with fancy edges, such as scalloped, looped, or picot. Plush elastics use a bulky filament yarn on the side next to the skin that creates a soft texture for skin contact.

Knit elastics are warp knits that produce lengthwise elongation and crosswise stability, so that the elastic does not narrow when stretched. Knit elastics are less expensive because production rates are higher. They are lighter weight compared to woven elastics and can be made in open structures for better comfort features for warm weather and active sportswear. Filling insertion yarns can be used to add greater stiffness to the elastic. Sewing channels or lengthwise spaces in the elastic structure allow for stitching the elastic to the fashion fabric without altering elasticity.

TRIMS

Trims include a wide range of materials and treatments that enhance the aesthetics of a textile product. They can be selected based on color matching or accent requirements. Trims are used to bind and finish raw fabric edges. Woven, knit, or braid trims can be cut from broad fabrics or made in narrow widths for this specific application. When used on curved shapes, they require good flexibility. For that reason, many bindings are cut on the bias, made from braids, or knit. The width of the binding relates to the sharpness of the curve—wider bindings on shallow curves and narrow bindings on sharp curves.

Knit Trims

Knit trims can be cut from circular knits or flat-bed knits and made or cut to the dimension needed. For example, neckbands and cuffs can be knit in a tube of the specified diameter, cut as specified, and applied to the product producing a circular cuff or turtleneck collar with no seam. With flatbed knits, the trim piece may be knit to a shape of specific dimensions and with finished edges. The machine in Figure 5-17 produces knit trim. The manner in which the trim pieces are connected is important, because they may need to be separated by cutting, application of steam, or pulling of connecting yarns. Equipment available in the production facility needs to be addressed when writing specs for trims so that costs for separating them can be considered.

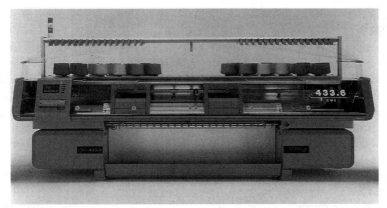

Figure 5-17
Flatbed knitting machines that produce knit trims. (*Courtesy of Stoll America Knitting Machinery, Inc.*)

Warp knit trims are used for racing stripes on athletic apparel and as trim on lingerie and sleepwear. Rib knit trims are used on sweaters and other garments, such as coats at necklines and sleeve edges. The structure of the rib knit (1 × 1 or 2 × 2) determines the bulk and stretch of the trim. These trims may be used in single or double layers. Some rib trims include elastomeric fibers, such as spandex, to improve fit, give better recovery from stretch, and enhance shape retention.

Edgings

Edgings accentuate style features such as details, shapes, or colors. Edgings include piping, lace, ribbon, fringe, tape, and picot trim. The specific nature of the edging—its structure, dimensions, color, fiber content, and requirements for application—must be considered when developing specifications.

Flat Trims

Flat trims are applied to flat surfaces of the product to add visual interest. Examples include braid, tapes and ribbons, embroidery, and appliqué. Most trims are stitched in place either during production of the components or as a separate production step. However, some trims may be held in place with adhesives or glues. This is the case with some trims used on wedding dresses and veils. The problem with adhesives used in this manner is that they may not be durable to cleaning solvents and age.

Embroidery and Appliqués

Embroidery makes use of close or overlapping stitches to form intricate patterns on fabric or product surfaces. Multithread, multihead machines are commonly used to create embroidered surfaces on product shells or components. A number of embroidery threads are available in a variety of fiber or structural types, colors, lusters, sizes, and textures. Most threads are either rayon or polyester. Thread size ranging from 70 to 600 denier is important in terms of developing the design. Finer threads (smaller denier) allow for greater detail, but require more stitches to cover the surface. Ply threads may be used for added strength or texture. Metallic threads add luster, but are less flexible, more sensitive to abrasion, and less comfortable.

Backing fabric is used to support the embroidered area and to prevent distortion of the design. These are usually nonwoven fiberwebs of an appropriate weight and hand for the fashion fabric and the embroidery pattern.

Many companies develop exclusive embroidered designs for use with their products. A variety of stitches are used to create the pattern. Different stitches are used to create compact surfaces, fill in design areas, create surface texture, or outline the design. When specifying embroidery, the pattern, thread, and stitch type should be considered.

Appliqués are designs that are sewn or fused to product components. Appliqués include single layers of fabric, pieces of lace, preembroidered sequins or beads, emblems, leather patches, and other items. They are used on many items of apparel, as well as on such accessories as baseball hats. Appliqués may include a fusible interlining to facilitate application to the fashion fabric. Some of the adhesives used with fusible interlinings may be heat activated. Backing minimizes raveling or stretching of edges during application.

Embroidery and appliqué materials may not be compatible with the other materials in the product. Some of the biggest problems relate to colorfastness of the thread or other materials used and their requirements for care. For example, consider a garment that is covered with appliqués that have sequins that dissolve in dry cleaning solvents. If the garment is made of a fabric that requires dry cleaning, the use of the sequins creates a garment that is impossible to clean. Garments of this nature labeled "dry clean only, remove sequins before cleaning" present unrealistic demands for care.

INTERLININGS, LININGS, AND OTHER SUPPORT MATERIALS

These materials provide a foundation for product shape, support areas subjected to stress, help maintain a product's appearance, enhance comfort, or enclose interior parts for aesthetic or performance reasons. These materials must be compatible with the fashion fabric. Although they contribute to the overall quality of the finished product, they may not be visible at point of sale. Often many types of support materials are combined in one product because each material has a different function. These materials come in a variety of different types, are made from many different materials, and may have different application methods and care requirements.

Interlinings

Interlinings or interfacings are sewn or fused to specific areas of the product to shape, support, stabilize, reinforce, and improve performance. Many different types are available and influence the aesthetics, performance, cost, comfort, and care of the finished product. For example, the hand and drape of a fabric can be altered by the selection of the interlining. Handling and sewability of interlinings are other important factors to consider. Interlinings that are easy to handle and sew are less expensive in terms of production costs than are those that require more effort and attention to detail. Fiber content, fabric weight, fabrication method, and method of application probably need to be specified. For products where a soft hand is important, cotton and rayon may be the fibers of choice. Where resiliency is needed, wool and hair fibers may be preferred. Nylon provides a stiff, resilient, lightweight interlining. Weights range from 0.4 to 4.0 oz/yd^2. The heavier the weight, the more support provided to the fashion fabric. Lighter weight interlinings produce a softer hand.

Fiberwebs are the most widely used fabrication method for interlinings. Webs can be made with no special orientation (random or all-bias) or oriented in lengthwise, crosswise, or both directions. Oriented webs provide greater stability in the direction of orientation. Because of their nature, fiberwebs have a tendency to pill with abrasion. Hence, the web should be covered or protected with a layer of fabric in the final product. Woven interlinings of many basic structures are also available. They are more expensive and grain characteristics are more important with these types. Knit interlinings are usually warp tricots, raschels, or weft-insertion raschels. They are highly stable with minimal stretch, low bulk, and low weight. Lightweight and stable foams may be used with some products, such as car interiors and some upholstery fabrics, to shape and support the fashion fabric.

Interlinings can be fused to the fashion fabric quickly and inexpensively. Fusible interlinings incorporate a bonding agent that is heat, pressure, or steam activated. Several types of bonding agents can be applied in a pattern to or all over the back of the interlining. Several problems with fusible interlinings occur. The bonding agent may strike back through the interlining and adhere to the fusing press. **Strikethrough** occurs when the bonding agent appears on the face of the fashion fabric. Differential shrinkage occurs when the fashion and interlining fabrics do not shrink at the same rate. In delamination, the layers of interlining and fashion fabric separate. Sometimes this is complete, and sometimes it occurs as bubbles or puckers in certain areas. Boardiness or an unattractive change of hand is another problem that can occur with fusible interlinings.

Linings

Linings are used to present a finished appearance, protect the user from internal structure, add comfort to the product, or protect the fashion fabric. For example, draperies are often lined to protect the more expensive fashion fabric from exposure to harmful sunlight. Lining fabrics may be selected for a particular appeal. For example, linings in sleeping bags and winter coats are added for warmth and comfort. Linings for suit jackets finish the garment's interior and make it easier to slide on over shirts or blouses. Linings are more like traditional fashion fabrics than they are like interlinings. Many different fiber types, fabrication methods, and finishes are used to produce lining fabrics. Cotton, nylon, acetate, rayon, polyester, wool, silk, and blends are used depending on the product type. For example, acetate, nylon, and silk are used in suit jackets of different qualities and prices. Wool is used to line gloves, boots, and hats. Polyester fiberfill and fiber batting are used in sleeping bags and coats. Cotton and polyester blends are used in products where comfort and durability are needed. Weight of the lining fabric relates to the function of the lining. Heavier weight linings are used for warmth. Lighter weight linings may provide comfort, opacity (especially important for swimwear and draperies), hand, and drapeability. Fabrications range from balanced plain weave fabrics to warp faced twills for greater durability to satins to quilted and bonded fabrics. Higher-density fabrics may contribute wind resistance, slip ease (facilitates layering of garments), flexibility, and durability. The location of the lining and the length of the lining should be considered. With some products, the lining fabrics differ by product parts. For example, with some coats, sleeve and body linings are of different fabrications and fiber types.

Other Support Materials

A variety of other materials are used in products. The type and purpose of each material should be considered when developing specifications.

Shoulder pads shape and support the shoulder area of apparel and functional clothing. Pads may range from those for business suit jackets and blouses to those that protect such as the ones used in hunting jackets. Pads may be made of fiberfill or foam. Types of pads may also differ with the target market. For example, pads used for menswear differs from those used for womenswear. Some shoulder pads are assembled from a variety of materials; others consist of foam only. The construction method for the shoulder pad should be specified, that is, sewn, molded, fused, or cut.

Sleeve headers of a fiber web or lamb's wool provide additional support for certain better quality tailored coats and jackets. Collar stays help retain the shape of collar points. They are available in several widths and weights. Different styles that are either sewn in or inserted after production are available.

Tapes of narrow plain or twill weave, knit, or braid fabrics provide shape retention and appeal. Tapes are used to stabilize seams in knits and bias-cut products, cover or protect stitching, retain shape of fabric edges, outline product features, or bind raw edges. Tapes can be cut from fashion fabric to ensure that colors, textures, and weights match between the fashion fabric and the tape.

Bra cups support, shape, and smooth the breast area of womenswear that may be worn without support garments. Bra cups are often included in swimwear and some evening gowns. They may contain materials like foam or fiberfill to enhance breast size and shape.

OTHER MATERIALS

Nail heads, rivets, beads, sequins, rhinestones, grommets, D-rings, ties and drawstrings, and buckles are other trims used in producing some textile products. Often special equipment is needed to attach these materials to the fabric. They may be held in place with prongs, special attaching devices, or adhesives. Application needs to be done carefully; otherwise these materials may cut yarns or tear holes in the fabric. Materials include metals such as brass, pewter, stainless steel, and plated zinc or nickel; plastics such as melamine or polyester; glass; or composites combining aluminum with plastic coatings. Some trims, such as sequins, may be soluble in dry cleaning solvents. Ties and drawstrings may be covered with fabric or made from cords or yarns of various fiber types. Color, weight, and flexibility are important for ties and drawstrings.

LABELS

Labels are used to provide information to the manufacturer, retailer, and consumer. Some information, such as fiber content (generic name and percentage), care information, country of origin, and brand name or RN/WPL number, are required. The manner in which the information is presented may be regulated. For example, the Textile Fiber Products Identification Act states that fiber blends be listed as a percentage in descending order by generic fiber name and that, if trade names are used, they be presented in the same type and color font as the fiber name. Other information, such as size, color, style number, construction features, trade name, and use of union labor, are voluntary (see Chapter 4). Sometimes the information is combined on one label, but this can create problems. For example, even though everything a company produces may be 100% cotton, not all items may require the same care.

Specifications should identify the number and type of labels, information to be included on each label, location of each label (that is, center back of neck, waistband, attached to sleeve, or looped around a button) presentation method (that is, sewn-in, attached to garment, or as part of the packaging), fabrication method (that is, woven in, printed, textile, or paper), and size.

Sewn-in Labels

Sewn-in labels must be compatible with the other materials used in the product and the care as stated on the care label. For sewn-in labels, location may be specified in the Care Label Regulation and is based on product type. For example, pants and slacks generally have the label located at the waistband of the center back seam. Sewn-in labels should be comfortable to the user, durable, easy for the operator to handle and attach, permanently legible, and appropriate in cost. Many different types are available in terms of fiber content, fabric structure, size, color, and information. Some labels are jacquard weaves; others are printed. If wet or chemical finishing is to be done, labels should be resistant to alterations from these processes. Because the Care Label Regulation specifies that the labels are permanent, it might be worthwhile to determine the manner in which the label responds to use and care and how long the label remains legible.

Hangtags

Hangtags include information at point of sale, but they are not required to be a permanent part of the product. They often include fiber content information, disclaimers or cautions regarding fabric appearance or performance, extra buttons or yarn, size, color, styling information, and brand name or company information. Some hangtags are used by a specific product industry to assist consumers in their purchase decisions. For example, SWIM, the Swimwear Industry Manufacturers Division of AAMA, promotes use of their hangtags to member companies to help consumers select flattering swimwear.

Hangtags are usually printed on paper or board that may be made from recycled materials. Because recycling is an important issue with some companies and consumers, that information is often indicated on the tag. Weight, color, and finish of the paper should be specified, as should the design and information to be included.

PACKAGING

The type and amount of materials in which the finished product is to be packaged when it is delivered to the buyer may also need to be specified. Weight and type of plastic bags, amount of pins or tissue paper, use of and type of hangers, and presence or absence of cardboard for retaining product shape are aspects that should be considered. In addition, the specs should indicate the number of finished products to be combined in a box or carton, the label information to be included on the box or carton and, if applicable, the use of bar codes.

CONCLUSIONS

When developing specifications for materials, it is necessary to understand the elements that should be considered. Identifying types of materials, the way specs can be verified, terms and dimensions of importance, and a general understanding of standard procedures is critical to being able to develop, interpret, and use materials specifications. Specific components for basic materials were discussed to identify why specifications are important. Example specs with units were cited to illustrate the nature of these specifications.

Specifications describe and define the nature and physical characteristics of importance for every material to be used in a product. Specs help in selecting appropriate materials for the product in terms of its appearance, cost, compatibility, and appeal to the target market.

SUGGESTED READINGS

American Association of Textile Chemists and Colorists. (1996). *AATCC Technical Manual, 71.* Research Triangle Park, NC: Author.

American Society for Testing and Materials. (1996). *Annual Book of ASTM Standards, Vol. 7.1 & 7.2.* West Conshohocken, PA: Author.

American Standards Association. (1960). *American Standard Performance Requirements for Textile Fabrics.* Vol. 1. New York: Author.

Anderson, S. L. (1983). *Textile Fibres: Testing and Quality Control.* Manchester, England: Textile Institute.

Annis, Patricia A., Thomas W. Quigley, & Karen E. Kyllo. (1992, September). Hand Techniques for Cross-sectioning Fibers and Yarns. *Textile Chemist and Colorist, 24(9),* 78–82.

Annis, Patricia A., Thomas W. Quigley, & Karen E. Kyllo. (1992, August). Useful Techniques in Textile Microscopy. *Textile Chemist and Colorist, 24(8),* 19–22.

Anon. (1995, July). Monitoring, Testing, and Quality Control. *Textile Month,* 17–34.

Anon. (1997, January). Hang Tag Programs Offer Consumers More Options. *AAMA News,* 1, 7.

Avondale's Fiber Evaluation Hones Plant Process Control. (1992, October). *Textile World,* 66, 68.

Barella, A. (1993). The Hairiness of Yarns. *Textile Progress, 24(3),* 1–48.

Bona, Mario. (1990). *Textile Quality: Physical Methods of Product and Process Control.* Rome: Texilia.

Brenner, Kurt. (1991, August). Knitting Needles: Their Role in Determining Fabric Quality. *Knitting Times,* 82–84.

Brown, Patty. (1992). *Ready-to-Wear Apparel Analysis.* New York: Macmillan.

Bryne, M. S., A. P. W. Gardner, & Anne M. Fritz. (1993). Fibre Types and End-uses: A Perceptual Study. *Journal of the Textile Institute, 84(2),* 275–288.

Convery, S., T. Lunney, A. Hashim, & H. McGinnity. (1994). Automated Fabric Inspection. *International Journal of Clothing Science and Technology, 6(5),* 15–19.

Crook, Alan. (1991). Sewing Threads. *Textiles, (2),* 14–16.

Day, Melissa Phillips, & Billie J. Collier. (1997). Prediction of Formaldehyde Release from Durable Press Fabrics. *Textile Chemist and Colorist, 29(1),* 33–36.

Felix, E. & K. Douglas. (1983). Yarn Quality Specifications for Woven and Knitted Cloth. In *Quality, Design, and the Purchaser.* Manchester, England: Textile Institute.

Fortess, Fred. (1986, August). The Ultimate Objective: No Inspection Required. *Bobbin, 27,* 54–56, 58, 60.

Ghosh, T. K., H. Peng, P. Banks-Lee, H. Hamouda, & D. H. Shin. (1991). Analysis of Fabric Deformation in a Roll-Making Operation. *Textile Research Journal, 61,* 153–161.

Glock, Ruth E., & Grace I. Kunz. (1995). *Apparel Manufacturing: Sewn Products Analysis,* 2nd ed. Englewood Cliffs, NJ: Prentice-Hall.

Goetz, Arthur. (1985, September). Procedures for Identifying Dyes and Pigments. *Textile Chemist and Colorist, 17(9),* 171–176.

Goldberg, J. B. (1957). *Fabric Defects.* New York: J. B. Goldberg.

Hall, David M., Robert P. Walker, & Emilio C. Mora. (1992, June). Scanning Electron Microscopy for Problem Solving in Textiles. *Textile Chemist and Colorist, 24(6),* 15–18.

Henry, M. Frances. (1958, December). Straight Thinking About Off-Grain Fabrics. *What's New in Home Economics,* 1–6.

Jacobsen, Donald M. (1985, August). A Formula: Fabric Inspection Savings—Fact or Fiction? *Bobbin, 26,* 70, 72, 74, 76, 78.

Judd, Peter. (1991). Interlinings. *Textiles, 20(3),* 11–16.

Kadolph, Sara J., & Anna I. Langford. (1998). *Textiles,* 8th ed. Englewood Cliffs, NJ: Prentice-Hall.

Koenig, Sharon K., & Sara J. Kadolph. (1983, June). Comparison of Performance Characteristics of Seven Fusible Interfacings. *Textile Research Journal, 53,* 341–346.

Little, Trevor J. (1988, November). The TALC Report Card. *Bobbin, 30,* 96, 98, 100, 102.

Material Quality Committee. (1972, April). *Sears Fabric Defect Threshold Scales.* Atlanta: American Apparel Manufacturers Association.

Mehta, Pradip V. (1992). *An Introduction to Quality Control for the Apparel Industry.* Milwaukee: ASQC Press.

Merkel, Robert S. (1991). *Textile Product Serviceability.* New York: Macmillan.

Monitoring, Testing, and Quality Control. (1995, July). *Textile Month,* 17–34.

Moore, Carolyn, & Lois M. Gurel. (1987, Summer). Fabric Defect Tolerances in First Quality Piece Goods. *Journal of Home Economics,* 49–51.

Moore, Carolyn. (1992, Fall). Factors That Affect Undesirable Garment Drape. *Journal of Home Economics,* 31–34.

Morgan, Tom, & Cheryl McDaniel. (1994, May). Choosing Hardware Not a Snap. *Bobbin, 35,* 70, 72, 74–75.

Mori, Miyuki., & Masako Niwa. (1994). Investigation of the Performance of Sewing Thread. *International Journal of Clothing Science and Technology, 6(2/3),* 20–27.

Pantone, Inc. (1992). *The Pantone Textile Color Selector—Cotton Edition, Textile Color Swatch Card/Cotton, Textile Color Guide—Paper Edition,* or *Textile Color Specified—Paper Edition.* Moonachie, NJ: Author

Parker, Alan. (1993, March). Yarn: The Strengths and Weaknesses. *Textile Month,* 25, 27, 29, 31.

Powderly, Dan. (1987, March). International Fabric Quality. *Bobbin, 28,* 122.

Powderly, Dan. (1985, January). U. S. Fabric Improvements Unnoticed. *Bobbin, 26,* 72, 74, 76, 78, 168, 170, 172, 174.

Powderly, Daniel. (1983, February). Better Fabrics—Higher Production. *Bobbin, 24,* 110, 112, 114.

Powderly, Daniel. (1987). *Fabric Inspection and Grading.* Columbia, SC: Bobbin International.

Powderly, Daniel. (1983, March). First or Second Quality? A Fabric Grading Overview. *Bobbin, 24,* 126, 128, 130.

Powderly, Daniel. (1988, March). Mine Eyes Have Seen the Defect. *Bobbin, 29,* 100, 102, 104.

Powderly, Daniel. (1987, September). The New Worth Street Rules. *Apparel Industry Magazine,* 104–110.

Powderly, Daniel. (1988, March). Three Approaches to Scoring Fabric Quality. *Bobbin, 29,* 107.

Quality Management in the Spinning Mill. (1994, May). *Canadian Textile Journal, 11(4),* 26.

Rebenfeld, Ludwig. (1991). Fiber Requirements and Challenges for the Future. In *Textile World at a Crossroad.* Manchester, England: Textile Institute.

Scannapieco, Mary. (1985, January). Evaluating Fabric Suppliers. *Bobbin, 26,* 65–68.

Sette, S., L. Boullart, & P. Kiekens. (1995). Self-Organizing Neural Nets: A New Approach to Quality in Textiles. *Textile Research Journal, 65,* 196–202.

Shaw, H. V., & J. M. Bailey. (1991). The Changing World of Spinning—Trends in Technology and Economics. In *Textile World at a Crossroad.* Manchester, England: Textile Institute.

Shishoo, Roshan. (1990, March). Interaction Between Fabric Properties and Garment Making. *Apparel International,* 3–4, 6.

Slater, K. (1993). Chemical Testing and Analysis. *Textile Progress, 25(1/2)*, 1–168.

Srinivasan, K., P. H. Dastoor, P. Radhakrishnaiah, & Sundaresan Jayaraman. (1992). FDAS. A Knowledge-Based Framework for Analysis of Woven Textile Structures. *Journal of the Textile Institute, 83(3)*, 431–448.

Suh, Moon W. (1992). Quality, Process, and Cost Control—A "Random Walk" in Textile Profitability. *Journal of the Textile Institute, 83(3)*, 348–360.

Textile Institute, The. (1991). *Textile Terms and Definitions,* 9th ed. Manchester, England: Author.

Tortora, Phyllis G., & Robert S. Merkel. (1996). *Fairchild's Dictionary of Textiles,* 7th ed. New York: Fairchild.

Tsai, I-Shou, Chung-Hua Lin, & Jeng-Jong Lin. (1995). Applying an Artificial Neural Network to Pattern Recognition in Fabric Defects. *Textile Research Journal, 65,* 123–130.

Ukponmwan, Joshua O. (1987). Appraisal of Woven Fabric Quality. *Textile Research Journal, 57,* 283–298.

Vigo, Tyrone L. (1994). *Textile Processing and Properties: Preparation, Dyeing, Finishing, and Performance.* New York: Elsevier.

Warner, Steven B. (1995). *Fiber Science.* Englewood Cliffs, NJ: Prentice-Hall.

Weissenberger, W., & E. Frick. (1992, September). Quality Assurance from Yarn to Fabric. *Textile Month,* 47–50.

Worth Street Textile Market Rules. (1986). Washington, DC.: American Textile Manufacturers Institute.

Zhang, Yixiang Frank, & Randall R. Bresee. (1995). Fabric Defect Detection and Classification Using Image Analysis. *Textile Research Journal, 65,* 1–9.

REVIEW QUESTIONS

1. Explain the connections among specifications for materials, product quality, and consumer satisfaction.

2. Identify the differences and similarities between these pairs of terms:
   a. qualitative and quantitative procedures
   b. crimp and takeup
   c. bow and skew
   d. patent and latent defects
   e. defect and grade

3. Specify five characteristics for each component of the fabrics listed and explain how those characteristics affect product quality and performance.
   a. fiber
   b. yarn
   c. fabric
   d. finishes (including dyeing or printing)

4. Identify two characteristics that can be specified for the materials listed and explain how each affects product quality and performance.
   a. closures
   b. trim and elastics
   c. thread
   d. support materials
   e. packaging

ACTIVITIES

1. Select a sample product and target market and write materials specs for it.

2. Measure selected material characteristics for a product.

3. Discuss the affect on product quality and customer satisfaction when specs are not met or when specs are lowered.

4. Read this article (Powderly, Daniel. [1987, September]. The New Worth Street Rules. *Apparel Industry Magazine,* 104–110) and discuss how its use in business is related to product quality.

5. Describe the elements that would need to be considered when writing specs for labels and hangtags and explain their importance.

6. Discuss how labeling and packaging is used to promote products to consumers.

7. Visit several retail store types and analyze how packaging facilitates handling of merchandise by employees and promotes the product to consumers.

Chapter 6

DURABILITY TESTING

OBJECTIVES

- To understand the dimensions used to describe the durability of materials.

- To understand basic science and procedures related to durability testing.

- To develop specifications related to durability of materials.

- To interpret durability specifications for product development.

- To conduct durability testing of materials.

KEY TERMS

durability testing

constant rate of extension (CRE) machine

constant rate of traverse (CRT) machine

constant rate of load (CRL) machine

tensile strength

breaking force

breaking strength

breaking elongation

tenacity

grab test

effective strength

jaw break

modified grab test

raveled strip test

cut strip test

stress-strain curve

stress

strain

breaking point

yield point

Young's modulus

tearing strength

trapezoid test

tongue test

bursting strength

ball burst test

diaphragm bursting test

thread strength

friction

abrasion resistance

flat or planar abrasion

flex abrasion

edge abrasion

endpoint

percentage loss in breaking force

visual change

pile retention	protrusion	shear strength
pilling resistance	bean bag snag test	bond strength
pilling propensity	mace test	impact resistance
Martindale pressure test	yarn distortion	crosswise strength
	frosting	element pull-off
snagging	screen wire method	element slippage
distortion	emery method	holding strength
snag	peel strength	

Chapter 5 examined the nature and characteristics of materials. The focus was on writing specifications to describe the materials used in a product. Chapters 6 to 9 focus on assessing how these materials (fashion fabrics, closures, and so on) perform in testing. Testing performance of materials in a lab is assumed to help determine the suitability of materials for products, predict material performance in products in consumer use, and guarantee consumer satisfaction with the product.

In laboratory performance testing of materials, a material is subjected to a procedure or condition of use, and its behavior or reaction is measured. Performance testing consists of a series of tests that assess various dimensions of serviceability in terms of durability, colorfastness, appearance retention, care, comfort, and safety.

Durability testing evaluates how the various materials used in a product perform when subjected to conditions that are assumed to measure their durability. The conditions of interest are ones that measure strength and abrasion resistance and help us understand how a material withstands various forces applied to it.

For durability testing, the procedures often subject the material to stress of some kind, such as a pulling force, and measures the amount of force at which a material fails. These procedures focus on the physical-mechanical aspects of materials. This means that performance characteristics of materials are analyzed by subjecting them to a physical or mechanical force. The tests often subject the material to an ever-increasing amount of force or friction until the weakest or most vulnerable component fails. From a durability perspective, failure occurs when a material ruptures or tears apart or when it cracks, snags, or pills to the degree that would be unacceptable to consumers.

Results reflect the amount of force the material experienced at failure. For example, in measuring fabric strength, the results are listed as the number of pounds, such as 150 pounds, that were needed to pull the fabric apart. The higher the number, the stronger, more abrasion resistant, or more durable the material is.

The practice of testing materials until they fail is used only in two areas of materials testing: durability and safety. In other areas, such as care, comfort, and appearance retention, procedures more closely resemble consumer use and do not test the materials until the failure point is reached.

Because standard test methods do not include pass/fail scales, no industry-wide values describe the point of acceptable or unacceptable performance. However, material specifications that describe acceptable measures of performance for individual companies often include minimum values for various measures of durability (see Table 6-1). These values are used in testing materials to determine their suitability when selecting materials for specific products. Thus, one measures the actual value at which the material failed and states that the material is or is not acceptable for use in a particular product.

Several aspects of durability testing are used to determine whether a material is acceptable to the buyer. Most common are measures of material strength and abrasion resistance. Testing these two dimensions is a common practice within the industry because it checks in a comprehensive way the interactions among material components and finishing. Even so, these measures are not necessarily the best measures of performance. Forces encountered in use are rarely sufficient to break or otherwise destroy the materials.

As with most testing, durability testing is conducted with materials that have been conditioned to avoid discrepancies as a result of moisture content. Durability testing measures one dimension of one material at a

---

Table 6-1
MINIMUM PERFORMANCE STANDARDS FOR TWO CATALOG RETAILERS.*

| Property | Company A | | Test method |
	Knit shirts	Woven shirts	
Bursting Strength (psi)		60	ASTM D 3786
Tensile Strength (lbf)		40	ASTM D 5034, Grab Method
Pilling Resistance	4.0		ASTM 3512, IVA, 3 cycles

| Property | Company B | | Test Method |
	Knit shirts	Woven shirts	
Bursting Strength (psi)	60		ASTM D 3786
Tensile Strength (lbf)		30	ASTM D 5034, Grab Method
Pilling Resistance			

*These values are company standards, but permission to use the company names was not given.

time, with the material in the new and unused condition. Thus, for example, the strength of a material is evaluated without subjecting it to abrasion or laundering. Even though products are abraded and laundered when used and changes because use may influence a product's durability, product use is not often addressed in standard test methods. This omission is deliberate; conditions of use vary tremendously across consumers.

Determining a standard set of use conditions adds complexity, time, and cost to materials testing. The results probably would not provide any more usable information than current practice. Although test methods may not reflect actual use situations, they do provide measures of durability that are helpful in determining which materials to use in a product, in comparing similar products or materials, and in checking to see that materials meet specifications. Keep in mind that in the area of durability, products rarely fail during their early stages of use. Thus, durability testing of new materials is a reasonable approach to use in developing a basic understanding of how the materials will endure when used by consumers.

The art of writing performance specifications so that they truly reflect consumers' expectations for durability performance is a very complex, difficult, and poorly understood task. However, it is one component of quality assurance that companies attempt on a daily basis.

Factors affecting durability are discussed in most introductory textile books. For information on the effect of fiber type, yarn and fabric structure, fabric weight, and finishes, consult one of these books (Hatch, 1993; Hudson, Clapp, & Kness, 1993; Kadolph & Langford, 1998; Price & Cohen, 1994).

This chapter considers durability of fabric and other materials used in a textile product. Most of these procedures are standard test methods that focus on the durability of fabrics, especially the fashion fabric, although some focus is placed on interlinings and other uses of nonwovens. The few test methods that focus on other materials, such as closures and trims, will also be discussed.

STRENGTH TESTING

Strength testing evaluates several dimensions by which failure related to durability can occur. Most strength tests measure the fashion or other fabrics to be used in the product. These tests subject the fabric to forces under carefully controlled conditions. The amount of force exerted on the fabric is a measure of the energy expended to produce a specific type of failure. Force is measured as the amount of mass required for something to happen. In the United States, this is expressed in pounds and is often referred to as pounds of force (lbf). Thus, lbf is used to describe one measure of material durability. For example, if a fabric splits apart when weights totaling 157 lb. are suspended from one end, it is reported as the fabric ruptured at 157 lbf.

Because most fabrics are two dimensional in their characteristics (lengthwise and crosswise, warp and filling, or wale and course), many procedures require testing of two sets of fabric specimens. One set reflects the lengthwise dimension; the other reflects the crosswise dimension. For woven fabrics, these two dimensions would be selected to focus on warp yarns (the lengthwise dimension) or filling yarns (the crosswise dimension). Because specimens are selected to represent the general nature of the fabric, multiple specimens (often 5 or more) are used for each dimension. Thus, a total of 10 specimens might be used for a fabric: 5 warp and 5 filling specimens. Because some fabrics may be used while wet, several strength tests may be done with wet and dry specimens, and a total of 20 specimens may be needed.

The location from which specimens are removed from the fabric is important. Because of the way fabrics are made and finished, the portions of fabric closest to selvages may differ more than portions near the center of the fabric. Thus, specimens for strength testing are often restricted to the center part of the fabric. This restriction is sometimes referred to as the 10 percent rule: fabric within 10 percent of the width closest to either selvage should not be used in these procedures. In addition, specimens should be cut so that they do not represent the same lengthwise or crosswise components of the material. Figure 4-2 illustrates the issues related to cutting specimens. These rules are of special importance for durability testing because those performance measures deal with interactions among yarn structure, fabrication, fabric density, and finishing.

Two ASTM documents provide basic information related to strength testing. Several important definitions are listed in ASTM D 4848, Terminology Related to Tensile Properties of Textiles. ASTM D 76, Specifications for Tensile Testing Machines for Textiles, addresses characteristics for the three major types of tensile testing machines: constant-rate-of-extension (CRE), constant-rate-of-traverse (CRT), and constant-rate-of-loading or force (CRL). With all three types of machines, a fabric specimen is held in place by clamps attached to opposing ends of the specimen (see Figure 6-1). Each machine may be equipped with several types of clamps or jaws. The clamp type is usually specified in the test method. Specimens may need to have an on-grain jaw alignment mark so that the specimen is clamped in place correctly.

With a **constant-rate-of-extension** (CRE) tensile testing machine, the pulling clamp moves at a uniform rate and the force-measuring mechanism moves a negligible distance with increasing force. As load is applied, the specimen elongates. As the pulling clamp moves, an increasing force is applied to the fabric. The force is recorded until the fabric ruptures. The force at which the fabric ruptured is recorded in lbf. CRE machines are preferred for many standard test methods. They are common in testing labs because of their versatility, but they are expensive. When equipped with a computer interface, the operator must receive training.

The **constant-rate-of-traverse** (CRT) machine is designed so that the pulling clamp moves at a uniform rate, and the force is applied

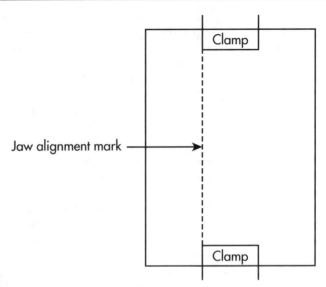

Jaw alignment mark

Figure 6-1
A tensile strength specimen is held in place by clamps at opposite ends. The specimen illustrated here is for the grab test.

Figure 6-2
CRT Tensile Testing Machine.

through the other clamp (see Figure 6-2). This produces a rate of increase of force or extension. The rate of increase of force or extension is not constant and is dependent on the fabric's elongation characteristics. Once again, the force is recorded in lbf until the fabric ruptures. CRT machines are the second most common type used in the industry. They are less expensive, less versatile, and do not require as much operator training as CRE machines.

The **constant-rate-of-loading** (CRL) or force is designed so that the rate of increase of force is uniform with time after the first three seconds, and the specimen elongates in a fashion related to its individual characteristics (see Figure 6-3). The force in lbf is recorded until the fabric ruptures. CRL machines are not all that common in testing labs primarily because their use in standard test methods and their versatility are limited.

TENSILE STRENGTH (BREAKING FORCE AND ELONGATION)

Tensile strength is the strength of a material under tension and is expressed in terms of force. Tensile strength usually refers to fiber performance. **Breaking force,** or **breaking strength,** is the force needed to rupture a fabric. **Breaking elongation** is the elongation corresponding to the breaking force (ASTM, 1996). It describes the increase in specimen length that had occurred up to rupture and it is usually expressed as a percentage.

Many strength specifications are written as breaking force values even though they may be described by the terms tensile strength or **tenacity.** These tensile tests measure the resistance of a material to stretching in one direction (Textile Institute, 1991). Two standard test methods may be used depending on the size and preparation of the specimens. Both procedures allow for testing wet specimens, which may be an important performance consideration for some materials. CRT, CRE, or CRL equipment can be used if the machine operates at a speed of 12 ± 0.5 in./min and obtains the required 20 ± 3 sec time to break, but the CRE and CRT machines are preferred. Machines for each type include the Instron tester and the Universal Testing Machine for CRE types, the Scott tester for CRT, and the inclined plane tester for CRL (see Figure 6-2 and 6-3).

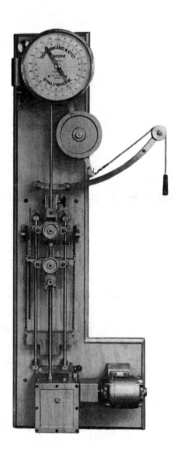

GOODBRAND

Tensile Tester for Fabric
Model Number L(a)

Machine Size: Up to 300 lbs. capacity

English	Metric
6′ 5″ × 2′ 2″ × 1′ 1″	192 cms. × 62.5 cms. × 32 cms.
Up to 1000 lbs. capacity	
6′ 10″ × 2′ 11″ × 1′ 1″	205 cms. × 87 cms. × 32 cms.
Extra width for graph motion	
7″	18 cms.

Figure 6-3
CRL Tensile Tester for fabric (used for strip, grab, and tear tests) up to 1000 lbs. capacity. (*Courtesy of SDL International Ltd*)

GOODBRAND

Tensile Tester for Fabric

Model Number L(a)

Capacities: The machine is normally arranged to have one load reading but can be supplied with additional readings. The standard readings are suitable for tests up to $100 \times \frac{1}{2}$ lb.; 200×1 lb.; 300×2 lbs.; 500×5 lbs.; 700×5 lbs. and 1000×5 lbs.; also intermediate or metric readings.

Specimens: Standard machines are arranged for testing strip samples up to 4″ or 10 cms. wide and 7″ to 9″ or 18 to 23 cms. long between grips with allowance for stretch.

Rates for Traverse:

    (a) For strip tests = 18″ or 46 cms. per minute; alternatively 4″ or 10 cms. per minute.

    (b) For grab tests = 12″ or 30 cms. per minute.

    (c) For tear tests = $4\frac{1}{2}$″ or 11.5 cms. per minute.

Unless otherwise ordered the machine will be arranged to have a rate of traverse suitable for strip tests at 18″ per minute.

Drive: Motor drive through worm reduction gearbox controlled by direct-on-line push-button starter.

Grips: For strip tests the grips are marked suitably to take up to the maximum width of sample to be used. The grip faces are serrated to give maximum holding ability.

Specimen Extension: This is indicated on the stretch rule alongside the sample, which is engraved 0–6″ × $\frac{1}{8}$″ or 0–15 × $\frac{1}{10}$ cm., and shows actual extension of specimen.

Indicator: The readings are shown on a clearly marked dial by a finger pointer. The pointer mechanism is in direct contact with a dead-weight pendulum arm. Pawls on the pendulum arm are in constant engagement with teeth on the quadrant arm rack with the result that an accurate reading continues to be shown until the pendulum is reset by hand.

Construction and fittings: The machine is arranged on a base suitable for wall-mounting. A locking or locating-box is fitted to hold the upper grip stationary whilst the samples are positioned. A half turn of a small lever releases the bottom grip follower from the traverse screw allowing instantaneous resetting at starting position. Also fitted with rod guides to ensure vertical movement of jaws.

Extras:

    (1) Other grips (e.g., for tear tests and grab tests), either fixed or interchangeable. (Unless otherwise ordered grips for strip tests will be arranged.)

    (2) Grips for different widths and lengths of samples.

    (3) An autographic recording unit can be fitted.

    (4) Other rates of traverse, multiple, or infinitely variable speed drives.

When ordering: Please state:

    (a) Load reading and sample size settings.

    (b) The rate of traverse required.

    (c) Full details of the electrical supply available.

Goodbrand and Company Limited
Clarence Street, Stalybridge, Cheshire
Telephone: ASHton-under-Lyne 1631-2-3

Figure 6-3 (continued)

Breaking force specifications are generally written as minimums. This indicates that any performance exceeding the minimum value is acceptable. When specs list one value, it applies to both fabric directions. These specs depend on the product type and user (see Table 6-2).

Grab Test

In the grab test, the specimen is wider than the clamps or jaws of the machine. This procedure, ASTM D 5034, Breaking Force and Elongation of Textile Fabrics (Grab Test), is applicable to woven, nonwoven, and felted fabrics and evaluates the fabric's effective breaking force. It is not recommended for knit fabrics because of their high stretch. However, very stable

Table 6-2
DURABILITY PERFORMANCE SPECIFICATIONS FOR SAMPLE PRODUCT CATEGORIES.*

Category	Upholstery	Curtains Draperies	Vocational Apparel	Blankets	Toweling	Regular Apparel
Breaking Force[1]	50	15/20[2]	60/70[3]	20	40	30/70/40/25[4]
Tearing Strength[1]	6.0	1.0/1.5[2]	4.5/6.0	—	—	3.0/2.5[5]
Bursting Strength	—	20/20	—	50 psi	50 lbf	30 lbf/60psi[6]
Abrasion Resistance	3000[7]	—	—	—	—	750/1000[8]
Pilling[9]	—	—	—	—	—	3.5

*(From ASTM Recommended Performance Specifications, 1996.)

[1]In lbf.
[2]The first number refers to sheer curtains and the second number to draperies.
[3]The first number refers to career dress apparel, the second to vocational apparel.
[4]The first number refers to dress shirts; the second, to men's pants and shorts; the third to women's pants and shorts; and the last to lining materials.
[5]The first number refers to men's pants and shorts; the second number, women's pants and shorts and outerwear.
[6]The first number refers to women's knit shirts; the second to men's knit shirts, shorts, and pants. The different units reflect different machines used in the assessment.
[7]Cycles for light duty upholstery fabrics using the oscillatory cylinder method.
[8]The first number refers to the number of cycles for shirts and the second number to pants, shorts, and outerwear. Both use the rubber abrasive wheel and the Taber Abraser.
[9]The value after 30 minutes of tumbling in the random tumble pilling tester for skirts, pants, shorts, and outerwear..

knits (with less than 11 percent stretch), such as some warp knits, are sometimes tested in this manner because their stretch is similar to that of some woven fabrics.

Because fabric portions adjacent to the area under stress contribute to overall fabric strength, the **grab test** may be most realistic in terms of assessing consumer performance. This contribution from adjacent areas is sometimes described as the **effective strength** of the fabric. The results from this test will not replace results from yarn strength testing because of the assistance from yarns not directly between the clamps. Figure 6-1 shows how the specimen extends beyond both sides of the clamps.

In this procedure, rectangular specimens are cut on grain, with the long direction parallel to the direction of testing. For example, if the specimen has the longer side parallel to the warp yarns, this is a warp specimen. Jaw alignment marks are used to place the specimen properly between the clamps. Specimens are clamped in place. The bottom edge of the top clamp is marked to determine if any slippage occurred during the test. The machine is started and the breaking force and any other information needed is recorded. When both wet and dry testing is conducted, the specimen number is doubled. The results for any specimens that slipped in the jaws or broke at the jaws is discarded. A **jaw break** occurs when specimens break within 0.25 inch of the jaw edge.

Modified Grab Test

In the **modified grab test,** lateral slits or cuts are made mid-length on the long edges of the specimen. The cuts will sever all yarns bordering the portion held between the clamps (see Figure 6-4). Thus, fabric assistance is reduced significantly. The modified grab test is used for fabrics that are likely to ravel during testing, such as high-strength fabrics and some smooth filament yarn fabrics.

Results of the grab test and the modified grab test cannot be compared or used to replace results from any other breaking force tests, such as either of the strip test methods. Advantages of both grab tests are that specimens can be prepared quickly, but the larger specimens require more fabric.

Strip Tests

A procedure similar to the grab test is ASTM D 5035, Breaking Force and Elongation of Textile Fabrics (Strip Test). It includes both raveled and cut strip specimens. The **raveled strip test** is applicable to woven fabrics, and the **cut strip test** is applicable to nonwoven, felted, and dipped or coated fabrics. The same restrictions for knitted fabrics apply to this test method. Raveled and cut strips determine the force required to break a specific width of fabric. They are useful because they describe the effective strength of yarns in the fabric.

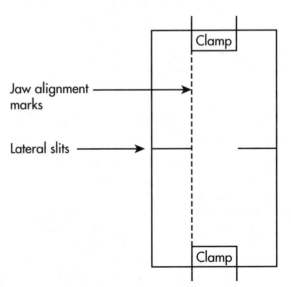

Figure 6-4
Modified grab test.

The cut strip test is used for heavily fulled fabrics and other types of woven fabrics that can not be raveled easily. The cut strip test is not recommended for fabrics that can be raveled because they tend to unravel during testing as a result of the force exerted on the yarns along the lengthwise edges.

Raveled strips are cut on grain and yarns on both long sides are raveled out. Note that the two short edges of each specimen are not raveled and remain as cut edges. Cut strips are cut on grain and require no further preparation. Specimens for both strip tests are placed in the jaws with the long cut or raveled edge, parallel to one edge of each clamp. Machine operation and recording of the results are the same as for the grab test.

Stress-Strain Curves

Some machines are equipped to produce a stress-strain curve during tensile testing. A **stress-strain curve** is a graphical representation of a material's resistance to deformation (**stress**) and its deformation or elongation caused by an external force (**strain**). Stress is recorded as force per unit area, and strain is recorded as percent elongation. Figure 6-5 shows a stress-strain curve for a material. The **breaking point** is the point at which the curve stops and the material ruptures. The breaking force is the value of the strain at that point. Stress-strain curves are used to identify yield point and Young's modulus that provide information regarding processing properties and performance. Beyond the **yield point,** deformation can not be completely recovered. It is the point at which some degree of deformation becomes permanent. **Young's modulus** is the ratio of change in stress to change in strain within the elastic limits of the material (ASTM, 1996). Young's modulus can be calculated by dividing the stress at any point by the strain at the same point.

TEARING STRENGTH

Tearing strength measures a material's resistance to the continuation of a tear. It reflects the strength of individual yarns. As the force increases on a tear, the yarns distort until they rupture. If a tear is closely examined, yarn distortion can be seen (see Figure 6-6). The procedures used to evaluate tearing strength begin with a small slit cut in the fabric and apply the force perpendicular to the yarns so that tearing continues from the slit. This perpendicular orientation of the force relative to the yarns differs from breaking elongation where the force is applied parallel to the yarns that will be pulled apart. Breaking force procedures do not measure the force required to initiate or start a tear.

Several procedures and pieces of equipment are used to assess tearing strength. CRE machines are preferred to CRT machines. However, some companies continue to use CRT machines for this assessment. Criteria re-

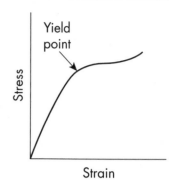

Figure 6-5
Stress-strain curve that shows the yield point.

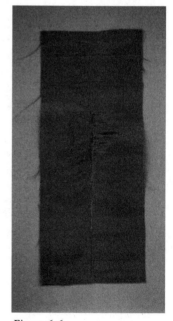

Figure 6-6
Yarn distortion at a tear. Note the puckering in the center of this sample.

lated to equipment specs and specimen preparation in terms of the 10 percent rule and representing as great an area of the material as possible are similar to those for breaking force methods. Tearing strength specs are also written as single minimum values that apply to both fabric directions (see Table 6-2).

Trapezoid Method

ASTM D 5587, Tearing Strength of Fabrics by the Trapezoid Procedure, can be used for most fabrics, including knitted, woven, and composite types. Tearing strength can be recorded as a single peak force or as the mean of the five highest peak forces. The specimen is cut as shown in Figure 6-7, with a small slit on one edge. When cutting the small slit on the narrow side of the isosceles trapezoid, the slit must be on-grain, so that only yarns in one direction are severed. The specimen is placed in the jaws so that the narrow side of the trapezoid forms a straight line with the edge of the clamp and so that the angled sides of the trapezoid are lined up with the clamp edge. The machine is run until the tear is several inches long.

The force may increase to a single maximum value, or it may demonstrate a short cycle for each yarn. The force increases until a yarn tears and may decrease slightly before increasing again and tearing the next yarn. Figure 6-8 shows two sample charts. Either the single value or an average of the five highest peaks is recorded. ASTM D 5733, Tearing Strength of Nonwoven Fabrics by the Trapezoid Procedure, is essentially the same procedure and is used for most nonwoven fabrics regardless of their finish.

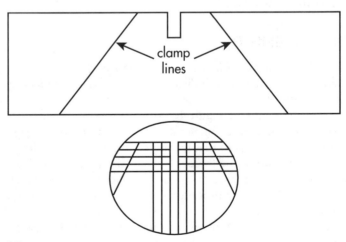

Figure 6-7

Trapezoid Test Specimen. The fabric is clamped in place so that the clamps abut and are parallel to the clamp lines.

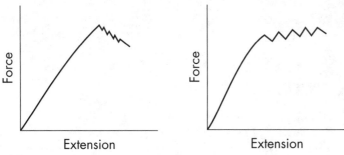

Figure 6-8
Examples of charts from the tear test, single peak (left) and multiple peaks (right).

Tongue Test

ASTM D 2261, Tearing Strength of Woven Fabrics by the Tongue (Single Rip) Method (Constant-Rate-of-Extension Tensile Testing Machine), and ASTM D 1424, Tearing Strength of Woven Fabrics by Falling Pendulum (Elmendorf) Apparatus, have many similarities to the trapezoid tear test. The major differences relate to the specimen size and equipment used in the procedure. The tongue method uses either a CRE or CRT machine. In the center of the short edge of the rectangular specimen, a slit, parallel to the yarns in the long direction, creates a two-tongue shape somewhat reminiscent of a pair of pants. Each side or tongue of the slit is clamped in a separate jaw so that when force is applied, the two tongues form a straight line. The falling pendulum, or Elmendorf tear tester, is shown in Figure 6-9. It uses smaller specimens with a shorter slit in the center of one long side. Very similar procedures for nonwovens are ASTM D 5735, Tearing Strength of Nonwoven Fabrics by the Tongue (Single Rip) Method (Constant-Rate-of-Extension Tensile Testing Machine), and ASTM D 5734, Tearing Strength of Nonwoven Fabrics by Falling-Pendulum (Elmendorf) Apparatus.

BURSTING STRENGTH

Bursting strength is the force or pressure required to rupture a textile by distending it with a force that is applied at right angles to the plane of the fabric. As the force increases, the fabric distorts and forms a bubble until it finally ruptures or tears apart. Sometimes a loud popping or snapping noise accompanies the rupture.

Results from bursting strength tests are not indicative of breaking force results. A different type of force is exerted on the fabric in bursting strength. Both lengthwise and crosswise aspects of the fabric are subjected to the force simultaneously so that separate directional specimens are not needed. Bursting strength specs are written as minimums.

Figure 6-9
Elmendorf tear tester. (*Courtesy of Thwing-Albert Instrument Company*)

Figure 6-10
Ball burst attachment for a CRT machine used to test bursting strength.

Ball Burst Test

ASTM D 3787, Bursting Strength of Knitted Goods—Constant-Rate-of-Traverse (CRT) Ball Burst Test, is used in the bursting strength assessment of knitted fabrics. The ball burst device shown in Figure 6-10 is attached to the CRT machine and replaces the clamps normally used in testing breaking force. Specimens are cut 5 inches in diameter or 5 inches square and then placed flat in the center of a ring clamp. In the **ball burst test,** a polished steel ball is forced through the specimen. The force at rupture is recorded.

Diaphragm Bursting Test

ASTM D 3786, Bursting Strength, Hydraulic, of Knitted Goods and Non-woven Fabrics—Diaphragm Bursting Strength Tester Method, is similar to the ball burst test in many ways. The major difference is related to how the

Figure 6-11
Diaphragm bursting strength tester.

equipment operates. In the **diaphragm bursting test,** a rubber diaphragm is distended because the hydraulic force steadily increases until the fabric ruptures. This method is used to test knit and nonwoven fabrics. Figure 6-11 shows a machine that records bursting strength in pounds per square inch (psi).

Thread Strength

Thread strength and elongation are two characteristics related to durability that are included as part of ASTM D 204, Sewing Threads. It includes procedures for assessing straight, loop, and knot strength and elongation characteristics at sewing forces using a CRE machine. Conditions for testing both dry and wet thread are included.

FRICTION TESTING

As two surfaces come into contact, they move relative to each other in a sliding or rolling action. **Friction** describes the resistance to relative motion between two objects in physical contact with each other. Smooth materials of the same chemical compound create less friction and are more resistant to abrasion than rougher materials of the same substance. It takes less energy to move two smooth materials together than it takes if one or both materials are rough. Because rough materials have more surface area in contact with each other, more force is needed to move them relative to each other. In other words, friction is greater and abrasion resistance lower when materials are rough. Friction between moving objects wears away each object.

Textile materials performance in terms of friction is related to abrasion resistance, pile retention, pilling, and snagging. Most friction testing of materials used in textile products involves movement and an assessment of how a material withstands friction. The performance is often assessed as a measure of loss of some portion of the material or a measure of loss of aesthetic appeal or appearance.

ABRASION RESISTANCE

Abrasion resistance is the ability of a material to resist erosion as a result of rubbing against a surface or other material. Because some fiber characteristics are humidity dependent, abrasion resistance is assessed using conditioned specimens. For most procedures, the 10 percent rule and admonition to not test the same lengthwise and crosswise components also apply here.

Abrasion occurs to fibers held under tension in the fabric or product. Breakdown occurs as a result of abrasion as transverse cracks appear on the fiber. The performance is related to the type of abrasion in terms of direction and pressure, the type of abrading material (fabric, skin, concrete, or other material), and the condition of the fabric, such as the amount of tension on the fabric and whether the material is wet or dry. Abrasion occurs during wear or use and during agitation in cleaning. Abrasion with a lot of pressure may distort the fabric, cause fibers or yarns to be pulled to the surface, or remove fiber ends from the surface of a napped fabric. These changes in appearance may affect consumer satisfaction with the product, just as much as wearing away of the material.

There are three general types of abrasion—edge, flat, and flex. Completely planar or flat abrasion resistance is not too common in textile products. **Flat or planar abrasion** occurs when a flat object is rubbed against a flat material. An example of planar abrasion is the flat area of a tablecloth. Planar resistance tends to be good for most materials because the force of rubbing is distributed over a wide area. However, for many products, flat abrasion resistance is assumed to occur when the curve is gradual or the bend is shallow, such as what occurs in a shirt or jacket as it bends across the back of the wearer, in the area between the arm and the body of the wearer, or on the seat of an upholstered chair.

Flex abrasion is the most common type of abrasion to which a textile product is subjected. In flex abrasion, the material is bent or flexed during rubbing. Flex abrasion occurs with apparel, furnishings, and many industrial products. Very little of the surface of most products is completely flat during use. So, flex abrasion tests may address the conditions of use most realistically.

In **edge abrasion,** the material is folded back on itself while it is being abraded. In products, pleats, folds, cording, cuffs, and hems are most subject to edge abrasion. Edge abrasion is a harsh measure of a fabric's resistance to wear. Most products show damage along edges before damage elsewhere in the product becomes apparent because the force is concentrated on a small portion of the material.

Most products and materials are subjected to varying amounts of each type of abrasion. However, most standard test methods focus on only one type of abrasion. Because abrasion resistance is so dependent on numerous factors, seven standard test methods have been developed. The differences among the procedures include the type of equipment, abradant (the material that rubs against the specimen), materials used, and assessment method. Each standard test method identifies aspects related to verifying the settings of the machine and changing the abradant on a regular basis.

Evaluation

The means by which abrasion resistance is evaluated depends on the procedure. Several options exist. One option is **endpoint** which counts the number of cycles until the fabric ruptures, two or more yarns have broken, or a hole appears. The point at which the fabric ruptures may be described in some test methods by the term failure.

A second option is percentage loss in breaking force. Some older procedures may refer to this as percentage loss in breaking load. Breaking force of the untreated fabric is measured. In evaluating abrasion using **percentage loss in breaking force,** the fabric is subjected to a specified number of cycles. Then, the breaking force of the abraded fabric is measured. Results are calculated using Equation 6-1.

Equation 6-1

$$\text{Loss in breaking force, \%} = 100\,(A - B)/A$$

where, A = breaking force before abrasion and
B = breaking force after abrasion

The third option is evaluating any visual change that occurred as a result of the test. Evaluation for **visual change** considers the effect that a specified number of cycles has on the luster, color, surface nap or pile, pilling, matting, or any other change resulting from abrasion. The change may be described by comparing the appearance of the abraded specimen to a standard rating scale and expressing the loss of appearance as a numerical value.

Abrasion specs are written as minimums (see Table 6-2). They identify the procedure, settings, and other pertinent factors for the specific procedure.

Flat Abrasion Resistance

In these procedures, the specimen is held flat and horizontal while subjected to abrasion. ASTM D 4966, Abrasion Resistance of Textile Fabrics (Martindale Tester Method), may not be usable for some fabrics, especially those that are thick or those with a long pile, because they cannot be mounted in the specimen holder. The Martindale Tester used in this procedure (see Figure 6-12) subjects the fabric to abrasion with known pressure that begins as a straight line and then gradually widens into an ellipse until it forms another straight line. This abrasive action is repeated a specified number of times, such as 5,000, until the full number of cycles has been reached, particularly if visual change is to be assessed. For endpoint or failure assessment, the number of cycles between examinations will decrease as wear appears, so that the number of cycles recorded at endpoint reflects the true, and not an inflated, value.

The rotary platform double-head method uses a machine called a Taber Abraser (ASTM D 3884, Abrasion Resistance of Textile Fabrics [Rotary Platform, Double-Head Method]) (see Figure 6-13). It can be used for most fabrics and subjects the fabric to multidirectional abrasion using a rotary rubbing action and controlled conditions of pressure. Abrasive heads of a rubber-base compound or a vitrified compound simulate mild and harsh abrasion. Specimens are dropped over the mounting post on a rotating platform against which two abrasive wheels slide—one toward the specimen's periphery and the other toward the specimen's center. The resulting ring-shaped area of abrasion is evaluated based on percentage loss of breaking force, using Equation 6-1 or a specified endpoint, such as a hole or broken yarns.

In ASTM D 4158, Abrasion Resistance of Textile Fabrics (Uniform Abrasion Method), the uniform abrasion testing machine (the Schiefer ma-

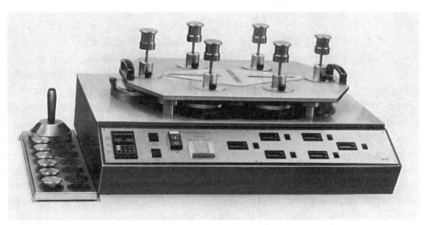

Figure 6-12
Martindale Abrasion Tester. (*Courtesy of SDL International Ltd*)

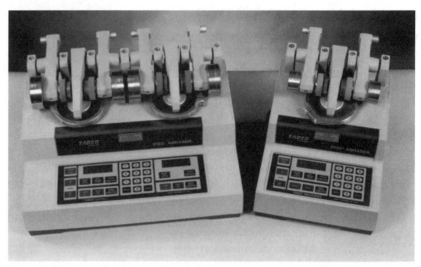

Figure 6-13
Taber Abraser. (*Courtesy of Taber Industries*)

chine) is used on a wide range of textile materials, including woven and knit textiles, socks, carpeting, and heavy felt (see Figure 6-14). In this procedure, abrasion is applied uniformly in all directions in the plane of the specimen's surface. Machine settings, mounting of specimens, and conditions of abrasion can be varied depending on the nature of the specimen and its conditions of use. Evaluation is based on change of some specified criteria after a specified number of cycles. Change criteria possibilities include thickness, weight, electrical capacitance, or some other factor of interest.

Flex Abrasion Resistance

In flex abrasion resistance, the material is bent, curved, or flexed during the test. In ASTM D 4157, Abrasion Resistance of Textile Fabrics (Oscillatory Cylinder Method), the material is subjected to a unidirectional rubbing under specified pressure, tension, and abrasive action. The oscillatory cylinder holds the fabric in a flexed or curved condition while it is abraded over a specified arc at a rate of 90 cycles per minute. Abrasion resistance of a material using this machine, also known as a Wyzenbeek abrasion tester, can be assessed by abrasion to rupture, percentage loss in breaking force, or by evaluation of visual changes. The procedure often is used to assess abrasion resistance of upholstery fabrics, leather, and other materials. For upholstery, light duty fabrics may be required to resist 3,000 cycles before failure has occurred, medium duty fabrics 9,000 cycles, and heavy duty fabrics 15,000 cycles.

The Stoll-Quartermaster abrasion tester is the machine used for ASTM D 3886, Abrasion Resistance of Textile Fabrics (Inflated Di-

Figure 6-14
Schiefer abrasion machine. (Reprinted, with permission, from the Annual Book of ASTM Standards, copyright American Society for Testing and Materials, 100 Barr Harbor Drive, West Conshohocken, PA 19428-2959)

aphragm Method). This procedure is used for woven and knitted fabrics, but is not applicable to floor coverings. Abrasion of a unidirectional or multidirectional type on a fabric held in a fixed, flexed position and supported by an inflated diaphragm is evaluated by failure or by visual rating. Failure occurs when the specimen is so worn at the center of the abrasion area that the contact pin in the abradant plate comes in contact with the pin in the diaphragm. This stops the machine and the number of cycles is reported. One problem is that lint may accumulate in the contact pin area and lead to a false reading.

ASTM D 3885, Abrasion Resistance of Textile Fabrics (Flexing and Abrasion Method), is used to assess the abrasion resistance of woven fabrics, excluding floor coverings. Specimen size is based on fabric density. The specimen is clamped in place in a Stoll-Quartermaster flexing and abrading machine and subjected to unidirectional reciprocal folding and rubbing over a bar as one clamp arm moves backward and forward. Evaluation is based on failure, percentage loss of breaking force using Equation 6-1, or visual assessment.

Edge and Flex Abrasion Resistance

Even though AATCC usually focuses on wet tests, the organization has developed AATCC 93, Abrasion Resistance of Fabrics: Accelerotor Method. This procedure uses a machine called an accelerotor in which the specimen is tumbled by a rotor in a cylindrical chamber lined with an abrasive material (see Figure 6-15). Each specimen is subjected to flexing, rubbing, shock, compression, and other mechanical forces while it is tumbling. Evaluation is based on loss of weight, loss of breaking force, or on visual change.

In the procedure for loss of weight, the specimen is weighed just before and just after testing. Loss of weight is calculated using Equation 6-2. In the procedure for loss of breaking force, a piece of fabric twice the length of the specimen is cut. One half of the length is removed and tested for breaking force. The other half is folded and the fold is stitched in place

Figure 6-15
Accelerotor. *(Courtesy of Atlas Electric Device Co.)*

Specimen as cut

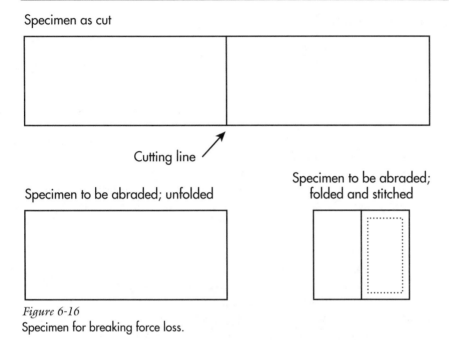

Cutting line

Specimen to be abraded; unfolded

Specimen to be abraded;
folded and stitched

Figure 6-16
Specimen for breaking force loss.

to simulate an edge in the product (see Figure 6-16). After abrasion, the stitching is removed and the specimen's breaking force is evaluated and compared to the value for the unabraded portion using Equation 6-1.

Equation 6-2

$$\text{Loss in weight, \%} = 100\,(A - B)/A$$

where, A = weight before abrasion and
$\quad\quad\ B$ = weight after abrasion

PILE RETENTION

Pile retention refers to the degree to which cut-pile yarns are held secure and intact to wear and resist pile loss as a result of pile pull-out. Pile retention was developed to assess performance of corduroy fabrics, but may be of interest with some other cut pile fabrics. ASTM D 4685, Pile Retention of Corduroy Fabrics, suggests testing fabric before and after laundering or drycleaning. In this procedure, specimens are subjected to a specified number of abrasion cycles on the face and back of the fabric. Evaluation of pile pull-out, not alteration of surface pile appearance, is based on a visual comparison between photographic standards and specimens that are viewed over a lightbox. An example spec is a minimum rating of 3.5 for corduroy slacks, pants, and skirts.

PILLING RESISTANCE

Pilling resistance measures resistance to the formation of pills on a textile surface. Pills result from abrasion, when fiber ends or other fiber debris is broken away from the surface, but becomes entangled with fibers that are still attached to the material. Pilling is most common with spun yarn fabrics, but some filament yarn fabrics that have received excessive wear also exhibit pilling. Pills are most likely to form when fibers with good flex abrasion resistance are combined with fibers of poorer flex abrasion resistance, as in polyester/cotton blends. Because pilling is related to abrasion resistance, the 10 percent rule applies when cutting specimens, as does the recommendation to take specimens so that they do not represent the same lengthwise and crosswise components. Specimens should be conditioned before testing.

Pilling occurs as fiber ends work to the fabric surface, become abraded, break off, and entangle with other fibers. Eventually pills break or are abraded off the fabric surface. Unfortunately, as one pill breaks off, many others are forming, so fabric appearance generally does not improve with use. Measuring pilling resistance is another means of evaluating a fabric's resistance to abrasion. Pills composed of fiber from the fabric are referred to as regular pills and are much less visible than pills from other fabrics or lint. These other fiber pills are collectively referred to as lint pills.

In pilling testing, a fabric is exposed to conditions that are likely to result in the formation of pills or some other objectionable surface change. **Pilling propensity** describes the ease and extent of pilling. Often fabrics are tested first when new and then after cleaning. Finishes present on new fabric prevent fiber ends from escaping from yarns and minimize pilling. Testing new fabric may give a false measure of product performance. Cleaning removes the residue of these finishes and brings fiber ends to the surface so that pilling is more likely to occur with fabrics that have been cleaned at least one time. Thus, testing for pilling after cleaning gives a more realistic assessment of product performance.

In addition to pill formation, other unacceptable surface changes such as matting and fuzzing also may occur with abrasion. Test methods to be discussed in this section also examine these related surface changes.

Evaluation is based on a visual comparison between the specimen and a five-point photographic rating scale, where 5 corresponds to no pilling or surface change and 1 corresponds to very severe pilling or surface change (see Figure 6-17). In some procedures, lint is used to form the pills since it is easier to see than regular pills. Pilling specs are written as minimums (see Table 6-2).

Martindale Pressure Test

When using the Martindale pressure tester (ASTM D 4970, Pilling Resistance and Other Related Surface Changes of Textile Fabrics [Martindale Pressure Tester Method]), rubbing is in the same pattern as for abrasion

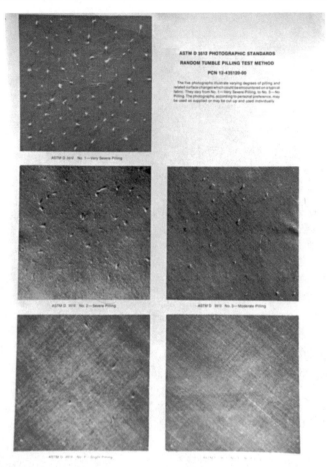

Figure 6-17
Rating scale for pilling.

resistance testing. The same piece of equipment is used; however, with pilling testing, the test specimen is rubbed against a layer of the same fabric (see Figure 6-14). The same restrictions in terms of pile height and fabric thickness apply to this procedure as for the abrasion resistance procedure.

Random Tumble Pilling Tester

ASTM D 3512, Pilling Resistance and Other Related Surface Changes of Textile Fabrics; Random Tumble Pilling Tester Method, describe uses of the random tumble pilling tester (Figure 6-18), which is similar to the accelerotor in that a rotor tumbles the fabric inside a cylinder lined with cork. With the pilling tester, the rotation rates are slower and the liner is softer compared to the one used in the accelerotor. Small amounts of lint fiber are

Figure 6-18
Random Tumble Pilling Tester. (*Courtesy of SDL International Ltd*)

added to each chamber for each specimen to generate lint pills on the fabric. Pills are evaluated using the photographic rating scale discussed earlier.

Brush Tester

ASTM D 3511, Pilling Resistance and Other Related Surface Changes of Textile Fabrics; Brush Pilling Tester Method uses a brush tester with two rotating platforms. On one platform, a flat-topped nylon brush is mounted so that it brushes against specimens mounted on the second platform. After several minutes of contact with the brush, the brush is removed and the specimens are remounted so that one specimen rubs against another specimen forming regular pills on the fabric. The visual rating scale is used to assess pilling.

SNAGGING

Snagging is a special type of abrasion. With snagging, a portion of the fabric structure catches on an abradant material with some resulting change in fabric appearance, fabric structure, or yarn structure. Snagging is most likely to occur with fabrics with long floats, large yarns, or a lower fabric density. Snagging resistance also recognizes that fabrics may be distorted during snagging or that a portion of a yarn may be snagged. Thus, **distortion** is defined as a visible defect in the texture of the fabric. A **protrusion** describes a visible group of fibers, yarn portion, or yarn that extends above the normal fabric surface. A **snag** is a yarn portion or a yarn that is pulled up from the normal surface of the fabric. A protrusion is different from a snag, but nevertheless creates problems in terms of the visual appreciation of the product. A snag occurs when a surface pulls, plucks, scratches, or catches on a component or portion of a fabric pulling it from its normal pattern.

Testing for snagging is recommended both before and after cleaning. Snags are classified as (1) those with a protrusion and no distortion; (2) those with a distortion and no protrusion; and (3) those with both a protrusion and a distortion. In addition, other changes in appearance can occur such as color contrasts in printed and yarn dyed fabrics.

Evaluation is based on comparison to a photographic standard (see Figure 6-19). A second option is to perform a visual assessment, whereby points are assigned to each of the three types of snags, totaled, and a rating assigned based on the total. Once again, for both evaluation options, a rating of 5 can be interpreted as no or insignificant snagging and a rating of 1 can be interpreted as very severe snagging.

Bean Bag Snag Test

ASTM D 5362, Snagging Resistance of Fabrics (Bean Bag Snag Test Method), is used to assess a range of woven and knitted fabrics. It is not recommended for open fabrics like net, tufted or nonwoven fabrics, or heavy or stiff fabrics that cannot be made into a small bag because of their stiffness or thickness. The **bean bag snag test** uses a small bean bag covered with the test fabric. The bean bag is placed inside a rotating chamber with inward-pointing needles that catch at the tumbling fabric bag (see Figure 6-20). Evaluation is based on comparison to the photographic rating scale or visual assessment using the point system.

Figure 6-19
Photographic standards for snag testing. (*Courtesy of SDL International Ltd*)

Mace Test

ASTM D 3939, Snagging Resistance of Fabrics (Mace Test Method), is used for a wide range of fabrics made from many different yarn types, including smooth and textured filament and spun yarns. The same restrictions that apply to the bean bag test apply here for fabrics for which this procedure is not suitable. With the **mace test,** a tube of fabric is constructed and placed over a cylinder on the mace tester (see Figure 6-21). A spiked ball or mace bounces randomly against the fabric as the tube rotates. Evaluation is based on a comparison with a set of photographic or fabric standards.

YARN DISTORTION TESTING

Yarn distortion refers to a condition of woven fabrics in which the symmetrical surface of a fabric is altered by shifting or sliding of warp

Figure 6-20
Bean Bag Snag Tester. (*Courtesy of Atlas Electric Device Co.*)

or filling yarns. Distortion is likely to occur as force is exerted laterally on the fabric. The force is the result of pulling forces, friction, or both. Distortion is more likely to occur with fabrics that have low yarn density per inch and with fabrics in which yarns and interlacing patterns offer little friction resistance to distortion. Yarns of this type tend to be tiny in size and smooth in nature, such as the filament yarns found in satin and taffeta. Fabric structures most likely to distort are basket, twill, and satin weave fabrics with long floats. Yarn distortion alters the appearance of the fabric and may create an irregular bubble effect. Fabrics that distort easily are sometimes described as sleazy. ASTM D 1336, Distortion of Yarn in Woven Fabrics, was dropped in 1995 because no action on reapproval of the procedure was taken by the appropriate committee. Because some organizations continue to assess yarn distortion, it is possible for the test method to be reinstated. For these reasons, it will be discussed briefly here. A fabric shift tester is used to apply surface friction to the fabric (see Figure 6-22). After the test, the physical distance of distortion is measured. Figure 6-23 shows several examples of yarn distortion.

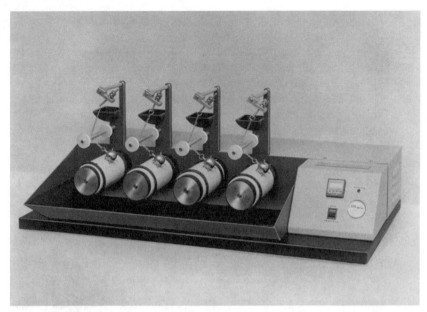

Figure 6-21
Mace Tester. (*Courtesy of SDL International Ltd*)

Figure 6-22
Fabric shift tester. (*Courtesy of Instrument Marketing Services, a subsidiary of SGS US Testing Company Inc.*)

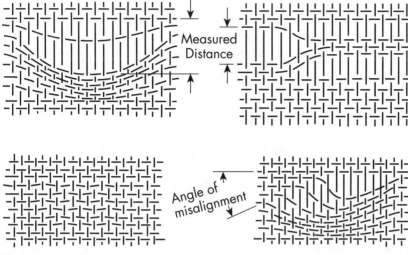

Figure 6-23
Examples of yarn distortion. (*Reprinted, with permission, from the Annual Book of ASTM Standards, copyright American Society for Testing and Materials, 100 Barr Harbor Drive, West Conshohocken, PA 19428-2959*)

FROSTING

Frosting is a change in fabric color caused by localized abrasion. Frosting examines the interaction between colorant penetration into the fiber and abrasion resistance. Colorants that do not penetrate deep into fibers are more likely to exhibit frosting. For example, vat dyes such as indigo concentrate on the fabric's surface. Thus, as it is abraded, the colored portion is worn away and a white or light cast appears in the areas of heaviest abrasion. Although this procedure could be discussed in Chapter 8, it really is more a measure of abrasion resistance than a measure of colorfastness.

Frosting can occur as a result of natural wear, use of excessive force when removing a stain, or deliberately developed during finishing to create a worn look for certain products. Frosting is evaluated by subjecting the fabric to controlled wear and comparing the abraded specimen to a new unfrosted specimen. The change in color between the two is compared to a standard color rating scale, where 5 is no color loss and 1 is severe color loss.

The two standard test methods are AATCC 119, Color Change due to Flat Abrasion (Frosting): Screen Wire Method, and AATCC 120, Color Change due to Flat Abrasion (Frosting): Emery Method. Both methods can be used for all colored fabrics. The **screen wire method** is especially sensitive to changes in durable press cross-dyed fabrics. The **emery**

method is especially sensitive to poor dye penetration in all cotton fabrics and to union-dyed blends. Both methods use the CSI surface abrader. In the mildly abrasive screen wire method, a slightly flexed specimen is abraded by screen wire. In the emery method, the slightly flexed specimen is subjected to a severe abrasion from an emery polishing paper. For both methods, the fabric is evaluated by comparison to the rating scale after a specified number of cycles.

DURABILITY TESTING OF OTHER MATERIALS

Several methods have been developed to assess the durability of other materials used in a product. Methods that focus on nonwoven materials were discussed earlier because the procedures are very similar to those used for fashion and lining fabrics. Other methods developed specifically for other types of material will be discussed in this section.

HOOK AND LOOP FASTENERS

Two procedures are used to assess the durability performance of hook and loop touch fasteners. Peel strength (ASTM D 5170, Peel Strength ["T" Method] of Hook and Loop Touch Fasteners) is assessed using a CRE machine. **Peel strength** is a measure of the force required to separate the two parts of the fastener. A standardized procedure is used to bond the two layers together because the strength of the bond is related to the force with which they are adhered. One free end of the mated tape is placed in each clamp of the machine and the force in lbf required to separate the layers is recorded.

Shear strength (ASTM D 5169, Shear Strength [Dynamic Method] of Hook and Loop Touch Fasteners) is the amount of force required to cause the two parts to slide on each other causing separation. Specimens are prepared so that they overlap by several inches and mate with the other part. The unmated part of each layer is clamped in place in the CRE machine and the force in lbf required to separate the mated layers is recorded.

SNAP FASTENERS

The ability of snap fasteners to resist a pull perpendicular to and parallel with the plane of the fasteners is addressed in ASTM D 4846, Resistance to Unsnapping of Snap Fasteners. Either a CRE or a CRT machine is used to test snaps attached near the end of two layers of fabric. A suggestion is made to test the snaps before laundering and after a specified number of launderings. The force required to separate the two parts of a snap is recorded in lbf.

FUSIBLE INTERLININGS

ASTM D 2724, Laminated, Bonded, and Fused Apparel Fabrics, is used to examine the bond strength of composite fabrics. **Bond strength** is the force required to separate the fabric layers of a laminated, bonded, or fused composite fabric. It may be done on fabric before or after a specified number of cleaning cycles. The layers are separated by hand for several inches so that the clamps of a CRE or CRT machine can be attached to each layer. The fused or bonded fabric portion forms a right angle to the separated portions that are clamped in the jaws. Results are reported in ounces per inch of specimen width.

BUTTONS

ASTM D 5171, Impact Resistance of Plastic Sew-through Flange Buttons, is of special importance for buttons that are likely to be subjected to commercial pressing on a regular basis. **Impact resistance** measures the button's resistance to fracture when subjected to sudden application of an external force. An impact resistance tester is used. One button at a time is centered on a surface under a long tube through which a specified mass is dropped onto the button (see Figure 6-24). After the impact, the button is

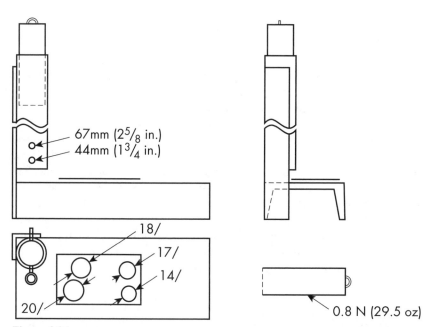

Figure 6-24

Impact resistance tester for buttons. (*Reprinted, with permission, from the Annual Book of ASTM Standards, copyright American Society for Testing and Materials, 100 Barr Harbor Drive, West Conshohocken, PA 19428-2959*)

removed and examined visually with a magnifying glass to determine breaking, cracking, or chipping. The number of buttons that exhibited each problem is reported.

ZIPPERS

Several dimensions of the strength of zippers and zipper parts are assessed using ASTM D 2061, Strength Tests for Zippers. **Crosswise strength** refers to the ability of a zipper chain to resist a lateral pulling force using a CRE or CRT machine. **Element pull-off** measures the gripping strength of elements around the bead. **Element slippage** examines the resistance of an element to longitudinal movement along the bead. Both of the procedures that examine the elements of a zipper use a tensile testing machine equipped with a specially designed device for that procedure. **Holding strength** of stops is addressed by subjecting the stops to five dimensions of use: to prevent the slider from moving beyond the stop, to resist failure applied longitudinally to the bottom, to hold two stringers of chain together at the bottom, to resist separation, and to remain in place. The slider's ability to resist crushing, spreading at the end during use, twisting in use, and pull-off are addressed. Other measurable aspects of zipper durability include holding strength of separable zippers and the holding strength of the slider lock.

CONCLUSIONS

Durability testing of materials frequently focuses on the fashion fabric, but several standard test methods have been developed for examining the performance of such other materials as fusible interlinings, nonwovens, and various fasteners. Durability procedures can be categorized as those that focus on strength aspects and those that focus on the effect of friction in the form of abrasion on the material. Each category includes several different procedures. For almost all of these procedures, the values describing performance to one procedure can not be assumed to describe performance for another procedure. Many of these procedures expose the material to a steadily increasing force or condition until the material fails. Evaluation may be based on a measure of force, a change in performance, a change in appearance, or a comparison to standard rating scales where a number is assigned to represent the change that occurred.

SUGGESTED READINGS

Adanur, Sabit. (1995). *Wellington Sears Handbook of Industrial Textiles*. Lancaster, PA: Technomic Publishing Company.

American Association of Textile Chemists and Colorists. (1996). *AATCC Technical Manual, 71*. Research Triangle Park, NC: Author.

American Society for Testing and Materials. (1996). *Annual Book of ASTM Standards, Vol. 7.1 & 7.2.* West Conshohocken, PA: Author.

Bona, Mario. (1990). *Textile Quality: Physical Methods of Product and Process Control.* Rome: Texilia.

Booth, J. E. (1969). *Principles of Textile Testing.* New York: Chemical Publishing Company.

Brown, Patty. (1992). *Ready-to-Wear Apparel Analysis.* New York: Macmillan.

Constant, F. Woodbridge. (1967). *Fundamental Principles of Physics.* Reading, MA: Addison-Wesley.

Dittman, Richard, & Glenn Schmieg. (1979). *Physics in Everyday Life.* New York: McGraw-Hill.

Elmasri, M. T., J. W. S. Hearle, & Brenda Lomas. (1983). Product Quality and Durability in Workwear. In *Quality, Design, and the Purchaser.* Manchester, England: Textile Institute.

Glock, Ruth E., & Grace I. Kunz. (1995). *Apparel Manufacturing: Sewn Products Analysis, 2nd ed.* Englewood Cliffs, NJ: Prentice-Hall.

Hatch, Kathryn L. (1993). *Textile Science.* Minneapolis: West Publishing Company.

Hudson, Peyton, Anne C. Clapp, & Darlene Kness. (1993). *Joseph's Introductory Textile Science, 6th ed.* New York: Harcourt Brace Jovanovich.

Kadolph, Sara J., & Anna I. Langford. (1998). *Textiles, 8th ed.* Englewood Cliffs, NJ: Prentice-Hall.

Lyle, Dorothy Siegert. (1977). *Performance of Textiles.* New York: John Wiley & Sons.

McAngus, E. J., & W. W. Adams. (1967–1968). *Physical Textile Testing at Westpoint Pepperell.* Atlanta: Textile Industries.

March, Robert H. (1970). *Physics for Poets.* New York: McGraw-Hill.

Mehta, Pradip V. (1992). *An Introduction to Quality Control for the Apparel Industry.* Milwaukee: ASQC Press.

Merkel, Robert S. (1991). *Textile Product Serviceability.* New York: Macmillan.

Morton, W. E., & J. W. S. Hearle. (1993). *Physical Properties of Textile Fibers,* 3rd ed. Manchester, England: Textile Institute.

Naik, A., & E. Carrera. (1994). Friction and Wear in Fabrics. *Textile Month,* 21–24.

Pile, John F. (1995). *Interior Design.* New York: Harry N. Abrams.

Price, Arthur, & Allen C. Cohen. (1994). *J. J. Pizzuto's Fabric Science, 6th ed.* New York: Fairchild.

Ramgulam, R. B., J. Amirbayat, & I. Porat. (1993). The Objective Assessment of Fabric Pilling. Part I: Methodology. *Journal of the Textile Institute, 84(2),* 221–226.

Stone, Janis K., & Carol Warfield. (1975). Measuring Textile Durability. *Illinois Research, 17(1),* 14–15.

Textile Institute, The. (1991). *Textile Terms and Definitions, 9th ed.* Manchester, England: Author.

Tortora, Phyllis G., & Robert S. Merkel. (1996). *Fairchild's Dictionary of Textiles, 7th ed.* New York: Fairchild.

Warfield, Carol, & Janis F. Stone. (1979). Incremental Frictional Abrasion. Part III: Analysis of Abrasion Effects Using Photomicrographs of Fabric Cross Sections. *Textile Research Journal, 49(5),* 250–259.

Weiss, Richard J. (1990). *Physics of Materials.* New York: Hemisphere Publishing Corporation.

REVIEW QUESTIONS

1. Why do some procedures require testing of specimens that represent both directions of the material?

2. Why are there restrictions in terms of where or how the specimens are removed from the fabric?

3. Explain how breaking force and breaking elongation are measured.

4. Explain how CRT, CRE, and CRL machines differ.

5. Why is friction important in assessing materials performance?

6. Define three types of abrasion resistance and their means of evaluation.

7. Why is pile retention important for corduroy?

8. How is pilling performance evaluated?

9. Why are snagging and pilling considered measures of durability?

10. How is the durability of closures assessed?

11. Identify four measures of durability performance that would be important for each product below. Identify the procedure and evaluation method to be used.
    a. shirt for office work
    b. tent for weekend camp-outs
    c. shorts for an active three-year-old
    d. towel for household bathroom
    e. upholstery for theater seats

ACTIVITIES

1. Study Table 6-2 and discuss why some performance measures are blank for some product types and suggest why the recommendations differ.

2. Write durability specs for a selected product and target market and explain your choices.

3. Test the durability of a product in the lab and discuss what its performance would mean in terms of consumer satisfaction.

4. Bring in a product that failed in terms of durability and discuss why it failed.

5. Visit a testing lab and watch durability testing. Discuss with managers and technicians their role in quality assurance.

6. Explore the world wide web for information related to durability testing. Discuss how the information would be used in materials testing.

7. Explore the printed technical literature for information on durability testing of materials and discuss the application of results in product performance.

8. Examine catalog copy and store displays for information related to material or product durability. Explain what this information would mean to consumers.

Evaluating Material Contributions to Comfort, Safety, and Health

Chapter 7

OBJECTIVES

- To use reference scales to evaluate material performance.

- To understand the dimensions, units, and terms used to describe material performance for comfort, safety, and health.

- To understand scientific principles applied to performance evaluation.

- To develop specifications for comfort, safety, and health that describe material performance requirements.

- To interpret performance specifications for product development.

- To assess material performance for adherence to specifications for comfort, safety, and health issues.

KEY TERMS

comfort	conduction	water repellency
stretch	convection	water resistance
comfort stretch	radiation	waterproof
elongation	phase change	water vapor transmission
elastic fabric	evaporation	
stretch yarn fabric	condensation	desiccant
low-power stretch	absorption	thickness
fabric stretch	moisture absorbency	hand
fabric growth	absorbent	skin contact
calorie	absorbate	KES
heat	saturation point	stiffness
heat transfer	specular reflectance	flexural rigidity

drape	char length	impact resistance
air permeability	thermal protection	health
wind resistance	chemical resistance	allergens
electrostatic propensity	penetration	irritants
	permeation	formaldehyde release
electrostatic clinging	breakthrough time	ultraviolet or UV protection
safety	permeation rate	
flammability	degradation	biological resistance

This chapter continues to explore how materials are evaluated to determine if they are suitable for use in a product. Comfort, safety, and health are serviceability dimensions that are important in product performance and consumer satisfaction. These three areas of serviceability fit together nicely. In fact, at times, it may be difficult to separate them completely. Products that are not comfortable may pose a safety or health risk, thereby adversely affecting consumer use and satisfaction with a product.

Many issues related to comfort also relate to and affect the aesthetics of the materials. The connection between comfort and aesthetics should be kept in mind in discussing the evaluation and measurement of performance.

Safety issues for some products are regulated by federal, state, or local laws (see Chapter 3 for a detailed discussion of regulatory issues). In end uses for which safety and health regulations must be met, other performance dimensions may be sacrificed. Those dimensions that are affected adversely by safety and health requirements will be identified in this discussion.

Measuring a material's reaction to conditions of use provides information that can be used to predict product performance. Thus, manufacturers are better able to combine appropriate materials to create a product. This chapter deals with issues that may be more important for some products than for others, but do contribute to the success or failure of a product. For example, when buying shorts to wear while exercising, comfort may be of primary interest. Yet, although comfort may not be as important in selecting slacks or pants for work, this factor will affect the wearer's work, attitude, and satisfaction with the product. Consumers seldom consider safety and health issues when selecting apparel or items for general household use, yet these factors can be of critical importance. This chapter focuses on evaluating the performance of materials related to the comfort, safety, and health of users of textile products.

Most basic textile books discuss the effects of various components (fiber content, yarn and fabric structure, and finishes) on these performance factors. Consult one of these books if such a review is needed (Hatch, 1993; Hudson, Clapp, & Kness, 1993; Kadolph & Langford, 1998; Price & Cohen, 1994). The effect of other individual materials, such as closures, support materials, and trims, on these performance measures is most often negligible. However, when the effect could be significant, it is discussed, such as in the discussion of flammability.

COMFORT ASPECTS

Comfort is complex and includes physical, physiological, and psychological factors. Environmental conditions can influence comfort significantly. The next time you are caught in the rain, notice how quickly your perception of comfort is altered! Comfort is often described as a neutral sensation. Nothing in the near or far environment is irritating. The individual is not especially conscious or aware of such elements as ambient temperature, wind speed or air movement, noise, light, moisture, or movement. It is not too hot, too cold, too wet, too dry, too breezy, too stuffy, too noisy, too quiet, too bright, or too dim. Discomfort occurs when we are too aware of our environment, our clothing, our psychological presence, or our emotional state.

Comfort describes how materials interact with the body and addresses how the body's functional environment can be expanded. For example, rainwear makes it easier for us to walk, play, or perform work outside on rainy days. Gripper treads on shoes and boots makes it easier and safer to walk on slick or icy surfaces. Flannel sheets and insulation in walls and roofs help us keep warm, when the outside temperature drops below 0°F and the wind howls.

The relationship between comfort and materials includes how a material moves with or restricts body movement, retains or conducts body or environmental heat, absorbs or repels moisture, feels next to the skin, allows or restricts access of still or moving air to the skin, conforms to a three-dimensional shape, and conducts static electricity. Most of the evaluation procedures for comfort dimensions are based on mechanical-physical actions done to a material and its measured change or reaction. A few procedures use trained individual raters or judges to evaluate or assess a performance characteristic of a material.

These procedures attempt to simulate some dimension or aspect of consumer use. Once again, these laboratory procedures measure one dimension of performance at a time in carefully controlled conditions, so that the laboratory results are precise and reliable. Often the measures of performance are based on fewer specimens than are used in durability tests, and there are fewer restrictions in terms of where and how the specimen should be cut from the material and prepared for the test method.

ELONGATION AND ELASTICITY

The discussion in Chapter 6 on durability established that fabrics elongate when a force of any kind is exerted on them. To test durability, the force on the fabric was increased until it failed and the force and elongation at rupture were measured. Breaking elongation is one measure of durability. This chapter further examines the fabric's ability to elongate under force, but it considers elongation as a measure of comfort. The force exerted on the fabric to cause it to elongate is significantly less than the force needed to rupture it. Measuring how a fabric responds to a smaller amount of force will be measuring its comfort elongation rather than its breaking elongation. Breaking elongation is almost always referred to by that term, but comfort elongation usually is referred to as just elongation. One needs to be sure of the type of elongation that is being discussed or described.

Stretch is another term that is used in more than one way. Chapter 8 will discuss how fabrics react to the chemical and mechanical action of cleaning. Although it is not common, some materials increase in size or stretch during cleaning. Stretch, however, is also used to describe the comfort elongation of materials. Stretch in terms of care refers to an increase in size because of some action of cleaning; **stretch** in terms of comfort refers to an increase in one dimension because of force exerted on the material. This increase is usually accompanied by a decrease in another dimension. For example, if a material becomes wider, it also probably becomes shorter. **Comfort stretch** refers to the small amounts of increase in material dimensions that occur with movement. Because the increases are relatively small, the wearer may not be aware that a small change in another direction has also occurred. Stretch and elongation are often used as synonyms, especially by consumers, but to the specialist, the terms describe different material behaviors.

In comfort elongation, **elongation** is expressed as a percentage that refers to the ratio of the extension of a material to its length before stretching. Force exerted on the material causes it to deform. The nature of the material, its structure, and the amount of force determine the degree and type of deformation. Figure 7-1 shows a close-up of a knit fabric in relaxed and elongated conditions. Note how the shape of the loop structure changes when a force pulls it out of its relaxed form. As a force is exerted on a material, changes in the material in the direction parallel to the pulling force occur most dramatically, but changes in other dimensions may also occur.

Most tests that measure elongation focus on elastic fabrics or fabrics made with stretch yarns. An **elastic fabric** is made with an elastomeric material or is a blend of elastomeric and other materials, such as a nylon/spandex blend tricot used in swimwear. A **stretch yarn fabric** is made using at least some yarns with a high degree of potential elastic stretch and rapid recovery. Several standard test methods evaluate elongation and elasticity of

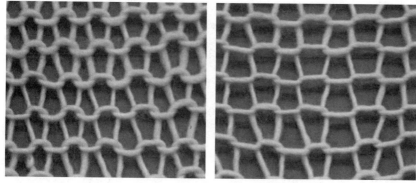

A.   B.

Figure 7-1
Close-up of a knit fabric: normal, relaxed condition (a) and elongated condition
when a force is applied (b).

materials. Some focus on elastic fabrics; some focus on stretch yarn fabrics;
and still others focus on knits. Although no standard test exists for measuring comfort stretch or elongation of regular woven fabrics, many companies
use one of the existing standard procedures for this purpose. In several
cases, a test method may suggest laundering the material and testing its performance in both the new and laundered conditions.

ASTM D 1775, Tension and Elongation of Wide Elastic Fabrics, incorporates two procedures: tension at a specified elongation and elongation at a specified tension. Both procedures use a constant rate of load
(CRL) machine. This method is not recommended for testing the performance of narrow elastic fabrics. ASTM D 4964, Tension and Elongation
of Elastic Fabrics (Constant-Rate-of-Extension Type Tensile Testing Machine), is a similar procedure that uses a constant rate of elongation (CRE)
machine. This procedure can be used with wide and narrow elastic fabrics.
Results from these two ASTM methods are not comparable, because the
operating principles for each machine differs.

For the tension at specified elongation procedure described in ASTM
4964, a conditioned specimen is sewn into a circular loop and mounted in
a CRL machine. The loop is elongated under a specified tension and returned to zero tension. The cycle is repeated a total of three times and
recorded by a plotter. Tension elongation is calculated based on the extension recovery plot using Equation 7-1.

Equation 7-1

$$L = F/W$$

where L = loop tension in lbf/in.
$\quad F$ = observed loop tension from the plot in lbf
$\quad W$ = specimen width in inches

For the elongation at specified tension procedure described in ASTM 4964, the same size loop and cycle procedure is used, but tension-recovery curves are plotted. Elongation at specified tension is calculated from the plot using Equation 7-2.

Equation 7-2

$$E = 100(2L/C)$$

where L = extension in inches
E = elongation in percent
C = loop circumference

Knit fabric elongation is determined following the procedure in ASTM D 2594, Stretch Properties of Knitted Fabrics Having Low Power. The knit static extension tester used in this procedure is shown in Figure 7-2. In this procedure, static means that the fabric is held stationary while a weight is attached to it. This procedure measures **low-power stretch,** which describes a material that exhibits high stretch and good recovery under a small force or low load. **Fabric stretch,** usually expressed as a percentage, is the increase in length of a fabric specimen

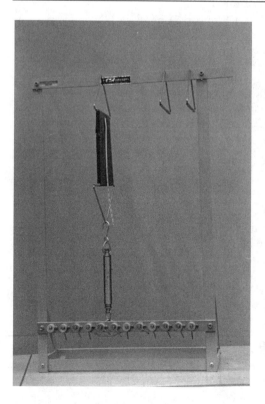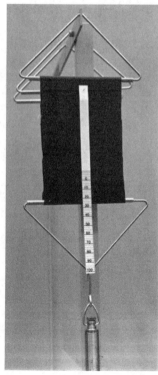

Figure 7-2 (left)
A knit static extension tester.

Figure 7-3 (right)
Specimen with hanger assembly for the knit static extension tester.

resulting from a load applied under specified conditions. **Fabric growth,** also expressed as a percentage, is the difference between the original length of a specimen and its length immediately after removal of a specified load for a prescribed time. This test method also includes two procedures. In fabric stretch, each specimen is sewn into a tube and marked with benchmarks a specified distance apart. The tube and hangers are assembled as shown in Figure 7-3, and a specified load is applied to the lower hanger. The length of the elongated specimen is measured with the marked pin-hook rule, marked in percentage, so no calculations are needed. Fabric stretch is calculated using Equation 7-3, if the pin-hook rule is not used.

Equation 7-3

$$\text{Fabric Stretch, \%} = 100 \left[(C - A)/A \right]$$

where A = distance between benchmarks before extension, (usually 5 in. or 50 in. depending on the machine used)
C = distance between benchmarks during extension

Fabric growth uses a similar specimen and procedure. The specimen is extended for a specified percentage stretch, held at that stretch for a prescribed time, and allowed to recover under no load. During recovery, the length is measured at preselected times and fabric growth is calculated using Equation 7-4.

Equation 7-4

$$\text{Fabric Growth, \%} = 100 \left[(B - A)/A \right]$$

where A = distance between benchmarks before extension (usually 5 in.)
B = distance between benchmarks after release of load/recovery from extension

Test method ASTM D 3107, Stretch Properties of Fabrics Woven from Stretch Yarns, is similar to ASTM 2594, except that the focus is on fabrics with high stretch and good recovery properties when exposed to a low load. A woven static extension tester is used (see Figure 7-4). Specimens are marked with benchmarks a specified distance from each short end (see Figure 7-5). Equations 7-3 and 7-4 are used to calculate fabric stretch and fabric growth. The test method also allows for determining both immediate fabric growth and fabric growth after stretching. To determine fabric growth after stretching, the same procedure is followed as for determining immediate fabric growth, except that recovery length is measured at predetermined time intervals. For each time interval, the recovery length used in the calculation is specific to that interval.

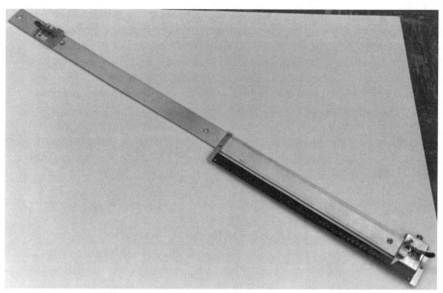

Figure 7-4
A woven static extension tester.

HEAT RETENTION/CONDUCTION

One aspect of comfort is the way materials affect heat transfer. The body produces heat by metabolizing ingested food, which is converted into energy, and by exercising the muscles. The energy in food and in physical exercise is measured in calories. Food with a higher-caloric value has more internal energy than food with a lower-caloric value. Activities with a higher-caloric value use up, or burn, more energy than activities with a lower-caloric value. Calories can be used to measure energy as heat, which is simply energy in another form. A **calorie** is the amount of energy (the heat) needed to raise 1 g of water 1°C.

Thus, **heat** is one way of defining the internal energy within an object. Hot objects have more internal energy than cool objects. Heat always travels or flows from the hotter object to the cooler object; it never travels from a cool object to a hot object. One common method for measuring the heat in an object is to measure the object's temperature.

Heat generated by the body is distributed evenly by the circulating blood. The body loses excess heat by exhaling hot air, touching a cold object, and fanning air over the surface of moist skin. These several mechanisms enable the body to maintain the fairly narrow range of internal temperature required for proper function. (One of the ways we know we are ill is an elevated internal temperature.) When the body generates more heat than it loses, people feel hot and perspire. Perspiration is a highly efficient means of speeding up heat loss. When the body is not generating heat as quickly as it is losing heat, we feel cold and shiver. Shivering is an involuntary muscle action that generates heat.

Textiles can be used to block undesirable heat loss. For example, heavy or bulky coats help slow down heat loss in the winter. This slowing down of the rate of heat transfer is referred to as the ability of a material to insulate. Conversely textiles can be used to speed up heat loss by absorbing or wicking moisture that is at body surface temperature away by facilitating the evaporation of moisture or by increasing air movement across the body. By using absorbent fibers or those with good wicking characteristics, moisture loss and the heat it contains can be increased.

In addition to the body's ability to produce heat from food, heat from objects in the environment, such as the sun, an oven, a fire, or a furnace, is another factor that needs to be considered in terms of comfort. For example, textiles such as pot holders are used to protect us from hot pans. **Heat transfer** deals with the flow of internal energy between a hot object and a cold object. This heat transfer can occur through several mechanisms.

Conduction describes heat transfer by direct contact. In conduction, energy is transferred directly between objects that touch. If you touch a hot pan with your bare hand, you will experience a burn. The energy transfer was so quick that the skin was not able to dissipate the energy before tissue damage (a burn) occurred.

In **convection,** hot molecules mix with cool molecules. We make use of this physical behavior when we add cold water or ice to hot coffee or tea. We also see forced convection when we stir or blow on hot soup to cool it or when we use a fan to cool off. In forced convection, warm air molecules directly above the hot object are mixed with cool molecules farther away from the surface. Thus, the hot surface loses heat to the now cooler air more quickly and the hot object cools more quickly as a result of moving air over its surface. This concept also applies in the winter when temperature and wind speed combine to create rapid heat loss referred to as wind chill.

Heat transfer by **radiation** involves the transmission of energy between objects that are in straight lines of sight. We experience radiant heat transfer when we sit in front of a fire or stand in direct sunlight. If anything comes between the fire and the individual or the sun and the individual, radiant heating does not occur. If you have ever sat in front of a fire on a cold night, you know that the side facing the fire may be very warm while the side away from the fire may be very cool. This is an example of radiant heat transfer or radiation.

Phase change heat transfer occurs when an object changes its physical state. Several types of phase change occur: from a liquid to a vapor (**evaporation** of water), from a solid to a liquid (melting of ice), from a liquid to a solid (freezing of water), from a vapor to a liquid (**condensation** of water), or from a solid to a vapor or gas (sublimation of dry ice). Cooling by evaporation is an important mechanism used by the body to keep internal temperatures from becoming too high. When a liquid, such as perspiration evaporates, it absorbs a significant amount of energy (heat) as it changes phase from a liquid to a gas. Conversely, when a gas, such as water vapor condenses as droplets of water on a glass filled with ice and a cold bever-

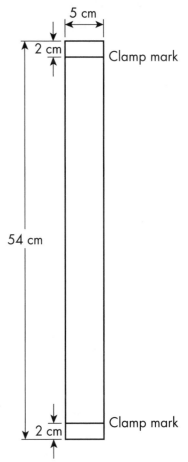

Figure 7-5

Fabric specimen prepared for the woven static extension tester. (*Reprinted, with permission, from the Annual Book of ASTM Standards, copyright American Society for Testing and Materials, 100 Barr Harbor Drive, West Conshohocken, PA 19428-2959)*

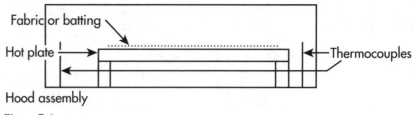

Figure 7-6
Diagram of apparatus for measuring thermal transmittance.

age, it loses a significant amount of energy (heat). If you have ever experienced a steam burn, you have absorbed energy into your skin. The burning sensation is a result of tissue damage by this rapid influx of heat. Evaporation and condensation are two types of heat transfer that occur as materials change their physical state. There are no standard test methods to evaluate phase change heat transfer.

Two standard test methods have been developed to assess how materials affect the transfer of heat using the mechanisms of conduction, convection, and radiation. ASTM D 1518, Thermal Transmittance of Textile Materials, is used to assess the performance of fabrics, battings, fiberfill, and other insulating materials for use in cold weather wear and gear such as sleeping bags. The method also can be used to assess performance of product components where fabric and batting or fiberfill are layered. This test method acknowledges the complexity of measuring thermal comfort and indicates that results should be used for relative comparisons when materials are exposed to the same conditions in the test. In this procedure, the time for heat to transfer up through a material from one side of a hot plate where conditions are warm and dry to the other side where conditions are cool is measured. Figure 7-6 shows a diagram of the arrangement of materials and hot plate. The other procedure will be discussed later in this chapter in the section on safety.

MOISTURE ABSORBENCY

Absorption, also known as **moisture absorbency,** is the ability of one material (the **absorbent**) to take in or absorb another material (the **absorbate**). For example, the absorbency of a cotton towel is related to the amount of water (the absorbate) the cotton fibers (the absorbent) absorb. Moisture absorption includes the ability of a material to retain a liquid, such as water, in its interstices, pores, and internal portions. Some fibers with irregular surfaces can hold liquids along the surfaces, almost like potholes on a road hold moisture when snow melts or when it rains. Fibers with high-absorption characteristics are made of polymers that form temporary hydrogen bonds with water molecules. Moisture absorption is one measure of a material's performance in terms of comfort.

Fibers with good moisture absorption characteristics absorb dyes and chemical finishes readily. These fibers tend to be used in apparel that is in direct contact with the skin because they help cool the body by readily absorbing perspiration. Thus, many highly absorbent fibers are used in apparel designed for exercise and warm weather wear. Materials made of these fibers are used in products that require a high degree of absorbency, such as towels, diapers, wipes, and other related products. Materials used to make these products can be evaluated in terms of how quickly they absorb liquid moisture and the quantity they have absorbed when reaching the **saturation point.** A material is saturated when it can no longer absorb additional moisture. Excess moisture may either pool around the material or pass through it. Notice that when a saturated towel is used to mop up a spill, it simply spreads the spill around.

Absorbing water from the skin or other surfaces is a prime function of toweling. ASTM D 4772, Surface Water Absorption of Terry Fabrics (Water-Flow Test Method), is specific to terry toweling; it does not apply to other toweling fabrics, such as huck, crash, honeycomb, or nonwoven materials. This procedure can be used for terry materials or terry towels that have been hemmed or that incorporate the selvage as part of the towel's edge treatment. It is suggested that specimens be washed and dried before testing because finishes on new fabric may interfere with absorbency. Each specimen is placed in an embroidery hoop, so that tension is controlled, and placed at a 60° angle on the water flow tester as shown in Figure 7-7. Because the procedure is nondestructive, the specimen does not need to be removed from the towel for testing if tests are to be conducted on finished products. Distilled or deionized water flows over the specimen. After a short time, the water that ran off the specimen is recorded. The water retained by the specimen is calculated using Equation 7-5.

Equation 7-5

$$W_{A \text{ or } B} = 50 - P_{A \text{ or } B}$$

where W = water retained (ml)
P = water from pan (ml)
A = the face of the fabric
B = the back of the fabric

AATCC 79, Absorbency of Bleached Textiles, can be used for bleached, dyed, or printed materials. In this procedure, a single drop of water falls 1 cm onto a conditioned material held under tension. The time in seconds for the drop to lose its specular reflectance is measured. **Specular reflectance** is the shiny reflective surface of a drop of water when it beads up on a surface. Complete loss of specular reflectance occurs when the drop has been absorbed into the material until it appears as a dull wet

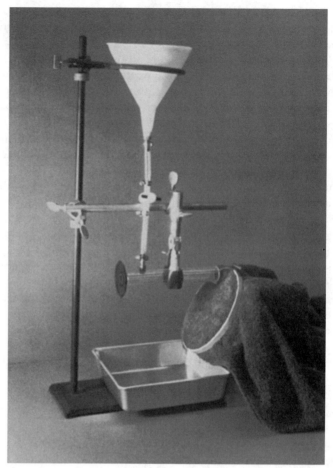

Figure 7-7
Water flow tester with specimen.

spot. Figure 7-8 shows a progression from full specular reflectance to complete loss of specular reflectance.

WATER REPELLENT, WATER RESISTANT, AND WATERPROOF MATERIALS

The opposite of water absorption is water repellency. This performance characteristic is important for protective apparel, outerwear, accessories, awnings, textile covers for objects, portable shelters, and other applications in which a textile product is intended to protect an object from wetting. Most products with this characteristic are made from materials that possess the desirable performance behavior by a combination of their physical structure and a finish.

Water repellency describes the relative resistance of a material to any single aspect or combination of surface wetting, water penetration, or

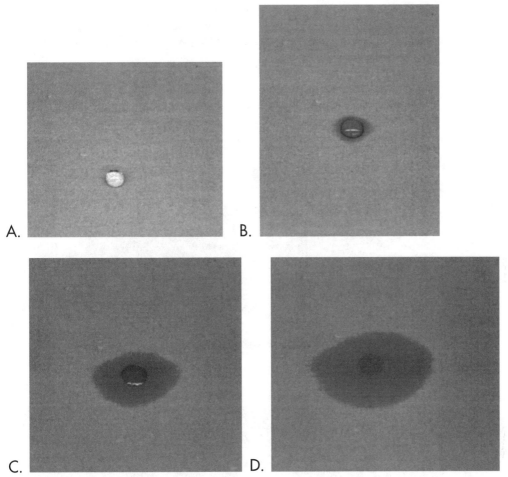

Figure 7-8
Water drop on fabric surface from full specular reflectance (a) to full absorption (d).

water absorption. Water repellency is usually achieved by combining a dense fabric structure with a finish that resists, but does not prevent, water penetration at interstices within the fabric structure. **Water resistance** refers to the ability of a material to withstand penetration by water under pressure or water that drops from a distance and strikes against a material with a known amount of force, such as driving rain. **Waterproof** materials are usually coated composite materials that have closed pores or very tiny interstices that are resistant to the penetration of water regardless of its pressure or force. These terms differentiate among the degree of resistance to wetting or penetration of water. Waterproof materials are most resistant, followed by water resistant materials, and then water repellent materials.

The degree to which a material resists wetting also affects comfort associated with any product made of it. Waterproof materials tend to be air impermeable unless they incorporate a poromeric structure. Thus, these materials can become hot and clammy when used in outerwear. The resistance of a material to wetting by water is especially important to determine because many products that incorporate these materials are designed to keep an object or person dry.

The test methods used to assess this performance characteristic attempt to simulate real-use conditions. These methods can be used for any material whether it has been treated to be water resistant or not. AATCC 22, Water Repellency: Spray Test, is a quick and simple procedure. Water

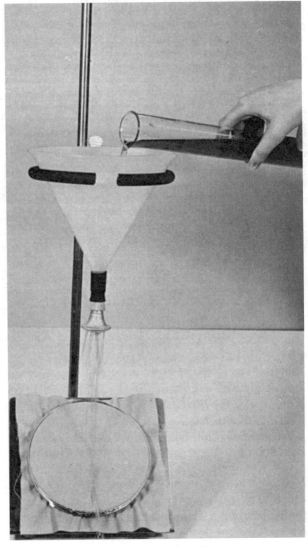

Figure 7-9
AATCC Spray Tester. *(Reprinted with permission from the American Society of Textile Chemists and Colorists, P.O. Box 12215, Research Triangle Park, NC 27709)*

penetration is not measured, so it is not recommended as a measure of rain penetration resistance. In this method, a specimen is placed in an embroidery hoop. The hoop is placed on the spray tester and distilled water is poured through the spray nozzle (see Figure 7-9). The pattern produced by the wetting of the surface from the water spray is evaluated using the spray test rating scale illustrated in Figure 7-10. The official spray test rating chart is a 14" × 17" chart available from AATCC. The numerical grade is reported.

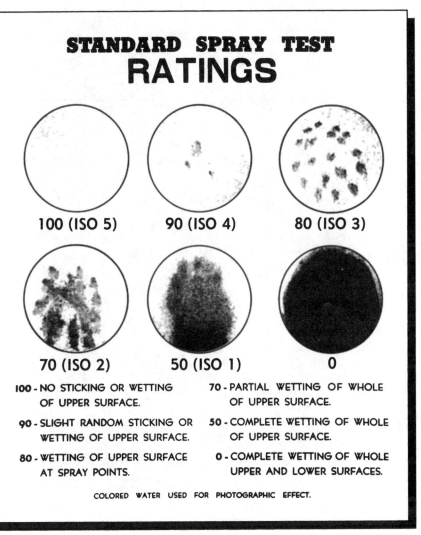

STANDARD SPRAY TEST
RATINGS

100 (ISO 5)   90 (ISO 4)   80 (ISO 3)

70 (ISO 2)   50 (ISO 1)   0

100 - NO STICKING OR WETTING OF UPPER SURFACE.

90 - SLIGHT RANDOM STICKING OR WETTING OF UPPER SURFACE.

80 - WETTING OF UPPER SURFACE AT SPRAY POINTS.

70 - PARTIAL WETTING OF WHOLE OF UPPER SURFACE.

50 - COMPLETE WETTING OF WHOLE OF UPPER SURFACE.

0 - COMPLETE WETTING OF WHOLE UPPER AND LOWER SURFACES.

COLORED WATER USED FOR PHOTOGRAPHIC EFFECT.

Figure 7-10
AATCC Spray Tester Rating Scale. (*Reprinted with permission from the American Society of Textile Chemists and Colorists, P.O. Box 12215, Research Triangle Park, NC 27709*)

AATCC 35, Water Resistance: Rain Test, is most often used to predict rain penetration for apparel fabrics. As such, it is used to assess the suitability of materials for umbrellas, rainwear, and hats. The rain tester shown in Figure 7-11 can be set at different intensities so that the performance of the material over a range of exposures can be assessed. Thus, different pressure heads or

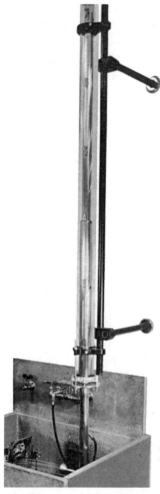

Figure 7-11
AATCC Rain Tester. *(Reprinted with permission from the American Society of Textile Chemists and Colorists, P.O. Box 12215, Research Triangle Park, NC 27709)*

Figure 7-12
Impact Penetration Tester. *(Reprinted with permission from the American Society of Textile Chemists and Colorists, P.O. Box 12215, Research Triangle Park, NC 27709)*

heights of water in the tube can be used during testing. In this method, separate specimens are used to assess performance at each intensity. Each specimen is backed by a piece of blotter paper of known weight. The specimen is sprayed with water under controlled conditions. The weight gained by the blotter paper is calculated in grams (the difference between the original weight of the blotter paper and the final or wetted weight of the blotter paper).

AATCC 42, Water Resistance: Impact Penetration Test, is another procedure for evaluating rain penetration. Distilled water is sprayed from a height onto a taut specimen backed by a weighed blotter paper and its weight gain is calculated (see Figure 7-12).

Conditioned and weighed specimens are tumbled in water in the AATCC 70, Water Repellency: Tumble Jar Dynamic Absorption Test (see Figure 7-13). After the excess water is removed, the percentage weight gain is calculated using Equation 7-6. This method is ideal for fabrics

Figure 7-13
The Dynamic Absorption Tester. (*Courtesy of Atlas Electric Device Co.*)

treated to be water resistant because the tumbling process is designed to simulate dynamic use conditions.

Equation 7-6

$$\%I = 100(W_W - W_O)/W_O$$

where I = weight increase in percent
W_W = weight of the specimen after wetting
W_O = original weight of the specimen

AATCC 127, Water Resistance: Hydrostatic Pressure Test, tests the performance of materials when they are exposed to standing water for a period of time. Materials of duck and canvas to be used in tarpaulins, covers, and awnings are examples of such applications. In this process, a specimen is subjected to steadily increasing water pressure (measured in inches or centimeters), until three points of leakage appear on its reverse side.

WATER VAPOR TRANSMISSION

Water vapor transmission, which is especially important for outerwear, measures the speed with which water vapor passes through a material. Two nonstandard procedures can be used to measure this characteristic. The first takes place in a humid environment. A known weight of dried calcium chloride or other desiccant is placed in a container that is covered by a specimen of the material. A **desiccant** is a compound that absorbs water vapor from the air, thereby maintaining a low relative humidity in its immediate environment. At prescribed time intervals, the calcium chloride is weighed and the moisture content is determined by subtraction.

The second procedure occurs in a dry environment. A specimen of the material covers a pan containing a known amount of water. Water loss by evaporation is measured at prescribed intervals. These two procedures measure grams of water transmitted per square meter of material in a 24-hour period (Adanur, 1995).

THICKNESS

The thickness of a material affects comfort in terms of heat transfer (thicker fabrics transfer heat more slowly than thinner fabrics of comparable components), flexibility (thicker fabrics tend to be less flexible than thinner fabrics of comparable components), bulk, and drape. Material thickness is also important in terms of planning for production, shipping, packaging, and handling. For example, if two products are identical in terms of the yardage of material used, the product made from the thicker material will require a larger volume of space and more packaging materials than the product made from the thinner material. Thickness of materials helps determine the number of fabric lays or layers possible in a cutting room and appropriate settings for sewing machines. In some end uses, thickness is critical. For example, air bags must be able to withstand their explosive expansion during an accident, but they must be compact enough to fit in the space in which they are stored.

Thickness is measured following ASTM D 1777, Measuring Thickness of Textile Materials. It is applicable to most fabrics in a wide range of structures and finishes. **Thickness** refers to the distance through the fabric from one surface to the other. A smooth, unwrinkled, conditioned specimen is placed flat on the base of the instrument and compressed as a weighted pressure foot is lowered slowly. Thickness is measured as the final distance between the base and pressure foot. A thickness gauge, such as the one shown in Figure 7-14, is used in this procedure.

Figure 7-14
Thickness gauge.

HAND AND SKIN CONTACT

Hand of materials is an important aesthetic and comfort characteristic. It also affects spreading, cutting, sewing, and handling operations during manufacturing. **Hand** is the tactile sensations or impressions that arise when materials are touched, squeezed, rubbed, or otherwise handled. Hand is not synonymous with skin contact. **Skin contact** occurs when the surface of the skin touches a material, but it is a static condition in which neither the material nor the body is required to move or interact for any sensation to occur. Examples of skin contact sensations include prickling, itchiness, roughness, clamminess, and cling. Hand involves a more dynamic situation in which at least one component (the skin/body or the material) moves. At present, no standard test methods exist for evaluating hand or skin contact. However, a substantial amount of research during the past 25 years has resulted in a much better understanding of the factors that contribute to hand. Kawabata, a Japanese researcher, was responsible for much of this research. He and his coworkers developed a list of dimensions that are used to describe hand. A better understanding of fabric hand and an ability to measure hand accurately are absolutely essential in terms of developing automatic production equipment, in which robots, rather than human operators, are used to produce products.

Based on the work of Kawabata and others, AATCC has developed a protocol or procedure that should be followed in assessing hand (Evaluation Procedure AATCC 5, Subjective Evaluation of Fabric Hand). The protocol can be used when different individuals rate materials at different times, when raters are being trained to detect and distinguish the constituent elements or components of hand, when a previous analysis is to be duplicated, or when a panel of raters evaluates the same material.

In this protocol, the individual's hands should be clean, but not recently washed, and should not be contaminated with hand lotion or cream. The room should be free of distractions. The individual should not look at the material while assessing its hand. Materials can be hidden behind a screen or drape or the individual can close his or her eyes or use a blindfold. The material to be evaluated is placed on a smooth nonmetal surface in a predetermined orientation, such as face side up and warp pointing toward the individual. Elements of hand relate to compression, bending, shearing, and fabric surface. Results may be recorded on a form, on a tape recorder, or to an assistant who records the results.

Several instruments have been developed to be used in assessing hand. A series of four instruments are used in the KES-F system (**KES** stands for Kawabata Evaluation System): a shear/tensile tester, a compression tester, a pure bending tester, and a surface tester. Table 7-1 describes the mechanical properties and their relationship to performance. Figure 7-15 illustrates the principles involved in the objective measurement of hand.

A combination of instruments are used in the FAST (Fabric Assurance by Simple Testing) system. The extension meter measures warp and filling tensile properties and shear behavior. The compression meter measures

Table 7-1
BASIC FABRIC MECHANICAL PROPERTIES AND RELATED QUALITY AND PERFORMANCE ATTRIBUTES OF MATERIALS AND PRODUCTS.

Fabric Mechanical Properties	Quality and Mechanical Performance
Uniaxial tension	Material handle and drape
Biaxial tension	Material formability and tailoring properties
Shear under tension	Product appearance and seam pucker
Pure bending	Mechanical stability and shape retention
Lateral compression	Relaxation shrinkage, dimensional stability, and hygral expansion
Longitudinal compression and buckling	Wrinkle recovery and crease retention
Surface roughness	Abrasion and pilling resistance
	Mechanical and physiological comfort

From S. C. Harlock. (1989, July). Fabric Objective Measurement: 2, Principles of Measurement. Textile Asia, 66–71. (Reprinted by permission from Textile Asia, the Asian Textile & Apparel Monthly, GPO Box 185, Hong Kong.)

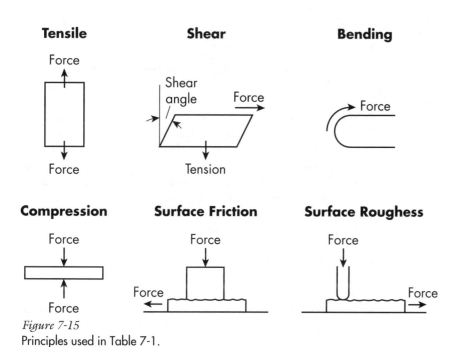

Figure 7-15
Principles used in Table 7-1.

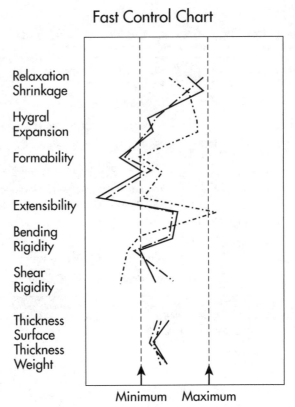

Fast Control Chart

Relaxation
Shrinkage

Hygral
Expansion

Formability

Extensibility

Bending
Rigidity

Shear
Rigidity

Thickness
Surface
Thickness
Weight

Minimum   Maximum

Figure 7-16
A FAST control chart.

fabric thickness under a variety of loads. The bending meter measures bending length. Surface friction and dimensional stability to heat and moisture also are assessed.

Both the KES and the FAST systems enter the data from the instrumental analysis into a computer program and plot the results on a control chart to determine appropriateness of a material for production and end-use demands. The control chart shows a "snake" diagram plotted between minimum and maximum values for each dimension that has been measured or calculated. If the "snake" lies between these identified extremes, problems in production as a result of the way the material handles and discomfort for consumers should be low. Figure 7-16 illustrates an example FAST control chart.

STIFFNESS

Although stiffness is one element assessed in hand, it also relates to other performance measures. Stiffness affects fabric drape, resistance to roll such as in waistbands, resistance to wrinkling, and other aspects related to comfort and aesthetics. **Fabric stiffness** is a measure of a fabric's resistance to bending or flexing. More force, energy, or work is needed to bend a material that is described as being stiff compared to that required to bend a material that is described as being pliable.

Two options are presented in ASTM D 1388, Stiffness of Fabrics. The first option is the cantilever test. The specimen is slid parallel to its horizontal axis at a specified rate until its leading edge projects from the edge of a horizontal surface or cantilevers over space. Figure 7-17 shows the stiffness tester used with the cantilever option. The length of the overhang is measured at the point where the leading edge bends under its weight to form a 41.5° angle. Bending length and flexural rigidity are measured using the sequence of equations listed in Equation 7-7. **Flexural rigidity** is a measure of material stiffness that is calculated using fabric mass and length of overhang.

Equation 7-7a

$$c = o/2$$

where c = bending length in cm and
o = length of overhand in cm.

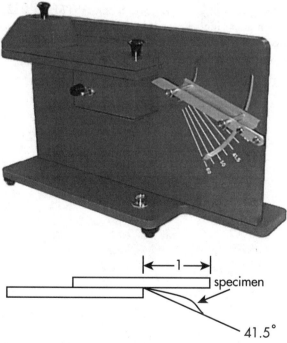

Figure 7-17
Cantilever stiffness tester. (*Courtesy of Instrument Marketing Services, a subsidiary of SGS US Testing Company Inc.*)

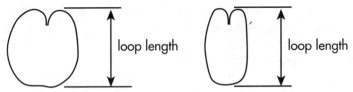

Figure 7-18
Heart loop test and loop lengths: stiff fabric (left) and pliable fabric (right).

Equation 7-7b

$$G = Wc^3$$

where G = flexural rigidity in mg cm
$\quad W$ = fabric mass per unit area in mg/cm^2
$\quad c$ = bending length in cm

The second option is used for fabrics that tend to curl, such as jersey knits, or that would cling to the stiffness tester, such as nylon tricot. In this procedure, called the heart loop test, a strip of fabric is formed into a loop with a shape somewhat reminiscent of a heart (see Figure 7-18). The length of the loop as it hangs under its own mass is measured and flexural rigidity is calculated.

A final procedure for measuring stiffness is ASTM D 4032, Stiffness of Fabric by the Circular Bend Procedure. This procedure is applicable to all fabrics and measures the force in lbf (pounds of force) needed to push a flat, folded-in-half specimen through an opening in a platform (see Figure 7-19).

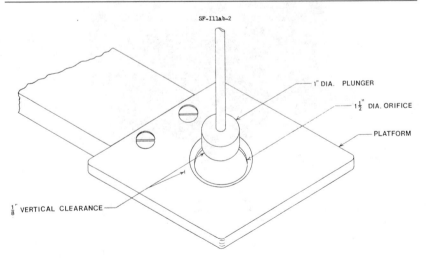

Figure 7-19
Platform, plunger, and specimen for the circular bend procedure for stiffness. (*Adapted, with permission, from the Annual Book of ASTM Standards, copyright American Society for Testing and Materials, 100 Barr Harbor Drive, West Conshohocken, PA 19428-2959*)

DRAPE

Drape is a behavior characteristic of a material that describes how the material falls or hangs or flows over a three-dimensional form. No standard test methods are used to determine drape for a material. However, a nonstandard procedure that uses the drapemeter shown in Figure 7-20 has

Figure 7-20

Drapemeter and diagram showing specimen placement and paper ring. (*Courtesy of SDL International Ltd*)

been developed. In this procedure, a circle specimen is draped over a cylinder. A light shines down from the top, so that the material casts a shadow over a preweighed paper ring that is placed around the base of the cylinder. The shadow is traced onto the ring. The shadow trace on the ring is cut out and weighed and the drape coefficient is calculated using Equation 7-8. Several example tracings of shadows and the corresponding drape coefficients are shown in Figure 7-21. Drape coefficients closer to 100 percent represent stiffer and less drapeable materials. Drape coefficients closer to zero represent pliable and more drapeable materials. Digital analysis of drape using photovoltaic cells that measure the light being absorbed is an alternative procedure (Collier, 1991).

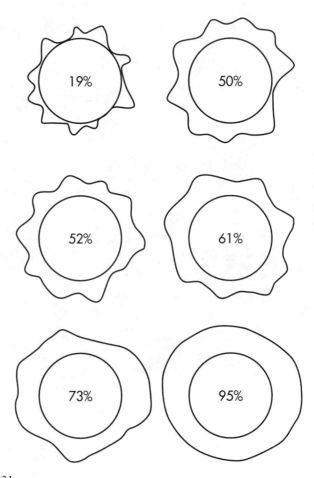

Figure 7-21
Drape shadows and drape coefficients for stiff fabric (bottom right), pliable fabric (center), and very pliable fabric (top left).

Equation 7-8

$$F = 100 \; (W_s/W_r)$$

where F = drape coefficient in percent
  W_s = weight in grams of the shadow
  W_r = weight in grams of the paper ring

AIR PERMEABILITY

Air permeability is especially important for comfort for outerwear, tents, sleeping bags, blankets, and other protective textile products. Material performance in terms of air permeability is also important for the functioning of many industrial products, such as vacuum cleaner bags, parachutes, hot air balloons, air bags, and sails. **Air permeability** is the rate of air flow passing vertically through a known area of material when an air pressure difference exists between the two sides of the material. Air flow is not the same thing as wind resistance. **Wind resistance** affects the behavior of material that is confronted by or exposed to a dynamic condition of rapidly moving air (wind). Air permeability deals with material behavior when exposed to still or slowly moving air. At present, no standard test method measures wind resistance.

Air permeability is measured using ASTM D 737, Air Permeability of Textile Fabrics. In this procedure, conditioned specimens are clamped in place and air pressure is increased on one side of the material. The change in air pressure on the other side is measured in $ft^3/min/ft^2$, which is the volume of air flowing each minute through the exposed fabric (see Figure 7-22).

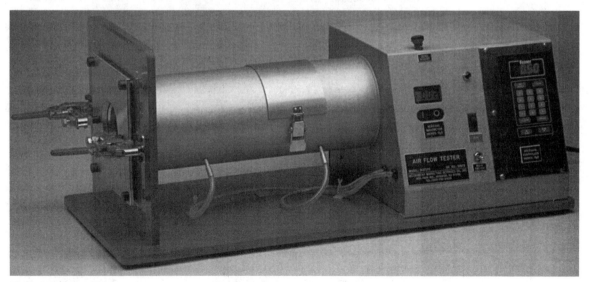

Figure 7-22
Air flow tester. (*Courtesy of Instrument Marketing Services, a subsidiary of SGS US Testing Company Inc.*)

ELECTROSTATIC PROPENSITY

To understand electricity and electrical charge, it is necessary to understand the basic structure of the atom. The internal structure of an atom can be compared to a sun, with planets in orbit around it. An atom has a central section called a nucleus, which is composed of positively charged particles called protons. Around this nucleus are small orbiting negatively charged particles called electrons. In its neutral state, an atom has an equal number of electrons and protons, and therefore, no charge. However, under some circumstances, such as the frictional sliding of materials, some atoms lose electrons while others gain electrons. As a result, some atoms become positively charged and others become negatively charged. This difference in charge becomes significant when billions of atoms are grouped together to form an object.

A basic law of physics states that materials with opposite charges attract each other. Thus, when the difference between two objects becomes great enough and they are close enough to each other, a rapid and spontaneous flow of electrons will occur that neutralizes the electron charge difference between the two objects. If this occurs in the dark, this flow appears as a spark or tiny moving streak of light. An electrical charge differential can develop when materials slide across each other, as when a slip and skirt slide when the wearer walks or sits, when clothes tumble in a dryer, when a person slides in or out of a chair, or when materials slide across surfaces in production facilities.

Static build-up can create comfort problems through static cling and static discharge. It creates manufacturing problems with raw and processed materials because static interferes with the efficient handling and movement of materials. Static also can create safety problems, especially in areas where fine dust accumulates, such as the bale opening area in spinning mills or where oxygen and other highly flammable materials, such as gas stations (gas vapors), hospitals (oxygen), and petroleum refineries (petroleum distillates), are used. Static problems are most pronounced when relative humidity levels are low, materials are very dry, or materials have low regain properties. **Electrostatic propensity** is a measure of the capacity of a nonconducting material to acquire and hold an electrical charge through friction or other means. Measuring this behavior allows us to determine when it is likely to occur so that materials can be substituted that are less likely to develop problems of this nature, or take steps to minimize the problem in terms of comfort, productivity, and safety.

In ASTM D 4238, Electrostatic Propensity of Woven Fabrics, the specimen is clamped to a rotating metal disk. A direct current potential is applied to a needle electrode that is positioned above it. A detecting electrode measures the electrostatic charge on the specimen. Low-humidity conditions are recommended for this test to simulate worst-case scenario conditions.

Several AATCC procedures have been developed to measure static build-up on materials. In AATCC 76 Electrical Resistivity of Fabrics and

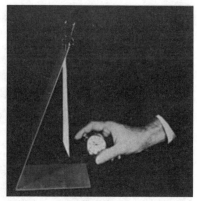

Figure 7-23
Fabric-to-metal cling plate, showing fabric cling (left) and decay (right). (*Reprinted with permission from the American Society of Textile Chemists and Colorists, P.O. Box 12215, Research Triangle Park, NC 27709*)

AATCC 84 Electrical Resistivity of Yarns, a conditioned specimen is measured for electrical resistance using an electrical resistance meter. The specific problem of fabric cling is measured using AATCC 115, Electrostatic Clinging of Fabrics: Fabric-to-Metal Test. **Electrostatic clinging** is the propensity of one material to adhere to another because of an electrical charge on one or both surfaces. The procedure measures the time required for an induced charge on a material to decay to the point where the electrical attractive forces causing a specimen to cling to a metal surface are overcome by the gravitational forces pulling the specimen away from the metal. A metal plate shown in Figure 7-23 is used in this procedure. Time in seconds for the material to hang free from the metal plate is recorded.

Because walking on carpets is likely to trigger a static discharge when relative humidity is low, AATCC 134, Electrostatic Propensity of Carpets, was developed to assess performance of carpets in this regard. In this procedure, a carpet is brought to environmental equilibrium in specified conditions of temperature and humidity. A technician wearing sandals with specified shoe soles and heels, as shown in Figure 7-24, walks in a controlled manner on the carpet specimen. The charge build-up on the technician is recorded.

LIGHT REFLECTANCE, TRANSMITTANCE, AND ABSORPTANCE

ASTM E 1175, Determining Solar or Photopic Reflectance, Transmittance, and Absorptance of Materials Using a Large Diameter Integrating Sphere, is used to access optical properties of window blinds, draperies, and other window coverings. The ability of these materials to allow light to

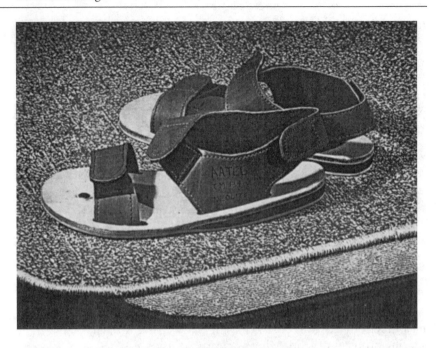

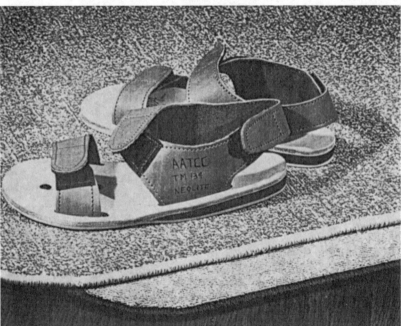

Figure 7-24
Sandals with the specified soles and heels used in measuring static build-up on carpet specimens. (*Reprinted with permission from the American Society of Textile Chemists and Colorists, P.O. Box 12215, Research Triangle Park, NC 27709*)

enter a structure is assessed by illuminating a specimen and measuring the light reflected, transmitted, or absorbed. Photopic in the title refers to the "spectral response of the average human eye when fully adapted to daylight conditions" (ASTM, 1996, p. 666).

SAFETY

Safety addresses the physical risks to which the user of a textile product is exposed. Safety includes a few applications involving strength and durability characteristics. For example, the strength and abrasion resistance of ski tow ropes, parachute cords, and rope ladders are important measures of their safety. These performance procedures were discussed in Chapter 6. However, for the majority of textile products, the major safety issue is flammability.

FLAMMABILITY

Flammability is the way a material reacts to heat, the manner in which it ignites and burns, the ease or difficulty with which a burning textile is extinguished, the type of ash or melt remaining, and the amount of smoke produced. Materials that are described as flammable tend to ignite quickly, burn rapidly, and extinguish with difficulty. Flammability is a common property of most materials used for apparel, furnishings, and some industrial products. Flame resistant or flame retardant materials are made in several ways. They may incorporate fibers that are less likely to ignite, that burn more slowly, or that self-extinguish. Or, materials may be treated with a finish that decreases the likelihood of ignition or the speed of burning or increases the likelihood of the material self-extinguishing. Some test methods simulate accidental ignition and measure the time it takes for the material to burn. Other test methods expose the material to a small flame and measure the time until a specified amount of material has burned. Still other methods measure different aspects of a burning material, such as the amount of oxygen consumed or the amount of heat generated.

Test methods that measure a material's flammability are usually designed to simulate normal use conditions or to reflect a common means of ignition. For example, careless smoking is often the cause of a fire in upholstered furniture and mattresses. Thus, a cigarette is used as the ignition source. Some procedures use a small specimen; other procedures work with a prototype or a full-scale sample product in which fashion fabric and support materials are used. The results of one method cannot be compared with results of another method because the condition of the material, specimen orientation, ignition source, performance measured, and time of exposure to heat or ignition source may vary.

Mandatory Procedures

Over the last fifty years, epidemiological studies of textile products have helped researchers and public health officials identify several textile product categories that have an unacceptably high risk factor for personal injury, property damage, or death because of their flammability. These high-risk product categories are subject to regulations that define a specific acceptable performance level in terms of flammability behavior under carefully defined and described conditions. These screening procedures are designed to remove items and materials from interstate commerce that are deemed to be unsafe and unsuitable for the public.

Mandatory testing procedures are indicated in the Flammable Fabrics Act and the Amended Flammable Fabrics Act. Records of the results of testing must be kept. If a material does not meet the minimum acceptable level of performance, it cannot be used in a product that fits within that product category. For example, if a material does not meet the minimum requirement for children's sleepwear, the material cannot be used in any type of children's sleepwear. The material can, however, be used in other products, such as pants, tops, or jackets.

Mandatory tests are described in detail in the laws and regulations. Included in the law or regulation are defined limits for acceptable performance. These pass/fail scales are binding and nonnegotiable. The intent of mandatory testing is to remove unsafe materials and products from the market. Several standard test methods discussed in the next section resemble mandatory tests, but testing should be done following the procedure described in a specific law or regulation.

ASTM D 4723, Index and Descriptions of Textile Heat and Flammability Test Methods and Performance Specifications, includes summary tables for approximately 75 procedures used in the United States and Canada. The procedures include those developed by ASTM, governmental agencies, and various trade and professional organizations. Many procedures include performance specification criteria. Procedures developed by governmental agencies often include pass/fail criteria for specific materials or products in order to ensure a certain level of public safety. For example, pass/fail scales are included for materials used in buses, cars, planes, trains, taxis, and ferries. Pass/fail scales are included for furnishings used in public areas, such as museums, theaters, health care facilities, and schools. ASTM D 4391, Standard Terminology Relating to Burning Behavior of Textiles, defines terms used to describe the flammability of materials.

The Consumer Product Safety Commission (CPSC) is the division of the Federal Trade Commission that is responsible for most of the mandatory testing procedures for consumer products. Procedures for other materials should be consulted for camping tents, textile building materials, vehicle interiors, interior furnishings, aircraft, tarpaulins, and electric blankets. Textiles used in interior furnishings for public areas should be evaluated to ensure that they meet building code requirements as specified for the geographic area, funding agency, and end-use classification. For example, if a building uses federal funds for part or all of the construction costs, federal code requirements apply. Some of these procedures use mock-up products or full-scale furnishings to determine the hazard.

16 CFR 1610, Standard for the Flammability of Clothing Textiles (General Wearing Apparel), is a mandatory procedure for all apparel materials except some accessories and interlinings. By experimenting with a material, the face, orientation, and pattern portion that produces the most rapid flame spread is determined and used in specimen preparation. Each specimen is dried, cooled, and exposed to a flame for 1 second at a 45° angle. The time of flame spread and identification of damage to the base structure are noted. Figure 7-25 shows the testing apparatus, and Table 7-2 describes the specification criteria. A similar procedure, without the details regarding sampling, is found in ASTM D 1230, Flammability of Apparel Textiles.

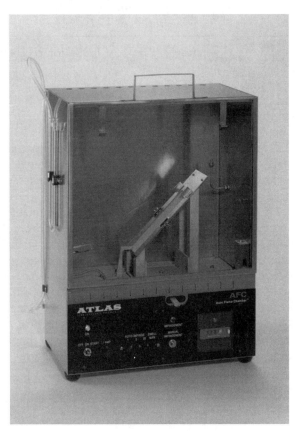

Figure 7-25
The 45° angle tester. (*Courtesy of Atlas Electric Device Co.*)

Table 7-2
SPECIFICATION CRITERIA FOR THE 45° ANGLE TESTER.

For plain surface textiles:

Class 1—'Normal flammability' is (a) average burn time of 3.5 s or more, (b) ignited but extinguished, (c) did not ignite.

Class 2—Not applicable.

Class 3—'Rapid and intense burning' is average burn time of less than 3.5 s for 10 specimens.

For raised fiber surface textiles:

Class 1—'Normal flammability' is (a) average burn time of 0–7.0 s with less than 2 specimens of 10 burning the base fabric, (b) average burn time of more than 7.0 s for 5 to 10 specimens, (c) no burning of the base fabric, disregarding the average burn time for 5 specimens.

Class 2—'Intermediate flammability' is average burn time of 4.0–7.0 s for 5 or 10 specimens with 2 or more base burns.

Class 3—'Rapid and intense burning' is average burn time of less than 4.0 s and when more than 2 of the 10 specimens have base burns.

Reprinted, with permission, from the Annual Book of ASTM Standards, copyright American Society for Testing and Materials, 100 Barr Harbor Drive, West Conshohocken, PA 19428-2959.

A second mandatory procedure using the 45° angle tester is 16 CFR 1611, Standard for the Flammability of Vinyl Plastic Films (General Wearing Apparel). The criteria for acceptable performance is an average burn rate of less than 1.2 in./s for both lengthwise and crosswise directions.

Children's sleepwear is covered by two mandatory standards: 16 CFR 1615, Standard for the Flammability of Children's Sleepwear; Sizes 0 through 6x and 16 CFR 1616, Standard for the Flammability of Children's Sleepwear; Sizes 7 through 14. The two procedures are similar. Underwear and diapers are excluded, but every other item, including nightgowns, pajamas, robes, or similar items intended for sleeping, are covered by these standards. A vertical tester and a 3 s ignition time are used (see Figure 7-26). Minimum conditions for a passing grade include an average char length of 7.0 in. or less and no individual specimen with a char length of 10 in. **Char length** is the amount of fabric consumed or damaged by the flame. Damage is assessed by the material's ability to support a weight without tearing. With both standards, materials are required to meet the minimum performance as listed in the pass/fail scale at any point up to and including fifty care cycles.

Textile floor coverings are also the subject of two mandatory standards: 16 CFR 1630, Standard for the Surface Flammability of Carpets and Rugs, and 16 CFR 1631, Standard for the Surface Flammability of Small Carpets and Rugs. The major difference between the two standards is the

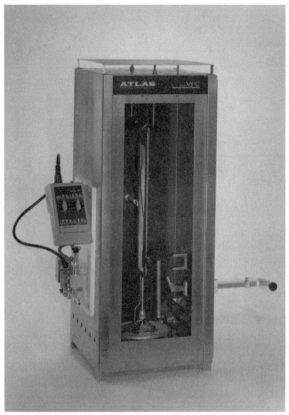

Figure 7-26
The vertical flammability tester. (*Courtesy of Atlas Electric Device Co.*)

size of the product that falls within its purview. These procedures are similar to ASTM D 2859, Flammability of Finished Textile Floor Covering Materials. The methenamine timed-burning tablet ignition source is used in all three procedures. The carpet specimen is placed in a frame and the methenamine pill is placed in the center of the specimen and ignited. To pass the federal standards, the charred area must not extend any closer to the edge of the frame than 1 inch for at least 7 of the 8 specimens (see Figure 7-27). If a carpet or rug has had a topical flame-retardant finish applied, a refurbishing or cleaning treatment is required before testing for flammability to be sure that the finish is durable to whatever cleaning procedure is recommended.

A final mandatory standard is 16 CFR 1632, Standard for the Flammability of Mattresses (and Mattress Pads). This procedure uses a mattress or prototype in a horizontal position and addresses the all-too-frequent hazard associated with smoking in bed. Lighted cigarettes are placed on the smooth tape edge or in quilted or tufted locations on a bare mattress,

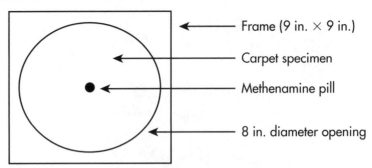

Figure 7-27
The methenamine pill test for carpets.

and more lighted cigarettes are placed between two sheets on the mattress surface. The mattress passes if none of the cigarette locations has a char length greater than 2.0 in. in any direction from the nearest point of contact with the cigarette.

Voluntary Procedures

Conformance to the specifications for procedures discussed in this section is not mandatory. However, several procedures do include performance specification criteria. A few select methods for apparel, furnishing, and industrial materials will be discussed here.

A voluntary procedure for testing apparel fabrics is ASTM D 3659, Flammability of Apparel Fabrics by the Semi-Restraint Method. This vertical method measures burn time, mass lost, rate of area flame spread, and average area destroyed by burning. A method sponsored by the National Fire Protection Association (NFPA) is NFPA 1971, Protective Clothing for Structural Fire Fighting. Also a vertical method, it measures char length and afterflame time.

ASTM D 4151, Flammability of Blankets, is a horizontal procedure that uses a flame and measures damage to a paper tab or monitor. Performance specification criteria include two classes based on the condition of the paper monitor: Class 1, no damage and suitable or Class 2, damage and unsuitable.

Because of problems with smoldering cigarettes and ignition of upholstered furniture, several procedures have been developed. ASTM E 1352, Cigarette Ignition Resistance of Mock-Up Upholstered Furniture Assemblies, is used to test materials to be used in furnishings for public facilities, such as hospitals and educational facilities. ASTM E 1353, Cigarette Ignition Resistance of Components of Upholstered Furniture, is used to test the performance of cover and interior fabrics, welt cords, and filling, padding, decking, and barrier materials. Each procedure works with materials that are assembled to resemble a small chair seat and back. The assembly's performance is assessed by noting if ignition occurred and measuring any char that developed. Materials are classified based on their performance. For example, cover fabrics are classified as either Class I (did not obviously ignite and has a char length of less than 1.8 in.) or Class II (ignited and has a char length exceeding 1.8 in.). The Upholstered Furniture Action Council (UFAC) and the National Fire Protection Association (NFPA) have similar procedures.

ASTM E 1537, Fire Testing of Real Scale Upholstered Furniture Items, is used to assess performance of items intended for public areas. A full-size manufactured item, a prototype, or a mock-up is ignited. Several measurements are made—the rate of heat and smoke release, total amount of heat and smoke, rate and concentration of selected gases released during burning, and the rate and amount of mass lost.

Ignition Characteristics of Finished Textile Floor Covering Materials (ASTM D 2859) is used to identify carpets, rugs, and other textile floor coverings that can be rated as flame resistant. In this procedure, the specimen is exposed to a standard ignition source (a methenamine pill) in a draft-protected environment and the resulting char length is measured.

Flame resistant materials are required in some states for camping tents and several standard procedures exist for this assessment. ASTM D 4372, Specification for Flame-Resistant Materials Used in Camping Tents, works with several specimens—new and after exposure to weathering, leaching, or both. Specimens representing flooring, walls, and tops are tested. Performance measurements include extent of damage, afterflame time, and flame time of burning specimen droppings.

THERMAL PROTECTION

A final issue related to both safety and flammability focuses on the use of textile materials to protect individuals from heat from an open flame. ASTM D 1408, Thermal Protective Performance of Materials for Clothing by Open-Flame Method, measures heat energy transmitted through a material to a thermocouple up to the amount of heat that is sufficient to cause a second-degree burn injury. This procedure is particularly applicable for materials used in apparel for firefighters and others whose work requires close proximity to an open flame. **Thermal protection** is the amount of heat transfer protection (insulation) provided by a material when it is exposed to an open flame.

CHEMICAL RESISTANCE

Chemical resistance is a material's ability to block the transmission of chemicals through it. Chemicals can be in the form of gases, dusts, powders, granular substances, solids, or liquids. These chemicals may be toxic, corrosive, carcinogenic (causing cancer), mutanagenic (causing mutations in a fetus), teratogenic (causing birth defects in a fetus), or hazardous.

Some chemicals, such as insecticides, herbicides, cleaning agents, and solvents, may be widely available and used by consumers for gardening, cleaning, maintenance, and repairing property.

Water penetration resistance, oil repellency, water vapor transmission, and air permeability tests are often used to determine some measure of the material's resistance to chemicals. In many cases, these procedures are modified to ensure the safety of the technician or researcher or to more closely simulate real conditions in which a chemical is used. Other procedures have been developed to simulate real-use conditions. For example, significant research has been undertaken to replicate conditions in which exposure to pesticides may occur. Most of these procedures are designed to assess the ability of the material to present a barrier to penetration or permeation of the chemical through the material. **Penetration** is the flow of chemical through closures, porous materials, seams, pinholes, and other imperfections of a material on a nonmolecular level (ASTM, 1996).

Methods tend to be of two types. AATCC Methods 42 (impact penetration test to water) and 118 (oil repellency test) are examples of run-off penetration tests in which the liquid impacts the material from a stationary source, where the material is at an angle to the liquid contact point, and where blotter paper is used to absorb the penetrating liquid. AATCC Method 127, Hydrostatic Pressure Water Repellency Test, is an example of procedures in which the liquid is under pressure when it comes in contact with a material.

Permeation involves chemical movement through the material at a molecular level. Permeation resistance is measured as breakthrough time and permeation rate. **Breakthrough time** is measured by exposure to the first detectable presence of the chemical on the other side of the material. **Permeation rate** is the volume of chemical that passes through the material in a given time unit. ASTM F 739, Resistance of Protective Clothing Materials to Permeation by Liquids or Gases under Conditions of Continuous Contact, is one standard test method that provides a means of evaluating permeation. In this procedure, the material is exposed to a chemical and its transmission through that material, absorption by the material, damage to the material, or some other factor is measured. Often spectrophotometry is used to assess a chemical's transmission through or absorption by a material specimen.

Some procedures examine a material's resistance to degradation because of exposure to a specific chemical. **Degradation** is a "change in a material's physical properties as a result of chemical exposure" (ASTM, 1996, Vol. 11.03, p. 849). Changes in weight, appearance, dimensions, tensile strength, and hardness can be assessed after a specific exposure to determine the level of damage.

IMPACT RESISTANCE

Materials used in some functional clothing and industrial products must be able to withstand impact from projectiles, sharp or blunt objects, or an instantaneous heavy load. **Impact resistance** is the ability of a material to withstand high-speed loading or a significant force applied to a small area. Seat belts, sewing thread, body armor, aircraft carrier arrestation cables, tire cords, and tie ropes for animals are products that use materials that must be able to absorb tremendous amounts of energy quickly without rupturing, tearing, or disintegrating. Testing for impact resistance may take one of several forms: dropping weights on the specimen, where the mass and shape are determined by end use; falling pendulums, where the load can be adjusted as desired; high-speed revolving flywheels that at prescribed intervals elongate the specimen; and guns that fire one of several projectiles at the specimen (Adanur, 1995).

HEALTH ISSUES

Textile materials should also be considered in terms of their impact on the health of the individual. **Health** is the interaction of physical, mental, emotional, and social aspects of the individual. Health issues also imply the effect of long-term exposure to a material. Health issues do not necessarily imply a risk in terms of injury and death, but they may imply a loss of comfort or efficiency or the general feeling of wellness. Some issues discussed in this section relate to materials used in functional clothing for specific occupations, leisure activities, or athletic events. Standard test methods do not yet exist for all areas that may be of interest for some applications or occupations.

ALLERGENS AND IRRITANTS

Allergens are foreign materials that cause a physical reaction by the body after exposure. The sensitization period can be as short as a week or as long as several years. Allergies can result from surface contact, inhalation, or ingestion. Most problems with textile materials relate to surface contact issues. Individuals may be allergic to fibers, finishes, dyes, detergents, or other materials added to or used to clean a textile. Most allergic reactions are the result of exposure to dyes, finishes, and fibers. The symptoms include skin redness, a skin rash, sneezing, watery eyes, and hives.

    Irritants are materials that produce a very mild pain sensation, such as rough materials that abrade, poke, or stab the skin. They produce more localized problems with textile products. An example is a red area that develops where a rough material touched the skin.

    Allergy tests are conducted for a wide range of materials, such as strawberries, plant materials, and dust mites, that are known to cause allergic responses in people. Patch or scratch tests are used to assess these health problems. In these procedures a tiny amount of material such as wool is taped to the skin or slightly scratched into the skin. The area is then examined after a specified length of time, usually 24 to 48 hours, to see if any physical reaction occurred.

FORMALDEHYDE

Formaldehyde is a chemical compound that had been used often in finishing of cotton and cellulosic materials in the 1980s and earlier. A toxic compound, it is also a sensory irritant. The problems with exposure to formaldehyde, which are most critical in terms of the manufacturing and retailing industry, are related to **formaldehyde release.** This is the amount of formaldehyde evolved from textiles in accelerated storage conditions and includes free (unbonded) formaldehyde as well as formaldehyde released by the degradation of finishes.

In AATCC 112, Determination of Formaldehyde Release from Fabric: Sealed Jar Method, a weighed specimen is suspended over water in a sealed jar and heated in an oven at a specified temperature for a prescribed time (see Figure 7-28). The amount of formaldehyde released is determined using a spectrophotometer.

ULTRAVIOLET PROTECTION

Ultraviolet radiation is a source of damaging energy to organic materials, including hair, fiber, and skin. Exposure to sunlight results in damage to skin cells, sunburns, and, in some cases, skin cancer. This damage can be seen by the difference in wrinkles between the skin of areas frequently exposed to the sun and areas usually covered by clothing and protected from sunlight expo-

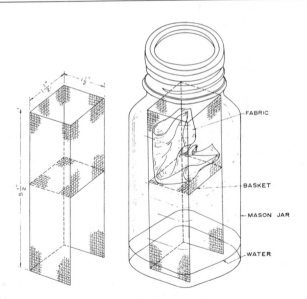

Figure 7-28

The sealed jar method for determining formaldehyde release. (*Reprinted with permission from the American Society of Textile Chemists and Colorists, P.O. Box 12215, Research Triangle Park, NC 27709*)

sure. People expose their skin to the damaging effects of UV radiation, when they sun tan, use tanning booths, and work and play outdoors. The number of people with skin cancer has grown at alarming rates during the past 15 years and that disastrous growth rate is expected to increase.

Concern with sunlight damage has created a demand for products that provide protection, such as lotions and creams. Some textiles also claim to provide extra protection from sunlight damage. The Food and Drug Administration has assigned responsibility for regulating textile materials and products to the Consumer Product Safety Commission and the Federal Trade Commission. The FTC insists that manufacturers prove that their products function as claimed in terms of **ultraviolet (UV) protection.** The FTC also indicated that if the industry did not develop standards addressing UV protection, terms, and evaluation procedures, the FTC would develop standards and impose them on the industry.

Thus, in 1996 ASTM formed a new subcommittee on UV Protective Clothing to address these issues. The FTC imposed early guidelines for materials in terms of protection provided and ruggedness conditions under which materials were to be tested. Guidelines of 40 launderings and 200 hours of accelerated UV exposure will be used as starting points in developing standards for UV protective materials.

Four task groups have been formed. One group on test method development will focus on conditions and procedures for exposure. They will consider wetness, dryness, stretch, durability, and abrasion factors to which materials are exposed in use and care. A second group on test method development will focus on measuring biological end points, such as changes in the skin described as burning, wrinkling, or tanning. A third group will focus on development of a classification standard that examines appropriate use of UV protective apparel. The final group will work on developing consistent and effective labeling for UV protective products.

Various nonstandard procedures have been used to evaluate the UV blocking effect of materials. These methods expose a material to a UV light source and measure the amount of UV transmitted through the material.

BIOLOGICAL RESISTANCE

Biological resistance is a material's ability to block the transmission of organisms through it. It has become a major concern for health care workers, researchers, veterinarians, farmers, and others who work with blood, urine, and other body fluids of people and animals. With the recognition of the hazards of blood-borne pathogens, such as hepatitis B virus (HBV) and human immunodeficiency virus (HIV), and the health risks associated with them, this issue is one of major importance. Because clothing items are the last line of defense against exposure to these pathogens, evaluation of their ability to protect is critical.

ASTM F 903, Resistance of Materials Used in Protective Clothing to Penetration by Liquids, uses synthetic blood and a surrogate virus to determine the resistance of occupational clothing, such as barrier gowns used in emergency rooms, to blood that may be infested with pathogens. In the procedure, the liquid is in contact with the specimen for one hour and at varying pressures for several additional minutes (see Figure 7-29). Visual detection of the red liquid is one parameter that is measured. A second parameter is an assay measure used to detect viable virus penetration even when liquid penetration did not occur. Because viruses can be much smaller than even the tiniest droplet of a liquid, the assay measure is one of special importance.

Other procedures include working with bovine (cow) blood in a strike through procedure in which droplets of blood are placed on a specimen and pressure is applied until the blood shows through on the other side of the material. This is referred to as visible strike through. In the elbow lean test, the technician layers a presoaked blotter containing synthetic blood, a specimen, and a film barrier, and then presses an elbow on the film layer until visible penetration occurs.

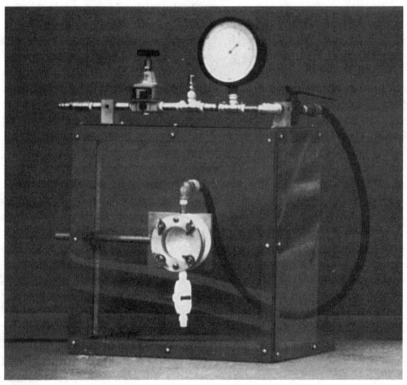

Figure 7-29
The penetration test apparatus. (*Courtesy of Wilson Road Machine Shop*)

MATERIAL SPECIFICATIONS

Material specifications often identify the test method by organization and number, the desired measure of performance, the option within the procedure, and the unit by which that performance characteristic is measured. Specs often include the conditions under which the test is conducted, if more than one combination of conditions is possible. Specifications are normally listed as minimums. Several example specifications for comfort and safety are listed in Table 7-3.

CONCLUSIONS

This discussion concerns comfort, safety, and health issues. Many performance characteristics that affect comfort also relate to aesthetics. Assessing performance of materials related to comfort, safety, and health issues is conducted much less often when compared to tests for durability, care, and colorfastness. When comfort, safety, or health aspects of a material are assessed, it is often because of the high demand for comfort in some end-uses where high performance claims are made or because the use of some certified or trademarked materials in a product means that testing is required by the supplier of the material in order to use the certification or trademark. Comfort testing is not considered as critical by the apparel and furnishings industry as is the testing described in the other chapters in this part. However, all too

Table 7-3
PERFORMANCE SPECIFICATIONS FOR SAMPLE PRODUCT CATEGORIES.*

Category	Upholstery	Sheer Curtains	Vocational Apparel[1]	Blankets	Toweling	Regular Apparel[2]
Air permeability	—	4	10	—	—	—
Water repellency	—	—	90/70[3]	—	—	—
Water resistance	—	—	No leaks[4]	—	—	—
Absorbency	—	—	—	—	90% or better	—
Flammability	Passing[5]	Passing[5]	Class 1	—	Class 1	Class 1
Thermal transmission	—	—	—	Acceptable	Class 1	—

[1]Outerwear.
[2]Except children's sleepwear and some occupational apparel.
[3]First number refers to ratings for new materials; second number refers to materials washed three times.
[4]Within one minute at a specified pressure.
[5]Based on the procedure as specified in the appropriate building codes.

—No values listed in the ASTM recommended performance specifications for the product type.

often product failure can be traced to use of materials that were inappropriate to satisfy consumer expectations for comfort, safety, and health.

Flammability testing is mandatory for certain product categories. Records are kept by firms that produce or sell materials used in those products to verify that materials met the requirements for safety as mandated by law or regulation.

Few standardized procedures exist at present for some health and safety issues. During the past few years, several procedures have become standardized as interest in and demand for standard procedures increases. Health and safety issues related to general use products and those for specialized occupations are driving this demand for standard evaluation procedures.

SUGGESTED READINGS

Adanur, Sabit. (1995). *Wellington Sears Handbook of Industrial Textiles*. Lancaster, PA: Technomic Publishing Company.

American Association of Textile Chemists and Colorists. (1996). *AATCC Technical Manual, 71*. Research Triangle Park, NC: Author.

American Society for Testing and Materials. (1996). *Annual Book of ASTM Standards, Vol. 4.07*. West Conshohocken, PA: Author.

American Society for Testing and Materials. (1996). *Annual Book of ASTM Standards, Vol. 7.01 & 7.02*. West Conshohocken, PA: Author.

American Society for Testing and Materials. (1996). *Annual Book of ASTM Standards, Vol. 11.03*. West Conshohocken, PA: Author.

American Society for Testing and Materials. (1996). *Annual Book of ASTM Standards, Vol. 12.02*. West Conshohocken, PA: Author.

Anon. (1996, July). New Subcommittee on UV Functional Clothing Formed. *ASTM Standardization News, 24*, 16–17.

Bona, Mario. (1990). *Textile Quality: Physical Methods of Product and Process Control*. Rome: Texilia.

Booth, J. E. (1969). *Principles of Textile Testing*. New York: Chemical Publishing Company.

Brown, Patty. (1992). *Ready-to-Wear Apparel Analysis*. New York: Macmillan.

Campbell, Hugh J. (1993, March). Flammability Testing of Textile Products. *Canadian Textile Journal, 111(2)*, 20–22, 26–27.

Capjack, L., S. Davis, & N. Kerr. (1994, April). Textiles and UV Radiation. *Canadian Textile Journal, 111(3)*, 14–15.

Cary, Richard T. (1976). A Comparison of Selected Test Methods for Measuring the Prime-Moisture Absorbency of Terry Toweling. Unpublished Doctoral Dissertation, Purdue University, West Lafayette, IN.

Collier, Billie J., Yongping Chen, & John R. Collier. (1992, October). A Dynamic Method for Measuring Formaldehyde Release from Durable Press Fabrics. *Textile Chemist and Colorist, 24(10)*, 26–29.

Collier, Billie J. (1991). Measurement of Fabric Drape and Its Relation to Fabric Mechanical Properties and Subjective Evaluation. *Clothing and Textiles Research Journal, 10(1)*, 46–52.

Constant, F. Woodbridge. (1967). *Fundamental Principles of Physics*. Reading, MA: Addison-Wesley.

Dittman, Richard, & Glenn Schmieg. (1979). *Physics in Everyday Life*. New York: McGraw-Hill.

Fourt, Lyman, & Norman R. S. Hollies. (1970). *Clothing Comfort and Function*. New York: Marcel Dekker.

Frank, Tom. (1991). Testing Materials for Water Repellency and Air Permeability. *Textiles, 20(2)*, 18–19.

Gioello, Debi. (1985, April). Hand of Fabric Primer. *Bobbin, 26*, 122, 124–126.

Glock, Ruth E., & Grace I. Kunz. (1995). *Apparel Manufacturing: Sewn Products Analysis*. Englewood Cliffs, NJ: Prentice-Hall.

Govmark Organization, Inc., The. (1995,

August 24). *Flammability Testing Information for Apparel and Apparel Fabrics*. Bellmore, NY: Author.

Harlock, S. C. (1989, July). Fabric Objective Measurement: 2, Principles of Measurement. *Textile Asia*, 66–71.

Hatch, Kathryn L. (1993). *Textile Science*. Minneapolis: West Publishing Company.

Hatch, Kathryn L., Nancy L. Markee, & Howard I. Maibach. (1992). Skin Response to Fabric: A Review of Studies and Assessment Methods. *Clothing and Textiles Research Journal, 10(4),* 54–63.

Hearle, John W. S. (1992, April). Can Fabric Hand Enter the Dataspace? Part 1. *Textile Horizons,* 14–16.

Hearle, John W. S. (1993, June). Can Fabric Hand Enter the Dataspace? Part 2. Measuring the Unmeasurable. *Textile Horizons,* 16–20.

Henry, Norman W. (1992, May). Biological Resistant Clothing. *ASTM Standardization News, 20,* 32–33.

Henry, Norman W. (1994, February). Standardized Biological Test Methods for Functional Clothing. *ASTM Standardization News, 22,* 38–41.

Hewson, Mike. (1994, April). Formaldehyde in Textiles. *Journal of the Society of Dyers and Colourists, 110,* 140–142.

Holme, Ian. (1994, December). Flammability—the Environment and the Green Movement. *Journal of the Society of Dyers and Colourists, 110,* 362–366.

Hollies, Norman R. S., & Vera R. Usdin. (1980). The Skin Barrier—How Does It Handle Materials Lost from Clothing? In the American Association of Textile Chemists and Colorists, *Textiles: Toxicological and Environmental Concerns.* Research Triangle Park, NC: Author, 33–35.

Hudson, Peyton, Anne C. Clapp, & Darlene Kness. (1993). *Joseph's Introductory Textile Science,* 6th ed. New York: Harcourt Brace Jovanovich.

Ito, K., & M. Nitta. (1994). Some Difficult Issues in Recent Apparel Manufacturing and a Counter-Measure for the Future. *International Journal of Clothing Science and Technology, 6(2/3),* 14–16.

Kadolph, Sara J., & Anna I. Langford. (1998). *Textiles,* 8th ed. Englewood Cliffs, NJ: Prentice-Hall.

Kalyanaraman, A. R., & A. Sivaramakrishnan. (1984, May). An Electronic Stiffness Meter—Performance Evaluation with the Known Instruments. *Textile Research Journal, 54,* 479–484.

Kawabata, Sueo. (1994). Difficulty with Shingosen: A View from an Analysis of Fabric Hand. *International Journal of Clothing Science and Technology, 6(2/3),* 17–19.

Kawabata, Sueo, & Masako Niwa. (1994). High Quality Fabrics for Garments. *International Journal of Clothing Science and Technology, 6(5),* 20–25.

Kawabata, Sueo, & Masako Niwa. (1996). Objective Measurement of Fabric Hand. In Raheel, Mastura. (ed.). *Modern Textile Characterization Methods.* New York: Marcel Dekker, pp. 329–354.

Kim, C. J., & E. A. Vaughn. (1975). Physical Properties Associated with Fabric Hand. In American Association of Textile Chemists and Colorists, *Book of Papers.* Research Triangle Park, NC: Author, pp. 78–95.

Kim, Jung-Jun, Hechmi Hamouda, Itzhak Shalev, & Roger L. Barker. (1993, August). Instrumental Methods for Measuring the Surface Frictional Properties of Softener Treated Fabrics. *Textile Chemist and Colorist, 25(8),* 15–20.

Krasny, John F. (1974, March). Fabric Flammability: Needs for Research. *Home Economics Research Journal, 2,* 160–166.

Luo, Cheng, & Randall R. Bresee. (1990, February). Appearance Evaluation by Digital Image Analysis. *Textile Chemist and Colorist, 22(2),* 17–19.

Ly, N. G., H. D. Tester, P. Buckenham, A. F. Roczniok, A. L. Adriaansen, F. Scaysbrook, & S. De Jong. (1991). Simple Instruments for Quality Control by Finishers and Tailors. *Textile Research Journal, 61,* 402–406.

Lyle, Dorothy Siegert. (1977). *Performance of Textiles.* New York: John Wiley & Sons.

McAngus, E. J., & W. W. Adams. (1967–1968). *Physical Textile Testing at Westpoint Pepperell.* Atlanta: Textile Industries.

McLaughlin, Joseph. (1980). Safety and Health Testing. In the American Association of Textile Chemists and Colorists, *Textiles: Toxicological and Environmental Concerns.* Research Triangle Park, NC: Author, pp. 31–32.

March, Robert H. (1970). *Physics for Poets.* New York: McGraw-Hill.

Mehta, Pradip V. (1992). *An Introduction to Quality Control for the Apparel Industry.* Milwaukee: ASQC Press.

Merkel, Robert S. (1991). *Textile Product Serviceability.* New York: Macmillan.

Minazio, Pier Giorgio. (1995). FAST—Fabric Assurance by Simple Testing. *International Journal of Clothing Science and Technology, 7(2/3),* 43–48.

Morton, W. E., & J. W. S. Hearle. (1993). *Physical Properties of Textile Fibers,* 3rd ed. Manchester, England: Textile Institute.

Oakland, B. G. M., & A. C. Stonebraker. (1987). A Survey Analysis of Attitudes Towards Voluntary/Mandatory Flammability Regulations by the Upholstered-Furniture Manufacturers in North Carolina, U.S.A., and Its Implications for Design. In The Textile Institute, *Textiles: Product Design and Marketing.* Manchester, England: Author, pp. 195–208.

Pile, John F. (1995). *Interior Design.* New York: Harry N. Abrams.

Potluri, Prasad, Isaac Porat, & John Atkinson. (1996). Towards Automated Testing of Fabrics. *International Journal of Clothing Science and Technology, 7(2/3),* 11–23.

Price, Arthur, & Allen C. Cohen. (1994). *J. J. Pizzuto's Fabric Science,* 6th ed. New York: Fairchild.

Rong, G.H., & K. Slater. (1993). A New Approach to the Assessment of Textile Performance, *Journal of the Textile Institute, 83(2),* 197–208.

Rudie, Raye. (1992, May). Love Affair with Lycra Spandex Far From Over. *Bobbin, 33,* 19–20.

Schoff, Clifford K. (1995, October). New Trends in Coatings Technology. *ASTM Standardization News, 23,* 24, 27.

Shishoo, Roshan L. (1995). Importance of Mechanical and Physical Properties of Fabrics in the Clothing Manufacturing Process. *International Journal of Clothing Science and Technology, 7(2/3),* 35–42.

Smith, Julia E. (1993). The Comfort of Clothing. *Textiles, 22(1),* 18–20.

Stull, Jeffrey O. (1996). Assessment of Chemical Barrier Properties. In Raheel, Mastura. (ed.). *Modern Textile Characterization Methods.* New York: Marcel Dekker, pp. 393–468.

Stylios, George. (ed.). (1991). *Textile Objective Measurement and Automation in Garment Manufacture.* New York: Ellis Horwood.

Tao, Weiying, & Billie J. Collier. (1994, February). The Environmental Scanning Electron Microscope: A New Tool for Textile Studies. *Textile Chemist and Colorist, 26(2),* 29–31.

Textile Institute, The. (1991). *Textile Terms and Definitions,* 9th ed. Manchester, England: Author.

Tortora, Phyllis G., & Robert S. Merkel. (1996). *Fairchild's Dictionary of Textiles,* 7th ed. New York: Fairchild.

Tull, Donald L. (1984, June). Quality Control of Hand and Finish. *American Dyestuff Reporter, 73,* 19–22.

Vigo, Tyrone L. (1994). *Textile Processing and Properties: Preparation, Dyeing, Finishing, and Performance.* Amsterdam: Elsevier.

Warner, Steven B. (1995). *Fiber Science.* Englewood Cliffs, NJ: Prentice Hall.

Warnock, Mary M., A. Majid Sarmadi, & Catherine R. Boy. (eds.) (1994, June). *Textile Fiber Systems for Performance, Protection, and Comfort.* Southern Cooperative Series Bulletin 379, Fayetteville: University of Arkansas.

Watkins, Susan M. (1984). *Clothing: The Portable Environment.* Ames: Iowa State University Press.

Weiss, Richard J. (1990). *Physics of Materials.* New York: Hemisphere Publishing Corporation.

Wilson, Cheryl A., & Rachel M. Laing. (1995). The Effect of Wool Fiber Variables on Tactile Characteristics of Homogeneous Woven Fabrics. *Clothing and Textiles Research Journal, 13(3),* 208–212.

Wilson, Cheryl A., & Rachel M. Laing. (1995). Investigation of Selected Tactile and Thermal Characteristics of Upholstery Fabrics. *Clothing and Textiles Research Journal, 13(3),* 200–207.

Winakor, G., C. J. Kim, & L. Wolins. (1980). Fabric Hand: Tactile Sensory Assessment. *Textile Research Journal, 50(10),* 601–610.

Zeronian, S. Haig. (1994). Chapter 6. Analysis of the Interaction Between Water and Textiles. In Weaver, J. William, (ed.). *Analytical Methods for a Textile Laboratory,* 3rd ed. Research Triangle Park, NC: American Association of Textile Chemists and Colorists, 117–128.

REVIEW QUESTIONS

1. Differentiate between these word pairs:
   a. breaking elongation and comfort elongation
   b. comfort stretch and power stretch
   c. fabric growth and fabric stretch
   d. water resistance and water repellency

2. Identify the performance measures and the methods that might be used in the assessment of materials to be used in these products:
   a. umbrella
   b. stadium blanket
   c. child's snowsuit
   d. work gloves for a winter tow truck driver
   e. cross country ski parka
   f. store front awning
   g. slip for women's wear
   h. blanket for baby bed
   i. gloves for gardeners
   j. bath towel
   k. leggings for use when using a chain saw
   l. raincoat
   m. hot pad for the kitchen
   n. hat for farmers
   o. surgical gloves

3. How does fabric thickness influence product comfort?

4. Explain why assessment of hand is of interest to producers and consumers of textile products.

5. Describe how air permeability is assessed.

6. Why is the measure of a material's flammability of interest?

ACTIVITIES

1. Write comfort and safety specs for a selected product and target market and explain your choices.

2. Test the comfort and safety of a product in the lab and discuss what its performance would mean in terms of consumer satisfaction.

3. Bring in a product that failed in terms of comfort and suggest reasons for its failure. Discuss how this problem could have been avoided by testing during product development.

4. Visit a testing lab and watch comfort, safety, and health testing. Discuss with managers and technicians their role in quality assurance.

5. Explore the world wide web for information related to comfort, safety, and health testing. Discuss how the information would be used in materials testing.

6. Explore the literature for information on issues related to safety and health testing of materials and discuss the application of results in specialized products, such as protective clothing used by people in the medical field.

Evaluating Care, Appearance Retention, Colorfastness, and Weather Resistance

Chapter 8

Objectives

- To use reference scales to evaluate visual components of material performance.

- To understand the dimensions, units, and terms used to describe material performance for care, appearance retention, colorfastness, and weather resistance.

- To understand the scientific principles that apply to performance evaluation.

- To develop specifications for care, appearance retention, and colorfastness that describe performance requirements.

- To interpret performance specifications for product development.

- To test materials for adherence to specifications for care, appearance retention, colorfastness, and weather resistance.

Key Terms

care instructions

care label

rating

grade

reference scale

rater

Gray Scale for Color Change

color change

gray scale

Gray Scale for Staining

colorant staining

multifiber test fabric

AATCC Chromatic Transference Scale

migration

bleeding

color loss

color transfer

growth

shrinkage

relaxation shrinkage

residual shrinkage

felting shrinkage

heat shrinkage

progressive shrinkage

consolidation shrinkage

dimensional restoration

dry cleaning	antibacterial finishes	cold water bleed
multiprocess wet cleaning	dye transfer	blue wool lightfastness standard fabric
	fulling	
soil redeposition	carbonizing	atmospheric fading unit (AFU)
stain	hot pressing	
wrinkle recovery	frosting	lightfastness
insect resistance	crocking	photochromism
mildew resistance	water spotting	weather resistance
rot resistance		

This chapter examines additional ways in which materials are tested to determine their suitability for use in manufacturing a specific product. By measuring the ways in which materials perform in terms of care, appearance retention, colorfastness, and weather resistance, a better understanding of the contributions materials make to product performance is achieved.

This chapter describes what happens to the appearance and performance of a material when it is exposed to conditions that simulate product use. Although most of the focus is on the fashion fabric, some of the discussion refers to closures, support materials, and trims. Many of the procedures apply as much to support materials and trims as they apply to fashion fabrics.

The discussion focuses on the cleaning practices of consumers and the ways in which materials react to storage conditions presented by manufacturers, retailers, or consumers. Once again, these procedures emphasize measuring one dimension of performance at a time. For example, one procedure focuses on measuring how a printed or dyed material reacts when it is exposed to steam pressing. Another procedure measures how a material wrinkles when it is twisted and compressed in use or storage. Still another procedure evaluates how a material withstands the chemical and mechanical action of laundering in terms of maintaining its original dimensions.

By measuring a material's reaction to these conditions that simulate use, we are better able to predict material performance in products. This understanding should help us determine which materials should be used to ensure that the consumer is satisfied with a product. Many of these issues are important to consumers: how a material responds to care, how well a material retains a new look, and how permanent the color is. Of course, the chapter continues to examine how the materials used in a product react to testing. Many product failures are related to poor performance in the areas of size or appearance retention or colorfastness. Consider the problems consumers have with textile products. Many such problems will be discussed in this chapter.

Factors affecting the performance of materials are discussed in most introductory textile books. For information on the effect of fiber type, yarn and fabric structure, fabric weight, and finishes, consult one of these books (Hatch, 1993; Hudson, Clapp, & Kness, 1993; Kadolph & Langford, 1998; Price & Cohen, 1994).

The serviceability components of care and appearance retention are related to each other. In addition, colorfastness is related to a large degree to the material's response to cleaning and to the use it receives. One aspect of appearance retention is the ability of a product to maintain its original color. Finally, weather resistance uses equipment, procedures, and exposure mechanisms similar to those used in some colorfastness procedures.

DEVELOPING AND EVALUATING CARE LABELS AND CARE INSTRUCTIONS

Care labels are required by the Care Label Regulation on most textile apparel products and are included on many textile furnishing products. Many companies, such as carpet and furniture manufacturers, include care labels, tags, or instructions with their products even though such information is not required. These companies provide this service because consumers have become so accustomed to seeing this information for many products, that they have begun to expect it on all textile products. Thus, much of the information provided voluntarily by manufacturers and retailers is a reaction to this consumer expectation.

Because many different terms can be used to describe proper care of a product, the industry has developed guidelines for explaining appropriate care or refurbishing procedures and has created definitions for terms and explanations for symbols that are used on care labels and tags. These standards are used in developing care labels and in evaluating the accuracy of the information included on such labels. The industry continues to work closely with the Federal Trade Commission to ensure that the efforts of both groups contribute to the same goal. In addition, standardizing the information helps to minimize misunderstandings by consumers, so that they interpret labels correctly and do not inadvertently produce or contribute to product failure during cleaning.

However, several major problems with care labels remain. Many consumers do not consult care labels before they clean soiled items. Clearly, the efforts of manufacturers, retailers, and industry organizations are useless if consumers do not read and follow the instructions on care labels. In addition, some companies continue to use labels that indicate procedures that are far more restrictive or mild than necessary. For example, a product that would survive machine washing and machine drying with no adverse effects should not be labeled dry clean only. A final problem with care labeling is that some instructions do not make any sense. For example, some denim jackets with leather collars are labeled "machine wash, machine dry; remove trim before washing." It is not realistic to expect that consumers will remove the collar before washing and reattach the collar before wearing. Unfortunately, labels with this kind of unrealistic or nonsense statement are far too common.

The ASTM guide (ASTM D 3938, Standard Guide for Determining or Confirming Care Instructions for Apparel and Other Textile Consumer Products) is used by manufacturers and retailers to ensure that correct information is included on care labels. The guide includes procedures for working with the complete product as well as working with all the materials to be used in manufacturing the product. **Care instructions** are a series of directions that describe procedures for refurbishing a product without adverse effects. Care labels should include warnings for those practices that are expected to have a harmful effect. A **care label** is a label that gives directions for cleaning a textile product.

The ASTM guide is used by companies to establish a reasonable basis for the care information provided on product labels. It addresses evaluation of materials or products after cleaning for changes in dimension, hand, appearance, and performance. Changes in performance address functional aspects, including durable press, water repellency, static buildup, flame resistance, and soil release. Although this chapter includes procedures for evaluating many aspects of performance, information related to hand assessment and some performance aspects related to comfort and safety were discussed in Chapter 7.

Another ASTM document (ASTM D 3136, Standard Terminology Relating to Care Labels for Textile and Leather Products Other Than Textile Floor Coverings and Upholstery) provides a uniform language for use on care labels, so that terms are used in a consistent fashion. A final document, ASTM D 5253, Standard Terminology of Writing Care Instructions and General Refurbishing Procedures for Textile Floor Coverings and Textile Upholstered Furniture, addresses terms used specifically for products that can not be cleaned by processes typically used for apparel and bed and bath linens.

With rapid changes in the global market and similar products being sold in many markets worldwide, care symbols are increasingly important and their use was recently approved in the United States (see Figure 8-1). Thus, many product labels include symbols. Manufacturers who sell the same or similar products in many markets outside the United States, need to keep inventory and management costs low. One set of care labels that incorporate information of the type and form required by laws in many markets is much cheaper than separate sets of care labels for each market. Labels with wider application also make it easier to get the right product to

Clothing Care Symbol Guide

Wash — Bleach — Dry — Iron — Dryclean

Produced by the Federal Trade Commission as part of Project CLEAN

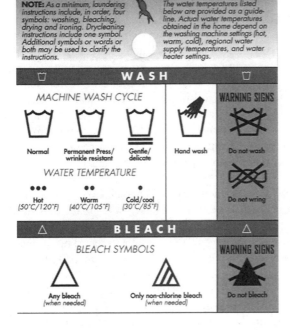

NOTE: As a minimum, laundering instructions include, in order, four symbols: washing, bleaching, drying and ironing. Drycleaning instructions include one symbol. Additional symbols or words or both may be used to clarify the instructions.

The water temperatures listed below are provided as a guideline. Actual water temperatures obtained in the home depend on the washing machine settings (hot, warm, cold), regional water supply temperatures, and water heater settings.

WASH

MACHINE WASH CYCLE
Normal — Permanent Press/wrinkle resistant — Gentle/delicate — Hand wash

WATER TEMPERATURE
Hot (50°C/120°F) — Warm (40°C/105°F) — Cold/cool (30°C/85°F)

WARNING SIGNS
Do not wash
Do not wring

BLEACH

BLEACH SYMBOLS
Any bleach (when needed) — Only non-chlorine bleach (when needed)

WARNING SIGNS
Do not bleach

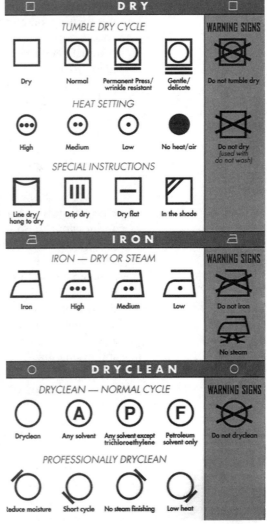

DRY

TUMBLE DRY CYCLE
Dry — Normal — Permanent Press/wrinkle resistant — Gentle/delicate

HEAT SETTING
High — Medium — Low — No heat/air

SPECIAL INSTRUCTIONS
Line dry/hang to dry — Drip dry — Dry flat — In the shade

WARNING SIGNS
Do not tumble dry
Do not dry (used with do not wash)

IRON

IRON — DRY OR STEAM
Iron — High — Medium — Low

WARNING SIGNS
Do not iron
No steam

DRYCLEAN

DRYCLEAN — NORMAL CYCLE
Dryclean — Any solvent — Any solvent except trichloroethylene — Petroleum solvent only

WARNING SIGNS
Do not dryclean

PROFESSIONALLY DRYCLEAN
Reduce moisture — Short cycle — No steam finishing — Low heat

Figure 8-1
Care symbols for home and commercial cleaning of textile products. (*Courtesy of the Federal Trade Commission*)

the right market. Ensuring that a product has the correct care for its intended market costs less if the same care label can be used in both products and both markets. ASTM has developed a guide (ASTM D 5489 Standard Guide for Care Symbols for Care Instructions Textile Products) that provides a uniform system of symbols for use on products including garments; piecegoods; and bath, kitchen, and bed linens.

RATING PROCESSES

Before discussing how a material reacts to various care procedures, the ways materials are rated or evaluated after testing so that visual changes that occurred can be defined or described in a quantitative and consistent manner need to be examined. Several processes help quantify or assign numbers to soil removal, amount of wrinkling, changes in color or appearance, and other visual changes that may occur during refurbishment. In materials evaluation, **rating** is the process of determining or assigning a grade to a material by comparing it to a standard reference scale. A **grade** is the symbol, number, or letter used for any step in a multistep standard reference scale for a quality characteristic. A **reference scale** consists of a series of photographs, plastic replicas, colored chips, or paired gray chips that represent a range of visual changes that are likely to occur on materials during testing. These representations are selected to illustrate a progressive alteration, as might be expected to appear with materials in consumer use or care.

Most of these procedures have several characteristics in common. First, most make use of one or more trained raters or evaluators. A **rater** is an individual who understands the procedure to be used in assigning the grade and the distinctions among the numerical ratings. This individual should have a good knowledge of textiles and of the test method for which a material's performance is being evaluated. Raters should have good vision and the ability to recognize minor differences in appearance or characteristics of materials. If more than one rater is used, raters should work independently in assigning grades. Using more than one rater improves the accuracy and precision of the results, but it requires more time for training and evaluation. The final grade for a specimen would be the mean of the individual grades assigned by each rater. If a rater is evaluating a specimen for color change, the rater should be checked for color blindness. Remember that colorblindness is far more common in men than women (approximately 8 percent of the male population and 0.5 percent of the female population are colorblind).

Second, the rating is conducted under carefully maintained conditions. Raters view a specimen at a consistent perception angle. The light source and direction of light are controlled so that the values assigned to a specimen are independent of the angle, type, or amount of light. Figure 8-2 illustrates a viewing set-up. Other light sources are removed, blocked,

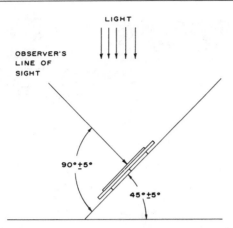

Figure 8-2
Illumination and viewing angles for rating specimens. *(Reprinted with permission from the American Association of Textile Chemists and Colorists, P.O. Box 12215, Research Triangle Park, NC 27709)*

or turned off. The area surrounding the specimen and the rating standard may be covered by a gray paper mask with cut-outs of the appropriate size. In addition, the background is controlled by using white of a defined type or another layer of the same new untested fabric. The mask and controlled background eliminate any influence from surrounding surfaces. Figure 8-3 shows a commercially available booth used in viewing and rating specimens that allows for control of many factors that might inappropriately influence results.

Third, the evaluation is based on comparisons to a standard rating scale. The reference standard, the specimen that has been tested, and a sample of untested material are used in assigning a rating. The tested specimen and an untested sample of the same material are aligned side by side in the same orientation in the viewing area. Thus, if a specimen is napped, nap for both pieces are in the same direction. Both pieces are in the same orientation such as filling oriented right to left and warp top to bottom with the "right" side of the sample fabric and the specimen facing the rater. If the specimen is printed, the same portion of the print is used and both pieces are placed in the same manner, so that the print is consistent when viewed. The paper mask exposes approximately equal amounts of both fabrics. It also exposes equal amounts of the reference standard. Figure 8-4 illustrates this concept.

Fourth, the evaluation is based on assigning a numerical value to the change between the untested sample and the specimen after testing. The amount of change represented in the reference scale should be approximately equal to the change demonstrated between the untested sample and the specimen that has been tested. Standard reference scales have been developed very carefully so that they represent essentially the same amount

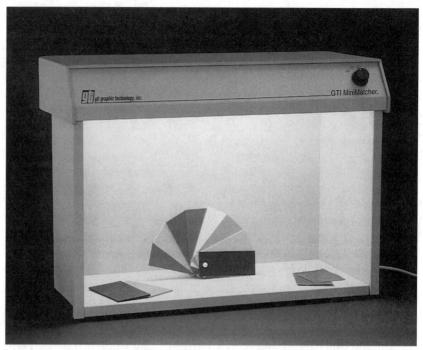

Figure 8-3
Light booth for rating specimens. (*Courtesy of Graphic Technology, Inc.*)

Figure 8-4
Colorfastness to washing: evaluation of color change: scale (left), washed specimen (top right), and unwashed specimen (bottom right).

of change between adjacent steps. For example, the change between steps 4 and 5 represents the same amount of change as that between steps 2 and 3—or any other two adjacent steps. With these scales, a grade of 5 always represents no change between the tested and untested specimens; a grade of 1 always represents the greatest amount of change between tested and untested specimens. In many instances, a half grade is used to rate a change that is not as severe as that represented by the lower grade, but not as small as that represented by the higher grade. For example, a rating of 4.5 indicates that the change was not as great as that represented by a grade of 4, but that some change was apparent and a grade of 5 would not have been an appropriate representation of the material's performance. In some instances, a grade of 0 (zero) may be assigned if the change is more severe than that represented by a grade of 1.

General comments in terms of using reference scales apply to the four evaluation procedures relating to color and appearance changes; other procedures discussed in this and several other chapters; and the evaluation procedures for evaluating visual change for pilling and snagging.

AATCC Evaluation Procedure 1, Gray Scale for Color Change, is used to evaluate changes in the color of textiles as a result of several different colorfastness tests. The **Gray Scale for Color Change** consists of paired chips varying from light to dark gray. This is a nine-step scale with half-points visually represented. **Color change** is an alteration in color of any kind, whether in lightness, hue, or chroma, or any combination of these, discernible by comparing the test specimen with a corresponding untested sample. A **gray scale** consists of pairs of standard gray chips; each pair represents a progressive difference in color or contrast that corresponds to a numerical colorfastness grade. Besides assigning a numerical grade to represent color contrast, a change in color also can be described using such qualitative terms as shift to another hue, lightening or darkening of the color, or a change of more or less chroma. For example, a sample might be graded as 3 redder, which means that the color change is represented by grade 3 in the red direction.

Individual scales for each of the possible combinations of lightness, hue, or chroma that make up the million or so colors that the human eye can see would not be practical. In addition, each scale would need to consider the ways in which any color changes when exposed to any one of many factors that affect the color of textile materials. Gray scales, however, allow for visual identification of color change with a minimal investment in training and rating scales. Although it takes some practice to learn to work with these scales and evaluating appearance based on the steps represented, most individuals adapt fairly quickly.

The second valuation procedure uses the **Gray Scale for Staining** (AATCC Evaluation Procedure 2, Gray Scale for Staining) to evaluate staining of undyed materials during colorfastness tests. **Colorant staining** is "the unintended pickup of colorant by a substrate due to 1) exposure to a colored or contaminated liquid medium or 2) direct contact with dyed or pigmented material from which colorant transfers by direct sublimation or

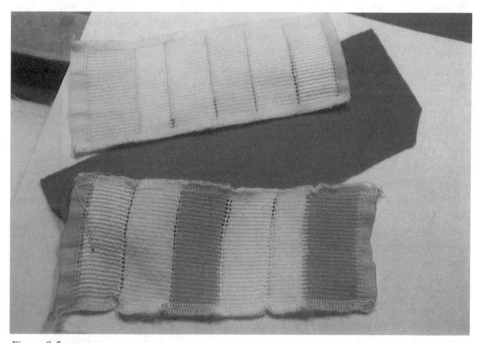

Figure 8-5
Examples of multifiber test fabrics: new samples (top) and samples after stain testing (bottom).
Note that some fiber bands have been stained during testing while other bands in the same
piece were less severely stained or not stained at all. (*Courtesy of Textile Innovators Corp.*)

mechanical action" (AATCC, 1996, page 344). The gray scale for staining consists of pairs of white and gray color chips, with the contrast between the chips corresponding to a grade.

Test methods that use this rating scale often make use of **multifiber test fabric.** The test fabric is made with filling-faced bands, in which the filling yarns in each band differ by fiber content. Multifiber test fabric makes use of the fiber specific nature of dyes. This means that a dye will bond only with certain chemical compounds. Because chemical composition is the basis of fiber generic types, any dye used in a specimen is not likely to stain all bands of the multifiber test fabric equally. Some bands will stain darker than others; some bands may not stain at all. The stained portion or band of the multifiber test fabric that has the greatest contrast is the band used to assign a grade. Figure 8-5 illustrates multifiber test fabrics in their new and stained condition. When evaluating staining, the new and stained pieces of multifiber test fabric should be oriented in the same direction and arranged so that the fiber stripes are in the same order.

The third evaluation procedure (AATCC Evaluation Procedure 3, AATCC Chromatic Transference Scale) is the only one that works with color chips. This scale uses 30 color chips from the Munsell Book of Color in gray and five hue families—red, yellow, green, blue, and purple—that are arranged in five rows and six columns with the lightest chips at the top (grade 5) and the darkest ones at the bottom (grade 1). Figure 8-6 illus-

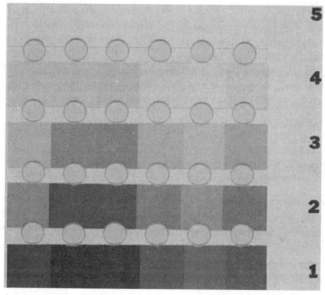

Figure 8-6
AATCC Chromatic Transference Scale. (*Reprinted with permission from the American Association of Textile Chemists and Colorists, P.O. Box 12215, Research Triangle Park, NC 27709*)

trates the **AATCC Chromatic Transference Scale** that is used to evaluate staining. This rating scale may be used with less experienced raters, but the results should be essentially the same as if the gray scale for staining were used.

AATCC Evaluation Procedure 7, Instrumental Assessment of the Change in Color of a Test Specimen, can be used as an alternate to Evaluation Procedure 1 (Gray Scale for Color Change). It is inappropriate for use with specimens that have been treated with or laundered with a compound that contains a fluorescent whitening agent (FWA). It uses a colorimeter or spectrophotometer that measures the color of the treated specimen and untreated fabric. Color differences are calculated and converted to a gray scale by a series of equations. Chapter 9 discusses instrumental assessment of color in detail.

These four procedures may be used to assess the effect of cleaning on textile products. Other appearance factors also may be evaluated. In these cases, even though color change is not assessed, many commonalties related to rating scales apply.

SPECIMEN SELECTION

Selecting specimens for use in evaluating performance related to care, appearance retention, colorfastness, and weather resistance may differ from the procedures discussed previously. Often fewer specimens are needed for these procedures. In addition, there are fewer restrictions related to the location from which the specimen is removed. For example, the 10 percent rule and the use of replica specimens that do not incorporate the same warp or filling yarns may not apply. These differences in selecting or cutting specimens relate to the component that is being evaluated. In many instances, it is the dye, print, finish, or process that is being evaluated. In these cases, problems or irregularities in performance may not be the result of the specific location from which the specimen was removed.

ASSESSMENT OF CARE PROCEDURES

Several procedures have been developed to simulate how a product is cared for by consumers. These practices include home laundering, as well as efforts by commercial establishments, such as dry cleaners and commercial launderers. Many problems can develop with a material used in a textile product when it is subjected to a cleaning process, including shrinkage, distortion, nonremoval of soil, wrinkling, color loss, staining, change in hue, change in hand or texture, and other alterations of appearance. Thus, it is important for manufacturers to examine procedures that measure a material's reaction to different cleaning processes that may lead to consumer dissatisfaction with the product.

UNDERSTANDING THE CLEANING PROCESS

Cleaning is a complex chemical and physical-mechanical process that involves the use of solvents, other chemicals, and soils on a substrate of varying chemical natures that may have had mechanical or chemical modifications made to it. Solvents include water and organic liquids used in dry cleaning and some stain removal agents. Detergents, water and fabric softeners, disinfectants, and other cleaning additives are used to restore a new appearance and fresh smell to textile products. Soil can include particulate matter, such as dust and powder; oily materials, such as body soil and fat or grease from food and engines; colored material, such as water-borne stains from beverages and fruit; and environmental soil, such as grit and leaf mold. Many soils are of an unknown type. Still others are combination soils, such as salad dressings that contain both oily soils and food dyes.

The substrate refers to the textile materials that are combined to produce the product. Although it is important to assess how individual materials react to cleaning, even simple products may be a combination of many materials. How each material reacts to different cleaning processes, soil types, and cleaning chemicals is as important as the interaction of the materials in the product to be cleaned. Even though each material may respond satisfactorily to the cleaning process, this does not guarantee that the product, which combines several materials, will be judged equally satisfactory after cleaning. Similar materials may differ in their reaction to cleaning, and materials of different chemical compositions may be combined in a product. For example, a cotton shirt may combine cotton fashion material, with polyester interlining, cotton/polyester thread, rayon or olefin sewn-in labels, and melamine thermoset resin buttons. The fashion material may have been treated with a wrinkle-free finish and fluorescent whitening agent so that it requires little care other than washing, but dye or pigment may have been used to add appeal and visual interest to the fashion material, labels, and buttons. Material testing evaluates the performance of each material and its finish. In addition, it is usually necessary to evaluate the manner in which materials interact in the product.

Dyes are large, complex organic molecules. One portion of the molecule produces color (the chromophore); another portion may alter the color within the general hue family (the auxochrome); and still another portion lends solubility to the molecule (the solubilizing group). Many dye classes exist because their use and performance differ. Dyes may differ in their fastness by fiber type. For example, a direct dye will exhibit different performance when it is used on cotton, rayon, linen, or lyocell. Solubility cycle dyes, such as the sulfur, vat, and indigo classes, form insoluble pigments close to the fiber's surface and exhibit poor fastness to crocking and abrasion. Reactive dyes form strong bonds within the fiber, but require good rinsing after dyeing to avoid bleeding problems. Other dye classes form bonds that are more easily broken. Disperse dyes tend to migrate under certain conditions. Direct and acid dyes have poor wet fastness.

Dyes are described as being fast or fugitive. Fast dyes are those in which a color change occurs very slowly. They also tend to bond well with the fiber or are trapped within the fiber so they will not bleed during normal use and care. Fugitive dyes may degrade and change color fairly quickly because of an environmental factor, such as sunlight, perspiration, or acid from cosmetics or deodorants. Fugitive dyes often form weak bonds with the fiber and therefore have a tendency to migrate, that is to leave the fiber readily and form a weak bond with another fiber. **Migration** is the nonuniform movement and distribution of colorants, finishes, or other chemicals from one part of a material to another or from one material to another material. For dyes to achieve a uniform color on a material, they must have some degree of migration. Without this tendency, a uniform or level color is difficult to achieve. Unfortunately, although migration makes it easy to achieve a level dye, it also makes it difficult to achieve a dye that does not bleed. Bleeding is a characteristic common with dyes that migrate well. **Bleeding** is the loss of color from textile materials during wet processing. During cleaning, the color migrates into the cleaning solution and may bond with other materials causing irregular stains on them.

Washing uses a water-detergent solution with heat and agitation to remove soil from textile products. Heat is in the form of water that is warmed to a desired temperature. Agitation provides mechanical action that assists in soil removal. The detergent and water work to add chemical energy that assists in soil removal. Other ingredients may be present to assist in cleaning, to disinfect, or to soften fabrics.

Effective cleaning depends on the machine cycle, proper sorting of textiles to be cleaned in the same cycle, and the appropriate amounts of chemical compounds to assist in cleaning, disinfecting, and softening. Incorrect choices in any of these areas can create problems with cleaning and satisfaction with the product's appearance.

The cleaning process is intended to remove only those foreign materials that we define as soil. Consumers want to keep the dyes, pigments, adhesives used to apply fusible interlinings, print inks on labels, and chemical finishes in their original location. For example, consumers do not want care label ink bleeding through the fashion fabric at the center back neck area of the shirt. In addition, consumers do not want the physical and aesthetic nature of materials to change. One exception to this occurs with stiff fabrics, which consumers often expect to soften with care. With many products, the hand is an important aesthetic characteristic of the product. In evaluating a material's reaction to cleaning during material testing, all changes should be identified and measured.

TEST METHOD PERSPECTIVES

Test methods to evaluate the effect of care on a material have been developed from two perspectives. The first approach subjects the material to a relatively severe condition, with the expectation that such extreme conditions are not likely to occur when the product is cleaned by the consumer. These conditions are sometimes referred to as worst case scenarios. This means that the material is subjected to the worst possible situation expected during consumer use. If a problem, such as color loss or staining is likely to occur, it will probably occur under these conditions. Thus, the test method first determines if the problem would occur under extreme conditions. If the answer is yes, then the test evaluates its severity.

The second approach subjects the material to conditions more normally encountered in use. The assessment also determines whether the problem will occur and, if so, the measure of its severity. The differences between the two procedures are the conditions of cleaning—extreme or normal.

In both approaches, the test conditions reflect some aspect of consumer use. In addition, both include instructions and techniques needed to measure the degree of change in the condition of the material. Once again, these procedures do not include any pass/fail scales. Companies develop specifications in terms of performance to describe when a material is acceptable and when a material is not acceptable for their needs and for their target market's expectations.

Many of the methods are described as being accelerated. This means that the results of one run of the procedure are equivalent to more than one consumer care cycle. Some accelerated procedures are identified as being equivalent to three consumer care cycles and others to five care cycles. Some test methods also recommend that the procedure be repeated two or more times before assessment to gain a more complete understanding of product performance in consumer use. This is especially important for products that are expected to be cleaned numerous times, such as bed linens and sportswear.

WASHING

Procedures and standard test methods assess how materials, such as fashion and support fabrics, linings, and trims, will withstand home or commercial washing or laundering. They are used to determine and confirm care label instructions. Many of these procedures use specially prepared detergents with and without fluorescent whitening agents. These standard reference detergents are more similar to traditional powder detergents than to the ultradetergents now common in the United States. Because these standard detergents have been used for years, their formulation is consistent across time and throughout the country. Home detergents change fairly frequently and vary throughout the country as a result of state or local laws and regulations, water conditions, and types of soil.

Colorfastness

One problem in washing is poor colorfastness, which appears as color loss, change, or transfer. New items may experience **color loss** when washing removes excess color that was not rinsed off after dyeing. In some cases, the loss of color is noticeable. In other cases, the product may look the same but color transfer has occurred. In **color transfer,** excess dye rinsed off of one material bonds with and stains another material.

Color loss may occur when weakly bonded dye molecules migrate out of the fiber. Both color loss and color change may occur when dye molecules are degraded. When a dye molecule is degraded or damaged, it may lose its ability to produce color or remain bonded to the fiber. Thus the total number of molecules coloring a material decreases. When this loss applies to a sufficiently high percentage of dye molecules, the product looks faded.

With some dye molecules, degradation changes the molecular structure. As a result, the dye produces a different perception of color and the material shifts hue. Many colors are achieved by mixing two or more dyes. If one component of the dye mixture is lost from the material or if one component is degraded, the color of the material is altered. For example, some green dyes may take on a bluish or yellowish cast with age, because they were created by mixing blue and yellow dyes. If the yellow component ages more quickly than the blue component, the material will take on a bluish cast.

One common test method that evaluates colorfastness to washing is AATCC 61, Colorfastness to Laundering, Home and Commercial: Accelerated. In this test method, the focus is on fabrics that are expected to be laundered on a frequent and regular basis. This procedure includes five test conditions that represent a home or commercial laundering situation. The variables in each condition are the mechanical action from small steel balls used in the process, chemical additives to the solution (bleach and detergent), water temperature, and water volume. The procedure uses a launder-ometer, a machine in which small containers are rotated around the center axis of a thermostatically controlled water bath (see Figure 8-7). Several materials can be tested simultaneously because each container is sealed and isolated from other materials.

The test condition that most closely approximates recommended care for a material or product is selected. Condition 1A approximates hand washing; condition 2A approximates home machine washing at cool temperatures; condition 3A approximates home washing under vigorous conditions; and conditions 4A and 5A approximate washing with different amounts of chlorine bleach added to the wash water. Individual containers are prepared for each material to be tested. A small piece of multifiber test fabric or bleached cotton cloth is cut and attached to each material specimen before it is added to the prepared container. After washing, specimens are rinsed, dried, and evaluated for color change and staining by assessing the color difference of the specimen before and after testing using the appropriate gray scale or an instrument.

Test results correlate with the results of five typical home or commercial launderings. Conditions such as temperature, abrasion, and low-water volumes are exaggerated in this procedure (see Table 8-1). The effects of

Figure 8-7
Launder-ometer and containers used for testing colorfastness to laundering. (*Courtesy of Atlas Electric Device Co.*)

Table 8-1
COLORFASTNESS TO WASHING TEST CONDITIONS.

Test Number	Temperature	Volume[1]	Detergent[2]	Chlorine[3]	Steel balls	Time
1A	40°C (105°F)	200	0.37	None	10	45 min
2A	49°C (120°F)	150	0.15	None	50	45 min
3A	71°C (160°F)	50	0.15	None	100	45 min
4A	71°C (160°F)	50	0.15	0.0115	100	45 min
5A	49°C (120°F)	150	0.15	0.027	50	45 min

(*From AATCC 61-1994, Colorfastness to Laundering, Home and Commercial: Accelerated.*)

[1]Total liquor volume in ml.
[2]Percent detergent of total volume.
[3]Available chlorine of total volume.

any cycle on color loss and fabric abrasion closely approximate consumer performance, but the effect on staining does not. Staining is influenced by many factors, including ratio of colored to uncolored fabric, fiber content of other items in the load, and end-use conditions.

A procedure that focuses on zippers is ASTM D 2057, Colorfastness of Zippers to Laundering, which uses an automatic washing machine and dryer with specific settings similar to some available to the consumer. The test method examines alteration of shade and staining that zipper tapes may experience during laundering.

Dimensional Change

Many problems are related to dimensional changes of materials. Poor dimensional stability can create problems with fit, size, appearance, and suitability for end use. Some types of dimensional change are explored in this section. Dimensional change assessment and problems more directly connected to products or components will be examined later.

Dimensional change refers to any alteration or modification in the dimensions of a material, component, or product during finishing, manufacture, or care. It refers to either an increase (**growth**) or to a decrease (**shrinkage**) in dimensions. Shrinkage is more common, especially in consumer use. Sometimes, materials such as some acrylic knits, may shrink in one dimension and grow in another.

Changes occur because tensions in some materials that developed during yarn spinning, fabrication, and finishing may be relaxed when a material is wetted and dried without tension. This type of shrinkage is known as **relaxation shrinkage.** However, because not all relaxation shrinkage problems are resolved during the first care cycle, it may be necessary to evaluate **residual shrinkage,** which is relaxation shrinkage that is not removed during the first care cycle. Although the residual shrinkage is often small, larger amounts can contribute to consumer dissatisfaction with a product. Thus, when testing performance of materials, many companies subject a material to two, three, or even five care cycles before they measure for dimensional change. This procedure produces a more realistic understanding of material performance in consumer use.

Other aspects of dimensional change may need to be examined for specific materials. **Felting shrinkage** is unique to wool and wool blend materials. Felting is a permanent type of shrinkage that results from the interlocking of the scales on the exterior of wool fibers. It occurs when materials are wet and subjected to agitation with heat, such as in laundering.

Heat shrinkage occurs with high temperatures and most often affects synthetic and manufactured goods that were improperly heat set during finishing. This problem is now much less common, because of computer control of heat setting ranges during finishing.

It is difficult to assess **progressive shrinkage** and to identify products that are likely to exhibit this problem. The material shrinks a little each time it is cleaned, and the problem tends to occur with some rayon fabrics and fabrics made of soft twisted cotton yarns. Often these fabrics are imported and may have been handcrafted. Fortunately, materials that exhibit progressive shrinkage are rare.

Besides the problems of product fit and appearance, poor dimensional stability also affects fabric density and drape. Materials may become more compact and stiff when they shrink. Dimensional stability problems may not be uniform in both lengthwise and crosswise directions or consistent from one part of the material to another. As a result, test methods often use several specimens cut from different areas of the conditioned fabric to avoid representing the same warp and filling yarns in any two specimens. The operator measures and marks with indelible ink the dimensions in both directions. Specimen size is larger than for many other tests so that the effects of agitation and twisting are more fully recognized. In addition, small changes in dimension that might be overlooked with a small specimen become more obvious in a larger specimen. Because dimensional stability can be significantly affected by heat, degree of agitation, and freedom from tension, washing machines and dryers similar to those found in consumer homes are often used. Three pairs of bench marks are marked on the fabric in both directions, as shown in Figure 8-8. A template (Figure 8-9) makes it easy to mark the fabric accurately and measure dimensional

Figure 8-8
Fabric sample marked for dimensional stability testing.

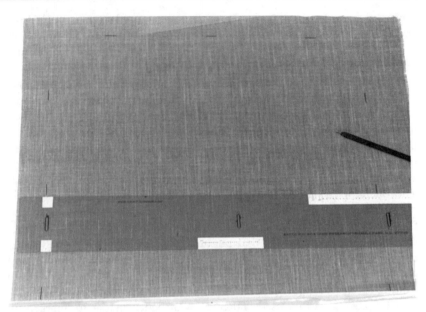

Figure 8-9
AATCC Shrinkage Scale on fabric washed one time.

change when the test is completed. The template numbers are in percentages, so no calculations are needed.

Two test methods are used to examine the behavior of fabrics that are normally labeled machine washable: AATCC 96, Dimensional Changes in Commercial Laundering of Woven and Knitted Fabrics Except Wool, and AATCC 135, Dimensional Changes in Automatic Home Laundering of Woven or Knit Fabrics. Neither procedure is considered accelerated, so to assess the effect of multiple cycles, the procedure must be repeated the requisite number of times. AATCC Method 96 is intended for materials that will be subjected to commercial laundry conditions. Five washing and five drying options can be combined to create the one most likely to be used for a particular product (see Table 8-2). In commercial laundering, higher temperatures, higher pHs, and longer cycle times are used than in home laundering. This method uses a cylindrical wash wheel.

AATCC Method 135 uses a home washer and dryer. Specimens are prepared as shown in Figure 8-8. Because a home washer and dryer are used, additional cotton or cotton/polyester fabric pieces (ballast or dummy pieces) are added to simulate a normal size load. Several washing and drying options are available so that the desired conditions can be simulated (see Table 8-3). After washing and drying, the distances between bench marks are measured, and dimensional change is calculated using Equation 8-1. Note that a positive number indicates growth, and a negative number indicates shrinkage. If the AATCC Shrinkage Scale is used,

Table 8-2
COMMERCIAL WASHING, DRYING, AND RESTORATION PROCEDURES.

Washing Temperatures	Total Time	Drying Type	Restoration
Ic 41° ± 3°C (105° ± 5°F)	30 min	A. Tumble	0. None
IIc 52° ± 3°C (125° ± 5°F)	45 min	B. Line	1. Tension presser
IIIc 63° ± 3°C (145° ± 5°F)	45 min	C. Drip	2. Knit shrinkage gauge
IVc 74° ± 3°C (165° ± 5°F)	60 min	D. Screen	3. Hand iron
Vc 99° ± 3°C (207° ± 5°F)	60 min	E. Flat bed press	

(From AATCC 96-1995, Dimensional Changes in Commercial Laundering of Woven and Knitted Fabrics Except Wool.)

the dimensional change is measured as a percent so no calculations are needed. However, note if the number on the scale is to the right of the zero (growth) or to the left (shrinkage).

Equation 8-1

$$\%DC = 100(B - A)/A$$

where DC = dimensional change
A = original dimension
B = dimension after laundering

Table 8-3
WASHING AND DRYING OPTIONS.

Machine Cycle	Washing Temperature	Drying Procedure
(1) Normal/Cotton Sturdy	(II) 27° ± 3°C (80° ± 5°F)	(A) Tumble
(2) Delicate	(III) 41° ± 3°C (105° ± 5°F)	i. Cotton sturdy
(3) Permanent Press	(IV) 49° ± 3°C (120° ± 5°F)	ii. Delicate
	(V) 60° ± 3°C (140° ± 5°F)	iii. Permanent Press
		(B) Line
		(C) Drip
		(D) Screen

(From AATCC 135-1995, Dimensional Changes in Automatic Home Laundering of Woven and Knit Fabrics.)

A modification of AATCC Method 135 has been developed for use in the cotton knit fabric industry. This procedure ensures that companies are using the same procedure for testing shrinkage of knit materials and is especially important for goods and products that are ready to be printed.

One test method examines the behavior of wool and wool blend fabrics that have been finished to be machine washable: AATCC 99, Dimensional Changes of Woven or Knitted Wool Textiles: Relaxation, Consolidation and Felting. This accelerated method tests materials for relaxation, consolidation, and felting shrinkage. Unlike tests for other fabrics, in which relaxation and consolidation shrinkage are assessed simultaneously, this procedure tests sequentially for each problem. Relaxation shrinkage is determined by soaking marked and measured specimens in a water solution, drying them in still air, and measuring. **Consolidation shrinkage** occurs when a fabric is gently agitated in water. Because wool and wool blend fabrics can be very sensitive to water, consolidation shrinkage is measured on a specimen only after relaxation shrinkage has been removed. This procedure also measures felting shrinkage by washing the specimen in a wash wheel after completing the consolidation method. This sequential test method is time consuming. The results are calculated using Equation 8-1. Note that the values used as the original dimension change depending

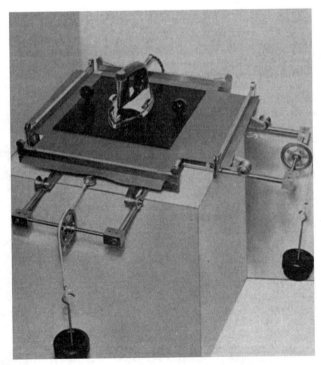

Figure 8-10
Tension presser. (*Reprinted with permission from the American Association of Textile Chemists and Colorists, P.O. Box 12215, Research Triangle Park, NC 27709*)

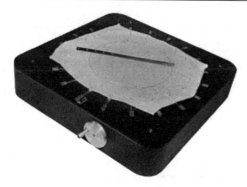

Figure 8-11
Knit shrinkage gauge. *(Reprinted with permission from the American Association of Textile Chemists and Colorists, P.O. Box 12215, Research Triangle Park, NC 27709)*

on the type of shrinkage being calculated. For consolidation shrinkage, the value is the measurement of the specimen after relaxation shrinkage has been removed. For felting shrinkage, the value is the specimen's measurement after consolidation shrinkage has been removed.

AATCC 160, Dimensional Restoration of Knitted and Woven Fabrics After Laundering, is used to ascertain if dimensional change can be reversed. **Dimensional restoration** is a material's return to its former, or original, length or width dimension. Some knits and materials used in tight fitting products, such as apparel and fitted bed sheets, may experience dimensional restoration during use. Restoration is most likely to occur in the width direction. Specimens are washed and dried, subjected to restoration forces, and then measured. This method is used with other techniques to determine the effect of washing and drying on dimensional stability. For example, restoration is an option identified in AATCC Method 135. The tension presser (Figure 8-10), knit shrinkage gauge (Figure 8-11), or hand iron are used in this method.

Appearance Alteration During Cleaning

Several test methods have been developed to quantify the possible alterations of appearance in a material that may occur during cleaning. Change in appearance can result from the abrasion of wet materials during washing and drying; such abrasion can be substantial, particularly with materials that are more sensitive to abrasion when wet. Another significant alteration is the appearance of wrinkles. Ideally, fabric should be smooth and wrinkle-free after cleaning. Unfortunately, this is not always the case.

AATCC 124, Appearance of Fabrics after Repeated Home Laundering, is designed to evaluate the smoothness of fabrics after at least one care cycle. Flat pieces of fabric representing different warp and filling yarns are washed and dried using options similar to those listed in Table 8-3. After washing and drying the specimens are conditioned and evaluated for visual

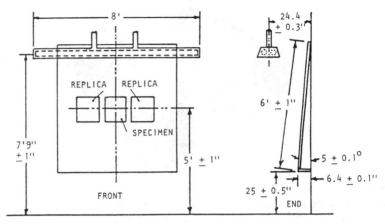

Figure 8-12
Diagram of the lighting area for visual evaluation of fabric appearance. (*Reprinted with permission from the American Association of Textile Chemists and Colorists, P.O. Box 12215, Research Triangle Park, NC 27709*)

change in appearance by trained raters. The rating is conducted in a lighting area, as illustrated in Figure 8-12. Grades are based on a comparison to the rating standards given in Figure 8-13. These standards sometimes are referred to as durable press standards, because this procedure originally was developed to assess claims for early durable press finishes.

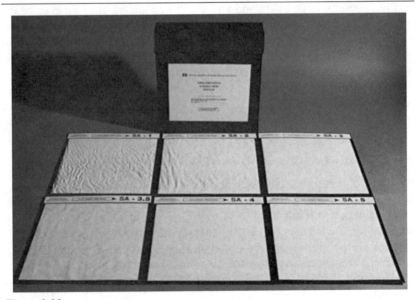

Figure 8-13
The AATCC smoothness appearance replicas. (*Reprinted with permission from the American Association of Textile Chemists and Colorists, P.O. Box 12215, Research Triangle Park, NC 27709*)

Printed and patterned fabrics may camouflage wrinkles. See the comparison in Figure 8-14 between two fabrics of similar weight, count, and structure. The earlier discussion of five-point rating scales applies to these standards and their use. For this reference scale, the grade assigned to a specimen is based on the degree and frequency of wrinkles. Some researchers are investigating computer assessment of appearance using image analysis to minimize the cost of performance assessment.

In Chapter 5, skew was identified as one quality characteristic of a fabric. The procedure used to measure the impact of skew on fabric performance is AATCC 179, Skewness Change in Fabric and Garment Twist Resulting from Automatic Home Laundering. In this procedure, specimens are cut so that no two specimens represent the same warp and filling yarns and are marked on the fabric face using one of the options illustrated in Figure 8-15. After being washed and dried using conditions selected from Table 8-3, specimens are measured.

The three measurement options are shown in Figure 8-16. In Option 1, diagonal lines connecting the corners are precisely measured, and skewness change is calculated using Equation 8-2. In Option 2, the bottom line of the square (line AD) is extended and a straight edge is lined up with each upper corner of the marked square, so that it connects with line AD at a right angle. The intersecting point is marked and the differences between the original square and the intersecting points are measured. Calcu-

A. B.

Figure 8-14

Wrinkling of patterned fabrics is more difficult to detect. Compare the appearance of these two fabrics that are identical in structure, weight, and fiber content: (a) solid, (b) print.

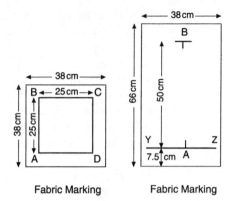

Fabric Marking   Fabric Marking

Figure 8-15
Marking options for skewness change in fabric: square option (left) and inverted T option (right). (*Reprinted with permission from the American Association of Textile Chemists and Colorists, P.O. Box 12215, Research Triangle Park, NC 27709*)

lations are done using Equation 8-3. In Option 3, a square is placed on the bottom line and lined up with the perpendicular section of line B. The intersection point on line YZ is marked, and the difference between the original point and the new intersecting point is measured. Calculations are made using Equation 8-4.

Equation 8-2

$$X = 100 \times [2(AC - BD)/(AC + BD)]$$

where X = percent change in skewness and AC and BD
refer to line segments

Equation 8-3

$$X = 100 \times [(AA' + DD')/(AB + CD)]$$

where X = percent change in skewness and AA', DD', AB,
and CD refer to line segments

Equation 8-4

$$X = 100 \times (AA'/AB)$$

where X = percent change in skewness and AA' and AB
refer to line segments

Durability of Finishes

ASTM D 2051, Durability of Finish of Zippers to Laundering, examines the performance of any enamel or decorative coating. A zipper specimen is laundered in a launder-ometer container, using AATCC Method 61, test condition 3A as described in Table 8-1. This is considered an accelerated test. The loss of any coating on the zipper chain or other components is evaluated.

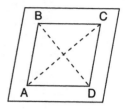

a. Diagonal lines for Option 1

DRY CLEANING

Dry cleaning is a process that uses organic solvents, rather than water, as the basis of the cleaning solution. Detergent and sometimes water are added to the solvent to aid in soil removal. Different equipment is used in the cleaning process, but the general principles are similar. The solvent and detergent remove soil while the items are tumbled. The amount of tumbling, additives to the solvent, and time of agitation differ. Products are sorted so that items of a similar nature are cleaned in the same cycle. The solvent is reclaimed, cleaned, and reused. Dry cleaning is especially good at removing oily and fatty soils, it does not swell the fiber as cleaning with water does, and it substantially reduces creasing and wrinkling.

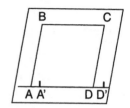

b. Offset marks for Option 2

An alternative to traditional dry cleaning is multiprocess wet cleaning, which offers several options for products, but it is not considered commercial laundering. **Multiprocess wet cleaning** uses controlled applications of heat, steam, natural soaps, and pressing techniques. This process is considered an environmentally safe alternative to traditional dry cleaning.

This section discusses procedures and standard test methods that assess how materials, such as fashion and support materials, linings, and trims, withstand commercial or coin-operated dry cleaning. Many procedures are used to determine and confirm care label instructions. Although no standard test methods currently claim applicability to the evaluation of materials cleaned by multiprocess wetcleaning, those methods that may be used for such assessment will be identified in the discussion.

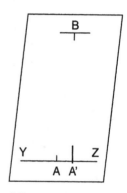

c. Offset mark for Option 3

Figure 8-16

Measurement options for calculating skewness change in fabric: Option 1 (top), Option 2 (center), and Option 3 (bottom). (*Reprinted with permission from the American Association of Textile Chemists and Colorists, P.O. Box 12215, Research Triangle Park, NC 27709*)

Colorfastness

The results from performance tests for colorfastness to laundering will not predict behavior during dry cleaning. Colorants act differently with different solvents. Thus, the effects of dry cleaning solvents on materials performance must be evaluated if dry cleaning is specified on care label instructions.

AATCC 132, Colorfastness to Dry Cleaning, is used to evaluate performance of materials, but it is not recommended for the evaluation of colorants when spot and stain removal agents are used by a dry cleaner. This accelerated test is the equivalent of three commercial cleanings. The procedure works with a launder-ometer, fabric specimens, cotton or multifiber test fabric, and cotton fabric bags. A piece of test fabric is attached to each specimen, which is then placed in a bag that contains steel discs to simulate abrasion. The bag is placed in a container with a solution of perchloroethylene and detergent and installed in the launder-ometer. After 30 minutes, the specimens are air dried before being evaluated for color change and staining. Because perchloroethylene is toxic by inhalation, skin contact, or ingestion, the safety precautions identified in the test method must be followed.

In ASTM D 2052, Colorfastness of Zippers to Dry Cleaning, a zipper specimen is sealed in a fabric bag that includes a piece of multifiber test fabric and cleaned three times using a coin-operated dry cleaning machine. Color change and staining are evaluated.

One common dry cleaning practice is treating spots before cleaning. This process uses various solvents depending on the combination of material and soil. One common solvent is perchloroethylene (commonly referred to as perc), which is particularly successful at removing certain soils and stains. AATCC 157, Colorfastness to Solvent Spotting: Perchloroethylene, evaluates the degree of color migration that occurs when a fabric is spotted with perc. In this procedure, a specimen is attached to white blotting paper, placed on a glass surface, and spotted with perc. The stain on the blotting paper is evaluated using the AATCC Chromatic Transference Scale. Some companies also evaluate the fabric to see if a ring remains on the fabric after the perc has dried.

Dimensional Change

Dimensional problems are less pronounced with dry cleaning than with laundering. However, dimensional change can be progressive, so three to five cleaning cycles are recommended before evaluating for dimensional change to produce a better and more realistic measure of material performance.

AATCC 158, Dimensional Changes on Drycleaning in Perchloroethylene: Machine Method, lists two options, one for sensitive materials and one for normal materials. Very sensitive materials that require special precautions are not included in this test. Multiple cycles are used to assess progressive dimensional change. The procedure uses a commercial dry cleaning machine and perc as the solvent. Specimens are cut, stitched along the sides to prevent raveling, and marked in a fashion similar to that shown in Figure 8-8. Dummy or ballast fabric is added to achieve the desired mass. After the machine is run, the load is rinsed and dried. Specimens are measured and dimensional change is calculated using Equation 8-1.

Durability of Finishes

Because finishes may not be durable to drycleaning, evaluating their performance after cleaning is important. AATCC 86 Drycleaning: Durability

Table 8-4
GRADING SCALES FOR DURABILITY OF APPLIED DESIGNS AND FINISHES.

Durability of Applied Design Grade	Durability of Fabric Handle Grade
A5 Negligible or no change in appearance	B5 Negligible or no change in handle
A4 Slightly changed in appearance	B4 Slightly changed in handle
A3 Noticeably changed in appearance	B3 Noticeably changed in handle
A2 Considerably changed in appearance	B2 Considerably changed in handle
A1 Much changed in appearance	B1 Much changed in handle

(From AATCC 86-1994, Dry cleaning: Durability of Applied Designs and Finishes.)

of Applied Designs and Finishes is used to assess the performance of both apparel and furnishing materials. It also assesses the resistance of colors to spot and stain removal agents used by dry cleaners, but it is not recommended for evaluating colorfastness. The performance of the single specimen is evaluated using the launder-ometer and perc. After dry cleaning, the specimen is rinsed, air dried, pressed, and evaluated for change in appearance and hand using the five point scales listed in Table 8-4. The performance of water repellency is evaluated using AATCC 22, Water Repellency: Spray Test (see Chapter 7).

ASTM D 2058, Durability of Finish of Zippers to Dry Cleaning, is very similar to ASTM D 2051, Durability of Finish of Zippers to Laundering. The major difference is that perchloroethylene and AATCC Method 86 are used to simulate dry cleaning. Evaluation is based on an assessment of coating loss to the zipper.

Cleaning Procedures for Floor Coverings

AATCC 138, Cleaning: Washing of Textile Floor Coverings, is a standardized cleaning procedure that can be used to assess wetfastness durability and permanency of antimicrobial properties, colorfastness behavior, permanency of finishes, and other topical treatments to the pile of textile floor coverings before, during, and after manufacturing and to procedures used to assess cleanability, and dimensional stability. A square of carpet or floor covering is wetted with water, scrubbed with a soap solution, rinsed, and oven dried. The wetting, scrubbing, and rinsing steps can be repeated as needed.

The hot water extraction method is used approximately 70 percent of the time in cleaning actual carpets. Thus, AATCC 171, Cleaning of Carpets: Hot Water Extraction Method, was developed to present a standardized means of cleaning carpets. Specimens cleaned by this technique can be tested for colorfastness, dimensional change, permanence of finishes, ease of cleaning, and other performance issues.

SOIL AND STAIN ASPECTS

Failure of the cleaning method to remove soil and stains is a major factor in product failure. Thus, standardized procedures have been developed to evaluate stain removal, effectiveness of stain resistant finishes, and degree of soiling. Some fibers, such as polyester, and some finishes, such as durable press finishes, hold on to oily soils tenaciously and create cleaning problems. As a result, soil resistant and soil repellent finishes were developed. This section examines test methods that measure the soiling of products, effectiveness of soil removal techniques, and effectiveness of soil and stain resistant finishes.

Standard test methods that measure soiling can be divided into those that assess soil redeposition during washing, those that measure soiling of carpeting, and those that measure staining of carpet backing. AATCC 151, Resistance to Soil Redeposition: Launder-Ometer Method, is an accelerated method that measures the degree of soil that may be redeposited on a fabric during laundering. The procedure is equivalent to 100 cycles if it is run for 30 minutes. In this procedure, a specimen is exposed to a soiling medium in a launder-ometer container under specified conditions, and the change in light reflectance is measured. Change in reflectance is a measure of **soil redeposition,** which is the soiling of relatively clean fabric during laundering by soil removed from another fabric.

The ability of fabrics to release oily stains is assessed following AATCC 130, Soil Release: Oily Stain Release Method. In this procedure, an oily stain is applied to a fabric and forced into the specimen with a weight. The stained material is laundered in a washing machine with sufficient ballast, and the remaining stain is evaluated using the AATCC Stain Release Replica or the 3M Stain Release Rating Scale shown in Figure 8-17.

Figure 8-17
The AATCC Stain Release Replica. (*Reprinted with permission from the American Association of Textile Chemists and Colorists, P.O. Box 12215, Research Triangle Park, NC 27709*)

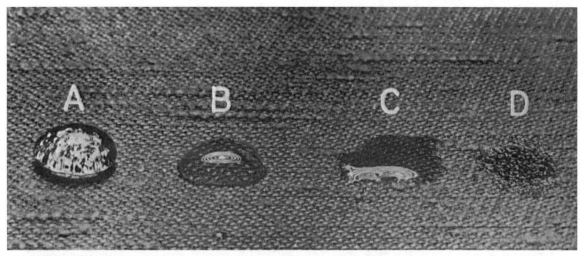

Figure 8-18
Different types of fabric wetting in the oil repellency–hydrocarbon resistance test. (*Reprinted with permission from the American Association of Textile Chemists and Colorists, P.O. Box 12215, Research Triangle Park, NC 27709*)

AATCC 118, Oil Repellency: Hydrocarbon Resistance Test, is used to detect the presence of a fluorochemical finish or other compound that makes a textile surface more difficult to wet, thus imparting soil resistance. In this procedure, a series of standard test liquids (oils) are dropped onto the fabric surface and observed for wetting, wicking, and contact angle. The grade assigned to the fabric corresponds to the highest number of test liquid that did not wet the surface. Thus, a grade of 2 indicates that oil grade number 2 wetted the surface, but oil grade number 1 did not. Figure 8-18 illustrates several possible outcomes for each oil.

Some research uses more sophisticated methods, such as electron microscopy, to determine soiling and soil residue on fabrics. These techniques are seldom applied to performance testing of materials because of the high cost of the equipment, sample preparation, and technician training.

Assessment of Floor Coverings

Soiling of floor coverings is especially problematic because of their semipermanent nature, high visibility, use in heavy traffic areas, exposure to different soils, and cost. The three carpet soiling tests (AATCC 121, Carpet Soiling: Visual Rating Method; AATCC 122, Carpet Soiling: Service Soiling Method; and AATCC 123, Carpet Soiling: Accelerated Soiling Method) measure the accumulation of soil on a carpet of any color, pattern, structure, or fiber content or the removal of soil from a carpet during cleaning. Assessment uses either the AATCC Gray Scale for Color Change or reflectance measurements. A jumbo version of this gray scale is available

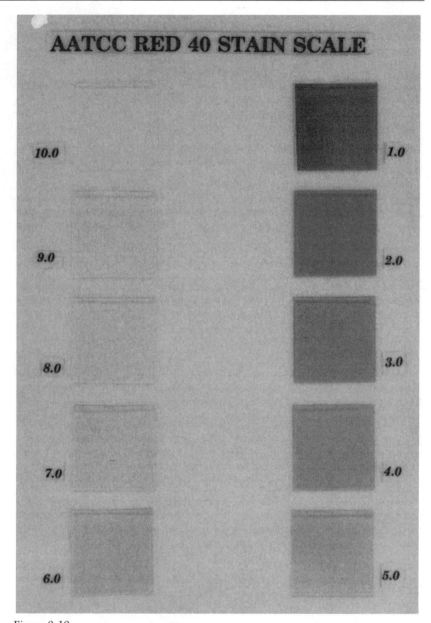

Figure 8-19
AATCC Red 40 Stain Scale used to assess staining of carpets. (*Reprinted with permission from the American Association of Textile Chemists and Colorists, P.O. Box 12215, Research Triangle Park, NC 27709*)

for use in carpet assessment. The visual rating method (AATCC 121) is used for carpets that are clean, as well as those that have a moderate degree of soiling. The service test (AATCC 122) is used for carpets exposed to normal foot traffic in a controlled test area, from which specimens are removed at predetermined intervals and visually rated for soiling. The accelerated soiling method (AATCC 123) is used to compare the soiling propensity of two or more carpets or as a preliminary screening method for measuring the effectiveness of a cleaning method or the cleanability of a carpet. AATCC method 123 should not be used as a replacement for floor testing. In this procedure, carpet samples are tumbled with a synthetic soil, vacuumed, and rated using the visual rating method.

Because color transference from rug backing to vinyl tile occurs with some rugs, a procedure has been developed to assess the potential for the problem to develop. AATCC 137, Rug Back Staining on Vinyl Tile, is an accelerated method that correlates with both dry and wet in-service use. A rug specimen is wet and placed between two pieces of vinyl tile. Weight is added to compress the sandwich of rug and tile, which is left for 24 hours. Color transference to the tile is assessed using the AATCC Chromatic Transference Scale or the AATCC Gray Scale for Staining.

Coloring agents used to add appeal to food are usually acid dyes. Because carpet is often made of nylon, which is both a color scavenger and receptive to acid dyes, food stains can really be a problem. A stain is a local deposit of soil or discoloration on a substrate that exhibits some degree of resistance to removal by laundering or dry cleaning. AATCC 175, Stain Resistance: Pile Floor Coverings, is a test method that determines carpet resistance to acid food color stains. A carpet specimen is stained with a red food dye solution, dried, rinsed in water, dried again, and assessed by comparing to the 10-point AATCC Red Stain Scale (See Figure 8-19). An alternate procedure using a chromameter to electronically measure carpet staining is being developed (Kissa, 1995).

BLEACHING

Bleaching is done during finishing of fabric as a preparation step to achieve level and uniform dyes and prints and to produce a bright, clear white. It is also used during cleaning to restore materials to a clean, new look. Bleaching chemicals include chlorinated compounds, peroxides, and sodium perborate or sodium percarbonate compounds. These compounds are designed to remove stains, but they also may remove or damage the color of a material.

Several procedures examine the effect of bleach on dyed and printed fabrics. AATCC 3, Colorfastness to Bleaching with Chlorine, is applicable to cotton, linen, and blends containing either cotton or linen that have been dyed or printed. Specimens are washed in a sodium hypochlorite solution (liquid chlorine bleach) in a launder-ometer and evaluated for color change and staining.

AATCC 101, Colorfastness to Bleaching with Hydrogen Peroxide, can be used for all textiles, except nylon and other polyamides. This bleaching agent, which is used in textile processing, is generally not used as a household bleach. Specimens are saturated with a hydrogen peroxide solution, steamed, rinsed, and evaluated for color change and staining.

Nonchlorine bleaches are widely used in home laundering. AATCC 172, Colorfastness to Non-Chlorine Bleach in Home Laundering, is used to evaluate their effect when used frequently on materials. The procedure looks at the interaction of the bleaching chemical, detergent solution, and abrasion during laundering. Because these nonchlorine bleach additives incorporate additional ingredients, such as whitening agents and bluing, it is the total effect that is evaluated in this accelerated method (equivalent to five home launderings). The conditions are based on the options listed in Table 8-1. The results of this procedure are used to determine the appropriateness of the instructions on care labels. After washing and drying, color change is evaluated.

Because chlorinated compounds can damage fabrics, two test methods have been developed that focus on the potential of fabric damage (AATCC 92, Chlorine, Retained, Tensile Loss: Single Sample Method, and AATCC 114, Chlorine, Retained, Tensile Loss: Multiple Sample Method). These accelerated tests are used with cotton and rayon fabrics. Specimens are

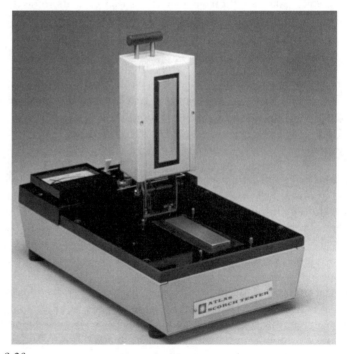

Figure 8-20
Scorch tester used for tensile loss as a result of retained chlorine and exposure to heat. (*Courtesy of Atlas Electric Device Co.*)

treated in a sodium hypochlorite (liquid chlorine bleach) solution, rinsed, dried, and pressed between hot metal plates using a scorch tester (see Figure 8-20). Tensile strength of specimens that are not heat treated (unscorched) and the strength of heat treated (scorched) specimens are compared using Equation 8-5.

Equation 8-5

$$\%R = 100\,(T_c - T_{cs})/T_c$$

where R = loss due to retained chlorine in %

T_c = average tensile strength of cholorinated specimens, unscorched, and

T_{cs} = average tensile strength of chlorinated specimens, scorched

APPEARANCE RETENTION

Appearance retention is a critical factor in the aesthetic appreciation of a textile product. Procedures that focus on the materials are designed to assess how a material changes in appearance during use. Procedures that focused on appearance changes during care were already discussed.

WHITENESS

The average consumer's perception of whiteness is based on a clear, bright, almost bluish white. This white can be dazzling when viewed under bright sunlight because so much of the light striking the object is reflected and seen by the eye. White materials that contain a small amount of another color, such as green or yellow, are not as desirable as a pure or just slightly bluish white material. Whiteness can be used to determine the degree to which a textile is free of impurities and to describe the presence of fluorescent whitening agents or blueing components. AATCC 110 Whiteness of Textiles uses a colorimeter or spectrophotometer to measure a fabric's whiteness. With many fabrics, as they age, are laundered, or are stored, a yellow cast or discoloration may appear. This procedure is used to evaluate the whiteness of new and used fabrics.

Whiteness problems also develop as a result of some aesthetic finishes, especially abrasion finishes. If the finishing agent is not neutralized after finishing, the material can yellow quickly. AATCC Method 110 is used to assess changes in whiteness after finishing so that problems of this nature can be minimized.

WRINKLE RECOVERY

Wrinkle recovery refers to a fabric's ability to recover from folding deformations. These deformations differ from those that occur during cleaning. To the consumer, both types of appearance alterations may be described as

Figure 8-21
Wrinkle recovery tester used in the recovery angle method.

wrinkles, but the means by which they are formed are quite different. The procedures discussed here focus on wrinkles that develop during use and storage.

In AATCC 66, Wrinkle Recovery of Fabrics: Recovery Angle Method, specimens are creased and compressed with a mass. Specimens are cut so that no two represent the same warp and filling yarns. Some specimens are folded face to face; and other specimens back to back. Each creased specimen is suspended in the wrinkle recovery tester for several minutes and the recovery angle is measured (see Figure 8-21).

In AATCC 128, Wrinkle Recovery of Fabrics: Appearance Method, each specimen is twisted and compressed by a mass in the AATCC wrinkle tester. After being hung in a vertical position for 24 hours, trained observers grade each specimen based on a comparison with the wrinkle recovery specimens (see Figure 8-22). Computer assessment of appearance using image analysis is being investigated by some researchers to minimize the cost of performance assessment of materials.

STORAGE

Many things can happen to materials in storage. Issues related to performance in storage are of interest to manufacturers, retailers, and consumers. Warehouses and distribution centers may store items for a long time in boxes or plastic. Consumers may store items in containers of similar mate-

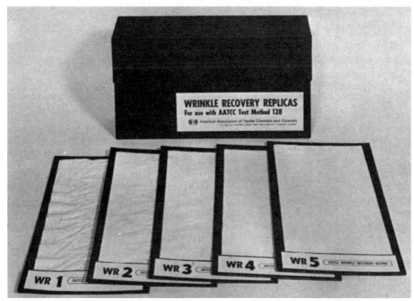

Figure 8-22
AATCC wrinkle recovery replicas. *(Reprinted with permission from the American Association of Textile Chemists and Colorists, P.O. Box 12215, Research Triangle Park, NC 27709)*

rials. In both cases, insect damage, mildew, and other negative conditions can create problems with subsequent use of a product.

RESISTANCE TO INSECTS

Many species of insects have been known to damage textile materials, particularly soiled textiles and those made of wool and other animal hair fibers, such as mohair, angora, and cashmere. The test methods discussed here assess insect damage on finished and unfinished materials. AATCC 24, Resistance of Textiles to Insects, uses larvae of two species of insects known for their attraction to textiles: the webbing clothes moth and the carpet beetle. This method uses two procedures to assess quantitatively the amount of feeding on the test specimen. The number and type of insects are specified, as are the time and conditions of the test. In the excrement weight method, carpet beetle larvae feed on a specimen for 14 days. At the end of the feeding period, excrement is removed and weighed. In the weight loss method, specimens are conditioned, weighed, exposed to insect larvae for 14 days, and weight loss is calculated.

AATCC 28, Insect Pest Deterrents on Textiles, is used to evaluate performance of fabrics treated to be insect resistant. **Insect resistance** is the capability to impede damage by insects by treating materials with chemicals. This procedure evaluates the effectiveness of the finish when it is new and again after conditions of ordinary service. Treated and untreated specimens are exposed to insects for a specified period. The fabric is examined for damage when new and again after washing, cleaning, hot pressing, or exposure to perspiration, light, abrasion, or other normal condition of use. Either the fabric weight loss method or the excrement weight method is used in this performance assessment.

RESISTANCE TO FUNGUS AND BACTERIA

When textiles are stored in high-humidity environments or when damp, they are subject to fungal, mold, and mildew growth and bacterial damage. Dark and stagnant storage spaces with warm and humid areas are especially likely to create problems. Irreparable damage and a distinct odor occur most frequently with cellulosic fiber fabrics. **Mildew resistance** is the resistance to the development of fungal growths and the accompanying unpleasant, musty odors on materials exposed to conditions favoring such growths. **Rot resistance** is a material's resistance to deterioration as a result of fungal growth.

One method, AATCC 30, Antifungal Activity, Assessment on Textile Materials: Mildew and Rot Resistance of Textile Materials, determines the susceptibility of materials to mildew and rot and the efficacy of fungicides on materials. This method offers several test options depending on the intended end use of the material and the likely conditions of use. The soil burial option buries the specimen in a soil bed for several weeks, and then measures the resultant loss of strength. This severe method is used for textile products, such as tents, that will be used in contact with the soil. In the agar plate options, the specimen is evaluated for resistance to rotting or to growth of other fungi that produce unpleasant odors. These procedures are used for textiles that will not be used in contact with the soil. Evaluation is based on strength loss or visual assessment of observed fungal growth. The humidity jar option is designed for outdoor textiles that are usually waterproofed. Evaluation is based on visual assessment of observed fungal growth.

In AATCC 100, Assessment of Antibacterial Finishes on Textile Materials, the effectiveness of finishes are assessed by a quantitative measure that identifies the percentage reduction between treated and untreated fabric specimens. **Antibacterial finishes** include any chemicals that kill bacteria (bactericide) or interfere with the multiplication, growth, or activity of bacteria (bacteriostat). AATCC 147, Antibacterial Activity Assessment of Textile Materials: Parallel Streak Method, is a quick technique for determining the antibacterial activity of finishing agents. An agar plate (agar is a gelatinous, nutrient-rich base in which bacteria activity or growth occurs) is streaked with or treated with a test bacterium culture. The textile specimen is placed on the agar and incubated at conditions that encourage the multiplication and growth of bacteria. A clear area around and under the textile indicates antibacterial activity.

Procedures similar to the parallel streak method and the quantitative analysis are used to assess antibacterial activity and mildew and rot resistance for carpets in AATCC 174, Antimicrobial Activity Assessment of Carpet.

RESISTANCE TO AGING

Textiles treated with sulfur dyes deteriorate dramatically under normal storage conditions if the dyes were not neutralized properly after dyeing. Because sulfur dyes often are used on cellulosic fibers that are sensitive to degradation by acids, it is not surprising to find that excess sulfur may combine with atmospheric moisture and form a weak acid. Over time, this weak acid creates a very brittle and tender fabric that tears easily. In this test method, AATCC 26, Ageing (sic) of Sulfur Dyed Textiles: Accelerated, specimens are steam aged in a controlled moist environment and tested for strength loss.

RESISTANCE TO DYE TRANSFER

Dye transfer can be a problem when materials of dissimilar color are stored in contact with each other. **Dye transfer** describes the movement of a chemical, dye, or pigment between fibers within a substrate or between substrates. The problem can be intensified as temperature and humidity increase or when products are steamed just before storage. Storage in plastic bags can exacerbate the problem. In AATCC 163, Colorfastness: Dye Transfer in Storage; Fabric-to-Fabric, dyed and finished specimens are sandwiched between a wetted multifiber test fabric and another fabric using the perspiration tester at room temperature (see Figure 8-23). Staining is evaluated.

COLORFASTNESS

The colorfastness procedures discussed in this section relate to production processes and consumer use of products. Colorfastness procedures can be divided into three categories. The first exposes colored material to a particular condition and evaluates the change in color. The second exposes both a colored material and a white material or multifiber test fabric to a particular condition and then examines the white material or test fabric for color stain transfer. The third combines the evaluation of color change and color stain transfer. Some colorfastness tests also include such conditions as heat and steam, because these may cause a dye to migrate within or between materials. In addition, conditions that may cause a dye to degrade or deteriorate are present in some tests. Several tests work with extreme conditions to ascertain if a problem is likely to develop.

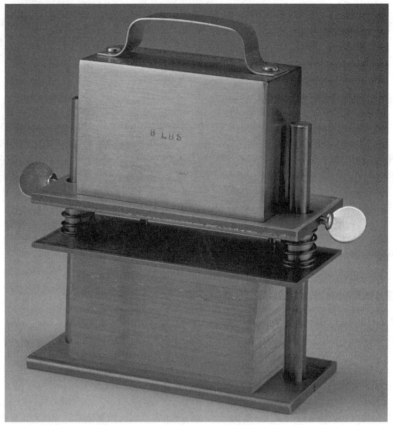

Figure 8-23
AATCC perspiration tester. (*Courtesy of Atlas Electric Device Co.*)

PRODUCTION PROCESSES

The colorfastness procedures discussed in this section focus on processes to which a material may be exposed during finishing or in the sewing facility. In **fulling**, the fabric, such as that used in boiled wool jackets, is subjected to moisture, heat, friction, and pressure. In AATCC 2, Colorfastness to Fulling, color change is evaluated after processing in a launder-ometer.

Carbonizing is a chemical process used in the processing of wool to eliminate plant matter by degrading the cellulosic material with acid. In AATCC 11, Colorfastness to Carbonizing, the specimen is exposed to a sulfuric acid solution and compared to standard dyed test controls.

Heat can cause major problems with staining, and some problems with color change. Several methods are used to evaluate colorfastness to heat. **Hot pressing** is a process for smoothing and perhaps shaping textile products by applying mechanical pressure with heat, sometimes in the presence of moisture. In AATCC 117, Colorfastness to Heat; Dry (Excluding Pressure), the test specimen is exposed to dry heat when in close contact with an undyed fabric. Color change and staining are evaluated. In AATCC 131, Colorfastness to Pleating: Steam Pressing, the specimen is steamed under specific pressure and time conditions and dried so that color change and staining can be evaluated. Three options are used in AATCC 133, Colorfastness to Heat: Hot Pressing. The effects of dry pressing, damp pressing, and wet pressing on color change and staining are evaluated. These colorfastness to heat test methods can also be applied to evaluating the ability of a material to be cleaned by multiprocess wetcleaning, because pressing, steaming, and heat are used in that process.

CONSUMER USE

Colorfastness to conditions or circumstances of use are of interest. These test methods consider how consumers use textile products and factors that may cause colorants on fashion and support materials, linings, and trims to change color or migrate from the fiber to which they are attached or bonded. Many of these procedures use extreme conditions of exposure, so that the potential for color problems under such circumstances, will be recognized. Other procedures are designed to more closely simulate normal consumer use and assess how a material is likely to perform under more realistic conditions.

Acid and Alkalis

Many consumers work around or use chemicals on a daily basis. For example, foods, beverages, cosmetics, deodorants, shampoos, soaps, body lotions, and medications, such as acne creme, contain acids, bases, and other chemicals may create problems with textile colorants. In AATCC 6, Colorfastness to Acids and Alkalis, specimens are steeped in (soaked) or spotted with several chemical solutions and evaluated for color change.

Frosting

Several dye classes and pigments are recognized for their inability to penetrate into the interior of a fiber. These dyes and pigments bond with or adhere to the surface or outer portions of the fiber. When the material is abraded, the colored portion of the fiber is removed and **frosting** or a whitish cast appears. Two procedures (AATCC 119, Colorfastness due to Flat Abrasion [Frosting]: Screen Wire Method, and AATCC 120, Colorfastness due to Flat Abrasion [Frosting]: Emery Method) that are used to assess frosting were discussed in Chapter 6.

Crocking

Color on the surface of a material may be transferred to another material by surface contact and rubbing. This problem, known as **crocking,** is usually more pronounced when one of the materials is wet. Dry crocking may

Figure 8-24
AATCC crockmeter. (*Courtesy of Atlas Electric Device Co.*)

occur, but wet crocking is more likely and is usually more severe. Three test methods examine material behavior in terms of crocking. In all cases, two pieces of standard white fabric, one dry and one wet, are rubbed across the material's surface. The white fabric is evaluated for color change.

In AATCC 8, Colorfastness to Crocking: AATCC Crockmeter Method, the AATCC crockmeter (see Figure 8-24) is used to test the colorfastness of fabric or yarn. In AATCC 116, Colorfastness to Crocking: Rotary Vertical Crockmeter Method, a different crockmeter, the rotary vertical crockmeter, is especially useful in evaluating the colorfastness of small surface areas within a material. It works with a smaller surface area so that one color in a print or area of a yarn dyed fabric is tested at a time (see Figure 8-25).

In AATCC 165, Colorfastness to Crocking: Carpets—AATCC Crockmeter Method, it is suggested that the procedure be carried out before and after cleaning and application of antistatic or antisoil topical finishes. This method also uses the AATCC crockmeter.

Perspiration

Perspiration is a saline, slightly acidic fluid secreted by sweat glands. The salt and acidic pH of perspiration can create problems with colorfastness. In a standard test method (AATCC 15, Colorfastness to Perspiration), a specimen is soaked in a simulated laboratory solution of perspiration. The wet specimen is stacked on top of a piece of multifiber test fabric of the

Figure 8-25
AATCC Rotary Vertical Crockmeter. (*Courtesy of Atlas Electric Device Co.*)

same size and placed in a perspiration tester or perspirometer so that the two pieces are pressed together (see Figure 8-23). The fabrics are oven dried at a temperature that simulates body surface temperature and evaluated for color change and staining.

Water

Because many dyes dissolve in water, which is a common solvent in dyeing, and because many dyes exhibit migration, bleeding is frequently encountered when materials are exposed to water. Thus, cleaning or spotting materials with a water-based solution can cause problems, some of which were discussed in the section on cleaning. Additional problems will be discussed here, particularly those affecting products designed to be used in or near water. It is necessary to determine if materials used in these products are suitable for that end use. In these test methods, the specimen is exposed to a specific type of water and evaluated for color change and or staining.

In the AATCC 104, Colorfastness to Water Spotting method, the specimen is spotted with distilled or deionized water and evaluated for color change. This procedure can be used with any color material. **Water spotting** describes a change in color, particularly at the periphery of an area wetted with water.

The procedure used in AATCC 107, Colorfastness to Water, is a simple one. The specimen is soaked in distilled or deionized water, backed with multifiber test fabric, placed in a perspiration tester, oven dried, and evaluated for color change and staining. Distilled or deionized water is used in this and other procedures because the quality of tap water varies widely among locations.

This procedure is a nonstandardized procedure. Although variations in the procedure exist among several large retailers, many use a procedure similar to the **cold water bleed,** which places damp fabrics in contact with other damp fabrics for 18 to 24 hours. The procedure simulates wet clothes left in the washer overnight, damp products placed next to each other in the hamper, or wet towels dropped onto clothes and left overnight. This process is similar to AATCC Method 107, except that the material is not oven dried. It remains damp until the two layers are finally separated. After separation, the layers are dried and evaluated for color change and staining.

These colorfastness to plain water methods also apply to the evaluation of a material's ability to be cleaned by multiprocess wetcleaning, as water may be used in that process.

In AATCC 106, Colorfastness to Water: Sea, the specimen is immersed in an artificial sea water solution. The specimen is backed with a multifiber test fabric, placed in a perspiration tester (see Figure 8-23), oven dried, and evaluated for color change and staining. This procedure is used with colored materials, such as towels, swimwear, sailing apparel, boat cushions, boat covers, and other products that will be used in or near sea water.

Because chlorine is used in most swimming pools to kill bacteria and other microorganisms, a test method has been developed to evaluate material performance when exposed to chlorinated water. AATCC 162, Colorfastness to Water: Chlorinated Pool, uses a dry cleaning cylinder into which a prepared dilute chlorine solution and the specimen are placed. This procedure is used to evaluate color change for swimwear, swimwear covers, deck furniture webbing, and some towels.

Environmental Conditions

Atmospheric contaminants present in the internal or external environment can cause colorfastness problems. These test methods examine the impact of atmospheric contaminants or pollutants on the performance of materials. Several of these procedures are of special importance for materials used in such furnishings as carpeting, upholstery, and draperies, because these products generally are used indoors and are exposed to that environment on a continuous basis.

In these procedures, specimens and a control fabric are exposed to fumes or gases. When the control fabric exhibits fading to a predetermined level, the specimen is evaluated for color change using the AATCC Gray Scale for Color Change. If no color change has occurred at the end of this exposure cycle, the specimen can be reevaluated after additional exposure to a specified number of cycles or the specimen can simply be exposed to additional cycles until a color change does occur. Exposure chambers for these test methods generally are constructed from blueprints purchased from AATCC.

Burnt gas fumes are present in the internal environment because of the combustion of natural gas products. Thus, materials used in structures that are heated with natural gas and liquid propane (LP) are more likely to have heightened exposure than materials used in structures that are heated with steam, electricity, or another source. In AATCC 23, Colorfastness to Burnt Gas Fumes, specimens are evaluated for their performance when exposed to this common environmental contaminant.

A related test method, AATCC 164, Colorfastness to Oxides of Nitrogen in the Atmosphere Under High Humidities, exposes the specimen and control fabric to humidities higher than 85 percent. Some colorants, such as some dyes used on nylon and acetate, are more likely to fade when exposed to oxides of nitrogen at higher humidities and should be evaluated using this procedure. Since many carpets are made of nylon and acetate is often used in draperies, this procedure can be especially important for assessing materials used in furnishings.

Ozone is another atmospheric gas that may fade colorants. In AATCC 109, Colorfastness to Ozone in the Atmosphere Under Low Humidities, specimens and control fabrics are exposed to ozone at relatively dry ambient conditions. This procedure can be used with laundered or dry cleaned specimens because cleaning affects how some materials react to ozone. In a similar procedure, AATCC 129, Colorfastness to Ozone in the Atmosphere Under High Humidities, conditions of exposure are more humid because some materials are more likely to fade at higher humidities.

Light

Light is readily recognized for its potential to damage colorants and materials. Because light is not constant in its characteristics, several tests allow for variation of the light source and intensity; other tests simulate a range of use conditions by combining light with several other environmental factors. Different light sources produce different types of light; some are more damaging than others. Light intensity is the amount of light striking an object. Sunlight is more intense on clear days than it is on cloudy or overcast days. When light exposure is combined with water or high humidities, changes in the color of materials may be accelerated.

Because of these variables, standard test methods have been developed. In addition, control fabrics, such as the **AATCC blue wool light-fastness standard fabrics,** have been developed to determine exposure of test specimens during testing (see Figure 8-26). The specimen and the control or standard fabric are exposed to light until the standard fabric reaches a predetermined level of fading. The exposure time is defined by a number of AATCC fading units. An **AATCC fading unit (AFU)** is the specific amount of exposure at specified conditions where one AFU is one-twentieth (1/20) of the light-on exposure required to produce a color

Figure 8-26
AATCC blue wool lightfastness standard fabrics L9 through L2 (left to right).

change equal to Step 4 of the AATCC Gray Scale for Color Change on AATCC blue wool lightfastness standard fabric L-4. **Lightfastness** is the property of material, often expressed as a number, that describes a ranked change in its color characteristics resulting from exposure to some designated light source. Testing lightfastness is especially important for furnishings, such as window treatments, carpeting, and upholstery, because of their frequent, if not continuous, and long-term exposure to light. Light damage in terms of fading, interactions with insecticides when buildings are fumigated, and tendering or weakening of materials as a result of light exposure is a common concern.

AATCC 16, Colorfastness to Light, is the test method that presents numerous options in terms of light source, including natural daylight, artificial carbon arc light, or artificial xenon arc, and in conditions of exposure (e.g., continuous light or alternating light and dark) to simulate conditions of use. These are not necessarily accelerated procedures because conditions of use and exposure can vary widely depending on the region and end use. In this procedure, specimens and a control fabric for comparison are placed inside a fadeometer (see Figure 8-27), weatherometer (see Figure 8-28), or daylight exposure cabinet. After testing, the specimens are evaluated for color change. The test method includes a report form because of the number of details that should be reported when lightfastness is tested.

Some materials display unique behavior when exposed to light. They change in color after a brief exposure, but return to their original color when stored in the dark. **Photochromism** is a qualitative designation for a reversible change in color of any kind that is immediately noticeable on termination of light exposure when exposed and unexposed portions of the material are compared. AATCC 139, Colorfastness to Light: Detection of Photochromism, is used to identify materials that exhibit this behavior. In this procedure, a material is exposed to a high-intensity light for a short time. Using the AATCC Gray Scale for Color Change, color change is as-

Figure 8-27 (Left)
Fadeometer. (*Courtesy of Atlas Electric Device Co.*)

Figure 8-28 (Right)
Weatherometer. (*Courtesy of Atlas Electric Device Co.*)

sessed immediately after exposure and again after the specimen is stored in specified conditions in the dark.

Two test methods alternate light exposure with darkness to simulate the day-night differences frequently encountered in consumer use. In both AATCC 125, Colorfastness to Water and Light: Alternate Exposure, and AATCC 126, Colorfastness to Water (High Humidity) and Light; Alternate Exposure, the basic principles discussed with AATCC Method 16 apply here. In AATCC Method 125, the specimen is soaked in a specified water solution before the exposure cycle. In AATCC Method 126, a dry specimen is first exposed in repeating cycles of short exposure to conditions of high humidity and darkness and longer exposure to conditions of light and low humidity until a color change occurs or until a specified number of cycles have passed.

Because light degradation of colorants can be accelerated at high temperatures and high-humidity or high-moisture levels, AATCC 177, Colorfastness to Light at Elevated Temperature and Humidity: Xenon Lamp Apparatus, sometimes is used to assess material performance. It is particularly applicable for materials that will be used in car, truck, and other vehicle interiors. In this procedure, the basic principles discussed with AATCC Method 16 also apply.

RESISTANCE TO WEATHERING

In addition to the color damage a material may experience after exposure to light, loss of strength and durability may also occur. Light damage is not limited to colorant damage. Often, it is combined with damage to durability performance because of moisture and heat action. Damage may be seen in fabrics that are weaker, brittle, or more sensitive to abrasion after exposure to light. **Weather resistance** is the ability of a material to resist degradation of its properties when exposed to real or simulated climatic conditions. These conditions are of great importance in evaluating such products as tents, awnings, outdoor furnishings, canvas covers for boats, tarpaulins, textiles and plastics used for the interiors of motor vehicles, many other industrial products, and outerwear.

A general discussion of issues related to weather resistance is included in AATCC 111, Weather Resistance: General Information. Five specific test methods focus on different light sources and conditions of exposure that are summed up in their titles: AATCC 111A, Weather Resistance: Sunshine Arc Lamp Exposure with Wetting; AATCC 111B, Weather Resistance: Exposure to Natural Light and Weather; AATCC 111C, Weather Resistance: Sunshine Arc Lamp Exposure without Wetting; AATCC 111D, Weather Resistance: Exposure to Natural Light and Weather through Glass; and AATCC 169, Weather Resistance of Textiles: Xenon Lamp Exposure. In each test method, specimens are exposed to specified conditions defined in terms of light source, relative humidity, wetting, or natural weather, with or without glass protection. After exposure, specimens are evaluated for their percentage of strength retained or lost, residual strength, and color change.

MATERIAL SPECIFICATIONS

Material specifications identify the test method, the desired measure of performance, and the unit by which performance is measured. Sometimes, specs might include the condition under which a test is conducted. For example, if a material is tested for light fastness, the exposure in AATCC fading units is often listed. Tables 8-5 and 8-6 provide recommended performance specifications for selected sample product categories (ASTM, 1996). It might also be helpful to compare the values for apparel with the values presented in Table 8-7 which lists the specs of woven and knitted shirts for two catalog retailers.

Table 8-5

COLORFASTNESS PERFORMANCE SPECIFICATIONS FOR SAMPLE PRODUCT CATEGORIES.

Category	Upholstery	Sheer Curtains	Vocational Apparel	Blankets	Toweling	Regular Apparel
Water	4	—	—	—	—	4/3.5[4]
Solvent	4	—	—	—	—	—
Crocking (dry/wet)	4/3	4/3	4/3	4/3	4/3	4/3
Burnt gas fumes	4[1]	4	4	4	—	—
Ozone	4	4	4	—	—	—
Light	4[2]	4	4	4	4	4
Perspiration[3]	—	—	4/3	—	—	4
Laundering[3]		4/3	4/3	4/3	4/3	3.5/3.5
Dry cleaning	—	—	4	4	—	—

(From ASTM Recommended Performance Specifications, 1996.)

[1]For 2 cycles.
[2]AFU values vary by category: 10 for upholstery; 60 for sheer curtains; 40 for outdoor and regular apparel; 20 for vocational apparel, blankets, and towels.
[3]The first number refers to shade change and the second, to staining.
[4]For swimwear exposed to chlorinated pool water.
—Indicates that no recommendation for this combination property and product category was listed.

Table 8-6

PERFORMANCE SPECIFICATIONS FOR CARE FOR SAMPLE PRODUCT CATEGORIES.

Category	Upholstery	Sheer Curtains[1]	Vocational Apparel[2]	Blankets[2]	Toweling[2]	Regular Apparel[2]
Dimensional Change[3]	5 x 5	3 x 3	—	3.5 x 3.5	10 X 6	variable[4]
Appearance[5]	—	3.0	—	Acceptable	Acceptable	3.5

(From ASTM Recommended Performance Specifications, 1996.)

[1]After 3 dry cleaning cycles.
[2]After 5 laundering cycles.
[3]Length by width, in percentage.
[4]Varies with fabric and product type.
[5]Durable Press Ratings, except where noted.
—Indicates that no recommendation for this combination property and product category was listed.

Table 8-7
MINIMUM PERFORMANCE STANDARDS FOR TWO CATALOG RETAILERS.

Company A

Property	Knit shirts	Woven shirts	Test method
Dimensional Change (washing)	7% x 7%	3% x 3%	AATCC 135, IVA, 3 cycles
Crocking (dry/wet)	4.0/3.0	4.0/3.0	AATCC 8
Colorfastness[1] to			
Washing	3.0	3.5/3.0	AATCC 135, IVA, 1 cycle
Dry cleaning	4.0/3.0	3.5/3.0	AATCC 132
Light (16 hr.)	4.0	4.0	AATCC 16E
Perspiration	4.0/3.0	4.0/3.0	AATCC 15

Company B

Property	Knit shirts	Woven shirts	Test method
Dimensional Change (washing)	7% x 7%	4% x 4%	AATCC 150, 3 cycles
Crocking (dry/wet)	3.5/3.0	3.5/3.0	AATCC 8
Colorfastness[1] to			
Washing	3.5/3.5	3.5/3.5	AATCC 61, 2A
Light (40 AFU)	4.0	4.0	AATCC 16E
Perspiration	3.5	3.5	AATCC 15

These values are company standards, but permission to use the company names was not given.
[1]The first number refers to shade change, the second to staining.

Although most specs are written as minimums, some specs are written as maximums. Each spec needs to be considered for the performance dimension it describes. For example, a minimum spec for colorfastness of 3.5 indicates that the material needs to be at least that fast. A maximum spec for dimensional change of 10 percent indicates that a change greater than 10 percent is not acceptable. Thus, both specs indicate an acceptable level of performance, but understanding what is meant by the level of performance is important in ensuring that consumers expectations are met.

CONCLUSIONS

Performance assessment of materials in terms of appearance retention includes examining the effects of care, the fastness of color and surface finishes to cleaning, and the fastness of color to use and environmental factors. The effect of exposure to light and weather conditions was also explored. These factors are of critical importance in producing products that meet consumer expectations. Far too many products disappoint consumers because they do not withstand cleaning. The failure is often the result of incorrect or unrealistic care labels. In other instances, the product does not maintain an acceptable appearance for a sufficient time period. The procedures discussed help manufacturers and retailers understand the ability of a material to contribute to the performance of a product.

Several basic concepts that are used frequently in material and product evaluation are the use of standard rating scales; tests that expose the material to extreme, accelerated, or normal test conditions; and use of control fabrics to assess exposure conditions.

SUGGESTED READINGS

Adanur, Sabit. (1995). *Wellington Sears Handbook of Industrial Textiles.* Lancaster, PA: Technomic Publishing Company.

American Association of Textile Chemists and Colorists. (1996). *AATCC Technical Manual, 71.* Research Triangle Park, NC: Author.

American Society for Testing and Materials. (1996). *Annual Book of ASTM Standards, Vol. 7.1 & 7.2.* West Conshohocken, PA: Author.

Angliss, Ian. (1991). The Quality of Colour. *Textiles, 20,* 17.

Anon. (1986). Residue Fact Sheet, Newton, IA: Maytag, Consumer Education Department.

Anon. (1994, July). Symbols Improve Communication for Textiles Industry. *ASTM Standardization News, 22,* 19–20.

Anon. (1996, September). Research Committee Highlights. *Textile Chemist and Colorist, 28(9),* 12–18.

Anon. (1997, March). Do Not Let Crockfastness Rub You the Wrong Way—A Study of the Parameters that Affect Pigment Prints. *Textile Chemist and Colorist, 29(3),* 13–15.

Baumert, Karen J., & Patricia Cox Crews. (1996, April). Influence of Household Fabric Softeners on Properties of Selected Woven Fabrics. *Textile Chemist and Colorist, 28(4),* 36–43.

Bellamy, Cindy. (1991). Relationship Between Dyestuff Selection and Garment Performance. In American Association of Textile Chemist and Colorists, *Book of Papers.* Research Triangle Park, NC: Author, pp. 60–64.

Bona, Mario. (1990). *Textile Quality: Physical Methods of Product and Process Control.* Rome: Texilia.

Booth, J. E. (1969). *Principles of Textile Testing.* New York: Chemical Publishing Company.

Bresee, Randall R., Patricia A. Annis, Mary M. Warnock. (1994, January). Comparing Actual Fabric Wear with Laboratory Abrasion and Laundering. *Textile Chemist and Colorist, 26(1),* 17–23.

Brown, Patty. (1992). *Ready-to-Wear Apparel Analysis.* New York: Macmillan.

Ford, J. E. (1993). Textile Product Specifications. *Textiles, 22(3),* 23–25.

Glock, Ruth E., & Grace I. Kunz. (1995). *Apparel Manufacturing: Sewn Products Analysis, 2nd ed.* Englewood Cliffs, NJ: Prentice-Hall.

Gore, Allan E. (1989, March). Testing for Crocking: Some Problems and Pitfalls. *Textile Chemist and Colorist, 21(3),* 17–18.

Hatch, Kathryn L. (1993). *Textile Science.* Minneapolis: West Publishing Company.

Hill, John W. (1984). *Chemistry for Changing Times,* 4th ed. New York: Macmillan.

Hudson, Peyton, Anne C. Clapp, & Darlene Kness. (1993). *Joseph's Introductory Textile Science,* 6th ed. New York: Harcourt Brace Jovanovich.

Ingamells, Wilfred. (1993). *Colour for Textiles: A User's Manual.* Bradford, England: Society of Dyers and Colourists.

Kadolph, Sara J., & Anna I. Langford. (1998). *Textiles,* 8th ed. Englewood Cliffs, NJ: Prentice-Hall.

Keyes, Norma M. (1995, January). Development of a New Test Method: Skewness Change and Garment Twist. *Textile Chemist and Colorist, 27(1),* 27–30.

Kim, Jong-Jun, Hechmi Hamouda, Itzhak Shalev, & Roger L. Barker. (1993, August). Instrumental Methods for Measuring the Surface Frictional Properties of Softener Treated Fabrics. *Textile Chemist and Colorist, 25(8),* 15–20.

Kissa, Erik. (1995, October). Determination of Stain on Carpets. *Textile Chemist and Colorist, 27(10),* 20–24.

Korona, Suzanne Dawn. (1994). An Evaluation of Variables in Accelerated and Home Laundering, *Conference Book of Papers.* Research Triangle Park, NC: American Association of Textile Chemists and Colorists, 78–82.

Ladisch, Christine M., & Shiang-Lan Rau. (1997, April). The Effect of Humidity on the Ozone Fading of Acid Dyes. *Textile Chemist and Colorist, 29(4),* 24–28.

Luo, Cheng, & Randall R. Bresee. (1990, February). Appearance Evaluation by Digital Image Analysis. *Textile Chemist and Colorist, 22(2),* 17–19.

Lyle, Dorothy Siegert. (1977). *Performance of Textiles.* New York: John Wiley & Sons.

McAngus, E. J., & W. W. Adams. (1967–1968). *Physical Textile Testing at Westpoint Pepperell.* Atlanta: Textile Industries.

Mehta, Pradip V. (1992). *An Introduction to Quality Control for the Apparel Industry.* Milwaukee: ASQC Press.

Merkel, Robert S. (1991). *Textile Product Serviceability.* New York: Macmillan.

Minazio, Pier Giorgio. (1995). FAST—Fabric Assurance by Simple Testing. *International Journal of Clothing Science and Technology, 7(2/3),* 43–48.

Morton, W. E., & J. W. S. Hearle. (1993). *Physical Properties of Textile Fibers,* 3rd ed. Manchester, England: Textile Institute.

Obendorf, S. Kay. (1988, May). Electron Microscopical Study of Soiling and Soil Removal. *Textile Chemist and Colorist, 20(5),* 11–15.

Patton, James P. (1989, March). Crock Test Problems Can Be Prevented. *Textile Chemist and Colorist, 21(3),* 13–17.

Price, Arthur, & Allen C. Cohen. (1994). *J. J. Pizzuto's Fabric Science,* 6th ed. New York: Fairchild.

Raheel, Mastura, & Maureen Dever Lien. (1985, May). The Use of Scanning Electron Microscopy for Studying Abrasion Phenomena in Laundered Fabric. *Textile Chemist and Colorist, 17(5),* 101–104.

Reagan, Barbara M., Shailendra Dusaj, Diana G. Johnson, & Diane M. Hodges. (1990, April). Influence of Aftermarket Carpet Protectors on the Soiling, Flammability and Electrical Resistivity of Nylon 6. *Textile Chemist and Colorist, 22(4),* 16–20.

Rucker, James W., Harold S. Freeman, & Whei-Neen Hsu. (1992, October). Evaluation of Factors Contributing to the Light-Induced Yellowing of Whitewashed Denim. Part 2. Effects of Various Treatments on Metal Content and Photoyellowing. *Textile Chemist and Colorist, 24(10),* 21–25.

Textile Institute, The. (1991). *Textile Terms and Definitions,* 9th ed. Manchester, England: Author.

Tortora, Phyllis G., & Robert S. Merkel. (1996). *Fairchild's Dictionary of Textiles,* 7th ed. New York: Fairchild.

Turner, John D. (1995, September). Stain Removal Methods for Washable Cotton and Cotton/Polyester Blend Fabrics. *Textile Chemist and Colorist, 27(9),* 21.

Vigo, Tyrone L. (1994). *Textile Processing and Properties: Preparation, Dyeing, Finishing, and Performance.* Amsterdam, The Netherlands: Elsevier.

Xu, Bugao. (1996, May). An Overview of Applications of Image Analysis to Objectively Evaluate Fabric Appearance. *Textile Chemist and Colorist, 28(5),* 18–23.

Xu, B., & Reed, J. A. (1995). Instrumental Evaluation of Fabric Wrinkle Recovery. *Journal of the Textile Institute, 86(1),* 129–135.

REVIEW QUESTIONS

1. Explain how materials analysis can contribute to the development and confirmation of care label instructions.

2. Describe the important elements of a standard reference scale and the scale's use. Give an example of such a scale.

3. Explain the differences and similarities among color change, staining, and migration.

4. Why is the term dimensional change used to describe material performance?

5. How is dimensional change assessed? Why do some procedures suggest more than one care cycle before dimensional change is assessed?

6. Explain each type of shrinkage listed below.
   a. relaxation shrinkage
   b. residual shrinkage
   c. progressive shrinkage
   d. felting shrinkage
   e. heat shrinkage

7. Why is the performance of some materials assessed for both washing and dry cleaning?

8. Describe the differences between wrinkle recovery and durable press.

9. Identify appearance retention and colorfastness problems that can develop while a material or product is being stored.

10. Identify the processes used to assess material performance for dimensions of performance listed below.
    a. crocking
    b. perspiration
    c. heat
    d. water
    e. acids and alkalis
    f. environmental conditions
    g. light

11. How are control or standard fabrics used in testing for colorfastness to light?

12. Why is weathering resistance important?

13. Select a product and develop appropriate specifications for assessing performance for appearance retention, care, and colorfastness.

ACTIVITIES

1. Review Tables 8-5 and 8-6 and discuss why some performance measures are blank for some product types and suggest why the recommendations differ.

2. Write care, appearance retention, colorfastness, and weather resistance specs for a selected product and target market and explain your choices.

3. Test the performance of a product in the lab in terms of care, appearance retention, colorfastness, and weather resistance and discuss what this would mean to a consumer and how it would affect their satisfaction.

4. Bring in a product that failed in terms of cleaning and discuss why it failed.

5. Visit a testing lab and watch testing for care, appearance retention, colorfastness, and weather resistance. Discuss the process and results with the technicians and managers.

6. Explore the world wide web for information related to cleaning and evaluating materials related to care, appearance retention, colorfastness, and weather resistance. Discuss how the information would be used in materials testing.

7. Read one of these articles (Reagan, Barbara M., Shailendra Dusaj, Diana G. Johnson, & Diane M. Hodges. [1990, April]. Influence of Aftermarket Carpet Protectors on the Soiling, Flammability and Electrical Resistivity of Nylon 6. *Textile Chemist and Colorist, 22(4),* 16–20; Ladisch, Christine M., & Shiang-Lan Rau. [1997, April]. The Effect of Humidity on the Ozone Fading of Acid Dyes. *Textile Chemist and Colorist, 29(4),* 24–28; or Anon. [1997, March]. Do Not Let Crockfastness Rub You the Wrong Way—A Study of the Parameters that Affect Pigment Prints. *Textile Chemist and Colorist, 29(3),* 13–15) and discuss its application in materials testing.

8. Examine catalog copy and store displays for information related to cleaning, appearance retention, colorfastness, and weather resistance. Explain what this information would mean to consumers.

9. Consider the information listed in Table 8-7. Explain what these specs would mean to consumer satisfaction. How would you explain these values to a consumer?

10. Interview consumers regarding their expectations for textile products and their reasons for dissatisfaction. How could these expectations be addressed in quality assurance?

Chapter 9

Specifying and Evaluating Color Requirements

OBJECTIVES

- To understand the basic principles related to light and color theory.

- To understand the concepts involved in color measurement, color matching, and shade sorting.

- To apply those concepts when writing specifications for color, color matching, and shade sorting.

- To interpret color specifications in product development.

- To evaluate materials for adherence to color specifications, using both objective and subjective assessment methods.

KEY TERMS

color	reflection	dimensioning color
wave	refractive index	saturation
wavelength	scattering	hue
frequency	selective spectral absorbers	brightness
amplitude	nonspectral colors	hueless or achromatic colors
visible light	spectral colors	
white light	fluorescence	chromaticity diagrams
infrared region (IR)	trichromatic or tristimulus color perception	CIE
ultraviolet region (UV)		additive color mixing
absorption	color theory	subtractive color mixing
transmission	metamerism	color fidelity
refraction	Bezold effect	color consistency

standardized light source	spectrophotometer	shade sorting
color measurement	colorimetry	CIELAB formula (CIE 1976 L*a*b* formula)
Maxwell triangle	Beer's Law	
spectral locus	color matching	DE or ΔE
color match	computer color match (CCM)	shade bank
spectroscopy	tristimulus colorimeter	strike-off

Color is an immediate and automatic part of our perception of the world. Often color is one of the first characteristics that people use to distinguish one item from another. Color helps people make many decisions throughout the day. The color helps determine the weather (storm clouds), safety issues in terms of driving or crossing the street (red light versus green light), and the flavor of food. For example, what flavor do you expect when you taste hard candy that is purple?

Color also is an important factor in consumer acceptance, demand, and purchase of textile products. Consumers feel strongly about the colors they like, wear, and use in decorating. Use of color makes very personal statements about the individual. Color is such a significant component of fashion that forecasters predict colors that will be in fashion several seasons in the future. Many companies pay for these predictions so that they can apply this information in developing new or modifying old products.

Not only does color attract consumers to products, but it influences them in making purchase decisions. Consumers focus on whether a color is attractive and fashionable, the correct color for a particular need, and consistent throughout the product. Color is one aspect of materials and products that are specified early in the product development process for two reasons. One, color is an important fashion attribute and, two, achieving the correct color is a time-consuming process.

Color consistency is another key element in meeting consumer expectations. Although most consumers would not make a statement to that effect when asked what they look for in a product, lack of consistency is one reason why products are rejected by manufacturers and retailers. Most color consistency problems are addressed by the supplier and manufacturer so that the consumer rarely needs to be concerned with this issue. This chapter focuses on color consistency. Two issues are of importance: producing the color as specified by the designer or product development team and meeting productivity demands in which color matches across a variety of materials within a single product regardless of each individual material's nature, texture, type, or chemical composition.

COLOR

Although it is difficult to define, understand, and measure, **color** is defined as the sensation resulting from the stimulation of the eye's retina by certain wavelengths of light. Light is a form of energy. The wavelengths of light that are absorbed by the retina determine the color that is seen. To perceive the color of an object, light must be reflected from the object. The reflected light is absorbed by the retina. The light energy becomes chemical energy and nerve impulses that carry the information to the brain, where it is interpreted as color. Color therefore depends on the light type, the object, the eye, and the brain.

Color is a physical component of a material that is usually added by dyeing, printing, coating, or painting. Some materials, such as some plastics and some fibers, are colored by incorporating colored pigments as the raw material is processed.

Understanding color assists in developing realistic performance expectations for materials, in writing specifications for color characteristics of materials, and in measuring and evaluating the color of materials and products. However, understanding color also requires some basic knowledge of the physics of energy and wave motion, the physiology of the human eye, and the psychology of perception.

PHYSICS OF LIGHT AND COLOR

Scientists distinguish two methods by which energy can be transported: by the transport of matter and by means of a wave. Wave motion can be demonstrated using a clear bowl partially filled with water. Place the bowl on a light-colored flat surface in bright light. Strike the edge of the bowl with a pencil or drop a small object into the water. Watch for waves that radiate from the area that has been struck or where the object was dropped. A **wave** is a form of energy represented by a series of crests and troughs. Waves can be differentiated by the qualitative characteristic of energy **wavelength** (λ), which is the distance from one crest to the next. Some energy wavelengths are very long and can be measured in meters, kilometers, feet, or miles; others are very short and can be measured in fractions of a meter or an inch. The metric system is most often used to measure wavelengths, so short wavelengths usually are measured as tiny fractions of a meter, such as a nanometer. One nanometer, usually abbreviated as nm, is equal to 1×10^{-9} meter or 0.000000001 meter.

The height of a wave and the number of waves passing over a given point in a unit of time describe a wave's quantitative characteristics. **Frequency** refers to the number of wave crests that pass a given point in one second. Because the speed of light is a universal constant, this means that as frequency increases, wavelength becomes shorter. **Amplitude** is the height of a wave crest. Higher amplitude waves are taller; lower amplitude waves are shorter. Figure 9-1 illustrates several characteristic features of waves.

The electromagnetic spectrum refers to wave energy carried in all directions throughout the universe. It is composed of a continuous range of frequencies and wavelengths of energy. The electromagnetic spectrum is shown in Figure 9-2 and consists of waves ranging in wavelength from very long to very short. All matter receives, absorbs, and radiates these waves, which move at a constant speed of approximately 186,000 miles per second in the vacuum of space. Our perception of objects depends on these waves and the manner in which we interpret them. It is only a narrow range of wavelengths that we perceive as light. See Figure 9-2 to determine where visible light is located in terms of other types of energy. **Visible light** is the portion of the electromagnetic spectrum that stimulates the sense of sight.

The visible part of the spectrum contains the wavelengths that the human eye is able to perceive. Some animals and insects can see wavelengths longer than or shorter than human perception allows. Visible light refers to the range of light wavelengths from 400 to 700 nm. **White light** is defined as light in which all portions or wavelengths of the visible spectrum are present in equal amounts. This definition of white light is an important one to understand in terms of color theory, color perception, and color measurement. Unfortunately, true white light is rare. Natural sunlight and incandescent light are shifted toward yellow. Indirect sunlight and fluorescent lights are shifted toward blue. Thus, our color perception may be shifted in one direction or another depending on the light source. For this reason, it is important to use a consistent light source when viewing and evaluating color.

The concept of color has meaning only in reference to light waves. Without light, people do not perceive color. Notice how dull colors appear at night when light intensity is low. Wavelengths in the **infrared region (IR)** are longer than visible light. This energy is perceived as heat. Wave-

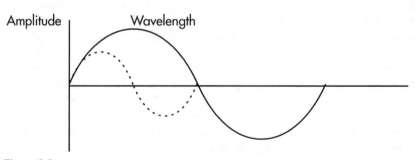

Figure 9-1
Two waves with different wavelengths (λ), frequencies, and amplitudes.

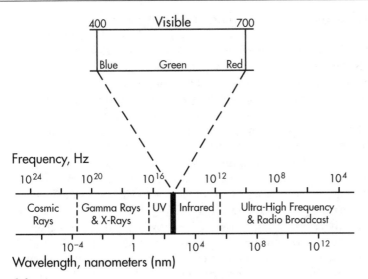

Figure 9-2
The electromagnetic spectrum.

lengths in the **ultraviolet region (UV)** are shorter than visible light. This causes molecular and cell damage. Neither of these two types nor any of the other types of energy are detectable by the human eye as light.

There are three stages in the life of a light beam. It is created by the conversion of matter into energy; the light energy then travels through space; and the light energy is destroyed or converted into another form of energy, such as chemical energy, as it is absorbed by matter. Light energy is created and destroyed only when it interacts with matter. For example, burning gases in the sun create light, while rhodopsin, a chemical in the eye, absorbs the light as it is converted to chemical energy and nerve impulses when we see an object.

Light energy interacts with matter in one of several ways. When light energy strikes an object, the energy is absorbed, transmitted, refracted, or reflected. In **absorption,** the energy is taken in or absorbed by the object. When light energy is absorbed, this energy is converted into another form of energy. Often, it becomes chemical energy, such as what is seen when green plants absorb light energy and produce chlorophyll. Sometimes, if the energy absorbed breaks molecular bonds within the material, light energy results in molecular damage to the object. This can be seen with light tendering of textile materials and the darkening (tanning) and wrinkling of human skin.

In **transmission,** the energy passes through the object with no change in either the energy or the object. Transmission of visible light occurs with transparent or clear objects, such as window glass. When light is transmitted through a clear object, the speed of light decreases. The amount of the decrease depends on the material. In refraction, the path of the light ray is bent as it passes through an object. Most materials that exhibit refraction are transparent in nature. **Refraction** occurs when light crosses the boundary between two different materials and bends because of a change in the speed with which light moves through each material. The **refractive index** is the ratio of the speed of light in space to its speed as it passes through matter. The refractive index of a material will be greater than 1.0. The larger the number, the slower the speed of light in that substance. A classic example of refraction occurs when a pencil is placed in a glass of water. The speed of light differs among the air, the glass, and the water. Thus, the refractive index of each material is different, and the pencil no longer appears as a straight object when viewed as it extends into the water, past the glass, and into the air.

In **reflection,** the direction of the movement of light is changed. The light is bounced or reflected away from the surface of the object. Light can be reflected in a controlled direction, or it can be scattered in many uncontrolled directions. Smooth objects tend to reflect most of the light in one direction. These objects often look shiny because of the higher percentage of light absorbed by the eye that is at essentially the same parallel angle. Rough or irregular objects reflect the light at many different angles. They often look dull or matte because the percentage of light entering the eye is less and the angle of the light varies widely. Figure 9-3 illustrates reflection on smooth and irregular surfaces.

Reflection is the process by which light arrives at the surface of a material and changes direction of travel on impact. If the reflecting surface is smooth, the angle at which the light is bounced back is equal to the angle at which the light arrived at the object's surface. This is referred to as the angle of incidence and is a basic law of physics. The angle of incidence for smooth objects is equal to the angle of reflection. Most light striking the object is bounced back and the object appears bright. Mirrors have a high percentage of light reflected from them, often in the range of 85 percent or higher.

However, most objects, including textile materials, are not perfectly smooth. Even satin fabrics have some irregularity on the surface because

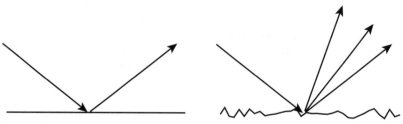

Figure 9-3
Light reflection from a smooth surface (left) and an irregular surface (right).

of the interlacing of yarns. **Scattering** is a special type of reflection in which the angle of reflection is multidirectional. This is usually caused by a rough surface or fine particles embedded in a material, as when bright synthetic fibers are delustered. Titanium dioxide particles are dispersed within the fiber and scatter light, thereby causing the luster or brightness of the fiber to decrease. We see the same thing when a brightly colored material is ground into a fine powder or when it is foggy outside. When the particles are large or when a large number of particles scatter light equally in all directions, the object is perceived as being white. This same principle applies when sunlight passes through a very humid atmosphere or when it is raining. Wavelengths of light in the blue region are scattered more than wavelengths in the red region, and a rainbow appears (see Figure 9-4).

The behavior of light is summarized in Equation 9-1. Incident light striking an object is either transmitted (or refracted), absorbed, reflected, or experiences some combination of these. If the object is opaque, transmission (or refraction) does not occur, and the amount of light transmitted or refracted equals zero.

Equation 9-1

$$I = T + A + R$$

where I is the incident light
T is the light transmitted or refracted
A is the light absorbed
R is the light reflected

Most objects are **selective spectral absorbers.** This means that they do not absorb all the light energy falling on them. They absorb only some wavelengths of the light. It is these selectively absorbed and reflected wavelengths that people see and interpret as colors; different wavelengths produce different color perceptions in the eye and brain.

Each color in the spectrum corresponds to a light wave of a particular wavelength. Longer wavelengths are toward the red end of the spectrum, and shorter wavelengths are toward the blue and violet end of the spectrum. Because the spectrum consists of all wavelengths from the shortest (400 nm) to the longest (700 nm) that the eye can perceive, a prism or rainbow shows a gradual flow from one color to another. However, if you examine a rainbow carefully, you will see that there is no brown or purple in the spectrum. These colors are referred to as **nonspectral colors,** because they do not occur in any natural spectra. A **spectral color** is a color that can be found in a spectrum. Figure 9-5 shows white light divided into the various colored portions of the spectrum. Note that the colors of Figure 9-4 and 9-5 are arranged in the same sequence. Whenever light is scattered or split into separate wavelengths, the shorter wavelengths are bent

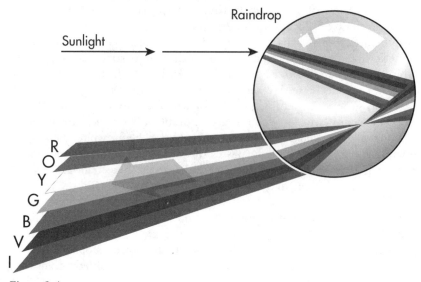

Figure 9-4
The spectrum of visible light.

more than the longer wavelengths. Thus, the resulting spectrum will always show the same arrangement and sequence of colors provided the light was a white light.

Fluorescence is another unique behavior of some compounds in terms of light. Objects that exhibit **fluorescence** emit light with a wavelength approximately 10 to 20 percent longer than the original incident light. Compounds that fluoresce essentially "convert" ultraviolet (UV) to visible light. This characteristic is used in many textiles and household detergents to produce a bright bluish white rather than a more natural, but unacceptable, yellowish white. Our concept of white as a bright, bluish white has been influenced significantly by the use of fluorescing compounds or fluo-

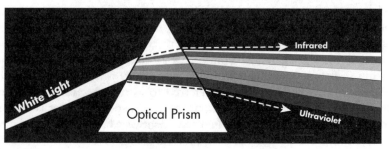

Figure 9-5
A prism will produce a rainbow spectrum from white light.

rescent whitening agents in paper, paint, plastics, fibers, detergents, and other materials.

Physiological Aspects of Color Perception

Only a small portion of the energy that strikes an object is in the visible portion of the spectrum. Of that portion, only a tiny fraction enters the eye to be processed into information regarding the object. The anatomical and physiological systems of the eye process an incredible amount of information from the relatively small amount of data or light energy that it receives.

When light energy is reflected from an object, it enters the eye through the clear cornea, the outer protective surface of the eye that helps focus the image as a result of its curvature and refractive index. From the cornea, the light passes through a transparent and somewhat elastic lens that changes shape slightly to modify the refraction of light and further focus the energy on the retina. The iris expands or contracts to control the amount of light entering the eye through the pupil. That is why in bright daylight the pupil is smaller than when the environment is dark and the amount of light low. The retina around the back of the eyeball contains light sensitive cells or photoreceptors called rods and cones. Nerve cells of the retina join to form the optic nerve that carries or transmits information to the brain.

Photoreceptors in the retina are small cells approximately 4 times the size of a wavelength of light. These cells are the end of the optical system and the beginning of the neural system of the eye. The retina includes two specialized types of cells. The rods are highly sensitive in dim light. These cells contain rhodopsin, which is more sensitive to low-light levels, flicker, and motion. The second type of cells are cones. They are less sensitive to low levels of light, but they provide high acuity and are sensitive to color. The macula is the most sensitive area of the retina in terms of color perception and the ability to perceive fine detail. Cones are concentrated in this central area of the retina. When you look intensely at an object, you concentrate the image on this central area where vision is the sharpest. This area is not useful in dim light, because no rods are present.

The optic nerve gathers neural messages and transports them to the region of the brain called the visual cortex. This is the portion of the brain that interprets the sensation of sight. The image seen is related to the rate at which the rods or cones fire or undergo a brief electric pulse triggered by the light being absorbed. The rate of firing produces a signal that is transmitted cell by cell along a neural pathway. Nerve cells can change the strength of their response charge. Thus, the eye not only processes information, but also works as an optical instrument.

Rhodopsin is a chemical in the eye that responds to light. One portion of this chemical is opsin, which is made up of many amino acids. According to the Young-Helmholtz theory of color vision, three minor variations exist in the cones; each differs in its response to different colors of light. One cone responds primarily to the wavelengths that produce the sensation of red, another to the wavelengths that produce green, and the third to the wavelengths that produce blue. These three types of color receptors are referred to as red (R), blue (B), and green (G). They give rise to the theory of three-color or **trichromatic or tristimulus color perception.** Each type of color receptor differs in its spectral sensitivity functions. In a given region of the spectrum, there must be at least two types of color receptors operating or functioning so that the spectral sensitivity functions differ over that region and produce a trichromatic perception of color. The brain processes this information into the abstraction called color.

Research in human color perception supports this theory of how the eye sees color. Researchers have found that three-colored lights are necessary and sufficient for most individuals to produce a match to a test color. In other words, people who have normal color vision can create any spectral color by using some combination of three-colored lights when they are able to control the amount of each light used. This discovery helps confirm that color is a three-dimensional perceptual phenomena. Thus, in theory, any three spectral colors can be used as primary colors to generate any other spectral color.

Color Theory

Color theory helps us understand the physics of light and energy and the manner in which the eye and brain interact with energy to perceive color. Color theory also explains why color measurement is so critical in terms of quality characteristics, why colors are hard to perceive in low light, and why it is so difficult to achieve a color match among materials of different compositions, types, and densities.

The color a person sees depends on the light source, the colorant used, and the human eye. Color vision or color blindness may restrict the perception of certain colors. When working with different materials, the color of each material may not always match the color of another material. Although both materials may be 100% cotton, the colorant, the preparation or density of the materials, and the way in which light is reflected probably differ. The result is that the two materials have different appearances. **Metamerism** (meh tam´ uhr izm) occurs when the color of two materials match when viewed under one light source, but not when viewed under any other light source.

The **Bezold effect** describes the merging of two or more tiny color areas into one new color. This effect is seen when small-scale prints or yarn-dyed fabrics are viewed from a distance. One does not see each color, but rather a new color that blends the individual colors together. This effect was used by Impressionist painters to create the unique look of their masterpieces. Today, it is used in color printers, such as ink jet printers. This effect is related to the ability of the cones in the eye to differentiate among very tiny objects. However, the cones' ability is limited. Thus, rather than seeing each colored component separately, the eye blends the components so that a person sees a color that is a combination of the two or more colors really present in the object. The Bezold effect occurs with small prints, plaids, and stripes, especially when they are viewed from a distance of several feet or more, and can create great difficulty in human assessment of color matches.

UNDERSTANDING COLOR DIMENSIONS

In trying to understand color, colored objects could be grouped and organized according to some set of criteria based on their colors. For example, all blue objects can be put together and then arranged from those that are the most intense blue to those that are the least intense blue. In addition, colored objects can be arranged from those that are darkest to those that are lightest. If objects are arranged in this fashion in a three-dimensional space, that arrangement could be described as dimensioning color. **Dimensioning color** is creating an arrangement of colors in some systematic method. It is a way of grouping together particular attributes of color. Color dimensions can be described in many different ways using different aspects of color. Color dimensions can be used to imply length, breadth, and thickness. These dimensions can be used to construct a solid three-dimensional body that represents all the possible colors that can be perceived by the human eye. Different color systems use different terms and define the terms differently, but all systems eventually reduce color to three dimensions and define color space by those three dimensions. Color can be described by these three terms: saturation, hue, and intensity.

Saturation is the dimension of color associated with the degree of purity of the light. There are many ways of describing or defining saturation. For example, in a color circle that varies from the least amount of color at its center to the greatest amount of color at its outer edge, saturation would describe the distance a specific color is located from the center of the circle. A saturated color is spectrally pure; it has not been mixed with another wavelength of light. Saturation describes the relative amount of the hue component of the color. For example, a fully saturated red, would be a color that is 100 percent red and that reflects light between 510 and 540 nm. Saturation also may be referred to as intensity, chroma, or grayness. It is the ratio of pure hue to grayness in the appearance of the color. The more saturated a color is, regardless of its hue or value, the more intense, pure, or strong the color appears. The amount of hue a color contains is in proportion to its grayness.

Hue is a qualitative aspect of color that describes pure spectral characteristics. It is the dominant color from within a mixture of wavelengths and is the quality that gives a color its name, such as red, blue, or yellow. The terms chromatic or chromaticity may also be used as a synonym for hue.

Brightness is the total intensity of the light wave. It describes the visual sensation related to the amount of reflected light of a color. Yellow is the lightest of the hues, with a corresponding high-reflectance value. Blue is the darkest of the hues, with a corresponding low-reflectance value. Blue darkens quickly to black, whereas yellow and orange are capable of enormous variations from pale tans all the way to very dark browns. The term value may be used as a synonym for brightness, which describes the amount of white or black added to a color. Monochromatic color schemes work with a single hue of varying values or varying amounts of white or black added to a color to change its brightness.

Whites, grays, and blacks, which may be thought of as desaturated versions of any color, are considered a part of most color systems. Most professionals who work with color describe the difficulty in matching whites and blacks when working with materials. Some whites, grays, and blacks are referred to as **hueless, or achromatic, colors** because they include no hue characteristic. The gray scales described in Chapter 8 are examples of achromatic colors. The distinction of the grays on a gray scale are a continuum from white to black that varies by brightness only.

THE INTERNATIONAL COMMISSION ON ILLUMINATION (CIE)

An international group of scientists belong to the International Commission on Illumination, which has studied the phenomena of color because of its importance in science, engineering, art, and industry. This organization is often referred to as the **CIE** (from the initials of the French version of its name, Commission Internationale de l'Eclairage). The CIE has defined three dimensions of color that it calls X, Y, and Z. The CIE system is based on the amount of a standard red (X), green (Y), and blue (Z) that would be needed to make a color match. Its selection of these dimensions is based on the trichromatic color theory already discussed.

Because it is simpler to use proportions of colors rather than actual amounts of color, the letters x, y, and z are used. Note that the difference between the two sets of dimensions is that upper case is used for one and lower case is used for the other. In this approach, x + y + z must total to one. This allows color to be reduced to two dimensions (x & y) into what are referred to as chromaticity diagrams or charts. Two-dimensional **chromaticity diagrams** make it easy to represent color in paper form, because pages in books are essentially two-dimensional objects. The problems with these charts are that light and dark colors of the same chromaticity are located at the same point, but are distinguished their Y values. In other words, if a chart were created with a different Y value for each page, light and dark values of the same chromaticity or hue would occur at the same location on different pages from the front cover of the book to its back cover. This two-dimensional system is used internationally in business, industry, and commerce to measure, describe, define, and identify color.

ADDITIVE COLOR MIXING

Additive mixing of colors adds wavelengths of light (colors) to create other colors. This system works primarily with monochromatic light sources, such as those used in the theater to light the stage, set the mood, or highlight stage characters. Primary colors in the additive system are red, green, and blue. When all three primary colors are combined in equal amounts, they produce white (see Figure 9-6). The absence of all three primary colors produces black. Secondary colors (yellow, magenta, and cyan) are created using equal combinations of two of the three primary colors. Tertiary colors are created by combining one primary and one secondary color (i.e., unequal amounts of two primary colors are added to produce a tertiary color). Additive mixing is used to create color on computer screens, television programs, and video images.

SUBTRACTIVE COLOR MIXING

Subtractive mixing of colors removes one or more colors from light to create other colors. A color is removed when a wavelength or band of wavelengths are absorbed by an object. The subtractive system works with objects whose surfaces absorb (remove) selected wavelengths of light incident on the object. Primary colors are yellow, magenta, and cyan. All three primary colors are combined in equal amounts to create black (see Figure 9-7). The absence of all three primary colors produces white. Secondary colors (red, blue, and green) are created using equal combinations of two of the three primary colors. Tertiary colors are created by combining one primary and one secondary color or by combining unequal amounts of two primary colors. Subtractive color mixing is used in applying color to most opaque objects, including fibers, plastics, and metal, and in dyeing and printing, and publishing.

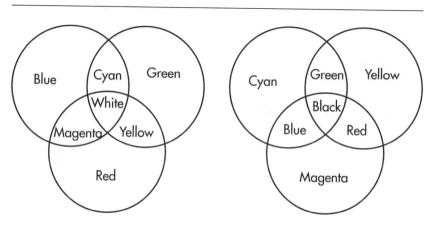

Figure 9-6 (Left)
Additive color mixing.

Figure 9-7 (Right)
Subtractive color mixing.

APPLICATION TO MATERIALS

The pigment or colorant used to color an object does not create or produce light, but absorbs light in a selective fashion. Subtractive mixing is used in the dyeing and printing of textiles and other opaque objects. Generally a material is dyed or printed to match a reference material that illustrates the desired color. Reference material provides the dye chemist or printer with a specific target toward which to work. It is important to recognize that when colorants are applied to textiles, the colorant changes the material's reflection properties. Specific colors are often achieved by using mixtures of colorants. This allows the dye chemist or printer to achieve a specific color without investing in a huge inventory of dyes or pigments. Unfortunately, use of mixtures also makes it more challenging to dye to shade or print to shade if another batch of materials of the same color is needed.

When a designer creates a product using a CAD system, the colors on the screen are produced through additive mixing. However, when the printed hard copy version of the image is made, the printer uses the subtractive system. No current software program accurately converts from one system to the other. Thus, the color seen on the screen may differ significantly from the color of the printed version. The same problem may occur when film or video images are made of real objects. The colors may not always be true. **Color fidelity** or color trueness between an image created using one color mixing system and an image created using the other system may not be a good match.

When materials are dyed or printed, the requirements for **color consistency or matching** to the standard or specification are high. This is especially true as demand for higher productivity and quality increases. For example, the demand for color consistency is higher when multiple plies or layers of material are cut at one time rather than just one or two.

Both additive and subtractive color mixing theories are equally important in terms of color perception, but subtractive color mixing is more important in color reproduction. Both theories continually interact, because light is the means by which people see color and opaque objects exhibit selective spectral absorption. It is this interaction between the two theories of color mixing that creates some of the most profound difficulties in duplicating color and achieving good color fidelity.

STANDARD LIGHT SOURCES

When an observer sees an object that is colored, the color that is actually seen depends on the light source. Thus, a **standardized light source** is necessary to work with color in a consistent and predictable manner. The CIE has considered this issue for decades and has selected several standard-

Table 9-1
STANDARD LIGHT SOURCES.

Type	Name	Characteristics
Ordinary incandescent light	Light source A CIE Illuminant A (CIE ILL A)	Light from a 500-W tungsten filament light bulb Strong in red, orange, and infrared
Noon sunlight	Light source B CIE Illuminant B (CIE ILL B)	Typifies the wavelength composition of direct sunlight at noon Strong in yellow
Average daylight	Light source D CIE Illuminant D (CIE ILL D)	Typifies average daylight over the range of 380–830 nm Replaces CIE Illuminant C (average daylight) Strong in blue

ized light sources. These sources are used because they are close replications of natural sunlight, they represent commonly used artificial light sources, or they produce something approximating pure white light. No single light source is considered perfect for all applications and end uses, but, different sources satisfy different industry and research needs. Selected standard light sources are identified in Table 9-1, and their spectra are diagrammed in Figure 9-8.

COLOR MEASUREMENT

Color measurement is the process of assigning numerical values to a color so that it can be assigned a specific location in a three-dimensional color solid. Thus, it is a means of describing color as a set of numbers. Color measurement, which can be done with the trained human eye or with instruments that assess color in three or more dimensions, assists in color matching and shade sorting. Many different instruments and systems may be used in this complex process, which is necessary because of the economic impact when colors are not as specified and do not match other materials to be used in the same products. Color measurement determines the specific colors of goods, but we need to know the process and theoretical system that will be used and the degree of accuracy and precision that are needed. How do we decide when a very small difference is critical and when a large difference would be acceptable?

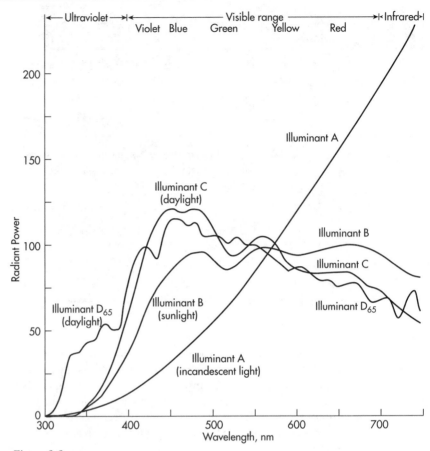

Figure 9-8
The spectrum of selected standard light sources.

THEORETICAL BASIS

In 1931 the CIE met to begin developing a three-dimensional coordinate system of color that eventually came to be called a chromaticity diagram. Chromaticity diagrams are based on an understanding of how the human eye sees color and on how color has been dimensionalized with the Munsell and other systems. The trichromatic or tristimulus system is based on the **Maxwell triangle.** In this right-angle triangle, the points represent the primary additive colors and the space enclosed represents all colors that can be mixed from monochromatic lights of these primary colors. The triangle, shown in Figure 9-9, is named after Scottish physicist James Clerk Maxwell.

Chromaticity coordinates theoretically describe light, but often they are used to characterize a colored surface, as with manufactured goods. These

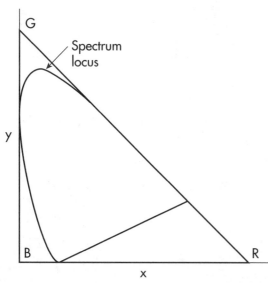

Figure 9-9
Maxwell's triangle.

coordinates refer to the light reflected by the surface of the object when it is illuminated by a standardized light source. The coordinates work with CIE XYZ tristimulus values, where X represents red, Y represents green, and Z represents blue, and x, y, and z are the relative proportions or fractional amounts of red, green, and blue needed to produce a specific color.

This approach led to the CIE Chromaticity Diagram. The diagram is often referred to as a tongue-shaped diagram. It uses imaginary primary colors and includes the gamut of real colors produced by mixing the imaginary primary colors. It represents both spectral and nonspectral colors. Maxwell's triangle encompasses the CIE diagram. The top represents greens, the bottom left blues, and the bottom right reds.

If the pure spectral colors from red to violet are plotted, they form a curve called the **spectral locus.** The curved line represents the chromaticities of all colors produced by monochromatic light. The wavelength scale can be located along the curved edge. The bottom straight edge connects red and blue and is called the purple line. (Remember, purple is a nonspectral color.) The location of any single point indicates something about the saturation of a perceived color. The closer a color is to the spectrum locus, the lower its saturation. Zero saturation (white) is located in the center of the diagram.

In most instances, absolute brightness of a color is of less interest than hue and saturation, so one of the three coordinates can be eliminated. The remaining two coordinates (x and y) may be plotted on a two-dimensional diagram, better known as a chromaticity diagram, where each point in the x-y plane is a unique color.

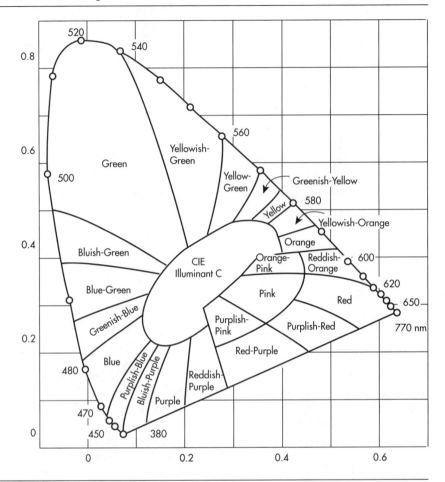

Figure 9-10
The CIE Chromaticity Diagram.

When two colors are mixed, a straight line connecting the two points identifies all possible colors resulting from the mixture, with different points along the line representing different ratios of each of the two colors. The straight line connecting the red and violet ends of the curve are nonspectral purples and constitute the outer boundaries of the diagram. The outer edge represents the saturated colors; inner portions are less saturated.

APPLICATION

Color measurement is usually correlated with one of the visual color systems that is based on the concept of three dimensions of color. The aim of color measurement is to improve the ability to predict the color sensations of the average viewer. The reason for measuring is to determine if the colors will be perceived as a match by the average consumer.

What do we mean when we say that a color matches? A **color match** occurs when both objects produce identical or near identical sensations. A color match is related to the light source, the visual or detection system (the eye or instrument), the nature and absorbing power of the colorant and the nature of the substrate, and the scattering properties of both the colorant and the substrate. For textile materials, scattering is significantly related to the fiber type and the structural nature of the fiber, yarn, and fabric.

Metamerism is a common problem with color matching. When metamerism occurs, two materials may produce the same visual perception under one light source, but a quite different sensation under another light source. To consumers this might appear as a match of materials in the store under fluorescent lights, but these same materials do not match when viewed under natural sunlight or incandescent light. A good example of a metameric color match occurs when materials match under natural daylight, but look quite different under the lights in many parking lots.

Human Perception

Several devices are used to measure color. One of the most common is the human eye. For human assessment to be reliable and precise, the light source and angle of viewing must be standardized. Even so, results depend on the individual. Human judgment tends to be conservative; judges are more likely to reject goods that would be acceptable to the average individual. The training that is required to produce a reliable judge can be significant, but, when instrument readings are questioned, it is the human eye that casts the final vote in determining the acceptability of colored materials.

Gray scales have been developed to have nearly identical intervals between the steps of each scale. These scales were discussed in Chapter 8. They are used by human judges to assess changes in color that occur when materials are used or exposed to environmental factors. The results obtained by using these scales tend to be somewhat subjective in nature, but the subjectivity can be decreased with better-trained raters and standardized light sources and procedures. These scales are difficult for untrained people to use, because most people are not comfortable with reducing color to light-dark or brightness dimensions.

Instruments

A common method for measuring color uses an instrument, such as a spectrophotometer, that has been specially designed for the purpose. **Spectroscopy** is the study of the emission and absorption of light and other portions of the electromagnetic spectrum. The production and analysis of the spectrum uses a light source that strikes the object, a disperser to differentiate wavelengths, a detector to sense the presence of light when it appears after the dispersion, and a recorder to make a temporary or permanent copy of the selected spectrum. A **spectrophotometer** measures the percentage of light transmitted or reflected at each wavelength in the visible spectrum by a colored surface. Each spectrum that is produced is specific to the colorant or mixture of colorants used in the object. Figure 9-10 shows fingerprint

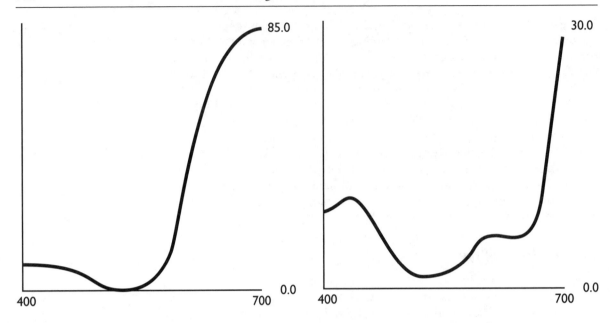

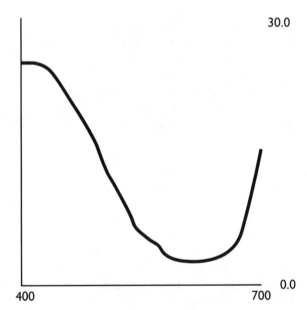

Figure 9-11
Fingerprint spectra for dyes.

spectra for specific dyes. The curve may be broad or narrow and may have one or more peaks depending on the colorant. The shape of the spectrum produced describes the color in a two-dimensional plot. Individuals experienced in reading these spectra can describe the color based on the wavelength locations of the peaks and their height and width.

Colorimetry acts on the subtractive principle, by which color is determined by the absorption or subtraction of light from an initially white beam of light. **Colorimetry** describes the measurement of color. A colorimeter usually is less expensive and slightly less accurate than a spectrophotometer. Often colorimeters are described as tristimulus because they have three sensors (red, green, and blue), while spectrophotometers may have somewhere between three and sixteen. Both instruments often include a computer program that calculates the degree of color matching based on various theoretical approaches to color measurement and assessment of color matches. After the operator selects an appropriate set of coordinates and a specific theoretical system, the colorimeter will perform the calculations. Many colorimeters also allow the operator to establish tolerances, or define a range of acceptable differences in terms of color match.

Colorimetry of this type is referred to as absorptiometric colorimetry because it measures the energy absorbed. It summarizes the work of several scientists, particularly Bouger (1929), Lambert (1760), and Beer (1852). **Beer's Law,** or the Lambert-Beer Law, states that the absorption of light in passage through any medium is proportional to the number of absorbing molecules in its path. Equation 9-2 is a mathematical representation of this law that is used to calculate $\log (I_O/I_T)$ as a convenient and practical measurement of absorption. Beer's Law is usually applied to such liquids as dyes, but it also relates to colored objects using the more complex phenomena of diffuse reflection, which is a special aspect of scattering. Table 9-2 reports the wavelengths absorbed by hue, the hue of the absorbed light, and the perceived hue for the full spectrum of visible light.

Equation 9-2

$$log\,(I_O/I_T)\ =\ elc$$

where I_O = the intensity of the original light
I_T = the intensity of the light leaving the medium
e = the molecular coefficient (a constant)
l = the thickness of the absorbing medium
c = the molar concentration of the absorbing substance

Greater advances have been made in the instrumental measurement of color than in the quantification of average color perceptions. Instrumental measurement is very important in industries, such as the textile industry complex, in which colorants are produced or used and where quality control of colored goods is critical.

Table 9-2
RELATIONSHIP BETWEEN ABSORBED WAVELENGTH OF STANDARD LIGHT AND HUE.

Absorbed Wavelength in nm	Hue of Absorbed Light	Perceived Hue
400–440	violet	greenish-yellow
440–480	blue	yellow
480–510	blue-green	orange
510–540	green	red
540–570	yellow-green	purple
570–580	yellow	blue
580–610	orange	greenish-blue
610–700	red	blue-green

COLOR MATCHING

In color matching, the main goal is to identify the point at which two materials produce a sufficiently similar visual sensation for the two colors to appear identical to the average individual. **Color matching** is the process of developing a formula to reproduce a color as many sequential times as needed, such as for reorders or carry-overs from one season to another. Color duplication is required when designers submit a color swatch or when coordinating fabrics or other materials are specified. Color matching may be done during product development or production or it may be done by suppliers. It ensures that the color specified by the designer or product development team is the color that will be used during production. In addition, color matching ensures that the various materials combined in a product produce the same visual sensation when viewed under a single light source.

Instrumental color formulation, also known as **computer color matching (CCM),** is the most successful commercial application of color science. A numerical method is used to define the color sensation caused by the reference material when viewed under standard conditions. CCM provides a rapid assessment of many possibilities in a short time period by using several combinations of colorants. The process uses a technique that evaluates all possible combinations of dyes or pigments until a combination is found that gives an almost perfect, or best possible, match. The technique requires a significant investment in capital and labor, as well as constant updating because fabrications and colorants change.

The **tristimulus colorimeter** was designed to respond to spectral distributions of light in the same manner as the human eye (see Figure 9-12).

Figure 9-12
A tristimulus colorimeter (left) and a spectrophotometer (top). Color measurement application (bottom left and right). (*Courtesy of HunterLab.*)

It provides rapid and precise measurements at a relatively low cost and makes it possible to quantify color differences. If two specimens have the same tristimulus value, they will be perfectly matched if standard observer, source, and viewing geometry do not change. Conversely, if any tristimulus value is different, the objects will not match and the overall difference will be at least a rough measure of the perceived color difference between them. Differences between similar colors can be determined by considering the XYZ values as coordinates in a three-dimensional color space.

Color differences are determined by a formula, of which several versions are in use. A simplified version—the **CIELAB formula** or the **CIE 1976 L*a*b* formula**—is based on the CIE color space shown in Figure 9-13. In this color space, L* refers to the lightness-darkness dimension, a* refers to the redness-greenness dimension, and b* refers to the yellowness-blueness dimension. L* has values ranging from 0 (black) to 100 (white); a* ranges from negative values (green) to positive values (red), and b* ranges from negative values (blue) to positive values (yellow).

The formula for color difference is recommended for use with textiles, paints, and plastics, and is used to match colors for materials needed in tex-

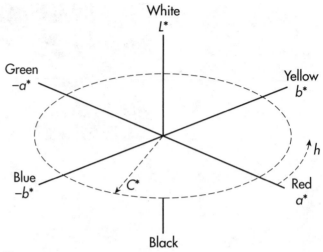

Figure 9-13
The CIE color space.

tile products, such as coatings for zippers, plastic buttons, and textile materials. The CIE formula allows the calculations of color differences from two sets of tristimulus values (XYZ). One set represents the standard color to be matched and the other set represents the specimen that is being evaluated. The CIELAB formula is used in many fields to determine differences in surface colors and work with perceived colors. Fortunately, colorimeters do the elaborate calculations automatically, so we simply have to know which equation is being used and why it was selected.

However, match predictions are not as easy to do as this discussion implies. Fiber-dye interactions have a major impact on the color sensation produced. The dyer needs access to a large library, with most variables present, to develop a good match to a preferred color. With computer color matching, the computer can perform this assessment quickly and accurately, but the operator needs to establish appropriate parameters and measures of quality in order for the system to work properly and efficiently.

SHADE SORTING

Shade sorting, which is the physical grouping of materials by color, is a regular part of quality assurance in most dyeing and printing facilities. It ensures that all fabric of one color purchased by a manufacturer matches. Thus, when fabric is spread in layers before product parts are cut out, there is less concern that parts from different layers will not match when sewn into a completed product. Each piece forming the lay has been accepted as a good commercial color match compared with the appropriate standard.

Visual shade sorting is time consuming and visual sorters generally "play it safe" by rejecting goods that probably are acceptable. As a result computer shade sorting, which identifies small segments of color volumes that would look the same to the average human eye, is becoming more common. These color volumes can be of any shape, but most are one of the shapes represented in Figure 9-14: cubic, rhombic dodecahedrons, or truncated octahedrons. Several different systems are used. One common system, the 555 system, uses a three-digit shade numbering system. The first five refers to the lightness-darkness dimension, the second five the redness-greenness dimension, and the final five the yellowness-blueness dimension. A color within the 555 space is an appropriate match to the standard and a number just outside, such as a 655 or a 545, is a just noticeable noncolor match in the dimension in which the difference occurs. For example, a sample with a 655 rating is just slightly lighter in color than the standard, or one tolerance unit outside the standard in the lightness dimension. See Figure 9-15 for an illustration of the 555 shade numbering system.

Another approach is the CCC (Clemson Color Cluster) system that works with the CIELAB formula and corrects some of the more pronounced problems associated with the 555 system. In particular, the CCC system is more flexible, so that fewer subgroups describing acceptable color match can be developed and color consistency within a matched subgroup can be adjusted so that all colors match.

STANDARD PROCEDURES

Two standard procedures have been developed in terms of color measurement. AATCC 6, Instrumental Color Measurement, covers three aspects of color measurement: reflectance, transmission, and calculations. In the reflectance measurement procedure, an opaque or nearly opaque material is measured by means of reflectance to obtain a numerical representation of the color of a specimen. Careful attention to equipment setup, use of standardized light sources, and preparation of and presentation of the specimen must be addressed. Color transmission most often is used for measuring solutions of dyes, rather than the color of a finished material. This procedure describes the equations used in calculating color and color differences, but the operator rarely needs to perform the calculations. Most instruments currently in use for color measurement perform this function.

Because the CIELAB formula does not always produce color difference values that correlate well with visual assessments, a modified formula can be used. Figure 9-16 illustrates the distortion that occurs with the CIELAB formula. AATCC 173, CMC: Calculation of Small Color Differences for Acceptability, is a standard procedure. CMC refers to the Colour Measurement Committee of a British organization, The Society of Dyers and Colourists, that developed the modification. The equation is used to

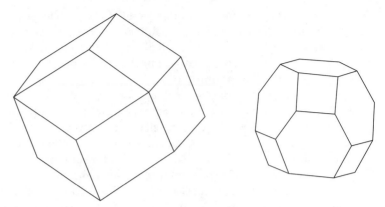

Figure 9-14
Examples of acceptable color match shapes.

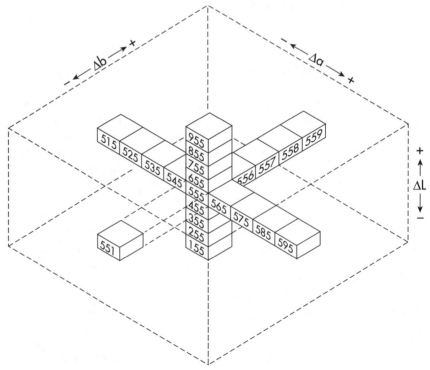

Figure 9-15
The "555" three-digit shade numbering system.

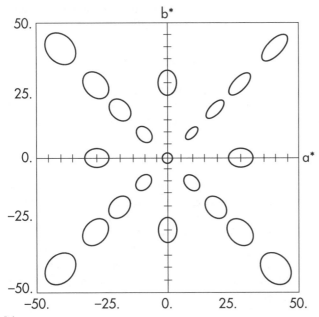

Figure 9-16

CMC (2:1) sections of acceptance volumes in CIE L*a*b* color space (shown 5 times actual size). If CIELAB were uniform, the shapes would be equal-sized circles. *(Reprinted with permission from the American Association of Textile Chemists and Colorists, P.O. Box 12215, Research Triangle Park, NC 27709.)*

calculate the color difference between a specimen and a color standard in a more nearly uniform color space. This allows for the use of a single number to determine color match and tolerances for materials.

The difference between the standard and the specimen is often referred to as delta E (ΔE, or DE) which signifies "difference in" and comes from the German Empfindung, meaning "sensation." **DE** or **ΔE** is a single number that defines the total color difference between the standard and the specimen. For example, a DE of 1.0 would define a volume of acceptable color. Any color difference greater than 1.0 would not be acceptable.

APPLICATION WITHIN PRODUCTS, PRODUCTION LOTS, AND COORDINATE PRODUCTS

Expectations for color match are highest within a single product because materials are usually in a similar orientation, connected in the same plane, and located directly next to each other. As a result of this close proximity, the eye is able to detect the smallest differences between the two portions of fabric or other materials. Greater differences tend to be tolerated when the materials differ in texture, weight, type, or reflectance characteristics.

However, color differences that are acceptable between garments are generally greater than acceptable color differences within a product. Thus, the range of acceptable color differences between parts of a product joined by a seam are expected to be minimal. When parts are joined by a seam, the eye is able to detect a much narrower color difference than when another color is imposed between two materials of the same color. For example, wider color variation is tolerated when the top of one color with a ribbed band of another color is combined with a pair of shorts of the first color. Slightly higher tolerances may exist in production lots of the same material because identical products are not likely to be used directly next to each other.

In coordinating products, the requirements are dependent on how close to each other coordinates are expected to be used. For example, if coordinates are expected to overlap on slightly different planes, such as with a top worn over a pair of pants, the color match can be slightly less strict than when two materials are connected across a seam. When coordinating colors are present in a print and a solid color, the color match can be less strict. When two prints are used in coordinates, the color match can be even less perfect.

Materials and Specifications

Material specifications for color match to standard might state something on the order of "the color of each material should be within the shade bank." **Shade bank** is a range of acceptable color shades for one color, such as classic navy blue, that has been sorted from lightest to darkest, greatest hue to least hue, or most saturated to least saturated. Shade banks usually consist of actual swatches of material so that texture and reflectance characteristics are included in the assessment. A shade bank usually implies that human assessment will determine the acceptability of a material.

Color match requirements within a product are often stated as "no objectionable shading" or "no mismatch among components." Sometimes, an acceptable DE of 1.0, or some other value, is specified. Color match requirements for a color specified by a designer or product development team often use the same or similar terminology.

The actual color that is required can be identified by a supplier's number or name designator or by supplying a physical sample of the material (although that material may not be a textile). For example, a piece of rock, wood, or other natural material might be used. In some cases, a textile swatch is provided, but the swatch usually differs in texture, weight, or fiber content from that of the desired material. In addition, some colors are described by referring to the color in a well-known color system, such as the Munsell System, or a published color atlas, as one of the PANTONE® publications (see Figure 9-17).

Hue
Colors of various hues are located at different angles on a circle around the neutral axis, with red as the starting point.

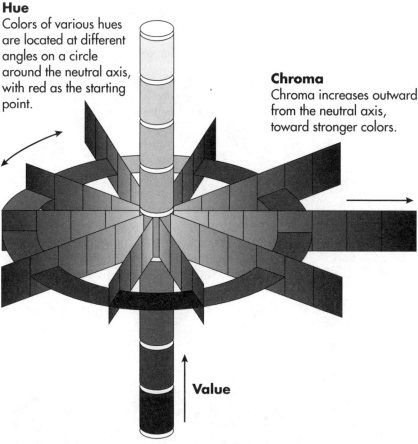

Chroma
Chroma increases outward from the neutral axis, toward stronger colors.

Value

Figure 9-17
The Munsell color system is used to specify the color of materials.

Specifications that are based on color systems or color atlases often identify the color by its numerical or alphanumerical description. For example, in the Munsell system, a color might be specified as hue 7.5 PB, value 4/, and chroma /12; this is written as 7.5 PB 4/12. Using the PANTONE Textile Color System®, a color might be specified as 11 for lightness-darkness, 52 for color, and 30 for saturation; this is written as 11-5230. When specs are written in this manner, the dyeing or printing facility needs access to the particular system or atlas used in defining a color. With some firms, once a dyeing or printing facility has produced a sample of the color or pattern in the correct fabrication, a **strike-off** or sample of the dyed or printed material is sent to the designer or product development team to be sure that the color is a good match.

Even though a color is specified, most firms do not specify the dye class or pigment type that should be used to achieve it. Designers and

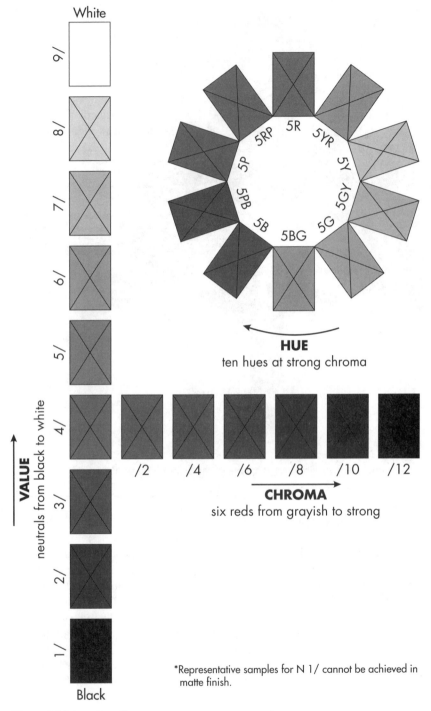

White

9/

8/

7/

6/

5/

4/

VALUE
neutrals from black to white

3/

2/

1/

Black

HUE
ten hues at strong chroma

5RP 5R 5YR

5P 5Y

5PB 5GY

5B 5G

5BG

/2   /4   /6   /8   /10   /12

CHROMA
six reds from grayish to strong

*Representative samples for N 1/ cannot be achieved in matte finish.

Figure 9-17 (continued)

product development teams usually leave that determination to the dyeing or printing firm. However, some firms do specify the use of a particular dye class, such as reactive dyes, or restrict the use of a particular dye class, such as sulfur dyes. These specifications could reflect a particular set of fastness requirements needed for the material, a special pureness or intensity of color desired, or a potential for tendering that may occur. Even when firms specify a dye class, they do not identify the specific dye that should be used to achieve a specific color. The major exceptions are specs that require the use of indigo, a vat dye, for some denims. In this situation, indigo produces a combination of color and performance characteristics, known as frosting, that is difficult to duplicate with other dye classes.

CONCLUSIONS

Color is a difficult attribute of a material to measure. Such measurement requires an understanding of how the color of an object is perceived and processed by the eye. Instruments used to assess color simulate human perception of color so that judgments and measures reflect human assessments and perceptions.

Color specifications describe the color desired in the materials by numerical descriptions, color swatches, material samples, or the style or color number used by a supplier. Many companies evaluate the degree to which materials meet specifications by a visual comparison to a standard using a shade bank to determine the acceptable range of colors. Instrumental assessment is also used to identify color matches in terms of the acceptable maximum difference between the standard and the material specimen.

As a result of this emphasis on producing the right color, shade sorting, and color matching, fewer materials and finished products are rejected on the basis of color. This means higher productivity rates, better quality merchandise, higher profits, fewer reworks, and fewer seconds. This also means fewer problems with pollution because fewer redyeings will be required. Doing things right the first time is a common quality assurance goal among many dyeing and printing facilities.

SUGGESTED READINGS

Albers, J. (1975). *The Interaction of Color.* New Haven, CT: Yale University Press.

Agoston, G. (1987). *Color Theory and Its Application in Art and Design.* New York: Springer-Verlag.

American Apparel Manufacturers Association Technical Advisory Committee. (No date). *Instrumental Shade Sorting.* Arlington, VA: American Apparel Manufacturers Association.

American Apparel Manufacturers Association Technical Advisory Committee. (No date). *Piece Goods Shading.* Arlington, VA: American Apparel Manufacturers Association.

American Association of Textile Chemists and Colorists. (1989). *Color Measurement Principles and the Textile Industry.* Research Triangle Park, NC: Author

American Association of Textile Chemists and Colorists. (1983). *Practical Applica-*

tions of Color Control. Research Triangle Park, NC: Author

American Association of Textile Chemists and Colorists. (1984). *Color Measurement Principles and the Textile Industry*. Research Triangle Park, NC: Author

American Association of Textile Chemists and Colorists. (1996). *AATCC Technical Manual, 71*. Research Triangle Park, NC: Author.

Aspland, J. R. (1993, November). Chapter 15: Color, Color Measurement and Control. *Textile Chemist and Colorist, 25(11)*, 34–42.

Aspland, J. Richard, Christine W. Jarvis, & James P. Jarvis. (1987, September). A Comparison of Four Approaches to Shade Sorting. *Textile Chemist and Colorist, 19(9)*, 67–68.

Bellamy, Cindy. (1991). Relationship Between Dyestuff Selection and Garment Performance. In American Association of Textile Chemist and Colorists, *Book of Papers*. Research Triangle Park, NC: Author, pp. 60–64.

Birren, F. (1982). *Light, Color, and Environment*. New York: Van Nostrand Reinhold.

Birren, F. (1980). *The Textile Colorist*. New York: Van Nostrand Reinhold.

Bona, Mario. (1990). *Textile Quality: Physical Methods of Product and Process Control*. Rome: Texilia.

Broadbent, Arthur D. (1994, March). Colorimetry: Part 1. Factors Involved in the Perception and Measurement of Colour. *Canadian Textile Journal, 111(2)*, 15–18.

Broadbent, Arthur D. (1994, May). Colorimetry: Part 2. The CIE Standard Observers and Calculation of Tristimulus Value. *Canadian Textile Journal, 111(4)*, 16–19.

Broadbent, Arthur D. (1994, June). Colorimetry: Part 3. The CIE X-Y-Z System and the y-x Chromaticity Diagram. *Canadian Textile Journal, 111(5)*, 18–21.

Broadbent, Arthur D. (1994, October/November). Colorimetry: Part 4. The CIELAB Colour Space. *Canadian Textile Journal, 111(7)*, 19–22.

Broadbent, Arthur D. (1995, April/May). Colorimetry: Part 5. Colour Difference Measurement and Their Use. *Canadian Textile Journal, 112(3)*, 14–18.

Brown, Patty. (1992). *Ready-to-Wear Apparel Analysis*. New York: Macmillan.

Celikiz, G. & R. Kuehni. (ed.). (1983). *Color Technology in the Textile Industry*. Research Triangle Park, NC: American Association of Textile Chemists and Colorists.

Chong, Patrick Tak Fu. (1996). Colorimetry for Textile Applications. In Raheel, Mastura. (ed.). *Modern Textile Characterization Methods*. New York: Marcel Dekker, pp. 355–392.

Constant, F. Woodbridge. (1967). *Fundamental Principles of Physics*. Reading, MA: Addison-Wesley.

Dittman, Richard, & Glenn Schmieg. (1979). *Physics in Everyday Life*. New York: McGraw-Hill.

Friedenberg, Ed. (1994, February). Cottech Conference Focuses on: Ecological Concerns, Quality. *Knitting Times, 35–36*, 38.

Gardner, Dennis. (1993, August). How to Select On-line Color Measurement. *Textile World, 143*, 86–87.

Glock, Ruth E., & Grace I. Kunz. (1995). *Apparel Manufacturing: Sewn Products Analysis, 2nd ed*. Englewood Cliffs, NJ: Prentice-Hall.

Gohl, E. P. G., & L. D. Vilensky. (1980). *Textile Science*. Melbourne, Australia: Longman Cheshire.

Harold, Richard W. (1987, December). Textiles: Appearance Analysis and Shade Sorting. *Textile Chemist and Colorist, 19(12)*, 23–31.

Harold, Richard W., & Gerald M. Kraal. (1996). Color: Control It in Production and Protect It in Court. *Textile Chemist and Colorist, 25*, 11–16.

Hatch, Kathryn L. (1993). *Textile Science*. Minneapolis: West Publishing Company.

Hudson, Peyton, Anne C. Clapp, & Darlene Kness. (1993). *Joseph's Introductory Textile Science*, 6th ed. New York: Harcourt Brace Jovanovich.

Ingamells, Wilfred. (1993). *Colour for Textiles: A User's Manual*. Bradford, England: Society of Dyers and Colourists.

Johnston, Chap, Al Joyner, & Rick Jarvis. (1993, December). Improving Quality Through Color Inventory. In *Proceedings from the Apparel Research Conference*, Atlanta.

Kadolph, Sara J., & Anna I. Langford. (1998). *Textiles*, 8th ed. Englewood Cliffs, NJ: Prentice-Hall.

Kuehni, R. G. (1983). *Color: Essence and Logic*. New York: Van Nostrand Reinhold.

Kuppers, H. (1972). *Color: Origin, Systems, Uses*. New York: Van Nostrand Reinhold.

MacAdam, D. L. (1981). *Color Measurement: Theme and Variations*. New York: Springer-Verlag.

March, Robert H. (1970). *Physics for Poets*. New York: McGraw-Hill.

Martin, Jimmy R. (1991). Dyeing Machines for Dyeing Garments: Not Just Adding

Color. In American Association of Textile Chemist and Colorists, *Book of Papers*. Research Triangle Park, NC: Author, pp. 276–277.

McGregor, Ralph. (1985, January). Coloration of Textiles: Methods, Models, and Misperceptions, *Textile Chemist and Colorist, 17*(1), 17–23.

McGregor, Ralph, Donald H. Mershon, & Christopher M. Pastore. (1994). Perception, Detection, and Diagnosis of Appearance Defects in Fabrics. *Textile Research Journal, 64(10),* 584–591.

McLaren, K. (1986). *The Colour Science of Dyes and Pigments,* 2nd ed. Boston: Adam Hilger.

Merkel, Robert S. (1991). *Textile Product Serviceability.* New York: Macmillan.

Nassau, K. (1983). *The Physics and Chemistry of Color.* New York: Wiley-Interscience.

Pantone, Inc. (1992). *The Pantone Textile Color System.* Moonachie, NJ: Author.

Park, James, & Kevin M. Park. (1994). Professional Colour Communicator (PCC)—The Definitive Colour Selector. In American Association of Textile Chemist and Colorists, *Book of Papers.* Research Triangle Park, NC: Author, 294–296.

Pensa, Ildo E. (1994). The Total Quality Concept in Garment Dyeing. In American Association of Textile Chemist and Colorists, *Book of Papers.* Research Triangle Park, NC: Author, 346–350.

Price, Arthur, & Allen C. Cohen. (1994). *J. J. Pizzuto's Fabric Science,* 6th ed. New York: Fairchild.

Rainwater, C. (1971). *Light and Color.* New York: Golden Press.

Randall, Dan. (1995, August). Integration in Color Development and Control. *American Dyestuff Reporter, 84,* 55–58, 96.

Reininger, D. Scott. (1994). Recent Developments in Portable Color Measurement Instruments and Applications in the Textile Industry. In American Association of Textile Chemists and Colorists, *Book of Papers.* Research Triangle Park, NC: Author, pp. 273–280.

Reininger, D. Scott. (1997, February). Textile Applications for Hand-Held Color Measuring Instruments. *Textile Chemist and Colorist, 29(2),* 13–17.

Rossotti, H. (1983). *Colour: Why the World Isn't Grey?* Princeton, NJ: Princeton University Press.

Sobel, M. (1987). *Light.* Chicago: University of Chicago Press.

Textile Institute, The. (1991). *Textile Terms and Definitions,* 9th ed. Manchester, England: Author.

Tortora, Phyllis G., & Robert S. Merkel. (1996). *Fairchild's Dictionary of Textiles,* 7th ed. New York: Fairchild.

Verity, E. (1980). *Colour Observed.* New York: Macmillan.

Vigo, Tyrone L. (1994). *Textile Processing and Properties: Preparation, Dyeing, Finishing, and Performance.* Amsterdam: Elsevier.

Weiss, Richard J. (1990). *Physics of Materials.* New York: Hemisphere Publishing Corporation.

Yang, Yiqi, & Shiqi Li. (1993, September). Instrumental Measurement of the Levelness of Textile Coloration. *Textile Chemists and Colorists, 25(9),* 75–78.

REVIEW QUESTIONS

1. Identify the factors that influence the way a colored object is perceived.

2. Describe what happens when you see a plaid fabric that is made of red, black, yellow, white, and green yarns.

3. Why do some materials look shiny and others do not?

4. How do fluorescent whitening agents work?

5. What is a chromaticity diagram, and why is it important to color measurement?

6. Explain why metamerism is important to designers, producers, and retailers.

7. Describe how additive and subtractive mixing theory relates to color perception.

8. Why is color measurement important to the textile industry complex?

9. Explain the differences between color matching and shade sorting.

10. Identify ways that color can be specified.

11. Explain the degree of acceptability represented by these situations:
    a. a 554 color match.
    b. ΔE of 0.8, when a specified level of 1.0 is required.

ACTIVITIES

1. Read this article (Reininger, D. Scott. [1997, February]. Textile Applications for Hand-Held Color Measuring Instruments. *Textile Chemist and Colorist, 29(2)*, 13–17) and discuss its application to quality assurance.

2. Select an object whose color you like and mix pigments or paints to match the color. Assess the degree of color match when it is wet and dry and under two or more light sources. Describe your success and the difficulties you encountered.

3. Find two or more different materials that are a good color match. Describe the degree of match when a different light source is used.

4. Visit a chemistry lab and see a demonstration of a spectrophotometer. Discuss how it is used and identify applications within the textile industry.

5. Examine coordinates in stores or catalogs and assess the success of the color matches. Pay particular attention to matches where the material or fabrication differ.

6. Experience the discrepancies between additive and subtractive mixing by developing a color using a CAD system. Print your design and compare the print-out with the screen image. Describe the color match and explain why the two do not match exactly.

7. Explore the various systems used in CAD programs to define color.

8. Assess your color perception using a color perception chart.

9. Collect samples of blue denim and create a shade bank describing an acceptable color range.

10. Select a color and work with dyes to create a color match. Explain the difficulties you encountered and your degree of success.

11. Specify color for a specific target market and textile product.

PRODUCT SPECIFICATIONS AND ANALYSIS

Part III focuses on the finished textile product by examining the interaction of materials in the product and the overall performance of the product. The finished product is assessed in terms of performance, appearance, size, fit, market suitability, and packaging. To present a product that appeals to the target market and performs at an appropriate level for that market, we must be able to describe the way the product should look, fit, and perform, and to evaluate products to determine when they meet these requirements.

Thus, Part III builds on the knowledge of materials testing developed in Part II, but it carries that knowledge to the next step. To assure the quality of a product, understanding the materials and their performance is not sufficient. We also must understand how the materials work together and how they combine with other product development, engineering, and merchandising activities to produce a product that appeals to and performs in a satisfactory manner for the target market.

To conclude the assessment and analysis of products and their performance with materials assessment is like saying that once athletes understand the rules of the sport, they are fully prepared to participate in it. To carry the analogy one step further, this part examines how players (the materials) work together and how the plays or actions (construction and fit) influence the game (product appearance and performance). Product evaluation uses several procedures to assess the quality, nature, characteristics, appeal, and performance of the finished product. Some procedures are similar to those used in material evaluation; others differ substantially.

This part contains four chapters. Chapter 10 identifies standards and specifications for products. Chapter 11 addresses the processes for inspecting products and the stages in development and production at which inspection is likely to occur. Chapter 12 assesses and evaluates product performance. Chapter 13 discusses how to ensure that the evaluation and assessment are based on a representative sample.

Major topics covered in Part III are:

- *specifying product characteristics;*

- *describing the desired appearance and performance levels for components and interactions of materials;*

- *assessing appearance and performance of product components and material interactions in finished products; and*

- *understanding the evaluation, testing, and sampling procedures used to assess product quality.*

Developing Standards and Specifications for Products

Chapter 10

Objectives

- To understand standards and specifications for products and their relationship to standards and specifications for materials.

- To use appropriate units and terms when writing product standards and specifications.

- To write standards and specifications that define an appropriate product for a specific target market.

- To apply standards and specifications to product development activities.

- To understand how standards and specifications affect product quality and cost.

Key Terms

product integrity	clo	construction
internal integrity	appearance	engineering specs
external integrity	workmanship	finishing
tolerance	size	product zoning
components	fit	zones
made-up	garment or product balance	packaging
design		
function		

Material standards and specifications help ensure that appropriate materials will be used in a product to meet the needs of the target market. These standards and specifications define expectations for each material's type, characteristics, quality, appearance, and performance. Standards and specifications are developed so that the materials in a product will not adversely affect consumer satisfaction.

Part II focused on understanding materials and assessing their performances. That discussion provided a partial understanding of quality assurance, because the quality of the materials cannot help but influence the quality of the finished product. However, it examined each material as a separate entity; it did not examine the interactions among materials in the product nor did it examine the relationship of materials to product construction, fit, and design. These three factors, which greatly influence product performance and consumer satisfaction, are affected by the materials used to make the product.

Most companies that work with standards and specifications identify minimum characteristics and quality and performance levels for materials. These companies also develop standards and specifications that focus on issues of quality and performance from a more holistic perspective because these factors are critical in terms of providing appropriate products. It is impossible to produce a satisfactory product from materials that do not incorporate desired characteristics, that are of an inappropriate or inadequate quality, or in which performance is less than specifications require. Dealing with materials performance is a critical step in quality assurance. However, standards and specifications for materials are only one portion of the total quality picture. Another part deals with the finished product. This chapter examines the complete product as a single entity and defines standards and specifications so that the product appeals to and performs at a satisfactory level for the target market.

Product integrity is the way the materials and other aspects of the product work together to affect consumer satisfaction (Clark & Kujimonto, 1990). Its two major components are internal and external integrity. **Internal integrity** addresses the consistency among the materials, the product's function, and its structure. Appendix C is a list of issues that address internal integrity. **External integrity** addresses the consistency between a product's performance and consumer expectations. This chapter defines measures of internal integrity that move beyond the materials used in the product.

STANDARDS AND SPECIFICATIONS

The definitions of standards and specifications given in Chapter 3 will be used here. To review briefly, a standard helps a company describe a quality level for the product it sells and ensures consistency in quality. Standards, which reflect the company's philosophy and business objectives and the target market expectations for the product, are often stated in general terms that describe characteristics and performance aspects for a product line.

Specifications include details for specific products. Specs reflect standards, but include more specific information describing exact characteristics and performance levels that must be met and procedures that describe the evaluation process.

Tolerances describe the acceptable range of variation from a specification. When reviewing specs for products, tolerances are more likely to be listed as ranges of behavior than as minimums, as was the situation with materials. There are several reasons for this. One important reason is that some product attributes are compartmentalized in the market. For example, size describes product dimensions in convenient and manageable compartments (sizes). If dimensions for any given size are too far above or below the specifications, the product will no longer fit within that size and will not meet customer expectations. In other words, if dimensions differ too much, a garment will no longer fit within the dimensions that define a size, such as medium.

A second reason for a range of tolerances is that the function of a product or component may be critical to its target market. **Components** are the product pieces that are sewn together or otherwise attached and treated as one piece in a later production stage, such as collars, cuffs, sleeves, and plackets. If a product or a component of a product is outside the acceptable range, it may no longer function or it may not function properly. For example, buttons and buttonholes must line up within a relatively narrow range or the closed placket will not have a smooth appearance. If the mismatch is too extreme, the buttons will not line up with the correct buttonhole, and the product will hang in a distracting or uncomfortable manner.

A third reason relates to the company's definition of quality for its products. If a product attribute or aspect falls below a specified level, the quality is too low. Conversely, if the attribute or aspect is above a specified level, the company cannot continue to earn a profit and its ability to meet its business objectives is compromised. For example, if a company that produces plaid shirts decides to expand its criteria for matching of plaids at center front to include matching plaids at pockets, yokes, and sleeves, more fashion fabric will be used when the pattern is cut, more time will be needed for spreading the material, more training of operators will be needed, production rates will probably slow down, and reworks or seconds may increase. The improved quality level may not be perceived by the target market, but the cost of producing the product will be higher. Thus, the company will need to either increase its price for the product and probably lose some sales or decrease its profit margin. In either case, overall company profits will likely be negatively affected.

A final reason for a range of tolerances is that some product aspects adversely affect product performance when they exceed a certain level. For example, if the stitches per inch for a seam are too high, the seam loses its ability to elongate slightly with use and is rigid and uncomfortable. In addition, too many stitches per inch may create problems in terms of seam pucker and snags or broken yarns in the fashion fabric from the needle.

RELATIONSHIP TO MATERIAL STANDARDS AND SPECIFICATIONS

Specifications and standards for products build on an understanding of the materials that will be used to manufacture the product. Often, changes in materials and products occur during the product development process, when team members begin to integrate material characteristics and performance with design, target market expectations, and business objectives. Materials evaluation ensures that they are able to produce a product that meets these requirements, but success also depends on the manner in which the materials interact with each other and the contributions each material makes to meeting the requirements for design, production, and the target market. Thus, the company and its suppliers must use product standards and specifications to determine the degree to which a product meets expectations.

Material specifications and standards describe what is expected from the materials. Although ASTM recommended performance specifications for materials address product type, their focus is on the performance of the materials and not the interaction of materials in the product or its overall performance (see Appendix G). In addition, there is no differentiation by target market and its expectations.

If materials are not able to perform at the desired level, then no amount of design modification or reengineering will overcome these shortcomings. Thus, the decision to use appropriate materials must be made relatively early in product development. If a material does not meet specifications, it is usually necessary to consider substituting another material in the product. Another option is to reexamine the specifications to see if they truly describe the performance required. Sometimes, specs can be modified without sacrificing product performance, product quality, or consumer satisfaction. In some cases, the evaluation process or testing procedure should be reexamined to see if it was done correctly. A final option is to discuss the matter with the material supplier to determine if modifications or alterations of the material so that it meets specs are possible.

Often, the designer or product development team specifies a certain fashion fabric for a product because its appearance, drape, texture, hand, print, color, or other aesthetic characteristic is related to the design of the product. A change in the material will alter the final product in a significant way. However, just as the material contributed to the look, fashion, and appeal of the product, so too will it contribute to a consumer's satisfaction or dissatisfaction. A material that is not able to meet minimum performance expectations for a given target market probably will not enhance the company's reputation with the target market.

In many cases, the performance and characteristics of the material, especially the fashion fabric, need to be known before several other steps in product development can occur. For example, the elongation and elasticity characteristics of knits influences pattern requirements. If a material is very stable, patterns need to incorporate ease. If the fabric is very stiff, it will not accommodate the three-dimensional body, chair, or object as well as if it were more pliable. Thus, pattern pieces may need to be adjusted depending on a material's hand, weight, bulk, drape, stiffness, or elongation potential. This adjustment will be needed even though a company may have used essentially the same pattern for several seasons.

Some companies evaluate the fashion fabric's dimensional change after one or more care cycles and try to incorporate that performance in their pattern work. This can be a dangerous practice because use of any support materials, such as interlining or reinforcing tapes, can alter the shrinkage of a material or result in a bubbled or puckered appearance when one material shrinks more than another. In addition, it is difficult to produce a pattern for any fabric that shrinks because shrinkage may not be uniform in all directions and among all pieces of the pattern. Even something as simple as a seam can alter the dimensional change of a material during care. Therefore, the appearance of the product after one or two care cycles may have been altered significantly simply as a result of shrinkage. This problem may happen even when pattern pieces are cut long, because of significant lengthwise shrinkage of the fashion fabric. Sometimes hangtags describe this adjustment of pattern pieces because of a material's reaction to care (see Figure 10-1).

WHAT TO DO, WHAT TO DO ...

Cotton shrinks. You know it, we know it. Our clothes shrink less than most, thanks to crack quality control, but the question remains: What to do about shrinkage? Well, we eased this garment just enough to fit after laundering. In other words, we made shrinkage work for us.

After all, if something fits before it shrinks, it only fits once. Our knits have the extra room they need to fit when you'll be wearing them: after they're washed. Simple, no?

So while this garment may look generous now, don't let that throw you. You ordered your usual size and you'll have it-once regular care and shrinkage do their work.

THANK YOU FOR YOUR PURCHASE!

Figure 10-1
Some hangtags suggest that a material may shrink and that the garment or product was cut large enough to allow for shrinkage of materials.

The tendency of a material to exhibit seam slippage may be used in determining seam and stitch type, as well as in selecting thread type for production. A sample product, prototype, or made-up may not always incorporate the materials, processes, and techniques that will be used when a product goes into production. **Made-up** is a prototype or sample product for any category other than apparel and refers to samples for medical, industrial, and furnishing applications.

Prototype garments and made-up furnishings may be produced in muslin to determine how a pattern needs to be adjusted to achieve the correct look and fit for the product. However, if a design is accepted for full production, a sample should be made up using the fashion fabric and other materials that will be used in production. Even when a sample uses appropriate materials and processes, the pattern maker will probably need to make some adjustments because materials can create a unique set of circumstances in terms of appearance and drape.

When the product is fitted onto the three-dimensional object, body form, or live fit model, further adjustments to the pattern may be needed. Finally, even more adjustments to patterns may be required when the pattern is graded in the appropriate size range for the company and its target market.

PRODUCT

This section focuses on significant attributes that contribute to the internal integrity of the finished product in terms of design, function, appearance, size, fit, construction, finishing, zoning, and packaging. This discussion does not replace the need for a basic understanding of product design, construction, engineering, pattern making, and other types of product knowledge. Instead, it examines these areas in terms of developing standards and specs for a product line within a company. Even though the discussion may focus on design and pattern making details, it will not define specific terms related to design and pattern making nor will it provide practice in developing the skills needed to produce a pattern or design a product.

The discussion assumes that the materials to be used in the product meet the required specifications and standards. This means that when evaluated individually, the materials were found to be of the appropriate type, quality, appearance and aesthetic characteristics, performance, and cost for the intended product and target market.

DESIGN

Design is the details, features, and characteristics of the finished product. Design works with the entire product from a holistic perspective and considers how the various parts of the product contribute to the aesthetic perception of the whole. Design specs are sometimes referred to as product specs or target specs depending on the specific area of interest: product type or target market.

The quality of the design is a significant factor in determining the appeal of the product to the target market. However, it is difficult to measure the quality of a design and identify those that will be successful. Some styles are popular in spite of their design; other products with good design fail to capture a significant share of the market.

Design standards and specs focus on the aesthetics and fashion characteristics of the product. Standards often address the position the company sees for itself in terms of fashion and the manner in which its products meet aesthetics requirements. For example, a company that prints graphic designs on T-shirts may describe its design standards as "we print T-shirts with slogans, patterns, logos, and graphics that appeal to the teen market."

Design specs address such features as collars, pockets, and fabric motifs that vary from product to product. Such specs identify the collar type and dimensions, material if it differs from the fashion fabric, treatment such as topstitching or appliqué or screen printing, and any other special details related to a particular feature. Design specs incorporate technical terms that differentiate one detail from another.

Individuals who write design specs must have a good understanding of the vocabulary used in the field. If a term is not well understood or if several features may be described with the same term, sketches with component dimensions can be used. For example, a design spec might include a close-up diagram of a particular detail with dimensions, features, and other aspects identified. Figure 10-2 shows a close-up sketch of a pocket that specifies its placement, dimensions, and other details.

When dimensions and details of larger components are an important part of the product's look, more information should be included. For example, the manner in which a skirt drapes depends on the grain (see Figure 10-3). Full skirts with side and center front and back seams drape differently when warp grain is parallel to side seams as compared to center front and back seams.

Design has a significant impact on the pattern for the product. Careful attention to detail in developing the pattern is required to ensure that the pattern pieces produce the identified style. In addition, the pattern needs to be sized correctly, oriented to fabric grain correctly, and reflect proper joining of all components.

FUNCTION

Function defines how well a product does what it is designed to do. It can address a specific set of performance requirements for a specialized end use, as for many functional clothing items, or it can address a more generalized set of requirements for a consumer product. Function or functional specs and standards address the ability of a product to perform well in its intended end use or to meet or exceed claims made in advertising or guarantees. Standards often describe the end use for a product line in terms of how the product is likely to be used by the consumer. For example, standards for outerwear and sleeping bags might describe temperature conditions under which the product will keep the user comfortable, such as

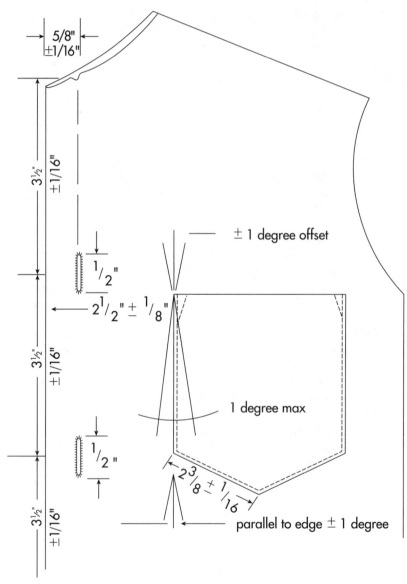

Figure 10-2
Design detail for pocket placement and structure.

Figure 10-3
Fabric grain affects skirt drape.

"comfortable to 0°F" or "designed to keep you warm and dry no matter how hard it rains." These standards address conditions of use in which the consumer is most likely interested.

Specs focus more on the evaluation procedure used in making this assessment or on details that help ensure that the product really will do what the company claims it will do. For example, specs for an outerwear item might address seam and stitch type, so that a hard-driving rain will not penetrate. Some design details might relate to function, because the design of the hood on a coat influences how well it stays in place and keeps the wearer warm or dry when the wind is strong.

Very few standard test methods exist for evaluating product performance. One procedure is ASTM F 1291, Measuring the Thermal Insulation of Clothing Using a Heated Manikin. Figure 10-4 illustrates a mannequin of this type used at Kansas State University in evaluating the performance of clothing.

Clo describes the comfort of clothing used to keep the body warm under adverse weather conditions. It defines the resistance to dry heat transfer provided by clothing. One clo is equal to $0.155°Km^2/W$. However, because this definition may be difficult to understand, one clo also may be interpreted as the "thermal insulation of a business suit as worn in Philadelphia, New Haven, or Toronto" (Fourt & Hollies, 1971, p. 9). Another more formal definition is "the amount of insulation necessary to maintain comfort and mean skin temperature of 92°F (33.3°C) in a 70°F (21.28°C) room with air movement less than 10 ft/min (3.05 m/min), relative humidity not over 50 percent with a body metabolism of 50 $Kcal/m^2/hr$" (Renbourn & Rees, 1972, p. 114). Specs for clothing may

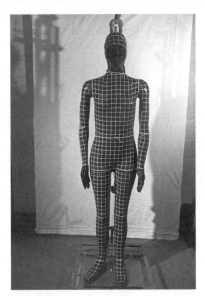 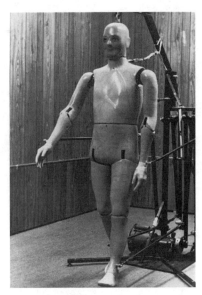

Figure 10-4
A heated mannequin used in evaluating the thermal insulation of clothing. (*Courtesy of Elizabeth McCullough, Kansas State University*)

describe insulation as 1 clo, 2.5 clo, or some other value depending on the amount of insulation required.

Specs for functional and protective clothing used in certain occupations often identify the ASTM procedure that would be used to evaluate the item's performance and the protection provided. Several procedures for protective clothing use the entire product to evaluate performance. For example, ASTM F 1052, Standard Practice for Qualitatively Evaluating the Comfort, Fit, Function, and Integrity of Chemical-Protective Suit Ensembles, evaluates protective garments when any contact with a hazardous chemical might have a significantly deleterious impact on the health or safety of the wearer.

APPEARANCE

Appearance is how the product looks when an individual views it from a near perspective. For example, appearance for an item of apparel is described in terms of what the viewer would see when standing a conversational distance away from the wearer of the product. Appearance not only includes hanger appeal, but also incorporates some quality issues and performance dimensions. Appearance addresses features that would be noticed when an individual walks into a room, has a conversation with someone, or engages in some other social or use interaction with the product or wearer of a product. Appearance standards do not address features that might be revealed under very close scrutiny or study of the product. Appearance standards emphasize the way the finished product looks from the outside and from a reasonably close position.

Appearance standards may describe the manner in which design details, plaids, stripes, or other material motifs match. These standards also address symmetry between two sides of a symmetrical product. Several examples illustrate these issues. When appearance standards address such issues as the matching of plaids, these standards also influence spreading and cutting operations. The product pieces must be cut in such a manner that operators are able to match motifs at seams during production.

Figure 10-5 shows a shirt where the pockets and collar are identical mirror images on the right and left sides. The pockets are identical in size, at the same vertical location on the shirt, and the same distance from the placket. The production of a shirt with this degree of symmetry was not done by accident or luck; the engineering specifications for construction addressed these details and ensured that the finished shirt met these requirements.

The plaids of the shirts shown in Figure 10-6 illustrate several options in terms of plaid symmetry and plaid matching in shirts. Note the difference in quality and appearance among the shirts illustrated. Often the degree of matching is related to the design of the plaid (balanced or unbalanced), its scale (large or small), and the degree or amount of contrast (high or low) among the colors present.

Figure 10-5
This shirt is symmetrical between right and left sides. Note that the symmetry extends to the size and placement of the pockets and the size and shape of the collar points.

Figure 10-6
Plaid shirts: (A) horizontal mismatch on pockets; (B) horizontal match, but not symmetrical (see the plaid pattern between right and left fronts) right to left; (C) horizontal match with right and left symmetry; and (D) horizontal and vertical match.

Product characteristics influence the way a product appeals to the consumer. Figure 10-7 illustrates two color block garments. In one top, the colors line up so that the seams meet at the same point at the center front of the shirt so that the eye flows from one side to the other and a pleasing appearance is created. In the other top, the colors do not quite line up, thereby altering the appearance and appeal of the top.

Appearance standards and specs also include factors related to workmanship. **Workmanship** is how the materials and construction used in

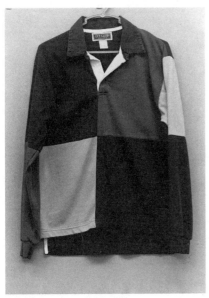

A.

B.

Figure 10-7
Shirts with color block yokes: match at center front (left) and mismatch at center front (right).

producing the product affect the appearance of the finished product. Figures 10-5, 10-6, and 10-7 also address workmanship, because engineering specifications in terms of production have to incorporate these standards in order for the finished product to achieve this level of workmanship.

Other factors that may relate to appearance and workmanship include such details as the way the seams and pleats fall, the appearance of hems, the visibility and uniformity of topstitching, and other aspects that the company has determined to be of importance. Figures 10-8 and 10-9 illustrate these points.

Appearance standards also specify the ability of closures to close the parts of the product and contribute to its appearance. For example, appearance standards for buttons may require that buttons and buttonholes match and that, when the placket is closed, this component is smooth and flat (see Figure 10-10). Appearance standards for separating zippers often require that they match at the bottom edge, that the slider of the zipper does not catch on materials that are too close to the teeth or coil, and that the zipper is smooth when opened or closed. Appearance standards for other closures often address similar requirements.

Appearance standards tend to emphasize the exterior of the product, but interior appearance may be of concern for certain products. In some cases, the interior may have a significant effect on the appearance of the finished product. For example, the interior or reverse side of some products, such as lined jackets and coats, bedding, window treatments, and sleeping bags will influence consumer satisfaction with the product (see Figure 10-11).

Figure 10-8
Appearance standards for skirts. The skirt on the left meets appearance standards because when the skirt is hanging, the pleats remain closed. The skirt on the right does not meet appearance standards because the pleats swing open slightly.

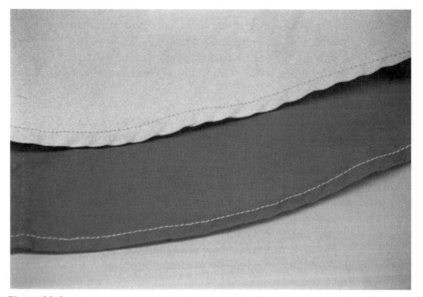

Figure 10-9
Appearance standards for hems: unacceptable because of roping of the hem (top) and acceptable (bottom).

A.   B.

Figure 10-10
(a) This shirt does not meet appearance standards: the collar is puckered, collar points are not the same length, and the placket is not smooth and flat. (b) This shirt meets appearance standards: flat and regular collar, smooth and flat placket, symmetrical right and left sides.

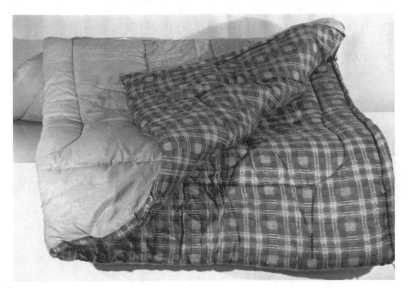

Figure 10-11
The appearance of the interior of a sleeping bag may be as important as the appearance of its exterior. Notice that no raw edges or edge finishes appear inside this bag.

SIZE

Size can be used to describe several aspects of a product. Essentially, **size** refers to the important length, width, depth, circumference, and vertical dimensions of a product. Vertical dimensions are the distance from one part of a product to another, such as the distance from the waistline to the fullest part of the hip for skirts and pants. The dimensions that are important for a product are based on the product type. For example, dimensions for a towel refer to length and width. If the towel has a woven-in decorative band, then added dimensions that are of importance are the distance of the band from the end of the towel, the width of the band, and its consistency for both ends of the towel.

For a garment, additional dimensions become important; in this case, **size** refers to a standard grouping of product dimensions based on a standard size chart. With garments, standard refers to the fact that the size chart is based on company standards. There are no industry-wide standards for describing or defining apparel size. Garment dimensions for a size M for children's wear in one company often differ from the dimensions for the same size in another company. Thus, a consumer may find that one company's size M product fits her/his figure better than another company's size M. Table 10-1 illustrates two sample standard size charts from different companies. Compare the dimensions listed for each size by the two companies.

Size specs include more detailed dimensions, tolerances allowed within a size range, and descriptions of the procedures to be followed in measuring product size. Table 10-2 shows size specs for the same two companies shown in the previous figure for the same size range. Notice the expanded number of dimensions of importance in the spec size charts compared to the standard size charts. Also notice that the dimensions for the standard size chart are based on body dimensions, whereas the spec size chart are based on product dimensions. The differences between these

Table 10-1
STANDARD SIZE CHARTS FOR CHILDREN, SIZES 4–6, BASED ON BODY MEASUREMENTS IN INCHES.

	Company A Size (Number)			Company B Size (Number)		
Measurement	4	5	6	4	5	6
Chest	23	24	25	22–24	—	26–28
Waist	21.5	22	22.5	21	—	22
Hips	23	24	25	23–24	—	25–26
Height	41	44	46	39–43	—	44–48

Table 10-2
SPECIFICATION SIZE CHARTS FOR CHILDREN, SIZES 4–6, BASED ON GARMENT MEASUREMENTS IN INCHES

| | Company A | | | | Company B | | | |
| | Size (Number) | | | | Size (Number) | | | |
Measurement	4	5	6	Tolerance	4	5	6	Tolerance
Chest	24	25	26	±0.5	23–25	—	27–29	±0.5
Waist	22	22.5	23	±0.25	21.5	—	22.5	±0.25
Hips	24	25	26	±0.5	24–25	—	26–27	±0.5
Total Torso	37.8	40.7	42.4	±0.5	38	—	42	±0.5
Neck Base	10.8	11.25	11.6	±0.25	10.5	—	11.5	±0.25
Armseye	9.75	10.4	11	±0.5	9.75	—	11	±0.5
Upper Arm	6.5	6.6	6.8	±0.25	6.5	—	6.75	±0.25
Thigh	12.6	13.25	13.8	±0.5	12.5	—	13.75	±0.5
Knee	9	9.5	10	±0.25	9	—	10	±0.25
Shoulder	2.8	3	3.1	±0.25	2.75	—	3	±0.25
Crotch	17.5	19.4	20	±0.5	17.75	—	19.75	±0.5
Arm Length	13.6	15	16.2	±0.25	13.5	—	16.25	±0.25
Waist Height	24.75	27	28.25	±0.5	25	—	28	±0.5
Waist-Knee	15.2	16.4	17.2	±0.5	15	—	17	±0.5
Waist-Hip	4.75	5.1	5.25	±0.25	4.75	—	5.25	±0.25
Crotch Height	17.5	19	20	±0.5	17.75	—	20.25	±0.5
Knee Height	10.25	11	11.5	±0.5	10.5	—	11.5	±0.5
Ankle Height	2.2	2.2	2.3	±0.25	2.25	—	2.5	±0.25

two companies occurs because they are catalog retailers. Standard size charts are used in their catalogs to assist customers in selecting the appropriate size. Companies who sell their products in stores may not use body dimensions in their standard size charts.

FIT

Fit is how the product dimensions relate to the three-dimensional form, body, or other object on which the textile product is to be used, worn, or displayed. For example, fit for apparel refers to how the garment relates to the individual's shape, while allowing for a general or specific range of movement. Fit for bedding addresses how the product's dimensions relate to the mattress or pillow, so that the bedding product stays in place, does not bunch up or pull loose during use, and is easy to fit around the mattress or pillow.

Fit standards include such features as how much ease or extra amount is needed for movement, how product features relate to the form, and how the product hangs on the form. The amount of ease needed depends on the type of product, the materials used, and body portion the product covers. For example, more ease is needed if the material is stiff, if it is woven, or if it covers a body part that has a wide range of movement such as the arm and shoulder area. Less ease is needed if the material is flexible, knit, or if it covers an area that does not require much movement, such as the waist. More ease would be expected in apparel for active sportswear or outerwear compared to apparel for more sedentary activities, such as office work. The amount of ease is also partly determined by product design. Some products are designed to have more ease than others.

Fit aspects related to product features and the body include such details as darts pointing towards the fullest part of the bust, pockets and their relationship to the scale of the bodice, amount of ease in the yoke across the back, and size of armseye and the diameter of the upper arm of the garment. Figure 10-12 shows a fit model during an evaluation session in which the fit of a garment is evaluated based on company standards.

Fit also addresses how the product drapes from the body or form. For apparel, it is not uncommon to verify that side seams fall essentially perpendicular to the floor. They should not twist to the front or back of the product. Garment skew or twist can develop when the fabric is skewed, when the pattern is not symmetrical, or when the pattern is rotated slightly when the marker is made so that grain is no longer straight with the original grain line as the designer wanted. Fit sessions on dummy models or live fit models may identify a problem with garment skew. Problems of this nature can be difficult to solve because so many possible reasons for or sources of skew exist.

Working with dummy models or fit models also helps identify **garment or product balance.** This is the point at which the garment will naturally ride on the body or form or drape from the body or form. Most shirts, tops, coats, and dresses balance from the shoulder. Pants, skirts, and other bottoms balance from the waist. Garment weight should be fairly evenly distributed between the front and back of the garment, especially if the garment is fairly simple without a significant amount of detail. For example, if a product, such as a T-shirt, has a tendency to slip towards the back so that the front neckline rides up with body movement, the balance is not correct. Checking fit on a live model helps correct problems of this nature.

Fit standards may reflect a variety of possibilities related to specific figure shapes. For example, for denim jeans sold by Lands' End, the company describes several degrees of fit for different figure types in their

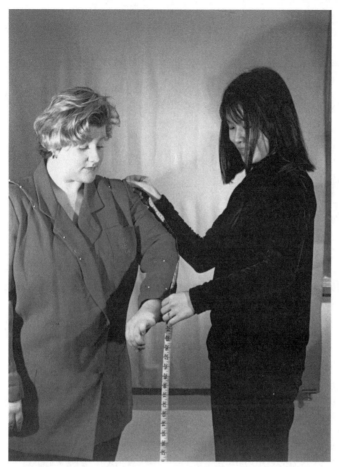

Figure 10-12
Use of live fit models help companies determine if a product meets company standards for fit.

catalog: regular, petite, tall, traditional, and relaxed. Figure 10-13 shows the difference in fit between Lands' End traditional fit and relaxed-fit jeans.

Fit standards often describe the general way a product should drape or hang on the form and the key elements used in identifying if a product has met fit standards. For example, a company might describe fit for a shirt as: shoulder seam bisects top shoulder when viewed from the side, side seam perpendicular to the floor, no excess bulk or tightness under the arms or across the back or chest, placket lies smooth and flat when closed, neck does not pull or gap when collar is closed, and the shirt is balanced from the shoulder seams.

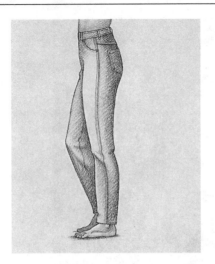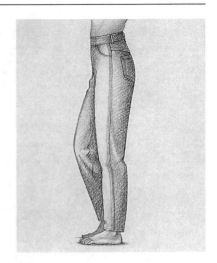

Figure 10-13
A Lands' End catalog shows the difference between traditional (left) and relaxed (right) fit for denim jeans. (*Courtesy of Lands' End*)

It is important that fit specs be described in terms of a specific set of figure dimensions or a standard dummy fit form. Unfortunately, some companies describe their fit based on an individual employee's figure. Thus, as Kim, the person on whom the company bases its standard size, ages, gains or loses weight, or changes because of gravity's tendency to shift body mass downward, fit for the company's product line may change. If Kim leaves the company, dies, or is on vacation or sick leave, significant problems with product consistency can develop.

CONSTRUCTION

Construction is the way the various parts, components, and materials of a product are combined or connected in a permanent fashion to create a finished product. Standards and specifications in the area of construction often focus on defining specific requirements. Sometimes minimums are listed, but in many cases the specs identify a process or construction requirement by name or designator, such as stitch type 301.

Although there is often overlap with design, function, and appearance areas, the main emphasis for construction standards and specifications is on the process of making the finished product. Construction standards may describe general requirements used to produce the product, such as 10–12 stitches per inch (spi). Construction specs should include details related to specific stitch and seam type, thread type, seam allowance, and other details related to joining two materials by stitching. Figures 10-14 and 10-15

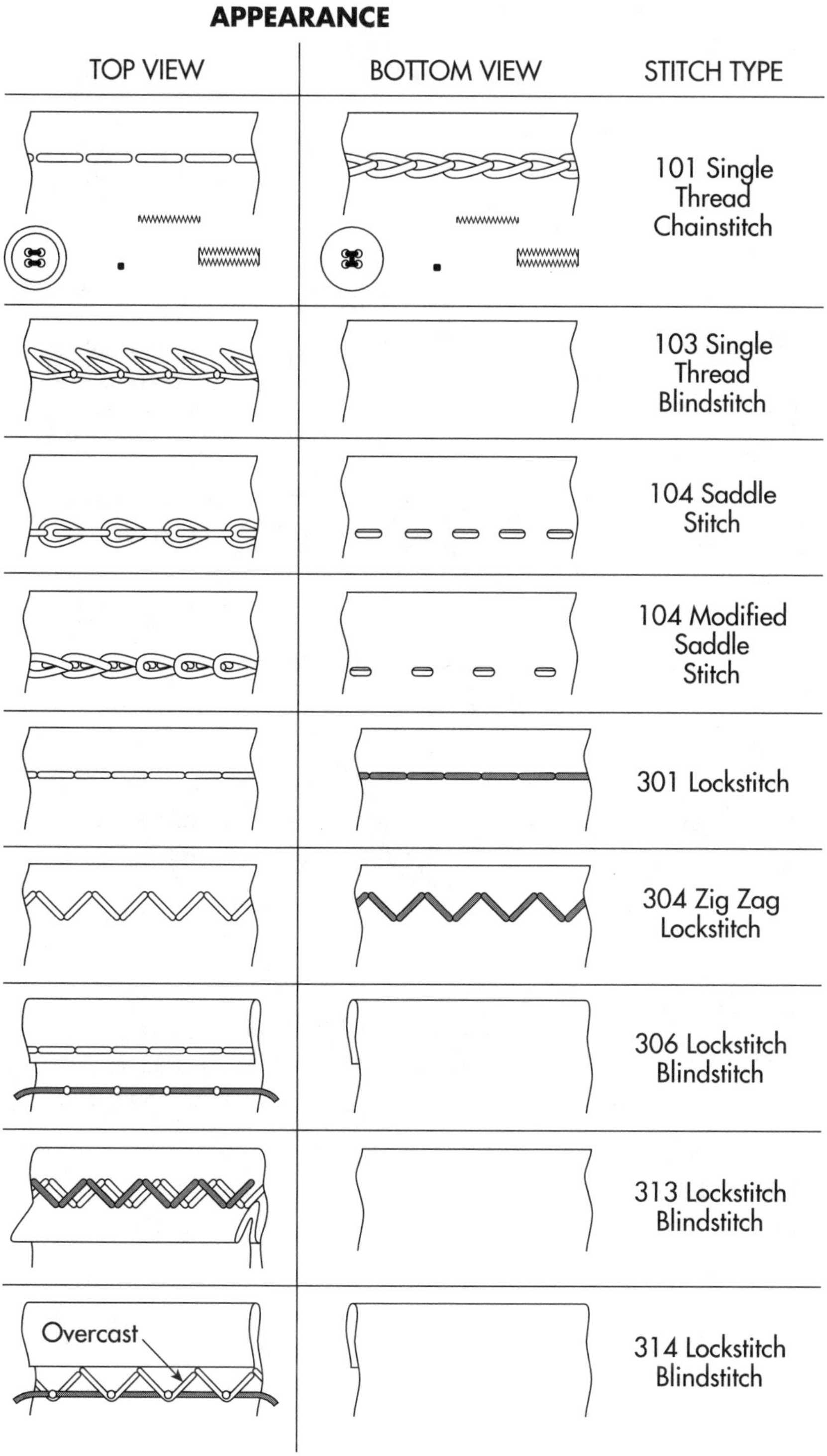

APPEARANCE

TOP VIEW	BOTTOM VIEW	STITCH TYPE
		101 Single Thread Chainstitch
		103 Single Thread Blindstitch
		104 Saddle Stitch
		104 Modified Saddle Stitch
		301 Lockstitch
		304 Zig Zag Lockstitch
		306 Lockstitch Blindstitch
		313 Lockstitch Blindstitch
Overcast		314 Lockstitch Blindstitch

Figure 10-14
Federal stitch specifications.

APPEARANCE

TOP VIEW	BOTTOM VIEW	STITCH TYPE
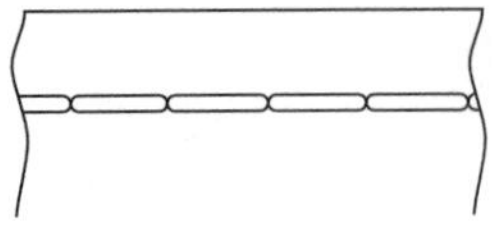		401 Two Thread Chainstitch
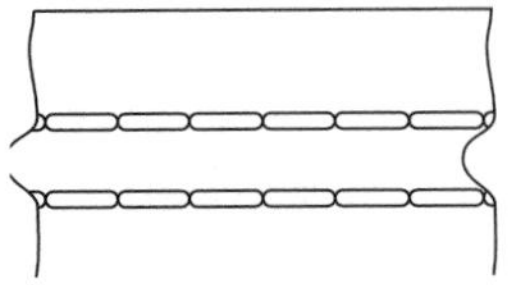 (Narrow Needle Spacing	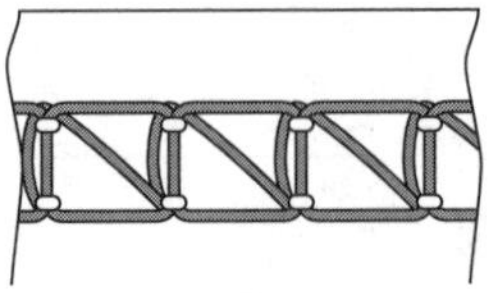	402 Cording Stitch for Permanent Creases
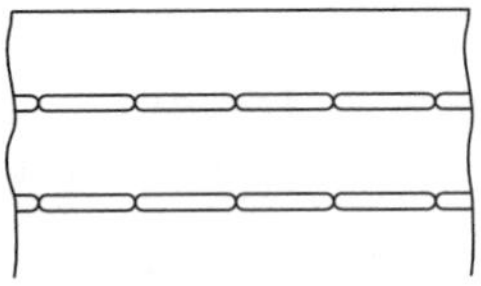	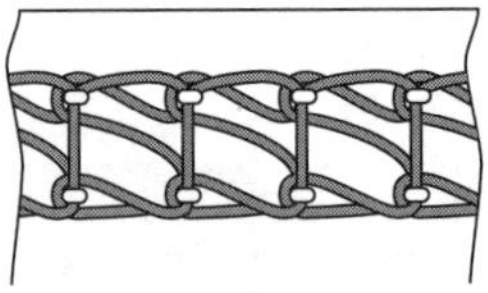	406 Coverseaming Stitch
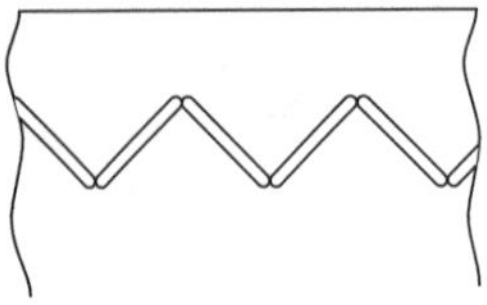	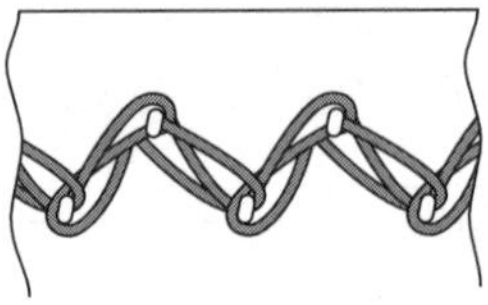	404 Zig Zag Chainstitch
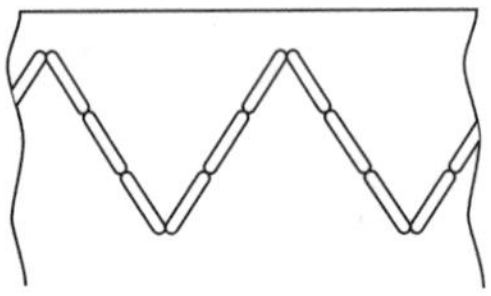	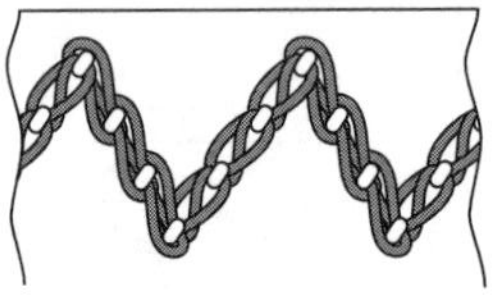	404 Mod. Multi-step Zig Zag Chainstitch
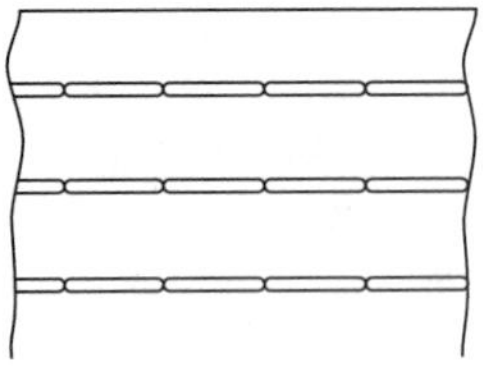	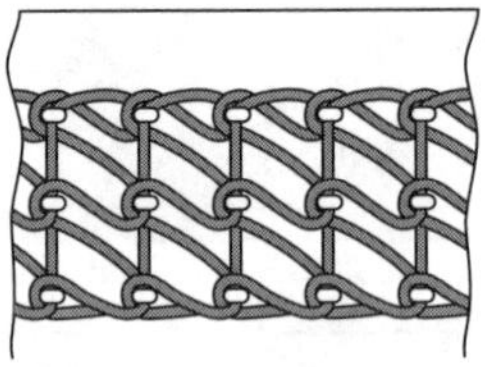	407 Coverseaming Stitch for Attaching Elastic

Figure 10-14 (continued)

APPEARANCE

TOP VIEW	BOTTOM VIEW	STITCH TYPE	APPLICATION
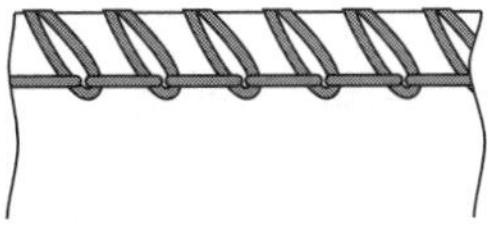 1 Thread	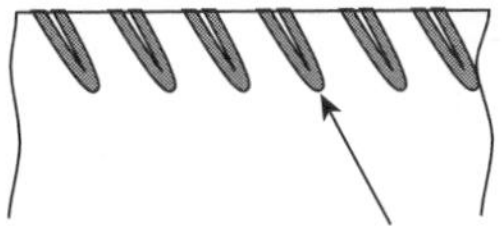 Ndl. Thds.	501	Break-open Seaming (easly unraveled) Note: No purl
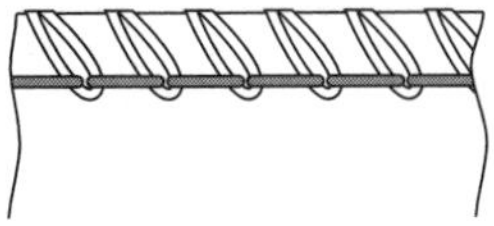 2 Threads	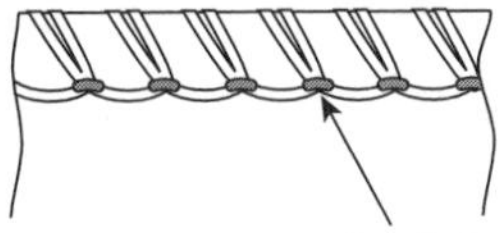 Ndl. Thds.	502	Seaming Bags, etc. Note: No purl
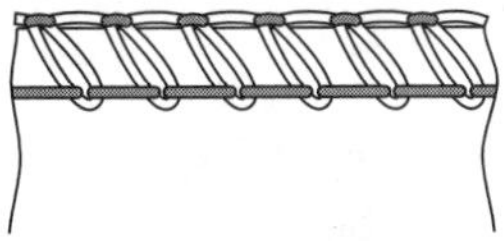 2 Threads	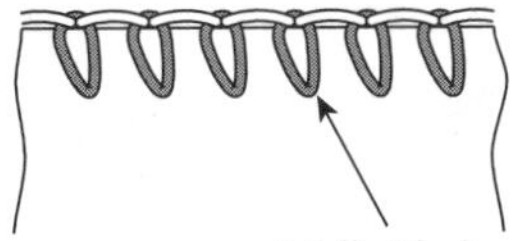 Ndl. Thds.	503	Serging Blindhemming Break-open Seaming Note: Purl on edge
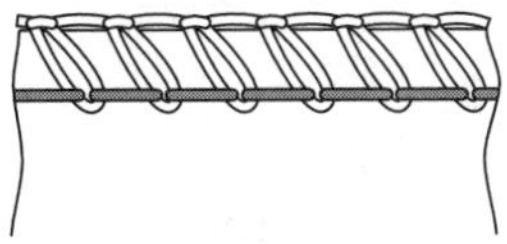 3 Threads	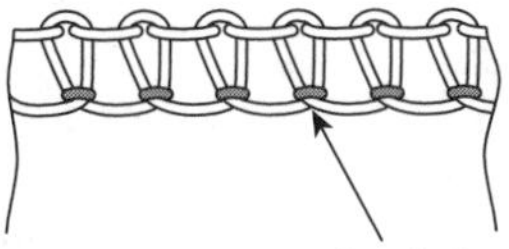 Ndl. Thds.	504	Seaming Knit Goods, etc. Serging Note: Purl on edge
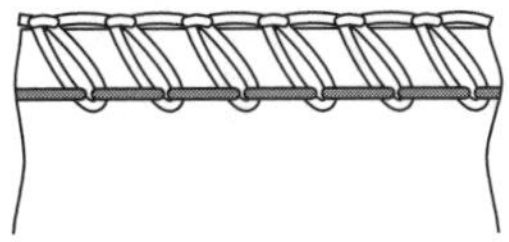 3 Threads	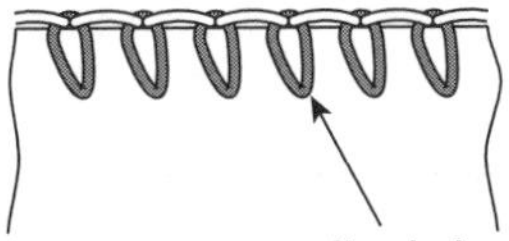 Ndl. Thds.	505	Serging Break-open Seaming Note: Double purl
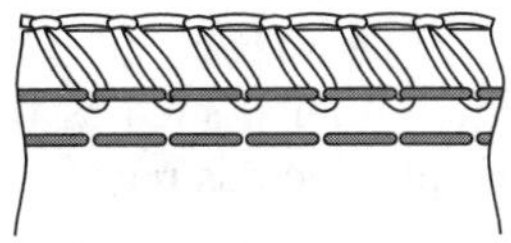 4 Threads	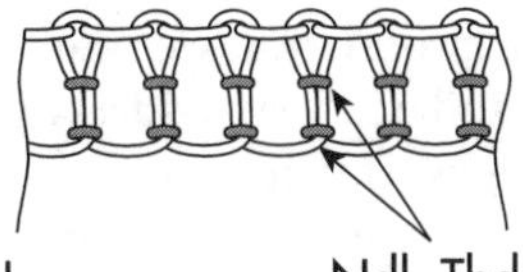 Ndl. Thds.	512 mock safety	Seaming Stitch (simulated safety stitch) Note: Purl on edge
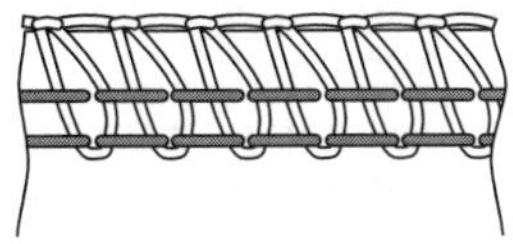 4 Threads	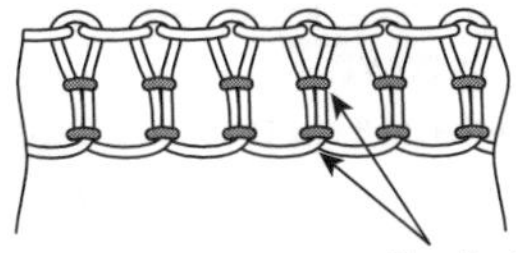 Ndl. Thds.	514	Seaming Stitch (produces strong seams on wovens or knits) same as 512 but with long Note: Upper looper

Figure 10-14 (continued)

APPEARANCE

TOP VIEW	BOTTOM VIEW	STITCH TYPE	APPLICATION
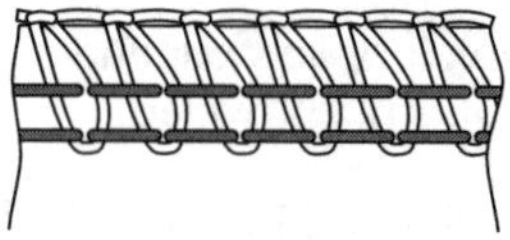 3 Threads	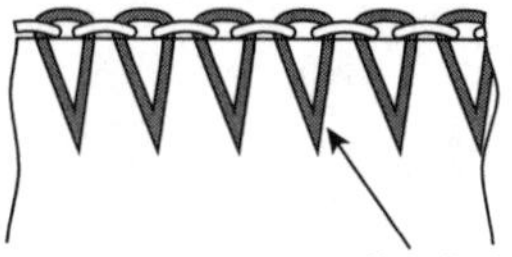 Ndl. Thds.	521	Hosiery Stitch Note: Break-open Stitch
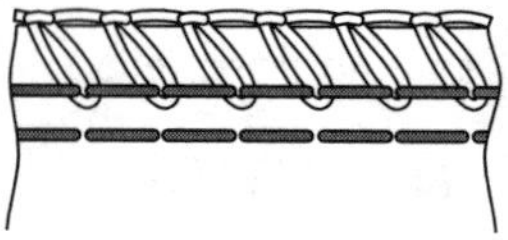 4 Threads	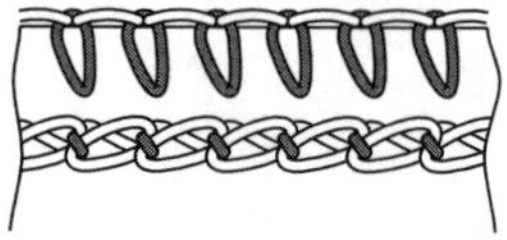	515 (401 & 503)	Safety Stitch Seaming
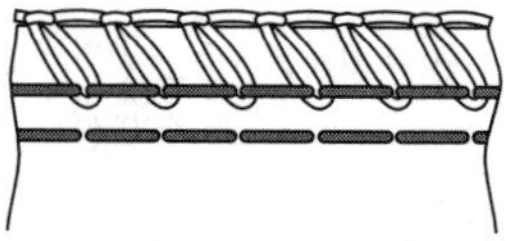 5 Threads	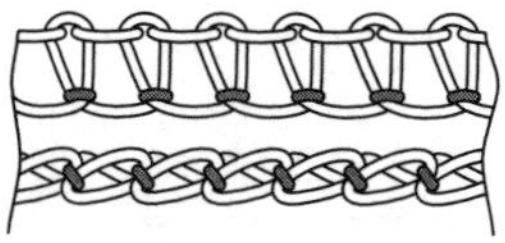	516 (401 & 504)	Safety Stitch Seaming
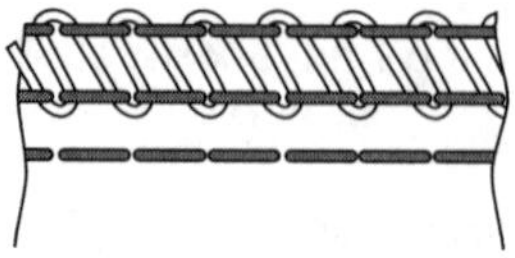 6 Threads	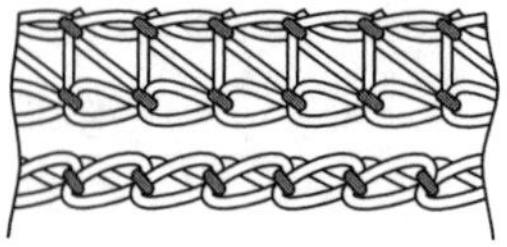	519 (401 & 602)	Safety Stitch Seaming

Figure 10-1 4 (continued)

present federal stitch and seam specs. These specs are widely used in the industry to describe seams in products and the general quality of construction. Construction or production specs are a type of process spec.

Construction standards may address other requirements, such as the treatment of seam edges so that no raw edges are visible. Details regarding finishing of seams may require that there are no thread ends at the ends of seams, that shoulder seams and armseye seams on dress shirts are stitched with a double needle, and that garments for children's wear include a two-inch hem to allow for growth.

Specifications for construction are sometimes referred to as **engineering specs** because they are often developed by apparel engineers. These professionals know the capabilities of sewing machines and other equipment used in producing products, understand the abilities of the operators in the production line, and are trained in a way that helps them interpret construction standards, design specs, and function specs. Figure 10-16 shows an engineering spec for a pocket.

PART I. GENERAL INFORMATION

Section 2A. Schematic Index of Seams and Stitchings in Alphabetical Order by Class

Seam Class SS (Superimposed)

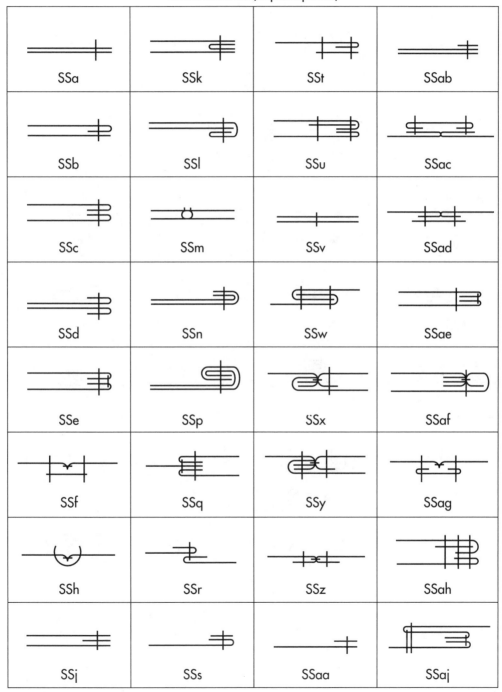

Figure 10-15
Federal seam specifications.

353

Seam Class SS (Superimposed)

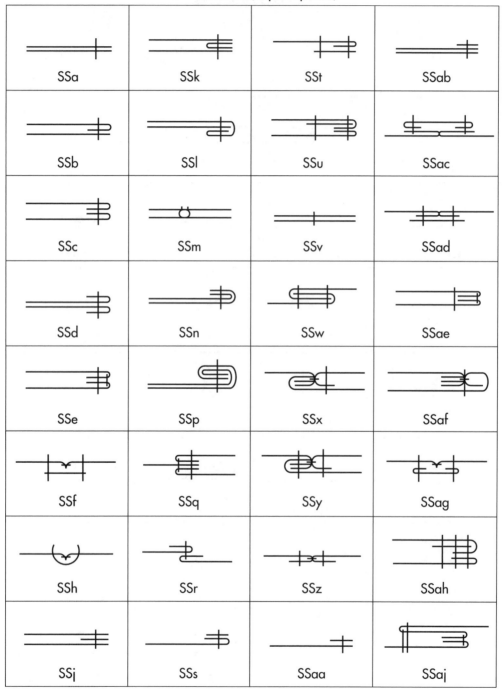

Figure 10-15 (continued)

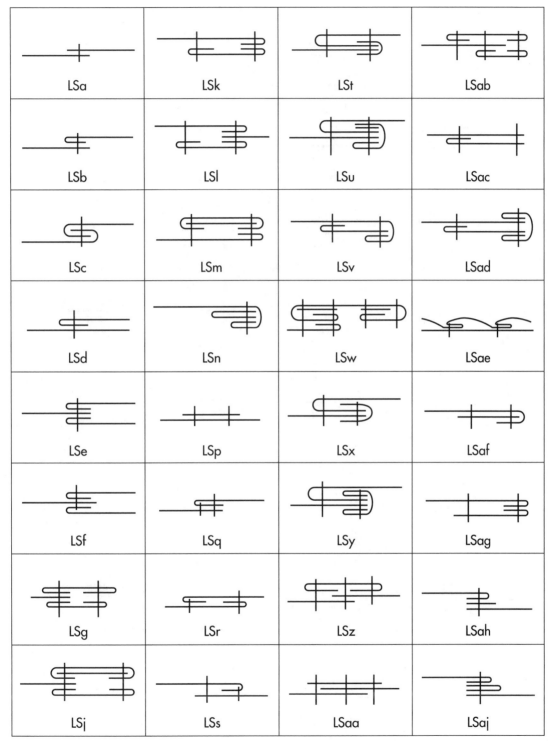

Figure 10-15 (continued)

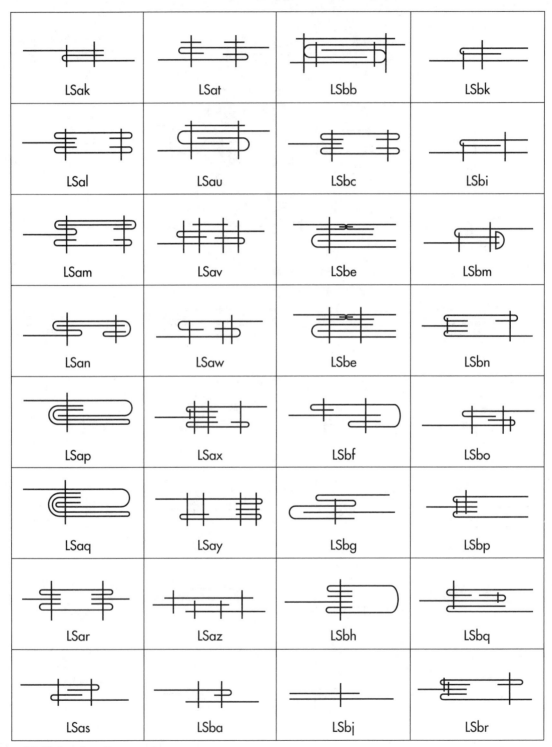

Figure 10-15 (continued)

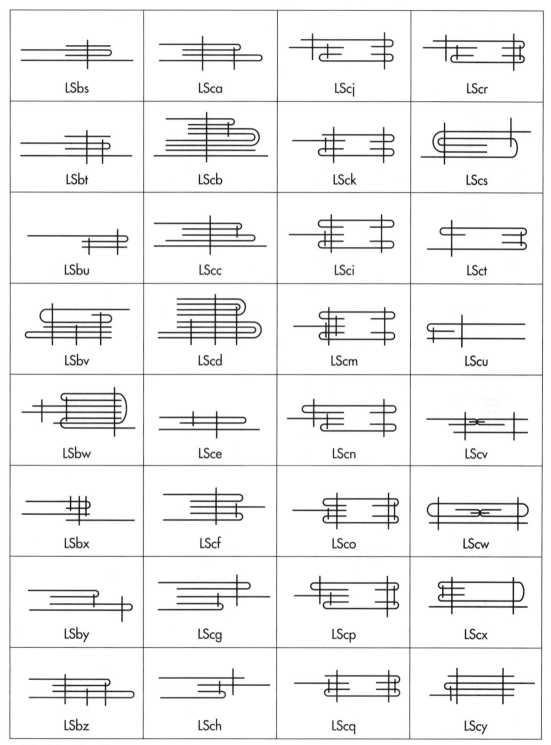

Figure 10-15 (continued)

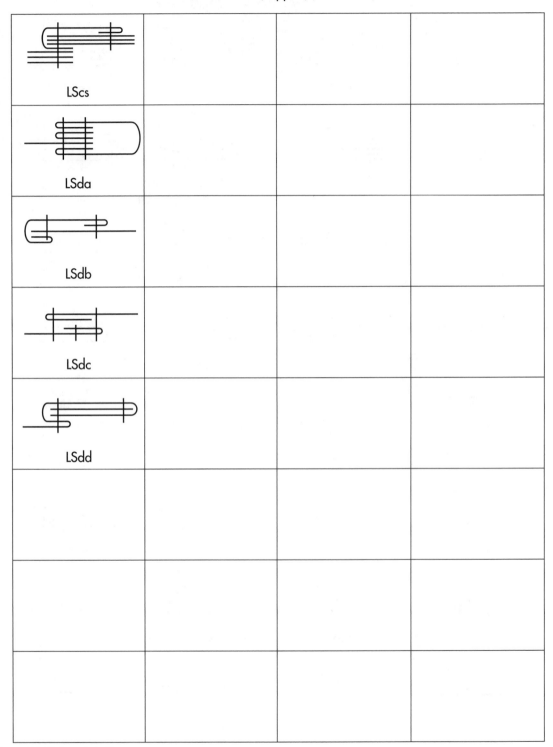

Figure 10-15 (continued)

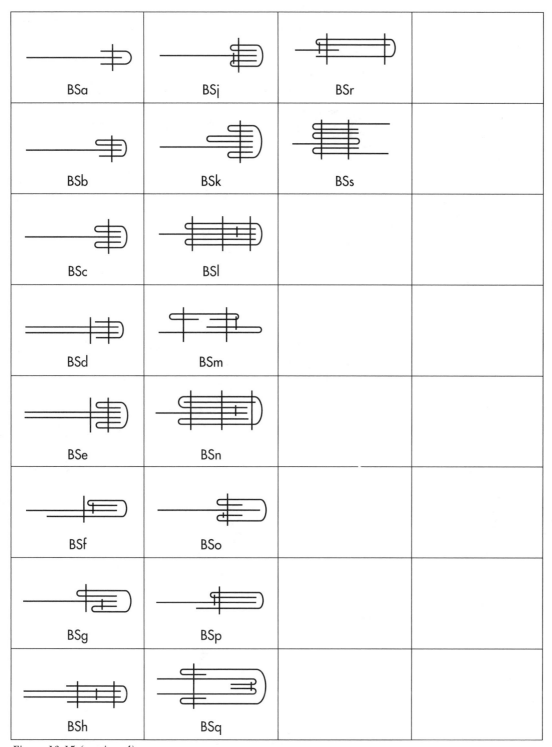

Figure 10-15 (continued)

Seam Class FS (Flat)

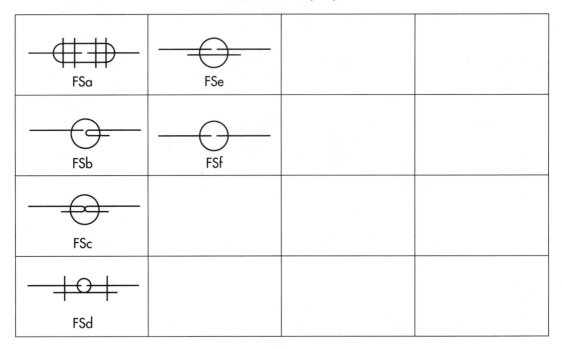

Stitching Class OS (Ornamental)

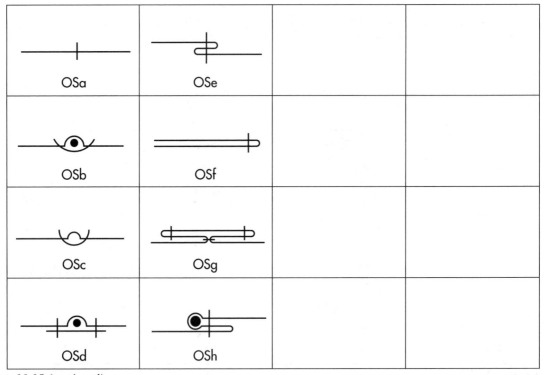

Figure 10-15 (continued)

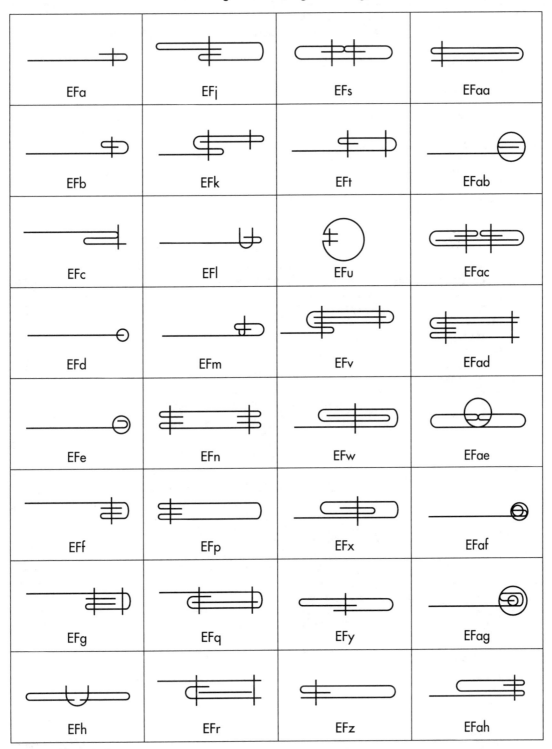

Figure 10-15 (continued)

361

ENGINEERING & STANDARDS SPECIFICATION		
OPERATION: BARTACK FRONT SLASH POCKET		PAGE: 11 OF 12
OPERATION NO: 340–01		DATE: 2/8/89
EQUIPMENT: JUKI LK 1852–5		RPM: 2350
ATTACHMENTS: THREAD WIPER, THROAT PLATE GUIDE, EYE SHIELD		
STITCHES PER INCH: 28	STITCH TYPE: 301	SEAM TYPE: SSa1

QUALITY SPECIFICATIONS

SPECIFICATIONS	REQUIREMENTS	TOLERANCE
TACK WIDTH	1/16"	± 1/32"
TACK LENGTH	3/8"	± 1/32"
ALIGNMENT TOP TACK	PARALLEL AND 9/16" FROM BAND SEAM EDGE	± 1/16"
ALIGNMENT BOTTOM TACK	PARALLEL TO BAND SEAM EDGE AND EXTENDING 1/32" OVER WELT EDGE	± 1/32"
	TACK SHOULD EXTEND 1/32" ONTO FACING	
	TOP EDGE OF FRONT AND WELT STITCH SHOULD MATCH TO NOTCH IN FACING	± 1/16"
	ATTACH FRONT POCKET NOTCH SHOULD MATCH NOTCH IN FACING	± 1/16"
	TACK SHOULD TOUCH WELT STITCH	NONE
THREAD COLOR	MATCH	NONE
APPEARANCE	LAYS FLAT AND SMOOTH	NONE
REPAIRS	DO NOT SEW OVER BAD WORK MUST BE PICKED CLEAN	

Figure 10-16
Engineering specifications for pocket placement for the shirt shown in Figure 10-5. (*Courtesy of* (TC)[2])

ENGINEERING & STANDARDS SPECIFICATIONS

OPERATION: BARTACK FRONT SLASH POCKET		PAGE:	12 OF 12
OPERATION NO: 340–01		DATE:	2/8/89
EQUIPMENT: JUKI LK 1852–5		RPM:	2350
ATTACHMENTS: THREAD WIPER, THROAT PLATE GUIDE, EYE SHIELD			
STITCHES PER INCH: 28	STITCH TYPE: 301	SEAM TYPE: SSa–1	

QUALITY SPECIFICATIONS

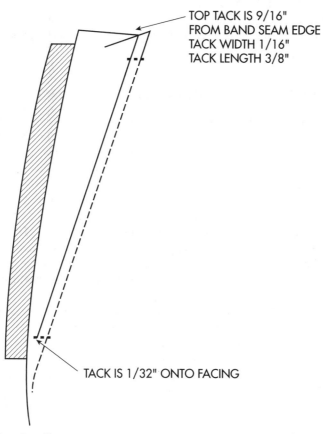

TOP TACK IS 9/16"
FROM BAND SEAM EDGE
TACK WIDTH 1/16"
TACK LENGTH 3/8"

TACK IS 1/32" ONTO FACING

Figure 10-16 (continued)

FINISHING

When construction is completed for a product, several additional steps may be needed to achieve the final look. **Finishing** is the procedures used to achieve a product's required final or finished appearance. It can include basic procedures related to the trimming of threads, pressing, steaming, turning products so they are right side out, and otherwise tidying up the product so that it looks neat and new. Finishing also refers to any product processing steps, such as abrasive washes, frosting, or product dyeing.

Standards relating to finishing often address expectations for the techniques or processes used to achieve this finished look. Specs address specific procedures, settings, materials, or ingredients that would be used in the finishing process. For example, standards might state that when product dyeing is used to color the product after production, the color must be level throughout the product, all parts, components, and materials must match the specified color and each other within the acceptable limits (see Chapter 9), and that labels cannot alter in appearance or accept dye. Specs would include specific numerical ratings for color limits, settings for the equipment, and additives used in dyeing. Finishing specs are a type of process spec.

ZONING FOR DEFECTS AND APPEARANCE

In **product zoning,** the company recognizes that some parts of a product are more crucial in terms of appearance than other parts. Those parts or **zones** that are most visible are of greater importance than parts that are less visible. Figure 10-17 illustrates sample zones for several different product types. A definition of each zone or priority area needs to be included in the specifications because terminology and designators for zones are not standard within the industry. For example, one company might use numbers, such as 1, 2, and 3, or roman numerals, such as I, II, and III, to describe zones and another company might use letters, such as A, B, and C, for their zones. Zone 1 for one company might be the part with the greatest demands for appearance, while another company might use zone C to describe similar requirements.

Typically, zones of the highest priority are those areas most likely to be viewed during face-to-face conversations with someone or those areas most likely to be seen when using the product. Thus, the areas of a garment closest to the face are of greatest importance for apparel. For furnishings, these areas would include backs, armrests, and cushions. Areas not as likely to be seen, but that remain visible, are assigned to the next zone in terms of priority. Areas that are generally not expected to be seen by others, such as under the arms, the crotch, and inside for apparel and areas under seat cushions and the bottom of upholstered furniture, are assigned lower zone priorities.

Product Zones

Explanation of Zones

When a construction flaw or defect occurs in a product, acceptance or rejection of the defective product is prioritized by the area, or zone, in which it occurs. Product zones that are more visible to a customer are more crucial in maintaining higher levels of quality.

Each product has specific zones that are more important than others, and guidelines are defined accordingly.

Zone 1

Areas with extremely high visibility that are likely to be viewed from a close distance at the time of purchase or receipt. Cosmetic flaws located in thus zone would be considered Major and would be cause for rejection of the product.

Zone 2

Areas which are not visibly dominant, but are visible in normal use. Cosmetic flaws in this zone would be evaluated based upon size of the defect, color, and intended end use of the product to determine acceptability.

Zone 3

Areas normally hidden in everyday use, but could be visible on occasion. Cosmetic flaws in this zone are more acceptable than in any other location on the garment. Flaws occurring in this zone would be evaluated product by product based upon the intended end use of the garment.

Knit Pants, Shorts & Slacks Zone Charts

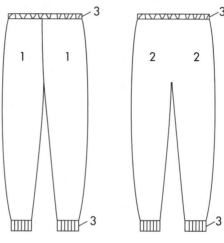

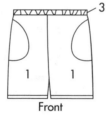

Front — Back

Woven Tops Zone Charts
Women's & Men's

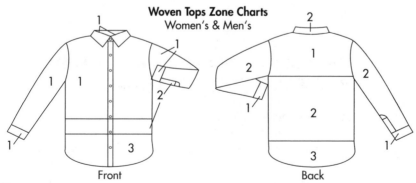

Front — Back

Figure 10-17
Zones for several products.

In addition to defining zones, many companies also identify types of defects that would be unacceptable in each area. For example, for men's dress shirts, a company may state that no fabric, construction, or appearance defects are allowed in Zone 1, which it has defined as the neckline, cuffs, and center front placket area. This company may further state that in Zone 1, an absence of thread ends, a button and buttonhole match within $\pm 1/16$ in., and collar points within $\pm 1/16$ in. of the specified length are required. If a shirt does not meet all these requirements for this zone, the shirt has not met specifications and is not acceptable according to its standards and specifications.

PACKAGING

Packaging is the manner in which a product is prepared for transportation, shipped, and presented to the customer. In some cases, packaging also describes how the product is presented to the ultimate consumer. Packaging standards often describe general aspects of how the product is packaged, whereas packaging specs describe the materials that should be used and the manner in which a product should be folded, blocked, supported, or otherwise manipulated when packaged (see Figure 10-18). In addition, packaging often indicates how many products will be shipped together in the same box or container and the kind of labeling or product information that is to be attached to the outside of individual product packages and on boxes, cartons, or other containers (see Figure 10-19).

Large retailers, catalog companies, and others who work from a distribution center often have very specific requirements for packaging because of their automation systems and the number of items that are processed on a daily basis. Use of bar-coding is absolutely essential in such circumstances. Suppliers who do not meet packaging specs may find orders refused, even though each individual product meets or exceeds minimum product specs.

RELATIONSHIP OF SPECS AND STANDARDS TO PRODUCT COST AND QUALITY

Standards and specifications for products have a significant impact on final costs. For example, when specifications indicate a high level of expectations in terms of construction and appearance, materials selection and construction techniques must ensure that the finished products meet that level of expectation. Production and material costs will probably be higher and, thus, the final cost for the product will be high. The same thing applies to standards. If production standards require that all shoulder seams be taped, then the additional cost for materials (the tape), labor, and attachments for machines that incorporate the tape into the seam must be included when

Sweaters, Blouses, Shirts, Wovens

Figure 1:
Lay item front down, flat and smooth with the sleeves extended.

Figure 2:
Sleeves must be folded flat and smooth with cuffs placed even with shoulders at top of package.

Figure 3:
Shirt must be folded neatly using hands to smooth out the bulkiness. Clips can be used to secure shirt in position, however pins of any sort are unacceptable.

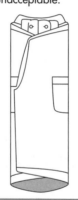

Figure 4:
The tail of the shirt must be tightened around the end of the folding template, extend slightly beyond the top of the shoulders and taper in on each side. The shirttail may then be tucked in between the sleeve fold and the sleeve cuffs.

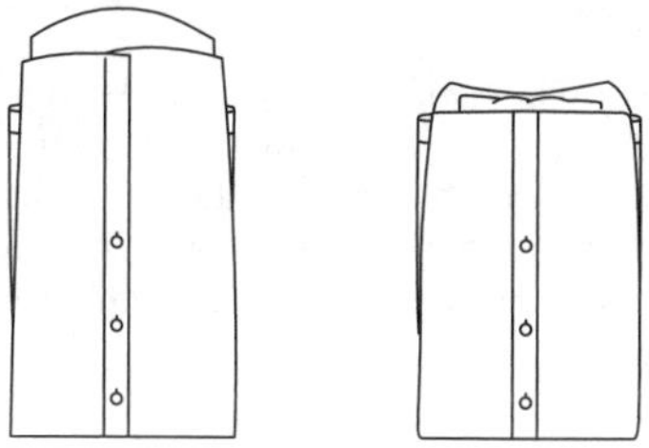

Figure 5:
Place folded item in an appropriately sized polybag. Seal and label with stock number, size, color, gender, vendor number and country of origin.

Figure 10-18
Diagram for packaging a shirt.

Apparel
Packing Merchandise

- Each <u>master shipping carton</u> must contain only one SKU (stock keeping unit). The buyer will not accept any Master Shipping carton that contains multiple SKUs.
- Merchandise must be bulk packed without multiple unit boxing or bagging inside of the master shipping carton.
- The merchandise inside the Master Shipping Carton must not be tied together in bundles with string, bands, ribbons, etc.
- Dot no ship merchandise on hangers or in hanger packs.
- The minimum case quantity is 4 selling units per master shipping carton.

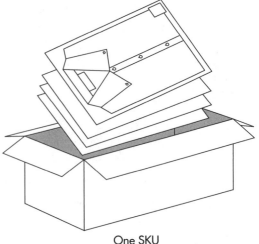

One SKU

No string,
bands, ribbons, etc.

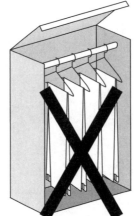

No hangers

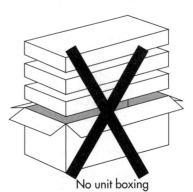

No unit boxing

The buyer encourages its vendors to send full cartons. If you are unable to fill a standard master shipping carton with one SKU, you may choose one of two options.

1. Reduced Carton Size (preferred)
If a shipment is small and a full case of one size and style is not possible, you can reduce the standard carton by no more than 6 inches, thus making the carton dimension 22 in. x 10 in. x 6 in., (minimum carton dimension).

2. Quantity Adjustment
Discuss order quantity adjustments with Inventory Control. For example, if you have a request for 20 units and the carton will hold 26 units, you may request increasing the quantity by 6 more units to make a full carton. Another example would be a request for 35 units, and the carton holds only 26. You may request a decrease in the quantity by 9, and include them in a subsequent order.

Figure 10-19
Diagram for packaging a shipping carton.

price is calculated. In addition, costs for operator training and time to meet these construction standards must be included.

Companies should have a reasonably good idea of the standards expected by their customers and the amount that these customers are willing to pay. Standards and specs that are higher than the target market demands cost the company money in terms of higher expenses and lower sales. Standards and specs that are lower than the target market demands also affect the company in terms of lower expenses and lower sales. Thus, the company needs to balance costs of producing and selling merchandise with the expectations of the target market. It is important to make sure that poor or low quality merchandise is not accepted or shipped out and that products are consistent in quality so that customers know what to expect.

The costs of managing standards and specifications for products is similar to that for materials. Many large companies have separate divisions that are responsible for managing standards and specifications. These costs are considered part of the cost of doing business and of maintaining a product of consistent quality.

CONCLUSIONS

Product integrity builds on the understanding of materials and material performance developed in Part II. A discussion of the various types of standards and specifications integrated materials with design, function, appearance, size, fit, construction, finishing, zoning, and packaging factors. Companies need to understand how the components of a product work together to produce an appealing and satisfactory product. Failure to address these significant issues can result in disaster. Regardless of how completely and carefully a material is specified and evaluated, if a company fails to develop product standards and specifications, well-understood and adequately performing materials can be combined in a product that fails to meet consumer expectations. Products may fail because of a poor appearance, inadequate understanding of functional demands put on it by the consumer, poor fit or size, inappropriate or poor construction, or failure to meet packaging requirements of the retailer. In other words, internal integrity was low or inconsistent. Regardless of the reason, product failure can amount to the same thing: loss of income for the company.

SUGGESTED READINGS

American Association of Textile Chemists and Colorists. (1996). *AATCC Technical Manual, 71.* Research Triangle Park, NC: Author.

American Society for Testing and Materials. (1996). *Annual Book of ASTM Stan-* *dards, Vol. 7.1 & 7.2.* West Conshohocken, PA: Author.

Amirbayat, J. (1993). Seams of Different Ply Properties. Part I. Seam Appearance. *Journal of the Textile Institute, 83(2),* 209–217.

Amster, Ruth Kutner. (1985, August). Sizing Up Apparel Standards, *Bobbin, 26,* 50, 52, 54–56.

Anfuso, Dawn. (1994, July). L. L. Bean's TQM Efforts Put People Before Processes. *Personnel Journal, 73(7),* 72–73, 75–78, 80, 83.

Apparel Quality Committee. (1985). *Elements of an Apparel Quality Control Program.* Arlington, VA: American Apparel Manufacturers Association.

Bass, Garnet. (1994, August). The Sun Also Rises. *North Carolina,* 44–46, 48–51.

Bhargava, Sunita Wadekar. (1993, May 17). Ann ReTaylored. *Business Week,* 70, 72.

Bona, Mario. (1990). *Textile Quality: Physical Methods of Product and Process Control.* Rome: Texilia.

Brown, Patty. (1992). *Ready-to-Wear Apparel Analysis.* New York: Macmillan.

Chisholm, Sandra Flora. (1995). Textile Quality Assurance: A Comparison Between Education and Industry. Unpublished Master's Thesis, Iowa State University, Ames.

Clark, Kim B., & Takahiro Kujimonto. (1990, November–December). The Power of Product Integrity. *Harvard Business Review, 68,* 107–118.

Cooklin, Gerry. (1991). *Introduction to Clothing Manufacture.* Oxford, England: BSP Professional Books.

Ford, J. E. (1993). Textile Product Specifications. *Textiles, 22(3),* 23–25.

Fourt, Lyman, & Norman Hollies. (1971). *Improvement of Firemen's Turnout Coats for Greater Comfort and Effectiveness in Work.* Washington, DC: U.S. Department of Commerce, National Bureau of Standards.

Fourt, Lyman, & Norman R. S. Hollies. (1970). *Clothing Comfort and Function.* New York: Marcel Dekker.

Gioello, Debi. (1985, April). Hand of Fabric Primer. *Bobbin, 26,* 122, 124–126.

Gladhill, Robert L. (1996, August). Conformity Assessment: What Is It, Why Do We Need It? *ASTM Standardization News, 24,* 30–33.

Glock, Ruth E., & Grace I. Kunz. (1995). *Apparel Manufacturing: Sewn Products Analysis, 2nd ed.* Englewood Cliffs, NJ: Prentice-Hall.

Glover, Brian. (1994). Kaizen, Kanban, or Common Sense. In American Association of Textile Chemist and Colorists, *Book of Papers.* Research Triangle Park, NC: Author, pp. 314–318.

Hatch, Kathryn L. (1993). *Textile Science.* Minneapolis: West Publishing Company.

Hearle, John W. S. (1992, April). Can Fabric Hand Enter the Dataspace? Part 1. *Textile Horizons,* 14–16.

Hearle, John W. S. (1993, June). Can Fabric Hand Enter the Dataspace? Part 2. Measuring the Unmeasurable. *Textile Horizons,* 16–20.

Hollies, Norman R. S., & Vera R. Usdin. (1980). The Skin Barrier—How Does It Handle Materials Lost from Clothing? In the American Association of Textile Chemists and Colorists, *Textiles: Toxicological and Environmental Concerns.* Research Triangle Park, NC: Author, 33–35.

Ito, K., & M. Nitta. (1994). Some Difficult Issues in Recent Apparel Manufacturing and a Counter-Measure for the Future. *International Journal of Clothing Science and Technology, 6(2/3),* 14–16.

JC Penney. (1996). *Minimum Construction Guidelines Manual.* Carrollton, TX: Author.

JC Penney. (1996). *Quality Control Guidelines of Apparel and Soft Home Furnishings.* Carrollton, TX: Author.

JC Penney. (1996). *Supplier Testing Guide.* Carrollton, TX: Author.

Kadolph, Sara J., & Anna I. Langford. (1998). *Textiles,* 8th ed. Englewood Cliffs, NJ: Prentice-Hall.

Karnes, Carol L., & John J. Karnes. (1994, February). How the Apparel Industry Measures Up to Quality Standards. *Quality Progress,* 25–29.

Kawabata, Sueo. (1994). Difficulty with Shingosen: A View from an Analysis of Fabric Hand. *International Journal of Clothing Science and Technology, 6(2/3),* 17–19.

Kawabata, Sueo, & Masako Niwa. (1994). High Quality Fabrics for Garments. *International Journal of Clothing Science and Technology, 6(5),* 20–25.

Kawabata, Sueo, & Masako Niwa. (1996). Objective Measurement of Fabric Hand. In Raheel, Mastura. (ed.). *Modern Textile Characterization Methods.* New York: Marcel Dekker, pp. 329–354.

Kim, Jong-Jun, Hechmi Hamouda, Itzhak Shalev, & Roger L. Barker. (1993, August). Instrumental Methods for Measuring the Surface Frictional Properties of Softener Treated Fabrics. *Textile Chemist and Colorist, 25(8),* 15–20.

Kowalski, Mike. (1991). Automotive Textiles to Date. *Textiles, 20,* 10–12.

Kutner Amster, Ruth. (1985, August). Sizing Up Apparel Standards. *Bobbin, 26,* 50, 52, 54, 56.

Lyle, Dorothy Siegert. (1977). *Performance of Textiles.* New York: John Wiley & Sons.

Mehta, Pradip V. (1992). *An Introduction*

to *Quality Control for the Apparel Industry*. Milwaukee: ASQC Press.

Merkel, Robert S. (1991). *Textile Product Serviceability*. New York: Macmillan.

Minazio, Pier Giorgio. (1995). FAST—Fabric Assurance by Simple Testing. *International Journal of Clothing Science and Technology, 7(2/3)*, 43–48.

Moore, Carolyn L. (1992, Fall). Factors That Affect Undesirable Garment Drape. *Journal of Home Economics, 31–34.*

Moore, Carolyn L., Lois M. Gurel, & Marvin Lentner. (1995). Effects of Fabric Skewness on the Drape of Four-Gore Skirts. *Clothing and Textiles Research Journal, 13,* 131–138.

Nike, Inc. (1988). *Nike Quality Assurance Manual*. Beaverton, OR: Author.

Pensa, Ildo E., (1994). The Total Quality Concept in Garment Dyeing. In American Association of Textile Chemist and Colorists, *Book of Papers*. Research Triangle Park, NC: Author, pp. 346–350.

Pile, John F. (1995). *Interior Design*. New York: Harry N. Abrams.

Potluri, Prasad, Isaac Porat, & John Atkinson. (1995). Towards Automated Testing of Fabrics. *International Journal of Clothing Science and Technology, 7(2/3),* 11–23.

Renbourn, E. T., & W. H. Rees. (1972). *Materials and Clothing in Health and Disease*. London: H. K. Lewis.

Rong, G. H., & K. Slater. (1992). A New Approach to the Assessment of Textile Performance, *Journal of the Textile Institute, 83(2),* 197–208.

Rudie, Raye. (1992, May). Love Affair with Lycra Spandex Far from Over. *Bobbin, 33,* 19–20.

Schoff, Clifford K. (1995, October). New Trends in Coatings Technology. *ASTM Standardization News, 23,* 24–27.

Shishoo, Roshan L. (1995). Importance of Mechanical and Physical Properties of Fabrics in the Clothing Manufacturing Process. *International Journal of Clothing Science and Technology, 7(2/3),* 35–42.

Shishoo, Roshan. (1990, March). Interaction Between Fabric Properties and Garment Making. *Apparel International,* 3–4, 6.

Siegel, Stan. (1992, January). Why We Need Checks and Balances to Assure Quality. *IEEE Software, 9,* 101–102.

Smith, Julia E. (1993). The Comfort of Clothing. *Textiles, 22(1),* 18–20.

Spiegel Quality Assurance Department. (1984). *The Spiegel Apparel Buyer's Guide to Quality Assurance*. Oak Brook, IL: Spiegel.

Spiegel Quality Assurance Department. (1983). *Spiegel Quality Standards*. Oak Brook, IL: Spiegel.

Spiegel Quality Assurance Department. (1984). *Spiegel Upscale Sizing*. Oak Brook, IL: Spiegel.

Stylios, George. (ed.). (1991). *Textile Objective Measurement and Automation in Garment Manufacture*. New York: Ellis Horwood.

Tamburrino, Nicola. (1992, April). Apparel Sizing Issues, Part 1. *Bobbin, 33,* 44–46.

Tamburrino, Nicola. (1992, June). Sized to Sell. *Bobbin, 33,* 68, 72–74.

Technical Advisory Committee. (1973). *Improving Apparel Performance*. Arlington, VA: American Apparel Manufacturers Association.

Tortora, Phyllis G., & Robert S. Merkel. (1996). *Fairchild's Dictionary of Textiles,* 7th ed. New York: Fairchild.

Vigo, Tyrone L. (1994). *Textile Processing and Properties: Preparation, Dyeing, Finishing, and Performance*. Amsterdam, The Netherlands: Elsevier Science B. V.

Watkins, Susan M. (1984). *Clothing: The Portable Environment*. Ames: Iowa State University Press.

REVIEW QUESTIONS

1. Explain each type of specs and standards and its relationship to product integrity and product quality.
   a. design
   b. function
   c. appearance
   d. size
   e. fit
   f. construction

g. zoning
h. finishing
i. packaging

2. Write standards and specs for workmanship for these products and explain why you selected those specific criteria for that product:
   a. T-shirt
   b. pillowcase
   c. bookbag
   d. shirt or blouse
   e. jeans or slacks

3. Identify product zones for the products in Question 2 and explain your rationale for the boundaries for the zones and the number of zones you developed for each product.

4. Describe how sample products, prototypes, or made-ups are used in assuring the quality of products.

ACTIVITIES

1. Discuss the relationships among materials, products, and customer satisfaction.

2. Examine several products of the same type and style, but at different price points. Discuss the relationships among materials, appearance, construction, size, and so on related to price. Is there a difference?

3. Write specs for a specific product and target market related to design, fit, size, construction, finishing, appearance, workmanship, zoning, and packaging (see Appendix C for ideas).

4. Explore the information available on the world wide web related to product specifications and standards. How does it apply to the information in this chapter?

5. Discuss how quality assurance relates to the information included in design, pattern making, and construction classes. Write standards and specifications for assignments in these classes. How does your work meet these standards and specifications?

6. Discuss how information related to internal integrity would be used by designers, merchandisers, retailers, buyers, and engineers.

7. Visit a design or product development company and ask how they use standards and specifications for design, construction, fit, size, finishing, appearance, workmanship, and packaging in their company.

8. Read these articles (Ford, J. E. [1993]. Textile Product Specifications. *Textiles, 22(3)*, 23–25; Kutner Amster, Ruth. [1985, August]. Sizing

Up Apparel Standards. *Bobbin, 26,* 50, 52, 54, 56; Tamburrino, Nicola. [1992, April]. Apparel Sizing Issues, Part 1. *Bobbin, 33,* 44–46; Tamburrino, Nicola. [1992, June]. Sized to Sell. *Bobbin, 33,* 68, 72–74) and discuss what they mean in terms of quality assurance.

9. Develop product zones and descriptions of acceptable and non-acceptable variations for specific products.

Chapter 11

INSPECTING PRODUCTS

OBJECTIVES

- To understand the purpose of each inspection type.
- To understand procedures and techniques used in product inspection.
- To apply the results of product inspection to decision making to ensure product quality.
- To inspect products for adherence to standards and specifications.

KEY TERMS

product inspection

product audit

inspection specifications

auditor or inspector

conformance

nonconforming goods

inspection

audit

materials inspection

patent defects

source inspection

incoming or receiving inspection

in-process inspection

during production inspection

du-pro inspection

process improvement

quality checkpoints

process control points

100% inspection

random or statistical sampling

vendor inspection

standard allowed minutes

standard allowed hours

exclusivity

final inspection

first quality merchandise

firsts

second quality merchandise

seconds

irregulars

imperfects

product inspection

pilot lot inspection

first piece inspection

shipment inspection

packed product inspection

packed product audit

buyer audit

supplier partnership

vendor certification

Determining when a product meets standards and specifications is a key element of quality assurance. It involves an in-depth understanding of the precise nature of the requirements and expectations for the product and the target market. The inspector must understand the measures used to assess performance, appearance, function, and size that are critical for the product and its ultimate success when used by consumers. The ability to determine if a product meets expectations is based on two basic procedures—inspection and evaluation. Both require a basic knowledge of standards, specifications, and customer expectations. Inspection, however, relies more on visual measures than on subjecting the materials or finished product to some physical or mechanical test (see Chapter 12).

Visual inspection is an important tool used at several stages to help assure the quality of the finished product. Inspection is done to assess materials to determine that they are free of patent defects. **Product inspection** implies the same search for nonadherence to characteristics, dimensions, and other required parameters that can be detected with the eye and the use of some simple measuring device, such as a tape measure, ruler, or template. The inspector compares the results for a product or sample of products to a set of standards and specifications that describe requirements for the product. **Product audit** is another term for product inspection.

Inspection specifications describe the procedures and stages of production at which inspection should occur. Thus, inspection specifications describe the inspection or audit process, whereas written specs and standards are the measures against which the materials and products that are being inspected are judged.

Visual inspection of products is often referred to as product inspection to differentiate this process from that used for materials inspection. Both types of inspection are important in ensuring product quality, but product inspection probably occurs at several different stages during production. It is not uncommon for both sample and finished products to be evaluated when a company is trying to identify the ability of a supplier or vendor to meet established standards and specifications. This chapter focuses on the visual assessment of products, but also it will review some basic elements related to material inspection.

Inspection is necessary in part because of the seasonal and fashion nature of many of the products produced by this industry. Product change tends to be rapid, deliberate product variation is wide, and production runs tend to be short in comparison to many other industries. In addition, this industry tends to be more labor intensive and the materials tend to be more flexible and easier to manipulate compared to materials used in production facilities in other industries. Thus, the potential for accidental product variation (defects or faults) can be great.

INSPECTOR TRAINING

Inspectors are the individuals who examine the product, material, component, or process to determine if it conforms to standards and specifications.

Inspectors are trained to conduct the inspection, to know what to look for, and in how to evaluate the item. Traditionally, on-the-job training is combined with more formal educational experiences. Many inspectors were originally production line employees, who worked for many years in the same company, often on the same production line. Other inspectors, especially those who conduct vendor inspections, are college graduates who have a knowledge of engineering, product performance, production, or related aspects. Inspectors are often referred to as auditors, but, in some companies, auditor is used for those individuals who work with basic processes, such as visual inspections, and inspector is used for those individuals engaged in more detailed analyses of products, processes, materials, or suppliers.

Desirable characteristics in an inspector or auditor include good vision and color perception, good attention to detail, thorough, self-directed, high-quality standards for individual work, the ability to get along with others, a reasonable knowledge of math, an interest in maintaining a company's reputation for quality merchandise, and the ability to communicate with others person to person or in more indirect forms using written memos or reports.

Conformance means that the materials, components, processes, or products meet requirements in terms of specifications and standards. They are within acceptable quality limits. **Nonconforming goods** are those that do not meet standards and specifications. Nonconforming goods may reflect a misunderstanding or misinterpretation of standards and specifications, poorly trained operators, poorly maintained machines, or incorrect machine settings. In some cases, nonconforming goods may need to be reworked to bring them up to the desired level of conformance. In other cases, the goods cannot be salvaged and the investment in them is lost in part or in total depending on the type of problem and the item involved.

INSPECTION

An **inspection or audit** is the visual examination or review of materials, product components, and finished products on the basis of their adherence to some established set of standards, specifications, or requirements. Inspection often includes a physical check of product dimensions or measurements to determine if the product is the appropriate size, shape, or proportion.

Thus, inspection implies a very careful examination of a material or product, sometimes with the assistance of a measuring device. The analysis is based on a comparison between the item under inspection and established requirements. Thus, a single product in the retail setting may have undergone numerous inspections, ranging from inspection of materials to in-process inspection during production to inspection of the finished product before packaging and after it arrives at the retailer's distribution center. Each inspection satisfies a particular need and is related to the established

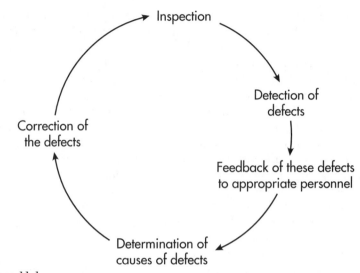

Figure 11-1
The inspection loop. (*Courtesy of the American Society for Quality*)

criteria against which each material, component, or product is to be inspected and when inspection is to be conducted during production.

The principle of inspection is relatively simple: examine the item of interest to detect defects, irregularities, and nonconformance as early in the process as possible, so that problems, inadequacies in production or materials, or inferior materials or components can be identified and corrected or replaced. Detection and correction are important in terms of individual products to guarantee that each and every product meets standards and specifications, thereby allowing it to be sold at full price. Detection and correction also are important to avoid production of additional nonconforming products and to keep overall production costs low and quality levels high. Figure 11-1 illustrates the principle involved in this detection-correction connection that is inherent in the inspection process.

The inspection of materials, components, and products during production is a key ingredient in a well-planned and complete quality assurance program that focuses on continuous improvement and has a goal of zero defects. Inspection helps companies detect problems and correct them in an efficient and timely manner. Sample inspection forms are included in Appendix B.

MATERIALS INSPECTION

Materials inspection identifies the presence of any patent defects with the materials that are to be combined in a product. Materials inspection is recommended as a means of increasing overall product quality and decreasing production costs. A company can avoid the investment of time, labor, or other resources when defective materials are identified before production begins. Thus, value will not be added to materials that fail to meet company requirements and costs related to working with unacceptable materials are kept low. Unfortunately, it is common practice within the textile industry complex to base the percentage of materials inspected on the value of the finished product. Thus, low-priced merchandise may have only a small percentage of its materials inspected before cutting and production begins. This practice is based on the incorrect assumption that the cost of inspection will improve profit margins for more expensive merchandise, but not for less expensive merchandise. Companies that revise their material inspection practices find that 100 percent inspection of materials pays for itself very quickly, regardless of the selling price of the goods produced.

Materials are inspected to determine their adherence to length, width, quality level, and uniformity requirements. Length and width requirements are related to cutting and marker aspects in terms of having sufficient material to meet production requirements. Uniformity can be considered another measure of fabric quality because a consistent material width and absence of patent defects contributes to cutting efficiency, product components that are free of material defects, lower production costs, and a higher profit margin. Quality level is based on the number, size, and type of patent defects identified during inspection. The AMTEX Partnership, a vertical textile industry research and development consortia, is working on a computer aided fabric evaluation (CAFE) project that will conduct automated inspection of fabric and mark and classify defects.

Other characteristics of materials may also be evaluated, such as yarn density and fabric grain, but these evaluations are not considered a part of the inspection process because they require more than a simple visual assessment or dimensional measurement. For example, evaluating fiber content, mass, or yarn count may be done but these procedures require more time, use of a balance, or calculations to determine adherence to requirements. Chapter 5 describes the process of material inspection in greater detail.

Companies that inspect materials when they arrive at the production or spreading and cutting facility may be more willing to refuse and return unacceptable materials and are better able to meet production deadlines compared to companies that inspect materials during spreading. In the latter case, materials are not inspected when they arrive, but by the individual spreading the fabric. Thus, the spreader is responsible not only for spreading the fabric correctly, but also for inspecting the fabric. Delaying material inspection until spreading can create problems if the fabric is found to be unacceptable because of poor width uniformity, insufficient amount or yardage, or poor quality as a result of patent defects. In addition, if a company only allows for inspection during spreading, then materials, such as buttons and zippers, that do not require spreading probably will not be inspected before being incorporated into a product.

When a fabric is determined to be unacceptable during spreading, spreading efficiency is compromised because the unacceptable material must be rewound and removed. In addition, spreading and production schedules will need to be modified and another material, hopefully one that will be acceptable, must be substituted. Changes in spreading and cutting because of unacceptable materials can create significant problems. New and appropriate materials must be received in a timely manner so that the company is still able to meet production deadlines. Thus, delaying inspection until materials are spread can result in disastrous delays in production and increased costs for the firm. Extra costs can include higher costs for rush delivery of finished merchandise, penalties for missing deadlines for delivery of finished goods, or increases in labor costs when operators must be paid overtime rates to meet production deadlines. However, many companies have recognized that material inspection must occur when goods are received if the company is to meet its required level of product quality.

SOURCE INSPECTION

Source inspection is the inspection of materials, components, products, or documents at the supplier's facility by an individual not employed by the supplier. Source inspection is not common in the textile industry complex. In some cases, companies may engage in source inspection because of the nature of the material, component, or product. Source inspection may be done because it is convenient or the buyer needs to identify the quality of the materials, components, or products immediately.

Source inspection also may refer to the inspection of results of specific requested procedures, such as from material or product testing, to determine if the appropriate level or range of performance was established before production. This means that the technical report from the materials testing division or independent company will be examined to determine the actual performance of the material or the process that was used in its assessment.

Another type of source inspection includes examination of documents related to inspection as a means of process improvement. Many companies require that their suppliers keep records of processes and inspection results so that problems can be traced to their sources and corrected. Keeping records of the inspection processes provides a means of identifying and documenting product quality.

Source inspectors perform many functions. They work with suppliers so that their materials, components, or goods are in compliance. Inspectors may train local individuals to be knowledgeable inspectors or plant managers, provide additional information regarding specs or standards, answer questions, and help interpret information so that it is used to improve quality. These inspectors also check documents to see that information is recorded consistently, logically, and completely. Finally, source inspectors may find it necessary to notify buyers when shipping of finished products is delayed for any reason, such as technical difficulties, disastrous weather conditions, or disruption of scheduling because of nonconforming materials. Source inspection is often used with government contracts.

INCOMING INSPECTION

It is not uncommon for product components to be assembled in separate facilities or in separate production lines and brought together in one plant or on one line for assembly. For example, cuffs, collars, or linings may be assembled in one place and shipped to another facility to be combined with other components, parts, and materials. Some processes, such as embroidery, require specialized equipment. As a result, they may be subcontracted to other companies and returned to the main assembly plant for incorporation into the finished product. In addition, some trims, such as bows or belts, may be purchased from other suppliers and require inspection to be sure that they are appropriate in characteristics and quality for the final product before they are attached or combined.

Incoming or receiving inspection is a visual examination of components and finished trims or other parts of a product. Inspection is especially important when components have been produced in another facility. If components and other parts are inspected immediately on arrival at the manufacturing plant, their acceptability can be determined at that point. If they are unacceptable, the supplier can attempt to minimize the negative impact of the inferior components on uninterrupted manufacturing, consistent quality, and production deadlines.

IN-PROCESS INSPECTION

In-process inspection is a general term that describes any visual evaluation or check of parts, components, or materials during production. This process concentrates on assessing conformance to standards and specifications for the assembly process. It is called in-process inspection because inspection occurs during the process of converting materials into finished products. In-process inspection means that individual parts or components of products are examined before they are assembled to determine if each part or component meets required specs and standards. Sometimes, this process is called **during production or du-pro inspection.**

In-process inspection occurs many times during production. Each inspection is designed to identify that each step in production has met specifications before anything further is done to the part or component or before additional parts or components are combined. In-process inspection detects and corrects problems before additional unacceptable work or processes are performed. This type of inspection detects nonconforming work or unacceptable materials before additional value has been added, so that work can be redone and unacceptable materials avoided. Thus, in-process inspection helps eliminate the production of unacceptable merchandise.

The concept of inspection during production is based on the work of Deming, Juran, and other quality experts, who state that quality can not be inspected into finished products. The goal is to identify and correct defects during production, thereby making it possible for products to meet specifications and standards at each stage in production. However, a conflict of interest will likely develop with in-process inspection when companies assign the same individual two simultaneous roles. Individuals who are responsible for the quality of production should not also be responsible for the rate of production. When rewards are based solely on production rates, the quality of the inspection will be compromised.

To avoid this conflict of interest, five basic elements must be present. First, each operation involved in the production of a finished product should have a set of written specifications that describe the requirements to be met. These specs must be carefully written so that the quality level is clearly defined.

Second, the individual(s) responsible for that operation must understand what is required of them and how their work will be evaluated. The specs should be in terms the operator understands. For example, translations into the appropriate language may be needed. In addition, if the operator is familiar with measurements in the metric system, measurements of a fraction of an inch, such as ¼ in. or .25 in. may not convey any sense of the width involved.

Third, these individuals should have received sufficient training to meet the stated requirements. Any questions from the operators regarding interpretation of the specs should have been addressed, and the operator should be able to perform the process correctly.

Fourth, the reward structure should emphasize meeting expectations rather than penalizing failure to meet production rates and specifications. In other words, pay should reflect how many items or processes were produced that met the specs and should not reflect how many in total were produced.

And fifth, the inspection process must incorporate a feedback mechanism so that problems related to incorrect handling of materials, incorrect machine settings, poor operator training or understanding, or other sources of defects can be identified and corrected. It is this final element, the feedback loop, that helps improve the process. This feedback is referred to as **process improvement** and is a key element to improving product quality. Thus, in-process inspection can be used as a diagnostic tool to help refine and improve the production process.

Often specific stages in production are identified as places where in-process inspection should occur. These **quality checkpoints** or **process control points** are identified on a master plan and ensure that inspection occurs at appropriate places during production. These points are usually places at which the next production step can compound the problem, as when components are joined or at which the next step cannot proceed until the error has been fixed without severely compromising the product. Sometimes, these checkpoints are also referred to as gatekeeping and the inspectors as gatekeepers, because additional processes do not take place until the item has been inspected, approved, and moved on to the next process.

These five elements are relatively basic for process control. Each step in production and its parameters need to be identified. Parameters describe requirements in terms of a standard and tolerances so that acceptable and unacceptable work is defined. For example, the requirements for producing a side seam should identify the stitch type, seam type, thread, seam allowance, stitches per inch, standards for appearance, placement of front and back pieces relative to each other, and amount of material to be trimmed. Operators must be informed of these requirements if they are to be expected to meet them. Because many facilities employ individuals who do not read, speak, or understand English, it may be necessary to include translations of specs in other languages or explain with diagrams or samples that illustrate what is acceptable and what is not.

Operators also need to know that their work will be inspected, the way in which this inspection will occur, and the criteria that will be used in the inspection process. When new specifications are introduced, operators must be trained so that they are able to meet them. Finally, rewards systems, such as pay rates, must be based on producing acceptable merchandise, not on piece rates that are based on producing a stated number of pieces per unit of time. Piece rates do not reward operators for acceptable work, but may penalize operators for poor work. Work force morale tends to be higher when the existing structure rewards acceptable work quality and production rates.

TYPES OF IN-PROCESS INSPECTIONS

After materials have been inspected and approved, they are moved into production. For fabrics, this means that they are ready to be spread and cut into the appropriate parts for a specific product. Inspection often occurs during spreading. Inspection at this stage is primarily another visual check, but during spreading the fabric is being manipulated so that some characteristics not apparent during materials inspection may be identified. For example, tight selvages may create problems in getting a flat layer thereby causing the fabric to bubble or pucker. This will create problems in cutting and sewing because some product pieces may be larger or slightly irregular in shape. Inspection after cutting is a quick examination of product pieces to make sure that notches and drill holes are correct, that edges are smooth and not fused, and that pieces are not distorted. Often the top, bottom, and middle plies are checked against the pattern to make sure they are correct.

In sewing, in-process inspection incorporates an evaluation of each operator's work based on the specifications and standards developed for that operation. This inspection often incorporates several evaluations. For example, a template may be used to quickly scan a shirt front to see that buttons or buttonholes are correctly placed, while a visual check will determine if the buttonholes are correctly sewn and that thread ends have been trimmed away. Checking thickness between thumb and forefinger will help determine that seams, hems, or pockets are not too thick or bulky. Thus, in-process inspection may involve appearance as observed by the trained eye, adherence to specifications as determined by a template, and touch based on an understanding of the standard.

In some companies, a floating inspector periodically checks work as it is proceeding through the production line. The inspector checks a random set of product parts to determine if they are meeting standards and specifications. In other companies, a more defined or formalized means of inspection takes place. For example, a formal inspector may inspect every fourth bundle of work by each operator or each operator's work is inspected every third hour. In still other companies, the work of each operator is inspected by the next operator in line. In all cases, incorrect items should be flagged or otherwise marked for rework. It is important that these inspections be thorough, regardless of who does them or the frequency at which they occur.

Inspections of all parts or components is referred to as **100% inspection.** With 100% inspection, costs are greater, but the possibility of inferior products being produced is reduced. Less than 100% inspection is referred to as **random or statistical sampling.** In random sampling, a few randomly selected items are inspected. This type of inspection is based on the assumption that product or process quality is consistent between samples. The problem is that quality can change drastically and quickly between items. Thus, the sample may reflect better or poorer quality compared with real quality. With random sample inspection, costs may be lower, but the risk of inferior products being produced and shipped out is greater.

When inspectors are identified as "police" within the facility, morale problems may develop. Management needs to help operators understand the role that inspectors play in terms of maintaining a consistent and desirable quality level for the company's products. Thus, training to help operators meet standards and specifications and developing reward systems for operators whose work consistently meets or exceeds standards and specifications promotes better morale. It is important that management work closely with operators, supervisors, engineers, and technicians. Machines and attachments must be properly set, adjusted, and maintained. Operators must receive appropriate training in terms of both the operation and the expectations for the amount and quality of work. When pay is based on the quality of work and not the quantity of work, operators are encouraged to do their best to produce work that meets specifications.

In-process inspection also occurs after finishing steps, such as dyeing, abrasive finishes, trimming, pressing, folding, or packaging. These inspections focus on a visual analysis to make sure that each product meets standards and specifications. In-process inspection can occur after each and every operation within a facility. Although many companies take shortcuts when it comes to inspection, attempts to reduce costs at the inspection level may, in fact, cost the company more in terms of rework (even though operators may not be paid for their rework), seconds, damaged components that must be recut, penalties for missed deadlines, or poor-quality merchandise.

VENDOR INSPECTION

In-process inspection by employees is done not just to benefit the manufacturer. In-process inspection of vendor's facilities has become a mainstay of many large retailers and others who contract production of manufactured textile and apparel items. Engineers or technical designers employed by these companies often visit the vendor's production facilities to inspect both the facility and its operations. A vendor inspection ensures that merchandise in production will meet standards and specifications developed by the buyer, that the merchandise will be available on time, and that sufficient documentation by the producer exists so that records can be examined when needed. In many ways, the documentation needed for suppliers is similar to that needed to qualify for ISO 9000 certification (see Chapter 3).

Vendor inspections may take place on a planned or scheduled basis or on an unscheduled, surprise basis. It is not uncommon for engineers and technical designers to spend a total of several months each year visiting and inspecting contract production facilities in the United States and elsewhere. When an inspector or auditor is visiting a plant, a significant amount of time may be spent observing sewing machine operators. When making these observations, the auditor should stand in front of the operator rather than behind and be aware that many operators are made uncomfortable when scrutinized in this fashion. Thus, many auditors have learned to watch operators closely while apparently strolling through the production floor. Auditors who would like to speak to operators should first ask permission from plant managers in order to not create problems with either management or operators.

Vendor inspections examine many dimensions beyond those operations directly connected to the production line. A partial list of areas to consider in a vendor inspection is included in Table 11-1. Often these inspections take place before a contract is signed with a vendor to determine if a legal agreement between the vendor and retailer is possible. Evaluations of this type are conducted at the vendor's manufacturing facility to determine if the company can produce the quantity of merchandise and meet standards, specifications, and production deadlines. The condition and cleanliness of the facility and equipment will help assess management's general approach. Dirty facilities in desperate need of repair often indicate a lax and uncaring managerial approach. Companies that cannot maintain their facility in an adequate fashion will have difficulty producing satisfactory merchandise in a timely manner.

Pattern making and design areas in plants, such as the cutting room supervisor, market layout, differences in markers among the contracting

Table 11-1
DIMENSIONS OF A VENDOR INSPECTION

General factory conditions and housekeeping
   Clean
   Well maintained
   Safety concerns
   Accessibility of machines
   General lighting
   Management access to production floor and
     employees

Standards and specifications
   Available and accessible to operators
   Knowledge of by operators
   Training systems in place

Pattern making and design
   Marker making
   Knowledge and experience
   Samples
   Knowledge of production floor
   Pilot lots

Spreading and cutting
   Knowledge of standards and specifications
   Production rates

Production
   Engineered flow
   Management of production
   Number of operators
   Skill level needed
   Knowledge of standards and specifications
   Production rates

Inspection procedures
   Materials

In-process
Final product
Record keeping
Number of and training of inspectors

Materials and product evaluation
   Equipment
   Training of personnel
   In-house facility or other
   Fit analysis
   Wear testing

Packaging and shipping
   Knowledge of standards and specifications
   Labels and packaging cartons

Management commitment
   Attitude toward vendor audit
   Attitude toward employees
   Knowledge of process
   Ability to delegate authority
   Ability to deal with problems and emergencies
   Concept of quality
   Attitude toward product quality

People
   Morale
   Knowledge
   Benefits
   Reward structure for meeting specs
   Attitude toward product quality

companies, and the location and availability of sample products, are considered. Sometimes, determining where sample products are made is also helpful.

An examination of annual production rates will identify the quantity of merchandise the facility is able to produce in a normal year. The price for sample products is a critical measure of importance to the retailer, because it helps determine product costs at the retail level. A list of current customers will help describe the quality of product that a facility normally produces. For example, facilities that produce at one quality level may find the transition to another quality level difficult to accomplish, especially if they are asked to increase quality substantially.

A vendor evaluation also assists the retailer to understand a contractor's current practices. For example, a company that engages in a series of 100% in-process inspections with a built-in feedback loop may have few adjustments to make in their internal processes to satisfy the retailer's quality assurance demands. A second company that does not conduct incoming materials inspections may have to develop a means of doing this, including employee training. Thus, the second company will need more time to prepare itself to meet quality demands.

Retailers probably do not want to be a vendor's sole customer because of the impact on the company and its employees if the retailer decides to source a product elsewhere. In addition, retail demand for one product is likely to be seasonal. If a vendor produces only one product for one retailer, it is not likely that they will be able to maintain a production work force all year round. Thus, trained operators will not be available when production is needed for the retailer.

Other aspects critical to retailers are the preseason and inseason lead times required by the vendor to meet production demands. The vendor's minimum requirements help determine order placement. In addition, the vendor's capability to meet EDI requirements for the retailer's distribution center are another dimension that must be determined.

A detailed examination of the production line will illustrate the usual production mix (styles, materials, colors, and so on) that a production facility can handle in its normal operation. The engineer or technical designer conducting the inspection should determine standard allowed minutes per day (SAMs) and standard allowed hours per day (SAHs). A **standard allowed minute** is a unit of measure for determining the time required for an operation and is the basis for production standards (Glock & Kunz, 1995). A **standard allowed hour** is used when costing in dozens instead of individual units and is converted from SAMs. These measures help the retailer determine the amount of business that can be placed with the vendor within the scheduled time frame.

In addition, vendor inspections may involve gathering information related to product development capability and timelines. For example, a retailer will want to assess the vendor's ability to produce patterns and engineer product requirements, as well as the vendor's interest in exclusivity requirements. **Exclusivity** indicates that a new product will be produced for the retailer only for a specified length of time or a specified number of seasons. Exclusivity is used to prevent a vendor from charging a retailer for product development costs on a new product, and then selling the product to competitors before the original retailer has earned a reasonable profit.

Many retailers have developed standard forms to be used in vendor evaluations so that the information collected is consistent and presented in a uniform fashion. The forms used to evaluate a potential vendor often differ from the forms used for an established vendor.

PRODUCT INSPECTION

The term product inspection can include several different types of inspection. Each is done for a specific reason. One type of product inspection occurs after all production operations have been completed. This **final in-**

spection ensures that a finished product meets required standards and specifications. Final inspection can be based on 100 percent of the products or on a statistical sample. Final inspection usually is done at the production facility, but in some cases and in some companies, it may be done at the distribution center or shipping facility. Final product inspection often means examining the product to see that it meets specifications related to design, size, fit, appearance, construction, and function as described in Chapter 10. A complete final inspection must be done before packaging. However, some companies refer to their inspection step after packaging as final inspection. In these cases, many product details, product size, and product fit cannot be evaluated. An earlier product inspection would have been able to assess adherence to these standards and specifications.

A final inspection based on a statistical sample is ideal if in-process inspection, training, and other quality assurance practices have been implemented, so that quality is incorporated into the product throughout the process. Companies that engage in 100 percent final inspection may do so because of insufficient in-process inspection during production. Companies that have used minimal in-process inspection tend to rely on final inspection to differentiate products that meet requirements (**first quality merchandise or firsts**) from those that do not (**second quality merchandise, seconds, irregulars, or imperfects**). These companies inspect all their products after production has been completed, they do not understand that quality is built into a product from the initial planning stages through production and attempt to "inspect quality into a product." This means that the company is separating production into two categories: products that will be sold for first quality price and products that will not be sold for first quality price. Unfortunately for these companies, their investment in each product is the same regardless of the price for which it is sold. Merchandise that undergoes this type of final inspection may carry an inspection sticker such as the one shown in Figure 11-2. Problems with imperfect merchandise may be identified on hangtags such as the one shown in Figure 11-3. Sometimes, these imperfect items are sold "as is" and the consumer is aware of the defect at point of sale.

Product inspection often involves a holistic visual analysis of the product to determine its adherence to requirements. Final inspection by the manufacturer is one example of product inspection. Several other types of product inspection are used to determine the acceptability of products. Many large retailers conduct product inspections for several reasons.

After the first sample or pilot lot of a product style has been produced, it should be inspected carefully. This pilot lot represents the quality from the production floor as it is expected to occur unless changes in the process are made. Thus, any flaws, defects, errors, and other problems should be identified during this inspection. A **pilot lot inspection** is a careful examination of the first sample production run in the facility for a specific style or product line. Basic or minor changes to the process and further refine-

Figure 11-2
Inspection stickers.

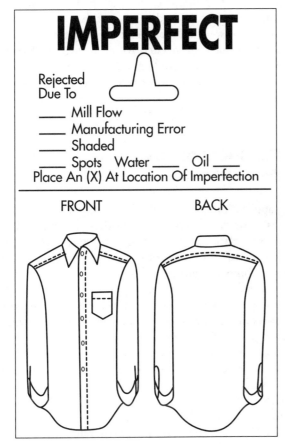

Figure 11-3
Imperfect label for shirts.

ments may become evident with a close examination of these sample products. Sometimes, this type of inspection is also referred to as **first piece inspection.** It is important that production not continue until the pilot lot inspection has been completed so that problems can be fixed at this stage. Thus, the pilot lot inspection helps detect problems, but some time may be needed to develop solutions so that subsequent production meets specs.

The entire pilot or sample lot requested from a contractor should be inspected (100% inspection) including any fine details included in the inspection specifications. The contractor should pay special attention to problems identified in the pilot lot inspection because full shipments of merchandise more than likely will be refused if these defects continue.

When products are shipped to the distribution center, another product audit or inspection may take place. This inspection is referred to as **shipment inspection, packed product inspection or audit,** or **buyer audit.** The entire shipment is unloaded at the distribution center and a predetermined number of sample products that represent all of the sizes and colors included in the shipment are pulled. The samples are 100% inspected for adherence to standards and specifications. Shipments whose samples do not pass inspection may be refused by the buyer and returned to the vendor. If products are needed to meet current customer demand, conforming products will be identified and sold; nonconforming products will be returned to the supplier. Most often, suppliers are charged for this 100% inspection.

Vendor Certification and Supplier Partnerships

One growing application of inspection is that companies are forming temporary alliances, formal partnerships, and other relationships with vendors or suppliers. These relationships are based on the recognition that vendors and buyers are dependent on each other for the continuation of their businesses. When a company engages in a quality assurance program, they must be able to assess the quality of the merchandise they sell. This is so whether the company sells materials to producers, manufacturers sell finished goods to retailers, or retailers sell products to consumers. Because of this dependence and the implementation of an inspection program, companies recognize that some vendors are better and more consistent at meeting specifications and standards. Thus, the concept of partnering with suppliers has developed.

With these partnerships, the traditional adversarial relationship between the vendor and the buyer has been replaced with a more cooperative relationship. In **supplier (or vendor) partnerships,** the buyer and supplier work together for the mutual benefit of both companies. This means that companies work together to meet specifications of and delivery requirements for materials and products. For example, suppliers may be notified more quickly that a product is being modified or a new product is being developed. Or, they may be invited to participate in various activities when a company changes the process, product, standards, or specifications. In some cases, the partnership is an informal one in which a buyer has a list of preferred vendors who deliver acceptable materials or products on time. Another example would be a company who works with a supplier or vendor because it generally keeps sufficient inventory on hand and is able to meet the buyer's demand. Still another example is the situation where the buyer and vendor work together to develop a better material for a product or write specifications that better reflect customer expectations. Supplier partnerships are also known as vendor partnerships.

Some partnerships are more formal. In these cases, the vendor has been certified by the buyer. **Vendor (or supplier) certification** is a formal agreement based on the quality of the materials or products received over an extended time span. With vendor certification, an in-depth, 100% inspection of goods as they are received by the buyer occurs less frequently. For example, if a vendor has provided the quality and quantity of materials as specified in the agreement for ten consecutive shipments and the materials have been tested and inspected and found to be acceptable, the buyer might certify the vendor. With vendor certification, the vendor must document its quality assurance procedures and maintain records to verify that it is meeting the buyer's expectations and requirements. The goods are still inspected, but the inspections occur less frequently and are less vigorous. Vendor certification is a measure of trust between companies, but it is subject to cancellation if quality deteriorates. However, in many instances, deteriorating quality means that the buyer and vendor work together to identify the problem and implement a solution. Vendor certification is also known as supplier certification.

CONCLUSIONS

Although inspection is used to check materials, processes, components, and products against standards to determine if they are acceptable, some defective merchandise may still be shipped. Inspection is not perfect because of human and system errors. For example, human inspectors may not remember specs and standards exactly, they may interpret them differently, they may be distracted and allow seconds to be identified as firsts, or they may misinterpret scales and templates.

Inspection can be used to detect errors and implement corrections. However, this is true only if a mechanism is in place to detect and correct an error. Correcting the unacceptable product, material, or component is good, but a better long-term solution is to minimize reoccurrence of the problem. Inspection can be used to implement corrective action so that problems of a specific nature do not recur. In addition, inspection can be used as a preventative measure by identifying potential problems that can be solved before production begins.

Inspection should not be viewed as the equivalent of quality assurance. Inspection is one component in the process of assuring the quality of a finished product. Inspection will never be able to ensure a certain level of quality in a product. Rather, it should ensure that products with defects or problems are much less likely to occur and that products with problems are much less likely to be purchased by the consumer.

SUGGESTED READINGS

Aft, Lawrence. (1992). *Fundamentals of Industrial Quality Control*, 2nd ed. Milwaukee: ASQC Press.

American Society for Testing and Materials. (1996). *Annual Book of ASTM Standards, Vol. 7.1 & 7.2*. West Conshohocken, PA: Author.

Anon. (1994, September). AMTEX: The American Textile Partnership. *Textile Chemist and Colorist, 26(9)*, 92–93.

Anon. (1995, April). Eight Projects Progressing as AMTEX Begins Third Year. *Textile World*, 27–28.

Arter, Dennis R. (1994). *Quality Audits for Improved Performance*. Milwaukee: ASQC Quality Press.

Beauregard, Michael R., Raymond J. Mikulak, & Barbara A. Olson. (1992). *A Practical Guide to Statistical Quality Improvement: Opening Up the Statistical Toolbox*. New York: Van Nostrand Reinhold.

Besterfield, Dale H. (1994). *Quality Control*, 4th ed. Englewood Cliffs, NJ: Prentice-Hall.

Bishara, Rafik H., & Michael L. Wyrick. (1994, October). A Systematic Approach to Quality Assurance Audit. *Quality Progress, 27*, 67–70.

Bona, Mario. (1990). *Textile Quality: Physical Methods of Product and Process Control*. Rome: Texilia.

Brown, Patty. (1992). *Ready-to-Wear Apparel Analysis*. New York: Macmillan.

Carter, C. L. (1990). *Quality Assurance, Quality Control, and Inspection Handbook*. Richardson, TX: C. L. Carter, Jr. and Associates.

Chisholm, Sandra Flora. (1995). Textile Quality Assurance: A Comparison Between Education and Industry. Unpublished Master's Thesis, Iowa State University, Ames.

Clark, Kim B., & Takahiro Kujimonto. (1990, November-December). The Power of Product Integrity. *Harvard Business Review, 68*, 107–118.

Cooklin, Gerry. (1991). *Introduction to Clothing Manufacture*. Oxford, England: BSP Professional Books.

Dale, B. G., & J. J. Plunkett. (1995). *Quality Costing*, 2nd ed. New York: Chapman & Hall.

Deming, W. Edwards. (1982). *Quality, Productivity, and Competitive Position*. Cambridge: Massachusetts Institute of Technology Center for Advanced Engineering Study.

Desai, Mahesh P. (1996, February). Implementing a Supplier Scorecard Program. *Quality Progress, 24,(2)*, 73–75.

Dickerson, Kitty G., Christopher C. Hooper, & Robert D. Boyle. (1995, April). The New Approach for Manufacturers. *America's Textiles International*, 28–31.

Fine, Edmund S. (1994, August). Zen and the Art of Quality Auditing. *Quality Progress, 22*, 192.

Ford, J. E. (1993). Textile Product Specifications. *Textiles, 22(3)*, 23–25.

Fortess, Fred. (1986, August). No Inspection Required. *Bobbin Magazine, 27*, 54–56, 58, 60.

Gladhill, Robert L. (1996, August). Conformity Assessment: What Is It, Why Do We Need It? *ASTM Standardization News, 24*, 30–33.

Glock, Ruth E., & Grace I. Kunz. (1995). *Apparel Manufacturing: Sewn Products Analysis, 2nd ed*. Englewood Cliffs, NJ: Prentice-Hall.

Goetsch, David L., & Stanley Davis. (1994). *Introduction to Total Quality: Quality, Productivity, Competitiveness*. New York: Macmillan.

Harrington, H. James. (1987). *Poor-Quality Cost*. Milwaukee: ASQC Press.

Ishikawa, Kaoru. (1985). *What is Total Quality Control? The Japanese Way*. Englewood Cliffs, NJ: Prentice-Hall.

Jacobsen, Donald M. (1985, August). Fabric: Inspection Savings—Fact or Fiction? *Bobbin, 26*, 70, 72, 74, 76, 78.

JC Penney. (1996). *Quality Control Guidelines of Apparel and Soft Home Furnishings.* Carrollton, TX: Author.

Johnson, Jay L. (1994, March). Target's New Vision: Total Quality. *Discount Merchandiser,* 38, 40, 42, 44, 46, 48, 50, 52, 66.

Juran, J. M., & Frank M. Gryna. (1993). *Quality Planning and Analysis: From Product Development through Use.* New York: McGraw-Hill.

Karnes, Carol L., & John J. Karnes. (1994, February). How the Apparel Industry Measures Up to Quality Standards. *Quality Progress,* 27, 25–29.

Knapton, Jim. (1990, February). How to Develop Your Own Unquality Costing Analysis. *Apparel Manufacturing,* 83–88.

McMurry, John W. (1994, June). AMTEX Spurs New Ways of Thinking. *Textile World,* 78, 80–82.

Mehta, Pradip V. (1992). *An Introduction to Quality Control for the Apparel Industry.* Milwaukee: ASQC Press.

Menon, H. G. (1992). *TQM in New Product Manufacturing.* New York: McGraw-Hill.

Merkel, Robert S. (1991). *Textile Product Serviceability.* New York: Macmillan.

Parsowith, B. Scott. (1995). *Fundamentals of Quality Auditing.* Milwaukee: ASQC Press.

Piccard, Lawrence G. (1992). *Fundamentals of Quality Control.* Milwaukee: ASQC Press.

Pond, Robert J. (1994). *Fundamentals of Statistical Quality Control.* New York: Macmillan.

Rabolt, Nancy J., Katrina Bothwell, Judith C. Forney, & Mary Barry. (1988). Quality Control in Overseas Apparel Manufacturing. *Journal of Consumer Studies and Home Economics,* 12(4), 389–397.

Sears, James A. (1983, July). Changing Role of the Quality Inspection Function. *Quality Progress,* 16, 12–17.

Scherkenback, William W. (1988). *The Deming Route to Quality and Productivity: Roadmaps and Roadblocks.* Washington, DC: Ceep Press Books.

Stylios, George. (ed.). (1991). *Textile Objective Measurement and Automation in Garment Manufacture.* New York: Ellis Horwood.

Technical Advisory Committee. (1973). *Improving Apparel Performance.* Arlington, VA: American Apparel Manufacturers Association.

Technical Advisory Committee. (1993, April). The Cutting Room of the Future. *Knitting Times,* K/A2, K/A4.

Tedaldi, Michael, Fred Scaglione, & Vincent Russotti. (1992). *A Beginner's Guide to Quality in Manufacturing.* Milwaukee: ASQC Quality Press.

Thompson Thome, Judy. (1987, January). TALC: A New Way of Doing Business. *Apparel Industry Magazine,* 24, 26.

Tortora, Phyllis G., & Robert S. Merkel. (1996). *Fairchild's Dictionary of Textiles,* 7th ed. New York: Fairchild.

United Nations Industrial Development Organization. (1972). *Quality Control in the Textile Industry.* New York: United Nations.

Weber, Richard T., & Ross H. Johnson. (1993). *Buying and Supplying Quality.* Milwaukee: ASQC Press.

Weller, Edward F. (1993, September). Lessons from Three Years of Inspection Data. *IEEE Software,* 10, 38–45.

REVIEW QUESTIONS

1. Explain why inspection helps ensure product quality.

2. Differentiate among these types of inspections in terms of when they occur, what they entail, and how they affect product quality:
   a. materials inspection
   b. source inspection
   c. in-process inspection
   d. pilot lot inspection
   e. shipment inspection
   f. final inspection

3. What is the difference between conformance and nonconformance?

4. Explain exclusivity. Why would this be a concern for manufacturers and retailers?

5. Why is final inspection not considered a key element in a general quality assurance program within the industry?

6. Explain how an inspection program can be both corrective and preventative in nature.

7. For a simple product, such as a towel, identify a sequence of inspections that may occur.

ACTIVITIES

1. Examine products for evidence that they were inspected. What does this mean in terms of product quality.

2. Visit a production facility, testing lab, or distribution center where product inspection occurs and discuss the process with the inspectors, auditors, and managers.

3. Discuss how inspection is used by, contributes to, or affects the work of designers, merchandisers, retailers, and engineers.

4. Compare the consistency of three products identical in size, color, and style in terms of size, construction, and appearance. Are these products exactly the same? How and why do they differ?

5. Explore the information available on the world wide web related to inspection. How does it apply to the information in this chapter?

6. Inspect your products from design, pattern making, and construction classes based on written standards and specifications and determine whether it would pass inspection.

7. Read these articles (Jacobsen, Donald M. [1985, August]. Fabric: Inspection Savings—Fact or Fiction? *Bobbin, 26,* 70, 72, 74, 76, 78 and Karnes, Carol L., & John J. Karnes. [1994, February]. How the Apparel Industry Measures Up to Quality Standards. *Quality Progress, 27,* 25–29) and discuss what they mean in terms of product quality.

Chapter 12

EVALUATING PRODUCTS

OBJECTIVES

- To understand the various procedures used to evaluate products.

- To integrate product evaluation with product quality expectations.

- To evaluate finished products for adherence to standards and specifications.

- To apply basic scientific principles to product testing.

KEY TERMS

material interactions

component testing

bond strength

foam tear

blister

bubble

crack mark

pucker

delamination

seam strength

seam slippage

seam failure

seam damage

seam pucker

seam jamming

tailorability

process-material interactions

sewability

formability

buckling

compressibility

shearing or shear stress

extensibility

hygral expansion

appearance of seams

needle damage

grin

shiners

color contrast

bleed-through

ridging

user-product interactions

wear or service testing

simulations

wearability

usability

mobility

dexterity

seam integrity

environment-product interactions

garment twist

torque

spirality

roping

flock rating scale

product integrity

Early in the product development process materials are evaluated to ensure that those used in the finished product will perform at the level specified. However, evaluation should not end with assessment of the materials. Although a company knows how individual materials react to stress or use, it does not know how these materials will react when they are fused, stitched, or otherwise attached to each other. Materials may create synergistic or antagonistic reactions when they are used together in a product. In addition, the manner or process of attachment often influences material performance.

Most material assessment focuses on new and flat fashion fabrics, interlinings, or closures. Sometimes a test method includes a suggestion or instruction to the operator to wash or clean the material, so that performance after one or more cleaning cycles can be examined. Nevertheless, the focus of material performance testing is on the material and not on the product or its use situations. Thus, material performance only describes one measure of a finished product's interaction with the environment and the user.

Product evaluation is based on a more holistic perspective. It incorporates material interactions; process-material interactions related to such production processes as stitching or fusing; user-product interactions, such as fit and function; and environment-product interactions, such as cleaning and some use situations.

To satisfy consumer needs and realize their business objectives, companies need to ensure that their products are able to perform at the level desired, that they meet standards for size and fit, and that they fulfill the desired appearance standards. These factors are important measures of product quality, for both the manufacturer and the consumer. Product evaluations are detailed processes. Figure 12-1 illustrates several broad categories of defects that may be identified by in-process or product inspection. This chapter focuses on how product components and products are evaluated through visual examination and product performance analysis.

MATERIAL INTERACTIONS

Even the simplest of constructed textile products usually contains more than one material. For example, a washcloth consists of cotton yarns interlaced in a warp pile weave to create terrycloth. The fabric is hemmed or overcast with one or more sewing threads. A label with fiber content, care, and producer information may be attached. Thus, this relatively simple object contains three separate materials: the fabric, the thread, and the label. We need to be sure that these three materials are compatible and that they do not interact in a way that creates dissatisfaction when the washcloth is used by a consumer.

Material interactions describes the way in which materials that are combined in a product act and react when their performance is influenced by the presence of another material. Three results are possible. The performance of any material might not change, may decrease measurably, or may

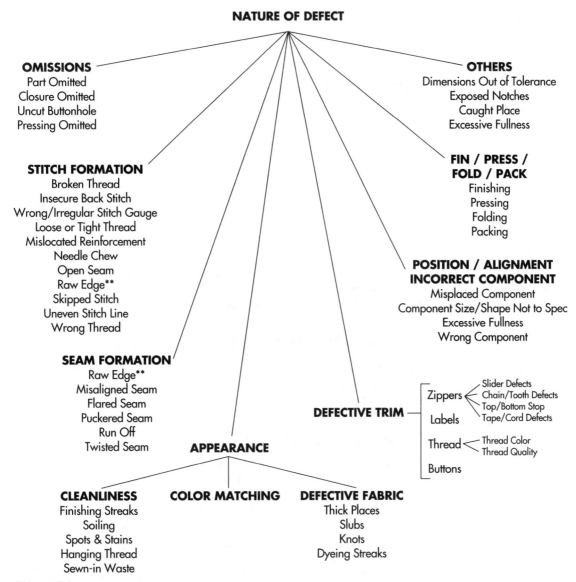

NATURE OF DEFECT

OMISSIONS
Part Omitted
Closure Omitted
Uncut Buttonhole
Pressing Omitted

OTHERS
Dimensions Out of Tolerance
Exposed Notches
Caught Place
Excessive Fullness

STITCH FORMATION
Broken Thread
Insecure Back Stitch
Wrong/Irregular Stitch Gauge
Loose or Tight Thread
Mislocated Reinforcement
Needle Chew
Open Seam
Raw Edge**
Skipped Stitch
Uneven Stitch Line
Wrong Thread

FIN / PRESS / FOLD / PACK
Finishing
Pressing
Folding
Packing

POSITION / ALIGNMENT INCORRECT COMPONENT
Misplaced Component
Component Size/Shape Not to Spec
Excessive Fullness
Wrong Component

SEAM FORMATION
Raw Edge**
Misaligned Seam
Flared Seam
Puckered Seam
Run Off
Twisted Seam

DEFECTIVE TRIM
Zippers — Slider Defects / Chain/Tooth Defects / Top/Bottom Stop / Tape/Cord Defects
Labels
Thread — Thread Color / Thread Quality
Buttons

APPEARANCE

CLEANLINESS
Finishing Streaks
Soiling
Spots & Stains
Hanging Thread
Sewn-in Waste

COLOR MATCHING

DEFECTIVE FABRIC
Thick Places
Slubs
Knots
Dyeing Streaks

Figure 12-1
Potential product defects grouped by class (from Dastoor, P. H., P. Radhakrishnaiah, K. Srinivasan, & S. Jayaraman. (1994). SDAS: A Knowledge-Based Framework for Analyzing Defects in Apparel Manufacturing. *Journal of the Textile Institute, 85,* 542–560). (Courtesy of the Textile Institute)

increase. These potential interactions cannot be predicted based solely on the evaluation of the individual performance of single materials. These interactions must be assessed by combining materials, subjecting them to some test condition, and evaluating the results.

Material interactions probably should be evaluated early in product development and should focus on working with sample materials. After the testing and evaluation has been completed, further testing of samples from the production floor may or may not be conducted depending on time and the focus of the firm.

COMPONENTS

Components are a likely place to begin an analysis of materials interactions, because components combine two or more product pieces into a portion of a finished product. Components identify real combinations of materials. Collars and cuffs for apparel might reasonably combine fashion fabric, interlining fabric, thread, and fusible adhesive. Thus, by testing the combination of materials in a component, the company can determine if these materials will produce a product that will satisfy consumer needs. Some companies that analyze interactions of materials refer to this phase of product testing as **component testing.**

Many different interactions may be evaluated, but the focus is often on a few key measures of performance. Some related measures will be discussed later in this chapter, as environment-product interactions, because they deal with interactions associated with cleaning.

STANDARD TEST METHODS

Several standard test methods are used to assess the manner in which components interact. These methods address a few limited areas, including performance of seams or performance of fused, bonded, and laminated fabrics.

Fabric Combinations

One of the most common uses of adhesives is to combine two or more materials together in textile products. This application is used in bonding, fusing, and laminating together layers of fabric such as fashion and interlining materials for apparel or fashion and shaping materials for furnishings and automotive interiors. The strength of the bond between materials is a measure of importance, as is the subsequent behavior of the now composite fabric.

AATCC 136, Bond Strength of Bonded and Laminated Fabrics, assesses the performance of these fabrics by one measure of durability. **Bond strength** is the tensile force, reported in oz/in. or g/cm, that is required to separate or pull apart the component layers. The procedure recommends measuring bond strength for newly adhered materials and for materials after the composite has been laundered or dry cleaned at least once. The instrument used is either a CRE or CRT type of tensile testing machine. One layer of the bonded specimen is placed in each clamp of a CRE or CRT tensile testing machine, as illustrated in Figure 12-2.

This procedure assesses if the clamped portion tore off, one or both of the material layers disintegrated, or the bond failed. Disintegration of a

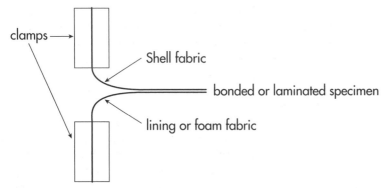

Figure 12-2
Side view of a bond strength specimen mounted in the clamps of a tensile testing machine.

material most often occurs with fiberweb or nonwoven interlinings. A thin layer or portion of the interlining remains adhered to the fashion material, but the remainder of the interlining tears loose. Behavior of this nature is not considered as a failure of the bond, because the bond was strong enough to cause the interlining to pull apart. A **foam tear** occurs when the foam portion of a laminated fabric ruptures before failure of the bond.

ASTM D 2724, Bonded, Fused, and Laminated Apparel Fabrics, assesses several aspects of performance involving materials combined by an adhesive. This specific procedure focuses on apparel fabrics and includes procedures for evaluating bond strength, dimensional stability, appearance, and permanence of the bond to washing and dry cleaning. The bond strength procedure is similar to the AATCC procedure discussed in the preceding paragraph.

The procedure for measuring dimensional stability is similar to that used for single materials. Benchmarks are placed on the material at specified distances. The material is marked, such as with the AATCC shrinkage gauge, cleaned (washed or dry cleaned) and dried one or more specified times. The distances between the benchmarks are then measured again. Equation 12-1 is used to calculate dimensional change.

Equation 12-1

$$\text{Dimensional Change, \%} = (A - B)100/A$$

where A = average original distance between bench marks
   B = average final distance between bench marks

Appearance is evaluated visually for several possible problems or conditions that might develop as a result of use or care (ATSM, 1996). A **blister** is a bulge, swelling, or similar alteration of a material's surface condition (either face or back). The material appears to be raised from the plane of the underlying component over a limited area, resulting in a puffy appearance. A blister—or bubble—often occurs when a small area of delamination develops in conjunction with shrinkage of the underlayers. A **crack mark** is a sharp break or crease in the surface contour of either layer that becomes evident when the composite is rolled, bent, draped, or folded. Crack marks often occur when the two parts of the composite material do not drape in the same manner. A **pucker** is a wavy three-dimensional effect typified by closely spaced wrinkles on either one or both sides of the fabric. Puckers most often develop because of a difference in shrinkage of the two layers of the composite. **Delamination** is a separation of at least a portion of the layers of the fabric. See Figure 12-3 for examples of these alterations in appearance.

Using a seam to combine materials of the same or different types also poses potential problems. **Tailorability** is the ease with which materials can be sewn together to form a product (Shishoo, 1990). Tailorability problems may occur if the materials are difficult to handle or they do not

Figure 12-3

Potential appearance problems with bonded, fused, and laminated materials: (A) crack marks, (B) delamination (C) poor abrasion resistance, and (D) loss of coating.

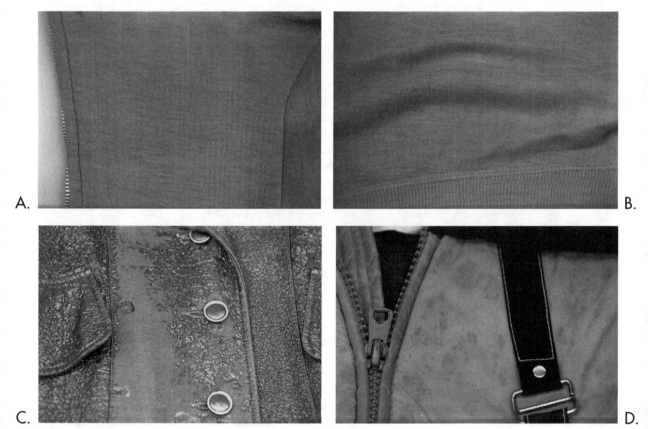

A.　　　　B.

C.　　　　D.

react well to sewing. For example, materials may have differences in natural body or handling. To produce a functional and attractive seam in such cases requires extra effort on the part of operators. The production engineer often addresses tailorability issues and determines appropriate settings for the sewing machine, the needle type and size, and the throat plate type. Quality of the final product is greatly influenced by tailorability. Experimentation and reliance on previous experience contribute to solving tailorability problems.

Thread

Thread is important because it is the principal method for joining the parts of most textile products. Threads can have a significant effect on the appearance of seams, decorative stitching, and embroidery. Several procedures assess the interactions between the thread and other materials after the completion of a seam or stitching. The sewing of seams will be discussed under process-material interactions.

Standard test methods evaluate several aspects of seams—strength, slippage, failure, damage, pucker, and jamming. **Seam strength** is the maximum resistance to rupture at the juncture formed by stitching together two or more planar materials. Seam strength is measured to assess seam durability. The greater the force needed to rupture the seam, the greater its strength. Strong seams are assumed to be more durable than weak seams. However, strength is only one measure of importance.

Seam slippage is the partial or complete loss of seam integrity manifested by yarn slippage parallel or adjacent to the stitch line (see Figure 12-4). Seam slippage occurs when yarns in the material react to force exerted on the seam and move away from their normal positions in the fabric. Seam slippage most often occurs in filament yarn fabrics, especially those

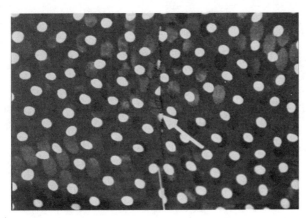

Figure 12-4
Seam slippage (at the arrow).

with a basket, twill, or satin interlacing pattern. In seam slippage, a band of only one set of yarns may appear parallel to the seam. This is especially problematic when warp and filling yarns are different colors, sizes, textures, or types. In severe cases, seam slippage compromises seam integrity and the seam fails. In these cases, the yarns slip beyond the cut edge of the fabric, thereby destroying the structure of the material and the seam.

Seam failure is the point at which an external force (1) ruptures the sewing thread, (2) ruptures the fabric, (3) causes excessive yarn slippage adjacent to the stitch line, or (4) causes any combination of these unacceptable conditions. When the seam fails, the force at that point is recorded as seam strength in lbf (pounds of force).

Seam damage is a reduction in seam efficiency caused by a change in the physical condition of one or more components in a seam (ASTM, 1996). For example, some amount of seam slippage would be viewed as seam damage. **Seam pucker** is caused by a distortion of the sewn fabric either during seam construction or later. Ideally, seams should be smooth and flat. When one or more of the materials present in a seam shrinks when cleaned, seam pucker is likely to occur (see Figure 12-5). **Seam jamming** is a special type of seam pucker that occurs if yarns in the fabric buckle. Seam jamming occurs with dense fabrics or when the tension of the thread is too high. In seam jamming, the space required for the sewing thread to penetrate the fabric distorts the yarns in a material. Depending on the fabrication method, yarns may deviate from an essentially straight, on-grain path or they may slip over or under an adjacent yarn. Either action alters the appearance of the material at the seam.

In ASTM D 1683, Failure in Sewn Seams of Woven Fabrics, a tensile testing machine (CRE type is preferred) is used to assess seam strength by applying a force longitudinal and perpendicular to the seam (see Figure 12-6). Seam slippage can be assessed by finding the differ-

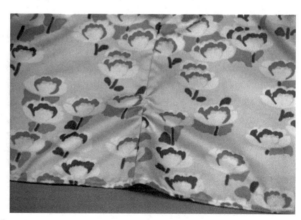

Figure 12-5
Seam pucker.

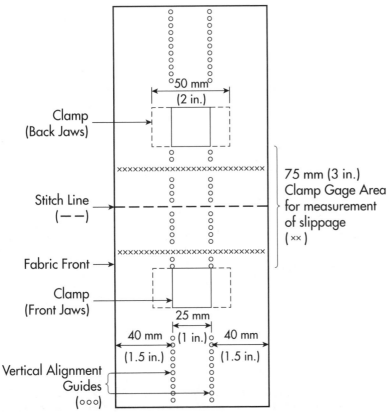

Figure 12-6
Specimen placement for seam strength measurements. (*Reprinted, with permission, from the Annual Book of ASTM Standards, Copyright © American Society for Testing and Materials, 100 Barr Harbon Drive, West Conshohocken, PA 19428-2959*)

ence between the elongation of the fabric alone and the elongation of the seamed fabric sample. Specimens can be removed from constructed products or they can be constructed from sample fabric.

Several standard test methods are used to assess resistance to seam slippage: ASTM D 434, Resistance to Slippage of Yarns in Woven Fabrics Using a Standard Seam; ASTM D 4034, Resistance to Yarn Slippage at the Sewn Seam in Woven Upholstery Fabrics—Plain, Tufted, or Flocked; and ASTM D 4033, Determining Yarn Slippage in Sewn Seams Made from Upholstery Fabrics (Dynamic Fatigue Method). Each method differs slightly. ASTM 434 uses a CRT (preferred) or CRE tensile testing machine and a process similar to that described for seam slippage in ASTM 1683. The distance between the fabric only and the seamed fabric force-extension curves are compared to assess seam slippage.

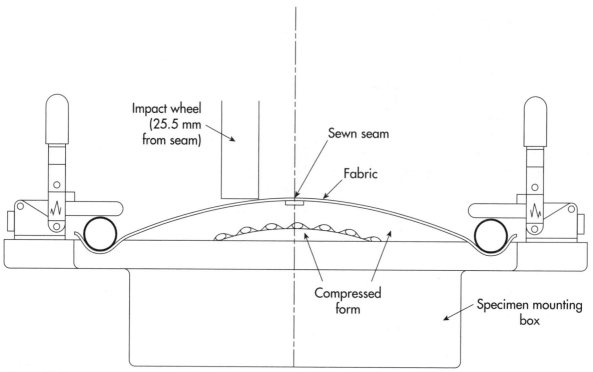

Figure 12-7
Diagram of seam slippage test for upholstered furniture. (*Reprinted, with permission, from the Annual Book of ASTM Standards, Copyright © American Society for Testing and Materials, 100 Barr Harbon Drive, West Conshohocken, PA 19428-2959*)

The other two procedures focus specifically on upholstery fabric seams. ASTM 4034 is similar to ASTM 434. ASTM 4033 uses a simulated portion of a chair or sofa. A seamed specimen is placed over a polyurethane foam composite that forms a simulated seam cushion. A fatiguing weight is dropped on the assembly from a standard height and removed (see Figure 12-7). This continuous, constant rate cycle is repeated until failure is observed or measured or until 7,000 cycles have been completed.

NONSTANDARD PROCEDURES

Nonstandard procedures are developed at the discretion of a company to address its specific needs in areas for which no standard test method exists. For example, if a company has experienced consumer satisfaction problems with a specific combination of materials, they are likely to develop a procedure to assess these interactions and minimize future problems. For example, if a company has had sufficient complaints over the years about zipper—fashion fabric interactions, it explores the nature of the problem and implements a solution.

Fabric Combinations

When two or more materials are adhered together, the hand of the resulting composite fabric can be significantly different from that of either single layer. Thus, some companies assess the hand of composites by using a modification of AATCC Evaluation Procedure 5, Subjective Evaluation of Fabric Hand.

CLOSURES

Different fasteners subject fashion and support fabrics to various stresses. Buttons may exert a tremendous amount of stress on a relatively few number of yarns in a fabric. This problem can be compounded by the type of thread used. It is important that the button and the thread be compatible. Some buttons, especially metal ones, are more likely to cut through the sewing thread with time. Further, a thread shank or backing button may improve serviceability with some materials and end uses. For instance, flat buttons used on a wool melton coat would be more serviceable with a thread shank and backing button.

Nonstandard procedures to evaluate the manner in which closures work with the shell, lining, and interlining or support materials focus on the material's resistance to distortion, which may be caused by the weight of the closure or by fabric rupture or yarn slippage as a result of a pulling force. In most instances, a modified tensile strength test is used. For example, in measuring zipper-material interactions, a zipper is sewn to the material as it would be in production; the tape is mounted in one clamp, and the material in the other. The force needed to tear the zipper-material component is measured and the location of the rupture is identified.

TRIMS AND OTHER MATERIALS

Elastic trims attached to shell materials can create problems if the components do not elongate in the same fashion. This can be especially problematic if the thread and type of stitch connecting the parts are too stable. Elongation potential can be measured in several ways. A common one is to grasp the component between the thumb and forefinger of each hand at a predetermined distance. Using "normal strength" pull each hand away from the other and measure the distance to which the component can be stretched without excessive force or rupture of the thread or other materials.

Recovery can be assessed in a similar fashion. After the component has been stretched, release the force and measure how much the fabric recovers from stretching. These simple procedures can be repeated a number of times if some measure of material fatigue is needed. These two, simple hand procedures are quick and inexpensive, but less accurate than similar procedures used in standard test methods for the elongation of materials discussed in Chapter 7. Other elongation assessments use a modification of one of several standard procedures in which the specimen incorporates a combination of materials.

Distortion because of the weight of the trim can also be assessed by a process similar to that used to determine distortion as a result of closures (see the previous section). Another concern is that some trims may stretch during application. As a result, the fashion fabric puckers when the trim relaxes. Appearance standards similar to the five-point rating scales are sometimes used to evaluate puckering.

PROCESS-MATERIAL INTERACTIONS

Stitching and fusing are the major production processes used to combine materials in one product. For some products, finishing steps may involve abrasive washes, wrinkle-resistant finishing, heat setting, or dyeing. These procedures often take place after sewing or fusing operations and they can have a profound effect on the quality and performance of the finished product. Many companies work closely with suppliers of thread, interlinings, and other materials to address such potential problems as sewability, fusing conditions, and abrasive washes, so that the serviceability of the product is not adversely affected by the production or finishing processes used to make it. In addition, concerns related to alteration of appearance or performance are addressed so that the product is more appealing to the consumer.

Process-material interactions describe the effects a production process has on the performance of individual materials, as well as the finished product. There are two approaches to research and evaluation in this area. In one, the production engineer determines the best procedures, equipment, and settings to be used in production to meet company specs and standards and to maximize productivity. At the same time, the quality assurance engineer evaluates the production engineer's choices in terms of product performance and its affect on product quality and serviceability. In some cases, compromises may be necessary between production requirements and performance specifications.

Process-material interactions usually are addressed later in product development, after the decision to incorporate a style in the line has been made by the merchandisers and designers. In this process, sample materials are used to evaluate interactions and establish settings and attachments for equipment, handling criteria, and other pertinent process information. Further evaluation may or may not occur depending on whether additional problems appear during production. For the evaluation of product wet finishing, full sample products usually are used.

SEWABILITY

A common problem in production is that the thread and the fashion or lining materials do not always combine well during assembly. **Sewability** is the ability of a thread to combine with another material in stitch and seam formation so that production and performance problems do not occur. Sewability examines the interactions among the thread, other materials, sewing machine, and needle. When sewability is good, all components and processes produce a smooth, attractive, and functional seam. Minimal maintenance or process adjustments are needed. When sewability is low, components or processes require high maintenance, and problems in seam appearance or performance are more frequent. Many of the factors that influence the sewability of a material are illustrated in Figure 12-8. Thus, sewability addresses material and process interactions, whereas tailorability emphasizes materials' reactions to the process of sewing. Both issues are important factors in terms of product quality and productivity.

When sewability or tailorability problems occur, the material is damaged or the machine does not work properly and jams or stops at unplanned intervals. Most thread manufacturers have a research and development division to help their customers solve problems when thread and

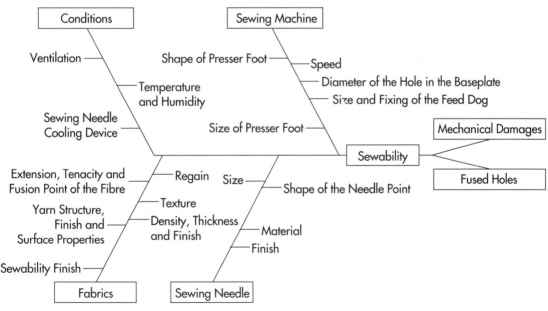

Figure 12-8
Factors that influence the sewability of materials (from Yonghua, Li, & Zhao Shujing. (1985). Fabric Sewability Assessment by Needle Temperature Test. *Journal of East China Institute of Textile Science and Technology (2)*, 94–104). (*Courtesy of Journal of China Textile University*)

materials are not compatible. Lubricants and other chemical treatments minimize problems with the sewability of threads.

Several aspects related to sewability are important: formability, buckling, compressibility, shearing, and hygral expansion. They address the manner in which materials handle the physical manipulations and mechanical forces to which they are subjected during sewing. **Formability** is the maximum compressibility before the onset of buckling. It describes the ease with which a two-dimensional material can be formed into a three-dimensional object, e.g., manufacturing a shirt from a cotton print cloth. Good formability means that the materials facilitate the creation of the three-dimensional product and that no distortion of the material or seam damage occurs in the process.

Buckling is the most common type of deformation found in apparel materials. In **buckling,** the material bends back on itself and forms an accidental fold, tuck, or pleat. When buckling and formability are combined, it is easy to work the excess material into the seam (formability) without a tuck developing (buckling) (see Figure 12-9). With shirts, for instance, the circumference of the sleeve cap is greater than that of the armseye of the shirt's body. Overfeeding is used during production so that the excess material in the sleeve cap edge is sewn into an armseye to provide ease of arm movement. However, with some materials, buckling may occur in the sleeve cap during sewing. Thus, the operator invests extra time and effort in minimizing the occurrence of buckling defects in the product.

Compressibility also describes the tendency of a material to buckle when overfed. **Compressibility** is the ability of a fabric to be compressed

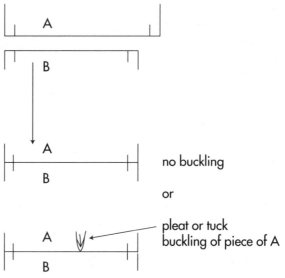

Figure 12-9
Buckling may occur when two different lengths of materials are sewn together.

or overfed without buckling. Materials that exhibit good compressibility are easier to sew in at sleeve caps, for example, than are materials that exhibit buckling.

Shearing or shear stress can result in yarn distortion if the force is applied at a particular angle to the warp or filling (see Figure 12-10). Even if the problem is not severe, it may be highly visible when the warp and filling are of different colors. Shearing is a problem that generally occurs during consumer use, unlike buckling, which creates problems during production.

Extensibility refers to a material's ability to stretch slightly. However, extensibility must be identified to ensure that problems in cutting do not develop. High extensibility is often related to high levels of hygral expansion. **Hygral expansion** is an increase in fabric dimension(s) with an increase in relative humidity. Materials with high levels of hygral expansion are prone to high extensibility. Part of the discussion in Chapter 7 about the KES and FAST systems also pertains to the sewability of materials.

The **appearance of seams** describes how a seam looks from the outside of the product after production. A seam should be smooth and flat and correspond to a visual rating of 5 (no puckering, buckling, or seam damage) when evaluated for appearance. Seams that are not smooth and flat after production are not likely to improve in appearance with pressing, but they are likely to exhibit even more puckering after cleaning. Products

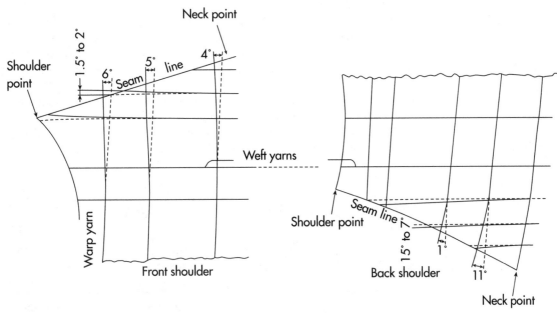

Figure 12-10
Shearing is a distortion of yarns in the material.

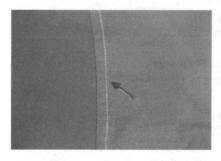
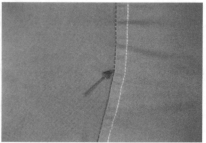

Figure 12-11 (Left)
Needle-related damage. (The arrow points to a severed yarn in the fashion fabric as a result of the top stitching.)

Figure 12-12 (Right)
Grin in a stressed seam.

with unattractive seams are less likely to sell than products with smooth, flat seams.

ASTM D 1908, Needle-Related Damage Due to Sewing in Woven Fabric is one procedure used to evaluate seam construction and examine seams for any damage as a result of sewing with needles. **Needle damage** is the partial or complete severance of yarns, deflection of yarns at the stitching line, or fusing of fibers caused by a needle passing through a material during sewing (see Figure 12-11). **Grin** occurs in stressed seams when the individual stitches can be seen (see Figure 12-12). **Shiners** are created at seams when the needle snags a yarn and pulls it tighter than the other yarns in the surrounding area of the material (see Figure 12-13). In addition, needle damage may not appear as shiners in the material, but may alter the appearance of printed or yarn dyed materials. This problem is sometimes referred to as **color contrast** (see Figure 12-14).

In this ASTM test method, seam specimens in the warp, filling, and bias directions are examined, and the number of needle damaged yarns are counted. The value is expressed as an index, or ratio, of damaged yarns to the total number of yarns or to the total number of needle penetrations in the seam. See Equation 12-2a and b. In addition, if excessive grin is present, it may also be considered a type of seam problem. Some companies examine seams for shiners and color contrast problems with prints and yarn dyed materials. Other companies consider only yarn severance or fusing problems as evidence of needle-related damage.

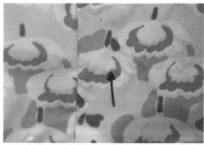

Figure 12-13 (Left)
Shiners occur when yarn tension in a material is tightened. The arrow points to an open seam (the seam has split). The shiner is just above the split.

Figure 12-14 (Right)
Color contrast problem as a result of seam formation.

Equation 12-2a

$$NF\% = 100(N_y/T_y)$$

where $NF\%$ = needle damage index due to fusing,
       severance, or deflection, %
    N_y = number of yarns damaged in direction evaluated
    T_y = total number of yarns in direction evaluated

Equation 12-2b

$$ND\% = 100(N_y/P_n)$$

where $ND\%$ = needle damage index due to fusing,
       severance, or deflection, %
    N_y = number of yarns damaged in direction evaluated
    P_n = number of needle penetrations

FUSING

Fusing of the interlining to fashion fabrics can create problems beyond those discussed under materials interactions. These additional problems relate to bleed-through of adhesive or ridging. In **bleed-through,** the adhesive appears on the technical face of the fashion fabric. Bleed-through, which is no longer common, is detected by visual examination. This problem may appear as a discoloration or grease spot on the fashion fabric in areas where the two materials were fused.

In **ridging,** a noticeable line appears on the face of the fashion fabric so that the point at which the interlining ends can be seen quite clearly when the product is used or worn. The ridge line can be unattractive and distract from the appearance of the product. Obviously, ridging is detected by visual examination of the product. This problem occurs most often when a significantly heavier interlining is used with a light and drapeable fashion material. Ridging is not common because of the wide variety of fusible interlinings available on the market.

FINISHING

Evaluation of product finishing most often focuses on one of two standards: evaluation of the wet process finish or examination of the product to see that it meets pressing and thread trimming specifications and standards. The assessment of pressing and thread trimming requires a simple visual examination. Wet processing evaluation often involves both a visual examination and testing of sample products to assess the effect of finishing on the performance of the product, especially in terms of durability and appearance factors.

Several types of wet processing may be done after the product has been created. For instance, product dyeing, abrasive washes, and some wrinkle-resistant finishes are applied to some sewn products. Items that have been product dyed are usually evaluated for colorfastness during specified use or environmental conditions, such as washing, perspiration, light exposure, and crocking. They are also evaluated for color levelness and color matching to standard for various materials present in the product. For example, buyers often specify that all components, except the label, be dyed the same color.

After abrasive washes, the overall appearance of the product should be examined to determine if it meets company standards. This is especially important in terms of color and streaking. The item in Figure 12-15 illustrates excessive streaking following an abrasive wash and does not meet company standards for appearance. Strength and abrasion resistance of materials, seam strength, and integrity of closures probably should be evaluated to ensure that the wash did not create excessive damage to these materials (see Chapter 6).

Some new wrinkle-resistant finishes are added to products after they have been produced. Other wrinkle-resistant finishes are added to the fash-

Figure 12-15
An abrasive wash product that no longer meets company standards because of excessive streaking.

ion fabric, but they are heat set after the products have been produced. In both cases, performance of the finish should be evaluated to ensure that the product was finished correctly and that the finish does not adversely affect product durability. These procedures were discussed in Chapters 6 and 8.

USER-PRODUCT INTERACTIONS

After the product has been produced and finished, further evaluations are needed to ensure that it will perform as expected. This holistic performance moves beyond that of individual materials or components and evaluates how the product and the user/customer interact. Product evaluation at this stage looks at **user-product interactions.** Here we work with the entire product to ensure that no process or material has created problems that will detract from its salability and performance. In addition, this evaluation verifies that the product will produce the desired effect when used by the consumer. Important elements include design, function, appearance, size, fit, construction, and packaging.

Complete products are used to evaluate user-product interactions. For evaluation of such factors as function, fit, and packaging, one or more sample products are usually sufficient. However, for design, appearance, size, and construction, each individual product may receive a final inspection to ensure that it meets requirements.

DESIGN

When design is evaluated, the entire product is judged according to a prototype standard to ensure that a finished product meets design criteria. It is evaluated visually to determine if all design standards and specifications were met during cutting, production, and finishing stages. Thus, each product is evaluated and identified as conforming or nonconforming according to the standards. For example, when the shirt in Figure 12-16 is evaluated for design, the inspector will examine the matching of stripes, the placement of pockets, the grain, the collar, the sleeves, the cuffs, and the entire shirt to see that each component meets specific criteria and that the overall effect is a positive one. The inspector is looking to see that all design criteria are met and that the entire shirt achieves the desired look for that particular style. Seam appearance is evaluated to ensure that seams do not pucker or that needle damage is not apparent. Seam appearance refers to the visual examination of any line of stitching present in the product and would include seams, hems, and topstitching.

In this assessment, zone definitions can be especially important for specific design criteria. For example, poor matching of plaids may be defined as a major defect when it occurs at the center front placket of a shirt. However, when poor matching of plaids exist at the side seams, it may not be defined as even a minor defect.

Figure 12-16
A shirt ready for inspection.

FUNCTION

Products should also be evaluated in terms of their ability to perform as expected. **Wear or service testing** is the process of evaluating finished products to determine whether they meet product performance criteria. It implies the use of the product in a real setting or environment, so that its performance can be evaluated by individuals who use or wear the product.

However, some wear testing uses simulations, in which a portion of the real environment is created or simulated in a laboratory setting. In **simulations,** the critical portion of the real environment is created, but extraneous elements are eliminated. In addition, a level of safety for the wearer or user is more likely to be ensured in a simulated environment. For instance, the water and slip resistance of workboots can be tested on wet floors and work surfaces in an environment that is safer than the deck of a fishing boat, where the risk of injury from a fall or falling overboard is greater.

Evaluation of function often focuses on products designed for extreme conditions of use, such as clothing for high risk occupations (e.g., haz-mat suits for cleaning up spills of hazardous materials, such as acids and solvents). However, even regular, less severe conditions of use also need to be evaluated. For example, some rainwear is evaluated to ensure that seams are resistant to the penetration of water in a heavy, wind-driven rain.

Function includes the general wearability or usability of the product. A product that meets **wearability** or **usability** criteria satisfies customer expectations for the end use. Wearability is the term used for apparel. Usability is the term used for furnishings and other textile products. Under all reasonable conditions of use, apparel products designed for regular or extreme conditions might need to be evaluated for function, mobility, comfort, dexterity, and related factors.

Mobility and dexterity are especially important in some situations. **Mobility** means ease of movement. It is often important that the clothing item not restrict limb or torso movement. For example, coats should have enough ease in the arm and shoulder area to allow the wearer to perform normal activities, such as driving a car. **Dexterity,** which is a more specific type of movement, is defined as fine motor control of the hands and fingers. For example, dexterity when wearing gloves may be measured by the wearer's ability to pick up a flat disk or coin.

To test the comfort level of apparel under extreme weather conditions, a mannequin is equipped with sensors that measure temperature change on the interior, or body, side of a garment (see Figure 12-17). This information is

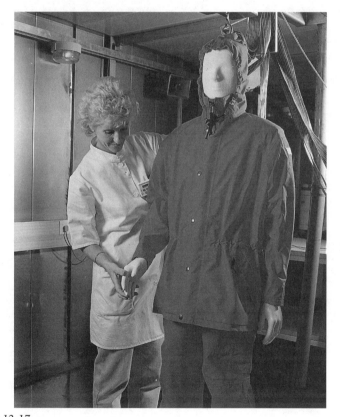

Figure 12-17
Coppelius, a mannequin equipped with sweat glands and sensors to measure body temperature, is part of the equipment used to test the comfort of products at the Center for Textile Protection and Comfort Research at North Carolina State University's College of Textiles. (Photo courtesy of VTT Chemical Technology, Finland.)

used to evaluate the heat or cold stress that a wearer would experience, thermal damage and burn injury to the body, and other measures of comfort and safety. Mannequins are also used to evaluate safety features, such as the ability of firefighter's apparel to protect the wearer from flames and heat. The mannequin, equipped with sensors and sweat glands, is used to evaluate the comfort characteristics of clothing in a range of conditions.

Furnishings may also need to be evaluated for proper functioning. For example, toweling absorbs water from the skin or other surfaces. ASTM D 4772, Surface Water Absorption of Terry Fabrics (Water-Flow Test Method) is specific to terrycloth and finished terrycloth towels that have been hemmed or incorporate the selvage as part of the edge treatment. The specimens are washed and dried before testing because finishes on a new fabric may interfere with absorbency.

In this procedure, the conditioned specimen is placed in an embroidery hoop so that tension is controlled and angled at 60° on the water flow tester (see Figure 12-18). A measured amount of distilled or deionized water is poured over the specimen, the runoff water is collected, measured, and the amount of water absorbed is calculated by subtracting the runoff volume from the original volume.

Figure 12-18
The water flow tester for testing absorbency of towels (left) and sampling plan for working with a finished bath towel (right). (*Reprinted, with permission, from the Annual Book of ASTM Standards, Copyright © American Society for Testing and Materials, 100 Barr Harbon Drive, West Conshohocken, PA 19428-2959*)

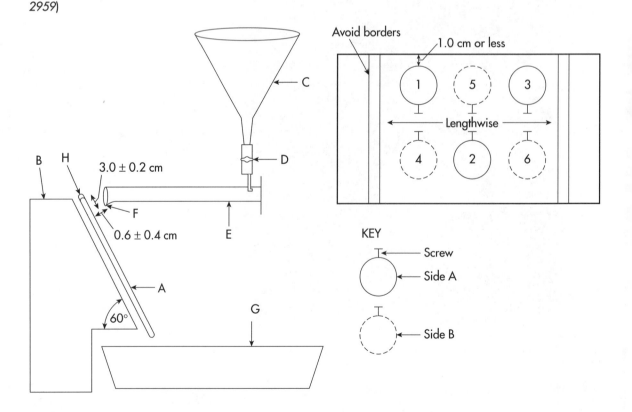

Other function tests relate to health and safety issues. Chapter 7 contains information about testing for flammability and chemical, impact, and biological resistance. In addition to these procedures, several tests have been developed for the evaluation of inflatable airbags in vehicles (see Appendix A).

APPEARANCE

The product is also examined visually to ensure that it falls within the tolerances established by the company for appearance. This procedure is another example of visual inspection by a trained inspector who understands the established criteria (see Chapters 10 and 11).

During this examination, the product is placed flat on a surface located at a comfortable height for the inspector. The front of the product, its back, and sometimes its sides and interior are inspected. Table 12-1 lists criteria related to the final appearance inspection for a shirt, such as the one shown in Figure 12-16. This set of inspection criteria examines specific components of the shirt as well as its overall appearance and impression. Note that product zones are considered when defects, flaws, irregularities,

Table 12-1
INSPECTION FAILURE CRITERIA FOR WOVEN SHIRTS.

Material Defects

Dyeing or printing
- unevenness of color within parts or between components or materials
- objectionable fading or shade bars
- objectionable out-of-register or misprints

Miscellaneous
- surface holes
- blemishes or weaknesses that could become a hole
- snagged or pulled yarns
- heavy barré or machine lines
- foreign material in fabric
- excessive stiffness
- technical back used as face
- nap not consistent in direction
- broken yarns
- any component not compatible with care instructions
- any material not in conformance with performance standards

Construction Defects

Irregular stitching
- hem or hidden stitching visible
- contrast stitching uneven
- broken stitches
- excessively tight or loose tension

Table 12-1
INSPECTION FAILURE CRITERIA FOR WOVEN SHIRTS. (CONTINUED)

Construction Defects
- parallel and straight topstitching
- use of monofilament thread
- skipped stitches
- needle cuts or needle damage
- excessive seam pucker

Irregular seams
- curled, puckered, crooked, pleated, twisted, wavy, or uneven seams
- open seams (stitching thread broken or absent)
- excessive grinning of seams
- uneven seam margins
- seam wrong side out

Closures
- buttonholes outside specs/tolerances for size, shape, stitch density, or location
- button-buttonhole or snap component misalignment
- buttons not securely sewn
- exposed or wavy zippers
- logo snaps upside down
- parts set improperly or backward
- color off when color match specified

Pockets
- noticeably uneven in size, shape, or location
- flap improperly shaped
- sewn in pleats or excessive puckers
- mismatch on front of bodice
- pocket stripes and plaids do not match horizontally and vertically when match is specified

Labeling
- incorrect labels
- incorrect label position
- labels or hangtags that are illegible, defaced, or missing
- labels positioned so entire label cannot be read
- miter fold not flush with bottom of collar
- printed, sewn, or adhesive identification or bundle marks on garment

Pressing
- excessively wrinkled garments
- any dampness in garment
- improperly pressed garments
- press marks from use of clamps, etc.
- burn, scorch, or related marks on garment

Hems
- puckered, twisted, or roped
- stitch with too deep a bite

Threads and yarns
- excessive or loose threads
- thread other than specified size, color, and type
- improper thread match

Table 12-1
INSPECTION FAILURE CRITERIA FOR WOVEN SHIRTS. *(CONTINUED)*

Dimensions
- poor product symmetry right to left
- top portion (front) of garment not equal to or longer (by ¼ in.) than underlying (back) portion

Mends and repairs
- threads on inside that interfere with wearability, comfort, or appearance
- loose ends from repairs on outside of garment
- poorly executed or noticeable repairs
- stitches must tie down original stitching in same stitch line

Construction
- incorrect bar tack
- raw or untrimmed edges, except as specified
- foreign objects sewn in or caught in seam
- parts or components sewn on unevenly or in wrong direction
- improper cuff turnings
- yoke uneven in location, shape, or size
- twisted sleeves

Collar and neck
- collar points improperly shaped or not uniform
- off-quarter or skewed collar
- collar band or under collar distinctly showing above top collar
- neck trim puckered or stretched
- neck opening off-center

Matching
- pattern side seam not matched when specified
- uneven stripe alignment (front straight, back not objectionable)
- plaids, checks, or horizontal stripes not matching at center front
- unmatched stripe at front seam or raglan sleeve armhole

Plackets
- placket crooked by more than ¼ in. top to bottom
- placket length not as specified
- placket sewn off grain
- placket width uneven top or bottom or distorted

General Defects

Soilage
- oil marks, soil marks, spots, ink, etc.
- rings left after cleaning soil spot

Not as specified
- any measurements not as specified or outside tolerances
- any item not conforming to construction or design specs
- substituted or missing parts unless approved by authorized personnel
- marked seconds
- shaded parts
- color off standard or not within shade bank

and problems appear. Part of the importance of the various zones is addressed in the specificity of the criteria for certain product parts compared to more general criteria for other parts. For example, five specific criteria are listed for collars and neck areas, but only two general criteria are listed for hems.

SIZE OR DIMENSIONS

Because size is a critical issue for apparel and many furnishing and industrial products, it must be evaluated after construction and finishing to ensure that the final product has the appropriate dimensions. In this evaluation, the product is also placed flat on the surface of a table. If the product is small and relatively flat, a template developed by the company may be used to determine if the product meets size or dimension specs.

Several basic practices are used to measure product dimensions. Metal or fiberglass rulers, tape measures, or other measuring devices are used because their dimensions do not change as relative humidity fluctuates and they do not stretch over time. These characteristics do not apply to wooden or fabric measuring devices.

Written or diagrammed instructions ensure that product measurements are evaluated in a constant and defined process. Figure 12-19 includes diagrams and instructions for measuring a woven shirt, such as the one shown in Figure 10-10b. Note that the instructions are designed to eliminate any irregularities in the measuring process.

Dimensions for woven products are sometimes based on full-circumference dimensions, that is the distance from side seam to side seam across the front of the product is added to the distance from side seam to side seam across the back of the product. This is especially true if company standards are written from a body size perspective. Dimensions for knit products may often be based on half widths, in which the distance from side to side across the product is measured.

FIT

Fit is sometimes evaluated using a random sample of products to ensure that selected sizes for a particular style continue to meet company standards. If a company uses a fit model to check the fit of their garments before production, it may select at random a sample product of the same size from the production line to ensure that fit remains constant. Some companies require that a single product of each size in a size range be evaluated for fit on fit models of the appropriate size. For example, for children's wear, a small, medium, and large product may be pulled from production to evaluate their fit on fit models that meet the company's criteria for those sizes. However, this practice is not common within the industry.

Measurement Instructions

1. Bust/ Chest*
- With front of garment facing you, measure straight across bust/chest from side to side at armholes seam.
- On garments with pleats, fully extend pleats without stretching fabric.

2. Across Chest
- With front of garment facing you, measure 5 in. down from high shoulder point parallel to center front.
- Measure straight across 5 in. from armhole to armhole.
- On garments with pleats, fully extend pleats without stretching fabric.

3. Sweep* - Garments with Vents or Shirttail Hems
- Lay garment flat in closed position.
- Measure straight across from side to side at top of vent or shirttail hem.

4. Sweep* - Garments with Straight Hems
- Lay garment flat in closed position.
- Measure from side to side along bottom of garment.

5. Front Length
- Measure from high shoulder point, down front body, to bottom of garment

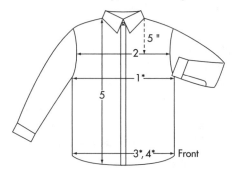

Take measurements with:
- *a dressmaker's or fiberglass coated tape measure (checked periodically against a metal ruler to assure accuracy).*
- *garments laid on a flat surface in a relaxed position.*
- *all wrinkles gently smoothed out.*
- *buttons and/or zippers fully closed (unless otherwise stated).*

6. Across Shoulder
- With back of garment facing you, locate shoulder points (where shoulder seam meets top of armhole, or where natural fold of shoulder meets top of armhole) on each side of garment.
- Measure straight across shoulders from point to point.
- If garment is sleeveless, measure excluding any trim at armhole.

7. Across Back
- With back of garment facing you, measure 4 in. down from high shoulder point parallel to center back.
- Measure across at 4 in. mark from armhole to armhole.

8. Center Back Length
- Measure from center of back neck seam, down center of the back, to bottom of garment.

9. Shoulder Slope
- Draw an imaginary line parallel with hem from high shoulder point out to shoulder width.
- From that point, measure straight down to shoulder point.

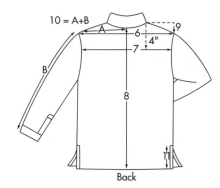

10. Sleeve Length - Garments with Set-In-Sleeves
- With back of garment facing you, measure half of shoulder width starting at center back neck, to shoulder point at top of armhole, then along center fold of sleeve to cuff edge.

11. Vent Height
- Measure from bottom edge of garment to top of vent opening.

Figure 12-19

Instructions and diagrams for measuring the dimensions of a shirt after production and finishing.

12. Sleeve Length - Garments with Raglan Sleeves
- Lay garment with back facing you
- Measure from center back neck at base of neck, in a straight line down sleeve, to sleeve edge.

13. Armseye - Raglan Back
- Lay back of garment facing you with body panel lying flat (without wrinkles at armhole seam).
- Measure from base of neck following contour of seam to armhole/side seam intersection point.

14. Armseye - Raglan Front
- Lay garment with front facing you and body panel lying flat (without wrinkles at armhole seam).
- Measure from base of neck following contour of seam to armhole/side seam intersection point.

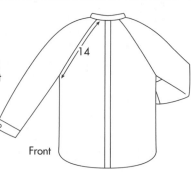

Front

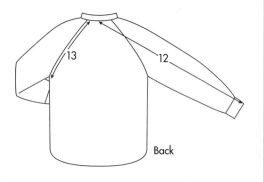

Back

17. Elbow*
- Fold sleeve in half, so edge of cuff is positioned at bottom of armhole.
- Measure straight across this fold from underarm to center fold.

18. Cuff Opening*
- Measure straight across bottom of sleeve from underarm side of cuff to center fold side of cuff.
- For button cuff, cuff should be measured closed and buttoned on first button.

19. Cuff Height
- Measure from cuff/sleeve seam down to edge of cuff.

15. Armseye - Sleeved & Sleeveless*
- Lay front of garment facing you with body panel lying flat (without wrinkles at armhole seam).
- Following armhole seam contour, measure from bottom of armhole to top of armhole keeping tape on body side of seam.
- Care must be taken to rotate tape measure so that measuring edge is absolutely flat along armhole seam.

16. Upper Arm*
- Measure 1 in. down from underarm, then from that point measure straight across sleeve perpendicular to center fold of sleeve.

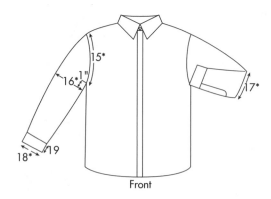

Front

Figure 12-19 (continued)

20. Neck Width
- Lay garment flat.
- Measure straight across from high shoulder point to high shoulder point at base of ribbing or collar.
- If there is no collar or trim, measure from edge to edge at high shoulder point.

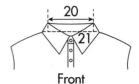

Front

21. Front Neck Depth
- Lay garment flat with front facing you.
- Draw an imaginary line at base of neck from high shoulder point to high shoulder point.
- From that center point, measure straight down to base of ribbing or collar at center front.

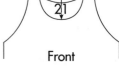

Front

22. Back Neck Depth
- Lay garment flat with back facing you.
- Draw an imaginary line at base of neck from high shoulder point to high shoulder point.
- From that center point, measure straight down to base of ribbing or collar at center back.

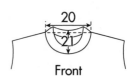

Front

23. Collar Height
- Measure at center back from base of collar to top outer edge of collar.

24. Collar Length at Outer Edge
- Undo all the buttons and lay collar flat so that inside of garment is facing you.
- Measure along collar edge from collar point to collar point

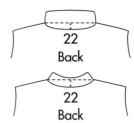

25. Collar Point
- Lay collar flat.
- Measure from base of collar to outer edge of collar point.
- If there is no collar band, measure from neck seam to collar point.

26. Collar Band Height
- Measure at center back from neck line seam to top of band.

27. Collar Base Edge - With or Without Band
- Undo all buttons and lay collar flat with inside of garment facing you.
- Measure along collar base from edge to edge.
- If garment has a zipper exclude the zipper from the measurement.

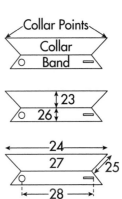

Figure 12-19 (continued)

28. Neck Circumference
- Undo all buttons and lay collar flat so that inside of garment is facing you.
- Measure from center of button to farthest end of buttonhole along inside of collar band.

29. Placket Width
- Measure placket on exterior of garment from seam or stitched edge to finished edge.

30. Placket Length
- Measure placket on exterior of garment from top edge to bottom seam or stitched edge.

31. Pocket Width - Exterior
- Measure the pocket across the top opening edge to edge.

32. Pocket Length - Exterior
- Measure at longest point from top opening edge to bottom finished edge.

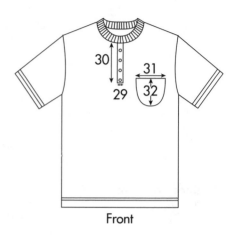

Front

Figure 12-19 (continued)

CONSTRUCTION

Products are also evaluated to ensure that construction specifications were adhered to during production. These specifications often incorporate details regarding stitch construction, pattern matching criteria, seam finishes, hem finishes, styling details, and such product shaping materials as shoulder pads, closures, and linings.

Seam and hem construction and finishes often vary by component or product location. **Seam integrity** becomes an important issue. It is the ability of a seam to join materials or components, to maintain an attractive appearance, to be durable, and to remain securely stitched during use and cleaning. Some stitch types are prone to unraveling and should be used only for applications in which seams are expected to unravel on demand. For example, some bags, such as those used to package livestock feed, have seam closures that are designed to unravel when one thread or string is pulled. This feature, while desirable when feeding a herd of cattle, is not desirable with most other products.

In evaluating construction, inspectors examine not only the sample products submitted to determine the ability of a supplier to produce at the appropriate quality level, but they also examine a randomly selected sample from the production line to ensure that the same care is used when lots are produced. Table 12-1 includes several criteria that are related to construction. Once again, a visual examination of the product determines if these specs and standards were met.

PACKAGING

Buyers of finished goods often have specific criteria for product packaging because of requirements in their distribution centers. Shipments that are not packaged according to specs may be refused because of the impact on time and labor at the distribution center. Thus, inspection of the packaging is one of the final checks performed at the production facility. The type and size of the container, the number of items in a container, its labeling, and bar coding are the types of criteria normally verified.

ENVIRONMENT-PRODUCT INTERACTIONS

One of the most significant problems with textile products is consumer dissatisfaction with how the product interacts with the environment. A major source of complaint is the way products respond to cleaning. Standard test methods that examine a finished product's response to cleaning are designed to check factors that go beyond the performance of individual materials.

After laundering or dry cleaning, seams and materials joined by seams are evaluated. If seam pucker occurred, it may be the result of shrinkage of either the material or thread or the recovery of the thread or material from elongation during sewing. Regardless of the source, the end result is a less desirable appearance.

AATCC 88B, Smoothness of Seams in Fabrics After Repeated Home Laundering, is used to evaluate interactions among materials in seams, hems, and topstitching during washing and drying. Specimens are washed and dried several times, with ballast fabric, under conditions similar to those described on the product's care label. Seam appearance is evaluated using one of two photographic rating scales: single needle seams or double needle seams (see Figure 12-20). Raters assign point

Figure 12-20
Photographic rating scales for evaluating appearance of seams after repeated washing and drying cycles: single needle (left) and double needle (right). *Reprinted with permission from the American Association of Textile Chemists and Colorists, P.O. Box 12215, Research Triangle Park, NC 27709.*

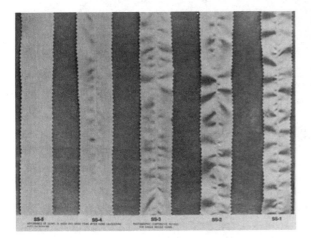
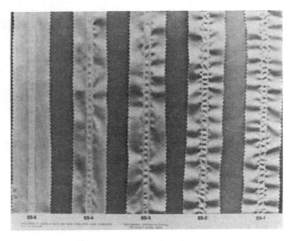

values to all or selected stitched areas based on the frequency and severity of the puckers.

A similar procedure examines style-related creases, such as pleats or center front creases in dress slacks. AATCC 88C Retention of Creases in Fabrics After Repeated Home Laundering uses the rating scale shown in Figure 12-21. Raters use the scale to assign point values based on the sharpness of the crease and the distinctness of its shadow.

Because garment components sometimes twist after washing and drying, AATCC 179, Skewness Change in Fabric and Garment Twist Resulting from Automatic Home Laundering, was developed to examine the likelihood of a product exhibiting this problem. **Garment twist** is a rotation, usually lateral, between different panels of a garment. It results from the release of latent fabric stresses during laundering of the woven or knitted fabric that forms the garment. Twist is also known as **torque** or **spirality**. The process for garments is similar to the procedure described in Chapter 8 for materials. The garment is marked as illustrated in Figure 12-22, washed, and then evaluated using one of three equations (see Equations 8-2, 8-3, and 8-4).

AATCC 150, Dimensional Changes in Automatic Home Laundering of Garments, is used to identify shrinkage, growth, or problems with unequal or differential shrinkage of materials combined in a product. This

Figure 12-21
Rating scale for evaluating appearance of creases after repeated washing and drying cycles. *Reprinted with permission from the American Association of Textile Chemists and Colorists, P.O. Box 12215, Research Triangle Park, NC 27709.*

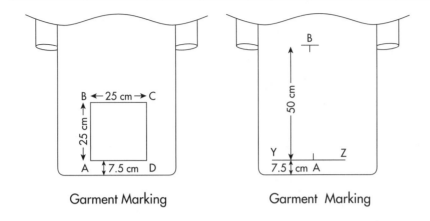

Garment Marking   Garment Marking

Figure 12-22
Marking methods for garments:
square marking option (left)
and inverted T marking option
(right). *Reprinted with
permission from the American
Association of Textile Chemists
and Colorists, P.O. Box 12215,
Research Triangle Park, NC
27709.*

procedure uses home laundering conditions. A wash-dry cycle is repeated a specified number of times. Some companies achieve reliable results with three cycles; other companies use five cycles. The product is marked in selected areas identified in the test method. Table 12-2, for example, identifies the recommended locations for bench marks for a shirt. In this procedure, pairs of bench marks are placed on the product, which is then washed and dried under conditions as similar as possible to those indicated on the care label. Then, the product is placed flat on a table, the dimensions between benchmarks are measured, and the shrinkage or growth is calculated using Equation 12-3. In addition to dimensional change, puckers and other changes that result from unequal shrinkage of materials are recorded.

Table 12-2
RECOMMENDED BENCH MARK LOCATIONS FOR DIMENSIONAL CHANGE IN SHIRTS.

Collar

Collar band

Body lengths

Sleeve lengths

Width at chest

Cuffs

(From AATCC 150, Dimensional Changes in Automatic Home Laundering of Garments.)

Equation 12-3

$$\%DC = 100\ (B - A)/A$$

where DC = dimensional change
A = original dimensions
B = dimensions after laundering

In AATCC 143, Appearance of Apparel and Other Textile End Products after Repeated Home Laundering, finished products are washed and dried five times according to their care label instructions (or in conditions as close as possible to the label's instructions), using standard home washing and drying machines. Products are assessed for overall appearance, which is then quantified by evaluating such individual components and features as hems, topstitching, seams, and creases according to the appropriate five-point rating scales. This procedure is especially useful when certain product features are critical to consumer satisfaction. For example, the appearance of the collar, cuffs, and center front button plackets on men's dress shirts are the most critical elements in evaluating appearance after washing and drying.

Besides comparing the product to seam and crease standard rating scales, unacceptable alterations in appearance also are noted. Potential problems include excessive wear from abrasion at collar points, cuffs, plackets, or button flaps; unraveling at seams, buttonholes, hems, or plackets; loss of body at supported areas such as collars, cuffs, or plackets; roping of hems; and other changes in the overall appearance or performance of the product. **Roping** is a hem that folds and twists along its edge. Roping often occurs in bias areas because of stretching or elongation during sewing. Pressing may temporarily remove the problem, but it reappears with washing and drying.

Flocked fabrics are especially sensitive to edge abrasion at cuffs and creases after laundering. For this reason, AATCC 142 Appearance of Flocked Fabrics After Repeated Home Laundering and/or Coin-Op Drycleaning was developed to evaluate a flocked fabric's performance during washing and dry cleaning using simulated pant leg specimens. AATCC has developed a **flock rating scale** (Figure 12-23) to assess the durability of an all-over flock fabric, such as flocked imitation velvet. Because all-over flocking is rarely used for apparel, this test method is not often implemented.

Two standard practices have been developed to evaluate the care of specific products. These procedures assess the success with which materials combined to form the product withstand the cleaning process. ASTM D 4721, Evaluation of the Performance of Bedcoverings and Accessories, Machine Washable and Drycleanable, includes instructions for evaluating seam strength, seam appearance, size consistency, and shade differences. After several care cycles, the bed covering is evaluated for durable press

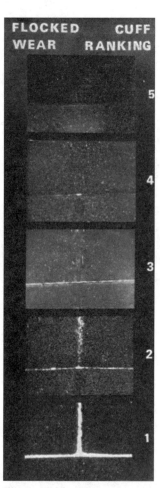

Figure 12-23
AATCC Flock Rating Scale.
Reprinted with permission from the American Association of Textile Chemists and Colorists, P.O. Box 12215, Research Triangle Park, NC 27709.

characteristics (smooth appearance of fabric and seams) and dimensional change, which is calculated using Equation 12-4.

Equation 12-4

$$\text{Percent change} = 100(F - O)/O$$

where F = final measurement
O = original measurement

ASTM D 4231, Evaluation of Men's and Boy's Home Launderable Woven Dress Shirts and Sport Shirts, is used to evaluate selected performance characteristics, such as seam failure, seam pucker, shade difference, dimensional change (using Equation 12-4), and the appearance of materials and shirt components (e.g., seams, pockets, collars, cuffs, and the top of the shirt button placket).

CONCLUSION

Product evaluation is necessary to assure consumers' satisfaction with the performance of the final product. Many aspects of the finished product, such as design, size, construction, fit, appearance, and packaging, are examined visually. Other characteristics, including function and the interaction of materials in laundering or dry cleaning cannot be predicted by assessing the performance of the individual materials in isolation. Evaluating the performance of materials or components in combination is needed to fully understand potential interactions. In some cases, randomly selected products are used in product evaluations. In others, all products or a sample set of products are examined during a final inspection to determine adherence to standards and specifications.

In addition, production processes are also evaluated to ensure that problems do not occur with product use. These procedures help ensure consistent product quality and consumer satisfaction.

Product evaluations are concerned with the overall integrity of the product. **Product integrity** is a product's ability to meet or exceed implied or stated guarantees in terms of performance and function. Companies that evaluate product integrity are more likely to realize their business objectives than companies that do not engage in detailed product analysis.

SUGGESTED READINGS

American Association of Textile Chemists and Colorists. (1996). *AATCC Technical Manual, 71*. Research Triangle Park, NC: Author.

American Society for Testing and Materials. (1996). *Annual Book of ASTM Standards, Vol. 7.1 & 7.2*. West Conshohocken, PA: Author.

Amirbayat, J. (1993). Seams of Different Ply Properties. Part I: Seam Appearance. *Journal of the Textile Institute, 83(2)*, 208–215.

Anfuso, Dawn. (1994, July). L. L. Bean's TQM Efforts Put People Before Processes. *Personnel Journal*, 72–73, 75–76, 78, 80, 83.

Anon. (1993). Seams Like a Good Idea. *Textiles, 22(1)*, 21.

Apparel Quality Committee. (1985). *Elements of an Apparel Quality Control Program*. Arlington, VA: American Apparel Manufacturers Association.

Bona, Mario. (1990). *Textile Quality: Physical Methods of Product and Process Control*. Rome: Texilia.

Bradbury, Mike, & John Kent. (1994, May/June). Dynamic Response: Its Impact on the Textile Marketing Chain. Part 1—The Fabric Supplier, Garment Maker, and Retailer. *Journal of the Society of Dyers and Colourists, 110*, 173–175.

Broadbent, Frank. (1992, July/August). The Need for Universal Seam Testing. *Textile Horizons*, 29.

Brown, Patty. (1992). *Ready-to-Wear Apparel Analysis*. New York: Macmillan.

Carruthers, Hamish. (1991). Design for the Market. In The Textile Institute (ed.). *Textile World at a Crossroads*. Manchester, England: Textile Institute.

Chmielowiec, Richard. (1995). Sewability in the Dynamic Environment of the Sewing Process. *Journal of the Federation of Asian Professional Textile Associations, 3(1)*, 83–94.

Chisholm, Sandra Flora. (1995). Textile Quality Assurance: A Comparison Between Education and Industry. Unpublished Master's Thesis, Iowa State University, Ames.

Cooklin, Gerry. (1991). *Introduction to Clothing Manufacture*. Oxford, England: BSP Professional Books.

Crook, Alan, & Ron Lloyd. (1991). Sewing Threads. *Textiles, 20(2)*, 14–16.

Dastoor, P. H., P. Radhakrishnaiah, K. Srinivasan, & S. Jayaraman. (1994). SDAS: A Knowledge-Based Framework for Analyzing Defects in Apparel Manufacturing. *Journal of the Textile Institute, 85(4)*, 542–560.

Dhingra, R. C., W. M. Chan, W. K. Liu, & H. Lo. (1995). Mechanical Properties of Fused Composites. *Journal of the Federation of Asian Professional Textile Associations, 3(1)*, 15–25.

Drinkman, M. (1990). Manufacture of High Performance Clothing with Breathable Membranes. In The Textile Institute (ed.). *Textiles: Fashioning the Future*. Manchester, England: Textile Institute, pp. 91–98.

Elmasri, M. T., J. W. S. Hearle, & B. Lomas. (1983). Product Quality and Durability in Workwear. In The Textile Institute (ed.). *Quality, Design, and the Purchaser*. Manchester, England: Textile Institute.

Fourt, Lyman, & Norman R. S. Hollies. (1970). *Clothing Comfort and Function*. New York: Marcel Dekker.

Gioello, Debi. (1985, April). Hand of Fabric Primer. *Bobbin, 122*, 124–126.

Glock, Ruth E., & Grace I. Kunz. (1995). *Apparel Manufacturing: Sewn Products Analysis, 2nd ed.* Englewood Cliffs, NJ: Prentice-Hall.

Hallberg, Jill. (1995, July). The Good Housekeeping Institute. *ASTM Standardization News, 23*, 32–35.

Harlock, S. C. (1989, July). Fabric Objective Measurement: 2, Principles of Measurement. *Textile Asia*, 66–71.

Hatch, Kathryn L., Nancy L. Markee, & Howard I. Maibach. (1992). Skin Response to Fabric: A Review of Studies and Assessment Methods. *Clothing and Textiles Research Journal, 10(4)*, 54–63.

Hearle, John W. S. (1993, April). Can Fabric Hand Enter the Dataspace? Part 1. *Textile Horizons, 13*, 14–16.

Hearle, John W. S. (1993). Can Fabric Hand Enter the Dataspace? Part 2. Measuring the Unmeasurable. *Textile Horizons, 13*, 16–20.

Hinckley, C. Martin, & Philip Barkan. (1995). The Role of Variation, Mistakes, and Complexity in Producing Nonconformities. *Journal of Quality Technology, 27(3)*, 242–249.

Hollies, Norman R. S., & Vera R. Usdin. (1980). The Skin Barrier—How Does It Handle Materials Lost from Clothing? In the American Association of Textile Chemists and Colorists, *Textiles: Toxicological and Environmental Concerns*. Research Triangle Park, NC: Author, pp. 33–35.

Howard, K. (1983). Computer Assisted Analysis of Consumer Complaints of Textile Items. *Journal of Consumer Studies and Home Economics, 7(4)*, 349–359.

Industrial Development Organization. (1972). *Quality Control in the Textile Industry*. New York: United Nations.

Ito, K., & M. Nitta. (1994). Some Difficult Issues in Recent Apparel Manufacturing and a Counter-Measure for the Future. *International Journal of Clothing Science and Technology, 6(2/3)*, 14–16.

JC Penney. (1996). *Minimum Construction Guidelines Manual.* Carrollton, TX: Author.

JC Penney. (1996). *Quality Control Guidelines of Apparel and Soft Home Furnishings.* Carrollton, TX: Author.

JC Penney. (1996). *Supplier Testing Guide.* Carrollton, TX: Author.

Jeffries, R. (1990). Functional Aspects of High Performance Clothing. In The Textile Institute (ed.) *Textiles: Fashioning the Future.* Manchester, England: Textile Institute, pp. 119–134.

Johnson, Jay. L. (1994, March). Target's New Vision: Total Quality. *Discount Merchandiser, 38,* 40, 42, 44, 46, 48, 50, 52, 66.

Kang, Tae Jin, & Chang Kyu Park. (1995). Practical Performance and Problem of Automated Pattern Design, Marking, and Cutting in Garment Manufacturing. *Journal of the Federation of Asian Professional Textile Associations, 3(1),* 95–101.

Kawabata, Sueo. (1994). Difficulty with Shingosen: A View from an Analysis of Fabric Hand. *International Journal of Clothing Science and Technology, 6(2/3),* 17–19.

Kawabata, Sueo, & Masako Niwa. (1994). High Quality Fabrics for Garments. *International Journal of Clothing Science and Technology, 6(5),* 20–25.

Kawabata, Sueo, & Masako Niwa. (1996). Objective Measurement of Fabric Hand. In Raheel, Mastura. (ed.). *Modern Textile Characterization Methods.* New York: Marcel Dekker, pp. 329–354.

Keyes, Norman M. (1995, January). Development of a New Test Method: Skewness Change and Garment Twist, *Textile Chemist and Colorist, 27(1),* 27–30.

Lyle, Dorothy Siegert. (1977). *Performance of Textiles.* New York: John Wiley & Sons.

Mehta, Pradip V. (1992). *An Introduction to Quality Control for the Apparel Industry.* Milwaukee: ASQC Press.

Merkel, Robert S. (1991). *Textile Product Serviceability.* New York: Macmillan.

Minazio, Pier Giorgio. (1995). FAST—Fabric Assurance by Simple Testing. *International Journal of Clothing Science and Technology, 7(2/3),* 43–48.

Mori, Miyuki, & Masako Niwa. (1994). Investigation of the Performance of Sewing Thread. *International Journal of Clothing Science and Technology, 6(2/3),* 20–27.

Pack, Howard. (1987). *Productivity, Technology, and Industrial Development: A Case Study in Textiles.* New York: Oxford University Press.

Peters, M. M. (1983). Fabric for Garments: Quality, Design, and the Purchaser. In The Textile Institute (ed.). *Quality, Design, and the Purchaser.* Manchester, England: Textile Institute.

Pile, John F. (1995). *Interior Design.* New York: Harry N. Abrams.

Potluri, Prasad, Isaac Porat, & John Atkinson. (1996). Towards Automated Testing of Fabrics. *International Journal of Clothing Science and Technology, 7(2/3),* 11–23.

Roach, A. R. (1994). Meeting Consumer Needs for Textiles and Clothing. *Journal of the Textile Institute, 85(4),* 484–495.

Rong, G. H., & K. Slater. (1993). A New Approach to the Assessment of Textile Performance. *Journal of the Textile Institute, 84(2),* 197–208.

Saville, N. (1990). Answers to Questions You Might Not Think to Ask. In The Textile Institute (ed.). *Textiles: Fashioning the Future.* Manchester, England: Textile Institute, pp. 99–118.

Schwartz, Peter. (1984, January). Effect of Jamming on Seam Pucker in Plain Woven Fabrics. *Textile Research Journal, 54(1),* 32–34.

Shishoo, Roshan L. (1995). Importance of Mechanical and Physical Properties of Fabrics in the Clothing Manufacturing Process. *International Journal of Clothing Science and Technology, 7(2/3),* 35–42.

Shishoo, R. L. (1990). Interactions Between Fabric Properties and Garment Making-Up Processes. In The Textile Institute (ed.). *Textiles: Fashioning the Future.* Manchester, England: Textile Institute, pp. 337–358.

Smith, Julia E. (1993). The Comfort of Clothing. *Textiles, 22(1),* 18–20.

Smith, Peter J. (1994). Colour Fastness Testing Methods and Equipment. *Review of Progress in Coloration, 24,* 31–40.

Spiegel Quality Assurance Department. (1984). *The Spiegel Apparel Buyer's Guide to Quality Assurance.* Oak Brook, IL: Spiegel.

Spiegel Quality Assurance Department. (1983). *Spiegel Quality Standards.* Oak Brook, IL: Spiegel.

Spiegel Quality Assurance Department. (1984). *Spiegel Upscale Sizing.* Oak Brook, IL: Spiegel.

Stylios, George. (ed.). (1991). *Textile Objective Measurement and Automation in Garment Manufacture.* New York: Ellis Horwood.

Tamburrino, Nicola. (1992, April). Apparel Sizing Issues, Part 1. *Bobbin, 33,* 44–46.

Tamburrino, Nicola. (1992, June). Sized to Sell. *Bobbin, 33,* 68, 72–74.

Technical Advisory Committee. (1973). *Improving Apparel Performance.* Arlington, VA: American Apparel Manufacturers Association.

Technical Advisory Committee. (1994). *New Yardsticks for Apparel.* Arlington, VA: American Apparel Manufacturers Association.

Tortora, Phyllis G., & Robert S. Merkel. (1996). *Fairchild's Dictionary of Textiles,* 7th ed. New York: Fairchild.

Tull, Donald L. (1984, June). Quality Control of Hand and Finish. *American Dyestuff Reporter, 73,* 19–22.

Vigo, Tyrone L. (1994). *Textile Processing and Properties: Preparation, Dyeing, Finishing, and Performance.* Amsterdam, The Netherlands: Elsevier Science B. V.

Waite, Denise M. (1973, February). Some Problems in Making-Up. *Textiles, 2(1),* 10–13.

Watkins, Susan. (1984). *Clothing: The Portable Environment.* Ames: Iowa State University Press.

Webster, J., & R. M. Laing. (1992). "A Stitch in Time " Studying Stitch Joining. *Textiles, 21(4),* 17–19.

Yonghua, Li, & Zhao Shujing. (1985). Fabric Sewability Assessment by Needle Temperature Test. *Journal of East China Institute of Textile Science and Technology, (2),* 94–104.

REVIEW QUESTIONS

1. Explain why product testing and product evaluation are needed even if material testing has been conducted.

2. Describe how each of these factors affects product evaluation and define a procedure that might be used in the evaluation of that factor:
   a. component testing
   b. design
   c. function
   d. appearance
   e. size
   f. fit
   g. construction
   h. finishing
   i. packaging

3. How are product zones incorporated in product evaluation?

4. How is wearability or usability of a textile product evaluated?

5. Why are mobility and dexterity important for apparel products?

6. Why is product evaluation related to laundering important even when shrinkage and colorfastness of shell materials has been conducted?

7. Explain how product testing and product integrity are related.

ACTIVITIES

1. Evaluate a product in terms of design, fit, size, construction, finishing, appearance, workmanship, and packaging. What would these results mean in terms of customer satisfaction?

2. Visit a testing lab and observe the evaluation of a product. Discuss with the technicians and management the relationship of their work to product quality.

3. Discuss the assessment of quality in terms of design, fit, size, construction, finishing, appearance, workmanship, and packaging for a specific product. How does this assessment relate to consumer satisfaction with that product?

4. Discuss complaints and returns with retailers. What factors are commonly mentioned by consumers when they are dissatisfied with a product?

5. Select a product you own and evaluate your satisfaction with it in terms of these criteria: design, fit, size, construction, finishing, appearance, workmanship, and packaging for a specific product.

6. Discuss how designers, merchandisers, retailers, engineers, and others would contribute to the evaluation of a product.

7. Discuss the ways in which designers, merchandisers, retailers, engineers, and others would use the information from a product evaluation.

8. Observe consumer-product interactions in a retail setting. (You will need to notify management that you are observing so that no problems develop.) Your observation may differ depending on the store type, your location within the store, and the type of merchandise. For example, observations in the dressing room area will probably differ from those nearer product displays. Summarize your observations and relate them to the factors related to product evaluation.

9. Read these articles (Broadbent, Frank. [1992, July/August]. The Need for Universal Seam Testing. *Textile Horizons*, 29; Hallberg, Jill. [1995, July]. The Good Housekeeping Institute. *ASTM Standardization News*, 23, 32–35; and Roach, A. R. [1994]. Meeting Consumer Needs for Textiles and Clothing. *Journal of the Textile Institute*, 85(4), 484–495) and discuss how they might be used in product evaluation.

SAMPLING A LOT AND DEVELOPING ACCEPTANCE LEVELS

Chapter **13**

OBJECTIVES

- To understand why samples are used to assess some aspects of product or material quality.

- To know the characteristics of a random sample.

- To select a representative sample from a production lot.

- To recognize the differences among sampling plans and their applications.

- To understand different inspection levels and their applications.

- To know the three types of defects.

- To describe the differences between defects and defectives.

- To establish acceptance levels and justify acceptance or rejection of goods.

- To integrate product standards and specifications with acceptance levels.

KEY TERMS

production lot

sampling

taking a sample

sample

bias

random sample

representative sample

convenience sample

stratified sample

constant percentage sample

systematic sample

sampling plan

acceptance sampling

ANSI/ASQ Z1.4 1993 or MIL STD 105E

operating characteristic curve (OC curve)

lot-by-lot sample

lot-by-lot acceptance sampling by attribute

attribute

skip lot sample

continuous production sample

standard or standard product

alpha or supplier risk (α)	destructive testing	major defect
	inspection levels	minor defect
beta or consumer risk (β)	normal inspection level	acceptable quality level (AQL)
Type 1 error	tightened inspection level	acceptance levels
Type 2 error		percentage defective
single sample plan	reduced inspection level	defects per hundred units
acceptance		
rejection	defect	
double sample plan	defective	
multiple sample plan	critical defect	

Most textile and apparel products are manufactured in facilities that use similar materials and processes in a given time frame to produce multiple copies of a product. In other words, a lot is composed of homogeneous products. They include the same materials, were produced by the same process, and perhaps were worked on by the same operator(s). Similar items form a **production lot** regardless of whether a few pieces or hundreds of pieces are produced. Ideally, lots should be as large as possible to reduce unit costs.

However, all products in a lot are not necessarily identical in all aspects. Minor variations in assembly or finishing may develop during production. Variations also may be present in materials. This can be especially problematic if 100% inspection of materials is not conducted.

This chapter explains how items are selected for inspection audits and the process by which unacceptable variations from standards and specifications are identified. Then, the manner in which inspectors determine when a production lot becomes unacceptable to the buyer will be discussed.

SAMPLING A LOT

The process of selecting items from a production lot to evaluate in a product audit is referred to as **sampling or taking a sample. A sample** is a subset of a production lot. It includes a few items removed from a production or shipping lot that are assumed to represent the overall range of quality. Selecting or taking a sample is a critical process in developing a reasonably confident picture of the quality and consistency of the entire lot. The selection process is based on common sense, an understanding of basic statistical analysis, and the application of scientific principles.

The sample depends on the size of the lot, the required acceptable level of quality, the buyer's confidence in the supplier or vendor, and the type of defects that may occur. In attribute sampling, the inspector examines products to determine whether they conform to specifications. There are only two outcomes. The product is either acceptable or deficient in one or more areas. Thus, for each criteria, a yes-no or acceptable-not acceptable scale exists. One of the challenges is identifying the point at which the deficiencies suggest that the entire lot is unacceptable to the buyer.

If a company's inspection plan includes in-process inspection during production and 100% materials inspection, then a final in-depth inspection of every item from production is probably not necessary. A sample of the lot, described as a statistical or random sample in Chapter 11, will help the company verify that quality is or is not acceptable. If the sample is drawn from the lot so that each item has an equal chance of being selected, then any problems, errors, or flaws will more than likely be present in the sample. Thus, the sample represents the lot and an evaluation of the sample will provide essentially the same type of information as a full inspection, with a minimal investment of time and labor.

In this case, a sample is a selected set of products that represent every style, color, and size in the production lot based on its distribution. Thus, the sample should reflect the numerical distribution of the lot. For example, if there are twice as many black products as green products, the sample should have twice as many black products. If the lot has one half as many products in size small as it does in size medium, then the sample should have twice as many size medium products.

Samples should be free of bias. **Bias** is a systematic error in how samples are selected. For example, a biased sample would be one where only the uppermost item was selected from each box or shipping carton or a sample where only one color or size was selected.

TYPES OF SAMPLES

Samples that are free of bias are called random samples. With a **random sample,** each product in the lot has an equal chance of being selected for inspection regardless of its sequence of production, color, size, style, location in boxes or crates, or any other factor of production, packaging, or convenience. The easiest way to select a random sample is to assign a separate number to each item in the lot. Next, randomly select a set of numbers and pull the corresponding products. This set of pulled samples is then used in assessing product quality. The number of sample products relates to the size of the lot and the type of inspection that is to be conducted.

A **representative sample** includes all styles, colors, sizes, and other planned variations in the product. For apparel and most furnishings, representative lots are usually selected, but they are not automatically random unless each item in the lot had an equal chance of being selected.

Products for a random or representative sample should be selected so that they are not all from the same box, location in a stack or box, produced on the same machine, or represent the same size or same color. Some companies use tables of random numbers, numbered cards from a deck, or some other means to assist in selection of a random sample. For example, take a production lot packaged in 40 boxes; each box contains the same number of items. All items in one box are the same style, color, and size. If the person pulling the sample selected the top item from each box, the sample would be a representative one by style, color, and size. However, the sample would not be random, because all items did not have an equal chance of being selected. Such a sample is a **convenience sample.** This means that the sample items were selected because they were easier to locate and select compared to other potential samples.

Convenience samples should be avoided whenever possible because they are not random and may not be representative of the entire lot. Using a convenience sample when conducting an audit may produce unreliable results. A random representative sample might have been selected in the example given above if the person used a random number table to determine which item should be chosen from each box. With a random sample, the assumption is that quality varies little from one product to the next. A convenience sample can be unreliable because some producers put their best items at the top of a box knowing that these are the samples easiest to select. Thus, the inspection is done using atypical examples and the results reflect a better quality level than may truly exist.

When a truly random sample is not practical, other options exist. One applies to products that are packaged in a consistent fashion. In this process, the random number table is used to identify the location of the product to be selected. For example, if the number 542 is selected to represent one item to be included in the sample, the first digit could represent the number of units stacked high in the carton, the second the width or the number of stacks from the carton's left side to its right side, and the final the depth or the number of stacks from the carton's front to its back. Thus, 542 would refer to the product 5 down from the top, 4 from the left edge of the carton, and 2 deep (see Figure 13-1). Variations of this process may be needed depending on the way in which items are packaged or on the size of the items. For instance, if products in a carton are only stacked 5 high, 5 across, and 4 deep, as in Figure 13-1, the numbers representing nonexisting locations, such as 758 for this carton, would be discarded.

Another option is a **stratified sample.** In this process, the lot is stratified into layers. Each layer is subdivided into cubes. If a cube is identified to be included in the sample, then every item within that cube is pulled for the sample. Stratified samples are used when a large, supposedly homogenous lot is sampled because it facilitates the process of pulling or taking the sample.

A **constant percentage sample** is one where the same percentage is used regardless of lot size to determine the number of units to be sampled.

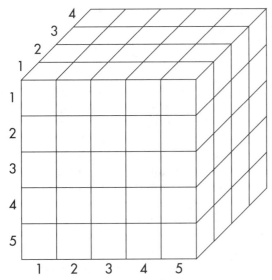

Figure 13-1
A shipping container that might be used with a random number table to select sample products.

For example, a constant percentage sample that uses a 1% sample would pull 1 item from a lot of 100 and 10 items from a lot of 1000. This type of sampling plan does not offer adequate protection for small lots (too few items are inspected) and offers too much protection for large lots (too many items are inspected). Statistically determined sampling plans are not dependent on the size of the lot. These plans are more efficient and less expensive to operate than constant percentage sampling plans.

A **systematic sample** selects units from equally occurring locations or at equal intervals of time. A systematic sample is most often used on continuously operating production lines where the same product is produced for weeks or months at a time. For example, a sample product may be pulled every eight hours to ensure that quality is consistent regardless of whether it was the first, second, or third production shift that produced a particular item.

SAMPLING PLAN

A **sampling plan** describes how to select a reasonable number of products to represent the production unit or lot based on color, size, style, and other dimensions of importance. Good sampling plans are critical to the process of acceptance sampling. **Acceptance sampling** is the inspection and evaluation of sample products selected from production lots for predetermined and defined quality characteristics after the product has been produced (Pond, 1994). Many industries, including the textile and apparel industry, use a document developed by the Department of Defense for purchasing supplies for the military and other government divisions. This document, which is referred to as the Military Standard 105E or **MIL STD 105E,** is used as the basis for sampling and for setting acceptable quality limits (Department of Defense, 1989). However, since that standard was cancelled by the Air Force in 1995, many companies use the commercial equivalent **ANSI/ASQ Z1.4–1993.**

If a sample consists of too few items, the sample is not representative, costs for inspecting the sample may be low, and results may not be valid. If a sample consists of too many items, the cost for inspecting the sample increases drastically without a corresponding increase in confidence in the results of the audit.

Sampling plans assume that the product represents a lot produced from the same materials, using the same assembly processes, based on the same specifications, and receiving the same processing. In this case, product could refer to materials, components, or end products. Thus, the major assumption of sampling plans is that products are homogeneous or essentially alike throughout the lot. Variations in materials, color, or styles that

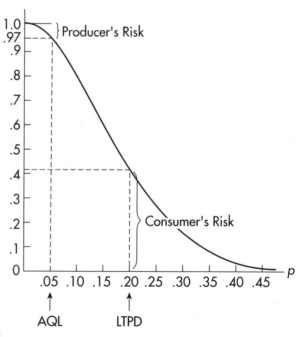

Figure 13-2

An OC curve (operating characteristics curve). (*Statistical Methods for Quality W/Applic. Eng./Mgmnt* by Miller/Miller, © 1985. Reprinted by permission of Prentice-Hall, Inc., Upper Saddle River, NJ)

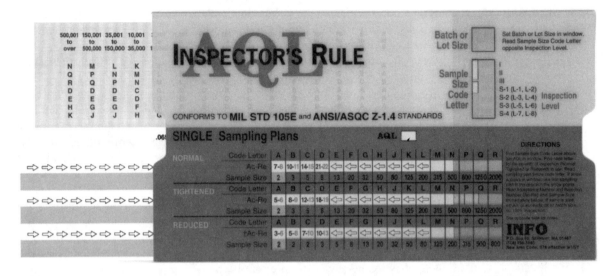

Figure 13-3
An inspector's rule. (*Reprinted by permission of INFO, P.O. Box 58, Stillriver, MA 01467*)

are included as a part of product specifications and standards are allowed and are considered part of the product description. Detection of variations in standards and specifications that are not allowed is the goal of the inspection. The audit is designed to determine the degree to which accidental variation within or between products exists. The audit is also used to determine when the number or amount of variation is extreme and adversely affects the quality, salability, or overall consumer satisfaction with the product, material, or process.

An **operating characteristic curve (OC curve)** is a plot of the probabilities of accepting a lot given the largest number of nonconformances allowed in a sample size n (see Figure 13-2). Standard tables are available to help identify the number of units to pull for a selected sample plan (see Figure 13-3). These readily available tables make it far easier to determine samples sizes than calculating the numbers using statistical equations.

TYPES OF SAMPLING PLANS

Several types of sampling plans are available. Selecting a specific sampling plan assumes that the receiving company maintains records of the results of inspections for each supplier of products, materials, or services. Record-keeping documents a performance and delivery history, which is consulted to determine the type of sampling plan to use. The specific plan selected by a company will depend on several factors. One of the most important is the previous history of a supplier, vendor, or production unit. If this is the first time a product has been purchased from this company, then the supplier's performance over time is not known. The risk of the supplier providing substandard products is greater than with a supplier who has a long history of providing consistent goods on time that meet standards and specifications. A larger sample would be used with the new, unknown supplier than with the trusted supplier.

If a supplier has recently experienced difficulty (e.g., within the last six months) in providing goods that meet standards and specifications, then each shipment will be examined closely to determine if the problems have been resolved. Conversely, if a company has provided goods for years that always exceed standards and specifications, then it is possible to examine a smaller sample to verify that the goods remain consistently high in quality. When suppliers expand into new product categories, a closer evaluation of a shipment may be warranted to be sure that standards and specifications are met.

Sampling plans also differ based on whether the inspection is done on a lot-by-lot basis, skip lot basis, or continuous production basis. When a **lot-by-lot sample** is used, samples are pulled from each production lot. Plans may differ for each lot if combinations between lots differ. A lot-by-lot basis generally is the preferred type of sampling plan, especially when the company is new and little history has been established. A lot-by-lot sample is commonly used with fashion goods because materials, styling, and assembly change frequently. Table 13-1 shows the distribution for a T-shirt lot by color and size and the corresponding sample plan.

Lot-by-lot acceptance sampling by attribute is the procedure commonly used in the textile industry complex. With this practice, a sample from each lot is inspected according to attributes. **Attributes** are specific criteria, such as size, appearance, function of closures, color matching, and seam appearance. Each product's adherence to standards and specifications is assessed. This type of acceptance sampling is used to identify differences among lots where the product is supposed to be uniform. It also is used when differences, such as color or fabric, or minor differences as a result of styling separate one lot from another lot. For instance, two shirt produc-

Table 13-1
A LOT OF T-SHIRTS CATEGORIZED BY COLOR AND SIZE AND THE CORRESPONDING SAMPLE PLAN.

Production Lot	Size				Sample* Size			
Color	Small	Medium	Large	Total	Small	Medium	Large	Total
Grey	25	50	35	110	3	5	5	13
White	25	50	35	110	3	5	5	13
Aqua	20	40	25	85	3	5	3	11
Dust	25	40	30	95	3	5	5	13
Total	95	180	125	400	12	20	18	50

*Based on normal single sampling plan for nondestructive inspection.

tion lots identical except for the pattern of the print probably would undergo lot-by-lot acceptance sampling by attribute.

In a skip lot basis, some production lots may not be sampled. A **skip lot sample** is used to decrease sampling. This type is especially common with producers of consistently high-quality products, when production history has been established at high levels, or when materials, styling, and assembly change infrequently, as with many basic goods. For example, basic bath linens, some undergarments, and basic T-shirts would be candidates for a skip lot basis sampling plan. Figure 13-4 shows examples of basic and fashion goods of consistently high quality.

A **continuous production sample** is used when products or processes are consistent for long periods of time. In continuous production, the assembly line may not stop for weeks or months at a time. The product is essentially unchanged within that time frame. The sample is inspected to verify that product quality has not changed and that products continue to meet standards and specifications. An example of continuous production in

Figure 13-4
Examples of merchandise that are of consistent quality.

the textile and apparel industry is that of basic nylon pantyhose. Samples are pulled from the line on a random basis to check for product consistency and to verify that product quality does not vary.

In an ideal sampling plan, the samples would represent fully and accurately the quality of the lot. The audit would result in the rejection of all lots worse than the standard and acceptance of all lots equal to or better than the standard. A **standard product or standard** is one that meets all specifications and company or product requirements. However, the possibility exists that acceptable lots will be rejected (**alpha or supplier risk (α)**) and inferior lots will be accepted (**beta or consumer risk (β)**). Supplier risk is also known as a **Type 1 error.** Consumer risk is also known as a **Type 2 error.**

A small sample size increases the possibility of either type of risk occurring. Some examples will help illustrate these types of risk. Alpha or supplier risk is possible when the inspection of a sample lot indicates that the lot does not meet standards and specifications. The samples exhibit too many instances of products that do not meet specs or standards for the lot to be considered first-quality merchandise. As a result, the entire lot is rejected by the buyer. In this situation, alpha risk implies that by random chance only the very poorest examples of the entire production lot were selected for the sample. As the problems were identified, the result was rejection of a lot that in reality was within a company's defined limits for product variation.

A beta or consumer risk is the opposite situation. In this type of risk, a sample indicates that the overall quality of the entire lot is better than it really is. The lot is accepted by the buyer and sold to the consumer. The consumer is the one who essentially identifies the unacceptably wide variation in the lot. Many retailers are more concerned with beta risk than they are with alpha risk because beta risk creates problems with consumer confidence and satisfaction. Of course, producers are more concerned with alpha risk because it affects their costs and income.

Single, double, and multiple sampling plans are used to determine product acceptability. In a **single sampling plan,** the total number of sample products inspected and the total size of the sample are equal. Only one sample is pulled for inspection. Acceptance or rejection of the production lot is based on adherence to standards. **Acceptance** means that the lot meets or exceeds standards and specifications and that the buyer agrees to buy or accept the lot. **Rejection** means that the lot did not meet standards and specifications and that the buyer refuses to buy or rejects the lot.

When a double sampling plan is used, it means that a problem was detected with the first sample. With a **double sampling plan,** the number of sample products that will be inspected is increased. The total number of sample products evaluated is related to the degree to which the original sample did not meet the standards. In other words, an additional sample is taken and evaluated. Acceptance or rejection is based on the cumulative results of both samples. **Multiple sample plans** may use as many as seven sample sets before a final decision regarding the acceptance or rejection of the production lot is reached. Multiple sample plans rarely are used with textile products. These plans (double and multiple) mean that more items will be inspected. It does not mean that the inspectors look at each item more closely or apply more stringent standards and specifications.

ADVANTAGES AND DISADVANTAGES OF SAMPLING

Working with a sample from a lot is more economical than 100% inspection. The inspection process is upgraded and incorporates more responsibility because the inspector is working with the fate of an entire lot, not just the fate of individual pieces. The impact of the inspection decision can be great, because the future of entire lots depend on the outcome. The economic value of the merchandise being inspected can be high. For large companies, the value of one lot can be in the hundreds of thousands of dollars. Thus, well-trained, knowledgeable, careful, and detail-oriented inspectors are essential.

Sampling is also used for **destructive testing.** Because the sample is destroyed in this process, only a few products or a tiny portion of a lot will be tested to ensure adherence to specific performance standards. Otherwise the company will not make a sufficient profit. For textile products, destructive testing is used for one of several reasons. It may be used to evaluate adherence to safety standards or to evaluate interactions of materials or processes (see Chapter 12). Destructive testing may also be applied to first production lot samples to ensure that the specific materials and processes were used before large numbers of the product are produced. This type of testing provides the buyer with one last opportunity to check for quality before the producer has invested significant resources in production (see Chapter 11).

Inspection of a sample means less risk of damage to the lot. If every finished product is inspected, the possibility exists that products will be damaged or soiled during the process. Sampling also improves delivery schedules because it takes less time to inspect a few items than to check each item in a lot.

Rejection or acceptance of entire lots emphasizes deficiencies as compared to sorting the lot into conforming or nonconforming units. Companies are more interested in taking preventive action when entire lots rather than a number of nonconforming units are rejected. In addition, the knowledge required to develop a properly designed sampling plan provides information companies can use to improve production, develop standards and specifications, and evolve a more timely and useful inspection policy.

Acceptance sampling is used when the cost of 100% inspection is high. This is especially true when the cost of passing a nonconforming product is low. Because many apparel and furnishing companies perceive this risk as low, consumer confidence in all textile products has decreased.

Acceptance sampling does not determine if a product is fit for use and that it will function as specified. That determination should have occurred much earlier during product development. Acceptance sampling either accepts or rejects a lot based on the inspection of a representative sample. Acceptance sampling refers to the inspection of lots after production or on receipt for conformance to characteristics defined by specifications or standards.

Disadvantages of sampling are the inherent alpha and beta risks already discussed. Planning and documenting the sampling process takes time and provides less information than 100% inspection. Finally, it is impossible to ensure that every item of a lot conforms to specifications. Thus, the possibility of an inferior product reaching the consumer is greater than with 100% inspection.

Inspection can be a tedious and boring process. Try this simple experiment. Read the next statement (in caps) one time only and count the number of Fs present. FIFSTEIN'S OFFERS FOR SALE A FINE SELECTION OF FIFTY-FIVE OLEFIN MICROFIBER FABRICS FROM FUSCHIA TO OFF WHITE FOR FURNISHINGS AND APPAREL. This exercise helps in recognizing the difficulties involved in understanding the criteria for inspection and measuring to that criteria. The tedious and detailed nature of inspection can create boredom. This is a common problem with acceptance sampling. When inspectors become bored or distracted, they may miss a critical element. By the way, there are 19 Fs in that sentence. How many did you count? Some inspectors count too few because they miss Fs in the middle of words or in prepositions; other inspectors count too many because they count Es or Vs.

INSPECTION LEVELS

Inspection level identifies the specific number of products pulled for the sample. It is another term used to describe the sample size. Charts, manuals, and inspector rules facilitate the identification of the correct inspection level. Figure 13-3 shows an AQL inspector's rule that conforms to the MIL STD 105E and ANSI/ASQ Z1.4–1993. These rules include information beyond that related to sample size.

Normal inspection is used when no evidence exists that the quality of the product submitted for evaluation is better or poorer than the specified quality level. Normal inspection is usually used at the beginning of the inspection process and at the beginning of one company's association with another company.

Tightened inspection is used when product inspection makes it apparent that product quality is deteriorating. Tightened inspection is usually implemented when two out of five consecutive lots have been rejected (Department of Defense, 1989). It generally requires the imposition of more stringent acceptance criteria, such as decreasing percentage defectives or defects per hundred units permitted in the sample. If quality levels drop, tightened inspection is generally mandatory until a specified improvement in the quality level of production lots has been demonstrated. After product quality has been reestablished, the sample lot will show that specs and standards are being met on a consistent basis. At this point, normal inspection is usually reinstated.

Tightened inspection does not mean any change in tolerance, standards, or specifications for products, materials, or components. The focus in tightened inspection is on examining a larger number of products. Because more items are inspected, a tightened inspection will probably also identify in more specific detail the kinds of problems that exist with the lot and should help isolate the specific factors that are contributing to the problems.

A **reduced inspection level,** which is used when it becomes apparent that product quality is very good, requires a smaller sample size. It is permitted under certain conditions relating to a consistent meeting of criteria for a lengthy time period. Reduced inspection is voluntary. For example, if a producer has a history of 10 or more consecutive inspections in which the quality level was met or exceeded, reduced inspection may be used. Reduced inspections involve a smaller investment in time and labor, but are done only when warranted by a long-established history with a supplier and confidence in its ability to provide a product that meets standards and specs.

TYPES OF DEFECTS

Lack of adherence to product standards or specifications creates problems with products. A **defect** is any nonconformance of a product with specific requirements (Department of Defense, 1989). Thus, a defect describes or refers to some feature or aspect of a product that is less than what was specified or that did not meet standards. Each company defines defects for its products. Something that one company would define as a defect might not be defined as a defect in another company. For example, a buttonhole that is located too far away from a placket edge would be considered a defect in Company A, but would not be considered a defect in Company B. Other examples of defects might be a noticeable yarn irregularity in a fabric, a broken thread in a seam, a material that shrinks more than the maximum specified, a color of button that does not meet specs, or a cuff that is not consistent in width.

A **defective** is a product with one or more defects (Department of Defense, 1989). For example, a T-shirt has a noticeable yarn irregularity by the neck band near the center front of the shirt. The irregularity is a defect; the shirt is a defective. If the company has identified product zones and defined acceptable and unacceptable appearance variations, the shirt may be considered a first- or second-quality product. Figure 13-5 shows a defective product with a noticeable defect.

Figure 13-5
This shirt has a defect (note the yarn-slub on the right front at pocket level).

Defects are divided into three general areas based on the nature, location, and degree of the defect. These three areas generally are referred to as critical, major, and minor. A **critical defect** results in hazardous or unsafe conditions for individuals using, maintaining, or depending on the product or prevents performance of a tactical function of a major end-use item (Department of Defense, 1989). Critical defects are not common with textile products, but they may occur with some occupational apparel, such as latex gloves for medical personnel. A critical defect in the glove would be a hole or tear that allows the individual wearing the glove to come into direct contact with blood and other body fluids, thereby increasing the risk of exposure to a fluid-borne pathogen or disease.

Children's sleepwear and some other textile products, such as mattresses and some furnishings, are required by law to meet mandatory pass/fail scales for flammability. Items in these categories that do not meet these specific performance requirements are also considered to have a critical defect. For example, if a pair of children's pajamas fails the flammability test, it has a critical defect and cannot be sold. Some companies use the term critical defect to describe a defect that makes it impossible for them to sell the product at full price. Thus, the term critical defect may be applied in several ways within the textile industry complex.

A **major defect** is likely to result in product failure or to reduce potentially the usability of the product for its intended purpose (Department of Defense, 1989). With textile and apparel products, major defects are those that adversely affect either the appearance of the product or its function and performance. For example, a company requires precise matching of center front stripes in its products. If a product is made where the stripes do not match, this product would be considered to have a major defect. Function and performance are not affected, but appearance is unacceptable.

A variety of defects can affect function, such as closures that do not work. When a product has been assembled in such a way that the zipper does not open, the defect usually is considered major. Another major defect related to function is a product that does not perform a specific end use properly or as the producer claims. For example, a raincoat that does not shed water or that shrinks significantly the first time it gets wet has a major defect.

Performance problems are difficult to determine except through testing. Visual inspection may not be sufficient to identify potential problems. For example, a pair of waterproof boots may have a poorly constructed seam, but the boots appear correct and look fine. As soon as the wearer walks through or stands in a puddle, however, water seeps into the boot. Testing product performance would have helped identify this major defect.

A **minor defect** is not likely to reduce materially the usability of a product for its intended purpose or is a departure from established standards that has little bearing on the effective use or operation of the product (Department of Defense, 1989). Minor defects are likely to occur in textile products. For example, many companies develop standards that describe the degree to which right and left sides of garments should match in terms of product dimensions. If the width of the right side differs from the width of the left side by one half inch, that difference might be considered only a minor defect.

Not all companies use these standard definitions of critical, major, and minor defects. Some may use other terms or may use these terms differently. For example, a company may describe any defect that renders a product unsalable as serious, while another company may define those same defects as critical. In neither case do these terms describe a defect that creates a physical risk. Thus, it is important to know the terminology used by each company to describe its specific hierarchy of defects.

When a product is zoned (see Chapter 10), a company usually categorizes defects as major or minor based on the area or zone of the product. Thus, a defect that might be considered minor in the interior of a product, such as a yarn slub in a pocket lining, might be considered major on the center front of a shirt near the collar in the fashion material. Thus, the location of a defect determines its severity and its impact on the ability of a company to sell that product at full price without creating consumer dissatisfaction.

ESTABLISHING ACCEPTANCE LEVELS

Establishing acceptance levels is a critical concept in identifying the point at which a sample's lack of adherence to standards and specifications is so extreme that the lot becomes unacceptable to the buyer. For the purpose of sampling inspection, **acceptable quality level (AQL)** is the minimal standard for a satisfactory process or product average (Department of Defense, 1989). It is the point at which a product sample can be considered a satisfactory representation of a process or product average. AQL, which is also called the **acceptance level,** is the maximum number of defects or defectives based on a specified number of units or products that is allowed within the sample before the lot is rejected. AQL can be defined by maximum percentage defective or maximum defects per hundred units (see Table 13-2).

Percentage defective is a percentage based on the number of defectives and the size of the sample or the number of units inspected (see Equation 13-1). Compared to the other methods, this one has less exacting acceptance criteria, lower costs, and is more apt to be used with processes or raw materials and components or products that have simple assembly and production requirements. Percentage defective in the textile and apparel industry is more likely to be found in material inspection and for very simple products or processes that use fusing or gluing rather than sewing. For example, the quality of fused collars and cuffs may be assessed using percentage defective. Another example are car mats made of composite materials in which the final product is simply cut from the appropriate material and the edges are heat sealed. No sewing is required. With percentage defective as the AQL, more defects may exist within a sample before the lot is rejected.

Equation 13-1

$$PD = (E \times 100)/(U)$$

where PD = percentage defective
E = number of defectives
U = number of units inspected

Table 13-2
An AQL Table.

Acceptable Quality Levels (normal inspection)

Sample size code letter	Sample size	0.010		0.015		0.025		0.040		0.065		0.10		0.15		0.25		0.40		0.65		1.0		1.5		2.5		4.0		6.5		10		15		25		40		65		100		150		250		400		650		1000	
		Ac	Re	Ac	Re	Ac	Re	Ac	Re	Ac	Re	Ac	Re	Ac	Re	Ac	Re	Ac	Re	Ac	Re	Ac	Re	Ac	Re	Ac	Re	Ac	Re	Ac	Re	Ac	Re	Ac	Re	Ac	Re	Ac	Re	Ac	Re	Ac	Re	Ac	Re	Ac	Re	Ac	Re	Ac	Re	Ac	Re
A	2	↓	↓	↓	↓	↓	↓	↓	↓	↓	↓	↓	↓	↓	↓	↓	↓	↓	↓	↓	↓	↓	↓	↓	↓	↓	↓	↓	↓	0	1	1	2	2	3	3	4	5	6	7	8	10	11	14	15	21	22	30	31
B	3	↓	↓	↓	↓	↓	↓	↓	↓	↓	↓	↓	↓	↓	↓	↓	↓	↓	↓	↓	↓	↓	↓	↓	↓	↓	↓	0	1	1	2	2	3	3	4	5	6	7	8	10	11	14	15	21	22	30	31	44	45
C	5	↓	↓	↓	↓	↓	↓	↓	↓	↓	↓	↓	↓	↓	↓	↓	↓	↓	↓	↓	↓	↓	↓	↓	↓	0	1	1	2	2	3	3	4	5	6	7	8	10	11	14	15	21	22	30	31	44	45	↑	↑
D	8	↓	↓	↓	↓	↓	↓	↓	↓	↓	↓	↓	↓	↓	↓	↓	↓	↓	↓	↓	↓	↓	↓	↓	↓	0	1	1	2	2	3	3	4	5	6	7	8	10	11	14	15	21	22	30	31	44	45	↑	↑	↑	↑
E	13	↓	↓	↓	↓	↓	↓	↓	↓	↓	↓	↓	↓	↓	↓	↓	↓	↓	↓	↓	↓	↓	↓	0	1	1	2	2	3	3	4	5	6	7	8	10	11	14	15	21	22	30	31	44	45	↑	↑	↑	↑	↑	↑
F	20	↓	↓	↓	↓	↓	↓	↓	↓	↓	↓	↓	↓	↓	↓	↓	↓	↓	↓	↓	↓	0	1	1	2	2	3	3	4	5	6	7	8	10	11	14	15	21	22	30	31	44	45	↑	↑	↑	↑	↑	↑	↑	↑
G	32	↓	↓	↓	↓	↓	↓	↓	↓	↓	↓	↓	↓	↓	↓	↓	↓	↓	↓	0	1	1	2	2	3	3	4	5	6	7	8	10	11	14	15	21	22	30	31	44	45	↑	↑	↑	↑	↑	↑	↑	↑	↑	↑
H	50	↓	↓	↓	↓	↓	↓	↓	↓	↓	↓	↓	↓	↓	↓	↓	↓	0	1	1	2	2	3	3	4	5	6	7	8	10	11	14	15	21	22	30	31	44	45	↑	↑	↑	↑	↑	↑	↑	↑	↑	↑	↑	↑
J	80	↓	↓	↓	↓	↓	↓	↓	↓	↓	↓	↓	↓	↓	↓	0	1	1	2	2	3	3	4	5	6	7	8	10	11	14	15	21	22	30	31	44	45	↑	↑	↑	↑	↑	↑	↑	↑	↑	↑	↑	↑	↑	↑
K	125	↓	↓	↓	↓	↓	↓	↓	↓	↓	↓	↓	↓	0	1	1	2	2	3	3	4	5	6	7	8	10	11	14	15	21	22	30	31	44	45	↑	↑	↑	↑	↑	↑	↑	↑	↑	↑	↑	↑	↑	↑	↑	↑
L	200	↓	↓	↓	↓	↓	↓	↓	↓	↓	↓	0	1	1	2	2	3	3	4	5	6	7	8	10	11	14	15	21	22	30	31	44	45	↑	↑	↑	↑	↑	↑	↑	↑	↑	↑	↑	↑	↑	↑	↑	↑	↑	↑
M	315	↓	↓	↓	↓	↓	↓	↓	↓	0	1	1	2	2	3	3	4	5	6	7	8	10	11	14	15	21	22	30	31	44	45	↑	↑	↑	↑	↑	↑	↑	↑	↑	↑	↑	↑	↑	↑	↑	↑	↑	↑	↑	↑
N	500	↓	↓	↓	↓	↓	↓	0	1	1	2	2	3	3	4	5	6	7	8	10	11	14	15	21	22	30	31	44	45	↑	↑	↑	↑	↑	↑	↑	↑	↑	↑	↑	↑	↑	↑	↑	↑	↑	↑	↑	↑	↑	↑
P	800	↓	↓	↓	↓	0	1	1	2	2	3	3	4	5	6	7	8	10	11	14	15	21	22	30	31	44	45	↑	↑	↑	↑	↑	↑	↑	↑	↑	↑	↑	↑	↑	↑	↑	↑	↑	↑	↑	↑	↑	↑	↑	↑
Q	1250	↓	↓	0	1	1	2	2	3	3	4	5	6	7	8	10	11	14	15	21	22	30	31	44	45	↑	↑	↑	↑	↑	↑	↑	↑	↑	↑	↑	↑	↑	↑	↑	↑	↑	↑	↑	↑	↑	↑	↑	↑	↑	↑
R	2000	0	1	1	2	2	3	3	4	5	6	7	8	10	11	14	15	21	22	30	31	44	45	↑	↑	↑	↑	↑	↑	↑	↑	↑	↑	↑	↑	↑	↑	↑	↑	↑	↑	↑	↑	↑	↑	↑	↑	↑	↑	↑	↑

↓ = Use first sampling plan below arrow. If sample size equals or exceeds lot or batch size, do 100 percent inspection.

↑ = Use first sampling plan above arrow.

Ac = Acceptance number
Re = Rejection number

(from MIL. STD 105E)

Defects per hundred units is a second way to define AQL. In **defects per hundred units (DHU),** the percentage is based on the number of defects and the size of the sample or the number of units inspected (see Equation 13-2). DHU provides for more exacting acceptance criteria than the percentage defective method, but the costs are higher. DHU is more likely to be used with complex products or completely assembled or finished textile products, particularly those that are sewn. For example, products evaluated by DHU may range from simple items, such as towels and draperies, to complex items, such as sports jackets and upholstered furniture.

Equation 13-2

$$DHU = (D \times 100)/(U)$$

where DHU = defects per hundred units
$\quad\quad D$ = number of defects
$\quad\quad U$ = number of units inspected

The inspection rule in Figure 13-3 indicates acceptable quality levels for single sampling plans for normal, tightened, and reduced sampling plans. (The use of the term "sampling plans" to describe several aspects of taking a sample is confusing, but is an inherent part of the MIL STD 105E or its commercial equivalent.) Such a rule also includes recommended batch or lot size, sample size, inspection level, directions for use, and accept-reject ranges. Samples with AQLs lower than the number to the left of the block of interest are accepted; AQLs higher than the number to the right are rejected. Samples with AQLs between the two numbers are processed using the double sampling plan discussed earlier. For example, 20 items selected from a production lot of 500 products, would be considered a normal inspection and have an AQL of 0.65. Double sampling would be required if the inspection results for the sample fell in the range between 0.65 and 1.0. The production lot would be rejected if the results exceeded 1.0. The block has an accept/reject range of 0–1.

AQL minimizes risk to suppliers and consumers. The process is as simple as it appears. Inspectors classify defects as major and minor, based on their location, type, size, and frequency. Appearance standards and performance specifications determine the levels of acceptable quality for a product. The steps involved in sampling a lot and developing acceptance levels are identified in Table 13-3.

It is important to note that AQL describes an acceptable level of defects. Companies that are unwilling to accept defects have a zero defects policy. Other companies use AQL applications to detect problems when product or materials run close to tolerance limits for specifications. Still other companies conduct 100% inspections of products or materials. Any defects in goods received from suppliers are cause for concern and could

Table 13-3
SEQUENCE OF OPERATIONAL STEPS.
1. Determine lot size.
2. Select inspection severity level.
3. Select sampling plan.
4. Determine sample size and acceptance level.
5. Select sample.
6. Inspect sample.
7. Tabulate and evaluate results.
8. Write report.

result in financial penalties, short shipments, or loss or cancellation of contracts.

APPLICATIONS

Sampling can be used for materials, processes, and finished goods with many different types of inspection. It refers to anything other than 100% inspection and to special types of samples used during product development.

Buyers are entitled to inspect goods to determine conformance to requirements before payment is made. However, unless specifications and standards are in writing, disagreements are difficult to resolve. Any problems in reaching an agreement may result in contractual disputes involving the legal system.

Standard test methods always include a section describing how samples are to be selected for destructive analysis. These procedures are based on ASTM D 4271 Standard Practice for Writing Statements on Sampling in Test Methods for Textiles. This procedure can be used for standard test methods related to raw materials (e.g., fibers), finished materials (e.g., fabrics), or finished products (e.g., furnishings or apparel). Standard test methods are often used for acceptance sampling to ensure that a material meets characteristics and performance specifications as determined by the buyer. Many of these standard business practices are described in the Worth Street Textile Market Rules (see Chapter 5). These procedures are based on attributes that describe a specific characteristic that can be measured or evaluated to determine if an item meets requirements.

Some companies require a specific type of sample for initial analysis. For instance, a buyer may require that a particular size or color sample be provided. Thus, the buyer may require the following samples: a size M garment for appearance analysis, two sample garments of every size for fit analysis, three sample products for performance assessment, three color submits to check for color matching and adherence to standard, two to three yards of production fabric for all new fabrics for analysis and performance evaluation, and two products of every color for photography for catalogs or advertising copy. These sample products are used in early inspections to be sure that pattern development work, material selection, and basic processes are appropriate. These sample products should not be confused with samples used in acceptance sampling of lots. However, these sample products are important in establishing the quality of the product and help ensure that the supplier understands standards and specifications.

CONCLUSIONS

Sampling is used when less than 100% inspection occurs. Special efforts are used to ensure that the sample represents the range of problems that may be present and the general quality of the lot. Different sample types may be used depending on the lot, the history with a specific company, and the type of defects that may occur.

AQL defines the number and severity of defects before an entire lot is rejected. Financial implications of such decisions are great. It is not uncommon for a retailer that deals with vendors to be making decisions on lots valued in the hundreds of thousands of dollars or more. Thus, recognition of the importance of setting reasonable standards and specifications, taking a sample, following standard practices, and keeping careful records is critical.

SUGGESTED READINGS

Aft, Lawrence. (1992). *Fundamentals of Industrial Quality Control,* 2nd ed. Milwaukee: ASQC Quality Press.

American Apparel Manufacturers Association. (1976). *Quality and Productivity—Cornerstone of Apparel Manufacturing.* AAMA Technical Advisory Committee Report. Arlington, VA: Author.

American Society for Testing and Materials. (1996). *Annual Book of ASTM Standards, Vol. 7.1 & 7.2.* West Conshohocken, PA: Author.

ANSI/ASQC A3. (1987). *Quality Systems Terminology.* Milwaukee: American Society for Quality Control.

Arter, Dennis R. (1994). *Quality Audits for Improved Performance,* 2nd ed. Milwaukee: ASQC Quality Press.

Barkman, William E. (1989). *In-Process*

Quality Control for Manufacturing. New York: Marcel Dekker.

Beauregard, Michael R., Raymond J. Mikulak, & Barbara A. Olson. (1992). *A Practical Guide to Statistical Quality Improvement.* New York: Van Nostrand Reinhold.

Bemowski, Karen. (1993, February). Quality, American Style. *Quality Progress, 26,* 65–68.

Besterfield, Dale H. (1994). *Quality Control,* 4th ed. Englewood Cliffs, NJ: Prentice-Hall.

Brush, Gary G. (1988). *How to Choose the Proper Sample Size, vol. 12.* Milwaukee: ASQC Quality Press.

Carr, Wendell E. (1992). *Statistical Problem Solving.* Milwaukee: ASQC Quality Press.

Carter, C. L. (Chuck). (1990). *Quality Assurance, Quality Control, and Inspection Book,* 5th ed. Richardson, TX: Author.

Chisholm, Sandra. (1995). Textile Quality Assurance: A Comparison Between Education and Industry. Unpublished master's thesis, Iowa State University, Ames.

Deming, W. Edwards. (1982). *Quality, Productivity, and Competitive Position.* Cambridge: Massachusetts Institute of Technology Center for Advanced Engineering Study.

Department of Defense. (1989, May 10). *Military Standard—105E: Sampling Procedure and Tables for Inspection by Attributes.* Washington, DC: Author.

Department of Defense. (1965, June 30). *Quality and Reliability Assurance Handbook H-53.* Washington, DC: Author.

Goetsch, David L., & Stanley Davis. (1994). *Introduction to Total Quality: Quality, Productivity, and Competitiveness.* New York: Macmillan.

Info. (1991). *AQL Inspection Manual.* Ayer, MA: Author.

Ishikawa, Kaoru, & David J. Lu. (translator). (1985). *What Is Total Quality Control? The Japanese Way.* Englewood Cliffs, NJ: Prentice-Hall.

JC Penney. (1996). *Quality Control Guidelines of Apparel and Soft Home Furnishings.* Carrollton, TX: Author.

Juran, J. M., & Frank M. Gyrna. (1993). *Quality Planning and Analysis: From Product Development Through Use.* New York: McGraw Hill.

Mehta, Pradip V. (1992). *An Introduction to Quality Control for the Apparel Industry.* Milwaukee, WI: Marcel Dekker (ASQC Quality Press).

Menon, H. G. (1992). *TQM in New Product Manufacturing.* New York: McGraw Hill.

Miller, Irwin, & Marylees Miller. (1995). *Statistical Methods for Quality with Applications to Engineering and Management.* Englewood Cliffs, NJ: Prentice-Hall.

Parsowith, B. Scott. (1995). *Fundamentals of Quality Auditing.* Milwaukee: ASQC Quality Press.

Pond, Robert J. (1994). *Fundamentals of Statistical Quality Control.* New York: Macmillan.

Tedaldi, Michael, Fred Scaglione, & Vincent Russotti. (1992). *A Beginner's Guide to Quality in Manufacturing.* Milwaukee: ASQC Quality Press.

Weber, Richard T., & Ross H. Johnson. (1993). *Buying and Supplying Quality.* Milwaukee: ASQC Quality Press.

REVIEW QUESTIONS

1. Differentiate between a random sample and a convenience sample.

2. Describe the circumstances under which a normal inspection and a reduced inspection should be conducted.

3. Define and identify examples of critical, major, and minor defects.

4. For the products listed here, identify an example of each type of defect. Why did you select those as examples? Under what circumstances might these defects make the product unacceptable for its intended use?
   a. 100% cotton jersey T-shirt
   b. 100% cotton terry cloth washcloth
   c. 100% nylon braided dog leash
   d. sleeping bag with a 100% nylon taffeta shell, 100% polyester fiberfill, 65% cotton/35% polyester flannelette inner lining, and a two-way full length zipper.

5. Establish acceptance levels for each of the products listed in Question 4.

ACTIVITIES

1. Experiment with taking samples from lots by using items such as boxes of crackers, cookies, or bandages. Inspect them for consistency of size, freedom from defects, number of chips, size of gauze patch, and so on. Compare your results for several sample types. What conclusions can you draw about the quality of the product and the information and use of each sample type? (Save this information for an activity suggested in Chapter 15.)

2. Visit a production facility or testing lab and discuss how it takes a sample and what it uses as an AQL.

3. Work with an inspector's rule and determine the number of products for a sample of a fictitious product lot. Compare sample sizes for normal, tightened, and reduced inspection levels.

4. Develop a list of possible defects from a specific product and target market. Categorize the defects as critical, major, or minor. Indicate if product zones would be important in your categories. Discuss why you defined these things as defects and why you categorized them as you did.

5. Establish an AQL for the product in Activity 4. Explain your decision.

6. Inspect a sample lot, identify defects, and determine AQL. Is the lot acceptable? Explain why you made this decision.

Part IV

INTEGRATION AND DATA ANALYSIS

This final part consists of two chapters. Chapter 14 focuses on integrating all of the factors that influence product quality. It deals with total quality management in terms of the interactions among the people, the materials, and the processes that are necessary for a quality product or service to be delivered. This chapter also examines new technologies and their relationship to process and product quality.

Cross-functional teams have become a major technique for conducting business within the textile industry complex. Because of their wide use, Chapter 14 defines the role of such teams and describes several aspects of their work. The concept of continuous improvement in quality assurance is also discussed, as are ethical issues related to quality assurance.

Chapter 15 examines several ways of presenting data related to product or process quality and the manner in which the data are analyzed to determine quality levels, variations, and trends. Although this chapter is not a complete review of the many analytical tools used in measuring and assessing quality, it provides an introduction to several commonly used methods for analyzing product and process quality.

Thus, this part focuses on these key aspects of quality assurance:

- *integration of issues regarding product or process quality with other functions of organizations,*

- *presentation and analysis of data,*

- *continuous improvement of products and processes, and*

- *ethical behavior of professionals.*

Chapter 14

TOTAL QUALITY MANAGEMENT

OBJECTIVES

- To understand the role of quality assurance within a business setting.

- To understand the integration of technical and people systems on process improvement and quality assurance.

- To examine future applications of technology to process improvement and quality assurance.

- To explore the role of cross-functional teams in terms of product quality.

- To discuss the importance of professional ethics in terms of directing behavior.

KEY TERMS

total quality management (TQM)

technical systems

people systems

preventive perspective

policies

procedures

processes

objective

continuous improvement

sporadic problem

chronic problem

quality function deployment (QFD)

benchmarking

competitive analysis

cross-functional teams

specific-purpose team

self-managing team

ethical behavior

ethics

robotics

CIM (computer integrated manufacturing)

Producing a product that is known for its quality is not an accident. Rather, it requires the integration of many activities, builds on several knowledge bases, and incorporates a variety of production processes. It involves coordination of various activities and careful attention to analysis, evaluation, and planning. Everyone who works for the company as well as the people who work for suppliers have an impact on a product's quality. This is true regardless of whether the product is a material incorporated into the finished product, a service that facilitates communication among companies, or a machine. It is important to understand how these various factors influence the quality of the finished product.

Total quality management (TQM) refers to activities that involve everyone in an organization in an integrated effort to improve performance at every level. The goal of TQM is to maintain the organization's competitiveness in the world market. Several key factors are present in a TQM perspective: a customer focus, an emphasis on quality, teamwork, individual empowerment, training and education, involvement of all employees, commitment by management, and continuous process improvement. Several of these factors have already been discussed. This chapter integrates these factors and explores some of them in greater detail. Specifically, this chapter focuses on the interactions between the technical systems and the people systems that are present within businesses in the textile industry complex.

A key element in TQM is that quality must be built into the product or service; it cannot be inspected in or controlled. Companies that engage in final inspection as a means of controlling product quality are engaged in a self-defeating process. Many companies have undergone major revision of focus and organization to ensure that quality is a driving force within the company.

WORKING WITH THE TECHNICAL SYSTEMS

Technical systems are the equipment and procedures already in place within the organization to assist in meeting its objectives. Technical systems are also concerned with those factors of production that require significantly detailed knowledge about processes, materials, or techniques. Technical systems include design and product development, pattern making, spreading and cutting, materials selection and evaluation, inspection and product evaluation, production, packaging, and shipping.

Technical systems are designed to extend and enhance human productivity and maintain an organization's competitive edge. These systems rely on the expertise of selected individuals who are knowledgeable about specific areas and possess the necessary skills to perform the required work. Individual employees are expected to be creative in developing solutions to specific problems. They should be able to determine the information needed to make an informed decision, collect the data, and evaluate or analyze this material. In many cases, experts or teams of experts must be able to theoretically solve a problem, develop a practical application of that solution, and then successfully implement the process.

For TQM to work, the various technical areas must use terminology consistently, apply the same techniques in terms of measuring for the same parameter, and adapt the same criteria to define quality and to accept or reject products. For example, the inspector who is evaluating work in the cutting room should use the same location for measuring dimensions of a product part as is used in the specs for the piece. If the inspector measures the piece at a different location, parts may be accepted that should be rejected and parts that should be accepted may be rejected. If inspection and specification personnel communicate before inspection occurs, such problems as these are less likely to occur. Thus, communication and training are key elements in TQM of the technical systems.

When divisions within an organization work together to minimize problems, they tend to be more efficient and synergistically work to produce a better and more consistent product. Continuous improvement is more probable when teams of experts evaluate the process from several different perspectives. Each expert tends to see or evaluate things differently. Aspects that may appear correct and even ideal to one person may represent an area of possible improvement to another expert. Thus, the use of teams often minimizes problems with the processes of designing, engineering, producing, shipping, and marketing products. Techniques used to measure performance and to evaluate a process to determine areas for improvement are identified in Chapter 15.

PRODUCT DEVELOPMENT ASPECTS

Product development is a general term that often includes design, pattern making, and related activities. The designer and the pattern maker communicate so that the final pattern correctly interprets the design, uses materials efficiently without sacrificing design integrity, and allows for efficient production sequencing. Sometimes, the designer and pattern maker need to reach compromises on specific elements of the design. For example, with some apparel items the amount of flare along the hem can make a significant difference in material utilization rates. In some cases, a small change in flare may still allow the design to be expressed as the designer wants but improve material utilization. In other cases, a change in hem flare would compromise the design too much and material utilization rates must remain less than ideal. In these cases, fashion dictates and, ultimately, consumer appeal are more important than efficient material utilization rates.

The pattern maker may need to work with material specialists to determine material weight, drape, and stiffness. Materials that are heavy or stiff often require more ease to drape and form around three-dimensional objects such as the human figure or the frame of a chair. In these cases, the pattern must incorporate the appropriate amount of ease so that the finished product is able to meet size and fit requirements as well as functional demands.

Fit of the product is evaluated to be sure that the materials and the pattern work together and create the desired look and function in terms of the customer's needs. Fit is a critical issue, especially in apparel. Companies are preferred by some consumers because of the way their products fit specific figure types and avoided by other consumers for the same reason.

SPREADING AND CUTTING

Important aspects of spreading include layering or plying the material so that each ply is properly aligned. This includes such details as matching patterns or plaids. Ply tension is another important element, if the material is stretched too much, the excess will buckle in a ply. The operator should also examine the material during spreading to detect any bow or other grain problems that may exist. Finally, the operator is responsible for laying the ply so that splices that join lengths of fabric together are not incorporated in product parts.

Most pattern pieces must be cut in a straight vertical orientation of the cutting blade, so that the edges of each piece are sharp and not ragged and so that all pieces are the same dimensions. Plies of thermoplastic materials should not be fused together. Product pieces should be the same dimensions as the pattern pieces. Notches to facilitate location and placement of other product parts or components are correctly and precisely marked. Drill holes are the correct size and in the correct location.

MATERIALS

Materials used in the product are often selected at the same time that the product development team or designer is creating individual designs for the line. The same fashion material may be used in several products within the line so that materials inventory and investment in material evaluation is kept within reasonable limits. The manner in which materials are handled in storage, spreading, cutting, sewing, and finishing often have a significant impact on the quality of the final product. Thus, a basic knowledge of the materials facilitates the process and helps ensure that the final product meets specs and standards.

Materials evaluation was discussed extensively in Part II, and material interactions and material-process interactions were discussed in Part III. However, keep in mind that materials greatly influence productivity, product quality, product appeal, and consumer satisfaction with the finished product. Thus, understanding the materials to be used in a product is an important component of TQM. Evaluation of materials and their interactions are not the only factors in quality assurance, but they are a major element in contributing to the quality of finished products.

PRODUCTION

Production is another major element in product quality. Although it plays a critical role, activities before and after production also influence product quality. Specifications and standards should be identified for each production step. Operators must know company expectations for quality regarding their individual production processes and must have received proper training to reach the specified level for quality and productivity. In addition, the production process should be evaluated on a continuous basis, so that variations are kept within reasonable limits and so that product quality is not compromised at any stage.

Evaluation of the performance of the finished product is also important. The company should ensure that the various materials and processes combined in the product are compatible and produce a reasonably serviceable product for the price. Customer satisfaction is very much related to the product as a whole as well as the interactions of materials and processes inherent within the product. Product testing is a critical aspect that examines these interactions. It is important to remember that many consumers equate price with product quality and performance expectations. Thus, consumer satisfaction with a specific textile product is very much related to the price paid for the item. Thus, it is important that price be kept as low as possible while meeting consumer expectations and producing a consistent product that meets or exceeds standards and specifications.

PACKAGING AND SHIPPING

The manner in which a product is packaged and shipped is an additional factor in quality assurance. Packing the product correctly, adhering the right labels to the container, and shipping the container at the specified time to the appropriate company help ensure that the product is available for sale to the consumer at the best time. For example, children's clothing sells especially well during the few weeks before school starts. Retailers and manufacturers work to have store shelves fully stocked during this ideal selling time. Correct package labels, meeting specs in terms of packaging, and shipping the product on time are all factors used in assessing quality of products and process.

WORKING WITH THE PEOPLE SYSTEMS

People systems are the individuals and the roles they fill within the organization. They are involved with hiring individual employees, maintaining a positive morale within the company, empowering individuals and teams to correct problems, developing trust within the company, and working toward well-understood goals in terms of quality so that business objectives are met. People systems focus on the individual employees—on educating and training them to understand the organization's emphasis on and commitment to quality and their role in that process. A team approach to problem solving is a key element of the people system.

People systems incorporate formal and informal training and education programs that contribute to improved understanding of individual positions, expectations for productivity, and roles in helping the division or department meet its goal in terms of quality and productivity. Individuals and teams are empowered to identify problems or areas that require focused efforts, develop a plan that addresses an identified need, and implement the plan so that the problem is corrected.

These systems often take a **preventive perspective,** which means that potential problem areas are identified and a plan is developed and implemented to prevent a foreseeable problem from occurring. Many training programs also have this goal. In the people system, individuals are encouraged to establish specific goals for their work and to undertake or participate in training programs.

People systems are dependent on several key factors. Empowerment is one. Another is good lines of communication within the company, with suppliers, and with buyers, so that all interested individuals and organizations are aware of and involved in problem solving. Third, all participants should agree on goals and objectives that enable them to work together in a unified and directed fashion. A final requirement is that adequate resources need to be available.

SUPPLIERS

Many organizations recognize that their suppliers significantly influence the quality of the final product. As a result, these companies have begun to include suppliers in their chain of communication. This empowers the supplier by helping it understand how its goods or services influence product quality. This, in turn, helps the supplier provide goods or services of an appropriate quality in a timely manner. It is important to realize that suppliers also have an investment in the competitive stature of their buyers. If a buyer of a supplier's goods or services loses market share, then the supplier is likely to suffer loss of revenue as well. Thus, it behooves buyers and suppliers to work together for their mutual benefit. Many organizations have developed a certification program with their suppliers to facilitate communication and understanding. These certification programs frequently benefit both the supplier and the buyer.

MANAGEMENT

Management is responsible for five major functions within an organization—planning, organizing, commanding, coordinating, and controlling activities. Management tends to focus on developing organizational **policies.** These broad guides to action differ from **procedures or processes,** which provide details describing how a given activity is to be accomplished (Juran & Gryna, 1993).

Management's primary purposes are to establish objectives for the organization, to identify resources available to assist in meeting objectives, and to provide assistance in planning and implementing procedures and programs that will facilitate meeting specific objectives. An **objective** is a statement of a desired result to be achieved within a specified time (Juran & Gryna, 1993). It is based on policies developed by management, but it identifies a specific measurable target for the organization.

Management is often involved in negotiating and clarifying objectives. It may need to work with divisions within the organization to help reconcile apparently conflicting objectives. For instance, an organization may want to improve product quality without increasing product cost. In this instance, some clarification or reconciliation may be needed because these objectives may, on first examination, appear to be mutually exclusive.

It is equally important that sufficient resources be devoted to planning and implementing programs, including training programs, so that each member of the organization understands her or his role in meeting these objectives. Training and educational programs help ensure that each employee has sufficient knowledge and skill to be able to perform at the level needed to meet objectives.

In TQM, management at all levels must be involved in and committed to defining and achieving a specified level of quality in the process and in the finished product. Without a clear commitment on the part of management, the organization will probably fail to meet its objectives for quality. Management must have a clear vision of the direction the organization should take and the ability to see beyond the present. Management also must foster an attitude of change and demonstrate a commitment to continuous improvement in order for TQM to be effective.

Management is also involved with the identification and assignment of major responsibilities within the organization. As a first step, objectives are usually divided into subobjectives. Subobjectives are assigned to divisions or teams within an organization whose members then focus on those specific activities or responsibilities. Evaluation and assessment of programs, progress towards meeting objectives or subobjectives, and corrective actions are often part of management's responsibilities. In short, management evaluates the organization's ability to reach specific objectives.

This may mean that management establishes objectives that are then restated in "do-able" terms. For example, an objective such as "We will produce a product that is competitive in terms of cost, performance, and quality" does not include information that can be readily evaluated. The organization must define terms and performance measures and implement procedures that will allow the organization to meet these stated goals. Each objective is restated so that it reflects specific quality standards. By establishing standards and specifications, the organization is able to measure progress toward meeting the objective. One measure would be the establishment of specifications and standards for the product. A second measurement would be a count of the number of finished products that meet standards and specifications.

Sharing standards and specifications for materials with suppliers is another implementation procedure that could be measured by assessing the change in the number of nonconforming products because of material-related problems. Thus, it becomes clear that many factors are interconnected when an organization adapts a TQM perspective.

CONTINUOUS IMPROVEMENT

Continuous improvement is a constant effort to refine processes so that the result is an overall increase in the quality of products or services. This may mean striving for better levels of performance or identifying and implementing corrective action so that problems decrease in occurrence or cease to occur. Problems can be identified as either sporadic or chronic.

Sporadic problems are sudden adverse changes in the product or process. They are remedied by identifying why the problem occurred and restoring the product or process to its normal condition. For instance, a new shipment of material that previously had performed well in colorfastness testing arrives. Testing shows that it is no longer fast to washing. Investigation reveals that the dye house had changed suppliers and the new dye was not as fast as the previous dye. There are several possible solutions to this problem including reevaluation of the dyeing process to determine if conditions can be modified to improve wash fastness, returning to the original source of the dye, or investigating other dyes or sources until one with adequate wash fastness is found. Selecting the appropriate solution will resolve this sporadic problem.

Continuous improvement focuses on finding solutions to chronic problems. A **chronic problem** is a long-term adverse situation in which the remedy is related to changing or modifying the status quo. For instance, modifying specifications or standards so that they better reflect customer expectations would be a solution to a chronic problem.

Continuous improvement usually requires an organized approach that focuses on a specific chronic problem. After the problem has been recognized, a plan is developed to diagnose the problem so that a solution can be designed and implemented. Diagnosis is based on understanding the problem and how it occurs. Some of the analytical tools described in Chapter 15 are useful in identifying sources of chronic problems. Several teams or divisions within the organization may be involved in the analysis of the problem and development of theories that suggest causes for the problem.

Development and selection of possible solutions also involves several departments within the organization. Once the solution has been implemented, the process should be analyzed to verify that the solution success-

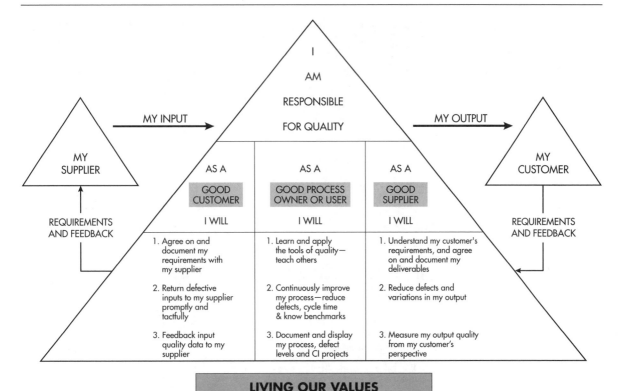

Figure 14-1
Continuous improvement
practices. (*Reprinted from J. M.
Juran and Frank M. Gyrna,
Quality Planning and Analysis:
From Product Development
Through Use, p. 8, 1993,
McGraw Hill, with permission
of the McGraw-Hill companies*)

fully solved the chronic problem and did not introduce new problems. Figure 14-1 illustrates communication and documentation aspects that contribute to continuous improvement.

DESIGN AND PRODUCT DEVELOPMENT

Significant portions of the textile industry complex are involved in continuous modification of products to satisfy customer needs. Much of this change is related to the fashion nature of some parts of the industry. Additional modifications are based on laws and regulations related to trade, production, labeling, or environmental issues. Still other changes result from the dynamic and everchanging nature of the materials. Many organizations have research programs that are designed to improve performance and expand markets for specific materials or to develop new materials and create markets for them. Thus, design and product development issues apply to all types of textile products, even basic and nonfashion goods.

A basic understanding of quality issues is necessary to satisfy the customer. Table 14-1 organizes the components of quality from the manufacturing and service perspectives. In this model, wholesalers and retailers are

Table 14-1
COMPONENTS OF QUALITY.

Manufacturing	Service (Retailing)
Product Features	
performance	accuracy
reliability	timeliness
durability	completeness
ease of use	friendliness and courtesy
serviceability	anticipating customer needs
aesthetics	knowledge of server
availability of options & expandability	aesthetics
reputation	reputation
Freedom from Deficiencies	
Products free of defects and errors at delivery, during use, and during cleaning or other servicing	Service free of errors during original and future transactions
Sales, billing, and other business processes error free	Sales, billing, and other business processes error free

(Modified from Juran, J. M., & Frank M. Gyrna. [1993]. Quality Planning and Analysis: From Product Development Through Use. New York: McGraw Hill, p. 4.)

considered service industries. With many retailers now involved in private label merchandise, these companies are affected by design and product development issues. Thus, both manufacturers and retailers need to understand several key factors in product development and product or service quality.

Figure 14-2 illustrates relationships among the various activities that contribute to continuous improvement in the product or service provided to the customer. From this model, it is clear that interactions must occur among the various segments of the industry in order to provide the customer with a product or service that meets their needs.

ENGINEERING AND PRODUCTION

Customer or user needs are translated into product design requirements for production. It is not uncommon for product failures to be traceable to inadequate engineering, production, or design specifications. For example, seam failure that results from the incorrect seam, stitch, or thread type in

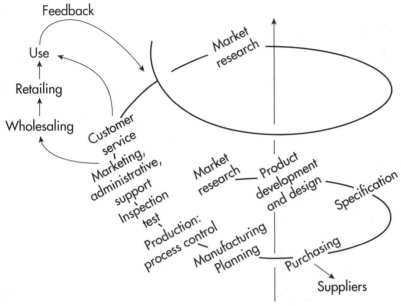

Figure 14-2
The spiral of progress in quality. (*Reprinted from J. M. Juran and Frank M. Gyrna, Quality Planning and Analysis: From Product Development Through Use, p. 6, 1993, McGraw Hill, with permission of the McGraw-Hill companies*)

relation to the stress to which a seam may be subjected is an example of inadequate design specifications. To avoid this problem, the individuals developing specs must have a good understanding of customer expectations and performance aspects of seams, stitches, threads, and the interactions among them.

Quality function deployment (QFD) is a technique in which a series of interlocking matrices translate customer needs into product and process characteristics. Figure 14-3 illustrates the process. With QFD, it is more likely that customer needs are incorporated into product and process design. In Figure 14-2 direct communication with customers is one important means of understanding what the customer wants. If communication with the customer is blocked, then satisfying customer needs becomes more difficult. Unfortunately, some organizational policies limit communication with customers. This is especially common with retail organizations that discourage customer returns, those retailers that fail to notify suppliers of product returns because the product did not meet consumer expectations, or those suppliers whose return policies make it difficult for retailers to return merchandise because of consumer dissatisfaction or product failure.

SPREADSHEETS IN QUALITY PLANNING

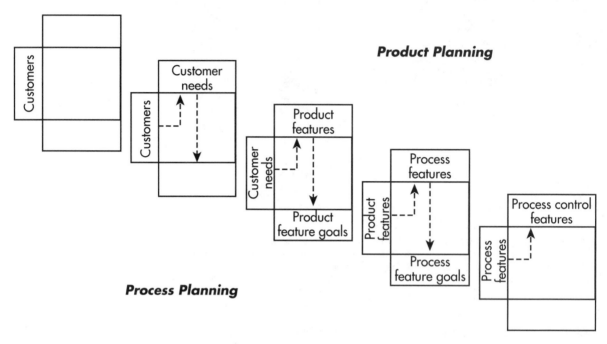

Figure 14-3
Generic planning spreadsheets. *(Reprinted with permission from J. M. Juran et al. [1990]. "Planning for Quality" course notes, 2nd ed. Wilton, CT: Juran Institute, p. 256)*

BENCHMARKING

Benchmarking is becoming increasingly popular as a process improvement tool. **Benchmarking** is the "process of comparing and measuring an organization's operations or internal processes against those of a best-in-class performer from inside or outside its industry" (Goetsch & Davis, 1994, pp. 414). In benchmarking, two organizations agree to share information about process or operations. The two companies often are not competitors, but both are interested in improving operations.

Benchmarking is not competitive analysis. In benchmarking, one organization takes the information about any given activity that has been shared by another organization and improves upon it. In **competitive analysis,** an organization compares a competitor's product against its own so that it can improve its product and make it more competitive. Consumers often conduct competitive analysis when they investigate several similar products before making a purchase. Competitive analysis is similar to comparative testing. The major difference is that competitive analysis does not necessarily involve physical testing while comparative testing does.

In benchmarking, the emphasis is on the basic processes used to produce, distribute, and support a product. The goal is to understand how to do a particular job better and more efficiently, so that the result is a better product at the same or a lower cost. Benchmarking is particularly beneficial in determining the allocation of resources for process improvement. With benchmarking, identifying processes that require major change can be made easier.

COMPETITION

Competition in the global market is more intense than in local or regional markets. For this reason, organizations that focus on improving product and process quality are more likely to compete in the global market. Global competition requires products or services that satisfy customer needs at reasonable and competitive prices. Establishing benchmarks, focusing on continuous improvement, and utilizing cross-functional teams are some of the ways that organizations have been able to maintain a competitive edge in the expanding global market.

WORKPLACE CROSS-FUNCTIONAL TEAMS

Cross-functional teams are becoming more and more common in the textile industry complex, as job responsibilities combine what were once traditionally separate areas. Cross-functional teams may be the standard operating procedure in some organizations, or they may be created for specific purposes such as solving chronic problems within the organization. In either case, the **cross-functional team** consists of a group of individuals who work together but who represent different departments or different areas of specialization. Teams vary in size depending on the organization and the role they are serving, but most teams range in size from four to twenty members. Larger teams may be divided into subteams that interact frequently.

In **specific-purpose teams,** the individual members continue to serve in their regular roles within an organization. Team members meet together on a periodic basis to deal with a specific issue. Special purpose teams usually disband after the specific issue has been resolved.

Permanent teams are often organized to deal with a general issue of interest to the organization, such as business process quality or a broad product category such as women's separates. These teams are often self-managing. The **self-managing team** plans, implements, and controls its work to reach a defined business objective.

For example, a retailer that develops its own private label merchandise and uses self-managed teams will probably have designers, production engineers, material specialists, and pattern makers work together so that all the products developed by the team meet company specifications and are directed toward meeting organizational objectives. Individual members of the team meet together on a regular basis and interact with each on an as-needed basis. They may travel to production facilities to ensure that suppliers are able to meet specifications, standards, and delivery deadlines. Designers and pattern makers work with production engineers to develop specifications and other criteria so that suppliers have correct information to use when purchasing materials and producing finished products. Each individual within the team has an area of specialization, but the flexibility inherent in such a team means that members are able to perform more than one role.

Several characteristics of cross-functional teams must be understood for the teams to function efficiently. One, team members are responsible to the team for their work. The work should be done correctly and on time because the work of all members is interconnected and time is usually critical. If something is done incorrectly, it may seriously detract from meeting deadlines and may require that other team members redo work. Incorrect work increases costs.

Two, members should have confidence in each other. If one team member does not have the confidence of the others, the entire output of the team can be adversely affected.

Three, team members are interdependent and share information as it becomes available. A significant amount of teamwork is based on the most current and correct information. Thus, team members need to be informed of any changes in information as soon as possible, so that their work will be correct and up to date. The results of completed work may need to be modified. Interdependence also implies that some tasks may be handled by more than one person at any one time. For example, team members may assist with tasks outside of their particular specialization in order to meet a fast-approaching deadline.

It takes time for teams to learn to work together efficiently and reliably. Teams that work best build on each member's strengths. Good communication skills are critical in maintaining the information flow among members. Documentation of decisions and processes is also critical, as teams need a record of activities. Data should be recorded and analyzed to determine the impact of decisions on processes and to develop and implement appropriate product or process improvements.

Individual members need to identify with the team and feel that they are a valued member of it. It is ideal if team members trust each other and support each other's work. Loyalty among team members is an ideal outcome of a strong and well-functioning team.

Teams often go through several stages as the team matures and learns how to work together. These stages are sometimes referred to as forming, storming, norming, and performing (Scholtes, 1988). Each stage has several key elements. In the forming stage, team members get to know each other, identify each other's working style and strengths, and explore the boundaries of acceptable group behavior. This stage may not make great strides toward accomplishing team goals. The forming stage often is marked by feelings of anticipation and anxiety and lofty, abstract discussion of concepts and issues.

In the storming stage, teams experience resistance to individual approaches, conflict with the team, and rapidly changing attitudes about the team or individual members. Teams may argue, experience disunity, and feel increased tension about working together. Individual members may be defensive and competitive.

In the norming stage, members develop a sense of team cohesion and begin to actively work to achieve team goals. Team members have begun to work out their differences and have developed the ability to critique work without seeming to attack individuals. Critiques may incorporate both positive and negative issues without generating feelings of hostility or choosing sides.

In the performing stage, the team is truly focused on diagnosing problems, implementing changes, and performing its work in order to reach organizational objectives. Teams have established group dynamics, understand each other, and are able to work through problems that may arise. Loyalty to team members is present, and team members work well and efficiently together as a cohesive unit.

Cross-functional teams offer great potential to most organizations, but only if each member is willing and able to work with the other members of the team. Disharmony can create significant problems with productivity and job satisfaction. Individuals who are not experienced with cross-functional teamwork may have some difficulty in adjusting to this kind of work environment. It does require that individual members be responsible and self-motivated. Most teamwork decisions are based on consensus after discussion and exploration of several options. It is important for team members to accept consensus decisions and work to reach specific objectives rather than dwelling on options that were discarded by the team.

With teamwork, fewer people and fewer resources tend to get more accomplished than when individuals work by themselves. Synergism is created such that the need for management and support staff is reduced. Productivity increases frequently are seen when teams have learned to work together.

ETHICAL BEHAVIOR

Business practices should operate within acceptable legal and ethical standards. TQM is based on three factors: trust, integrity, and values. Because this is true, ethical behavior becomes a critical element in professional in-

Table 14-2
TESTS OF ETHICAL BEHAVIOR.

Morning after test: How will you feel about this behavior in the morning?

Front-page test: What would your reaction be if this behavior were the lead article on the front page of your hometown newspaper?

Mirror test: How will you feel about this behavior when you look in the mirror?

Role reversal test: How would you feel if you were on the receiving end of this behavior?

Common sense test: What does everyday common sense say about this behavior?

(Modified from Goetsch, David L. [1992]. Industrial Supervision in the Age of High Technology. New York: Macmillan, p. 135.)

teractions. **Ethical behavior** is following and demonstrating personal behavior and professional practices that subscribe to the values of society.

Ethics refers to the rules or standards for behavior governing the conduct of professionals. The ASQC Code of Ethics is included in Appendix F. Terms such as trust, responsibility, and integrity often are used when ethical behavior and ethics are discussed.

Management should ensure that an organization's internal environment promotes, expects, and rewards ethical behavior. It should set an example of ethical behavior in all external and internal dealings (Goetsch & Davis, 1994). Corporate-sponsored training programs may focus on a variety of issues related to ethics, including drug and alcohol abuse, conflict of interest, misuse of proprietary information, abuse of expense accounts, misuse of company property, false or misleading advertisements, bribery, employee theft, and receiving excessive gifts from professional or governmental contacts.

It is important to recognize that legal and ethical do not mean the same thing. Although some practices may be legal, they may not be ethical. However, all illegal behaviors are also unethical and should always be avoided. Table 14-2 identifies several tests to determine if any questionable behavior would be considered ethical. These questions should help anyone determine when behavior would not be considered ethical by the majority of the population. It is also important to note that behavior that leaves one feeling good about oneself is behavior that is consistent with one's personal value system.

THE FUTURE

In the future, organizations will be influenced greatly by the technical system and the people system. Recently, manufacturing has undergone tremendous change as computer systems are increasingly used to facilitate design, production, engineering, and manufacturing. These computer systems are used to enhance both product quality and productivity of specific processes.

In some cases, such as computer aided design (CAD) systems, basic components can be replicated quickly, easily, and accurately. Modifications of colors, motifs, or design lines are made so that the designer can explore several alternates. In computer aided pattern making, lengths of seams, amount of ease, and other pattern characteristics can be measured or adjusted quickly and accurately. Markers can be modified with minimal effort so that grain is correct and material utilization rates are optimized. The effect of CAD systems on the textile industry complex has been significant. However, additional changes are expected as robotics and computer integrated manufacturing are implemented at increasing rates in design and production facilities. In many cases, processes are integrated so completely that it may be difficult to delineate between specific or traditional roles.

ROBOTICS

Robotics refers to automated systems that are designed to perform repetitive tasks quickly, accurately, and correctly. Often robotics are developed with the expectation that they will decrease assembly costs and increase productivity rates so that over time these systems eventually will pay for themselves in lower costs and higher sales. However, current robotic systems are not able to match the speed with which human operators are able to pick up, identify, and orient materials and perform the sewing operation. Even simple robotic systems are not able to provide good returns for the investment. In some systems, a human operator is used to pick up, identify, and orient the components or pieces, while the robotic device does the sewing. Thus, these systems have continued to rely on the people system for the most difficult part and the technical system for the simplest part of the process.

With the current industry trend of shifting labor intensive operations to geographic regions where labor costs are low, robotics are not expected to become a significant part of production for most textile products. Low transportation costs and improving transportation facilities worldwide are contributing to this trend.

CIM (COMPUTER-INTEGRATED MANUFACTURING)

CIM (computer-integrated manufacturing) refers to a variety of activities including, but not limited to, design, pattern making, receiving, manufacturing, scheduling, communications, inventory, shipping, and inspection. CIM deals with the gathering, manipulation, and distribution of process and management information throughout a facility or organization in a manner that facilitates meeting deadlines. CIM systems are designed to process and share information so that delays, misinterpretation, and problems are eliminated.

These systems tend to be fairly complex and need to process incredible amounts of information efficiently. CIM is part of the technical system of an organization that works with the people systems. Thus, although CIM may not be user friendly, the most useful systems are the ones that provide information in a useable manner and that can readily interface with the people systems. Usually, numerous subsystems interact with different departments or divisions within the organization to provide practical solutions to specific problems. The difficulty lies in developing subsystems that can communicate with other subsystems and share information.

For example, a subsystem might be responsible for maintaining records of equipment used within the cutting room. The database probably includes lists of vendors, prices, parts, distributors, repair facilities, and related information. Different pieces of equipment are likely to be used for spreading or cutting different types of materials, so the equipment list might need to be linked to certain product types or specific styles or seasons. Equipment probably should be monitored to identify life-cycle characteristics, the need for rework or repair, and related information. Thus, a subsystem could be used to create a history for each piece of equipment. This history would be used to project equipment replacement needs and develop a repair and maintenance schedule.

CIM may incorporate a number of management subsystems that focus on coordinating a variety of activities. Such subsystems might include one that orders materials so that specific production schedules can be met without accumulating excessive inventory and another that schedules work in an efficient manner. Figure 14-4 illustrates several subsystems that might be used in a textile product manufacturing facility.

CIM systems commonly are found in pattern production, marker making, and cutting rooms, but they are not well established in assembly operations. The problems relate to automated handling of flexible and limp materials where sewability and tailorability characteristics differ drastically from one material to another. Minor changes in material characteristics, such as in yarn size or twist, can alter handling characteristics substantially. The Kawabata evaluation system and related systems discussed in Chapter 7 are an attempt to predict handling characteristics so that automated handling devices can be programmed for variations among materials. However, the constant changes inherent in fashion goods will continue to limit full application of CIM in production facilities until a much more complete and comprehensive data base is available.

CONCLUSION

Producing a product that meets customer expectations, that is consistent in characteristics and performance aspects, and that meets standards and specifications is the result of deliberate, planned interactions between

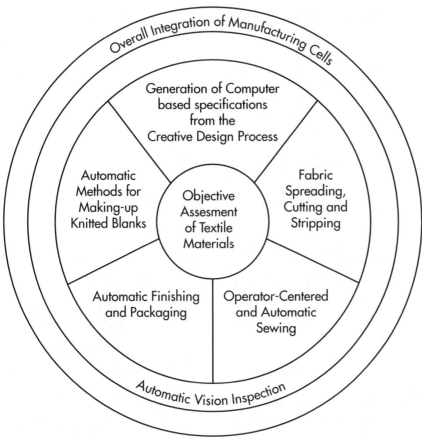

Figure 14-4

Management subsystems for computer-integrated manufacturing. (*Reprinted with permission from Munden, D. L., W. J. Loweth, & M. J. Ryan. [1990]. The Cimtex Centre for Automated Garment Production. In The Textile Institute (ed.). Textiles: Fashioning the Future. Manchester, England: Textile Institute, p. 390*)

technical systems and people systems. Various quality programs, such as TQM, continuous improvement, cross-functional teams, and benchmarking, are common strategies used to make organizations competitive in the global marketplace. A basic understanding of and adherence to personal and professional ethics is also critical to success in the textile industry complex.

Changes within the textile industry complex are occurring at ever-increasing rates. Computer integrated manufacturing and robotics are two techniques that are expected to become increasingly useful.

SUGGESTED READINGS

Aft, Lawrence. (1992). *Fundamentals of Industrial Quality Control,* 2nd ed. Milwaukee: ASQC Quality Press.

Anderson, John C., Kevin Dooley, & Manus Rungtusanatham. (1994, December). Training for Effective Continuous Quality Improvement. *Quality Progress,* 57–61.

Anon. (1993, April). The Cutting Room of the Future. *Knitting Times,* K/A 2, K/A 4.

Anon. (1985, October). The Case for Quality Control. *American Dyestuff Reporter,* 14, 16, 18, 42.

Anfuso, Dawn. (1994, July). L. L. Bean's TQM Efforts Put People Before Processes. *Personnel Journal,* 72–73, 75–76, 78, 80, 83.

Apparel Quality Committee. (1985). *Elements of an Apparel Quality Control Program.* Arlington, VA: American Apparel Manufacturers Association.

ASQC Futures Team. (1996, July). Quality and Its Environment in 2010. *Quality Progress,* 71–79.

Barkman, William E. (1989). *In-Process Quality Control for Manufacturing.* New York: Marcel Dekker.

Beauregard, Michael R., Raymond J. Mikulak, & Barbara A. Olson. (1992). *A Practical Guide to Statistical Quality Improvement.* New York: Van Nostrand Reinhold.

Bentley, J. (1991). Manufacturing Strategy—Investing Through the 90s. In The Textile Institute (ed.). *The Textile World at a Crossroads.* Manchester, England: Textile Institute, pp. 64–73.

Besterfield, Dale H. (1994). *Quality Control,* 4th ed. Englewood Cliffs, NJ: Prentice-Hall.

Bezold, Clement. (1996, July). On Futures Thinking: Trends, Scenarios, Visions, and Strategies. *Quality Progress, 29,* 81–83.

Bicknell, Barbara A., & Kris D. Bicknell. (1995). *The Road Map to Repeatable Success: Using QFD to Implement Change.* Boca Raton, FL: CRC Press.

Bona, Mario. (1990). *Textile Quality: Physical Methods of Product and Process Control.* Rome: Texilia.

Boznak, R. G. (1994, July). When Doing It Right the First Time Is Not Enough. *Quality Progress, 27,* 74–78.

Bradbury, Mike, & John Kent. (1994, May/June). Dynamic Response: Its Impact on the Textile Marketing Chain. Part 1—The Fabric Supplier, Garment Maker, and Retailer. *Journal of the Society of Dyers and Colourists, 110,* 173–175.

Brown, Patty. (1992). *Ready-to-Wear Apparel Analysis.* New York: Macmillan.

Buban, Margaret. (1995, October). Factoring Ethics Into the TQM Equation. *Quality Progress, 28,* 97–99.

Cahill, Neil. (1993, September). Textiles: Where Will the Industry Be in 2018? *Textile World, 143,* 102–103, 105, 108, 110, 112.

Caplan, Frank. (1990). *The Quality System: A Sourcebook for Managers and Engineers,* 2nd ed. Radnor, PA: Chilton Book Company.

Carrere, Carol G., & Lisa Cedrone. (1995). Pre-Production: The Race is on for New Integrated Technology. Paper presented at the 1995 Apparel Research Conference, Atlanta, GA., November, 1995.

Carruthers, Hamish. (1991). Design for the Market. In The Textile Institute (ed.). *The Textile World at a Crossroads.* Manchester, England: Textile Institute.

Chisholm, Sandra Flora. (1995). Textile Quality Assurance: A Comparison Between Education and Industry. Unpublished Master's Thesis, Iowa State University, Ames.

Clark, Kim B., & Takahiro Fujimoto. (1990, November–December). The Power of Product Integrity. *Harvard Business Review,* 107–118.

Connors, Jeanne L., & Thomas A. Romberg. (1991). Middle Management and Quality Control: Strategies for Obstructionism. *Human Organization, 50(1),* 61–65.

Cooklin, Gerry. (1991). *Introduction to Clothing Manufacture.* Oxford, England: BSP Professional Books.

Cotton, Ronald J. (1993). *Total Engineering Quality Management.* Milwaukee: Marcel Dekker (ASCQ Quality Press).

Crosby, Philip B. (1989). *Let's Talk Quality: 96 Questions You Always Wanted to Ask Phil Crosby.* New York: Penguin.

Dastoor, P. H., P. Radhakrishnaiah, K. Srinivasan, & S. Jayaraman. (1994). SDAS: A Knowledge-Based Framework for Analyzing Defects in Apparel Manufacturing. *Journal of the Textile Institute, 85(4),* 542–560.

Derringer, George C. (1994, June). A Balancing Act: Optimizing a Product's Properties. *Quality Progress,* 51–58.

Dickerson, Kitty, Christopher C. Hooper, & Robert D. Boyle. (1995, April). The New Approach for Manufacturers. *America's Textiles International*, 28–32.

Dighe, Atul, & Clement Bezold. (1996, July). Trends and Key Forces Shaping the Future of Quality. *Quality Progress*, 89–98.

Emerson, Gary L. (1991). *A How-To Manual for Material Review and Corrective Action in Industry*. Milwaukee: ASQC Quality Press.

Finch, Bryon J. (1997, May). A New Way to Listen to the Customer. *Quality Progress, 30(5)*, 73–76.

Friedenberg, E. (1995, April). Flynt Quality Conference Told Customer Response Will Replace QR. *Knitting Times*, 40–41.

Fujisawa, Y. (1991). Far East Quality Management of Textiles Between East and West. In The Textile Institute (ed.). *The Textile World at a Crossroads*. Manchester, England: Textile Institute, pp. 32–40.

Gilbert, Ross J. (1987, November). A Values-Oriented Approach to Quality. *Quality Progress, 20*, 38–40.

Gladhill, Robert L. (1996, August). Conformity Assessment: What Is It, Why Do We Need It? *ASTM Standardization News, 24*, 30–33.

Glock, Ruth E., & Grace I. Kunz. (1995). *Apparel Manufacturing: Sewn Products Analysis, 2nd ed.* Englewood Cliffs, NJ: Prentice-Hall.

Goetsch, David L. (1992). *Industrial Supervision in the Age of High Technology*. New York: Macmillan.

Goetsch, David L., & Stanley Davis. (1994). *Introduction to Total Quality: Quality, Productivity, and Competitiveness*. New York: Macmillan.

Grafton, P. M. (1989). Computer Integrated Sewing Systems from Near Myth to CIMple Reality. In The Textile Institute (ed.). *Textiles: Fashioning the Future*. Manchester, England: Textile Institute, pp. 373–378.

Gryna, Frank M. (1991, May). The Quality Director of the 90s. Part 2. Assisting Upper Management with Strategic Quality Management. *Quality Progress*, 51–54.

Hall, Hazel. (1994). Information Strategy: A New Item for the Textile Industry's Agenda. *Journal of the Textile Institute, 85(4)*, 533–541.

Harari, Oren. (1993, February). The Lab Test: A Tale of Quality. *Management Review*, 55–58.

Harrington, H. James. (1987). *Poor-Quality Cost*. Milwaukee: ASQC Quality Press.

Hawkyard, C. J., & I. McShane. (1994). The Quest for Quality in the British Textile Industry. *Journal of the Textile Institute, 85(4)*, 469–475.

Hawley, John K. (1995, October). Where's the Q in TQM? *Quality Progress*, 63–64.

Henry, Jane E., & Meg Hartzler. (1997, May). Virtual Teams: Today's Reality, Today's Challenge. *Quality Progress, 30(5)*, 108–109.

Hohner, Gregory. (1993, May). Integrating Product and Process Designs. *Quality Progress, 26*, 55–61.

Holland, Charles. (1993, October). Puzzled by Your Quality Plan? Go for Results. *America's Textiles International*, 98–101.

Howe, Roger J., Dee Gaeddert, & Maynard A. Howe. (1993). *Quality on Trial*. St. Paul: West Publishing Company.

Huckett, J. (1991). CIM—The Key to Quality Performance. In The Textile Institute (ed.). *Total Quality for Higher Profit*. Manchester, England: Textile Institute.

Hudson, Peyton B. (1982, February). Q. C. Profile. *Bobbin*, 21–25.

Industrial Development Organization. (1972). *Quality Control in the Textile Industry*. New York: United Nations.

Ishikawa, Kaoru, & David J. Lu. (translator). (1985). *What Is Total Quality Control? The Japanese Way*. Englewood Cliffs, NJ: Prentice-Hall.

Ito, K., & M. Nitta. (1994). Some Difficult Issues in Recent Apparel Manufacturing and a Counter-Measure for the Future. *International Journal of Clothing Science and Technology, 6(2/3)*, 14–16.

JC Penney. (1996). *Supplier Testing Guide*. Carrolton, TX: Author.

Johnson, Jay L. (1994, March). Target's New Vision: Total Quality. *Discount Merchandiser*, 38, 40, 42, 44, 46, 48, 50, 52, 66.

Juran, J. M., & Frank M. Gyrna. (1993). *Quality Planning and Analysis: From Product Development Through Use*. New York: McGraw Hill.

Juran, J. M. (1992). *Juran on Quality by Design: The New Steps for Planning Quality into Goods and Services*. New York: Free Press.

Juran, J. M., et al. (1990). *"Planning for Quality" course notes*, 2nd ed. Wilton, CT: Juran Institute.

Kang, Tae Jin, & Chang Kyu Park. (1995). Practical Performance and Problem of Automated Pattern Design, Marking, and Cutting in Garment Manufacturing. *Journal of the Federation of Asian Professional Textile Associations, 3(1)*, 95–101.

Karnes, Carol L., & John J. Karnes. (1994, February). How the Apparel Industry Measures Up to Quality Standards. *Quality Progress, 27,* 25–29.

Knapton, Jim. (1990, February). How to Develop Your Own Unquality Costing Analysis: Management by Knowing in the Sewing Plant. *Apparel Manufacturer,* 83–88.

Kolbeck, Wayne B. (1984, August). Quality Assurance: Is Your Program Up to Date? *Bobbin, 25,* 81, 82, 84, 86, 88, 90, 92.

Koksal, Gulser, William A. Smith, & C. Brent Smith. (1992). A System Analysis of Textile Operations: A Modern Approach for Meeting Customer Requirements. *Textile Chemist and Colorist, 24(10),* 30–35.

Krenz, Keith. (1995). Introduction to the One Company Concept. Paper presented at the 1995 Apparel Research Conference, Atlanta, GA., November, 1995.

Lupo, John. (1995). Wal-Mart: Building Better and More Effective Partnerships. Paper presented at the 1995 Apparel Research Conference, Atlanta, GA., November, 1995.

Luther, David B. (1996, July). Quality, the Future, and You. *Quality Progress, 29,* 68–69.

Magohazy, Yehia E. El. (1992). Using Off-Line Quality Engineering in Textile Processing: Part I. Concepts and Theories. *Textile Research Journal, 62(5),* 266–274.

Mehta, Pradip V. (1992). *An Introduction to Quality Control for the Apparel Industry.* Milwaukee: ASQC Press.

Menon, H. G. (1992). *TQM in New Product Manufacturing.* New York: McGraw Hill.

Merkel, Robert S. (1991). *Textile Product Serviceability.* New York: Macmillan.

Mills, Charles A. (1986, June). Marketing Quality Assurance. *Quality Progress, 19,* 20–23.

Modarress, Batoul, & A. Ansari. (1989, second quarter). Quality Control Techniques in U.S. Firms: A Survey. *Production and Inventory Management Journal, 30(2),* 58–62.

Mundel, August B. (1991). *Ethics in Quality.* Milwaukee: ASQC Quality Press.

Munden, D. L., W. J. Loweth, & M. J. Ryan. (1990). The Cimtex Centre for Automated Garment Production. In The Textile Institute (ed.). *Textiles: Fashioning the Future.* Manchester, England: Textile Institute, pp. 387–400.

Nadkarni, R. A. (1995, November). A Not-So-Secret Recipe for Successful TQM. *Quality Progress, 28,* 91–96.

O'Mara, Kevin J., & W. Oxenham. (1995, December). CIM in Spinning. *Textile Asia,* 47–48, 53.

Pack, Howard. (1987). *Productivity, Technology, and Industrial Development: A Case Study in Textiles.* New York: Oxford University Press.

Picard, Lawrence G. (1992). *Fundamentals of Quality Control.* Milwaukee: ASQC Quality Press.

Peters, M. M. (1983). Fabric for Garments: Quality, Design, and the Purchaser. In The Textile Institute (ed.). *Quality, Design, and the Purchaser.* Manchester, England: Textile Institute.

Potluri, Prasad, Isaac Porat, & John Atkinson. (1996). Towards Automated Testing of Fabrics. *International Journal of Clothing Science and Technology, 7(2/3),* 11–23.

Provost, Lloyd P., & R. M. Sproul. (1996, August). Creativity and Improvement: A Vital Link. *Quality Progress, 29,* 101–107.

Rabolt, Nancy J., Katrina Bothwell, Judith C. Forney, & Mary Barry. (1988). Quality Control in Overseas Apparel Manufacturing. *Journal of Consumer Studies and Home Economics, 12,* 389–397.

Rao, Vittal A. (1985, June). Total Quality: A Commitment to Excellence. *Bobbin, 25,* 40, 42, 44, 46, 48, 50–52.

Reda, Susan. (1994, March). Quality Control: K-Mart Commits to Product Testing. *Stores, 76,* 47–49.

Rhodes, Ed. (1995). Divergent Technological Development in the European Apparel Sectors. Paper presented at the 1995 Apparel Research Conference, Atlanta, GA., November, 1995.

Roach, A. R. (1994). Meeting Consumer Needs for Textiles and Clothing. *Journal of the Textile Institute, 85(4),* 484–495.

Rose, Kenneth H. (1995, February). A Performance Measurement Model. *Quality Progress,* 63–66.

Rong, G. H., & K. Slater. (1993). A New Approach to the Assessment of Textile Performance. *Journal of the Textile Institute, 83(2),* 197–208.

Rubinstein, Sidney P. (1991, May). The Evolution of U.S. Quality Systems. *Quality Progress, 24,* 46–49.

Rupp, Roger O., & James R. Russell. (1994, December). The Golden Rules of Process Redesign. *Quality Progress, 27,* 85–90.

Saibel, Mahlon. (1991). CIM in American Apparel Manufacturing. In The Textile Institute (ed.). *The Textile World at a Crossroads.* Manchester, England: Textile Institute, pp. 150–157.

Saraph, Jayant V., & Richard J. Sebastian. (1993, September). Developing a Quality Culture. *Quality Progress, 26,* 73–78.

Saville, N. (1990). Answers to Questions You Might Not Think to Ask. In The Textile Institute (ed.). *Textiles: Fashioning the Future.* Manchester, England: Textile Institute, pp. 101–118.

Scherkenback, William W. (1986). *The Deming Route to Quality and Productivity: Road Maps and Roadblocks.* Washington, DC: Ceep Press Books.

Scholtes, Peter R. (1988). *The Team Handbook: How to Use Teams to Improve Quality.* Madison, WI: Joiner Associates.

Shishoo, Roshan L. (1995). Interactions between Fabric Properties and Garment Making-up Processes. In The Textile Institute (ed.). *Textiles: Fashioning the Future.* Manchester, England: Textile Institute, pp. 337–358.

Siegel, Stan. (1992, January). Why We Need Checks and Balances to Assure Quality. *IEEE Software,* 102–103.

Stebbing, Lionel. (1989). *Quality Assurance: The Route to Efficiency and Competitiveness,* 2nd ed. New York: John Wiley & Sons.

Stylios, George. (1995). Living Without Frontiers: The Global Retailer. *International Journal of Clothing Science and Technology, 7(4),* 5–8.

Stylios, George. (ed.). (1991). *Textile Objective Measurement and Automation in Garment Manufacture.* New York: Ellis Horwood.

Taguchi, Genichi, & Seiso Konishi. (1994). *Taguchi Methods: On-Line Production.* Dearborn, MI: American Supplier Institute.

Tamburrino, Nicola. (1992, April). Apparel Sizing Issues, Part 1. *Bobbin, 33,* 44–46.

Technical Advisory Committee. (1973). *Improving Apparel Performance.* Arlington, VA: American Apparel Manufacturers Association.

Technical Advisory Committee. (1994). *New Yardsticks for Apparel.* Arlington, VA: American Apparel Manufacturers Association.

Tedaldi, Michael, Fred Scaglione, & Vincent Russotti. (1992). *A Beginner's Guide to Quality in Manufacturing.* Milwaukee: ASQC Quality Press.

Villa, Kay M. (1996, November). Weaving a Fabric of Cooperation: ASTM and ATMI's Relationship. *ASTM Standardization News, 24,* 19–23.

Weber, Richard T., & Ross H. Johnson. (1993). *Buying and Supplying Quality.* Milwaukee: ASQC Quality Press.

Weir, George. (1995, June). Management by Knowing: My Customer Doesn't Know Quality. *Knitting Times, 43.*

Winchester, S. C. (1994). Total Quality Management in Textiles. *Journal of the Textile Institute, 85(4),* 445–459.

Wood, Freddie. (1993, September). Succeeding in Textiles in the Nineties. *Textile World, 45,* 51, 53, 54, 56–59.

Zangwill, Willard I. (1994, June). Ten Mistakes CEOs Make About Quality. *Quality Progress,* 43–48.

REVIEW QUESTIONS

1. Describe TQM and its role in quality assurance.

2. Discuss the role that management plays in quality assurance.

3. Explain how technical systems and people systems interact.

4. Define continuous process improvement and explain its role in quality assurance.

5. Differentiate between chronic and sporadic problems.

6. Describe how quality function deployment and customer satisfaction are connected.

7. Explain the process of benchmarking.

8. Identify the stages that cross-functional teams go through as the members learn to work together.

9. Explain how CIM affects product or process quality.

ACTIVITIES

1. Explore ways TQM is used by local educational institutions, businesses, and governments.

2. Visit a business and discuss their use of TQM and its impact on quality.

3. Discuss how TQM and continuous improvement could be used to avoid product failure or reduce consumer dissatisfaction with products.

4. Evaluate the way teams in which you have been a member have functioned. Analyze how your behavior contributed to or detracted from the team's performance and productivity. How could you have improved the team's work?

5. Develop a plan that would apply TQM and continuous improvement to your education and work. Implement your plan and evaluate its effectiveness.

6. Read these articles (Anfuso, Dawn. [1994, July]. L. L. Bean's TQM Efforts Put People Before Processes. *Personnel Journal,* 72–73, 75–76, 78, 80, 83; Hawkyard, C. J., & I. McShane. [1994]. The Quest for Quality in the British Textile Industry. *Journal of the Textile Institute, 85(4),* 469–475; Johnson, Jay L. [1994, March]. Target's New Vision: Total Quality. *Discount Merchandiser,* 38, 40, 42, 44, 46, 48, 50, 52, 66) and discuss how they relate to TQM and continuous improvement.

Chapter 15

ANALYTICAL TOOLS

OBJECTIVES

- To understand the variety of techniques used to analyze data.
- To select the appropriate analytical tool for specific problems.
- To use the analytical tool correctly.
- To interpret results based on the analysis.
- To implement improvements based on the results of data analysis.

KEY TERMS

statistical process control (SPC)

variation

normal variation

unacceptable variation

abnormal variation

random variation

assignable variation

key product variables

key process variables

flow chart

process map

special cause

common cause

local cause

assignable cause

system cause

control limits

specification limits

upper specification limit

lower specification limit

variable data

continuous data

attribute data

discrete data

independent variable

dependent variable

normal distribution

mean

mode

median

kurtosis

bimodal distribution

skewness

scatter diagram

correlation

cause-and-effect diagram

fishbone diagram

histogram

range

frequency

Pareto chart

Pareto principle

80/20 rule

check sheet

box plot	rule of sevens	probability
box-and-whisker plot	rule of thirds	standard deviation
control chart	attribute control chart	in control
variable control chart	p chart	out of control
$\overline{X}$ control chart	np chart	upper control limit (UCL)
R control chart	c chart	lower control limit (LCL)
point out	u chart	

Improving quality and productivity are two major goals of many companies in the textile industry complex. This is true whether they are involved in producing materials or finished products or they are involved directly with the consumer. Information about the process, equipment, and materials is required for understanding which aspects of quality and productivity can be improved upon and the steps necessary for this improvement. The information is collected so that data analysis can be used to identify possible improvements and suggest strategies for successful implementation.

Analytical tools are used to collect, organize, present, and understand data so that appropriate action can be taken. These same tools are used in planning and analyzing experiments. This is especially true for complex, multistep processes, such as those involved in producing materials and finished textile products and in presenting them to the consumer.

STATISTICAL PROCESS CONTROL (SPC)

Analysis of materials, processes, and products is part of the current emphasis on continuous quality improvement found in many industries worldwide. The textile industry complex is no exception to this trend. **Statistical process control (SPC)** refers to using a variety of statistical and other analytical techniques to identify and minimize unacceptable variations in a company's products or processes. **Variation** refers to characteristics or measurements that differ from specifications or standards. **Normal variation** assumes that no two items will ever be completely identical. **Unacceptable variations** are those that fall outside the maximum tolerance level for specifications and standards established by the company or by the customer. Unacceptable variations are also known as **abnormal variations.** SPC is used to discover areas that require action, to identify and correct those factors that cause or contribute to problems, and to identify aspects that indicate lax inspection.

Variations can be random or assignable. **Random variation** has many individual causes, any one of which usually produces only a small amount of variation. If many causes occur simultaneously, the amount of random variation can be significant. Random variation is difficult to control and can never be eliminated completely from a process.

Assignable variation is the result of a definite cause or a set of causes. It is not always present, but when it occurs the cause or causes can be identified by studying the process and collecting data about it. Thus, action to eliminate these variations can be undertaken. However, because any one cause may not contribute to a large amount of variation, it may not always be economically feasible to attempt a solution, especially if the variation is small.

SPC is based on the assumption that all products possess specific characteristics that are designed or incorporated to meet customer needs. These characteristics are known as **key product variables.** Inspection of materials and inspection during production help ensure that standards and specifications for product characteristics are met. Thus, it is necessary to identify the factors involved in production that impact on or contribute to product characteristics. These factors are known as **key process variables.**

The initial stages of an SPC system include the identification of key process and key product variables. Sometimes a **flow chart** or **process map** helps to identify these key points for inspection and the key measurements that should be made of the process or product. A flow chart, such as the one illustrated in Figure 15-1, should assist a company in identifying when

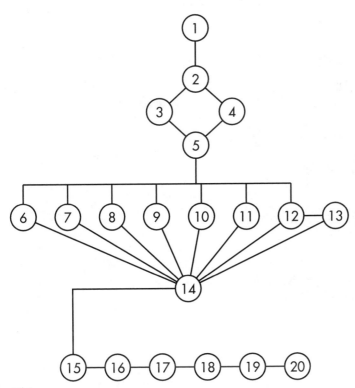

Figure 15-1
A flow chart or process map for a man's dress shirt. (Reprinted with permission from Mehta, Pradip V. [1992]. *An Introduction to Quality Control for the Apparel Industry.* Milwaukee: Marcel Dekker [ASQ Quality Press]).

inspection should occur and what measurements should be taken to ensure that the final product meets customer expectations.

Variations in products usually can be traced to one of the five areas described in Table 15-1. The reason for identifying a variation is so that the company can correct the cause, which is described as either special or common. **Special causes** of variations are specific conditions that, once identified, can be corrected. **Common causes** of variations are conditions that exist because of the general system in place within the company. Table 15-1 includes examples of common and special causes related to each of the five areas of product variations. Special causes are also known as **local causes** or **assignable causes.** Common causes are sometimes referred to as **system causes.**

Some history of the process in data form is needed to apply SPC. These data are used to establish control limits. **Control limits** describe an acceptable range of values from the lowest acceptable value to the highest acceptable value. Values outside the control limits are not acceptable and may be the result of special causes. With SPC, points outside the control limits signal that both a check of the process and efforts to eliminate the cause of the problem should be undertaken.

Control limits are not the same as specification limits. **Specification**

Table 15-1
VARIATIONS IN PRODUCTS AND PROCESSES.

Input Factors	Potential Sources	Examples of Causes
Human resources	Training, experience, physical and mental ability, morale, attitude, fatigue	Special cause: operator not trained properly Common cause: absence of operator training program
Machines	Component parts, preventive maintenance, parts inventory, wear, age, repair, vintage, technology	Special cause: worn belt Common cause: absence of belt inspection program
Methods	Procedures, compliance to procedures, controls, measurements, auditing, techniques	Special cause: operator did not follow procedure Common cause: written job procedure does not exist
Materials	Composition, storage, compliance to specifications, suppliers	Special cause: poor quality material approved by material inspectors Common cause: absence of material inspection system
Environment	Indoor, outdoor, humidity, temperature, sunshine, rain, atmosphere	Special cause: humidity increased moisture content of materials Common cause: materials not stored in controlled environment

(Modified from Parsowith, B. Scott. [1995]. Fundamentals of Quality Auditing. Milwaukee: ASQ Quality Press, p. 61, 62.)

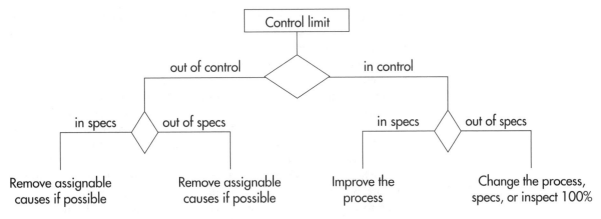

Figure 15-2
Control limits and suggested actions.

limits indicate the specified value for a measurable parameter, characteristic, or performance criteria, plus or minus an allowable tolerance. **Upper specification limits** describe the highest or greatest acceptable value; **lower specification limits** describe the lowest or least acceptable value. Thus, specification limits indicate the spread over which a measurable value is determined to be acceptable. Products, materials, or processes with values above the upper specification limit or values below the lower specification limit are not acceptable. Control limits describe the point at which a process in control becomes out of control. Thus, control limits are used to monitor a process, while specification limits are used to determine when a product, process, or material is acceptable to the buyer. Both types of limits are important in terms of product quality, but their uses and applications differ. Figure 15-2 illustrates the ways in which control and specification limits may influence action. Remember, the goal from a quality assurance perspective is to produce a product that is both within specification and in control.

In SPC, several basic tools are commonly used to assess process quality. They include the scatter diagram, the cause-and-effect or fishbone diagram, the histogram, the Pareto chart, the check sheet, variable control charts, and attribute control charts. The tools are grouped so that similar types are discussed together.

DATA TYPES

Key process and product variables can be evaluated based on either variable or attribute data. **Variable data** describe values derived from actual measurements using instruments or measuring equipment, such as tape measures or balances for determining mass or weight of materials. Mass of materials and product dimensions are examples of variable data. Sometimes the term **continuous data** is used because the precision of the measuring device is related to the precision of the data. For example, product dimensions are usually measured to the nearest ¼ inch, but with a more precise tape measure, measurements could be made to ¹⁄₆₄ inch. Thus, variable data can be determined to several decimal points depending on the instrument used.

Attribute data are based on a count of the number of times a particular characteristic exists. Another way of considering attributes is that they refer to quality characteristics that meet, exceed, or fail to meet specifications. There are two possible types of attributes: those for which measurements are not possible, but for which acceptance is determined on a yes-no basis, such as soil or stains on a product, and those for which measurements are possible, but for which time, cost, or need restricts their use, such as for the precise location of labels in a product to the nearest 0.1 inch.

Discrete data is another term for attribute data. Attribute data are reported only in whole numbers. For example, the number of buttons on a shirt would be attribute data, but the distance between buttons would be variable data. It is not possible to have 5.8 buttons on a shirt, but the space between buttons could be 2.9 in., 2.95 in., or 2.951 in. depending on the fineness of the measuring device.

With SPC, it is also helpful to know the difference between independent and dependent variables. An **independent variable** is the variable manipulated during the experiment or process. When plotted on X-Y coordinates, the independent variable is usually plotted on the X-axis. For example, needle or sewing speed could be considered an independent variable. The speed could be increased or decreased during sewing to determine a speed that provides the longest life for the needle.

A **dependent variable** is a measurable variable that is assumed to be dependent on the independent variable. For example, needle life is a dependent variable related to needle or sewing speed. Dependent variables usually are plotted on the Y-axis.

The data used in analyzing a material, process, or product should be collected so that it measures the variable of interest. It is important that the results are measured and recorded free of bias.

DISTRIBUTION CURVES

A **distribution curve** plots the frequency that a value occurs within a sample or population. Several different types of distribution curves exist. Several of the more common types will be considered.

A **normal distribution curve** is bell shaped (see Figure 15-3). It most often is found when a variable measurement is made, especially of a natural process. Data tend to cluster around the center point with fewer data points occurring as one moves away from the center point to the left or to the right. For example, the length of cotton fibers in a bale should produce a normal distribution ranging from a tiny fraction of an inch to

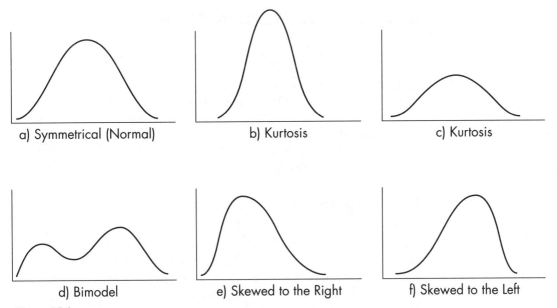

Figure 15-3

Distribution curves: (A) normal, (B) and (C) kurtosis, (D) bimodal, (E) and (F) skewed.

two or more inches in length. Very short fibers and very long fibers will occur less frequently than average length fibers. Thus, the curve will be lower at the extreme ends and higher at the center (see Figure 15-3a). In a normal curve, the **mean** (average) is the same value as the **mode** (most frequently occurring value) and the **median** (middle value when the data are arranged from smallest to largest value). The tails are symmetrical.

Curves that are more peaked (Figure 15-3b) or flatter (Figure 15-3c) than normal are said to display **kurtosis.** Curves of this nature generally are not as desirable as normal curves. Kurtosis may indicate that many factors are operating simultaneously and affecting the measurements.

A curve that is well centered but displays two peaks or modes reflects **bimodal distribution.** Bimodal distribution (Figure 15-3d) occurs when two different causes are influencing production, such as when different operators or different methods are being used.

Curves that have an elongated tail on one side or the other exhibit **skewness.** The type of skewness may be influenced either by a measurement characteristic that ends in zero or by sorting. When the tail is to the right of the distribution curve, it is positively skewed (Figure 15-3e). This kind of problem can happen with some measurement characteristics or could be the result of sorting when nonconforming products are removed from the sample. When the tail is to the left of the curve, it is negatively skewed (Figure 15-3f). Left skew occurs as a result of sorting.

ANALYSIS OF DATA USING GRAPHS

Graphs present data in a visual form; this discussion focuses on a few selected types. Although other possibilities exist, they are not commonly used to present data regarding quality of products or processes for a variety of reasons. One is that they require working with one variable at a time, while holding all other variables constant. That approach is not practical for complex cut and sewn textile products. Another reason is that some graphs do not provide information as efficiently as the types presented here which are relatively easy to produce and comprehend.

SCATTER DIAGRAMS

Scatter diagrams identify relationships between variables. A **scatter diagram** plots many points on the X-Y coordinates. These diagrams are more reliable when more rather than less data are plotted. When the data are plotted, it may show no correlation, a positive correlation, or a negative correlation between variables. The three possibilities are illustrated in Figure 15-4. A **correlation** describes what happens to one variable as the other variable changes. For example, a positive correlation indicates that as one variable increases, so does the other variable. The amount of increase (or decrease in the case of a negative correlation) is related to the slope of the line.

In developing a scatter diagram, it is important to define the independent and dependent variables carefully and to label and scale the X- and Y-axes properly. Both a correlation analysis and a linear regression can be calculated using the data plotted on the diagram. For information on these two statistical procedures, consult an introductory statistics book.

Figure 15-4
Scatter diagrams: (A) null correlation, (B) positive correlation, and (C) negative correlation. (FUNDAMENTALS OF STATISTICAL QUAL. CTRL. by Pond, © 1994. Reprinted by permission of Prentice-Hall, Inc., Upper Saddle River, NJ)

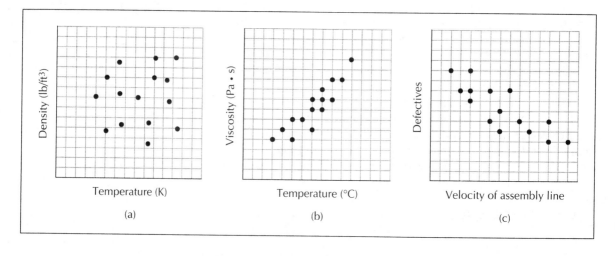

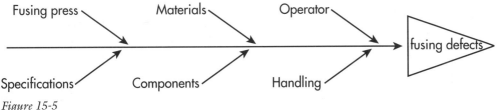

Figure 15-5
A simple cause-and-effect diagram: Fusing step for a shirt.

CAUSE-AND-EFFECT DIAGRAM

A **cause-and-effect diagram** reflects the relationships among processes, materials, and variations within products. These diagrams are used to improve processes and decrease variation of processes or products. Areas of interest are identified in the diagram. Another term for a cause-and-effect diagram is a **fishbone diagram.** Figure 15-5 illustrates such a diagram for fusing. Specific details could be added to each portion of the diagram. For example, for the fusing press portion, an engineer might add such items as maintenance, settings for heat and pressure, cleanliness, and so on as potential areas for investigation. A diagram of this type helps to define potential causes of problems and to propose an investigatory plan to determine which are creating or contributing to nonconformities or defects.

HISTOGRAMS

A **histogram** is a bar chart on which variable data is plotted. It is essentially an illustration of the distribution of the data by frequency (see Figure 15-6). **Range** describes the values present in the distribution, from lowest to highest. Determining the number of cells or classes is based on the number of observations (see Table 15-2). **Frequency** indicates the number of times

Table 15-2
NUMBER OF CELLS IN A HISTOGRAM.

Number of Data	Number of Cells
20–50	6
51–100	7
101–200	8
201–500	9
501–1000	10
over 1000	11–20

(From Pond, Robert J. [1994]. Fundamentals of Statistical Quality Control. New York: Macmillan, p. 48.)

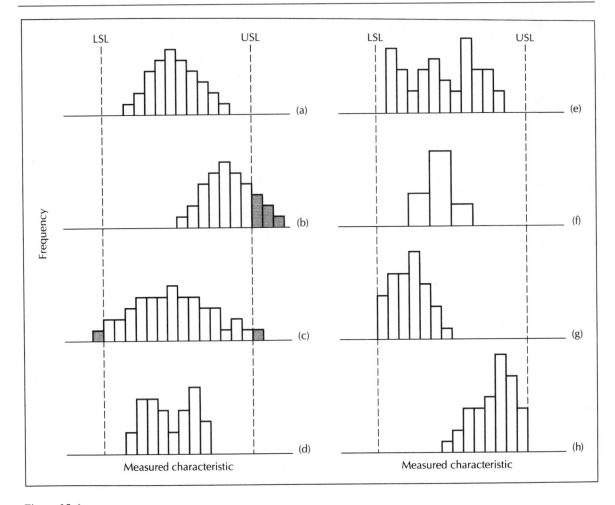

Figure 15-6

Histogram types.
(FUNDAMENTALS OF
STATISTICAL QUAL. CTRL. *by
Pond, © 1994. Reprinted by
permission of Prentice-Hall,
Inc., Upper Saddle River, NJ)*

a value falls within each segment of the range. Values towards the low and high end of the range tend to have lower frequencies than values near the center of the range. This distribution of values often follows a normal distribution or bell-shaped curve (see Figure 15-6a). Lower and upper specification limits (LSL and USL) are sometimes shown on histograms to assist in the assessment of the data.

The shape of the histogram helps identify the type of variation that is occurring within the data. For example, a histogram with two or more significant frequency peaks indicates that more than one cause is operating as the products are produced. If the distribution is skewed, then products may be being sorted before measurements are made. In sorting, nonconforming products are removed after 100 percent inspection reveals that they fail to meet specs (see Figure 15-7).

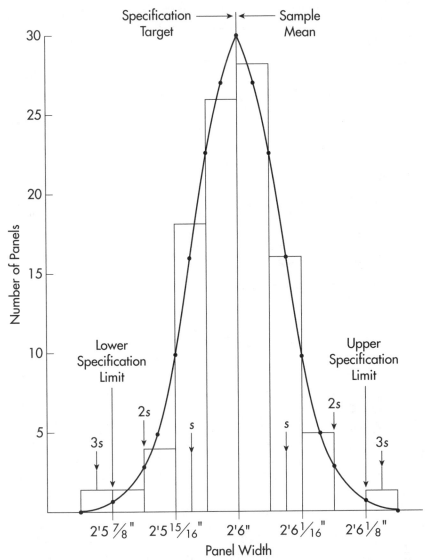

Figure 15-7
Histogram and normal distribution curve. (*From Tedaldi, Michael, Fred Scaglione, Vincent Russotti [1992]. Milwaukee: ASQ Quality Press, p. 137; reprinted with permission of the American Society for Quality*)

PARETO CHARTS

Pareto charts are histograms that graph the data in descending order of occurrence. The Pareto chart, or diagram, usually provides a clear picture of troubleshooting priorities. The curve was named for the Italian economist Vilfredo Pareto, who discovered that 80 percent of the wealth in Italy

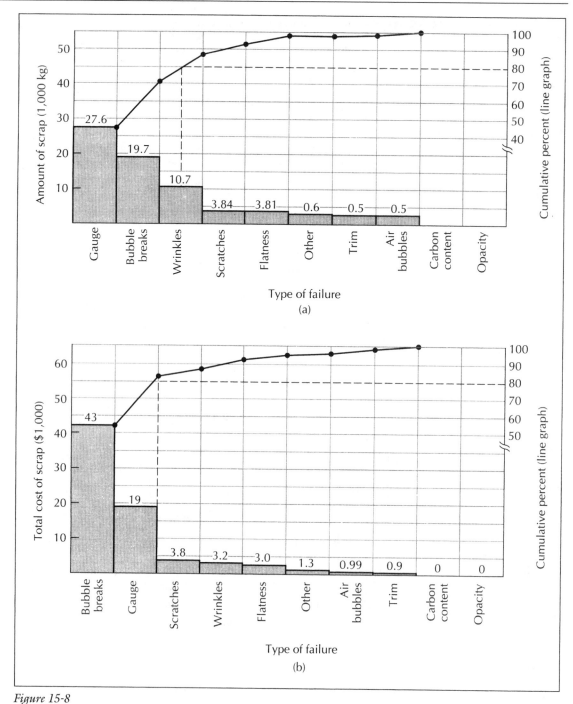

Figure 15-8
A Pareto chart with a cumulative frequency distribution. The dashed line indicates when 80 percent of the problem has been accounted for. (FUNDAMENTALS OF STATISTICAL QUAL. CTRL. *by Pond, © 1994. Reprinted by permission of Prentice-Hall, Inc., Upper Saddle River, NJ)*

was held by 20 percent of the population. The **Pareto principle** is often referred to as the **80/20 rule:** "20 percent of the process quality characteristics cause 80 percent of the problems with a product or service" (Pond, 1994, pp. 61).

A cumulative frequency distribution graphs the total frequency of cells to the left of the cell of interest. Thus, a quick glance at a Pareto chart will help the observer identify the major causes of variation. The dashed line in Figure 15-8 is the point at which 80 percent of the problems are identified.

CHECK SHEET

Nonconformance can be evaluated on a yes-no basis; the item is acceptable or not. Specific guidelines or check sheets help inspectors determine conformity or nonconformity. **Check sheets** describe in detail the characteristics and parameters that must be measured or examined during inspection of a material, component, or product. Check sheets often indicate on a drawing of the product the specific areas that must be evaluated; a check-off list ensures that the product is properly inspected. On some check sheets, a check mark indicates nonconformities, flaws, or errors. For example, a check sheet for a towel would describe through words or diagrams the critical appearance areas, measurements, and other aspects of importance in determining conformance or nonconformance. If a specific towel is acceptable in every criteria except for the hem, the appearance of the towel would be described as nonconforming. The check sheet for this towel would include a check mark on the hem and a verbal description of the appearance problem detected by the inspector.

BOXPLOT

A **boxplot** or **box-and-whisker plot** is a simple way to summarize data. In this graph, five values are plotted: the median, maximum value, minimum value, first quartile, and third quartile (see Figure 15-9). To create a boxplot, the data are arranged in rank order from smallest to largest value and divided into fourths of equal sizes. The box, whose end points correspond to the upper limit for the first quartile and the lower limit for the third

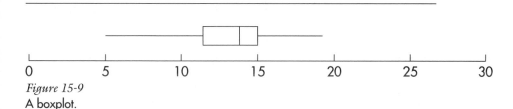

Figure 15-9
A boxplot.

quartile, summarizes the two middle quartiles of the data. The vertical line in the box is the median. The line to the left of the box begins at the minimum value and, to the right of the box, ends at the maximum value. Thus, a quick glance at a boxplot provides a fair amount of information about the data. In Figure 15-9, the boxplot indicates that some values are much lower than others, but that the data are grouped more closely above the median than below the median.

CONTROL CHARTS

Control charts are major tools used in studying process variation. They identify variation within a process and the allowable variation of the process over time. Control charts help identify when it is appropriate to take action regarding a variation that has become excessive within a process.

VARIABLE CONTROL CHARTS

Variable control charts are a graphical representation of the average measurement of samples taken over time. These charts are used to plot values so that a visual assessment of the data can be made quickly. (In statistical process control, $\overline{X}$ (read as X single bar or as X bar) refers to the mean of a sample, while $\overline{\overline{X}}$ (read as X double bar) refers to the mean of the population. It is important to remember that distinction.)

Two basic types of variable control charts are used. Each differs in terms of the type of data charted and the application of the chart in terms of studying and identifying variation. $\overline{X}$ control charts illustrate the means of the samples taken. R control charts illustrate the range of measurements of the samples taken. Figure 15-10 shows a sample form often used to collect and chart data. Calculations for control limits require use of statistically derived standard factors found in some statistical process control reference books. For more information, consult one of these reference books.

Several possible signs on a control chart (either variable or attribute) indicate when a process is out of control. These are point out, rule of sevens, and rule of thirds. It is wise to consider both R and $\overline{X}$ charts before attempting to bring a process back into control. In **point out**, at least one data point extends beyond the upper or lower control limit (see Figure 15-11).

Figure 15-10
A control chart form. (*Adapted with permission of the American Society for Quality*)

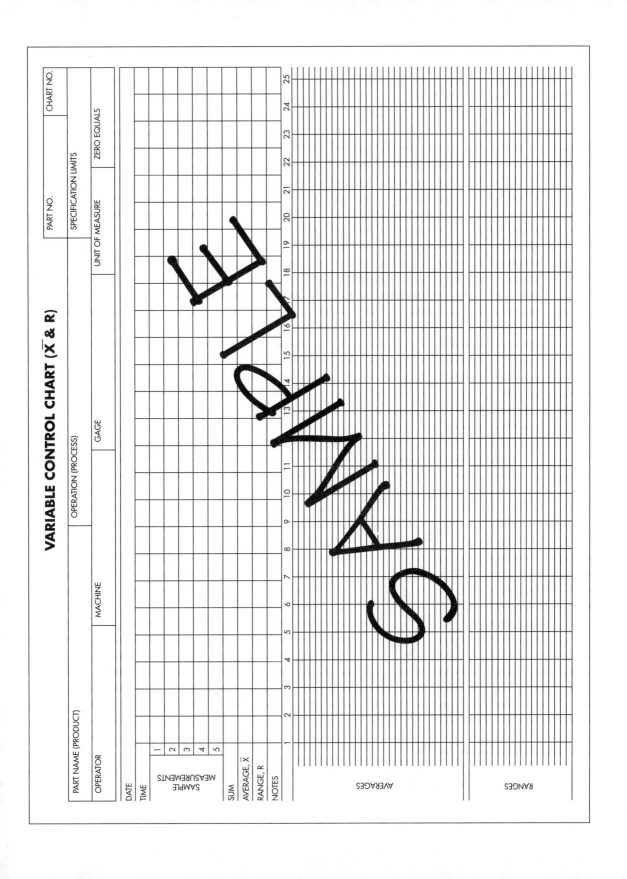

VARIABLE CONTROL CHART ($\bar{X}$ & R)

PART NAME (PRODUCT)		OPERATION (PROCESS)		PART NO.		CHART NO.
OPERATOR	MACHINE	GAGE	UNIT OF MEASURE	SPECIFICATION LIMITS	ZERO EQUALS	

		1	2	3	4	5	6	7	8	9	10	11	13	14	15	16	17	18	19	20	21	22	23	24	25
DATE																									
TIME																									
SAMPLE MEASUREMENTS	1																								
	2																								
	3																								
	4																								
	5																								
SUM																									
AVERAGE, $\bar{X}$																									
RANGE, R																									
NOTES																									

AVERAGES

RANGES

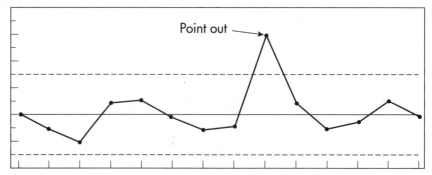

Figure 15-11
A control chart with a point out signal. (From Parsowith, B. Scott. [1995]. *Funda-*
mentals of Quality Auditing. Milwaukee: ASQ Quality Press, p. 68.) (*Adapted with*
permission of the American Society for Quality)

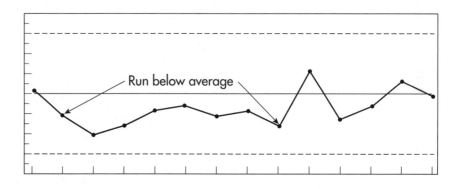

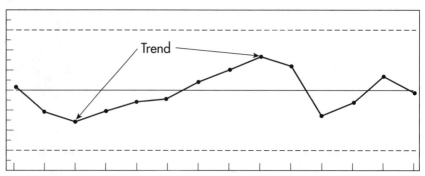

Figure 15-12
Two control charts with a rule of sevens signal. (From Parsowith, B. Scott. [1995].
Fundamentals of Quality Auditing. Milwaukee: ASQ Quality Press, pp. 69, 70.)
(*Adapted with permission of the American Society for Quality*)

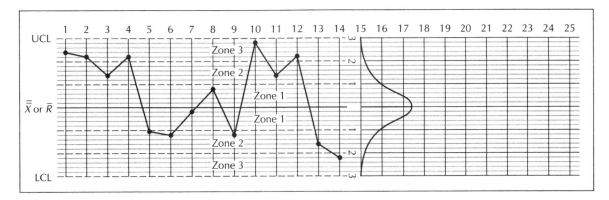

Figure 15-13
A control chart with a rule of
thirds signal.
(FUNDAMENTALS OF
STATISTICAL QUAL. CTRL. *by
Pond, © 1994. Reprinted by
permission of Prentice-Hall,
Inc., Upper Saddle River, NJ)*

The **rule of sevens** can appear in two forms: seven points in a row above or below the mean or seven points in a row that have a positive or negative slope. Figure 15-12 illustrates two examples of this signal. Trends of this nature indicate that a process problem is likely to exist.

The **rule of thirds** describes a normal probability in which approximately two thirds of the points should be within one standard deviation of the mean and approximately one third of the points should be relatively near the control limits (see Figure 15-13). If the distribution of points is significantly different from the two-thirds/one-third rule, it means that the process is out of control.

Variable control charts are used to plot variable data, but they cannot be used to plot attribute data. The reverse does not hold true; attribute control charts can be used to plot attribute and variable data, as long as the variable data are reported as numbers of units that are conforming or nonconforming. Variable control charts are also not realistic to use when many variables exist, because charting each variable would be time consuming and expensive. Attribute control charts minimize the time and expense factors and provide useful information quickly and relatively inexpensively.

ATTRIBUTE CONTROL CHARTS

Attribute control charts report the number of nonconforming units or the number of each occurrence of nonconformance in products. Thus, one needs to be able to identify the existence of a nonconforming unit in order to create an attribute control chart. There are four types of attribute control charts: p (proportion), np (number nonconforming), c (count of nonconformities), and u (count of nonconformities per unit). The type selected depends on whether the subsample size is variable or not and whether it is a nonconformity or nonconforming unit that is being studied (see Figure 15-14). Figure 15-15 shows a form used for developing attribute control charts.

	Sample size (n)	
	n varies	n is constant
Nonconforming unit	p	np
Nonconformity	u	c

Figure 15-14
Attribute chart selection diagram.

For the p control chart, we need to calculate p, which is the proportion of nonconforming units using Equation 15-1, the average for the p chart ($\bar{p}$), using Equation 15-2, and the upper and lower control limits (UCL and LCL), using Equations 15-3 and 15-4. **Upper control limits** and **lower control limits** for p and most other types of control charts are usually set at plus or minus three standard deviations from the average. The average subsample size is calculated using Equation 15-5.

Equation 15-1

$$p = np/n$$

where p = the proportion or fraction nonconforming
in the sample or subgroup
np = the number nonconforming in the sample or subgroup
n = the number inspected in the sample or subgroup

Equation 15-2

$$\bar{p} = \Sigma\, np/\Sigma n$$

where $\bar{p}$ = the average for the p chart
n = the number nonconforming in a sample or subgroup
np = the number nonconforming in the sample or subgroup

Equation 15-3

$$UCL_p = \bar{p} + 3\,\{\bar{p}(1 - \bar{p})/n\}^{1/2}$$

where UCL_p = the upper control limit
$\bar{p}$ = average for the p chart
n = the number in a sample or subgroup

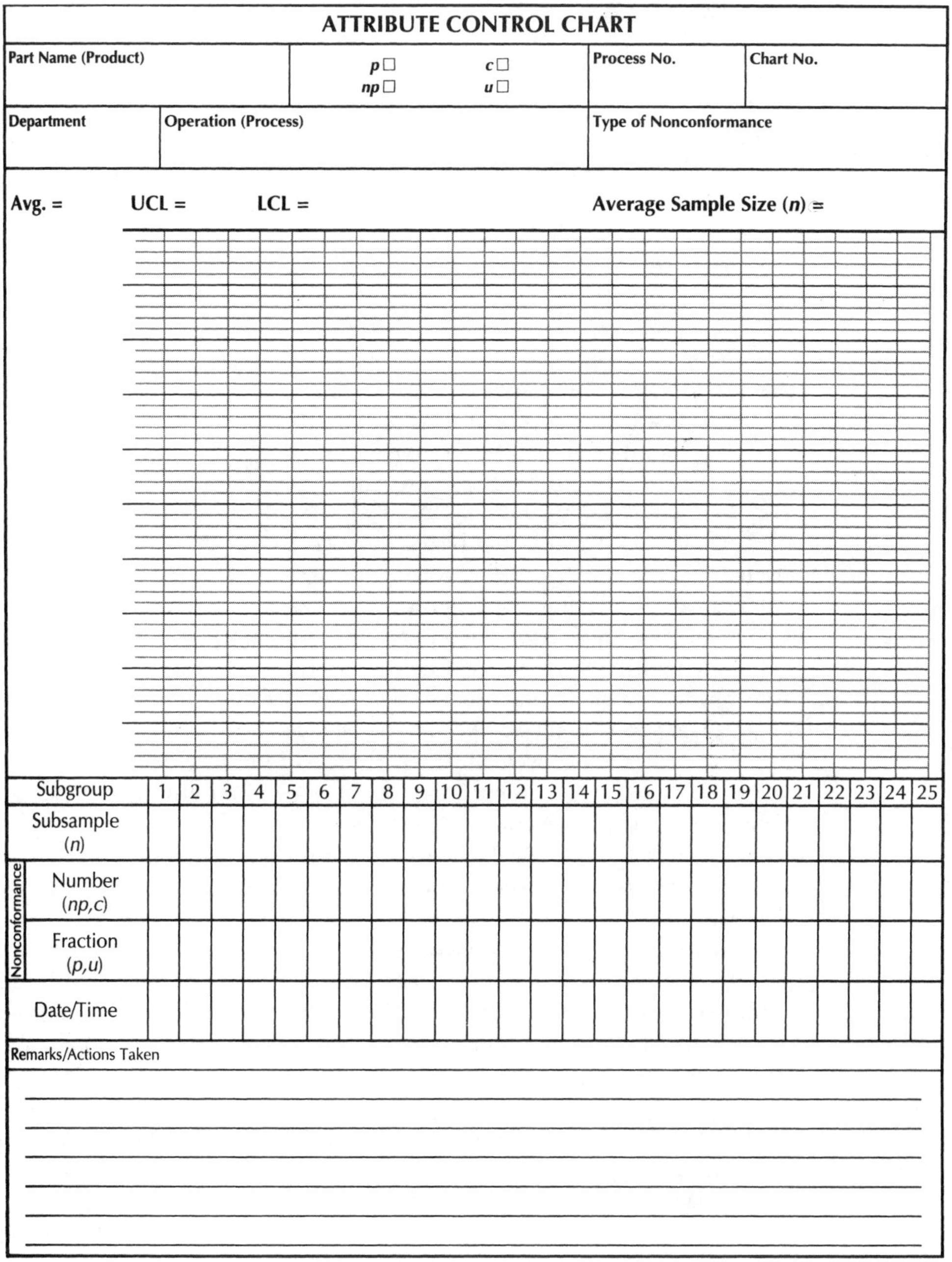

ATTRIBUTE CONTROL CHART

Part Name (Product)		$p\ \square$ $np\ \square$	$c\ \square$ $u\ \square$	Process No.	Chart No.
Department	Operation (Process)			Type of Nonconformance	

Avg. =   UCL =   LCL =   Average Sample Size (*n*) =

Subgroup	1	2	3	4	5	6	7	8	9	10	11	12	13	14	15	16	17	18	19	20	21	22	23	24	25	
Subsample (*n*)																										*
Number (*np,c*)																										*
Fraction (*p,u*)																										
Date/Time																										

(Nonconformance)

Remarks/Actions Taken

Figure 15-15

A sample form used to construct attribute control charts. (FUNDAMENTALS OF STATISTICAL QUAL. CTRL. *by Pond, © 1994. Reprinted by permission of Prentice-Hall, Inc., Upper Saddle River, NJ*)

Equation 15-4

$$LCL_p = \bar{p} - 3\,\{\bar{p}(1-\bar{p})/n\}^{1/2}$$

where LCL_p = the upper control limit
  $\bar{p}$ = average for the p chart
  n = the number in a sample or subgroup

Equation 15-5

$$\bar{n} = \Sigma\, n/k$$

where $\bar{n}$ = average subsample size
  n = the total number of units inspected
  k = number of samples or subgroups

The **p chart** can be quite useful. It can assess control of one characteristic, a group of characteristics of the same type or of the same nature, the finished product, or the quality of work done by a production unit, a work center, a work shift, or an entire production facility. It is frequently used to evaluate performance of operators, groups of operators, or management.

Nonconforming charts help determine the average quality level of a given product, material, or process. These charts help bring to the attention of management any changes in the average. They also assist in identifying areas where improvement in the process, product, or materials may have a significant impact on product quality. A p chart also helps management determine if a shipment should be released to a buyer. Finally, p charts identify areas in which variable charting should be done. Although variable charts are more expensive and time consuming to prepare, they are more sensitive than attribute charts.

The **np chart** (number nonconforming) is similar in many ways to the p chart. The major difference is that the sample size is constant. Thus, calculations are easier and less frequent. Values for np can be posted directly on the chart after they are measured. It is generally easier for operating personnel to understand the np chart than the p chart.

Count of nonconformities are used in the last two types of attribute control charts: **c charts** (count of nonconformities) and **u charts** (count of nonconformities per unit). These charts focus on nonconformities. A product that has one nonconformity would generate a value of one and a product that has four nonconformities would generate a value of four for these charts. The p and np charts work with products; c and u charts with nonconformities within products.

Nonconformities are based on two major assumptions. One, that the opportunity for nonconformity is large, but the chance of any one nonconformity occurring is small. Two, the incident of nonconformity is independent of another nonconformity (Besterfield, 1994). The c and u charts are used to establish benchmarks, or average quality levels, identify and bring to management's attention changes in the average, improve product quality, evaluate performance of operating and management personnel, provide information regarding the acceptability of a product before shipment, and suggest possible uses of variable control charts.

To calculate $\bar{c}$ (read as c-bar), use Equation 15-6. The c chart is used when the inspected unit can be any constant size, such as one or 100, and provides the information desired. To calculate upper and lower control limits, use Equations 15-7 and 15-8.

Equation 15-6

$$\bar{c} = \Sigma \, c/g$$

where $\bar{c}$ = the average count of nonconformities for
         a number of subgroups
   c = the count of nonconformities
   g = the number of subgroups

Equation 15-7

$$LCL_c = \bar{c} - 3\bar{c}^{1/2}$$

where LCL_c = lower control limit for a number of nonconformities
     $\bar{c}$ = the average count of nonconformities for a
            number of subgroups

Equation 15-8

$$UCL_c = \bar{c} + 3\bar{c}^{1/2}$$

where UCL_c = lower control limit for number of nonconformities
     $\bar{c}$ = the average count of nonconformities for a number
            of subgroups

If the number of inspected units varies, then a u chart should be used. To calculate u or $\bar{u}$, use Equations 15-9 or 15-10. To calculate upper and lower control limits, use Equations 15-11 and 15-12.

Equation 15-9

$$u = c/n$$

where u = the count of nonconformities in a subgroup
   c = the count of nonconformities of the units inspected
   n = the number inspected in a subgroup

Equation 15-10

$$\overline{u} = \Sigma c / \Sigma n$$

where $\overline{u}$ = the average count of nonconformities/
    unit for many subgroups
  c = the count of nonconformities of the units inspected
  n = the number inspected in a subgroup

Equation 15-11

$$LCL_u = \overline{u} - 3(\overline{u}/n)^{1/2}$$

where LCL_u = lower control limit for number of
    nonconformities/unit
  $\overline{u}$ = the average count of nonconformities/
    unit for many subgroups
  n = the sample or subgroup size

Equation 15-12

$$UCL_u = \overline{u} + 3(\overline{u}/n)^{1/2}$$

where UCL_u = lower control limit for number of
    nonconformities/unit
  $\overline{u}$ = the average count of nonconformities/
    unit for many subgroups
  n = the sample or subgroup size

OTHER ANALYTICAL TOOLS

Other analytical tools are used to work with data. These tools may identify sources of variations and points at which variation is too great to be acceptable. In some cases, further analysis of data may be needed.

PROBABILITY

Probability describes the likelihood of a given result occurring when an action is done. Consider a coin toss as an example. The chance of a tossed coin landing with the head side up is 0.5. Because the coin has only two sides, there is one chance out of two, or a probability of 0.5, that it will land heads up.

Probability is useful in predicting the occurrence of specific events in the future. It is based on a knowledge of the possible outcomes of an event. Thus, one needs to know something about the process in order to predict possible outcomes. Probability is useful in determining the likelihood of variation occurring within a process.

MEAN AND STANDARD DEVIATION

When several data of the same type have been measured, it can be helpful to know two things about the data: their mean or average and the manner in which the data cluster around the mean. The mean is calculated by using Equation 15-13. This requires totaling the individual data points and dividing them by the number of data points. (Σ is a symbol that means that all the data should be totaled.) It is important to recognize that this calculation is based on a sample of the population and not the entire population. This distinction is especially important when calculating the way the data clusters around the mean.

Equation 15-13

$$\overline{X} = (\Sigma\ X_i)/n$$

where $\Sigma\ X_i$ = all the data from the first value to the ith or last value
  n = the number of data points
  $\overline{X}$ = the mean

Standard deviation describes the manner in which the data clusters around the mean. It is a mathematical expression of the width of the data distribution. Equation 15-14 is used to calculate standard deviation for samples. In this equation, the difference between the mean and each data point is determined, the difference is squared, the total for all the squared differences is calculated, that value is divided by the number of data points minus 1 to get the dividend, and the square root of the dividend is determined.

Equation 15-14

$$s = [\Sigma\ (X_i - \overline{X})^2/(n - 1)]^{1/2}$$

where s = the standard deviation for a sample of a population
  X_i = each individual data point
  $\overline{X}$ = the mean for the sample
  n = the number of data points

In a normal distribution, 68.26 percent of the sample population should fall within one standard deviation of the mean, 95.46 percent should fall within two standard deviations of the mean, and 99.73 percent should fall within three standard deviations of the mean. Because standard deviation is a square root of a number, the value is reported as a ± value. When we plot one, two, or three standard deviations from the mean, we move to the left and to the right along the X-axis. Figure 15-7 shows a normal distribution curve superimposed over a histogram with the mean, specification target, upper and lower specification limits, and one, two, and three standard deviations identified.

CONTROLLING VARIATION

Before production begins, specifications and standards for processes and products should have been identified. Ideally, the process has been established to produce products according to specifications that maintain established quality levels. In addition, acceptable control limits for the process have been determined. When the process consistently produces products that fall within the control limits, the process is said to be **in control.**

However, a process occasionally produces a product that is outside the control limits. When the out-of-control product is rare, it is generally not a cause for concern. However, when the process begins to consistently produce products that are outside control limits, then it is **out of control**. This type of problem could be the result of many causes such as variations in materials, equipment setting, or other problems described in Table 15-1. Identifying the reason for the process being out of control can be done using one or more of the analytical procedures described in this chapter.

Once the problem is identified, a review of the process is needed to determine how the problem occurred. A reasonable second step is to verify that the control limits first defined as allowable in the process remain acceptable. If control limits were not defined initially, then definition at this point is suggested, with upper and lower control limits. A careful analysis of the process will identify any changes that would help ensure that the process is more carefully controlled. Monitoring the process is the final step. Control charts are often used to monitor processes and products to ensure that they are consistently acceptable in terms of quality, characteristics, and performance.

CONCLUSION

Analytical tools are used to identify the point at which variation in a material, process, or product is so great that some action needs to be taken to correct the problem. Some of these tools are used to help identify the factor that is contributing to the excessive variation. Use of the correct tool is often critical to identify the cause and determine how to effect a change that will bring the process back in control.

Many of these tools measure quality on a regular basis, so that any change can be quickly identified and corrected. Analytical tools are useful in identifying averages of processes, determining quality of work of operators, identifying where improvements in a process can have a positive impact on product quality, and determining when shipments are appropriate for release to a buyer. Additional information regarding statistics and other analytical tools are covered in more detail in statistics and statistical process control reference books.

SUGGESTED READINGS

Aft, Lawrence. (1992). *Fundamentals of Industrial Quality Control*, 2nd ed. Milwaukee: ASQC Quality Press.

Beauregard, Michael R., Raymond J. Mikulak, & Barbara A. Olson. (1992). *A Practical Guide to Statistical Quality Improvement*. New York: Van Nostrand Reinhold.

Besterfield, Dale H. (1994). *Quality Control*, 4th ed. Englewood Cliffs, NJ: Prentice-Hall.

Carr, Wendell E. (1992). *Statistical Problem Solving*. Milwaukee: ASQC Quality Press.

Carter, C. L. (Chuck). (1990). *Quality Assurance, Quality Control, and Inspection Book*, 5th ed. Richardson, TX: Author.

Department of Defense. (1989, May 10). *Military Standard—105E: Sampling Procedure and Tables for Inspection by Attributes*. Washington, DC: Author.

Department of Defense. (1965, June 30). *Quality and Reliability Assurance Handbook H-53*. Washington, DC: Author.

Goetsch, David L., & Stanley Davis. (1994). *Introduction to Total Quality: Quality, Productivity, and Competitiveness*. New York: Macmillan.

Hahn, Gerald J. (1993, October). Improve Quality with Data-Driven Analytics. *Quality Progress, 26*, 83–86.

Hare, Lynne B., Roger W. Hoerl, John D. Hromi, & Ronald D. Snee. (1995, February). The Role of Statistical Thinking in Management. *Quality Progress, 28*, 53–60.

Hinckley, C. Martin, & Philip Barkan. (1995). The Role of Variation, Mistakes, and Complexity in Producing Nonconformities. *Journal of Quality Technology, 27(3)*, 242–249.

Hoyer, Robert W., & Wayne C. Ellis. (1996, January). A Graphical Exploration of SPC, Part 2. The Probability Structure of Rules for Interpreting Control Charts. *Quality Progress, 29*, 57–64.

Hoyer, Robert W., & Wayne C. Ellis. (1996, May). A Graphical Exploration of SPC, Part 1. SPC's Definitions and Procedures. *Quality Progress, 29*, 65–73.

Ishikawa, Kaoru, & David J. Lu. (translator). (1985). *What Is Total Quality Control? The Japanese Way*. Englewood Cliffs, NJ: Prentice-Hall.

Juran, J. M., & Frank M. Gyrna. (1993). *Quality Planning and Analysis: From Product Development Through Use*. New York: McGraw Hill.

Kaminsky, Frank C., Robert D. Davis, & Richard J. Burke. (1993). *Statistics and Quality Control for the Workplace*. Milwaukee: ASQC Quality Press.

Kenett, Ron S. (1994, May). Making Sense Out of Two Pareto Charts. *Quality Progress, 27*, 71–73.

McAngus, E. H., & W. W. Adams. (1969). *Physical Textile Testing at Westpoint Pepperell*. Atlanta, GA: Textile Industries.

Mehta, Pradip V. (1992). *An Introduction to Quality Control for the Apparel Industry*. Milwaukee, WI: Marcel Dekker (ASQC Quality Press).

Menon, H. G. (1992). *TQM in New Product Manufacturing*. New York: McGraw Hill.

Merkel, Robert S. (1991). *Textile Product Serviceability*. New York: Macmillan.

Miller, Irwin, & Marylees Miller. (1995). *Statistical Methods for Quality with Applications to Engineering and Management*. Englewood Cliffs, NJ: Prentice-Hall.

Mills, David. (1993). *Quality Auditing*. London: Chapman & Hall.

Nickols, Frederick W. (1996, January). Yes, It Makes a Difference! *Quality Progress, 29*, 83–87.

Parsowith, B. Scott. (1995). *Fundamentals of Quality Auditing*. Milwaukee: ASQC Quality Press.

Pond, Robert J. (1994). *Fundamentals of Statistical Quality Control*. New York: Macmillan.

Tedaldi, Michael, Fred Scaglione, & Vincent Russotti. (1992). *A Beginner's Guide to Quality in Manufacturing*. Milwaukee: ASQC Quality Press.

Weber, Richard T., & Ross H. Johnson. (1993). *Buying and Supplying Quality*. Milwaukee: ASQC Quality Press.

Zaciewski, Robert D., & Lou Németh. (1995, October). The Multi-Vari Chart: An Underutilized Quality Tool. *Quality Progress, 28*, 81–83.

REVIEW QUESTIONS

1. Describe the differences between key process and key product variables, and give an example of each.

2. How does statistical process control influence product quality?

3. Describe each of these basic tools, give an example of each, and explain how it is used in statistical process control.
   a. scatter diagram
   b. cause-and-effect diagram
   c. histogram
   d. Pareto chart
   e. check sheet
   f. variable control chart
   g. attribute control chart

4. Explain the differences between control limits and specification limits.

5. Explain why mean and standard deviation are important in terms of statistical process control.

ACTIVITIES

1. Work through this problem.
   A company is interested in determining the strength of the seams in its chambray work shirts. They have measured the values in lbf:

123.4	131.9	125.7	121.8	130.1
129.3	128.4	119.5	126.6	132.5
129.3	127.3	129.0	126.2	124.1
124.5	128.1	127.1	128.7	123.4
124.3	128.3	129.8	125.6	120.8

   Create a histogram that represents these data. Calculate the mean and standard deviation and plot these values on the histogram. Identify the mode and median and draw a boxplot.

2. For the cracker, cookie, or bandage activity in Chapter 13, plot your data and identify the type of distribution curve present. Identify the mean, mode, and median. Create a boxplot to represent these data.

3. Discuss how the results from a statistical analysis would be used by designers, merchandisers, retailers, and engineers.

4. Select a specific product and identify those aspects that would be considered variable and those that would be considered attribute data. Explain your choices and categories.

5. Develop a cause and effect diagram for a simple task, such as hemming a towel. Make it as detailed as possible. How would these factors be measured?

6. Develop a check sheet for a specific product.

Selected ASTM and AATCC Procedures

ASTM Procedures

Volume 7.01 and 7.02

ASTM D 123	Standard Terminology Relating to Textiles
ASTM D 204	Sewing Threads
ASTM D 276	Identification of Fibers in Textiles
ASTM D 434	Resistance to Slippage of Yarns in Woven Fabrics Using a Standard Seam
ASTM D 629	Quantitative Analysis of Textiles
ASTM D 737	Air Permeability of Textile Fabrics
ASTM D 1059	Yarn Number Based on Short-Length Specimens
ASTM D 1117	Nonwoven Fabrics
ASTM D 1230	Flammability of Apparel Textiles
ASTM D 1244	Designation of Yarn Construction
ASTM D 1388	Stiffness of Fabrics
ASTM D 1408	Thermal Protective Performance of Materials for Clothing by Open-Flame Method
ASTM D 1422	Twist in Single Spun Yarns by the Untwist-Retwist Method
ASTM D 1423	Twist in Yarns by the Direct-Counting Method
ASTM D 1424	Tearing Strength of Fabrics by the Falling-Pendulum Type (Elmendorf) Apparatus
ASTM D 1518	Thermal Transmittance of Textile Materials
ASTM D 1683	Failure in Sewn Seams of Woven Fabrics
ASTM D 1775	Tension and Elongation of Wide Elastic Fabrics
ASTM D 1777	Measuring Thickness of Textile Materials
ASTM D 1908	Needle-Related Damage Due to Sewing in Woven Fabric
ASTM D 2261	Tearing Strength of Fabric by the Tongue (Single Rip) Procedure (Constant Rate-of-Extension Tensile Testing Machine)
ASTM D 2594	Stretch Properties of Knitted Fabrics Having Low Power
ASTM D 2724	Bonded, Fused, and Laminated Apparel Fabrics
ASTM D 2859	Flammability of Finished Textile Floor Covering Materials
ASTM D 3107	Stretch Properties of Fabrics Woven from Stretch Yarns
ASTM D 3512	Pilling Resistance and Other Related Surface Changes of Textile Fabrics; Random Tumble Pilling Tester Method

ASTM D 3659	Flammability of Apparel Fabrics by the Semi-Restraint Method
ASTM D 3775	Fabric Count of Woven Fabric
ASTM D 3776	Mass per Unit Area (Weight) of Woven Fabric
ASTM D 3773	Length of Woven Fabric
ASTM D 3774	Width of Woven Fabric
ASTM D 3786	Bursting Strength, Hydraulic, of Knitted Goods and Nonwoven Fabrics—Diaphragm Bursting Strength Tester Method
ASTM D 3882	Bow and Skewness in Woven and Knitted Fabrics
ASTM D 3884	Abrasion Resistance of Textile Fabrics (Rotary Platform, Double-Head Method)
ASTM D 3990	Standard Terminology Relating to Fabric Defects
ASTM D 4032	Stiffness of Fabric by the Circular Bend Procedure
ASTM D 4033	Determining Yarn Slippage in Sewn Seams Made from Upholstery Fabrics (Dynamic Fatigue Method)
ASTM D 4034	Resistance to Yarn Slippage at the Sewn Seam in Woven Upholstery Fabrics—Plain, Tufted, or Flocked
ASTM D 4151	Flammability of Blankets
ASTM D 4231	Evaluation of Men's and Boys' Home Launderable Woven Dress Shirts and Sport Shirts
ASTM D 4238	Electrostatic Propensity of Woven Fabrics
ASTM D 4271	Standard Practice for Writing Statements on Sampling in Test Methods for Textiles
ASTM D 4391	Standard Terminology Relating to Burning Behavior of Textiles
ASTM D 4721	Evaluation of the Performance of Bedcoverings and Accessories, Machine Washable and Drycleanable
ASTM D 4723	Index and Descriptions of Textile Heat and Flammability Test Methods and Performance Specifications
ASTM D 4772	Surface Water Absorption of Terry Fabrics (Water-Flow Test Method)
ASTM D 4964	Tension and Elongation of Elastic Fabrics (Constant-Rate-of-Extension Type Tensile Testing Machine)
ASTM D 5034	Breaking Force and Elongation of Textile Fabrics (Grab Test)
ASTM D 5035	Breaking Force and Elongation of Textile Fabrics (Strip Test)
ASTM D 5362	Snagging Resistance of Fabrics (Bean Bag Snag Test Method)
ASTM D 5426	Visual Inspection and Grading Fabrics Used for Inflatable Restraints
ASTM D 5427	Accelerated Aging of Inflatable Restraint Fabrics
ASTM D 5428	Evaluating Performance of Inflatable Restraint Modules
ASTM D 5430	Visually Inspecting and Grading Fabrics

ASTM D 5446   Determining Physical Properties of Fabrics in Inflatable
               Restraints
ASTM D 5587   Tearing Strength of Fabrics by the Trapezoid
               Procedure
ASTM D 5807   Evaluating the Overpressurization Characteristics of
               Inflatable Restraint Cushions

Volume 4.07

ASTM E 1352   Cigarette Ignition of Mock-Up Upholstered Furniture
               Assemblies
ASTM E 1353   Cigarette Ignition Resistance of Components of
               Upholstered Furniture
ASTM E 1474   Determining the Heat Release Rate of Upholstered
               Furniture and Mattress Components or Composites
               Using a Bench Scale Oxygen Consumption
               Calorimeter
ASTM E 1537   Fire Testing of Real Scale Upholstered Furniture Items

Volume 11.03

ASTM F 739   Resistance of Protective Clothing Materials to
               Permeation by Liquids or Gases under Conditions of
               Continuous Contact
ASTM F 903   Resistance of Materials Used in Protective Clothing to
               Penetration by Liquids
ASTM F 955   Evaluating Heat Transfer Through Materials for
               Protective Clothing Upon Contact with Molten
               Substances
ASTM F 1001   Standard Guide for Selection of Chemicals to Evaluate
               Protective Clothing Materials
ASTM F 1052   Standard Practice for Qualitatively Evaluating the
               Comfort, Fit, Function, and Integrity of Chemical-
               Protective Suit Ensembles
ASTM F 1060   Thermal Protective Performance of Materials for
               Protective Clothing for Hot Surface Contact
ASTM F 1154   Standard Practices for Qualitatively Evaluating the
               Comfort, Fit, Function, and Integrity of Chemical-
               Protective Suit Ensembles
ASTM F 1291   Measuring the Thermal Insulation of Clothing Using a
               Heated Manikin.
ASTM F 1342   Protective Clothing Material Resistance to Puncture
ASTM F 1358   Effects of Flame Impingement on Materials Used in
               Protective Clothing Not Designated Primarily for Flame
               Resistance
ASTM F 1359   Standard Practice for Determining the Liquid-Tight
               Integrity of Chemical Protective Suits or Ensembles
               Under Static Conditions

ASTM F 1383	Resistance of Protective Clothing Materials to Permeation by Liquids or Gases Under Conditions of Intermittent Contact
ASTM F 1407	Resistance of Chemical Protective Clothing Materials to Liquid Permeation—Permeation Cup Method
ASTM F 1414	Measurement of Cut Resistance to Chain Saw in Lower Body (Legs) Protective Clothing
ASTM F 1449	Standard Guide for Care and Maintenance of Flame Resistant and Thermally Protective Clothing
ASTM F 1458	Measurement of Cut Resistance to Chain Saw of Foot Protective Devices
ASTM F 1494	Standard Terminology Relating to Protective Clothing
ASTM F 1670	Resistance of Materials Used in Protective Clothing to Penetration by Synthetic Blood
ASTM F 1671	Resistance of Materials Used in Protective Clothing to Penetration by Blood-Borne Pathogens Using Phi-X174 Bacteriophage Penetration as a Test System

Volume 12.02

| ASTM E 1175 | Determining the Solar or Photopic Reflectance, Transmittance, and Absorptance of Materials Using a Large Diameter Integrating Sphere |

Volume 15.04

ASTM D 1516	Width of Leather
ASTM D 1517	Standard Definitions of Terms Relating to Leather
ASTM D 1815	Water Absorption (Static) of Leather
ASTM D 1912	Cold-Crack of Upholstery Leather
ASTM D 1913	Resistance to Wetting of Garment-Type Leathers (Spray Test)
ASTM D 2096	Colorfastness and Transfer of Color in the Washing of Leather
ASTM D 2097	Flex Testing of Finish on Upholstery Leather
ASTM D 2098	Dynamic Water Resistance of Shoe Upper Leather by the Dow Corning Method
ASTM D 2099	Dynamic Water Resistance of Shoe Upper Leather by the Maeser Water Penetration Tester
ASTM D 2209	Tensile Strength of Leather
ASTM D 2210	Grain Crack and Extension of Leather by the Mullen Test
ASTM D 2211	Elongation of Leather
ASTM D 2212	Slit Tear Resistance of Leather
ASTM D 2213	Compressibility of Leather
ASTM D 2214	Estimating the Thermal Conductivity of Leather with the Cenco-Fitch Apparatus

ASTM D 2322	Resistance of Chrome-Tanned White Shoe Upper Leather to Artificial Perspiration
ASTM D 2821	Measuring the Relative Stiffness of Leather by Means of a Torsional Wire Apparatus
ASTM D 2941	Measuring the Break Pattern of Leather (Break Scale)
ASTM D 4705	Stitch Tear Strength of Leather, Double Hole
ASTM D 4786	Stitch Tear Strength, Single Hole
ASTM D 4831	Buckle Tear Strength of Leather
ASTM D 5552	Resistance of Colored Leather to Bleeding

AATCC Evaluation Procedures

AATCC 1	Gray Scale for Color Change
AATCC 2	Gray Scale for Staining
AATCC 3	AATCC Chromatic Transference Scale
AATCC 4	Standard Depth Scales for Depth Determination
AATCC 5	Fabric Hand: Subjective Evaluation of
AATCC 6	Instrumental Color Measurement
AATCC 7	Instrumental Assessment of the Change in Color of a Test Specimen

Selected AATCC Procedures

AATCC 6	Colorfastness to Acids and Alkalis
AATCC 8	Colorfastness to Crocking: AATCC Crockmeter Method
AATCC 15	Colorfastness to Perspiration
AATCC 16	Colorfastness to Light
AATCC 20	Fiber Analysis: Qualitative
AATCC 20A	Fiber Analysis: Quantitative
AATCC 22	Water Repellency: Spray Test
AATCC 35	Water Resistance: Rain Test
AATCC 61	Colorfastness to Laundering, Home and Commercial: Accelerated
AATCC 66	Wrinkle Recovery of Fabrics: Recovery Angle Method
AATCC 76	Electrical Resistivity of Fabrics
AATCC 79	Absorbency of Bleached Textiles
AATCC 88B	Smoothness of Seams in Fabrics After Repeated Home Laundering
AATCC 88C	Retention of Creases in Fabrics After Repeated Home Laundering
AATCC 92	Chlorine, Retained, Tensile Loss: Single Sample Method
AATCC 93	Abrasion Resistance of Fabrics: Accelerotor Method
AATCC 96	Dimensional Changes in Commercial Laundering of Woven and Knitted Fabrics Except Wool
AATCC 104	Colorfastness to Water Spotting
AATCC 106	Colorfastness to Water: Sea

AATCC 107	Colorfastness to Water
AATCC 136	Bond Strength of Bonded and Laminated Fabrics
AATCC 114	Chlorine, Retained, Tensile Loss: Multiple Sample Method
AATCC 115	Electrostatic Clinging of Fabrics: Fabric-to-Metal Test
AATCC 116	Colorfastness to Crocking: Rotary Vertical Crockmeter Method
AATCC 117	Colorfastness to Heat; Dry (Excluding Pressure)
AATCC 118	Oil Repellency: Hydrocarbon Resistance Test
AATCC 119	Colorfastness due to Flat Abrasion (Frosting): Screen Wire Method
AATCC 120	Colorfastness due to Flat Abrasion (Frosting): Emery Method
AATCC 124	Appearance of Fabrics after Repeated Home Laundering
AATCC 128	Wrinkle Recovery of Fabrics: Appearance Method
AATCC 130	Soil Release: Oily Stain Release Method
AATCC 132	Colorfastness to Drycleaning
AATCC 133	Colorfastness to Heat: Hot Pressing
AATCC 135	Dimensional Changes in Automatic Home Laundering of Woven or Knit Fabrics
AATCC 142	Appearance of Flocked Fabrics After Repeated Home Laundering and/or Coin-Op Drycleaning
AATCC 143	Appearance of Apparel and Other Textile End Products after Repeated Home Laundering
AATCC 150	Dimensional Changes in Automatic Home Laundering of Garments
AATCC 162	Colorfastness to Water: Chlorinated Pool
AATCC 173	CMC: Calculation of Small Color Differences for Acceptability
AATCC 179	Skewness Change in Fabric and Garment Twist Resulting from Automatic Home Laundering

SAMPLE DOCUMENTS AND RECORD KEEPING FORMS

PIECE GOODS QUALITY CONTROL INSPECTION REPORT

FABRIC SUPPLIER _____

DATE OF INSPECTION _____

PURCHASE ORDER # _____

STYLE # _____

TOTAL ROLLS RECV'D. _____

TOTAL YARDS INSP. _____

TOTAL PENALTY POINTS _____

POINTS PER 100 yds. _____

REJECT SHIPMENT _____

ACCEPT SHIPMENT _____

ROLL NUMBER	COLOR	WIDTH ORDERED	WIDTH ACTUAL MIN.	WIDTH ACTUAL MAX.	LENGTH ON ROLL	LENGTH ACTUAL	COLOR DYE YARDS	SHADE DEF. YARDS	PENALTY POINTS HOLE	PENALTY POINTS SOIL	PENALTY POINTS FAB. DEF.	TOTAL POINTS	POINT PER 100YD.	REJ. (X)	COMMENTS

Approval Design Appraisal Report			Brand/Label		Input Date		ADAR NO.	

Supplier			Sample Size		Description			Import	Date / /

Buyer			Subdivision	Made/Season	Fabric	Color	F.O.B. Branch Office	

Grade Rule No.		How to Measure No.		Size Range	Retail Lot Number	Catalog Lot Number	

Grade Rule No.		How to Measure No.					

Construction Spec No. /1001-590		Main Spec. Sheet ☐	Live Modeled ☐				

WEIGHT
LBS./OZ.

Ident. No.	MT. PT.	Point of Measurement	Sample Received	Should Measure	Sample Received	Should Measure	Comments
209		Bust/Chest					
210/139		Waist/Half Waist					
213		Sweep					
217/176/ 184		Armhole Circ./ Depth/Raglan					
206		Upper Arm					
207		Cuff Opening					
132/114 115/116		Sleeve Lgth./Inseam					
102		Across Shldr.					
103		Across Bk.					
105/206		Across Chest/Elbow					
104		Back Waist Lgth.					
101		CB Length					
122/141		Front Lgth. HPS/Front Lgth					
118/130		Rel. Neck Circ./Collar Lgth					
218		Ext. Neck Circ.					
131/178		Side Lgth./Neck Width					
236/175		Torso Lgth./Neck Drop					
865/999		Bk. Neck Scoop/ Side Neck Scoop					
237/136 196/162		Belt Length/Strap Length					
210		Waist-Rel.					
210/213		Waist-Ext./Sweep Ext.					
211		High Hip					
212		Hip/Seat					
223		Thigh					
126		Outseam					
127		Inseam					
251/777		Total Crotch Lgth./ True Piece					
224		Knee					
225		Bottom Opening					
126		Fr. Piece					
129		Bk. Piece					
119		Center Bk. Lgth.					
213		Sweep					

☐ Production Sample Requested
☐ Approved With Corrections
☐ Not Approved–Resubmit Required

N O T E — All merchandise must conform to this report. Failure to comply with JCPenney procedures and the terms and conditions of all other documentation issued by JCPenney with respect to the merchandise will be cause for the return of all merchandise by JCPenney.

Supplier's Signature		Date	Date Faxed
JCPenney Designer's Signature		Designer No.	Date

JCP 7576 (Rev. 10/90)
TOC# 006-8840-4001

Distribution: White-Quality Control.   Canary-Supplier   Green-Inspection   Goldenrod-Buyer

Quality Audit Report

Quality Control Department

Sub   Lot #/7 Digit Cat. #   Audit Date   Inspector # Name   Supplier #   Supplier Name

Audit Location (City, State)   Contractor Name   Domestic   807   Imp   Contractor Location (City, State, Country)

Audit Location   Brand Code   Brand/Supplier Label Name/Style
Final FOB   Store   JCP Warehouse

Retail   Both   Acceptable Quality Level _____   Defective Units Allowed
Catalog   Media #_____   Sample Table   A   C

Initial Audit   Factory Eval.   Sell Price Per Unit   Actual   Production Quantity/Lot Size   Quantity Sampled
Re-audit #_____   _____   Estimate

Product   Cut #/Date Code   Factory Rating   Buyer

		Number of Major Defects	
Defect Code	Description of Major Quality Defect	Counting Space	Total

Number of Units With Major Defects   Total Major Defects

Status of Quality Audit   _____   P = Pass   Contacted/Date
Status of Size Audit   _____   F = Fail
Status of Packaging Audit   _____   O = Override   _____
Status of Color Audit   _____   N = Not Applicable   _____
Status of Label Audit   _____   _____
                                                                                          NRP _____

Corrective Action: (Include reaudit date if applicable)

Size Comments: ☐ Size Sheet Attached

Packaging Comments: Unit/Protective Pack   Master Carton

General Comments: (Include Color and Label Information)

TOC = 006-2246-0002 (rev. 7/91)

Samples forwarded
MTC   Yes   No
Other   Yes   No

DATE _____

INSPECTOR _____

SUPERVISOR _____

WORK-IN PROCESS INSPECTION RECORD

X-FOR REJECTED BUNDLE
0-FOR PASSED BUNDLE

NAME	OPERATION	TIME	AQL 1.5 INSPECT-7 REJECT FOR 1 DEFECT	PLACE A "J" FOR EACH PASSING BUNDLE THREE CONSECUTIVE REQUIRED	RESERVED FOR FOLLOW UP BUNDLE THAT FAILED	DESCRIPTION OF DEFECTS AND REASONS FOR REJECTIONS
		8-10				
		10-12				
		12-2				
		2-4				
		8-10				
		10-12				
		12-2				
		2-4				
		8-10				
		10-12				
		12-2				
		2-4				
		8-10				
		10-12				
		12-2				
		2-4				
		8-10				
		10-12				
		12-2				
		2-4				

ASSESSMENT GUIDES

Size: to assess adherence to size specs, the following items should be considered.

1. Areas that are essential to measure
2. Procedure to be followed in measuring
3. Measurement dimensions and tolerances acceptable for each area
4. Diagrams of product or component showing area to be measured

Material Performance: to assess material performance, the following items should be considered.

1. Performance measures that are essential to customer satisfaction with the product
2. Procedures or standard test methods to be used and any modifications to standard procedures
3. Performance requirements and tolerances acceptable for each measure of performance

Product Performance: to assess performance of the product, the following items should be considered.

1. Performance measures that are essential to customer satisfaction with the product
2. Procedures or standard test methods to be used and any modifications to standard procedures
3. Performance requirements and tolerances acceptable for each measure of performance
4. Interactions of materials that may adversely affect product performance and customer satisfaction.

Product Fit: to assess adherence to fit specs, the following items should be considered.

1. Company specs and standards for the product type
2. Customer expectations for the product type
3. Relationship of product type and function

Workmanship and Construction: to assess adherence to workmanship specs, the following items should be considered.

1. Company specs and standards for the product type
2. Customer expectations for the product type
3. Visibility of the various parts of the product in terms of consumer use

Product Zones: to identify and define product zones, the following items should be considered.

1. Product type and end use
2. Customer expectations for the product
3. Visibility of the various parts of the product during normal use by the customer

Criteria for Critical, Major, and Minor Defects: to identify and define defect types, the following items should be considered.

1. Product type and end use
2. Function of the product and each component or material
3. Customer expectations for the product
4. Visibility of the various parts of the product during normal use by the customer

Possible Defect Descriptions

Materials/Fabric

1. Hole or surface flaw that could develop into a hole
2. Slubs that are easily distinguishable
3. Distinctive shading
4. Dye spots, misprints, or out-of-register prints
5. Cuts, tears, or visible surface repairs
6. Bow or skew exceeding 1.5 percent
7. Plaids, checks, or horizontal stripes that are conspicuously out of match at center front or back of a product

Cleanliness

1. Soil, spots, or stains
2. Attached thread clusters

Pressing

1. Burn or scorch marks
2. Glaring shine marks
3. Press marks from clamps
4. Absence of pressing when specified
5. Products packaged moist after steam pressing
6. Improper pressing
7. Seams not lined up when specified for center leg crease
8. Loops twisted after pressing
9. Pressed-in creases uneven

Seams and Stitching

1. Twisted, roped, buckled, or puckered seams
2. Open or broken stitches

3. Raw edges when covered edges are specified
4. Seams not back stitched or bar tacked when specified
5. Irregular or uneven top stitching
6. Seam grin-through
7. Any part of product caught in seam or stitches
8. Any exposed drill holes
9. Length of legs off by more than 3/8 in.
10. Stitch count not conforming to specs
11. Stitch or seam type not conforming to specs
12. Label correctly attached
13. Sewn on design attached in correct place and sewn on according to specs
14. Double needle stitch on crotch seam
15. Use of monofilament thread other than where specified

Buttonholes

1. Size within specs
2. Ragged edges
3. Uncut buttonhole
4. Out of alignment or improper spacing
5. Thread shade not to specs
6. Broken stitches in buttonhole
7. Density too high or low
8. Stitch depth too narrow or wide

Button/Button Sewing

1. Button not securely attached
2. Button missing
3. Broken or damaged button
4. Out of alignment or improper spacing
5. Button not to specs
6. Lack of support materials on fragile fabric
7. Buttons that crack, chip, discolor, rust, bleed, melt, or otherwise cause consumer dissatisfaction when care label is followed

Waistband

1. Uneven in width
2. Excessive fullness, puckering, or twisting
3. Closure misaligned
4. Belt loops are crooked

Belt Loops

1. Not fully secure
2. Extend above waistband
3. Missing tacks

4. Color shade not to specs
5. Thread shade not to specs
6. Raw edges showing

Collars and Lapels

1. Excessive fullness, puckers, or twisting of top collar
2. Collar points not well shaped and not symmetrical right and left
3. Uneven or irregular top stitching
4. Length of collar points uneven
5. Cording, piping, or trim on collar uneven
6. Under collar shows above top collar
7. Collar off center when attached to garment
8. Loose thread or lint inside collar and shows through to surface
9. Buttons or buttonholes not aligned.

Front and Back

1. Uneven at bottom hem
2. Underfacing showing
3. Pockets conspicuously uneven
4. Darts uneven in length
5. Darts poorly shaped
6. Spot shirring not even right and left sides

Sleeves and Armholes

1. Pleats at sleeve head unless specified
2. Sleeves set in improperly, backward, or twisted
3. Sleeve head stay stitching showing on outside
4. Excessive puckering in sleeve seam
5. Underarm seam out of alignment specs
6. Cuffs attached incorrectly
7. Hem uneven or roped
8. Facing uneven or twisted

Cuffs

1. Uneven by more than ¼ in.
2. Left and right cuffs do not match
3. Interlining or lining exposed
4. Buttons or buttonholes not aligned
5. Ends of cuffs not symmetrical
6. Stay stitching showing on outer surface

Hems

1. Twisted, roped, puckered, pleated, or excessively visible from exterior
2. Uneven in width

3. Side seams busted open when specified
4. Uneven length of product unless specified

Pockets

1. Not uniform in size and shape
2. Misaligned horizontally or vertically
3. Crooked
4. Missing bartack, backtack, or rivet where specified
5. Bartack or rivet not as specified
6. Sewn-in pleats or puckers

Zippers

1. Any malfunction in operation
2. Tape does not match color specs
3. Wavy zipper
4. Exposed zipper that detracts from product's appearance
5. Irregular or uneven stitching
6. Crooked or uneven placket
7. Bartack missing or incorrectly located at bottom or base of zipper

Gripper

1. Misaligned
2. Missing or incorrect
3. Defective in operation

Fly area

1. Width is uniform
2. Bottom stop not securely clinched
3. Top of zipper not caught in band
4. Either side of fly extends past other side by excessive amount

Labels

1. Labels are correct
2. Located in correct location
3. Care labels are permanent

ADDRESSES FOR ORGANIZATIONS

American Society for Quality (ASQ)
310 West Wisconsin Ave.
Milwaukee, WI 53203
phone 414-272-8575 fax 414-272-1734

American Society for Testing and Materials (ASTM)
100 Barr Harbor Drive
West Conshohocken, PA 19428
phone 610-832-9500 fax 610-832 9555

American Association of Textile Chemists and Colorists (AATCC)
PO Box 12215
Research Triangle Park, NC 27709
phone 919-549-8141 fax 919-549-8933

SOURCES FOR EQUIPMENT AND MATERIALS

SDL International Ltd.
PO Box 162 Crown Royal
Shawcross Street
Stockport SK1 3JW England
phone 0161-480-8485
fax 0161-480-8580

Defect Rating Scale
Department 817, FC-517B
3333 Beverly Road
Sears Merchandise Group
Hoffman Estates, IL 60179
fax 708-286-5991

Joseph Pernick Manufacturing
Corp.
74-10 88 Street
Glendale, NY 11385
phone 718-894-8001
fax 718-894-6204

Alfred Suter Co.
PO Box 350
Ramsey, NJ 07446-0350
phone 201-818-0113
fax 201-818-0654

Thwing-Albert Instrument Co.
10960 Dutton Road
Philadelphia, PA 19154
phone 215-637-0100
fax 215-632-8370

Ahiba
2175 Hawkins Street
Charlotte, SC 28293

Taber Industries
455 Bryant Street
North Tonawanda, NY 14120
phone 716-694-4000
fax 716-694-1450

Polyspec, Inc.
2301 South Tyron Street
Charlotte, NC 28203
phone 704-376-3766

Custom Scientific Instrument, Inc.
see Atlas Electric Device Co.

Atlas Electric Device Co.
4114 North Ravenswood Avenue
Chicago, IL 60613
phone 312-327-4520
fax 312-327-5787

International Wool Secretariat
  Development Centre
Testing Materials Supply Service
Valley Drive, Ilkley
West Yorkshire LS29 8PB,
  England
phone 01-943-60155
fax 01-943-816692

SGS US Testing Co. Inc.
291 Fairfield Avenue
Fairfield, NJ 07004
phone 973-575-5252
fax 973-575-8271

GTI Graphic Technology Inc.
PO Box 3138
Newburgh, NY 12550
phone 914-562-7066
fax 914-562-2543

MacBeth
405 Little Britain Road
New Windsor, NY 12553-6148
phone 800-MACBETH
or 914-565-7660

HunterLab
Hunter Associates Laboratory
11491 Sunset Hills Road
Reston, VA 22090
phone 703-471-6870
fax 703-471-4237

Datacolor International
Applied Color Systems Inc.
5 Princess Road
Lawrenceville, NJ 08648
phone 609-794-2189
fax 609-896-3804

Tailored Lighting, Inc.
9 Tobey Village Office Park
Pittsford, NY 14534
phone 800-2LIGHTS
fax 716-383-8453

Testfabrics, Inc.
PO Box 420
Middlesex, NJ 08846
phone 908-469-6446
fax 908-469-1147

Textile Innovators Corp.
PO Box 115
Dallastown, PA 17313
phone 919-794-9703
fax 919-794-9704

3M Co.
Bldg 53-1S-02
367 Grove Street
St. Paul, MN 55144
phone 612-778-5879
fax 612-778-5397

T. J. Edwards Co.
33 Dover Street
Brockton, MA 02401
phone 508-583-9300
fax 207-786-2810

Crosrol Inc.
PO Box 6488
Greenville, SC 29606
phone 803-235-2981

Orange Machine and Mfg. Co.
1503 Bay Avenue
Point Pleasant, NJ 08742
phone 732-295-2262

William Harrison Co.
4595 East 10th Court
Hialeah, FL 33013
phone 305-681-8381
fax 305-685-0407

Precision Scientific Co.
3737 West Cortland Street
Chicago, IL 60647

E. H. Benz Co.
73 Maplehurst Avenue
Providence, RI 02908
phone 401-331-5650
fax 401-331-5685

Precision Machine and
  Development Co.
340 New Churchmans Road
New Castle, DE 19720
phone 302-328-1511
fax 302-328-1954

Instrument Marketing Services
A Subsidiary of SGS US Testing
   Co. Inc.
291 Fairfield Avenue
Fairfield, NJ 07004
phone 973-575-5252
fax 973-575-8271

Wilson Road Machine Shop
1170 Wilson Road
Rising Sun, MD 21911
phone 410-658-5633

Minolta Corp.
Instrument Systems Div.
101 Williams Drive
Ramsey, NJ 07446
phone 800-724-4075

Labsphere Inc.
PO Box 70
North Sutton, NH 03260
phone 603-927-4266
fax 603-927-4694

Pantone, Inc.
590 Commerce Blvd.
Carlstadt, NJ 07072-3098
phone 201-935-5500
fax 201-896-0242

INFO
PO Box 606
Ayer, MA 01432
phone/fax 978-456-3848

NRD, Inc.
2937 Alt. Boulevard, North
Grand Island, NY 14072
phone 716-773-7634

The ASQ Code of Ethics

To uphold and advance the honor and dignity of the profession, and in keeping with high standards of ethical conduct, I acknowledge that I:

Fundamental Principles

I. Will be honest and impartial; will serve with devotion my employer, my clients, and the public.

II. Will strive to increase the competence and prestige of the profession.

III. Will use my knowledge and skill for the advancement of human welfare and in promoting the safety and reliability of products for public use.

IV. Will earnestly endeavor to aid the work of the Society.

Relations with the Public

1.1 Will do whatever I can to promote the reliability and safety of all products that come within my jurisdiction.

1.2 Will endeavor to extend public knowledge of the work of the society and its members that relates to the public welfare.

1.3 Will be dignified and modest in explaining my work and merit.

1.4 Will preface any public statement that I may issue by clearly indicating on whose behalf they are made.

Relations with Employers and Clients

2.1 Will act in professional matters as a faithful agent or trustee for each employer or client.

2.2 Will inform each client or employer of any business, connections, interests, or affiliations that might influence my judgment or impair the equitable character of my services.

2.3 Will indicate to my employer or client the adverse consequences to be expected if my professional judgment is overruled.

2.4 Will not disclose information concerning the business affairs or technical processes of any present or former employer or client without his or her consent.

2.5 Will not accept compensation from more than one party for the same service without the consent of all parties. If employed, I will engage in supplementary employment of consulting practice only with the consent of my employer.

Relations with Peers

3.1 Will take care that credit for the work of others is given to those to whom it is due.

3.2 Will endeavor to aid the professional development and advancement of those in my employ or under my supervision.

3.3 Will not compete unfairly with others; will extend my friendship and confidence to all associates and those with whom I have business relations.

From ASQ Auditor Certification, page 9.

ASTM RECOMMENDED SPECIFICATIONS FOR PRODUCT TYPES

Number	Title
4847	Awning and Canopy Fabrics, Woven
4110	Bathrobe, Dressing Gown, and Pajama Fabrics, Knitted, Men's and Boys'
3784	Bathrobe and Dressing Gown Fabrics, Woven, Men's and Boys'
4154	Beachwear and Sport Shirt Fabrics, Knitted and Woven, Men's and Boys'
4037	Bedspread Fabrics, Woven, Knitted, or Flocked
5432	Blanket Products for Institutional and Household Use
4235	Blouse and Dress Fabrics, Knitted, Women's and Girls'
4233	Brassiere Fabrics, Knitted and Woven, Women's and Girls'
4232	Career Apparel Fabrics, Dress and Vocational, Men's and Women's
3995	Career Apparel Fabrics, Knitted, Dress and Vocational, Men's and Women's
3781	Coat Fabrics, Knitted Rainwear and All-Purpose, Water Repellent, Men's and Boys'
3779	Coat Fabrics, Woven Rainwear and All-Purpose, Water-Repellent, Women's and Girls'
4769	Comforter Fabrics, Woven and Warp Knitted
4116	Corset-Girdle Combination Fabrics, Knitted and Woven, Women's and Girls'
4109	Coverall, Dungaree, Overall, and Shop Coat Fabrics, Woven, Men's and Boys'
4118	Coverall, Dungaree, Overall, and Shop Coat Fabrics, Woven, Women's
4152	Dish, Huck, and Terry Bath Towel Fabrics, Woven, Institutional
4038	Dress and Blouse Fabrics, Woven, Women's and Girls'
3778	Dress Coat Fabrics, Drycleanable Woven, Women's and Girls'
4115	Dress Glove Fabrics, Knitted and Woven, Women's and Girls'
3477	Dress Shirt Fabrics, Woven, Men's and Boys'
4119	Dress Shirt Fabrics, Knitted, Men's and Boys'
3782	Dress Suit Fabrics and Sportswear Jacket, Slack, and Trouser Fabrics, Knitted, Men's and Boys'
3780	Dress Suit Fabrics and Sportswear Jacket, Slack, and Trouser Fabrics, Woven, Men's and Boys'
3562	Dress Topcoat and Dress Overcoat Fabrics, Woven, Men's and Boys'

4522   Feather-Filled and Down-Filled Products

3783   Flat Lining Fabrics, Woven, for Men's and Boys' Apparel

4114   Flat Lining Fabrics, Woven, for Women's and Girls' Apparel

4153   Handkerchief Fabrics, Woven, Men's, Women's, and Children's

3993   Household Blanket Fabrics, Woven, Thermal, Flocked, Nonwoven, and Knitted

3691   Household Curtain and Drapery Fabrics, Woven, Lace, and Knit

4111   Household and Institutional, Napery and Tablecloth Fabrics, Woven

3821   Household Kitchen and Bath Towel Fabrics, Woven Terry

4036   Household Pillowcase, Bed Sheet, and Crib Sheet Fabrics, Woven and Knit

4035   Necktie and Scarf Fabrics, Knitted

3785   Necktie and Scarf Fabrics, Woven

3655   Overcoat and Jacket Fabrics, Sliver Knitted, Men's and Women's

3819   Pajama Fabrics, Woven, Men's and Boys'

4234   Robe, Negligee, Nightgown, Pajama, Slip, and Lingerie Fabrics, Knitted, Women's and Girls'

4117   Robe, Negligee, Nightgown, Pajama, Slip, and Lingerie Fabrics, Woven, Women's and Girls'

4113   Slipcover Fabrics, Woven

4156   Sportswear Fabrics, Woven, Women's and Girls'

4155   Sportswear, Shorts, Slacks, and Suiting Fabrics, Woven, Women's and Girls'

3782   Sportswear Jacket, Slack, and Trouser Fabrics, Dress Suit Fabrics, Knitted, Men's and Boys'

3996   Swimwear Fabrics, Knit, Men's, Women's, and Children's

3994   Swimwear Fabrics, Woven

5433   Towel Products for Institutional and Household Uses

4112   Umbrella Fabrics, Woven

3820   Underwear Fabrics, Woven, Men's and Boys'

3690   Upholstery Fabrics, Indoor, Vinyl-Coated and Urethane-Coated

4771   Upholstery Fabrics, Knitted, for Indoor Use

3597   Upholstery Fabrics, Woven—Plain, Tufted, or Flocked

5431   Woven and Knitted Sheeting Products for Institutional and Household Uses

5378   Woven and Knitted Shower Curtains for Institutional and Household Uses

UNITS OF MEASURE AND SYMBOLS

Measures of temperature

°C = degrees centigrade or Celsius   °F = degrees Fahrenheit

Measures of heat

cal = calories

Measures of distance

cm = centimeter

m = meter

in. = inch

ft = foot (feet)

yd = yard

Measures of area

cm^2 = square centimeter

m^2 = square meter

$in.^2$ = square inch

ft^2 = square foot (feet)

yd^2 = square yard

Measures of volume

cm^3 = cubic centimeter = cc

L = liter

ml = milliliter

Measures of time

sec or s = second

Measure of force and pressure

psi = pounds of force per square inch

lbf = pound of force

Measures of mass or weight

oz/yd^2 = ounces per square yard g/m^2 = grams per square meter

Other measures

mg-cm = milligram-centimeter (measure of stiffness)

%rh = percentage, relative humidity (measure of the amount of moisture the atmosphere holds compared to how much it could hold at saturation)

ΔE = delta E (measure of color match)

Other symbols

Σ = summation symbol used in statistics

CONVERSION FACTORS

Length

1 cm = 0.394 in.	1 in. = 2.54 cm
1 m = 3.28 ft	1 ft = 0.305 m
1 m = 1.093 yd	1 yd = 0.914 m

Area

$1 \text{ cm}^2 = 0.155 \text{ in}^2$	$1 \text{ in}^2 = 6.45 \text{ cm}^2$
$1 \text{ m}^2 = 10.76 \text{ ft}^2$	$1 \text{ ft}^2 = 0.093 \text{ m}^2$
$1 \text{ m}^2 = 1.195 \text{ yd}^2$	$1 \text{ yd}^2 = 0.837 \text{ m}^2$

Volume

$1 \text{ cm}^3 = 0.061 \text{ in}^3$	$1 \text{ in}^3 = 15.4 \text{ cm}^3$
$1 \text{ m}^3 = 35.3 \text{ ft}^3$	$1 \text{ ft}^3 = 0.028 \text{ m}^3$
1 L = 1000 ml	$1 \text{ ml} = 1 \text{ cm}^3$
$1 \text{ m}^3 = 264 \text{ gal}$	1 gal = 3.79 L
1 L = 1.06 qt	1 qt = 0.95 L

Mass

1 kg = 2.22 lb	1 lb = 454 g = 0.45 kg
1 g = 0.035 oz	1 oz = 28.37 g
$1 \text{ g/m}^2 = 0.42 \text{ oz/yd}^2$	$1 \text{ oz/yd}^2 = 33.9 \text{ g/m}^2$

Force

1 N = 0.225 lb	1 lb = 4.45 N

Temperature

0 °C = 32 °F Water freezes, ice melts
100 °C = 212 °F Water boils, steam condenses

$$°C = (°F\text{-}32)5/9 \qquad\qquad °F = 9/5(°C) + 32$$

INFORMATION SOURCES FOR LOCATING INDEPENDENT TESTING LABS

Independent Testing Laboratories, Inc. *Directory of Independent Testing Laboratories.* Washington, DC: Author. (*The Directory* lists approximately 30 labs that deal with textiles.)

American Society for Testing and Materials. *International Directory of Testing Laboratories.* West Conshohocken, PA: Author. (*The Directory* lists approximately 115 labs in 28 states and 25 labs in 14 countries that focus on textile mill products and approximately 110 labs in 30 states and 40 labs in 16 countries that focus on textile products, finished products, and apparel.)

Both sources include such information for individual labs as their addresses, phone and fax numbers, email addresses, directors, areas of specialization by products and materials, laboratory services offered, equipment available, testing capabilities (test methods by organization and designator number), applications or end uses, accreditation, number and education of staff, and branch offices.

GLOSSARY

AATCC Chromatic Transference Scale: a rating scale that consists of 30 color chips from the Munsell Book of Color in gray and five hue families: red, yellow, green, blue, and purple

abnormal variations: unacceptable variations in a material, product, or process

abrasion resistance: the ability of a material to resist the wearing away of any part of it by rubbing against a surface or other material

absorbate: a material that is absorbed by another material

absorbent: a material that takes in or absorbs another material

absorption: with colored objects, it is the light energy incident on the object that is taken in or absorbed by the object; *See also* moisture absorbency

acceptable quality level (AQL): in sampling inspection, the limit of a satisfactory process or product average (Department of Defense, 1989)

acceptance: the decision that the lot meets or exceeds standards and specifications and the buyer agrees to buy the lot

acceptance levels: *see* acceptable quality level

acceptance sampling: the inspection and evaluation of sample products selected from production lots for specified predetermined and defined quality characteristics after the product has been produced (Pond, 1994)

acceptance specification: the various criteria that will govern the acceptance of a product at various stages of production and on completion of production

accuracy: the agreement between the true value of the property being tested and the average of many observations made according to the test method, preferably by many observers

achromatic colors: colors that include no hue characteristic

additive color mixing: adding wavelengths of light (colors) to create other colors

aesthetics: how a textile product satisfies the customer's needs in terms of appearance, fashionability, fit, and styling

air permeability: the rate of air flow passing vertically through a known area of material when an air pressure difference exists between the two sides of the material

allergens: foreign materials that cause a physical reaction by the body after exposure to the material

alpha (α) risk: the possibility that good lots will be rejected

American Apparel Manufacturers Association (AAMA): a national organization that deals with issues of interest to the sewn products industry

American Association of Textile Chemists and Colorists (AATCC): a professional organization that works with the textile wet processing industry

American Society for Quality (ASQ): a professional organization that works to improve the quality of manufactured goods, services, and related aspects, formerly American Society for Quality Control (ASQC).

American Society for Quality Control (ASQC): *see* American Society for Quality

American Society for Testing and Materials (ASTM): an international organization that develops and promotes use of standard documents and procedures

amplitude: the height of a wave crest

ANSI/ASQ Z1.4-1993: a standard (similar to the former Military Standard 105E) widely used in quality assurance that directs taking a sample, developing acceptable quality levels, and ultimately ensuring a satisfactory level of product or process quality

antibacterial finishes: any chemical that kills bacteria or interferes with the multiplication, growth, or activity of bacteria

appearance: how the product looks when an individual views it from a near distance

appearance of seams: *see* seam appearance

appearance retention: the degree to which a textile product retains its original appearance during storage, use, and care

assignable cause: *see* special cause

assignable variation: an anomaly with a definite cause or a set of causes

atmospheric fading unit (AFU): the specific amount of exposure at specified conditions of which one AFU is one-twentieth ($\frac{1}{20}$) of the light-on exposure required to produce a color change equal to Step 4 of the AATCC Gray Scale for Color Change on AATCC blue wool lightfastness standard fabric L-4

attribute: a specific criterion of a product or material

attribute control chart: a tool for measuring the number of nonconforming units or the number of each occurrence of nonconformance in products

attribute data: a count of the number of times a particular characteristic exists

audit: *see* inspection

auditor: *see* inspector

ball burst test: a polished steel ball is forced through a specimen to determine the force required to rupture the fabric

barré: the optical result of physical or dye differences in the yarns, geometric differences in fabric structure, or any combination of the differences (AATCC, 1996, p. 335).

bean bag snag test: a small bean bag covered with the fabric of interest is tumbled in a chamber with sharp needles spaced periodically around the interior

Beer's Law: the absorption of light in passage through any medium is proportional to the number of absorbing molecules in its path

benchmarking: the process of comparing and measuring an organization's operations or internal processes against those of a best-in-class performer from inside or outside its industry (Goetsch & Davis, 1994, pp. 414).

beta (β) risk: the possibility that bad lots will be accepted

Bezold effect: a characteristic of color perception that merges two or more tiny color areas into one new color

bias: a systematic error in how samples are selected; a constant and systematic error in results

bimodal distribution: a distribution curve that is well centered but displays two peaks or modes

biological resistance: a material's ability to block the transmission of organisms through it

bleeding: loss of color from textile materials during wet processing including cleaning and washing

bleed-through: with fusible materials, the adhesive appears on the technical face of the shell fabric

blister: a bulge, swelling, or similar alteration of a material's surface condition characterized by its being raised from the plane of the underlying component over a limited area giving a puffy appearance

blue wool lightfastness standard fabric: a control fabric used in determining the light exposure of test specimens

bond strength: the force required to separate the layers of a laminated, bonded, or fused composite fabric

bow: a condition in which the crosswise yarn forms one or more arcs as it moves across the fabric

boxplot: a diagram that plots five bits of information about a data set: the median, maximum value, minimum value, first quartile, and third quartile

box-and-whisker plot: *see* boxplot

breaking elongation: the elongation corresponding to the breaking force

breaking force: the strength of a material under tension expressed in terms of force

breaking point: in a stress-strain curve, the point at which the curve stops and the material ruptures

breaking strength: *see* breaking force

breakthrough time: the time from initial exposure to a chemical to its first detectable presence on the reverse side of the material

brightness: the total intensity of a light wave or color

bubble: *see* blister

buckling: a defect that occurs when material bends back on itself and forms an accidental fold, tuck, or pleat

bursting strength: the force or pressure required to rupture a textile by distending it with a force that is applied at right angles to the plane of the fabric

buyer audit: *see* shipment inspection

c chart: a type of attribute chart in which the count of nonconformities is reported

calibration: the process of fixing, checking, or correcting the gradations of a measuring instrument

calorie: the amount of energy (the heat) needed to raise 1 gram of water 1°C

carbonizing: a chemical process used to eliminate plant matter in wool by degrading the cellulosic material with acid

care: the procedure(s) recommended for returning a soiled item to its clean and as near to new condition as possible

care instructions: a series of directions that describe practices that should refurbish a product without adversely affecting it

care label: a tag that gives directions for cleaning a textile product

cause-and-effect diagram: a diagram that reflects relationships among processes, materials, and variations within products

char length: the distance at which the physical strength of a material was damaged by exposure to flame

check sheet: a list used by an inspector that details the characteristics and parameters that must be measured or examined for a material, component, or product

chemical resistance: a material's ability to block the transmission of chemicals through it

chromaticity diagrams: a two-dimensional representation of color

chronic problem: a long-term adverse situation in which the remedy is related to changing or modifying the status quo

CIE: International Commission on Illumination (Commission Internationale de l'Eclairage)

CIELAB formula (CIE 1976 L*a*b* formula): a color difference formula based on the CIE color space

CIM (computer integrated manufacturing): a variety of activities including, but not limited to, design, pattern making, receiving, manufacturing, scheduling, communications, inventory, shipping, and inspection

classification: a systematic arrangement or division of materials, products, systems, or services into groups based on similar characteristics, such as origin, composition, properties, or use

clo: the resistance to dry heat transfer provided by clothing

closed specification: the exact material, component, or product of a manufacturer or vendor, including style numbers, tradenames, and other specific identifiers

closures: the mechanical devices used to hold two parts of a textile product together

cold water bleed: a colorfastness problem that may occur when damp fabrics are in contact with other damp fabrics for 18 to 24 hours

color: the sensation resulting from the stimulation of the eye's retina by certain wavelengths of light

color change: a change in color of any kind whether in lightness, hue, or chroma, or any combination of these, discernible by comparing the test specimen with a corresponding untested sample

color consistency: *see* color match

color contrast: irregularities in the colors in a print or patterned fabric due to needle-related damage at a seam or yarn snags; *see* shiners

color fidelity: the color match between two images created by different mixing systems

color loss: a noticeable loss of color in a material or product

color match: the ability of a material to register the same color as the standard; the condition that occurs when two or more objects produce identical or near identical sensations

color matching: the process of measuring a color to determine if it registers the same as the standard; the process of developing a formula to accurately reproduce a color as many times as needed

color measurement: the process of assigning numerical values to a color so that it can be assigned a specific location in a three-dimensional color solid

color theory: explanations that help us understand the physics of light and energy and the manner in which the eye and brain interact with energy to perceive color

color transfer: dye or other colorant from one material bonds with and stains another material

colorant staining: the unintended pickup of colorant by a substrate because of (1) exposure to a colored or contaminated liquid medium or (2) direct contact with dyed or pigmented material from which the colorant transfers by direct sublimation or mechanical action (AATCC, 1996)

coloration: the process of adding color to a material

colorimetry: the measurement of color

comfort: positive interaction between the textile product and the body; includes aspects related to physical, physiological, and psychological factors

comfort stretch: the small amounts of increase in material dimensions that occur with movement

common cause: variations that exist because of the general system in place within the firm

company standard: a consensus among a business's employees concerning products or services provided

comparative testing: testing to compare two or more products from the same plant, different plants owned by the same company, or competitive products

competitive analysis: comparison between a company's product and that of a competitor to determine how to improve the product and make it more competitive

component testing: a laboratory analysis of the way(s) in which materials interact and influence the performance of each other

components: product pieces that are sewn together or otherwise attached and treated as one piece in a later production stage

compressibility: the ability of a material to be compressed or overfed without buckling

computer color match (CCM): a numerical method that defines a color sensation created by a reference material when viewed under standard conditions

condensation: a phase change that occurs when a gas changes into a liquid

conduction: heat transfer by direct contact

conformance: the condition that occurs when the materials, components, processes, or products meet requirements in terms of specifications and standards

consolidation shrinkage: a type of shrinkage that occurs when a wool fabric is gently agitated in water

constant percentage sample: a consistent percentage is used regardless of lot size to determine the number of units to be sampled

constant rate of extension (CRE) machine: a piece of equipment in which the pulling clamp moves at a uniform rate, and the force-measuring mechanism moves a negligible distance with increasing force

constant rate of load (CRL) machine: a piece of equipment in which the rate of increase of force is uniform with time after the first three seconds, and the specimen elongates in a fashion related to its individual characteristics

constant rate of traverse (CRT) machine: a piece of equipment in which the pulling clamp moves at a uniform rate, and the force is applied through the second clamp producing a rate of increase of force or extension

construction: the way the various parts, components, and materials of a product are combined or connected in a permanent fashion to create a finished product

consumer (β) risk: *see* beta risk

continuous data: *see* variable data

continuous improvement: constant efforts to refine processes so that the end result is an overall increase in the quality of products or services

continuous production sample: a sample used when products or processes are consistent for long periods of time

contract testing: *see* independent testing

control chart: a data analysis tool that identifies variation within a process and its allowable variation over time

control limits: an acceptable range of values from the lowest acceptable value to the highest acceptable value

controls: means by which a process is kept within established limits; treatment to which experimental results are compared

convection: a heat transfer mechanism that occurs when hot molecules mix with cool molecules

convenience samples: samples selected because they were easier to locate than other possible items

correlation: the relationship between two variables as one variable changes

cost: the amount of money exchanged for a textile product

count: the number of yarns in the lengthwise and crosswise directions of the fabric in one unit of measure, such as one inch

crack mark: a sharp break or crease in the surface contour of a layered material that becomes evident when it is rolled, bent, draped, or folded

crimp: the additional amount of yarn needed to interlace with other yarns when producing a fabric

critical defect: a defect resulting in hazardous or unsafe conditions for individuals using, maintaining, or depending on the product, or a defect that prevents performance of a tactical function of a major end-use item

crocking: a colorfastness problem in which color on the surface of a material transfers to another material by surface contact and rubbing

cross-functional teams: a group of individuals who work together, but who represent different departments or areas of specialization

crosswise strength: the ability of a zipper chain to resist a lateral pulling force using a CRE or CRT machine

customer satisfaction: a measure of how well a product or service meets customer expectations

cut strip test: a breaking force test using a narrow cut strip of material

DE: a single number defining the total color difference in a color space

defect: the departure or nonconformance of some characteristic from its intended level or state

defect: any nonconformance of a product with specific requirements

defect point: the penalty assigned based on the length of the defect

defective: a product with one or more defects

defects per hundred units: a percentage based on the number of defects and the size of the sample or the number of units inspected

degradation: a change in a material's physical properties as a result of chemical exposure (ASTM, 1996)

delamination: a separation of at least a portion of the layers of a material

demerit point: *see* defect point

dependent variable: the measurable variable whose value is assumed to be dependent on the independent variable

desiccant: a compound that absorbs water vapor from the air maintaining a low relative humidity in its immediate environment

design: the details, features, and characteristics of a finished product

destructive testing: a type of testing in which the sample is destroyed or damaged in the process

dexterity: fine motor control of the hands and fingers

diaphragm bursting test: a rubber diaphragm is distended because of hydraulic force that steadily increases until the fabric ruptures

dimensional change: either an increase in dimensions (growth) or a decrease in dimensions (shrinkage)

dimensional restoration: a material's return to its former or original length or width dimension

dimensioning color: an arrangement of colors in some systematic method

discrete data: *see* attribute data

disposal specification: any special requirements for disposal of the product

distortion: a visible defect in the texture of the fabric

distribution curve: a plot of the frequency with which a value occurs within a sample or population

double sample plan: a technique used when the first sample was marginal in terms of meeting acceptance levels

drape: a behavior characteristic of a material that describes how the material falls, hangs, or flows over a three-dimensional form

dry cleaning: a process that uses organic solvents rather than water as the basis of the cleaning solution

du-pro inspection: an abbreviation of during-production inspection

durability: the length of time a textile product will be useable for its intended purpose

durability testing: procedures designed to evaluate how the various materials used in a product perform when subjected to conditions that are assumed to measure their durability

during production inspection: *see* in-process inspection

dye transfer: the movement of a chemical, dye, or pigment between fibers within a substrate or between substrates

ΔE: a single number defining the total color difference in a color space

edge abrasion: a condition that occurs when material is folded back on itself while being abraded

effective strength: *see* grab test

80/20 rule: *see* Pareto principle

elastic: a material that exhibits good elongation when subjected to a force and good recovery after the force is released; a narrow fabric used to create an expandable opening in a product

elastic fabric: a fabric made with an elastomeric material or a blend of elastomeric materials that have been combined in one fabric with other materials

electrostatic clinging: the propensity of one material to adhere to another because of an electrical charge on one or both surfaces

electrostatic propensity: a measure of the capacity of a nonconducting material to acquire and hold an electrical charge through friction or other means

element pull-off: the gripping strength of elements around the bead of a zipper

element slippage: the resistance of an element to longitudinal movement along the bead of a zipper

elongation: the ratio of the extension of a material to its length prior to stretching, expressed as a percent

emery method: a method used to evaluate the likelihood of a material exhibiting frosting

endpoint: the number of cycles until the fabric ruptures, two or more yarns have broken, or a hole appears

engineering specs: specifications for construction of a textile product

environment-product interactions: the manner in which the product interacts with the environment after it has been purchased by the consumer

ethical behavior: following and demonstrating personal conduct and professional practices that subscribe to the values of society.

ethics: the rules or standards for behavior governing the conduct of professionals

evaporation: a phase change that occurs when a liquid becomes a gas

exclusivity: the restrictions of time or seasons during which a new product will be produced for only one retailer or manufacturer

extensibility: a material's ability to stretch slightly with use or manipulation

external integrity: the consistency between a product's performance and consumer expectations

fabric count: *see* count

fabric density: the number of components in the fabric per unit measure

fabric growth: the difference between the original length of a specimen and its length immediately after removal of a specified load for a prescribed time

fabric mass per unit area: the mass (listed as grams or ounces) per unit of area (listed as square meters or square yards)

fabric quality: a measure of the degree to which a material is free of visual defects or irregularities, usually based on a numeric point system

fabric stretch: the increase in length of a fabric specimen resulting from a load applied under specified conditions

fabric weight: *see* fabric mass

fabrication: a method used to produce a fabric; the process of producing a fabric

fabrication method: the techniques used to produce the fabric

failure: sometimes used to describe the point at which the fabric ruptures

felting shrinkage: a permanent type of shrinkage unique to wool fibers as a result of the interlocking of scales on their exterior

fiber analysis: procedures used to identify qualitative and quantitative aspects of the fibers present in a material

final inspection: an evaluation to ensure that a finished product meets required standards and specifications

finishes: chemical or physical treatments of materials to enhance appearance or performance

finishing: the procedures used to achieve a product's required final or finished appearance; the addition of a chemical or physical finish to a material

first piece inspection: *see* pilot lot inspection

first-quality merchandise: products that meet requirements

first-quality product: products that meet the standards and specifications

firsts: *see* first-quality merchandise

fishbone diagram: *see* cause-and-effect diagram

fit: the relationship between product dimensions and the three-dimensional form, body, or other object on which the textile product is to be used, worn, or displayed

flammability: the capacity of a material to react to heat; the manner in which a material ignites and burns, and the ease or difficulty with which a burning textile is extinguished

flat abrasion: the type of abrasion that occurs when a flat object is rubbed against a flat material

flex abrasion: the type of abrasion that occurs when the material is bent or flexed during rubbing

flexural rigidity: a measurement of material stiffness that is calculated using fabric mass and length of overhang

flock rating scale: a rating scale used to assess the durability of an all-over flock fabric

flow chart: a detailed procedural diagram that helps identify key points for inspection and key measurements that should be made of the process or product

fluorescence: the emission of light with a wavelength approximately 10 to 20 percent longer than the original incident light

foam tear: a rupture that occurs when the foam portion of a laminated fabric fails before failure of the bond

formability: the maximum compressibility that can occur before the onset of buckling

formaldehyde release: the amount of formaldehyde emitted from textiles in accelerated storage conditions, includes free (unbonded) formaldehyde as well as formaldehyde released by the degradation of finishes

frequency: the number of wave crests that pass a given point in one second; the number of times a value falls within each segment of the range within a set of data

friction: the resistance to relative motion between two objects in physical contact with each other.

frosting: a change in fabric color caused by localized abrasion; a color problem that occurs when the dyed or printed portion of a material is abraded away and the material takes on a whitish look

FTMS: standard procedures used in government procurement of materials and products (Federal Test Methods and Standards)

fulling: a finish in which the fabric is subjected to moisture, heat, friction, and pressure to compress the fabric structure

function: how well a product does what it is designed to do

functional specification: the intended functional requirements for a product; may identify limitations

garment balance: the point at which the garment will naturally ride on the body or drape from the body

garment twist: a rotation, usually lateral, of panels in a garment

grab test: a breaking force procedure in which the fabric portions adjacent to the area under stress contribute to overall fabric strength

grade: the process of assigning a numerical value based on the number, size, and severity of defects observed during a visual inspection; the symbol, number, or letter used for any step in a multistep standard reference scale for a quality characteristic

gray scale: a scale consisting of pairs of standard gray chips that represent progressive differences in color or contrast corresponding to numerical colorfastness grades

Gray Scale for Color Change: a rating scale that consists of paired chips varying from light to dark gray that are used to evaluate the effect of a particular treatment on the color of a material or product

Gray Scale for Staining: a rating scale that consists of pairs of chips of white and gray varying from light to dark gray that are used to evaluate staining of undyed materials during colorfastness tests

grin: a condition that occurs in stressed seams when individual stitches are visible from the outside of a product

growth: an increase in product or material dimensions

guarantee: a pledge or an assurance that something is as represented and that it will be replaced if it does not meet specifications

guide: a series of options or instructions that do not recommend a specific course of action

hand: the tactile sensations or impressions that arise when materials are touched, squeezed, rubbed, or otherwise handled

hangtag: a label that includes information at point of sale, but is not a permanent part of the product

health: the interaction of physical, mental, emotional, and social aspects of the individual

heat: the internal energy within an object

heat shrinkage: a type of shrinkage that occurs with high temperatures; it most often occurs with synthetic and manufactured goods that were improperly heat set during finishing

heat transfer: the flow of internal energy between a hot object and a cold object

histogram: a type of bar chart that is used to plot variable data

holding strength of zipper stops: a measurement of the force that causes the slider to move beyond the stop, a measurement of the force at which failure applied longitudinally to the bottom occurs, a measurement of the force that holds two stringers of chain together at the bottom, a measurement of the force that causes chains to separate

hot pressing: a process for smoothing and perhaps shaping textile products by applying mechanical pressure with heat, sometimes in the presence of moisture

hue: a qualitative aspect of color that describes the dominant color from within a mixture of wavelengths; pure spectral characteristics; the quality that gives a color its name

hueless colors: *see* achromatic color

hygral expansion: an increase in a material's dimension(s) that occurs because of an increase in relative humidity

impact resistance: the ability of a material to withstand high-speed loading or a significant force applied to a small area; a measure of a button's resistance to fracture when subjected to sudden application of an external force.

imperfects: *see* second-quality merchandise

in control: the situation that occurs when the process consistently produces products that fall within the control limits

incoming inspection: *see* receiving inspection

independent testing: testing that is done by a separate business that tests materials for other firms

independent variable: the variable manipulated during the experiment or process

industry standard: the consensus among many companies in an industry or among individuals members of a profession

infrared region (IR): the portion of the energy spectrum in which wavelengths are longer than visible light

in-house testing: the process of evaluating materials or products within the firm that produced them

in-process inspection: any visual evaluation or check of parts, components, or materials during production

insect resistance: the capability to impede damage by insects by treating materials with chemicals

inspection: the visual examination or review of materials, product components, and finished products on the basis of their adherence to some established set of standards, specifications, or requirements

inspection levels: the type of examination and acceptance levels established for materials or products based on a supplier's history

inspection specifications: the details of the various inspections that have to be carried out on the product at various stages of production

inspector: the individual who examines the product, material, component, or process to determine if it conforms to standards and specifications

installation specification: detailed instructions necessary for installing products on site ready for use

interfacing: *see* interlining

interlining: textile materials that are sewn or fused to specific areas of the product to shape, support, stabilize, reinforce, and improve performance

internal integrity: the consistency among the materials, function, and structure of a product

International Organization for Standardization (ISO): an organization that coordinates many worldwide voluntary standardization efforts

international standards: a condition in which a majority of the products or services conform to the same standard regardless of where a product was produced or a service was performed

irregulars: *see* second-quality merchandise

irritants: materials that produce a very mild pain sensation, such as rough materials that abrade, poke, or stab the skin

jaw break: a breaking situation that occurs when a specimen breaks with 0.25 in. of the jaw edge, creating an unusable result

KES: the Kawabata Evaluation System used to evaluate fabric hand using instruments

key process variables: factors involved in production that impact on or contribute to product characteristics

key product variables: specific characteristics that are designed or incorporated into a product to meet customer needs

kurtosis: a characteristic of some distribution curves that are flatter than normal or more peaked than normal

labels: item sewn in to apparel and other textile products used to provide information to the manufacturer, retailer, and consumer

laboratory testing: the process of evaluating characteristics or performance of materials using standard procedures in a specialized facility

latent defects: hidden defects that are not apparent until the material or product has been tested or used

length: the linear quantity of fabric delivered or used

lifetime testing: a type of testing in which the product remains in use until the user decides it is no longer serviceable

lightfastness: the property of material, often expressed as a number, that describes a ranked change in its color characteristics resulting from exposure to some designated light source

lining: a textile material used to present a finished appearance, protect the user from internal structure, or add comfort to the product

local cause: *see* special cause

lot-by-lot acceptance sampling by attribute: a procedure in which a sample from each lot is inspected according to attributes

lot-by-lot sample: a technique that pulls samples from each production lot

low-power stretch: a fabric that exhibits high fabric stretch and good recovery at a small force or low load

lower control limit (*LCL*): lowest acceptable value within a control range

lower specification limit: lowest acceptable value within specifications

mace test: a test in which a tube of fabric is constructed and placed over a cylinder against which a spiked ball (mace) bounces randomly as the tube rotates

made-up: a prototype or sample product for any category other than apparel; used for medical, industrial, furnishing, and other applications

maintenance specification: the procedures to be followed to ensure that the product receives correct maintenance at required intervals

major defect: a defect that is likely to result in product failure or to reduce potentially the usability of the product for its purpose

mandatory standard: the standard that is required, generally by a law or regulation

Martindale pressure test: a type of test for measuring pilling of materials

materials: items that require no additional processing before being used in the production of textile products; include fashion and support fabrics, thread, zippers, and other items used in making up or constructing textile products

material interactions: the way in which materials that are combined in a product act and react when their performance is influenced by the presence of another material

materials inspection: the process used to identify the presence of any patent defects with materials that are to be combined in a product

materials specification: details of materials used to produce a single product

materials testing: the process of evaluating each material used in a product to determine its characteristics and to measure its response to selected performance tests

maximum: the greatest or highest acceptable value for any given parameter or dimension

Maxwell triangle: the basis for trichromatic color perception theory

mean: the average of a set of data

median: the middle point in a set of data

metamerism: the condition that occurs when the color of two materials match when viewed under one light source, but they do not match when viewed under any other light source

migration: the nonuniform movement and distribution of colorants, finishes, or other chemicals from one part of a material to another or from one material to another material

MIL STD 105E: *see* ANSI/ASQ Z1.4-1993.

mildew resistance: the ability of a material to resist the development of fungal growths and the accompanying unpleasant, musty odors when exposed to conditions favoring such growths

minimum: the least or lowest acceptable value for any given parameter or dimension

minor defect: a defect that that is not likely to reduce materially the usability of a product for its intended purpose, or a departure from established standards having little bearing on the effective use or operation of the product

mobility: ease of movement

mode: the most frequent value in a set of data

modified grab test: a breaking force test in which lateral slits are made midlength on the long edges of the specimen

moisture absorbency: the ability of one material (the absorbent) to take in or absorb another material (the absorbate)

moisture equilibrium: the condition reached by a sample when it no longer takes up moisture from or gives up moisture to the surrounding atmosphere

moisture regain: the amount of water in a material determined under prescribed conditions and expressed as a percentage of the mass of the water-free material

multifiber test fabric: a fabric, used in testing for color bleeding and staining, made with filling-faced bands in which the filling yarns in each band differ by fiber content

multiple sample plan: *see* double sampling plan

multiprocess wet cleaning: a cleaning method that uses controlled applications of heat, steam, natural soaps, and pressing techniques to refurbish products

National Institute of Standards and Technology (NIST): a federal agency that coordinates U.S. activities in the areas of science and technology

needle damage: the partial or complete severance of yarns, deflection of yarns at the stitching line, or fusing of fibers caused by a needle passing through a material during sewing

nonconforming goods: items that do not meet standards and specifications

nonspectral colors: colors that do not occur in any natural spectra

normal distribution: the distribution curve with a bell shape

normal inspection level: a type of inspection that is used when there is no evidence that the quality of the product being submitted for evaluation is better or poorer than the specified quality level.

normal variation: the assumption that no two items will ever be completely identical

np **chart:** a type of attribute control chart in which the number nonconforming is reported

objective: a statement of the desired result to be achieved within a specified time (Juran & Gryna, 1993)

100% inspection: the process of evaluating all parts, components, or products

open specification: details for the consideration of multiple vendors, including a description of the character and/or performance desired in the product or material to be purchased

operating characteristic curve (OC curve): a plot of the probabilities of accepting a lot given the largest number of nonconformances allowed in a sample size

out-of-control: the condition that occurs when a process begins to consistently produce products that are outside control limits

p **chart:** a type of attribute control chart in which the proportion of nonconforming units is reported

packaging: a description of the manipulation of the product (i.e., folding) and the type and amount of materials to be used with the product to prepare it for shipping and/or sale to the consumer; the manner in which a product is prepared for transportation, shipping, and presentation to the customer

packed product audit: *see* shipment inspection

packed product inspection: *see* shipment inspection

Pareto chart: a histogram that graphs data in descending order of occurrence

Pareto principle: 20 percent of the process quality characteristics cause 80 percent of the problems with a product or service (Pond, 1994, p. 61).

pass/fail scale: the level of performance that meets or exceeds acceptable limits for a characteristic or condition

patent defects: irregularities that can be observed visually during examination or inspection of the material

peel strength: a measure of the force required to separate the two parts of a hook and loop fastener

penalty point: *see* defect point

penetration: the flow of a chemical through closures, porous materials, seams, pinholes, and other imperfections of a material on a nonmolecular level

people systems: the individuals and the roles they fill within the organization

percentage defective: a percentage based on the number of defectives and the size of the sample or the number of units inspected

percentage loss in breaking force: a calculation based on the difference between the original strength of a material and its strength after abrasion or exposure to sunlight or some other potentially damaging activity

permeation: chemical movement through a material at the molecular level

permeation rate: the volume of a chemical that passes through the material in a given time unit

phase change: a type of heat transfer that occurs when an object changes physical state

photochromism: a qualitative designation for a reversible change in color of any kind that is immediately noticeable on termination of light exposure when exposed and unexposed portions of the material are compared

pile retention: the degree to which cut-pile yarns are held secure and intact to wear and resist pile loss

pilling: formation of tiny balls of fiber on the surface of a material

pilling resistance: resistance to the formation of pills on a textile surface

pilot lot inspection: a careful examination of a first sample production run in a facility for a specific style or product line

planar abrasion: *see* flat abrasion

point out: the data point that extends beyond the upper or lower control limit on a control chart

policies: broad guidelines that help direct action within an organization

practice: a definitive procedure for performing one or more specific operations or functions that does not produce a test result

precision: the degree of agreement within a set of observations, or test results obtained as directed in a method

preventive perspective: an outlook in which potential problem areas are identified and a plan is developed and implemented so that a foreseeable problem is prevented from occurring

probability: the likelihood of a given result occurring when an action is done

procedures: details describing how a given activity is to be accomplished

process control points: specifically identified points or stages of production at which inspection should occur during production

process improvement: a continual process in which information from inspection and product or process evaluation is used to improve the process

process map: *see* flow chart

process specification: actions that need to be performed during the processing of materials to bring them to final product stage

processes: *see* procedures

process-material interactions: the effect of a production process on the performance of a material and its effects on the performance of the finished product

processed materials: *see* materials

procurement specification: a total picture of the what, where, when, and how expected of the product so that prospective suppliers know what is expected of them

product attributes: characteristics inherent in a product

product audit: another term for product inspection

product balance: the point at which the textile product will naturally ride on the form or drape from the form

product development: the design and engineering of products to be serviceable, producible, salable, and profitable (Glock & Kunz, 1995).

product inspection: a search for nonadherence to characteristics, dimensions, and other required parameters that can be detected with the eye and the use of simple measuring devices; a holistic visual analysis of a product to determine its adherence to requirements

product integrity: the way the materials and other aspects of the product work together to affect the consumer's satisfaction with the product; a product's ability to meet or exceed implied or stated guarantees in terms of performance and function

product quality: the total of a set of precise and measurable characteristics or components of the finished product

product specification: a description of the product to the extent necessary to make it

product testing: a type of testing in which sample products, prototypes, or several products from a limited production run are used or worn by a small group of users; the process of evaluating finished products to determine whether they meet product performance criteria

product zoning: the process of identifying those portions of a product that are most crucial in terms of appearance

production lot: items that include the same materials, were produced by the same process, and perhaps were worked on by the same operator

progressive shrinkage: a type of shrinkage in which the material shrinks a little each time it is cleaned

prototype testing: a type of product evaluation in which sample products, prototypes, or several products from a limited production run are used or worn by individuals

protrusion: a visible group of fibers, yarn, or portion that extends above the normal fabric surface

pucker: a wavy three-dimensional effect typified by closely spaced wrinkles on one or both sides of a material

put-up: a description of the length of fabric on the roll or bolt

qualitative procedures: techniques to determine which generic fibers are present in a material

quality: a complex concept used to describe the degree to which a process, material, product, or service possesses desirable physical or intangible attributes

quality assurance audit: *see* quality audit

quality audit: a term sometimes used to refer to inspection

quality checkpoints: *see* process control points

quality function deployment (QFD): a technique in which a series of interlocking matrices translate customer needs into product and process characteristics

quantitative procedures: techniques used to determine the percentage by weight of each generic fiber present in blends

R control chart: a variable control chart that illustrates the range of measurements of the samples taken

radiation: a type of heat transfer that involves the transmission of energy between objects that are in a straight line of sight with each other

random or statistical sampling: inspection of a select few materials, components, or products

random sample: a sample in which each product in a lot has an equal chance of being selected for inspection regardless of its sequence of production, color, size, style, location in boxes or crates, or any other aspect of production, packaging, or convenience

random variation: a type of variation that has many causes, but each cause contributes only a small amount to the variation

range: the values present in the distribution from the lowest to the highest possible values

rater: an individual who understands the procedure to be used in assigning a grade and the distinctions among the numerical ratings

rating: the process for determining or assigning a grade to a material by comparing it to a standard reference scale

raveled strip test: a breaking force test in which a narrow raveled strip of material is used

raw materials: fibers, yarns, dyes, finishing chemicals, and such other materials as plastics and metal that need to be processed into such items as buttons and zippers

receiving inspection: a visual examination of components and finished trims or other parts of a product

reduced inspection level: a type of product review that is permitted under certain conditions relating to a consistent meeting of criteria for a lengthy time period

reference scale: a series of photographs, plastic replicas, colored chips, or paired gray chips that represent a range of visual changes that are likely to occur with materials during testing

reflection: incident light bounced off an object

refraction: the behavior of light that is observed when light crosses the boundary between two different materials and bends because of a change in the speed with which light moves through each material

refractive index: the ratio of the speed of light in space to its speed as it passes through matter

rejection: the condition that occurs when the lot did not meet standards and specifications and the buyer refuses to buy it or rejects the lot

relaxation shrinkage: relaxation of tensions in materials that developed during yarn spinning, fabrication, and finishing that may occur when a material is wetted and dried without tension

reliability: the ability to repeat the exact process and get the same or very similar results

representative sample: a sample that includes all styles, colors, sizes, and other planned variations in the product in appropriate ratios

residual shrinkage: additional relaxation shrinkage that was not removed during the first care cycle

ridging: with fusible materials, a visually noticeable line that appears on the face of the shell fabric so that the point at which the interlining ends can be seen quite clearly when the product is used or worn

robotics: automated systems that are designed to perform repetitive tasks quickly, accurately, and correctly

roping: a hem that folds and twists along its edge

rot resistance: a material's resistance to deterioration as a result of fungal growth

rule of seven: on a control chart, seven points in a row above or below the mean or seven points in a row that have a positive or negative slope

rule of thirds: a normal probability in which approximately two thirds of the points should be within one standard deviation of the mean and approximately one third of the points should be relatively near the control limits

safety: a measure of the physical risks to which a user or wearer is exposed when a textile product is used or worn

sample: a subset of a production lot

sampling: the process of selecting items from a production lot to evaluate in a product audit

sampling plan: the process used to select a reasonable number of products to represent the production unit or lot based on color, size, style, and other dimensions of importance

saturation: the dimension of color associated with the degree of purity of the light

saturation point: the point at which a material is no longer able to absorb additional moisture

scatter diagram: a diagram that plots many points on X-Y coordinates

scattering: a specific type of reflection in which the angle of reflection is multidirectional

screen wire method: a method used to evaluate the likelihood of a material to exhibit frosting

seam appearance: a description (often numerical) of how a seam looks from the outside of the product after production

seam damage: a reduction in seam efficiency caused by a change in the physical condition of one or more components in a seam (ASTM, 1996)

seam failure: the point at which an external force (1) ruptures the sewing thread, (2) ruptures the fabric, (3) causes excessive yarn slippage adjacent to the stitch line, or (4) causes any combination of these unacceptable conditions

seam integrity: the ability of a seam to join materials or components, to maintain an attractive appearance, to be durable, and to remain securely stitched during use and cleaning

seam jamming: a special type of seam pucker that results from the buckling of yarns in a material

seam pucker: a distortion of the sewn fabric either during seam construction or later

seam slippage: the partial or complete loss of seam integrity manifested by yarn slippage parallel to or adjacent to the stitch line

seam strength: the maximum resistance to rupture at the juncture formed by stitching together two or more planar materials

second-quality merchandise: products that fail to meet requirements

seconds: *see* second-quality merchandise

selective spectral absorbers: objects that absorb only specific wavelengths rather than all the light energy falling on them

self-managing team: a group of individuals who plan, implement, and control the work to reach a defined business objective

service testing: *see* product testing

serviceability: the degree to which a product satisfies customers' needs

sewability: the ability of a thread to combine with another material in stitch and seam formation in such a fashion that production and performance problems do not occur

sewing thread: a special type of yarn that will pass through a sewing machine rapidly, form a stitch efficiently, and perform adequately in a textile product

shade bank: a range of acceptable color shades for one color

shade sorting: the physical grouping of similar materials by color

shear strength: the amount of force required to cause the two parts of a hook and loop fastener to slide on each other causing separation

shear stress: a type of yarn distortion that may occur when stress is applied at some angle to warp or filling

shearing: *see* shear stress

shiners: areas along seams that occur when the sewing needle snags a yarn and pulls it tighter than the other yarns in the surrounding area of the material

shipment inspection: an inspection of products after they have been received by a distribution center

shrinkage: a decrease in dimensions of a material or product

simulation: the recreation of the critical portions of the real environment

single sample plan: a plan in which the total number of sample products inspected and the total size of the sample are equal

size: the important length, width, depth, circumference, and vertical dimensions of a product; for garments, a standard grouping of product dimensions based on a standard size chart

skew: a condition in which the crosswise yarn forms some angle other than 90° as it moves across the fabric

skewness: a curve that has an elongated tail on one side or the other

skin contact: a static condition in which neither the material nor the body is required to move or interact, for any sensation to occur

skip lot sample: a sample in which some production lots may not be represented

snag: a yarn or portion of a yarn that is pulled up from the normal surface of the fabric

snagging: a portion of the fabric structure that has caught on an abradant material with some resulting change in fabric appearance, fabric structure, or yarn structure

soil redeposition: the soiling of a relatively clean fabric during laundering by soil removed from another fabric

source inspection: the examination of materials, components, products, or documents at a supplier's facility by an individual not employed by the supplier

spec: *see* specification

special cause: variations that result from specific conditions that, once identified, can be corrected

specific purpose team: a team whose members continue to serve in their regular roles within an organization while they work together to address an issue assigned to them

specification: a precise statement of a set of requirements to be satisfied by a material, product, system, or service that indicates the procedures for determining whether each of the requirements is satisfied

specification limits: the specified value for a measurable parameter, characteristic, or performance criteria plus or minus an allowable tolerance

specimen: the piece or portion of a material on which a test is conducted

spectral color: a color that can be found in a naturally occurring spectrum

spectral locus: curved line of a chromaticity diagram that represents the chromaticities of all colors produced by monochromatic light

spectrophotometer: an instrument that measures the percentage of light transmitted or reflected at each wavelength in the visible spectrum by a colored surface

spectroscopy: the study of the emission and absorption of light and other portions of the electromagnetic spectrum

specular reflectance: the shiny reflective surface of a drop of water when it beads up on a surface

spirality: *see* garment twist

sporadic problem: sudden adverse changes in the product or process

stain: a local deposit of soil or discoloration on a substrate that exhibits some degree of resistance to removal by laundering or dry cleaning

standard: commonly agreed on aid for communication and trade; a set of characteristics or procedures that provide a basis for resource and production decisions; a product that meets all specifications and company or product requirements

standard allowed hours: a unit of measure used when costing in dozens instead of in individual units

standard allowed minutes: a unit of measure for determining the time required for an operation

standard atmosphere: the conditions for testing textiles that is defined as air maintained at a relative humidity of 65 ± 2% and a temperature of 21 ± 1 °C (70 ± 2 °F).

standard calibration fabric: a fabric used because the operator knows the results that should be obtained with the fabric so that equipment can be adjusted accordingly

standard deviation: the manner in which the data cluster around the mean

standard test method: a procedure for evaluating materials or products that have been approved by a specific professional organization

standard product: a product that meets all standards and specifications

standardization: the process of developing and applying rules for a consistent and uniform approach to a specific activity for the benefit and with the cooperation of all concerned

standardized light source: a carefully controlled artificial light that is used in assessing and measuring the color of objects

statistical process control (SPC): a variety of statistical and other analytical techniques to identify and minimize unacceptable variations in a firm's products or processes

stiffness: a measure of a fabric's resistance to bending or flexing

strain: a material's deformation or elongation caused by an external force

stratified sample: a process of taking a sample when a large, supposedly homogenous lot exists

stress: a material's resistance to deformation

stress-strain curve: a graphical representation of a material's resistance to deformation (stress) and its deformation or elongation caused by an external force (strain).

stretch: an increase in one dimension because of force exerted on a material

stretch yarn fabric: a fabric made using at least some yarns with a high degree of potential elastic stretch and rapid recovery

strike-off: sample of a dyed or printed material

substandard product: a product that does not meet standards and specifications

subtractive color mixing: removing one or more colors from light to create other colors

supplier certification: *see* vendor certification

supplier partnerships: the condition in which the buyer and supplier work together for the mutual benefit of both companies

supplier risk (α): *see* alpha (α) risk

supplier testing: a process in which the firm that supplies a material tests it to make sure that it meets the requirements listed in the contract or agreement with the buyer

support materials: a variety of materials that are used to produce products beyond the fashion fabrics

system cause: *see* common cause

systematic sample: a sample that consists of items or units from equally occurring locations or at equal intervals of time.

tailorability: the ability and ease with which materials can be sewn together to form a product (Shishoo, 1990)

takeup: the additional length of yarn needed to make a piece of fabric

taking a sample: *see* sampling

target market: a group of customers or a segment of the population that is interested in and likely to purchase a particular product

target specification: the principal elements that should be considered during the design stage

tearing strength: a measure of a material's resistance to the continuation of a tear

technical systems: the equipment and procedures in place within an organization that assist in meeting organizational objectives

tenacity: *see* breaking force

tensile strength: the strength of a material under tension, expressed in terms of force

terminology: a document comprising definitions of terms; descriptions of terms; and explanations of symbols, abbreviations, or acronyms

test method: a definitive procedure for the identification, measurement, and evaluation of one or more qualities, characteristics, or properties of a material, product, system, or service that produces a test result

test specification: description of any tests that may be required during decision making, manufacturing, and inspection stages

testing: the analysis and evaluation of a material or product to assess its characteristics, quality, or performance

Textile/Clothing Technology Corporation [(TC)²]: a coalition of leaders in the U.S. textile and apparel industry, labor unions, and government organizations with an emphasis on improving the sewn products industry in the United States

textile quality assurance: the process of designing, producing, evaluating, and checking products to see that they meet the desired quality level for a firm's target market

thermal protection: the amount of heat transfer protection (insulation) provided by a material when it is exposed to an open flame

thickness: the distance through the fabric between its outer surface on one side and its outer surface on the opposite side

thread count: *see* count

thread strength: the force required to rupture a sewing thread

threshold levels: descriptions used in specifying materials and product that identify the greatest degree of irregularity that would be acceptable

tightened inspection level: a process for reviewing goods that is implemented when two out of five consecutive lots have been rejected

tolerance: the range of acceptable values

tongue test: a type of tearing strength test for materials

torque: *see* garment twist

total quality management (TQM): activities that involve everyone in an organization in an integrated effort to improve performance at every level

transmission: with colored objects, the light energy incident on the object that passes through the object with no change in either the energy or the object

trapezoid test: a type of tearing strength test for materials

trichromatic color perception: three types of color receptors present in the human eye that differ in their spectral sensitivity functions

trims: a wide range of materials and treatments that enhance the aesthetics of a textile product

tristimulus color perception: *see* trichromatic color perception

tristimulus colorimeter: an instrument that measures color by attempting to duplicate the perception of color of the human eye

turns per inch: *see* twist

twist: the number of times the fibers in the yarn turn around the length-wise central axis per unit measure

Type 1 error: *see* alpha (α) risk

Type 2 error: *see* beta (β) risk

***u* chart:** a type of attribute chart in which the count of nonconformities per unit is reported

ultraviolet or UV protection: the amount of protection provided by a material when the wearer is exposed to light containing ultraviolet rays

ultraviolet region (UV): the portion of the energy spectrum in which wavelengths are shorter than visible light

unacceptable variation: variations that fall outside the maximum tolerance level for specifications and standards established by the firm

upper control limit (*UCL*): highest acceptable value within a control range

upper specification limit: highest acceptable value within specifications

usability: the determination of a product's ability to meet customer expectations for the end use for which the item was designed and purchased

use specification: information and special instructions that users will need to enable them to use the product in its intended manner

user-product interactions: an examination of the ways in which product and user interact and influence customer satisfaction with the product

variable control chart: a graphical representation of the average measurement of samples taken over time

variable data: values derived from actual measurements using instruments or measuring equipment

variation: characteristics or measurements that differ from specifications or standards

vendor certification: a formal agreement based on the quality of the materials or products received over an extended time span

vendor inspection: an inspection of a production site

vendor partnership: *see* supplier partnership

verification: the process of fixing, checking, or correcting the gradations of a measuring instrument that is conducted periodically in an instrument's use location

visible light: the portion of the electromagnetic spectrum that stimulates the sense of sight

visual change: the effect that a procedure has on the luster, color, surface nap or pile, or other surface aspect of a material

voluntary standard: a standard that allows individuals or companies the right to determine on their own whether to adopt a standard

water repellency: the relative resistance of a material to surface wetting, water penetration, or water absorption

water resistance: the ability of a material to withstand penetration by water under pressure or water that drops from a distance and strikes against a material with a known amount of force

water spotting: a change in color, particularly at the periphery of an area wetted with water

water vapor transmission: the speed with which water vapor passes through a material

waterproof: a condition in which materials are resistant to the penetration of water regardless of its pressure or force

wave: a form of energy represented by a series of crests and troughs

wavelength (λ): the distance from one crest to the next crest of a wave of energy

wear testing: *see* product testing

wearability: the determination of a garment's ability to meets customer expectations for the end use for which it was designed and purchased

weather resistance: the ability of a material to resist degradation of its properties when exposed to real or simulated climatic conditions

white light: light in which all portions or wavelengths of the visible spectrum are present in equal amounts

width: the full usable distance across the fabric from one edge to the other

wind resistance: material behavior when it is confronted by or exposed to a dynamic condition of rapidly moving air

workmanship: how the materials and construction used in producing the product affect the way the finished product looks

Worth Street Textile Market Rules: a standard code of practices used in marketing of textile materials in the United States

wrinkle recovery: a fabric's ability to recover from folding deformations

$\bar{X}$ control chart: a variable control chart that illustrates the means of the samples taken

yarn defects: irregularities within the yarn that are not generally part of the nature of the yarn

yarn distortion: a condition of woven fabrics in which the symmetrical surface of a fabric is altered by shifting or sliding of warp or filling yarns

yarn number: a general term that describes the size of the yarn

yield point: the point on a stress-strain curve beyond which deformation can not be completely recovered

Young's modulus: the ratio of change in stress to change in strain within the elastic limits of the material

zones: differentiating areas of product in terms of critical appearance aspects related to materials, structure, and standards

INDEX